Current Controversies in Criminology

Ronald Weitzer, Editor

Prentice
Hall

Upper Saddle River, New Jersey 07458

DEC 1 6 2003

Library of Congress Cataloging-in-Publication Data

Current controversies in criminology / [edited by] Ronald Weitzer.—1st ed.
  p.   cm.
Includes bibliographical references.
  ISBN 0–13–094115–8
  1. Criminology.   2. Crime—United States.   3. Criminal justice,
Administration of—United States.   I. Weitzer, Ronald
  HV6025 .C86 2003
  364–dc21

                                                    2002011370

Publisher: Nancy Roberts
Senior Acquisitions Editor: Christopher DeJohn
Production Liaison: Joanne Hakim
Editorial/Production Supervision: Bruce Hobart (Pine Tree Composition)
Prepress and Manufacturing Buyer: Mary Ann Gloriande
Art Director: Jayne Conte
Cover Designer: Bruce Kenselaar
Cover Image Specialist: Karen Sanatar
Marketing Manager: Amy Speckman
Copy Editor: Carol Lallier

This book was set in 10/12 Times Roman by Pine Tree Composition, Inc.,
and was printed and bound by R.R. Donnelley.
The cover was printed by Coral Graphics.

© 2003 by Pearson Education, Inc.
Upper Saddle River, New Jersey 07458

Printed in the United States of America
10   9   8   7   6   5   4   3   2   1

ISBN: 0-13-094115-8

Pearson Education LTD., *London*
Pearson Education Australia, PTY. Limited, *Sydney*
Pearson Education Singapore, Pte. Ltd
Pearson Education North Asia Ltd, *Hong Kong*
Pearson Education Canada, Ltd., *Toronto*
Pearson Educación de Mexico, S.A. de C.V.
Pearson Education—Japan, *Tokyo*
Pearson Education Malaysia, Pte. Ltd
Pearson Education, *Upper Saddle River, New Jersey*

Contents

PART III: Controversial Crime-Fighting Methods

Preface

Current Controversies in Criminology offers readings on the causes of crime and on several important contested issues in American criminal justice. All of the articles are solid, scholarly examinations of key problems and issues in the field of criminology.

The book covers:

- Theories regarding the *causes* of crime;
- *Crimes* that are especially controversial or relatively new, poorly understood, and under-researched (hate crime, computer crime);
- *Crime-fighting methods* that have either a long and controversial history or new, cutting-edge measures that are equally controversial.

These readings are intended to stimulate critical thinking, dispel common myths about crime and crime-control practices, and generate informed class discussions about some of the most important issues in criminology today.

The book is divided into three parts. Part I, "What Causes Crime?" examines differing explanations of criminal behavior. Major perspectives are represented, including subcultural theory, conflict theory, routine activities theory, social disorganization theory, symbolic interactionist theory, and control theory. Some of these theories are presented as general explanations of crime, purportedly explaining all types of crime and thus competing with other theories, while other perspectives are less grandiose, being designed to explain certain types of crime or why crime occurs under certain kinds of conditions.

Part II, "Controversial Crimes," investigates several controversial or "new" types of crime that have generated heated debate in American society. Included are victimless crime, hate crime, child abuse, school shootings, date rape, computer crime, corporate crime, and government-sponsored crime. The featured articles examine offenders' motivations, harms to victims and to society, the criminal justice system's response, and some policy implications. Each article uses social science evidence to challenge popular misconceptions about these crimes.

Part III, "Controversial Crime-Fighting Methods," covers some of the most disputed crime-fighting techniques in America. Each reading critically evaluates one of these methods, raising questions about whether it does more harm than good. Included are measures that have a long history of controversy—such as gun control, the death penalty, and drug control—as well as some that have only recently begun to generate public concern and debate—such as "three-strikes and you're out" laws, racial profiling by the police, the crackdown on juvenile crime, community notification about sex offenders, and DNA testing.

ACKNOWLEDGMENTS

I would like to acknowledge the following reviewers:

- Ronald Burns, *Texas Christian University*
- Rebecca Cadima, *Fisher College*
- Keith Crew, *University of Northern Iowa*
- B. Grant Stitt, *University of Nevada*

Ronald Weitzer
George Washington University

INTRODUCTION TO # Part One:
What Causes Crime?

Theories are an essential part of any scientific enterprise. A *theory* may be defined as a set of testable propositions designed to explain a general class of phenomena, such as domestic violence or white-collar crime. Theories can advance our *understanding* of the social world and can also be used to *predict* both crime patterns and crime control practices. Part I of this book examines several leading theories that identify major causes of crime. Some theories purport to be *general* theories, explaining all types of crime, while others are *specific* to certain kinds of crime or certain contexts (such as neighborhoods). Each theory contains propositions that distinguish it from other theories, and each theory has attracted empirical research that appears to support at least some of the theory's propositions.

Causes of crime may be located at different levels of social reality. Some are *microsocial* factors at the level of face-to-face interactions between people, such as parental failure to properly socialize children or the dynamics of disputatious encounters between individuals; some focus on *macrolevel*

variables, such as social inequality or broad cultural and subcultural forces; and still others are intermediate, *mesolevel* approaches that explain crime at the neighborhood level or in particular kinds of organizations. Part I includes theories at each of these three levels.

Subcultural theory focuses on values and beliefs that depart from conventional standards and predispose people to commit crime. According to this theory, persons internalize the values, beliefs, and norms of deviant subcultures, including justifications for criminal conduct—all of which increases individuals' propensity to engage in criminal behavior. Subcultural theory has a long tradition in criminology. One example is Walter Miller's (1958) classic argument that distinctive cultural values explain gang delinquency among lower-class boys. The core values, what Miller called "focal concerns," of lower-class subculture include toughness, smartness, dealing with trouble, need for excitement, and quest for independence—values that clash with middle-class culture and the legal code and provide fertile

1

ground for delinquent behavior. A similar perspective is presented in Albert Cohen's book, *Delinquent Boys*. Cohen (1955) argues that delinquent subcultures arise among lower-class boys as a way of dealing with problems, particularly their need for *status* in a society whose conventional culture denies status to lower-class people. These boys deal with status frustration by substituting unconventional values, the pursuit of which increases individuals' status in the eyes of their peers. Delinquent subcultures stand in stark contrast to the middle-class values of ambition, good manners, self-restraint, and thrift; delinquent subcultures, argues Cohen, place a premium on values that are hedonistic (short-term "fun"), malicious (enjoying others' suffering), negativistic (inverting the normative standards of conventional society), and expressive (crime not as a means to a material end but instead offering thrills and earning offenders respect within the peer group). This value system leads to delinquent behavior among lower-class youth.

A subcultural explanation of homicide is presented in the reading "The Subculture of Violence" by Marvin Wolfgang and Franco Ferracuti. They argue that most homicides are conditioned by a distinctive value system that is more conducive to the use of violence than the larger, dominant culture of a society. According to Wolfgang and Ferracuti, the "groups with the highest rates of homicide" also have "in the most intense degree a subculture of violence." The subculture may be pronounced in certain small groups (juvenile gangs), in certain areas of a city (disadvantaged minority neighborhoods), and in certain regions of a country (the American South). Of course, the theory does not imply that all members of a subculture accept values and beliefs favorable to violence or that all members actually en-

gage in violent acts. But, in general, the existence of subcultures of violence helps explain why some groups are more prone to engage in violent crime than other groups; the law-abiding generally accept the dominant culture's normative prohibitions on violence, whereas those who reject conventional values are more predisposed to violent behavior.

How do subcultural values originate? And why do they resonate in some groups, communities, or regions and not in others? These questions are not addressed by Wolfgang and Ferracuti, though they briefly speculate about this in their final paragraph. The theory takes *as a given* the existence of subcultures of violence and then proceeds to explain violent crime through a cultural lens rather than asking how such subcultures arise in the first place. Another criticism of the theory takes issue with the very idea that criminogenic subcultures exist and contends that there is little evidence supporting the subculture of violence thesis (Erlanger 1974). Some classic works challenge the argument that offenders accept deviant values and beliefs (Merton 1938; Sykes and Matza 1957; Matza 1964), and argue that offenders accept the dominant value system and engage in crime because they have temporarily suspended or "neutralized" those values and moral constraints (Sykes and Matza) or because they face blocked opportunities in pursuing conventional values, like the hallowed goal of material success in American society, and believe they must break the law to achieve success (Merton). According to these theorists, crime is not rooted in deviant subcultures standing in opposition to convention; instead, crime can be committed by people who embrace *conventional* cultural values. Subcultural theorists would flatly reject this criticism. As Cohen (1955:129) insists, "The hallmark of the delinquent subculture is the explicit and wholesale repudiation of middle-class standards and the adoption of their very antithesis."

Subcultural explanations for crime are not limited to the values and norms of certain kinds of groups, neighborhoods, or regions of a country. Subcultures opposed to the dominant culture may be broader and diffused throughout a society, such as the youth "counterculture" of the late 1960s in America. Deviant values and behaviors are widely disseminated by the mass media, some of which may help to reinforce deviant and criminal behavior, at least for a segment of the population. In an April 2001 Harris poll, 55 percent of the American population thought that television contributes "a lot" to violence in society, and 53 percent felt the same way about movies. Similarly, 65 percent of Americans believe that rap music with violent lyrics "inspires" listeners to commit violence, according to a 1995 *Time/ CNN* opinion poll. Evidence indicates that media violence does indeed lead *some people* under *certain conditions* to act violently, though most people exposed to violence on television or in movies or to violent lyrics in music do not engage in aggressive behavior (Donnerstein and Linz 1995).

Whether exposure to media violence influences a viewer's behavior may be explained, at least in part, by Daniel Glaser's "differential identification" thesis, which holds that deviant behavior is *learned* when individuals positively identify with deviant others and their values, including people they know only via the mass media. Glaser (1956:440) writes that "a person pursues criminal behavior to the extent that he identifies himself with real or imaginary persons from whose perspectives his criminal behavior seems acceptable." Serial killers Jeffrey Dahmer and Ted Bundy and "Unabomber"

Ted Kaczynski, for instance, might be seen by some news viewers as role models whose behavior they want to emulate. However negatively such criminals are portrayed in the media, differential identification may nevertheless lead some people to follow in their footsteps and attack others. Popular music may have the same effect on some listeners who identify with the artist or the lyrics.

Subcultural theory, in a nutshell, holds that values, beliefs, and norms—whether limited to certain groups or more widely dispersed throughout a society—may contribute to criminal behavior.

Conflict theory centers on patterns of class, racial, and gender domination in society and the ways in which inequality gives rise to conflict, crime, and repressive social control. Conflict theory holds that the government and social institutions generally protect the interests of economic and political elites by imposing controls on powerless segments of society—such as the poor, the working class, and racial minorities. Elliott Currie's article, "Crime and Social Inequality," is a general analysis of class inequality and crime in America and Europe. He argues that violent crime rates are associated not with the level of absolute poverty in a society but instead with the *magnitude of the income gap* between rich and poor and the *level of economic support* available to people at the bottom of the class structure.

Currie attempts to prove his argument that socioeconomic inequality is a predictor of violent crime by comparing the United States to Europe. The United States is distinguished by a wider spread of income inequality than in European societies, less public assistance (welfare) for the poor, and a higher rate of violent crime. America's violent crime rate can be explained by these social and economic conditions. The existence of extreme poverty in a rich nation like the United States, coupled with a less generous welfare system than what exists in Europe, helps to account for America's high level of violent crime. It is no accident that nations with low levels of income inequality and generous welfare systems (the Netherlands, Scandinavia, etc.) also have the lowest violent crime rates. Currie is not asserting that socioeconomic inequality is the sole cause of crime, but he does see it as a *major* factor shaping crime rates.

Readers will notice that Currie is critical of strict cultural explanations of crime, including Wolfgang and Ferracuti's subculture of violence thesis. Currie argues that deviant values and beliefs are linked to structural variables, namely, unequal opportunities for achieving status and material success, which disadvantages certain racial groups and social classes. Currie calls his thesis "soft cultural," where values reflect socially structured opportunities, as opposed to the "hard cultural" approach that divorces cultural values and beliefs from structures of inequality in society, as in subculture of violence theory.

Currie restricts his comparative analysis to violent crime. It might be expected, however, that if income inequality and welfare levels predict violent crime across nations, they should also be especially strong predictors of economically motivated property crime. But property crime rates in many European nations are higher than in the United States. Why is it that economic factors explain violent crime rates but not property crime rates? Why does high income inequality and meager public assistance for the poor lead to *violent* crime? Shouldn't these economic factors generate higher rates of *property* crime in America? Currie provides no answers to these intriguing questions.

Classical theories portray crime as a rational course of action by offenders who seek to maximize pleasure and minimize pain. Criminals are thought to balance the costs and benefits of committing crimes; they do not act impulsively or unpredictably. **Routine activities theory** is influenced by the classical tradition. The theory, formulated by Lawrence Cohen and Marcus Felson ("Crime and Routine Activities"), attempts to explain why crime occurs in certain places under specific conditions by focusing on the convergence of three factors: (1) a motivated offender, (2) a suitable target, and (3) the lack of guardians capable of defending the target. It is assumed that offenders are motivated to commit crime out of self-interest and that many people might be motivated to break the law; the theory makes no attempt to explain why some people offend and others do not. The focus is on crime *events*, not on criminal *offenders* themselves.

A suitable target is something that is valued (e.g., a car) or an individual who, when attacked, provides pleasure or some other benefit to the perpetrator. Guardians are individuals or objects (e.g., car alarms, closed-circuit cameras) that have the capacity to protect possible targets. Their presence raises the costs of crime, making the target less attractive than unprotected targets to the offender.

Routine activities theory is primarily a microlevel perspective; its three variables converge to produce specific criminal events. But there is also a macro dimension, centered on large-scale growth over time in the opportunities for crime: Changes since World War II in the daily activities of work, leisure, and school have increased the number of people in public places, which increases their vulnerability as targets and keeps them away from home, where they might act as guardians. The increasing proportion of women in the workforce is one broad structural change that illustrates how a segment of the population may become more vulnerable to victimization over time.

One implication of the theory is that crime is hardly random, as some people think and as media reporting seems to suggest. Instead, crime is socially structured and somewhat predictable. Another implication is that the crime rate may increase over time for several reasons: more offenders, more targets, fewer guardians, or fewer convergences of offenders, targets, and absent guardians. It follows that crime rates can increase without any growth in the number of offenders, provided that their opportunities (more targets, fewer guardians) increase.

Unlike theories that attempt to explain why some people engage in crime while others do not—including most of the other theories featured in Part I—routine activities theory is concerned with criminal events rather than offenders. It is simply taken for granted that there will be a steady supply of offenders. But this leaves unexamined one of the three ingredients of criminal events. Does the idea of a "motivated offender" refer only to people with preexisting criminal motivations, or does it also include persons lacking such preexisting intentions who spontaneously decide to offend when an opportunity presents itself? The theory has been criticized for its ambiguity regarding offenders: "Since all persons are potentially motivated to commit crime, can the presence of a motivated offender simply be assumed from the presence of any person? If so, how does the theory distinguish between circumstances in which a motivated offender is present and those in which one is not?" (Akers 1997:31).

Social disorganization theory emphasizes "location, location, location." Un-like theories that focus on "kinds of people" explanations for deviant behavior (for instance, young males who commit violent crimes), the social disorganization approach examines the effects of "kinds of places" (specifically, different types of neighborhoods) in fostering conditions favorable or unfavorable to deviant behavior. Neighborhoods differ in their residents' capacity to control the behavior of people in public places, which is related to variables such as the transience of inhabitants, lack of community friendship networks, one-parent families, and unsupervised teenage peer groups. The more socially disorganized a neighborhood is along these dimensions, the greater the likelihood of local deviance. The theory was first advanced in the 1920s and 1930s and applied in Chicago by Clifford Shaw and Henry McKay (1942).

Rodney Stark's article, "Deviant Places," is a perfect example of the social disorganization perspective. He presents 30 propositions that seem to explain why deviance is more prevalent in some neighborhoods than in others. According to Stark, neighborhood poverty, transience, mixed residential/commercial use, population density, and dilapidation lead to moral resignation among residents, increased opportunities for disorderly behavior and crime, heightened motivation to engage in crime, and diminished social control over people in the community. This fuels a vicious circle, where law-abiding residents flee the neighborhood, greater numbers of crime-prone individuals are attracted to the neighborhood, and social control erodes further—begetting ever more crime and disorder.

It should be noted that even in the most socially disorganized and crime-ridden neighborhoods, only a minority of residents break the law. The theory does not predict that a majority of residents of such neighborhoods will commit crimes but only that disorganized communities will register a *higher rate* of crime than neighborhoods that are not disorganized.

One problem with the theory has to do with its central variable—the breakdown of social control in a neighborhood. The basic assumption is that weak social control fosters crime, but this proposition has rarely been tested directly, in part because it is somewhat difficult to measure the presence or absence of "social control."

The theories and perspectives sketched above all focus on general social causes of crime—subculture, social inequality, routine activities, and neighborhood characteristics. These factors may be considered either competing or complementary predictors, explaining why crime is more likely to occur within certain groups or in certain locations than in others. But how and why does crime unfold when it does, at the *microsocial* level? Routine activities theory offers a partial answer to this question, but it does not specifically address the *process* or *dynamics* of criminal events. What leads to a criminal act during face-to-face interaction between people? According to **symbolic interactionist theory**, crime is a situationally precarious outcome of social interactions—precarious because the outcome depends on individuals' subjective experiences and constructions of reality. From an interactionist perspective, therefore, the actions of offenders are more complex and less predictable than what is assumed by theories that link crime to the actor's social background, socialization, or economic opportunities. It is thus important to carefully analyze the interactional dynamics of face-to-face encounters between individuals, including "what it means, feels, sounds, tastes, or looks like to commit a particular crime" (Katz 1988:3).

David Luckenbill's article, "Criminal Homicide as a Situated Transaction," examines how homicide is produced in such microlevel social encounters, focusing on the interactions that take place immediately prior to a fatal attack. None of the homicides studied by Luckenbill were premeditated or planned in advance. All were preceded by fairly routine interactions between individuals, and in three-quarters of the cases, the offender and victim were initially involved in some pleasurable activity—partying, traveling, watching television, and so forth. Most of the offenders and victims knew each other as acquaintances, friends, or family members—which is consistent with homicide patterns in general, only about one-fifth of which involve strangers.

Luckenbill's central thesis is that in the course of ordinary social interaction a rupture occurs that transforms a normal encounter into a disputatious one. Typically, because of some perceived slight, one person will issue a challenge to the other, leading to a "character contest" in which one or both parties attempt to "save face" at the other's expense. Such transactions tend to escalate into increasingly belligerent verbal attacks or behaviors interpreted by the other party as offensive, even if they were not meant to be offensive. Luckenbill describes five stages of interpersonal exchanges that culminate in a fatal attack.

The interactionist perspective is a *situational* one. The question addressed is how and why a crime like murder happens in a particular setting with particular individuals. Again, this kind of analysis is very different from theories based on larger variables, such as the culture of violence, neighborhood disorganization, and social inequality. For interactionists, crime events are due to more immediate, situationally contingent factors like symbolic meanings and interpretations of others' behavior.

One problem with Luckenbill's study is the absence from his sample of cases of *premeditated killings*. This raises the question of whether the same situational dynamics he describes would be found when the killing was planned in advance. Premeditated killings differ from Luckenbill's in their lack of spontaneity and greater interactional predictability. Are premeditated killings also conditioned by "character contests," interpersonal challenges, and attempts to "save face," or is this process short-circuited when a murder is planned in advance and swiftly executed?

The last theory presented in Part I is another microlevel perspective on crime causation. Control theory, as presented by Travis Hirschi (1969) in his book, *Causes of Delinquency*, and then modified by Gottfredson and Hirschi in the form of **self-control theory** ("Crime and Low Self-Control") is presented as a general theory of crime: The theory purportedly explains all forms of criminal activity.

According to self-control theory, crime is rooted in the offender's psychic and emotional needs and desires, the gratification of which leads to criminal acts. According to Gottfredson and Hirschi, criminal acts "provide immediate gratification of desires" for money, sex, power, revenge, and so forth; are "exciting" and "thrilling"; and may provide "relief from momentary irritation." The theory identifies *low self-control* as the central cause of criminal behavior. Low self-control is defined as an individual's lack of restraint, predisposing him or her to pursue desires freed from conventional normative controls. It is *assumed* that people will be inclined to commit crime unless held in check by internal controls.

Low self-control is an individual, psychological trait, not a social phenomenon.

But the causes of low self-control are social. Why some individuals have low self-control and others have high self-control largely depends on socialization, mainly the *kind of child-rearing* the individual received in his or her early formative years. Effective child-rearing means that parents socialize children in accordance with conventional norms. Parents who supervise their children and who punish their misdeeds will instill self-restraint in them. Parental social control thus results in the child's self-control, which is likely to inhibit crime throughout the person's life. None of the other theories featured in Part I identify family relationships as the major determinant of criminal behavior, and most of them ignore the family altogether in favor of other causal variables.

In a nutshell, Gottfredson and Hirschi's theory posits the following cause–effect formula: ineffective child-rearing $\rightarrow$ low self-control $\rightarrow$ crime.

One problem with the theory is the apparent overlap between the concepts of low self-control and propensity to commit crime. Low self-control is posited as the *cause* of crime, but Gottfredson and Hirschi also use crime as an *indicator* of low self-control, which is tautological. They write that self-control is the "tendency of people to avoid criminal acts" (Gottfredson and Hirschi 1990:87). To test the proposition that low self-control causes a propensity to criminal behavior, operational measures of self-control—separate from crime—are needed but missing from the theory.

Gottfredson and Hirschi could have presented their propositions as complementary with other theories, that is, as identifying one important cause of crime. Instead, they take the bold position that low self-control is both a necessary and sufficient explanation for all crime and that all other explanations can be dismissed. Readers may find this extreme position unconvincing. Rather than replacing all other variables, low self-control could be theorized as one predictor, among others, of crime.

Part I is not an exhaustive survey of all possible causes of crime. The perspectives covered here are included because they are some of the *major sociological approaches* to understanding crime. Some popular "folk theories" are not included, such as the notion that guns or drugs cause crime. Guns, drugs, and alcohol may be considered "criminogenic commodities," as Mark Moore (1983) calls them, in that they are often present in criminal attacks and may increase the likelihood of a crime taking place. But to say that these commodities may be criminogenic in this sense is not to say that they are *causes* of crime in the sociological sense. Social scientists develop causal propositions based on social structural and situational variables, not on the basis of whether a specific commodity is present.

REFERENCES

Akers, Ronald. 1997. *Criminological Theories*. Los Angeles: Roxbury.

Cohen, Albert K. 1955. *Delinquent Boys: The Culture of the Gang*. Glencoe, IL: Free Press.

Donnerstein, Edward, and Daniel Linz. 1995. "The Media," in J. Q. Wilson and J. Petersilia (eds.), *Crime*, San Francisco: ICS Press.

Erlanger, Howard S. 1974. "The Empirical Status of the Subculture of Violence Thesis," *Social Problems* 22:280–291.

Glaser, Daniel. 1956. "Criminality Theories and Behavioral Images," *American Journal of Sociology* 61:433–444.

Gottfredson, Michael, and Travis Hirschi. 1990. *A General Theory of Crime*. Stanford, CT: Stanford University Press.

Hirschi, Travis. 1969. *Causes of Delinquency*. Berkeley: University of California Press.

Katz, Jack. 1988. *Seductions of Crime: Moral and Sensual Attractions in Doing Evil*. New York: Basic Books.

Matza, David. 1964. *Delinquency and Drift*. New York: John Wiley.

Merton, Robert K. 1938. "Social Structure and Anomie," *American Sociological Review* 3:672–682.

Miller, Walter B. 1958. "Lower-Class Culture as a Generating Milieu of Gang Delinquency," *Journal of Social Issues* 14:5–19.

Moore, Mark. 1983. "Controlling Criminogenic Commodities: Drugs, Guns, and Alcohol," in J. Q. Wilson (ed.), *Crime and Public Policy*, San Francisco: ICS Press.

Shaw, Clifford R., and Henry D. McKay. 1942. *Juvenile Delinquency and Urban Areas*. Chicago: University of Chicago Press.

Sykes, Gresham, and David Matza. 1957. "Techniques of Neutralization: A Theory of Delinquency," *American Journal of Sociology* 22: 664–670.

The Subculture of Violence

Marvin E. Wolfgang and Franco Ferracuti

Homicide is most prevalent, or the highest rates of homicide occur, among a relatively homogeneous subcultural group in any large urban community. Similar prevalent rates can be found in some rural areas. The value system of this group, we are contending, constitutes a subculture of violence. From a psychological viewpoint, we might hypothesize that the greater the degree of integration of the individual into this subculture, the higher the probability that his behavior will be violent in a variety of situations. From the sociological side, there should be a direct relationship between rates of homicide and the extent to which the subculture of violence represents a cluster of values around the theme of violence.

Except for war, probably the most highly reportable, socially visible, and serious form of violence is expressed in criminal homicide. Data show that in the United States rates are highest among males, non-whites, and the young adult ages. Rates for most serious crimes, particularly against the person, are highest in these same groups. In a Philadelphia study of 588 criminal homicides, for example, non-white males aged 20–24 had a rate of 92 per 100,000 compared with 3.4 for white males of the same ages. Females consistently had lower rates than males in their respective race groups (non-white females, 9.3; white females, 0.4, in the same study), although it should be noted, as we shall discuss later, that non-white females have higher rates than white males.[1]

It is possible to multiply these specific findings in any variety of ways; and although a subcultural affinity to violence appears to be principally present in large urban communities and increasingly in the adolescent population, some typical evidence of this phenomenon can be found, for example, in rural areas and among other adult groups. For example, a particular, very structured subculture of this kind can be found in Sardinia, in the central mountain area of the island. Pigliaru

From Marvin E. Wolfgang and Franco Ferracuti. 1967. *The Subculture of Violence*. London: Tavistock. Reprinted by permission of Taylor and Francis.

has conducted a brilliant analysis of the people from this area and of their criminal behavior, commonly known as the *vendetta barbaricina*.[2]

In Colombia, the well known *violencia* has been raging for the last 15 years, causing deaths of a total estimated between 200,000 and 300,000.[3] The homicide rate in several areas has been among the highest in the world, and homicide has been the leading cause of death for Colombian males aged between 15 and 45. Several causes, some political, initially associated with the rise of this phenomenon continue to exist, and, among them, a subcultural transmission of violence is believed to play an important role. More will be said later about the subcultural traditions of violence in Sardinia, Colombia, and elsewhere.

We suggest that, by identifying the groups with the highest rates of homicide, we should find in the most intense degree a subculture of violence; and, having focused on these groups, we should subsequently examine the value system of their subculture, the importance of human life in the scale of values, the kinds of expected reaction to certain types of stimulus, perceptual differences in the evaluation of stimuli, and the general personality structure of the subcultural actors. In the Philadelphia study it was pointed out that:

> . . . the significance of a jostle, a slightly derogatory remark, or the appearance of a weapon in the hands of an adversary are stimuli differentially perceived and interpreted by Negroes and whites, males and females. Social expectations of response in particular types of social interaction result in differential "definitions of the situation." A male is usually expected to defend the name and honor of his mother, the virtue of womanhood. . . and to accept no derogation about his race (even from a member of his own race), his age, or his masculinity. Quick re-

sort to physical combat as a measure of daring, courage, or defense of status appears to be a cultural expression, especially for lower socioeconomic class males of both races. When such a culture norm response is elicited from an individual engaged in social interplay with others who harbor the same response mechanism, physical assaults, altercations, and violent domestic quarrels that result in homicide are likely to be common. The upper-middle and upper social class value system defines subcultural mores, and considers many of the social and personal stimuli that evoke a combative reaction in the lower classes as "trivial." Thus, there exists a cultural antipathy between many folk rationalizations of the lower class, and of males of both races, on the one hand, and the middle-class legal norms under which they live, on the other.[4]

This kind of analysis, combined with other data about delinquency, the lower-class social structure, its value system, and its emphasis on aggression, suggest the thesis of a violent subculture, or, by pushing the normative aspects a little further, a *subculture of violence*. Among many juvenile gangs, as has repeatedly been pointed out, there are violent feuds, meetings, territorial fights, and the use of violence to prove "heart," to maintain or to acquire "rep."

It appears valid to suggest that there are, in a heterogeneous population, differences in ideas and attitudes toward the use of violence and that these differences can be observed through variables related to social class and possibly through psychological correlates. There is evidence that modes of control of expressions of aggression in children vary among the social classes. Lower-class boys, for example, appear more likely to be oriented toward direct expression of aggression than are middle-class boys. The type of punishment meted out by parents to misbehaving children is related to this class orientation toward aggression. Lower-class mothers report that they or their husbands are likely to strike their children or threaten to strike them, whereas middle-class mothers report that their type of punishment is psychological rather than physical; and boys who are punished physically express aggression more directly than those who are punished psychologically. As Martin Gold has suggested, the middle-class child is more likely to turn his aggression inward; in the extreme and as an adult he will commit suicide.[5] But the lower-class child is more accustomed to a parent–child relationship which during punishment is for the moment that of attacker and attacked. The target for aggression, then, is external; aggression is directed toward others.[6]

The existence of a subculture of violence is partly demonstrated by examination of the social groups and individuals who experience the highest rates of manifest violence. This examination need not be confined to the study of one national or ethnic group. On the contrary, the existence of a subculture of violence could perhaps receive even cross-cultural confirmation. Criminal homicide is the most acute and highly reportable example of this type of violence, but some circularity of thought is obvious in the effort to specify the dependent variable (homicide), and also to infer the independent variable (the existence of a subculture of violence). The highest rates of rape, aggravated assaults, persistency in arrests for assaults (recidivism) among these groups with high rates of homicide are, however, empirical addenda to the postulation of a subculture of violence. Residential propinquity of these same groups reinforces the socio-psychological impact which the integration of this subculture engenders. Sutherland's thesis of "differential association," or a psychological reformulation of the same theory in terms of learning process, could effectively be employed to describe more fully this impact in

its intensity, duration, repetition, and frequency. The more thoroughly integrated the individual is into this subculture, the more intensely he embraces its prescriptions of behavior, its conduct norms, and integrates them into his personality structure. The degree of integration may be measured partly and crudely by public records of contact with the law, so high arrest rates, particularly high rates of assault crimes and high rates of recidivism for assault crimes among groups that form the subculture of violence, may indicate allegiance to the values of violence.

We have said that overt physical violence often becomes a common subculturally expected response to certain stimuli. However, it is not merely rigid conformity to the demands and expectations of other persons, as Henry and Short seem to suggest, that results in the high probability of homicide.[7] Excessive, compulsive, or apathetic conformity of middle-class individuals to the value system of their social group is a widely recognized cultural malady. Our concern is with the value elements of violence as an integral component of the subculture which experiences high rates of homicide. It is conformity to *this* set of values, and not rigid conformity *per se*, that gives important meaning to the subculture of violence.

If violence is a common subcultural response to certain stimuli, penalties should exist for deviation from *this* norm. The comparatively nonviolent individual may be ostracized, but if social interaction must occur because of residential propinquity to others sharing in a subculture of violence, he is most likely to be treated with disdain or indifference. One who previously was considered a member of the ingroup, but who has rebelled or retreated from the subculture, is now an outgroup member, a possible threat, and one for the group to avoid. Alienation or avoidance takes him out of the normal reach of most homicide attacks, which are highly personal offenses occurring with greatest frequency among friends, relatives, and associates. If social interaction continues, however, the deviant from the subculture of violence who fails to respond to a potentially violent situation, may find himself a victim of an adversary who continues to conform to the violence values.

It is not far-fetched to suggest that a whole culture may accept a value set dependent upon violence, demand or encourage adherence to violence, and penalize deviation. During periods of war the whole nation accepts the principle of violence against the enemy. The nonviolent citizen drafted into military service may adopt values associated with violence as an intimately internalized reenforcement for his newly acquired rationalization to kill. War involves selective killing of an outgroup enemy, and in this respect may be viewed as different from most forms of homicide. Criminal homicide may be either "selective" or nondiscriminate slaying, although the literature on homicide consistently reveals its intragroup nature. However, as in wartime combat between opposing individuals when an "it-was-either-him-or-me" situation arises, similar attitudes and reactions occur among participants in homicide. It may be relevant to point out that in the Philadelphia study of criminal homicide, 65 percent of the offenders and 47 percent of the victims had previous arrest records. Homicide, it appears, is often a situation not unlike that of confrontations in wartime combat, in which two individuals committed to the value of violence came together, and in which chance, prowess, or possession of a particular weapon dictates the identity of the slayer and of the slain. The peaceful non-combatant in both sets of circumstances is penalized, because of the allelomimetic behavior of the group supporting violence, by his being ostracized as an outgroup member, and he is thereby segregated (imprisoned, in wartime, as a conscientious objector) from his original group. If he is not segregated, but continues to interact with his original group in the public street or on the front line that represents the culture of violence, he may fall victim to the shot or stab from one of the group who still embraces the value of violence.

An internal need for aggression and a readiness to use violence by the individual who belongs to a subculture of violence should find their psychological foundation in personality traits and in attitudes which can, through careful studies, be assessed in such a way as to lead to a differential psychology of these subjects. Psychological tests have been repeatedly employed to study the differential characteristics of criminals; and if a theoretical frame of reference involving a subculture of violence is used, it should be possible to sharpen the discriminatory power of these tests. The fact that a subject belongs to a specific subculture (in our case, a deviant one), defined by the ready use of violence, should, among other consequences, cause the subject to adopt a differential perception of his environment and its stimuli. Variations in the surrounding world, the continuous challenges and daily frustrations which are faced and solved by the adaptive mechanism of the individual, have a greater chance of being perceived and reacted upon, in a subculture of violence, as menacing, aggressive stimuli which call for immediate defense and counter-aggression.

We have said that overt use of force or violence, either in interpersonal relationships or in group interaction, is generally viewed as a reflection of basic values that stand apart from the dominant, the central, or the parent culture. Our hypothesis is that this overt (and often illicit) expression of violence (of which homicide is only the most extreme) is part of a subcultural normative system, and that this system is reflected in the psychological traits of the subculture participants. In the light of our discussion of the caution to be exercised in interpretative analysis, in order to tighten the logic of this analysis, and to support the thesis of a subculture of violence, we offer the following corollary propositions:

1. *No subculture can be totally different from or totally in conflict with the society of which it is a part.* A subculture of violence is not entirely an expression of violence, for there must be interlocking value elements shared with the dominant culture. It should not be necessary to contend that violent aggression is the predominant mode of expression in order to show that the value system is set apart as subcultural. When violence occurs in the dominant culture, it is usually legitimized, but most often is vicarious and a part of phantasy. Moreover, subcultural variations, we have earlier suggested, may be viewed as quantitative and relative. The extent of difference from the larger culture and the degree of intensity, which violence as a subcultural theme may possess, are variables that could and should be measured by known socio-psychological techniques. At present, we are required to rely almost entirely upon expressions of violence in conduct of various forms—parent–child relationships, parental discipline, domestic quarrels, street fights, delinquent conflict gangs, criminal records of assaultive behavior, criminal homicides, etc.—but the number of psychometrically oriented studies in criminology is steadily increasing in both quantity and sophistication, and from them a reliable differential psychology of homicides should emerge to match current sociological research.

2. *To establish the existence of a subculture of violence does not require that the actors sharing in these basic value elements should express violence in all situations.* The normative system designates that in some types of social interaction a violent and physically aggressive response is either expected or required of all members sharing in that system of values. That the actors' behavior expectations occur in more than one situation is obvious. There is a variety of circumstances in which homicide occurs, and the history of past aggressive crimes in high proportions, both in the victims and in the offenders, attests to the multisituational character of the use of violence and to its interpersonal characteristics.[8] But, obviously, persons living in a subcultural milieu designated as a subculture of violence cannot and do not engage in violence continuously, otherwise normal social functioning would be virtually impossible. We are merely suggesting, for example, that ready access to weapons in this milieu may become essential for protection against others who respond in similarly violent ways in certain situations, and that the carrying of knives or other protective devices becomes a common symbol of willingness to participate in violence, to expect violence, and to be ready for its retaliation.

3. *The potential resort or willingness to resort to violence in a variety of situations emphasizes the penetrating and diffusive character of this culture theme.* The number and kinds of situations in which an individual uses violence may be viewed as an index of the extent to which he has assimilated the values associated with violence. This index should also be reflected by quantitative differences in a variety of psychological dimensions, from differential perception of violent stimuli to different value expressions in questionnaire-type instruments. The range of violence from minor assault to fatal injury, or certainly the maximum of violence expected, is rarely made explicit for all situations to which an individual may be exposed. Overt violence may even occasionally be a chance result of events.

But clearly this range and variability of behavioral expressions of aggression suggest the importance of psychological dimensions in measuring adherence to a subculture of violence.

4. *The subcultural ethos of violence may be shared by all ages in a subsociety, but this ethos is most prominent in a limited age group, ranging from late adolescence to middle age.* We are not suggesting that a particular ethnic, sex, or age group all share in common the use of potential threats of violence. We are contending merely that the known empirical distribution of conduct, which expresses the sharing of this violence theme, shows greatest localization, incidence, and frequency in limited subgroups and reflects differences in learning about violence as a problem-solving mechanism.

5. *The counter-norm is nonviolence.* Violation of expected and required violence is most likely to result in ostracism from the group. Alienation of some kind, depending on the range of violence expectations that are unmet, seems to be a form of punitive action most feasible to this subculture. The juvenile who fails to live up to the conflict gang's requirements is pushed outside the group. The adult male who does not defend his honor or his female companion will be socially emasculated. The "coward" is forced to move out of the territory, to find new friends and make new alliances. Membership is lost in the subsociety sharing the cluster of attitudes positively associated with violence. If forced withdrawal or voluntary retreat are not acceptable modes of response to engaging in the counter-norm, then execution, as is reputed to occur in organized crime, may be the extreme punitive measure.

6. *The development of favorable attitudes toward, and the use of, violence in a subculture usually involve learned behavior and a process of differential learning, associa-*

tion,[9] or identification.[10] Not all persons exposed—even equally exposed—to the presence of a subculture of violence absorb and share in the values in equal portions. Differential personality variables must be considered in an integrated social-psychological approach to an understanding of the subcultural aspects of violence. We have taken the position that aggression is a learned response, socially facilitated and integrated, as a habit, in more or less permanent form, among the personality characteristics of the aggressor. Aggression, from a psychological standpoint, has been defined by Buss as "the delivery of noxious stimuli in an interpersonal context."[11] Aggression seems to possess two major classes of reinforcers: the pain and injury inflicted upon the victim and its extrinsic rewards. Both are present in a subculture of violence, and their mechanism of action is facilitated by the social support that the aggressor receives in his group. The relationship between aggression, anger, and hostility is complicated by the habit characteristics of the first, the drive state of the second, and the attitudinal interpretative nature of the third. Obviously, the immediacy and the short temporal sequence of anger with its autonomic components make it difficult to study a criminal population that is some distance removed from the anger-provoked event. Hostility, although amenable to easier assessment, does not give a clear indication or measure of physical attack because of its predominantly verbal aspects. However, it may dispose to or prepare for aggression.

7. *The use of violence in a subculture is not necessarily viewed as illicit conduct and the users therefore do not have to deal with feelings of guilt about their aggression.* Violence can become a part of the life style, the theme of solving difficult problems or problem situations. It should be stressed that the problems and situations to which we refer arise mostly within the subculture, for vio-

lence is used mostly between persons and groups who themselves rely upon the same supportive values and norms. A carrier and user of violence will not be burdened by conscious guilt, then, because generally he is not attacking the representatives of the non-violent culture, and because the recipient of this violence may be described by similar class status, occupational, residential, age, and other attribute categories which characterize the subuniverse of the collectivity sharing in the subculture of violence. Even law-abiding members of the local subculture area may not view various illegal expressions of violence as menacing or immoral. Furthermore, when the attacked see their assaulters as agents of the same kind of aggression they themselves represent, violent retaliation is readily legitimized by a situationally specific rationale, as well as by the generally normative supports for violence.

Probably no single theory will ever explain the variety of observable violent behavior. However, the subculture-of-violence approach offers, we believe, the advantage of bringing together psychological and sociological constructs to aid in the explanation of the concentration of violence in specific socioeconomic groups and ecological areas.

We are not prepared to assert how a subculture of violence arises. Perhaps there are several ways in different cultural settings. It may be that even within the same culture a collective conscience and allegiance to the use of violence develop into a subculture from the combination of more than one birth process, i.e. as a negative reaction to the communica-tion of goals from the parent culture, as a positive reaction to this communication coupled with a willingness to use negative means, and as a positive absorption of an indigenous set of subcultural values that, as a system of interlocking values, are the antithesis of the main culture themes.

NOTES

1. Marvin E. Wolfgang, *Patterns in Criminal Homicide*, Philadelphia: University of Pennsylvania Press, 1958.
2. A. Pigliaru, *La vendetta barbaricina come ordinamento giuridico*, Milano: Giuffrè, 1959.
3. G. Guzman Campos, O. Fals Borda, and E. Umaña Luna, "*La Violencia en Colombia: Estudio de un proceso social,*" Bogotá: Tercer Mundo, 1962.
4. Wolfgang, *Patterns in Criminal Homicide*, pp. 188–189.
5. Martin Gold, "Suicide, Homicide and the Socialization of Aggression," *American Journal of Sociology* (May, 1958) 63: 651–661.
6. *Ibid.*
7. Andrew F. Henry and James F. Short, Jr., *Suicide and Homicide*, Glencoe, IL: The Free Press, 1954, pp. 16–18, 91–92, 124–125.
8. Wolfgang, *Patterns in Criminal Homicide.*
9. Edwin H. Sutherland and Donald E. Cressey, *Principles of Criminology*, Philadelphia: Lippincott, 1955.
10. Daniel Glaser, "Criminality Theories and Behavioral Images," *American Journal of Sociology* (1956) 5:433–444.
11. A. H. Buss, *The Psychology of Aggression*, New York: Wiley, 1961, pp. 1–2.

Crime and Social Inequality

Elliott Currie

The debate over the relative importance of *cultural* versus material or *structural* factors in crime is a long one in American social science, but one that has shed more heat than light, in good part because the meager and inconclusive evidence it has generated has been overwhelmed by the ideological purposes to which it has been put. In order to make sense of that frustrating debate, it helps to distinguish between two different versions of the argument that criminal violence is the reflection of cultural attitudes or values—the *soft* version and the *hard*.

The *soft* version rests on the commonsense argument that there is inevitably an *interaction* between the structural and the cultural: the external conditions surrounding a group will have an effect, especially in the long run, on the attitudes and values they hold about themselves, about society as a whole, and about the moral weight of illegal activities and the use of violence. These attitudes, over time, may crystallize into more or less coher-

ent value systems that may persist to some extent even if the original conditions change. Nevertheless, the values cannot be usefully *detached* from the structural conditions that gave rise to them. It is therefore highly probable that significant changes in those conditions will be followed by shifts in the values as well.

Some variant of this soft cultural argument underlay much of the most influential criminological theory of the 1950s and 1960s. The chief problem that the theory sought to explain was the emergence of delinquent youth gangs in the cities of the "affluent" society. Beneath the specific concern over the troublesome behavior of the gangs was the deeper question of the reasons for the paradox noted in the previous chapter: the persistence—or indeed growth—of alienation and violence in the midst of abundance. Students of delinquency began to argue that the rise of the gangs reflected the growth of "subcultural" values stressing "toughness" and preda-

From Elliott Currie. 1985. *Confronting Crime*. New York: Pantheon. Reprinted by permission of Pantheon Books, a division of Random House,© 1985 by Elliott Currie.

tory behavior in place of legitimate achievement. These subcultural values in turn arose out of a crucial contradiction of postwar affluence: the fact that some groups were systematically blocked by race and economic disadvantage from achieving the goals of status and material well-being encouraged by the larger culture.

This argument drew to a great extent on the theoretical work of the Columbia sociologist Robert K. Merton (1957) and was most forcefully expressed in the classic study *Delinquency and Opportunity*, by Richard Cloward and Lloyd Ohlin (1960). In addition to offering an explanation of why delinquent gangs behaved as they did, the contention that blocked opportunities generated delinquent subcultures offered one answer to the question of how such widespread and virulent delinquency could appear in such a rich country. It suggested that more important than the sheer material impact of *absolute* deprivation was the social-psychological wound of *relative* deprivation—of being hindered from attaining what others were able to attain. The implications for social action seemed clear. Urban delinquency would continue and perhaps increase even in the face of economic growth and abundance unless the barriers to opportunity were removed. This theme was an important intellectual influence on the War on Poverty in the sixties, particularly its efforts at education, job training, and community organization.

A similar approach appears in Judith and Peter Blau's (1982) more recent study. The Blaus found strong associations between homicide rates and economic inequality, and even stronger ones for racial inequality. They also found that sheer poverty was a less powerful explanation for variations in homicide than inequality. Hence they, too, concluded that what most predictably generates violent crime is not the simple absence of material goods, but rather the deeper attitudes of hopelessness and alienation produced by inequalities that are perceived as unjust. Great inequalities of any kind, they argue, cause corresponding alienation in those at the bottom; but in professedly democratic societies, the experience of *ascribed* inequalities—justified by group membership rather than performance—are especially alienating. "Pronounced ethnic inequality in resources implies that there are great riches within view but not within reach of many people destined to live in poverty." The result is "resentment, frustration, hopelessness, and alienation." Once again, it is *relative* deprivation that is most salient—the sense of being unjustly deprived of what others have. Violence results "not so much from lack of advantages as from being taken advantage of." Those attitudes, moreover, often wreak havoc on close personal relations (especially in the family), thus compounding the problem by weakening some of the most important "informal" bulwarks against crime.

This sort of argument does not deny the importance of attitudes and values in understanding crime; far from it. To do so would amount to suggesting that human beings are simply automatons who respond in some visceral fashion to the bare fact of material conditions. But the soft cultural argument regards those values as the reflection of circumstances—in particular, the systematic exclusion of the poor and especially the minority poor from realistic chances of success and well-being in the terms prescribed by the larger culture.

The *hard* version of this argument, on the other hand, makes culture into something close to an independent force that shapes the fates of the minority poor. In the sixties this was often phrased in terms of a "subculture of violence" afflicting certain groups, most notably American blacks. The "subculture of violence" turned the norms of the larger culture upside down by placing a positive value on the use of violence to resolve personal problems. Sometimes this was just another expression of the soft argument that persistent discrimination often created tragically self-defeating attitudes among its victims, a line of reasoning that led logically to a sense of urgency about ending discrimination. But the harder version saw discrimination as mainly if not entirely in the past (indeed, the subculture was seen as primarily a legacy of slavery); by now it was the subculture itself, not current discrimination or the systematic blockage of opportunities through economic and technological change, that kept many blacks from achieving a successful and orderly life in the more open society of the sixties. A more recent variant of the argument has often been deployed by conservatives to explain the apparently paradoxical divergence in social conditions among American blacks since the 1960s—the glaring contrast between an increasingly successful majority and an increasingly impoverished, demoralized, and violent minority within a minority. That growing numbers of blacks have succeeded in the American economy in recent years is taken as evidence that there are no longer substantial racial barriers to success, and that what must therefore explain the demoralization and violence of the black poor is mainly their culture.

If all that was being said here was that a history of brutal discrimination and exclusion has often left its mark, fostering attitudes and behavior that can be brutal, self-defeating, and difficult to change, not many would now disagree. But the hard subculture argument says more; it says that these attitudes are no longer significantly generated by the current conditions of minority life in America, and thus that they are therefore unlikely to be much affected by improvements in those conditions.

Several crucial limitations of the hard view of crime and culture may be quickly stated. To begin with, it fits poorly with the historical trend in violent crime in recent decades—a fact noted by some critics as early as the sixties. It isn't unreasonable to argue that the inheritors of a legacy of slavery and harsh discrimination might carry a repertoire of violent responses with them as they moved away from their rural roots and into the cities. But the cultural argument is far less persuasive as an explanation of why criminal violence *worsened* as the descendants of slaves moved farther and farther from that experience, chronologically and geographically. (Studies of the careers of recent migrants to the cities drove home this objection; it was repeatedly shown that new entrants to the cities exhibited less social pathology than those who had been there longer and had thus been more heavily exposed to the demoralizing forces of urban conditions.) Moreover, the fact that some blacks have moved rapidly into the ranks of the stable and steady middle class while others remained trapped in instability and poverty would seem logically to contradict rather than support the hard cultural argument. After all, the culture at issue is presumably common to American blacks in general, most of whom are descended from slaves. Since the culture is common to the black community while the demoralization is not, it remains for us to explain—in terms *other* than the common culture—why some have managed to escape it and some not.

At the same time, there is an even more stubborn difficulty with the hard cultural argument: no one has yet been able to *find* the subculture of violence—and not for lack of trying. Many sophisticated quantitative studies have sought to determine just how much of the variation in criminal violence between different states or cities can be attributed to such cultural values versus the more *structural* forces of low income, poor education, and so on. Obviously, separating these things is harder in practice than in theory, and it is not surprising that the results have been inconclusive. Usually the research strategy is to use race itself (or sometimes Southern origin) as *indirect* indications of the subculture of violence—a dubious practice made necessary by the fact that the subculture itself has proven impossible to measure more directly. Several studies have concluded that once the structural factors have been accounted for, there is no remaining effect of race or region on the rate of violent crime; others find that some—usually small—effect remains. Yet it is difficult to attribute that differential—where it appears—reliably to culture without becoming circular, since we're never sure whether the research has managed to isolate and control for every structural feature of black life in America that might just as effectively explain it.

Again, however, the point is not to reject the influence of cultural forces on crime altogether, but to steer a middle course between the extremes of this increasingly fruitless debate between structure and culture. To say that there is little evidence for a distinctive subculture of violence is not to claim that violent attitudes and responses are not evident among the minority poor; that would be to fall once again—as liberals often have—into the trap of the denial of pathology. It *is*, however, to argue against the implications of intractability and permanence that pervade the hard version of the argument and the smug defeatism about the possibilities of social action that often accompanies it. The hard cultural argument exculpates contemporary institutions and policies far too blithely. It implicitly denies that society bears any responsibility to address these problems or has any realistic hope of doing so in ways that will prevent violence. The soft version is not only compatible with a more generous and active approach to the problems of the disadvantaged, but lends itself to it, as we've seen in the case of "opportu-

nity" theory. The existence of self-defeating values and attitudes among some of the poor thus becomes a signal for redoubled efforts to confront the mutable conditions that nourish them. The exact form those efforts should take is a complicated question; I do not think that the answers of the liberals of the 1960s were entirely adequate, but I will leave that issue for the final chapter. Suffice it to say here that the question of how stubborn the culture of the deprived may be is an empirical one. The answer is not dictated by fate or even by our tragic racial history; we will know it only when we begin to move decisively against the continuing inequalities of American life.

According to figures from the Organization for Economic Cooperation and Development (OECD), we had the widest spread of income inequality in the late sixties and early seventies of any comparable developed country. The narrowest spread was in Holland, where the share of total personal income going to the poorest fifth of the population was more than double that in the United States. During the same period, according to Dane Archer (1978), the homicide rate in America averaged more than thirteen times the Dutch rate, and the murder rate in New York City about ten times that in Amsterdam. In Denmark, where public expenditures amount to about half of the gross national product, versus a third in the United States (a comparison that greatly understates the real difference in social priorities, because so much of America's public spending—and so little of Denmark's—goes for defense), the homicide rate in the late seventies ranged between about one-tenth and one-nineteenth of the American rate.

Some conservative writers have argued that the relatively low Japanese crime rate is evidence that more market-based societies are relatively free of crime because they have eschewed the destructive lures of egalitarianism and public responsibility for the collective welfare. But this betrays a fundamental misconception about Japanese society. Among OECD countries, the Japanese are exceeded only by Holland, Sweden, and Norway in the extent to which they have narrowed the range of income inequality between rich and poor, and by Holland and Sweden alone in the proportion of personal income that goes to the bottom fifth of the population. Moreover, the elaborate provisions for job security and other private cushions against the impact of the market in Japan have been held up for years as models that the United States might wish to follow. In this respect, Japan is far closer to the welfare states of Western Europe than to the United States, which is uniquely lacking in the mechanisms of reciprocity and mutual obligation that have been developed in other industrial societies.

There are many ways to describe this difference in numbers; let me borrow a few from Robert B. Reich's (1983) powerful discussion of America's relative failure, among industrial societies, to develop effective social-service programs to ensure the well-being of its work force—worker's compensation and benefits for the unemployed, children, the aged, the handicapped, and the disabled. The United States spends just 14 percent of its GNP on these programs; Sweden spends 33.8 percent, West Germany 30.6 percent, the Netherlands 27.7 percent, France, 22 percent. The Japanese government spends 17 percent of its GNP on such services, but this figure is misleadingly low because it does not reflect the substantial contributions made by Japanese employers, in contrast to their American counterparts.

This isn't just a matter of levels of spending. What these figures represent is a historical commitment—often achieved through long and painful political struggle—to shift the moral balance of these societies toward greater concern for social solidarity and mutual support. The United States is the industrial country whose cultural and political traditions have been least favorable to that kind of commitment, the country in which the "forces of the market" have been least cushioned and regulated in the name of the wellbeing of its people. Can it be merely coincidental that it is also the country most torn by interpersonal violence?

These relatively crude comparisons, moreover, are supported by every sophisticated study we have of the cross-national relationships between inequality and violent crime. The problems in comparing different countries' crime rates are formidable, but—used carefully—international statistics on homicide are reliable enough to permit useful comparisons. The results have been consistent and revealing. Around the world, at every level of economic development, increasing equality goes hand in hand with lower risks of homicide.

Thus, in a careful analysis of murder rates in thirty-one countries, from poor ones in the Third World to advanced industrial societies, John and Valerie Braithwaite (1980) concluded that higher homicide rates were linked with several measures of economic inequality—a broad gap between the rich and the average wage earner, large disparities in income between workers in different sectors of industry, and a low per capita consumption of protein—usually indicating a "wide gulf between the poor and the remainder of the population." Using only slightly different measures, Stephen Messner (1980) arrived at similar conclusions in a study of thirty-nine countries, again spanning the range of economic development. Income inequality explained a very substantial 35 percent of the differences in homicide among these countries, even when several other factors—including population density, degree of urbanization, and level of economic development—were taken into account.

Historians and social scientists have often argued that growing welfare and growing crime in the sixties were both *responses* to the same set of underlying conditions—especially migration to the cities prompted by mechanization of agriculture (particularly in the South) and the resulting breakdown of traditional livelihoods and of patterns of informal social support and control. If welfare was a *cause* of crime, we'd expect crime to be worse where the welfare system was more generous and less so where it was more sparing (just as we'd have expected crime to rise in response to the public assistance programs of the thirties). But stubborn reality once again asserts itself. Not only is the American welfare state the least generous among modern industrial societies, but within the United States welfare is most meager in many of the states with the worst levels of criminal violence, and relatively generous in some of the most tranquil.

Consider two states whose approaches to social welfare have traditionally been at opposite extremes of generosity. In Texas, the average welfare payment for an AFDC family in 1980, one of the lowest in the country, amounted to all of $109 a month (and had dropped from its level of ten years before, even in constant dollars). In Wisconsin, the average AFDC payment was $366 a month, one of the country's highest—up by more than two-thirds since 1970. With three times the population and more than five times the number of poor people, Texas actually had only slightly more total AFDC families than Wisconsin. Few states left their citizens more at the beneficent mercy of the market system than Texas; few so cushioned them from its vicissitudes as Wisconsin—thus few presumably so wantonly exposed them to the risks of demoralization, depravity, and violence. And

the effect on crime? In 1980, the homicide rate in Texas was about six times that in Wisconsin; Houston's murder rate was five times higher than Milwaukee's.

What little specific research we have on how economic assistance to the poor affects crime supports these observations. James DeFronzo's (1983) analysis of AFDC levels and crime rates found that higher AFDC payments had a clear and consistent negative effect on rates of homicide, burglary, and rape. DeFronzo calculated that increasing the AFDC payment by just $10 a month for each member of a welfare family would reduce the murder rate by about one per one hundred thousand.

Those who argue that public assistance causes crime must also be prepared to explain why criminal violence rose in the late seventies and early eighties, when income supports were dropping significantly. It's more plausible to argue the other way around—that declining support may have been a factor in the surge of criminal violence in those years despite enormous increases in imprisonment. Precisely to what extent the shrinking of the American welfare state may help explain that phenomenon, we do not know. But it is difficult to maintain that our excessive generosity, fueled by misguided egalitarian zeal, was to blame.

I don't mean to exaggerate the achievements of the welfare state. Welfare in the United States remains a demeaning and alienating system that all too often is a mean-spirited and inadequate substitute for the provision of sustaining employment. Even in more generous countries, the welfare state has often represented a series of ad hoc, sometimes reluctant, attempts to moderate but not to correct the stresses and dislocations of a still largely unregulated market system. But in our time the more common and more destructive error is in the opposite direction—to deny or to minimize the important victories of the welfare state in humanizing life under modern industrial capitalism. Lowering the level of interpersonal violence is only one of those victories; but it is not a minor one.

It isn't accidental, then, that among developed countries, the United States is afflicted simultaneously with the worst rates of violent crime, the widest spread of income inequality, and the most severe public policies toward the disadvantaged. The industrial societies that have escaped our extremes of criminal violence tend either to have highly developed public sectors with fairly generous systems of income support, relatively well-developed employment policies, and other cushions against the "forces of the market," or (like Japan) to accomplish much the same ends through private institutions backed by an ethos of social obligation and mutual responsibility. By any measure we can construct, these countries have been less plagued by the extremes of inequality and economic insecurity. Our pattern of development into an advanced industrial society, on the other hand, has been unusually harsh and disruptive of the conditions that inhibit interpersonal violence.

This distinctly American pattern helps us to put in perspective another common argument—that prosperity causes crime. We've already examined the "paradox" of rising crime amid rising affluence. But some argue further that improvement in the material conditions of life, by itself, increases crime. Proponents of this view cite the rising crime rates in some affluent societies after the Second World War, especially the United States during the economic expansion of the sixties. Like the related argument that equality generates crime, this one implies that the crime problem cannot be made better by efforts to improve social conditions, particularly for the disadvantaged, and may be made worse. Sometimes this leads to a passive and fatalistic insistence that crime will always be with us, since it is caused by

trends we wouldn't want to interfere with, even if we could; sometimes, to regressive yearning for a past when there was more poverty but also less crime—a form of nostalgia that lends itself nicely to demands for the restoration of authoritarian controls in the family, the classroom, and the justice system.

In this simplistic form, the argument is quite wrong. It is not true that material prosperity, in itself, causes criminal violence or that violence is fostered by "improving social conditions." But there are different *varieties* of prosperity—and the variety we have encouraged in America powerfully intensifies the social conditions that do generate violent crime. Recognizing this will help us comprehend why the American experience with criminal violence has been so crucially different from that of other developed societies. It also has vital implications for social policy in the future.

The issue is complicated by the fact that prosperity may affect violent crime differently than it does property crime. Most evidence suggests that property crimes may increase with affluence (though those crimes have been reported so unreliably that conclusions must remain tentative). When there is more to steal, more will be stolen, other things being equal; the declining need for theft may be outstripped by increasing opportunity. But serious criminal violence is another story. It is hardly the prosperous, after all, who now fill the prisons—with a few spectacular exceptions. Nor is it among the prosperous countries—except for the United States—that we find those most afflicted with criminal violence. The worst violent crime is found in some Third World countries wracked by desperate poverty, especially parts of the Caribbean, Latin America, and Africa. In the late sixties, when some pundits were shaking their heads over the tendency of "affluence" to produce crime, Mexico's homicide rate was twenty-six times Holland's, Trinidad and Tobago's about eighty-eight times New Zealand's, and Manila's about twenty-seven times Vienna's (Archer 1978).

The evidence is strong that violence ordinarily *declines* as societies become more prosperous. A familiar sociological argument holds that the transition from the presumably more cohesive communities of the preindustrial era to the more fragmented ones of modern industrial societies *necessarily* involves a decline in social integration and a corresponding rise in crime and other social pathologies. But the record has actually been more complicated—and more encouraging. The best historical evidence shows that interpersonal violence was generally high in preindustrial Europe. It probably increased temporarily—at least in some places—with the first drastic disruptions wrought by early and harsh industrialization, which threw millions—especially the young—off the land and into the cities, without livelihoods, income, or the traditional supports of family and local community. But then, in most cases, things got better. In much of Europe and, with reservations, the United States, criminal violence seems to have declined in the late nineteenth century as the displaced were gradually, if imperfectly, integrated into stable occupational and communal roles in the industrial order and granted broader access to education and political participation. (One important reservation is that criminal violence remained high in urban black communities in America).

The "humanizing" effect of industrialization and democratization can also be observed in cross-national studies. As Messner (1982) has shown in a study of fifty countries, economic development—as measured by the growth of Gross National Product per capita—is associated, on balance, with declining rates of homicide. Why? Economic development ordinarily reduces the level of violence because, over the long run, it reduces economic inequality. As Messner puts it, "The more developed societies do not exhibit especially high levels of homicide, in part because the greater equality in the distribution of income accompanying development serves to deflate the homicide rate."

But it is true that economic growth in some countries *has* been accompanied by increasing criminal violence, even while the general level of affluence has been rising. What this tells us, though, is not that increasing affluence necessarily causes crime, but that something has gone badly awry in the process of growth itself.

To understand what has gone wrong, it is helpful to look at the social forces that keep crime relatively low in certain communities that are poor in material terms. Though the case is often overstated, it is true that some (though not all) poor countries have fairly low crime rates. This is not, however, a mysteriously benign effect of poverty; rather, as students of crime in the Third World have often pointed out, it is usually attributable to a strong and encompassing community life that offers meaningful work and family roles in the midst of material deprivation. In such a context, even the very poor may have socially valued occupations, as well as close, supportive relations with their families, religious associations, and other local institutions. These relationships provide not only material assistance, but also a less tangible but no less important sense of social purpose, cooperation, and mutual responsibility. (At the same time, in communities where *most* people are poor, inequalities of material well-being are likely to be less glaringly evident, and their implications for self-esteem and social status less encompassing.)

How these circumstances may influence crime is illustrated in a recent study of delinquency in rural India by Clayton Hartjen

(1982) who found a surprisingly low level of juvenile crime, despite widespread poverty. Why? According to Hartjen, part of the answer is that "Indians are immersed in a network of role relationships that involve a variety of obligations toward kin, *jati* [subcaste], and community." Children and youths are "included in almost all forms of social activity," notably meaningful work; this is especially true in agriculture, but "even in non-agricultural commercial enterprises, children are working: filling tires with air, packing groceries in the tiny shops along the streets, or working with their parents on construction and highway crews." Above all, the place of Indian citizens in the larger community is not so thoroughly dependent as in many wealthier societies on their economic performance. "Regardless of one's position in the economic structure," Hartjen writes, "one still belongs to the larger social system in terms of family, *jati*, and community membership. An Indian may be low on the membership hierarchy, but he or she is still a member."

Such relationships are important bulwarks against interpersonal violence both because they provide a fundamental sense of belonging to a larger supportive community and because they provide the setting in which informal social sanctions against aggression and crime can operate effectively. And this helps explain what has gone wrong in those countries where growth has, if anything, brought intensified violence. Economic development within the market system tends to undermine traditional institutions of support and mutual obligation; what is most crucial in influencing the pattern of violence and crime is the extent to which these traditional supports manage to survive in the face of that disruption (recall Japan's private mechanisms of social obligation) or are supplanted by new ones (Western Europe's welfare states). Where this happens, the overall effect is to decrease inter-

personal violence over time. Where it fails to happen, economic growth may weaken or destroy the supportive relations that existed in more traditional communities without putting anything of substance in their place. The result is an impoverished rural and urban underclass deprived of respectable livelihoods, torn away from personal attachments and informal controls, and dependent on an often inadequate labor market as the exclusive provider of social integration, material welfare, and self-esteem.

This is precisely what has happened in many Third World countries that have experienced the wrenching transformations of unregulated economic development. Rural livelihoods and ways of life have been eroded, often shattered, but there is no strong, labor-intensive industrial economy to absorb the displaced and to provide new occupations and new resources for stable community life. That condition—bad enough in itself—is typically exacerbated by the simultaneous growth of a small but glittering sector of extravagant affluence with which the displaced poor must necessarily compare themselves. The same profit-driven growth also tends to replace older values of mutuality and cooperation with a culture that encourages competitive, individual striving for a level of material consumption that only a fraction of the population can conceivably afford. The combination is volatile, and it goes a long way toward explaining why some cities of the developing countries are the most dangerous places in the world.

This process of disruptive development—in which a selective prosperity is accompanied by the persistence or even increase of inequality, the breakdown of communal bonds, and the destruction of stable work roles—not only helps account for the dreadful rates of criminal violence in places like Brazil, the Philippines, parts of the Caribbean, and

Africa, but it also illuminates the seeming paradox of violence amidst prosperity in the postwar United States, where these disruptions took place within a society and culture already deeply distorted by racial inequality.

The growth of the postwar American economy was unusual among advanced industrial societies in the extent to which it eliminated traditional livelihoods, yet failed to replace them with new opportunities. This helped ensure that the American distribution of income remained highly unequal in spite of the overall rise in the standard of living. To this aspect of economic deprivation must be added the fragmenting impact of a largely unbuffered market economy on less quantifiable but critical dimensions of communal life—local networks of support, traditions of mutual help, values of cooperation, and common provision of basic needs. In particular, the loss of agricultural employment and the large-scale movement from country to city broke older communities apart, while the relative absence of mechanisms to integrate the displaced into new jobs inhibited the development of a stable and supportive urban community life. In a familiar pattern, these transformations brought the unskilled of the rural South, Appalachia, and even the Caribbean and Latin America into American cities just as the capacity of the urban-industrial economy to absorb them was declining, trapping the newcomers in neighborhoods too rapidly changing to sustain strong networks of social support, and placing the marginal and uprooted poor in demoralizing proximity to the prosperous, while saturating them with the lures of an increasingly frenetic consumer culture.

As in the Third World, the combination was (and is) an explosive one—and one that sharply distinguishes the American pattern of economic development. Many other industrial societies suffered similar strains; none suffered them in such extreme form. It is precisely the minimization of inequality and unemployment and the preservation of strong communal institutions that, for example, help account for the experience of two modern industrialized countries noted for their low rates of serious crime—Switzerland and Japan. As Marshall Clinard (1978) has argued, Swiss economic development was far more decentralized than that in most other countries and took place in the context of a political system strongly based on local self-government and broad community participation. As a result, Switzerland's rise to affluence entailed considerably less disruption of local communal life than occurred in most industrial societies. Similarly, scholars have often pointed to the persistence of strong ties of community and kinship in the face of rapid industrialization in postwar Japan. In both cases, too, economic development was accompanied by a relatively narrow spread of income inequality and very low rates of unemployment, assuring a more egalitarian distribution of the fruits of growth.

It is important to be clear about what this evidence means and doesn't mean. That some forms of economic growth can generate crime doesn't mean that we should romanticize the supposedly harmonious life of poor countries—countries that are often both wretchedly deprived in material terms and ridden with their own forms of institutionalized violence and traditionally accepted brutality (Claiborne 1984). Nor does it suggest that poverty and material deprivation have nothing to do with crime (as comfortable observers in affluent nations sometimes prefer to believe) or justify a less-than-benign neglect of the material needs of the poor at home or overseas. It *does* tell us that if we want to understand the relationships between crime, inequality, and prosperity, we will need a broader conception of what we mean by impoverishment—and prosperity. It tells us that statistics on the growth of Gross National Product or personal income alone are not very precise guides to the extent of social deprivation; that the supports of community and kinship can inhibit violence even where there is little money and few material goods; and that the enforced separation of people from these communal supports in the name of economic growth can be among the worst forms of impoverishment of all. By the same token, it follows that if we wish to mount an effective attack on criminal violence, we cannot be satisfied with simply doling out funds, grudgingly and after the fact, to people who have been stripped of livelihoods and social networks by the dynamics of the private labor market.

This conclusion, most emphatically, does not mean that we should dismantle the welfare state and replace it with nostalgic calls for a revival of volunteerism and a vaguely defined community spirit; nor that we should diminish the role of government in the futile pursuit of an imagined vision of the industrial discipline of the nineteenth century or the traditional cohesiveness of the preindustrial village. Conservatives often forget that the unity and tranquility of these traditional communities—where they existed—depended on the stability of institutions that have increasingly been undermined by the market economy itself. In the face of that development, there are two logical responses. One is to try, through force and fear, to impose new forms of discipline and control on the uprooted and marginal poor of the cities, while allowing the disintegrative effects of a chaotic and disruptive economy to take their natural course. The other is to develop social and economic policies to forestall this volatile and tragic pattern in the first place, or to reverse it.

REFERENCES

Archer, Dane. 1978. "Cities and Homicide: A New Look at an Old Paradox," *Comparative Studies in Sociology* 1:73–94.

Blau, Judith, and Peter Blau. 1982. "The Cost of Inequality: Metropolitan Structure and Violent Crime," *American Sociological Review* 47:114–129.

Braithwaite, John, and Valerie Braithwaite. 1980. "The Effect of Income Inequality and Social Democracy on Homicide," *British Journal of Criminology* 20.

Claiborne, William. 1984. "India's Bride Burnings," *Washington Post* (National Weekly Edition), October 8.

Clinard, Marshall B. 1978. *Cities with Little Crime.* Cambridge: Cambridge University Press.

Cloward, Richard, and Lloyd Ohlin. 1960. *Delinquency and Opportunity.* Glencoe, IL: Free Press.

DeFronzo, James. 1983. "Economic Assistance to Impoverished Americans: Relationship to Incidence of Crime," *Criminology* 21.

Hartjen, Clayton. 1982. "Delinquency, Development, and Social Integration in India," *Social Problems* 29.

Merton, Robert K. 1957. "Social Structure and Anomie," in Merton, *Social Theory and Social Structure.* Glencoe, IL: Free Press.

Messner, Steven. 1980. "Income Inequality and Murder Rates: Some Cross-National Findings," *Comparative Social Research* 3:185–198.

———. 1982. "Societal Development, Social Equality, and Homicide," *Social Forces* 61.

Reich, Robert B. 1983. *The Next American Frontier.* New York: Random House.

Crime and Routine Activities

Lawrence E. Cohen and Marcus Felson

We consider trends in crime rates in terms of changes in the "routine activities" of everyday life. We believe the structure of such activities influences criminal opportunity and therefore affects trends in a class of crimes we refer to as *direct-contact predatory violations*. Predatory violations are defined here as illegal acts in which "someone definitely and intentionally takes or damages the person or property of another" (Glaser, 1971:4). Further, this analysis is confined to those predatory violations involving direct physical contact between at least one offender and at least one person or object which that offender attempts to take or damage.

We argue that structural changes in routine activity patterns can influence crime rates by affecting the convergence in space and time of the three minimal elements of direct-contact predatory violations: (1) motivated offenders, (2) suitable targets, and (3) the absence of capable guardians against a violation. We further argue that the lack of any one of these elements is sufficient to prevent the successful completion of a direct-contact predatory crime, and that the convergence in time and space of suitable targets and the absence of capable guardians may even lead to large increases in crime rates without necessarily requiring any increase in the structural conditions that motivate individuals to engage in crime. That is, if the proportion of motivated offenders or even suitable targets were to remain stable in a community, changes in routine activities could nonetheless alter the likelihood of their convergence in space and time, thereby creating more opportunities for crimes to occur. Control therefore becomes critical. If controls through routine activities were to decrease, illegal predatory activities could then be likely to increase. In the process of developing this explanation and

From Lawrence E. Cohen and Marcus Felson. 1979. "Social Change and Crime Rate Trends: A Routine Activity Approach," *American Sociological Review* v. 44: 588–608. Reprinted by permission of the American Sociological Association and the authors.

evaluating its consistency with existing data, we relate our approach to classical human ecological concepts and to several earlier studies.

The Structure of Criminal Activity

Sociological knowledge of how community structure generates illegal acts has made little progress since Shaw and McKay and their colleagues (1929) published their pathbreaking work, *Delinquency Areas*. Variations in crime rates over space long have been recognized (e.g., see Guerry, 1833; Quètelet, 1842), and current evidence indicates that the pattern of these relationships within metropolitan communities has persisted (Reiss, 1976). Although most spatial research is quite useful for describing crime rate patterns and providing post hoc explanations, these works seldom consider—conceptually or empirically—the fundamental human ecological character of illegal acts as *events* which occur at specific locations in *space* and *time*, involving specific persons and/or objects. These and related concepts can help us to develop an extension of the human ecological analysis to the problem of explaining changes in crime rates over time. Unlike many criminological inquiries, we do not examine why individuals or groups are inclined criminally, but rather we take criminal inclination as given and examine the manner in which the spatio-temporal organization of social activities helps people to translate their criminal inclinations into action. Criminal violations are treated here as routine activities which share many attributes of, and are interdependent with, other routine activities. This interdependence between the structure of illegal activities and the organization of everyday sustenance activities leads us to consider certain concepts from human ecological literature.

The Minimal Elements of Direct-Contact Predatory Violations

As we previously stated, despite their great diversity, direct-contact predatory violations share some important requirements which facilitate analysis of their structure. Each successfully completed violation minimally requires an *offender* with both criminal inclinations and the ability to carry out those inclinations, a person or object providing a *suitable target* for the offender, and *absence of guardians* capable of preventing violations. We emphasize that the lack of any one of these elements normally is sufficient to prevent such violations from occurring.[1] Though guardianship is implicit in everyday life, it usually is marked by the absence of violations; hence it is easy to overlook. While police action is analyzed widely, guardianship by ordinary citizens of one another and of property as they go about routine activities may be one of the most neglected elements in sociological research on crime, especially since it links seemingly unrelated social roles and relationships to the occurrence or absence of illegal acts.

The conjunction of these minimal elements can be used to assess how social structure may affect the tempo of each type of violation. That is, the probability that a violation will occur at any specific time and place might be taken as a function of the convergence of likely offenders and suitable targets in the absence of capable guardians.

The Ecological Nature of Illegal Acts

This ecological analysis of direct-contact predatory violations is intended to be more than metaphorical. In the context of such violations, people, gaining and losing sustenance, struggle among themselves for property, safety, territorial hegemony, sexual outlet, physical control, and sometimes for survival itself. The interdependence between offenders and victims can be viewed as a predatory relationship between functionally dissimilar individuals or groups. Since predatory violations fail to yield any net gain in sustenance for the larger community, they can only be sustained by feeding upon other activities. As offenders cooperate to increase their efficiency at predatory violations and as potential victims organize their resistance to these violations, both groups apply the symbiotic principle to improve their sustenance position. On the other hand, potential victims of predatory crime may take evasive actions which encourage offenders to pursue targets other than their own. Since illegal activities must feed upon other activities, the spatial and temporal structure of routine legal activities should play an important role in determining the location, type and quantity of illegal acts occurring in a given community or society. Moreover, one can analyze how the structure of community organization as well as the level of technology in a society provide the circumstances under which crime can thrive. For example, technology and organization affect the capacity of persons with criminal inclinations to overcome their targets, as well as affecting the ability of guardians to contend with potential offenders by using whatever protective tools, weapons and skills they have at their disposal. Many technological advances designed for legitimate purposes—including the automobile, small power tools, hunting weapons, highways, telephones, etc.—may enable offenders to carry out their own work more effectively or may assist people in protecting their own or someone else's person or property.

Not only do routine legitimate activities often provide the wherewithal to commit offenses or to guard against others who do so, but they also provide offenders with suitable targets. Target suitability is likely to reflect such things as value (i.e., the material or symbolic desirability of a personal or property target for offenders), physical visibility, access, and the inertia of a target against illegal treatment by offenders (including the weight, size, and attached or locked features of property inhibiting its illegal removal and the physical capacity of personal victims to resist attackers with or without weapons). Routine production activities probably affect the suitability of consumer goods for illegal removal by determining their value and weight. Daily activities may affect the location of property and personal targets in visible and accessible places at particular times. These activities also may cause people to have on hand objects that can be used as weapons for criminal acts or self-protection or to be preoccupied with tasks which reduce their capacity to discourage or resist offenders.

While little is known about conditions that affect the convergence of potential offenders, targets and guardians, this is a potentially rich source of propositions about crime rates. For example, daily work activities separate many people from those they trust and the property they value. Routine activities also bring together at various times of day or night persons of different background, sometimes in the presence of facilities, tools or weapons which influence the commission or avoidance of illegal acts. Hence, the timing of work, schooling and leisure may be of central importance for explaining crime rates.

RELATION OF THE ROUTINE ACTIVITY APPROACH TO EXTANT STUDIES

A major advantage of the routine activity approach presented here is that it helps assemble some diverse and previously unconnected criminological analyses into a single substantive framework. This framework also serves to link illegal and legal activities, as illustrated by a few examples of descriptive accounts of criminal activity.

Descriptive Analyses

There are several descriptive analyses of criminal acts in criminological literature. For example, Thomas Reppetto's (1974) study, *Residential Crime*, considers how residents supervise their neighborhoods and streets and limit access of possible offenders. He also considers how distance of households from the central city reduces risks of criminal victimization. Reppetto's evidence—consisting of criminal justice records, observations of comparative features of geographic areas, victimization survey data and offender interviews—indicates that offenders are very likely to use burglary tools and to have at least minimal technical skills, that physical characteristics of dwellings affect their victimization rates, that the rhythms of residential crime rate patterns are marked (often related to travel and work patterns of residents), and that visibility of potential sites of crime affects the risk that crimes will occur there. Similar findings are reported by Pope's (1977a; 1977b) study of burglary in California and by Scarr's (1972) study of burglary in and around the District of Columbia. In addition, many studies report that architectural and environmental design as well as community crime programs serve to decrease target suitability and increase capable guardianship (see, for example, Newman, 1973; Jeffery, 1971; Washnis, 1976), while many biographical or autobiographical descriptions of illegal activities note that lawbreakers take into account the nature of property and/or the structure of human activities as they go about their illegal work (see, e.g., Chambliss, 1972; Klockars, 1974; Sutherland, 1937; Letkemann, 1973; Jackson, 1969;

Martin, 1952; Maurer, 1964; Cameron, 1964; Williamson, 1968).

Evidence that the spatio-temporal organization of society affects patterns of crime can be found in several sources. Strong variations in specific predatory crime rates from hour to hour, day to day, and month to month are reported often (e.g., Wolfgang, 1958; Amir, 1971; Reppetto, 1974; Scarr, 1972; FBI, 1975; 1976), and these variations appear to correspond to the various tempos of the related legitimate activities upon which they feed. Also at a microsociological level, Short and Strodtbeck (1965: chaps. 5 and 11) describe opportunities for violent confrontations of gang boys and other community residents which arise in the context of community leisure patterns, such as "quarter parties" in black communities, and the importance, in the calculus of decision making employed by participants in such episodes, of low probabilities of legal intervention. In addition, a wealth of empirical evidence indicates strong spatial variations over community areas in crime and delinquency rates (for an excellent discussion and review of the literature on ecological studies of crimes, see Wilks, 1967). Recently, Albert Reiss (1976) has argued convincingly that these spatial variations (despite some claims to the contrary) have been supported consistently by both official and unofficial sources of data. Reiss further cites victimization studies which indicate that offenders are very likely to select targets not far from their own residence (see USDJ, 1974a; 1974b; 1974c).

Macrolevel Analyses of Crime Trends and Cycles

Although details about how crime occurs are intrinsically interesting, the important analytical task is to learn from these details how illegal activities carve their niche within the larger system of activities. This task is not an easy one. For example, attempts by Bonger (1916), Durkheim (1951; 1966), Henry and Short (1954), and Fleisher (1966) to link the rate of illegal activities to the economic condition of a society have not been completely successful. Empirical tests of the relationships postulated in the above studies have produced inconsistent results which some observers view as an indication that the level of crime is not related systematically to the economic conditions of a society (Mansfield et al., 1974: 463; Cohen and Felson, 1979).

It is possible that the wrong economic and social factors have been employed in these macro studies of crime. Other researchers have provided stimulating alternative descriptions of how social change affects the criminal opportunity structure, thereby influencing crime rates in particular societies. For example, at the beginning of the nineteenth century, Patrick Colquhoun (1800) presented a detailed, lucid description and analysis of crime in the London metropolitan area and suggestions for its control. He assembled substantial evidence that London was experiencing a massive crime wave attributable to a great increment in the assemblage and movement of valuable goods through its ports and terminals.

A similar examination of crime in the period of the English industrial expansion was carried out by a modern historian, J. J. Tobias (1967), whose work on the history of crime in nineteenth century England is perhaps the most comprehensive effort to isolate those elements of social change affecting crime in an expanding industrial nation. Tobias details how far-reaching changes in transportation, currency, technology, commerce, merchandising, poverty, housing, and the like, had tremendous repercussions on the amount and type of illegal activities committed in the nineteenth century. His thesis is that structural transformations either facilitated or impeded

the opportunities to engage in illegal activities. In one of the few empirical studies of how recent social change affects the opportunity structure for crime in the United States, Leroy Gould (1969) demonstrated that the increase in the circulation of money and the availability of automobiles between 1921 and 1965 apparently led to an increase in the rate of bank robberies and auto thefts, respectively. Gould's data suggest that these relationships are due more to the abundance of opportunities to perpetrate the crimes than to short-term fluctuations in economic activities.

Although the sociological and historical studies cited in this section have provided some useful *empirical* generalizations and important insights into the incidence of crime, it is fair to say that they have not articulated systematically the *theoretical* linkages between routine legal activities and illegal endeavors. Thus, these studies cannot explain how changes in the larger social structure generate changes in the opportunity to engage in predatory crime and hence account for crime rate trends. To do so requires a conceptual framework such as that sketched in the preceding section.

Microlevel Assumptions of the Routine Activity Approach

The theoretical approach taken here specifies that crime rate trends in the post-World War II United States are related to patterns of what we have called routine activities. We define these as any recurrent and prevalent activities which provide for basic population and individual needs, whatever their biological or cultural origins. Thus routine activities would include formalized work, as well as the provision of standard food, shelter, sexual outlet, leisure, social interaction, learning and childrearing. These activities may go well beyond the minimal levels needed to prevent a population's extinction, so long as their prevalence and recurrence makes them a part of everyday life.

Routine activities may occur (1) at home, (2) in jobs away from home, and (3) in other activities away from home. The latter may involve primarily household members or others. We shall argue that, since World War II, the United States has experienced a major shift of routine activities away from the first category into the remaining ones, especially those nonhousehold activities involving nonhousehold members. In particular, we shall argue that this shift in the structure of routine activities increases the probability that motivated offenders will converge in space and time with suitable targets in the absence of capable guardians, hence contributing to significant increases in the direct-contact predatory crime rates over these years.

DISCUSSION

Without denying the importance of factors motivating offenders to engage in crime, we have focused specific attention upon violations themselves and the prerequisites for their occurrence. However, the routine activity approach might in the future be applied to the analysis of offenders and their inclinations as well. For example, the structure of primary group activity may affect the likelihood that cultural transmission or social control of criminal inclinations will occur, while the structure of the community may affect the tempo of criminogenic peer group activity. We also may expect that circumstances favorable for carrying out violations contribute to criminal inclinations in the long run by rewarding these inclinations.

We further suggest that the routine activity framework may prove useful in explain-ing why the criminal justice system, the community and the family have appeared so ineffective in exerting social control since 1960. Substantial increases in the opportunity to carry out predatory violations may have undermined society's mechanisms for social control. For example, it may be difficult for institutions seeking to increase the certainty, celerity and severity of punishment to compete with structural changes resulting in vast increases in the certainty, celerity and value of rewards to be gained from illegal predatory acts.

It is ironic that the very factors which increase the opportunity to enjoy the benefits of life also may increase the opportunity for predatory violations. For example, automobiles provide freedom of movement to offenders as well as average citizens and offer vulnerable targets for theft. College enrollment, female labor force participation, urbanization, suburbanization, vacations and new electronic durables provide various opportunities to escape the confines of the household while they increase the risk of predatory victimization. Indeed, the opportunity for predatory crime appears to be enmeshed in the opportunity structure for legitimate activities to such an extent that it might be very difficult to root out substantial amounts of crime without modifying much of our way of life. Rather than assuming that predatory crime is simply an indicator of social breakdown, one might take it as a byproduct of freedom and prosperity as they manifest themselves in the routine activities of everyday life.

NOTES

1. The analytical distinction between target and guardian is not important in those cases where a personal target engages in self-protection from direct-contact predatory vio-

lations. We leave open for the present the question of whether a guardian is effective or ineffective in all situations. We also allow that various guardians may primarily supervise offenders, targets or both. These are questions for future examination.

REFERENCES

Amir, Menachem. 1971. *Patterns of Forcible Rape.* Chicago: University of Chicago Press.

Bonger, W. A. 1916. *Criminality and Economic Conditions.* Boston: Little, Brown.

Cameron, Mary Owen. 1964. *The Booster and the Snitch.* New York: Free Press.

Chambliss, William J. 1972. *Boxman: A Professional Thief's Journey.* New York: Harper and Row.

Cohen, Lawrence E. and Marcus Felson. 1979. "On estimating the social costs of national economic policy: a critical examination of the Brenner study." *Social Indicators Research.* In press.

Colquhoun, Patrick. 1800. *Treatise on the Police of the Metropolis.* London: Baldwin.

Durkheim, Emile. 1951. *Suicide: A Study in Sociology.* New York: Free Press.

———. 1966. *The Division of Labor in Society.* New York: Free Press.

Federal Bureau of Investigation (FBI). 1975. Crime in the U.S.: Uniform Crime Report. Washington, D.C.: U.S. Government Printing Office.

———. 1976. Crime in the U.S.: Uniform Crime Report. Washington, D.C.: U.S. Government Printing Office.

Fleisher, Belton M. 1966. *The Economics of Delinquency.* Chicago: Quadrangle.

Glaser, Daniel. 1971. *Social Deviance.* Chicago: Markham.

Gould, Leroy. 1969. "The changing structure of property crime in an affluent society." *Social Forces* 48:50–9.

Guerry, A. M. 1833. "Essai sur la statistique morale de la France." *Westminister Review* 18:357.

Henry, A. F., and J. F. Short. 1954. *Suicide and Homicide.* New York: Free Press.

Jackson, Bruce. 1969. *A Thief's Primer.* New York: Macmillan.

Jeffery, C. R. 1971. *Crime Prevention Through Environmental Design.* Beverly Hills: Sage.

Klockars, Carl B. 1974. *The Professional Fence.* New York: Free Press.

Land, Kenneth C. 1978. "Modelling macro social change." Paper presented at annual meeting of the American Sociological Association, San Francisco.

Letkemann, Peter. 1973. *Crime As Work.* Englewood Cliffs: Prentice-Hall.

Mansfield, Roger, Leroy Gould, and J. Zvi Namenwirth. 1974. "A socioeconomic model for the prediction of societal rates of property theft." *Social Forces* 52:462–72.

Martin, John Bower. 1952. *My Life in Crime.* New York: Harper.

Maurer, David W. 1964. *Whiz Mob.* New Haven: College and University Press.

Newman, Oscar. 1973. *Defensible Space: Crime Prevention Through Urban Design.* New York: Macmillan.

Pope, Carl E. 1977a. Crime-Specific Analysis: The Characteristics of Burglary Incidents. U.S. Dept. of Justice, Law Enforcement Assistance Administration. Analytic Report 10. Washington, D.C.: U.S. Government Printing Office.

———. 1977b. Crime-Specific Analysis: An Empirical Examination of Burglary Offense and Offender Characteristics. U.S. Dept. of Justice, Law Enforcement Assistance Administration. Analytical Report 12. Washington, D.C.: U.S. Government Printing Office.

Quètelet, Adolphe. 1842. *A Treatise on Man.* Edinburgh: Chambers.

Reiss, Albert J. 1976. "Settling the frontiers of a pioneer in American criminology: Henry McKay." Pp. 64–88 in James F. Short, Jr. (ed.), *Delinquency, Crime, and Society.* Chicago: University of Chicago Press.

Reppetto, Thomas J. 1974. *Residential Crime.* Cambridge: Ballinger.

Scarr, Harry A. 1972. *Patterns of Burglary*. U.S. Dept. of Justice, Law Enforcement Assistance Administration. Washington, D.C.: U.S. Government Printing Office.

Shaw, Clifford R., Henry D. McKay, Frederick Zorbaugh, and Leonard S. Cottrell. 1929. *Delinquency Areas*. Chicago: University of Chicago Press.

Short, James F., and Fred Strodtbeck. 1965. *Group Process and Gang Delinquency*. Chicago: University of Chicago Press.

Sutherland, Edwin H. 1937. *The Professional Thief*. Chicago: University of Chicago Press.

Tobias, J. J. 1967. *Crime and Industrial Society in the Nineteenth Century*. New York: Schocken Books.

U.S. Bureau of the Census (USBC). 1975–1976. Statistical Abstract of the U.S. Washington, D.C.: U.S. Government Printing Office.

U.S. Department of Justice (USDJ). 1974a. Preliminary Report of the Impact Cities, Crime Survey Results. Washington, D.C.: Law Enforcement Assistance Administration (NCJISS).

———. 1974b. Crime in the Nation's Five Largest Cities: Advance Report. Washington, D.C.: Law Enforcement Assistance Administration (NCJISS).

———. 1974c. Crimes and Victims: A Report on the Dayton-San Jose Pilot Survey of Victimization. Washington, D.C.: Law Enforcement Assistance Administration.

Washnis, George J. 1976. *Citizen Involvement in Crime Prevention*. Lexington: Heath.

Wilks, Judith A. 1967. "Ecological correlates of crime and delinquency." Pp. 138–56 in President's Commission on Law Enforcement and the Administration of Justice, *Task Force Report: Crime and Its Impact—An Assessment*. Appendix A. Washington, D.C.: U.S. Government Printing Office.

Williamson, Henry. 1968. *Hustler!* New York: Doubleday.

Wolfgang, Marvin E. 1958. *Patterns of Criminal Homicide*. Philadelphia: University of Pennsylvania Press.

Deviant Places

Rodney Stark

Norman Hayner, a stalwart of the old Chicago school of human ecology, noted that in the area of Seattle having by far the highest delinquency rate in 1934, "half the children are Italian." In vivid language, Hayner described the social and cultural shortcomings of these residents: "largely illiterate, unskilled workers of Sicilian origin. Fiestas, wine-drinking, raising of goats and gardens . . . are characteristic traits." He also noted that the businesses in this neighborhood were run down and on the wane and that "a number of dilapidated vacant business buildings and frame apartment houses dot the main street," while the area has "the smallest percentage of home-owners and the greatest aggregation of dilapidated dwellings and run-down tenements in the city" (Hayner, 1942:361–363). Today this district, which makes up the neighborhood surrounding Garfield High School, remains the prime delinquency area. But there are virtually no Italians living there. Instead, this neighborhood is the heart of the Seattle black community.

Thus we come to the point. How is it that neighborhoods can remain the site of high crime and deviance rates *despite a complete turnover in their populations?* If the Garfield district was tough *because* Italians lived there, why did it stay tough after they left? Indeed, why didn't the neighborhoods the Italians departed to become tough? Questions such as these force the perception that the composition of neighborhoods, in terms of characteristics of their populations, cannot provide an adequate explanation of variations in deviance rates. Instead, *there must be something about places as such* that sustains crime.

This paper attempts to fashion an integrated set of propositions to summarize and extend our understanding of ecological sources of deviant behavior. In so doing, the aim is to revive a *sociology* of deviance as an alternative to the social psychological ap-

From *Criminology* Vol. 25, No. 4 (1987): 893–909. Reprinted by permission of the American Society of Criminology and the author.

proaches that have dominated for 30 years. That is, the focus is on traits of places and groups rather than on traits of individuals. Indeed, I shall attempt to show that by adopting survey research as the *preferred* method of research, social scientists lost touch with significant aspects of crime and delinquency. Poor neighborhoods disappeared to be replaced by individual kids with various levels of family income, but no detectable environment at all. Moreover, the phenomena themselves became bloodless, sterile, and almost harmless, for questionnaire studies cannot tap homicide, rape, assault, armed robbery, or even significant burglary and fraud—too few people are involved in these activities to turn up in significant numbers in feasible samples, assuming that such people turn up in samples at all. So delinquency, for example, which once had meant offenses serious enough for court referrals, soon meant taking $2 out of mom's purse, having "banged up something that did not belong to you," and having a fist fight. This transformation soon led repeatedly to the "discovery" that poverty is unrelated to delinquency (Tittle, Villemez, and Smith, 1978).

Yet, through it all, social scientists somehow still knew better than to stroll the streets at night in certain parts of town or even to park there. And despite the fact that countless surveys showed that kids from upper and lower income families scored the same on delinquency batteries, even social scientists knew that the parts of town that scared them were not upper-income neighborhoods. In fact, when the literature was examined with sufficient finesse, it was clear that class *does* matter—that serious offenses are very disproportionately committed by a virtual under class (Hindelang, Hirschi, and Weis, 1981).

So, against this backdrop, let us reconsider the human ecology approach to deviance. To begin, there are five aspects of urban neighborhoods which characterize high deviance areas of cities. To my knowledge, no member of the Chicago school ever listed this particular set, but these concepts permeate their whole literature starting with Park, Burgess, and McKenzie's classic, *The City* (1925). And they are especially prominent in the empirical work of the Chicago school (Faris and Dunham, 1939; Shaw and McKay, 1942). Indeed, most of these factors were prominent in the work of 19th-century moral statisticians such as the Englishmen Mayhew and Buchanan, who were doing ecological sociology decades before any member of the Chicago school was born. These essential factors are (1) density; (2) poverty; (3) mixed use; (4) transience; and (5) dilapidation.

Each of the five will be used in specific propositions. However, in addition to these characteristics of places, the theory also will incorporate some specific *impacts* of the five on the moral order as *people respond to them*. Four responses will be assessed: (1) moral cynicism among residents; (2) increased opportunities for crime and deviance; (3) increased motivation to deviate; and (4) diminished social control.

Finally, the theory will sketch how these responses further *amplify* the volume of deviance through the following consequences: (1) by attracting deviant and crime-prone people and deviant and criminal activities to a neighborhood; (2) by driving out the least deviant; and (3) by further reductions in social control.

Proposition 1: The greater the density of a neighborhood, the more association between those most and least predisposed to deviance.

At issue here is not simply that there will be a higher proportion of deviance-prone persons in dense neighborhoods (although, as will be shown, that is true, too), rather it is proposed that there is a higher average level of interpersonal interactions in such neighborhoods and that individual traits will have less influence on patterns of contact. Consider kids. In low-density neighborhoods—wealthy suburbs, for example—some active effort is required for one 12-year-old to see another (a ride from a parent often is required). In these settings, kids and their parents can easily limit contact with bullies and those in disrepute. Not so in dense urban neighborhoods—the "bad" kids often live in the same building as the "good" ones, hang out close by, dominate the nearby playground, and are nearly unavoidable. Hence, peer groups in dense neighborhoods will tend to be inclusive, and all young people living there will face maximum peer pressure to deviate—as differential association theorists have stressed for so long.

Proposition 2: The greater the density of a neighborhood, the higher the level of moral cynicism.

Moral cynicism is the belief that people are much worse than they pretend to be. Indeed, Goffman's use of the dramaturgical model in his social psychology was rooted in the fact that we require ourselves and others to keep up appearances in public. We all, to varying degrees, have secrets, the public airing of which we would find undesirable. So long as our front-stage performances are credible and creditable, and we shield our backstage actions, we serve as good role models (Goffman, 1959, 1963). The trouble is that in dense neighborhoods it is much harder to keep up appearances—whatever morally discreditable information exists about us is likely to leak.

Survey data suggest that upper-income couples may be about as likely as lower-income couples to have physical fights (Stark and McEvoy, 1970). Whether that is true, it surely is the case that upper-income couples are much less likely to be *overheard* by the neighbors when they have such a fight. In dense neighborhoods, where people live in crowded, thin-walled apartments, the neighbors do hear. In these areas teenage peers, for example, will be much more likely to know embarrassing things about one another's parents. This will color their perceptions about what is normal, and their respect for the conventional moral standards will be reduced. Put another way, people in dense neighborhoods will serve as inferior role models for one another—the same people would *appear* to be more respectable in less dense neighborhoods.

Proposition 3: To the extent that neighborhoods are dense and poor, homes will be crowded.

The proposition is obvious, but serves as a necessary step to the next propositions on the effects of crowding, which draw heavily on the fine paper by Gove, Hughes, and Galle (1979).

Proposition 4: Where homes are more crowded, there will be a greater tendency to congregate outside the home in places and circumstances that raise levels of temptation and opportunity to deviate.

Gove and his associates reported that crowded homes caused family members, especially teenagers, to stay away. Since crowded homes will also tend to be located in mixed-use neighborhoods (see Proposition 9), when people stay away from home they will tend to congregate in places conducive to deviance (stores, pool halls, street corners, cafes, taverns, and the like).

Proposition 5: Where homes are more crowded, there will be lower levels of supervision of children.

This follows from the fact that children from crowded homes tend to stay out of the home and that their parents are glad to let them. Moreover, Gove and his associates found strong empirical support for the link between crowding and less supervision of children.

Proposition 6: Reduced levels of child supervision will result in poor school achievement, with a consequent reduction in stakes in conformity and an increase in deviant behavior.

This is one of the most cited and strongly verified causal chains in the literature on delinquency (Thrasher, 1927; Toby and Toby, 1961; Hirschi, 1969; Gold, 1970; Hindelang, 1973). Indeed, Hirschi and Hindelang (1977:583) claim that the "school variables" are among the most powerful predictors of delinquency to be found in survey studies: "Their significance for delinquency is nowhere in dispute and is, in fact, one of the oldest and most consistent findings of delinquency research."

Here Toby's (1957) vital concept of "stakes in conformity" enters the propositions. Stakes in conformity are those things that people risk losing by being detected in deviant actions. These may be things we already possess as well as things we can reasonably count on gaining in the future. An important aspect of the school variables is their potential for future rewards, rewards that may be sacrificed by deviance, but only for those whose school performance is promising.

Proposition 7: Where homes are more crowded, there will be higher levels of conflict within families weakening attachments and thereby stakes in conformity.

Gove and his associates found a strong link between crowding and family conflict, confirming Frazier's (1932:636) observations:

> So far as children are concerned, the house becomes a veritable prison for them. There is no way of knowing how many conflicts in Negro families are set off by the irritations

caused by overcrowding people, who come home after a day of frustration and fatigue, to dingy and unhealthy living quarters.

Here we also recognize that stakes in conformity are not merely material. Indeed, given the effort humans will expend to protect them, our attachments to others are among the most potent stakes in conformity. We risk our closest and most intimate relationships by behavior that violates what others expect of us. People lacking such relationships, of course, do not risk their loss.

Proposition 8: Where homes are crowded, members will be much less able to shield discreditable acts and information from one another, further increasing moral cynicism.

As neighborhood density causes people to be less satisfactory role models for the neighbors, density in the home causes moral cynicism. Crowding makes privacy more difficult. Kids will observe or overhear parental fights, sexual relations, and the like. This is precisely what Buchanan noted about the dense and crowded London slums in 1846 (in Levin and Lindesmith, 1937:15):

> In the densely crowded lanes and alleys of these areas, wretched tenements are found containing in every cellar and on every floor, men and women, children both male and female, all huddled together, sometimes with strangers, and too frequently standing in very doubtful consanguinity to each other. In these abodes decency and shame have fled; depravity reigns in all its horrors.

Granted that conditions have changed since then and that dense, poor, crowded areas in the center cities of North America are not nearly so wretched. But the essential point linking "decency" and "shame" to lack of privacy retains its force.

Proposition 9: Poor, dense neighborhoods tend to be mixed-use neighborhoods.

Mixed use refers to urban areas where residential and commercial land use coexist, where homes, apartments, retail shops, and even light industry are mixed together. Since much of the residential property in such areas is rental, typically there is much less resistance to commercial use (landlords often welcome it because of the prospects of increased land values). Moreover, the poorest, most dense urban neighborhoods often are adjacent to the commercial sections of cities, forming what the Chicago school called the "zone of transition" to note the progressive encroachments of commercial uses into a previously residential area. Shaw and McKay (1942:20) describe the process as follows:

> As the city grows, the areas of commerce and light industry near the center encroach upon areas used for residential purposes. The dwellings in such areas, often already undesirable because of age, are allowed to deteriorate when such invasion threatens or actually occurs, as further investment in them is unprofitable. These residences are permitted to yield whatever return can be secured in their dilapidated condition, often in total disregard for the housing laws. . . .

Shaw and McKay were proponents of the outmoded concentric zonal model of cities, hence their assumption that encroachment radiates from the city center. No matter, the important point is that the process of encroachment occurs whatever the underlying shape of cities.

Proposition 10: Mixed use increases familiarity with and easy access to places offering the opportunity for deviance.

A colleague told me he first shoplifted at age eight, but that he had been "casing the joint for four years." This particular "joint"

was the small grocery store at the corner of the block where he lived, so he didn't even have to cross a street to get there. In contrast, consider kids in many suburbs. If they wanted to take up shoplifting they would have to ask mom or dad for a ride. In purely residential neighborhoods there simply are far fewer conventional opportunities (such as shops) for deviant behavior.

Proposition 11: Mixed-use neighborhoods offer increased opportunity for congregating outside the home in places conducive to deviance.

It isn't just stores to steal from that the suburbs lack, they also don't abound in places of potential moral marginality where people can congregate. But in dense, poor, mixed-use neighborhoods, when people leave the house they have all sorts of places to go, including the street corner. A frequent activity in such neighborhoods is leaning. A bunch a guys will lean against the front of the corner store, the side of the pool hall, or up against the barber shop. In contrast, out in the suburbs young guys don't gather to lean against one another's houses, and since there is nowhere else for them to lean, whatever deviant leanings they might have go unexpressed. By the same token, in the suburbs, come winter, there is no close, *public* place to congregate indoors.

Thus, we can more easily appreciate some fixtures of the crime and delinquency research literature. When people, especially young males, congregate and have nothing special to do, the incidence of their deviance is increased greatly (Hirschi, 1969). Most delinquency, and a lot of crime, is a social rather than a solitary act (Erickson, 1971).

Proposition 12: Poor, dense, mixed-use neighborhoods have high transience rates.

This aspect of the urban scene has long attracted sociological attention. Thus, McKenzie wrote in 1926 (p. 145): "Slums are the most mobile . . . sections of a city. Their inhabitants come and go in continuous succession."

Proposition 13: Transience weakens extrafamilial attachments.

This is self-evident. The greater the amount of local population turnover, the more difficult it will be for individuals or families to form and retain attachments.

Proposition 14: Transience weakens voluntary organizations, thereby directly reducing both informal and formal sources of social control (see Proposition 25).

Recent studies of population turnover and church membership rates strongly sustain the conclusion that such membership is dependent upon attachments, and hence suffers where transience rates reduce attachments (Wuthnow and Christiano, 1979; Stark, Doyle, and Rushing, 1983; Welch, 1983; Stark and Bainbridge, 1985). In similar fashion, organizations such as PTA or even fraternal organizations must suffer where transience is high. Where these organizations are weak, there will be reduced community resources to launch local, self-help efforts to confront problems such as truancy or burglary. Moreover, neighborhoods deficient in voluntary organizations also will be less able to influence how external forces such as police, zoning boards, and the like act vis-à-vis the community, a point often made by Park (1952) in his discussions of natural areas and by more recent urban sociologists (Suttles, 1972; Lee, Oropesa, Metch, and Guest, 1984; Guest, 1984).

In their important recent study, Simcha-Fagan and Schwartz (1986) found that the association between transience and delinquency disappeared under controls for organizational participation. This is not an example of spuri-

ousness, but of what Lazarsfeld called "interpretation" (Lazarsfeld, Pasanella, and Rosenberg, 1972). Transience *causes* low levels of participation, which in turn *cause* an increased rate of delinquency. That is, participation is an *intervening variable* or *linking mechanism* between transience and delinquency. When an intervening variable is controlled, the association between X and Y is reduced or vanishes.

Proposition 15: Transience reduces levels of community surveillance.

In areas abounding in newcomers, it will be difficult to know when someone doesn't live in a building he or she is entering. In stable neighborhoods, on the other hand, strangers are easily noticed and remembered.

Proposition 16: Dense, poor, mixed-use, transient neighborhoods will also tend to be dilapidated.

This is evident to anyone who visits these parts of cities. Housing is old and not maintained. Often these neighborhoods are very dirty and littered as a result of density, the predominance of renters, inferior public services, and a demoralized population (see Proposition 22).

Proposition 17: Dilapidation is a social stigma for residents.

It hardly takes a real estate tour of a city to recognize that neighborhoods not only reflect the status or their residents, but confer status upon them. In Chicago, for example, strangers draw favorable inferences about someone who claims to reside in Forest Glen, Beverly, or Norwood Park. But they will be leery of those who admit to living on the Near South Side. Granted, knowledge of other aspects of communities enters into these differential reactions, but simply driving through a neighborhood such as the South Bronx is vivid evidence that very few people would actually *want* to live there. During my days as a newspaper reporter, I discovered that to move just a block North, from West Oakland to Berkeley, greatly increased social assessments of individuals. This was underscored by the frequent number of times people told me they lived in Berkeley although the phone book showed them with an Oakland address. As Goffman (1963) discussed at length, stigmatized people will try to pass when they can.

Proposition 18: High rates of neighborhood deviance are a social stigma for residents.

Beyond dilapidation, neighborhoods abounding in crime and deviance stigmatize the moral standing of all residents. To discover that you are interacting with a person through whose neighborhood you would not drive is apt to influence the subsequent interaction in noticeable ways. Here is a person who lives where homicide, rape, and assault are common, where drug dealers are easy to find, where prostitutes stroll the sidewalks waving to passing cars, where people sell TVs, VCRs, cameras, and other such items out of the trunks of their cars. In this sense, place of residence can be a dirty, discreditable secret.

Proposition 19: Living in stigmatized neighborhoods causes a reduction in an individual's stake in conformity.

This is simply to note that people living in slums will see themselves as having less to risk by being detected in acts of deviance. Moreover, as suggested below in Propositions 25–28, the risks of being detected also are lower in stigmatized neighborhoods.

Proposition 20: The more successful and potentially best role models will flee stigmatized neighborhoods whenever possible.

Goffman (1963) has noted that in the case of physical stigmas, people will exhaust efforts to correct or at least minimize them— from plastic surgery to years of therapy. Presumably it is easier for persons to correct a stigma attached to their neighborhood than one attached to their bodies. Since moving is widely perceived as easy, the stigma of living in particular neighborhoods is magnified. Indeed, as we see below, some people do live in such places because of their involvement in crime and deviance. But, even in the most disorderly neighborhoods, *most* residents observe the laws and norms. Usually they continue to live there simply because they can't afford better. Hence, as people become able to afford to escape, they do. The result is a process of selection whereby the worst role models predominate.

Proposition 21: More successful and conventional people will resist moving into a stigmatized neighborhood.

The same factors that *pull* the more successful and conventional out of stigmatized neighborhoods *push* against the probability that conventional people will move into these neighborhoods. This means that only less successful and less conventional people *will* move there.

Proposition 22: Stigmatized neighborhoods will tend to be overpopulated by the most demoralized kinds of people.

This does not mean the poor or even those engaged in crime or delinquency. The concern is with persons unable to function in reasonably adequate ways. For here will congregate the mentally ill (especially since the closure of mental hospitals), the chronic alcoholics, the retarded, and others with limited capacities to cope (Faris and Dunham, 1939; Jones, 1934).

Proposition 23:   The larger the relative number of demoralized residents, the greater the number of available "victims."

As mixed use provides targets of opportunity by placing commercial firms within easy reach of neighborhood residents, the demoralized serve as human targets of opportunity. Many muggers begin simply by searching the pockets of drunks passed out in doorways and alleys near their residence.

Proposition 24:   The larger the relative number of demoralized residents, the lower will be residents' perception of chances for success, and hence they will have lower perceived stakes in conformity.

Bag ladies on the corner, drunks sitting on the curbs, and schizophrenics muttering in the doorways are not advertisements for the American Dream. Rather, they testify that people in this part of town are losers, going nowhere in the system.

Proposition 25:   Stigmatized neighborhoods will suffer from more lenient law enforcement.

This is one of those things that "everyone knows," but for which there is no firm evidence. However, evidence may not be needed, given the many obvious reasons why the police would let things pass in these neighborhoods that they would act on in better neighborhoods. First, the police tend to be reactive, to act upon complaints rather than seek out violations. People in stigmatized neighborhoods complain less often. Moreover, people in these neighborhoods frequently are much less willing to testify when the police do act—and the police soon lose interest in futile efforts to find evidence. In addition, it is primarily vice that the police tolerate in these neighborhoods, and the police tend to accept the premise that vice will exist *somewhere*.

Therefore, they tend to condone vice in neighborhoods from which they do not receive effective pressures to act against it (see Proposition 14). They may even believe that by having vice limited to a specific area they are better able to regulate it. Finally, the police frequently come to share the outside community's view of stigmatized neighborhoods—as filled with morally disreputable people, who deserve what they get.

Proposition 26:   More lenient law enforcement increases moral cynicism.

Where people see the laws being violated with apparent impunity, they will tend to lose their respect for conventional moral standards.

Proposition 27:   More lenient law enforcement increases the incidence of crime and deviance.

This is a simple application of deterrence theory. Where the probabilities of being arrested and prosecuted for a crime are lower, the incidence of such crimes will be higher (Gibbs, 1975).

Proposition 28:   More lenient law enforcement draws people to a neighborhood on the basis of their involvement in crime and deviance.

Reckless (1926:165) noted that areas of the city with "wholesome family and neighborhood life" will not tolerate "vice," but that "the decaying neighborhoods have very little resistance to the invasions of vice." Thus, stigmatized neighborhoods become the "soft spot" for drugs, prostitution, gambling, and the like. These are activities that require public awareness of where to find them, for they depend on customers rather than victims. Vice can function only where it is condoned, at least to some degree. In this manner, McKenzie (1926:146) wrote, the slum "becomes the hiding-place for many services that are forbidden by the mores but which cater to the wishes of residents scattered throughout the community."

Proposition 29:   When people are drawn to a neighborhood on the basis of their participation in crime and deviance, the visibility of such activities and the opportunity to engage in them increases.

It has already been noted that vice must be relatively visible to outsiders in order to exist. Hence, to residents, it will be obvious. Even children not only will know *about* whores, pimps, drug dealers, and the like, they will *recognize* them. Back in 1840, Allison wrote of the plight of poor rural families migrating to rapidly growing English cities (p. 76):

> The extravagant price of lodgings compels them to take refuge in one of the crowded districts of the town, in the midst of thousands in similar necessitous circumstances with themselves. Under the same roof they probably find a nest of prostitutes, in the next door a den of thieves. In the room which they occupy they hear incessantly the revel of intoxication or are compelled to witness the riot of licentiousness.

In fact, Allison suggested that the higher social classes owed their "exemption from atrocious crime" primarily to the fact that they were not confronted by the temptations and seductions to vice that assail the poor. For it is the "impossibility of concealing the attractions of vice from the younger part of the poor in the great cities which exposes them to so many causes of demoralization."

Proposition 30:   The higher the visibility of crime and deviance, the more it will appear to others that these activities are safe and rewarding.

There is nothing like having a bunch of pimps and bookies flashing big wads of money and driving expensive cars to convince people in a neighborhood that crime pays. If young girls ask the hookers on the corner why they are doing it, they will reply with tales of expensive clothes and jewelry. Hence, in some neighborhoods, deviants serve as role models that encourage residents to become "street wise." This is a form of "wisdom" about the relative costs and benefits of crime that increases the likelihood that a person will spend time in jail. The extensive recent literature on perceptions of risk and deterrence is pertinent here (Anderson, 1979; Jenson, Erickson, and Gibbs, 1978; Parker and Grasmick, 1979).

CONCLUSION

A common criticism of the ecological approach to deviance has been that although many people live in bad slums, most do not become delinquents, criminals, alcoholics, or addicts. Of course not. For one thing, as Gans (1962), Suttles (1968), and others have recognized, bonds among human beings can endure amazing levels of stress and thus continue to sustain commitment to the moral order even in the slums. Indeed, the larger culture seems able to instill high levels of aspiration in people even in the worst ecological settings. However, the fact that most slum residents aren't criminals is beside the point to claims by human ecologists that aspects of neighborhood structure can sustain high rates of crime and deviance. Such propositions do not imply that residence in such a neighborhood is either a necessary or a sufficient condition for deviant behavior. There is conformity in the slums and deviance in affluent suburbs. All the ecological propositions imply is a substantial correlation between variations in neighborhood character and variations in crime and deviance rates. What an ecological theory of crime is meant to achieve is an explanation of why crime and deviance are so heavily concentrated in certain areas, and to pose this explanation in terms that do not depend entirely (or even primarily) on *compositional* effects—that is, on answers in terms of "kinds of people."

To say that neighborhoods are high in crime because their residents are poor suggests that controls for poverty would expose the spuriousness of the ecological effects. In contrast, the ecological theory would predict that the deviant behavior of the poor would vary as their ecology varied. For example, the theory would predict less deviance in poor families in situations where their neighborhood is less dense and more heterogeneous in terms of income, where their homes are less crowded and dilapidated, where the neighborhood is more fully residential, where the police are not permissive of vice, and where there is not undue concentration of the demoralized.

Finally, it is not being suggested that we stop seeking and formulating "kinds of people" explanations. Age and sex, for example, have powerful effects on deviant behavior that are not rooted in ecology (Gove, 1985). What is suggested is that, although males will exceed females in terms of rates of crime and delinquency in all neighborhoods, males in certain neighborhoods will have much higher rates than will males in some other neighborhoods, and female behavior will fluctuate by neighborhood too. Or, to return to the insights on which sociology was founded, social structures are real and cannot be reduced to purely psychological phenomena.

REFERENCES

Allison, Archibald. 1840. *The Principles of Population and the Connection With Human Happiness.* Edinburgh: Blackwood.

Anderson, L. S. 1979. The deterrent effect of criminal sanctions: Reviewing the evidence. In Paul J. Brantingham and Jack M. Kress (eds.), *Structure, Law and Power.* Beverley Hills: Sage.

Erickson, Maynard L. 1971. The group context of delinquent behavior. *Social Problems* 19:114–129.

Faris, Robert E. L., and Warren Dunham. 1939. *Mental Disorder in Urban Areas.* Chicago: University of Chicago Press.

Frazier, E. Franklin. 1932. *The Negro in the United States.* New York: Macmillan.

Gans, Herbert J. 1962. *The Urban Villagers.* New York: Free Press.

Gibbs, Jack P. 1975. *Crime, Punishment, and Deterrence.* New York: Elsevier.

Goffman, Erving. 1959. *Presentation of Self in Everyday Life.* New York: Doubleday.

———. 1963. *Stigma.* Englewood Cliffs, NJ: Prentice-Hall.

Gold, Martin. 1970. *Delinquent Behavior in an American City.* Belmont, CA: Brooks/Cole.

Gove, Walter R. 1985. The effect of age and gender on deviant behavior: A biopsychological perspective. In Alice Rossi (ed.), *Gender and the Life Course.* New York: Aldine.

Gove, Walter R., Michael L. Hughes, and Omer R. Galle. 1979. Overcrowding in the home. *American Sociological Review* 44:59–80.

Guest, Avery M. 1984. Robert Park and the natural area: A sentimental review. *Sociology and Social Research* 68:1–21.

Hayner, Norman S. 1942. Five cities of the Pacific Northwest. In Clifford Shaw and Henry McKay (eds.), *Juvenile Delinquency and Urban Areas.* Chicago: University of Chicago Press.

Hindelang, Michael J. 1973. Causes of delinquency: A partial replication and extension. *Social Problems* 20:471–478.

Hindelang, Michael J., Travis Hirschi, and Joseph G. Weis. 1981. *Measuring Delinquency.* Beverly Hills: Sage.

Hirschi, Travis. 1969. *Causes of Delinquency.* Berkeley: University of California Press.

Hirschi, Travis, and Michael J. Hindelang. 1977. Intelligence and delinquency: A revisionist view. *American Sociological Review* 42:571–587.

Jensen, Gary F., Maynard L. Erickson, and Jack Gibbs. 1978. Perceived risk of punishment and self-reported delinquency. *Social Forces* 57:57–58.

Jones, D. Caradog. 1934. *The Social Survey of Merseyside*, Vol. III. Liverpool: University Press of Liverpool.

Lazarsfeld, Paul F., Ann K. Pasanella, and Morris Rosenberg. 1972. *Continuities in the Language of Social Research*. New York: Free Press.

Lee, Barrett A., Ralph S. Oropesa, Barbara J. Metch, and Avery M. Guest. 1984. Testing the decline-of-community thesis: Neighborhood organizations in Seattle, 1929 and 1979. *American Journal of Sociology* 89:1,161–1,188.

Levin, Yale and Alfred Lindesmith. 1937. English Ecology and Criminology of the Past Century. *Journal of Criminal Law and Criminology* 27:801–816.

Mayhew, Heney. 1851. *London Labor and the London Poor*. London: Griffin.

McKenzie, Roderick. 1926. The scope of human ecology. *Publications of the American Sociological Society* 20:141–154.

Minor, W. William, and Joseph Harry. 1982. Deterrent and experimental effects in perceptual deterrence research. *Journal of Research in Crime and Delinquency* 18:190–203.

Park, Robert E. 1952. *Human Communities: The City and Human Ecology*. New York: The Free Press.

Park, Robert E., Ernest W. Burgess, and Roderick McKenzie. 1925. *The City*. Chicago: University of Chicago Press.

Parker, J., and Harold G. Grasmick. 1979. Linking actual and perceived certainty of punishment: An exploratory study of an untested proposition in deterrence theory. *Criminology* 17:366–379.

Reckless, Walter C. 1926. *Publications of the American Sociological Society* 20:164–176.

Shaw, Clifford R., and Henry D. McKay. 1942. *Juvenile Delinquency and Urban Areas*. Chicago: University of Chicago Press.

Simcha-Fagan, Ora, and Joseph E. Schwartz. 1986. Neighborhood and delinquency: An assessment of contextual effects. *Criminology* 24:667–699.

Stark, Rodney, and William Sims Bainbridge. 1985. *The Future of Religion*. Berkeley: University of California Press.

Stark, Rodney, Daniel P. Doyle, and Jesse Lynn Rushing. 1983. Beyond Durkheim: Religion and suicide. *Journal for the Scientific Study of Religion* 22:120–131.

Stark, Rodney, and James McEvoy. 1970. Middle class violence. *Psychology Today* 4:52–54, 110–112.

Suttles, Gerald. 1968. *The Social Order of the Slum*. Chicago: University of Chicago Press.

———. 1972. *The Social Construction of Communities*. Chicago: University of Chicago Press.

Thrasher, Frederick M. 1927. *The Gang*. Chicago: University of Chicago Press.

Tittle, Charles R., Wayne J. Villemez, and Douglas A. Smith. 1978. The myth of social class and criminality: An empirical assessment of the empirical evidence. *American Sociological Review* 43:643–656.

Toby, Jackson. 1957. Social disorganization and stake in conformity: Complementary factors in the predatory behavior of hoodlums. *Journal of Criminal Law, Criminology and Police Science* 48:12–17.

Toby, Jackson, and Marcia L. Toby. 1961. *Law School Status as a Predisposing Factor in Subcultural Delinquency*. New Brunswick: Rutgers University Press.

Welch, Kevin. 1983. Community development and metropolitan religious commitment: A test of two competing models. *Journal for the Scientific Study of Religion* 22:167–181.

Wuthnow, Robert, and Kevin Christiano. 1979. The effects of residential migration on church attendance. In Robert Wuthnow (ed.), *The Religious Dimension*. New York: Academic Press.

Criminal Homicide as a Situated Transaction

David F. Luckenbill

By definition, criminal homicide is a collective transaction. An offender, victim, and possibly an audience engage in an interchange which leaves the victim dead. Furthermore, these transactions are typically situated, for participants interact in a common physical territory (Wolfgang, 1958:203–205; Wallace, 1965). As with other situated transactions, it is expected that the participants develop particular roles, each shaped by the others and instrumental in some way to the fatal outcome (cf. Shibutani, 1961:32–37, 64–93; Blumer, 1969: 16–18). However, research, with few exceptions, has failed critically to examine the situated transaction eventuating in murder (Banitt et al., 1970; Shoham et al., 1973). At most, studies have shown that many victims either directly precipitate their destruction, by throwing the first punch or firing the first shot, or contribute to the escalation of some conflict which concludes in their demise (Wolfgang, 1958:245–265; Schafer, 1968:79–83; Goode, 1969:965; Toch, 1969; Moran, 1972). But how transactions of murder are organized and how they develop remain puzzles. What are the typical roles developed by the offender, victim, and possible bystanders? In what ways do these roles intersect to produce the fatal outcome? Are there certain regularities of interaction which characterize all transactions of murder, or do patterns of interaction vary among transactions in a haphazard fashion? Making the situated transaction the unit of investigation, this paper will address these questions by examining the character of the transaction in full.

METHOD

Criminal homicide is presently defined as the unlawful taking of a person's life, with the expressed intention of killing or rendering bodily injury resulting in death, and not in the course of some other criminal activity. This conceptualization excludes such forms of un-

From *Social Problems*, vol. 25, no. 2 (1977):176–186. Reprinted by permission of the University of California Press, the Society for the Study of Social Problems, and the author.

natural death as negligent homicide and vehicular manslaughter. This investigation will examine all forms of criminal homicide but felony murder, where death occurs in the commission of other felony crimes, and contract murder, where the offender conspires with another to kill in his behalf for payment.

The present data were drawn from all cases of criminal homicide over a ten-year period, 1963–1972, in one medium sized (350,000) California county. Sampling was of a multi-stage nature. Because criminal homicide may be mitigated through charging or plea negotiation to various types of manslaughter, it was necessary to gather all cases, for the years 1963–1972, found in the four charge categories of first and second degree murder, voluntary and involuntary manslaughter. In this way, ninety-four cases were gathered. Taking all cases of unnatural death except suicide documented in coroner's reports, those twenty-three cases not fitting the present conception of criminal homicide were eliminated. These consisted of fourteen vehicular manslaughters, eight felony murders, and one negligent homicide. The remainder, seventy-one deaths or seventy transactions (one double murder), were examined.

All official documents pertaining to these cases were secured. The character of the larger occasion as well as the organization and development of the fateful transaction were reconstructed from the content analysis of police, probation, psychiatric, and witness reports, offender interviews, victim statements, and grand jury and court testimony. These materials included information on the major and minor participants; who said and did what to whom; the chronology of dialogue and action; and the physical comportment of the participants.

In reconstructing the transaction, I first scrutinized each individual document for material relating only to the step-by-step development of the transaction. I then used the information to prepare separate accounts of the transaction. When all the individual documents for each case were exhausted, one summary account was constructed, using the individual accounts as resources. In the process of case reconstruction, I found that the various parties to the transaction often related somewhat different accounts of the event. Discrepancies centered, in large part, in their accounts of the specific dialogue of the participants. Their accounts were usually consistent with respect to the basic structure and development of the event.[1] In managing discrepancies, I relied on interparticipant consistency in accounts.

This methodological strategy should provide a fairly strong measure of reliability in case reconstruction. By using several independent resources bearing on the same focal point, particular biases could be reasonably controlled. In other words, possible biases in singular archival documents could be corrected by relying on a multitude of independently produced reports bearing on the transaction. For example, the offender's account could be compared with witnesses' accounts and with reports on physical evidence.

The Social Occasion of Criminal Homicide

Criminal homicide is the culmination of an intense interchange between an offender and victim. Transactions resulting in murder involved the joint contribution of the offender and victim to the escalation of a "character contest," a confrontation in which at least one, but usually both, attempt to establish or save face at the other's expense by standing steady in the face of adversity (Goffman, 1967:218–219, 238–257). Such transactions additionally involved a consensus among participants that violence was a suitable if not required means for settling the contest.

Before examining the dynamics of these transactions, it is useful to consider the larger context in which they were imbedded. A "situated transaction" refers to a chain of interaction between two or more individuals that lasts the time they find themselves in one another's immediate physical presence (Goffman, 1963:167). A "social occasion," in contrast, refers to a wider social affair within which many situated transactions may form, dissolve, and re-form (Goffman, 1963:18). And, as Goffman aptly demonstrates, social occasions carry boundaries of sorts which establish what kinds of transactions are appropriate and inappropriate.

Social occasions which encompassed transactions ending in murder shared several features. First, all such transactions occurred in occasions of non-work or leisure-time (cf. Bullock, 1955; Wolfgang, 1958:121–128; Wallace, 1965). The majority of murders occurred between the leisure hours of six p.m. and two a.m. and especially on weekends. More important, they were always found in leisure settings: almost half the cases occurred while members engaged in leisure activities at home; 15 percent occurred while members frequented a favorite tavern; another 15 percent occurred while members habituated a streetcorner or "turf;" a little over 12 percent occurred while the offender and victim drove or "cruised" about the city, highway, or country roads; the few remaining cases occurred while members engaged in activities in some other public place such as a hotel room.

Second, occasions of murder were "loose," informal affairs permitting a wide range of activities definable by members as appropriate (cf. Goffman, 1963:198–215). In contrast to work and such tighter occasions of leisure as weddings and funerals, where members are bound by rather strict sets of expectations, occasions of murder were permissive environs allowing the performance of various respectable and non-respectable activities. An "evening at home," the most prominent occasion in the cases, finds people engaging in many activities deemed suitable under the aegis of the private residence yet judged inappropriate for more formal affairs (cf. Cavan, 1963). Similarly, "an evening at the corner tavern," "hanging on streetcorner," or "cruising about town" have long been recognized as permissive settings providing access and opportunity to drink, take drugs, sell and purchase sex, or gamble without fear of censure by colleagues.

In the sample, members engaged in a variety of activities within such loosely structured occasions. In 75 percent of the cases, the offender and victim were engaged in pleasurable pursuits. They sought to drop serious or work roles and pursue such enjoyable activities as drinking alcoholic beverages, dancing, partying, watching television, or cruising main street. In the remainder of the cases, members were engaged in reasonably serious concerns. Here, conversations of marital or relational futures, sexual prowess, beauty, trust-worthiness, and integrity were central themes about which members organized.

A third feature of such occasions was their population by intimates. In over 60 percent of the cases, the offender and victim were related by marriage, kinship, or friendship. In the remaining cases, while the offender and victim were enemies, mere acquaintances, or complete strangers, at least one, but often both were in the company of their family, friends, lovers, or co-workers.

Dynamics of the Situated Performance

These are the occasions in which situated transactions resulted in violent death. But examination of the development of these situated interchanges is not to argue that such transactions have no historical roots. In almost half the cases there had previously occurred what might be termed rehearsals between the offender and victim. These involved transactions which included the escalation of hostilities and, sometimes, physical violence. In 26 percent of these cases, the offender and, sometimes, victim entered the present occasion on the assumption that another hostile confrontation would transpire.

The "offender" and "victim" are heuristic labels for the statuses that either emerge in the transaction or are an artifact of the battle. In 71 percent of the cases, the statuses of offender and victim are determined by one's statement of intent to kill or injure the other. Hence, in 63 percent of the cases, the victim initiates the transaction, the offender states his intention to kill or injure the victim, and the offender follows through by killing him. In 8 percent of the cases, the offender initiates the transaction, later states his intention to kill or injure the victim, and follows through by killing him. But in 29 percent of the cases, the statuses of offender and victim are determined by the results of the battle. Here, the initially cast victim initiates the transaction while the initially cast offender states his intention to kill or injure the victim. Due to strength or resources, the initially cast victim kills the initially cast offender in the course of battle. In discussing the first five stages, the labels of offender and victim will be used to refer to the statuses that emerge in the course of interaction and not the statuses resulting from the battle. Furthermore, the labels will be employed in a manner consistent with the pattern characteristic of the majority of the cases. Consequently, in 36 percent of the cases (those where the initially cast victim kills the initially cast offender and those where the offender initiates the transaction, later states his intention to kill or injure, and follows through), the adversary labeled "victim" kills

while the adversary labeled "offender" is killed. In the discussion of the sixth stage the labels of offender and victim will be used to refer to the statuses resulting from the battle.

Stage I. The opening move in the transaction was an event performed by the victim and subsequently defined by the offender as an offense to "face," that image of self a person claims during a particular occasion or social contact (Goffman, 1967:5). What constitutes the real or actual beginning of this or any other type of transaction is often quite problematic for the researcher. The victim's activity, however, appeared as a pivotal event which separated the previous occasioned activity of the offender and victim from their subsequent violent confrontation. Such a disparaging and interactionally disrupting event constitutes the initial move.

While the form and content of the victim's move varied, three basic types of events cover all cases. In the first, found in over 41 percent of the cases, the victim made some direct, verbal expression which the offender subsequently interpreted as offensive. This class of events was obviously quite broad. Included were everything from insults levied at some particular attribute of the offender's self, family, or friends to verbal tirades which disparaged the overall character of the offender:

Case 34 The offender, victim, and two friends were driving toward the country where they could consume their wine. En route, the victim turned to the offender, both of whom were located in the back seat, and stated: "You know, you really got some good parents. You know, you're really a son-of-a-bitch. You're a leech. The whole time you were out of a job, you were living with them, and weren't even paying. The car you have should be your father's. He's the one who made the payments. Any time your dad goes to the store, you're the first in line to sponge off him. Why don't you grow up and stop being a leech?" The offender swore at him, and told him to shut up. But the victim continued, "Someone ought to come along and really fuck you up."

A second type, found in 34 percent of the cases, involved the victim's refusal to cooperate or comply with the requests of the offender. The offender subsequently interpreted the victim's action as a denial of his ability or right to command obedience. This was illustrated in transactions where parents murdered their children. When the parent's request that the child eat dinner, stop screaming, or take a bath went unheeded, the parent subsequently interpreted the child's activity as a challenge to rightful authority. In other cases, the violent escalation came about after the victim refused to conciliate a failing or dead relationship. In yet other cases, the victim failed to heed the offender's demand that he not enter some "off limits" territory, such as the "turf" of a juvenile gang.

The third type of event, found in 25 percent of the cases, involved some physical or nonverbal gesture which the offender subsequently defined as personally offensive. Often this gesture entailed an insult to the offender's sexual prowess, and took the form of affairs or flirtation:

> *Case 10*   When the victim finally came home, the offender told her to sit down; they had to talk. He asked her if she was "fooling around" with other men. She stated that she had, and her boyfriends pleased her more than the offender. The offender later stated that "this was like a hot iron in my gut." He ripped her clothes off and examined her body, finding scars and bruises. She said that her boyfriends liked to beat her. His anger magnified.

Of course, the victim's activity was not always performed on the murderous occasion. In 15 percent of the cases, the event was performed on some previous occasion when the offender was not present. Nevertheless, it was on the murderous occasion that the event was made known to the offender by the victim or bystanders and so was symbolically re-enacted.

Although the content and the initial production of these events varied, each served to disrupt the social order of the occasion. Each marked the opening of a transformation process in which pre-homicide transactions of pleasurable, or serious yet tranquil, order came to be transactions involving an argumentative "character contest."

Stage II.   In all cases ending in murder the offender interpreted the victim's previous move as personally offensive. In some cases the victim was intentionally offensive. But it is plausible that in other cases the victim was unwitting. In Case 43, for instance, the victim, a five-week-old boy, started crying early in the morning. The offender, the boy's father, ordered the victim to stop crying. The victim's crying, however, only heightened in intensity. The victim was too young to understand the offender's verbal order, and persistent crying may have been oriented not toward challenging his father's authority, but toward acquiring food or a change of diapers. Whatever the motive for crying, the child's father defined it as purposive and offensive. What the victim intends may be inconsequential. What the offender interprets as intentional, however, may have consequences for the organization of subsequent activity.

In 60 percent of the cases, the offender learned the meaning of the victim's move from inquiries made of victim or audience. In reply, the offender received statements suggesting the victim's action was insulting and intentional. In 39 percent of the cases, the offender ascertained the meaning of the impropriety directly from the victim:

> *Case 28* As the offender entered the back door of the house his wife said to her lover, the victim, "There's _____." The victim jumped to his feet and started dressing hurriedly. The offender, having called to his wife without avail, entered the bedroom. He found his wife nude and the victim clad in underwear. The startled offender asked the victim, "Why?" The victim replied, "Haven't you ever been in love? We love each other." The offender later stated, "If they were drunk or something, I could see it. I mean, I've done it myself. But when he said they loved each other, well that did it."

In another 21 percent of the cases, however, the offender made his assessment from statements of interested bystanders:

> *Case 20* The offender and his friend were sitting in a booth at a tavern drinking beer. The offender's friend told him that the offender's girlfriend was "playing" with another man (victim) at the other end of the bar. The offender looked at them and asked his friend if he thought something was going on. The friend responded, "I wouldn't let that guy fool around with [her] if she was mine." The offender agreed, and suggested to his friend that his girlfriend and the victim be shot for their actions. His friend said that only the victim should be shot, not the girlfriend.

In the remaining 40 percent of the cases the offender imputed meaning to the event on the basis of rehearsals in which the victim had engaged a similar role. The incessant screaming of the infant, the unremitting aggressions of a drunken spouse, and the never-ending

flirtation by the lover or spouse were activities which offenders had previously encountered and assessed as pointed and deliberate aspersions:

> *Case 35* During a family quarrel the victim had broken the stereo and several other household goods. At one point, the victim cut her husband, the offender, on the arm. He demanded that she sit down and watch television so that he could attend to his wound in peace. On returning from the bathroom he sat down and watched television. Shortly after, the victim rose from her chair, grabbed an ashtray, and shouted, "You bastard, I'm going to kill you." As she came toward him, the offender reached into the drawer of the end table, secured a pistol, and shot her. On arrest, the offender told police officers, "You know how she gets when she's drunk? I had to stop her, or she would have killed me. She's tried it before, that's how I got all these scars," pointing to several areas on his back.

Such previous activities and their consequences served the offender as an interpretive scheme for immediately making sense of the present event.

> *Stage III.* The apparent affront could have evoked different responses. The offender could have excused the violation because the victim was judged to be drunk, crazy, or joking. He could have fled the scene and avoided further interaction with the victim by moving into interaction with other occasioned participants or dealt with the impropriety through a retaliatory move aimed at restoring face and demonstrating strong character. The latter move was utilized in all cases.

In countering the impropriety, the offender attempted to restore the occasioned order and reaffirm face by standing his or her ground. To have used another alternative was to confirm questions of face and self raised by the victim. He could have chosen from several options, each of which had important consequences both to the face he situationally claimed and to his general reputation. Thus, the offender was faced with a dilemma: either deal with the impropriety by demonstrating strength of character, or verify questions of face by demonstrating weakness (Goffman, 1969:168–169).

In retaliating, the offender issued an expression of anger and contempt which signified his opinion of the victim as an unworthy person. Two basic patterns of retaliation were found. In 86 percent of the cases, the offender issued a verbal or physical challenge to the victim. In the remaining cases, the offender physically retaliated, killing the victim.

For the latter pattern, this third move marked the battle ending the victim's life:

> *Case 12* The offender, victim, and group of bystanders were observing a fight between a barroom bouncer and a drunk patron on the street outside the tavern. The offender was cheering for the bouncer, and the victim was cheering for the patron, who was losing the battle. The victim, angered by the offender's disposition toward the fight, turned to the offender and said, "You'd really like to see the little guy have the shit kicked out of him, wouldn't you big man?" The offender turned toward the victim and asked, "What did you say? You want the same thing, punk?" The victim moved toward the offender and reared back. The offender responded, "OK buddy." He struck the victim with a single right cross. The victim crashed to the pavement, and died a week later.

Such cases seem to suggest that the event is a one-sided affair, with the unwitting victim engaging a passive, non-contributory role. But in these cases the third stage was preceded by the victim's impropriety, the offender's inquiry of the victim or audience, and a response affirming the victim's intent to be censorious. On assessing the event as one of insult and challenge, the offender elicited a statement indicating to participants, including himself, his intended line of action, secured a weapon, positioned it, and dropped the victim in a single motion.

While ten cases witness the victim's demise during this stage, the typical case consists of various verbal and physically nonlethal moves. The most common type of retaliation was a verbal challenge, occurring in 43 percent of the cases. These took the form of an ultimatum: either apologize, flee the situation, or discontinue the inappropriate conduct, or face physical harm or death:

> *Case 54* The offender, victim, and two neighbors were sitting in the living room drinking wine. The victim started calling the offender, his wife, abusive names. The offender told him to "shut up." Nevertheless, he continued. Finally, she shouted, "I said shut up. If you don't shut up and stop it, I'm going to kill you and I mean it."

In 22 percent of the cases, the offender's retaliation took the form of physical violence short of real damage or incapacitation:

> *Case 4* The offender, victim, and three friends were driving in the country drinking beer and wine. At one point, the victim started laughing at the offender's car which he, the victim, scratched a week earlier. The offender asked the victim why he was laughing. The victim responded that the offender's car looked like junk. The offender stopped the car and all got out. The offender asked the victim to repeat his statement. When the victim reiterated his characterization of the

car, the offender struck the victim, knocking him to the ground.

In an other 10 percent, retaliation came by way of countering the victim's impropriety with similar insults or degrading gestures. This response entailed a name-calling, action-matching set of expressions resembling that which would be found between boys in the midst of a playground argument or "playing the dozens" (cf. Berdie, 1947).

The remaining cases, some 11 percent of the sample, were evenly divided. On the one hand, offenders issued specific commands, tinged with hostility and backed with an aggressive posture, calling for their victims to back down. On the other hand, offenders "called out" or invited their victims to fight physically.

This third stage is the offender's opening move in salvaging face and honor. In retaliating by verbal and physically nonlethal means, the offender appeared to suggest to the victim a definition of the situation as one in which violence was suitable in settling questions of face and reputation.

Stage IV. Except for cases in which the victim has been eliminated, the offender's preceding move placed the victim in a problematic and consequential position: either stand up to the challenge and demonstrate strength of character, or apologize, discontinue the inappropriate conduct, or flee the situation and thus withdraw questions of the offender's face while placing one's own in jeopardy. Just as the offender could have dismissed the impropriety, fled the scene, or avoided further contact with the victim, so too did the victim have similar alternatives. Rather than break the escalation in a manner demonstrating weakness, all victims in the remaining sample came into a "working" agreement with

the proffered definition of the situation as one suited for violence. In the majority of cases, the victim's move appeared as an agreement that violence was suitable to the transaction. In some cases, though, the offender interpreted, sometimes incorrectly, the victim's move as implicit agreement to violence. A working agreement was struck in several ways.

The most prominent response, found in 41 percent of the cases, involved noncompliance with the offender's challenge or command, and the continued performance of activities deemed offensive:

> *Case 54* The victim continued ridiculing the offender before friends. The offender finally shouted, "I said shut up. If you don't shut up and stop it, I'm going to kill you and I mean it." The victim continued his abusive line of conduct. The offender proceeded to the kitchen, secured a knife, and returned to the living room. She repeated her warning. The victim rose from his chair, swore at the offender's stupidity, and continued laughing at her. She thrust the knife deep into his chest.

Similarly, a spouse or lover's refusal, under threat of violence, to conciliate a failing marriage or relationship served as tacit acceptance that violence was suitable to the present transaction.

Whether the victim's noncompliance was intentional or not, the offender *interpreted* the move as intentional. Take, for example, the killing of children at the hands of parents. In an earlier illustration, the first move found the parent demanding obedience and backed by a hostile, combative stance. In several of these cases, the child was too young to understand what the parent demanded and the specific consequences for noncompliance. Nevertheless, the child's failure to eat dinner or stop screaming was interpreted by the parent as a voluntary protest, an intentional challenge to authority. Consequently, the unwitting activities of victims may contribute to what offenders define as very real character contests demanding very real lines of opposition.

A second response, occurring in 30 percent of the cases, found victims physically retaliating against their offenders by hitting, kicking, and pushing—responses short of mortal injury:

> *Case 42* The offender and a friend were passing by a local tavern and noticed the victim, a co-worker at a food-processing plant, sitting at the bar. The offender entered the tavern and asked the victim to repay a loan. The victim was angered by the request and refused to pay. The offender then pushed the victim from his stool. Before the victim could react, the bartender asked them to take their fight outside. The victim followed the offender out the door and, from behind, hit the offender with a brick he grabbed from a trash can immediately outside the door. The offender turned and warned the victim that he would beat the victim if he wouldn't pay up and continued his aggressions. The victim then struck the offender in the mouth, knocking out a tooth.

In the remaining cases, victims issued counter-challenges, moves made when offenders' previous moves involved threats and challenges. In some cases, this move came in the form of calling the offender's bluff. In other cases, the counter came in the form of a direct challenge or threat to the offender, a move no different from the ultimatum given victims by offenders.

Unlike simple noncompliance, physical retaliation against offenders and issuance of counter-challenges signify an explicit accep-

tance of violence as a suitable means for demonstrating character and maintaining or salvaging face.

Just as the victim contributed to the escalation toward violence, so too did the audience to the transaction. Seventy percent of all cases were performed before an audience. In these cases, onlookers generally engaged one or two roles. In 57 percent of these cases, interested members of the audience intervened in the transaction, and actively encouraged the use of violence by means of indicating to opponents the initial improprieties, cheering them toward violent action, blocking the encounter from outside interference, or providing lethal weapons:

> *Case 23* The offender's wife moved toward the victim, and hit him in the back of the head with an empty beer bottle stating. "That'll teach you to [molest] my boy. I ought to cut your balls off, you motherfucker." She went over to the bar to get another bottle. The victim pushed himself from the table and rose. He then reached into his pocket to secure something which some bystanders thought was a weapon. One of the bystanders gave the offender an axe handle and suggested that he stop the victim before the victim attacked his wife. The offender moved toward the victim.

In the remaining cases, onlookers were neutral. They were neither encouraging nor discouraging. While neutrality may have been due to fear, civil inattention, or whatever reason, the point is that inaction within a strategic interchange can be interpreted by the opponents as a move favoring the use of violence (cf. Goffman, 1967:115).[2] Consider the statement of the offender in the following case:

> *Case 48* Police officer: Don't you think it was wrong to beat [your daughter] when her

hands were tied behind her back? [Her hands and feet were bound to keep her from scratching.]

Offender: Well, I guess so. But I really didn't think so then, or [my wife] would have said something to stop me.

Stage V. On forging a working agreement, the offender and, in many cases, victim appeared committed to battle. They contributed to and invested in the development of a fateful transaction, one which was problematic and consequential to their face and wider reputation. They placed their character on the line, and alternative methods for assessing character focussed on a working agreement that violence was appropriate. Because opponents appeared to fear displaying weakness in character and consequent loss of face, and because resolution of the contest was situationally bound, demanding an immediacy of response, they appeared committed to following through with expressed or implied intentions.

Commitment to battle was additionally enhanced by the availability of weapons to support verbal threats and challenges. Prior to victory, the offender often sought out and secured weapons capable of overcoming the victim. In 36 percent of the cases, offenders carried hand guns or knives into the setting. In only 13 percent of these cases did offenders bring hand guns or knives into the situation on the assumption that they might be needed if the victims were confronted. In the remainder of these cases such weapons were brought in as a matter of everyday routine. In either event, to inflict the fatal blow required the mere mobilization of the weapon for action. In 64 percent of the cases, the offender either left the situation temporarily to secure a hand gun, rifle, or knife, or transformed the status of some existing situational prop, such as a pillow, telephone cord, kitchen knife, beer mug,

or baseball bat, into a lethal weapon. The possession of weapons makes battle possible, and, in situations defined as calling for violence, probable.

The particular dynamics of the physical interchange are quite varied. In many cases, the battle was brief and precise. In approximately 54 percent of the cases, the offender secured the weapon and dropped the victim in a single shot, stab, or rally of blows. In the remaining cases, the battle was two-sided. One or both secured a weapon and exchanged a series of blows, with one falling in defeat.

CONCLUSION

On the basis of this research, criminal homicide does not appear as a one-sided event with an unwitting victim assuming a passive, noncontributory role. Rather, murder is the outcome of a dynamic interchange between an offender, victim, and, in many cases, bystanders. The offender and victim develop lines of action shaped in part by the actions of the other and focused toward saving or maintaining face and reputation and demonstrating character. Participants develop a working agreement, sometimes implicit, often explicit, that violence is a useful tool for resolving questions of face and character. In some settings, where very small children are murdered, the extent of their participation cannot be great. But generally these patterns characterized all cases irrespective of such variables as age, sex, race, time and place, use of alcohol, and proffered motive.

NOTES

1. Whenever detectives encountered discrepancies in accounts of the structure and development of the transaction, they would routinely

attend to such discrepancies and repair them through their subsequent investigation.

2. When the audience voices its dissatisfaction over the escalation of a character contest, it typically deteriorates. Of the thirty-two rehearsals found in the histories of the cases, about half did not result in death because of the intervention of a dissenting bystander. Discouragement usually took the form of redefining the victim's impropriety as unintentional, or suggesting that backing down at the outset of the escalation is appropriate given the occasion as one for fun and pleasure. While bystanders can be either encouraging or neutral in situations of murder, Wallace (1965) found that in 20 percent of the cases with an audience, some bystanders sought to discourage a violent confrontation, and would themselves often end in the hospital or city morgue. It cannot be determined if my findings are inconsistent with Wallace. He does not specify at what point in the development of the transaction discouraging bystanders intervene. While I found that bystanders were not discouraging in the escalation toward battle. I did find that several cases involved bystanders trying to discourage violence once opponents were committed to or initiated it. It was common in these cases for the bystander to suffer physical injury.

REFERENCES

Banitt, Rivka, Shoshana Katznelson, and Shlomit Streit. 1970. "The situational aspects of violence: A research model." Pp. 241–258 in *Israel Studies in Criminology*, edited by Shlomo Shoham. Tel-Aviv: Gomeh.

Berdie, Ralph. 1947. "Playing the dozens." *Journal of Abnormal and Social Psychology* 42 (January): 102–121.

Blumer, Herbert. 1969. *Symbolic Interactionism: Perspective and Method.* Englewood Cliffs, N.J.: Prentice-Hall.

Bullock, Henry A. 1955. "Urban homicide in theory and fact." *Journal of Criminal Law, Criminology and Police Science* 45 (January–February): 565–575.

Cavan, Sherri. 1963. "Interaction in home territories." *Berkeley Journal of Sociology* 8:17–32.

Goffman, Erving. 1963. *Behavior in Public Places: Notes on the Social Organization of Gatherings.* Glencoy, IL: Free Press.

———. 1967. *Interaction Ritual: Essays on Face-to-Face Behavior.* Garden City, N.Y.: Doubleday.

———. 1969. *Strategic Interaction.* New York: Ballantine.

Goode, William J. 1969. "Violence among intimates." Pp. 941–977 in *Crimes of Violence*, prepared by Donald J. Mulvihill and Melvin M. Tumin. Washington: U.S. Government Printing Office.

Moran, Alvin. 1971. "Criminal homicide: External restraint and subculture of violence." *Criminology* 8 (February): 357–374.

Shibutani, Tamotsu. 1961. *Society and Personality: An Interactionist Approach to Social Psychology.* Englewood Cliffs, N.J.: Prentice-Hall.

Shoham, Shlomo, Sara Ben-David, Rivka Vadmani, Joseph Atar, and Suzanne Fleming. 1973. "The cycles of interaction in violence." Pp. 69–87 in *Israel Studies in Criminology*, edited by Shlomo Shoham. Jerusalem: Jerusalem Academic Press.

Schafer, Stephan. 1968. *The Victim and His Criminal.* New York: Random House.

Toch, Hans. 1969. *Violent Men: An Inquiry into the Psychology of Violence.* Chicago: Aldine.

Wallace, Samuel E. 1965. "Patterns of violence in San Juan." Pp. 43–48 in *Interdisciplinary Problems in Criminology: Papers of the American Society of Criminology*, 1964, edited by Walter C. Reckless and Charles L. Newman. Columbus: Ohio State University Press.

Wolfgang, Marvin E. 1958. *Patterns of Criminal Homicide.* Philadelphia: University of Pennsylvania Press.

Crime and Low Self-Control

Michael R. Gottfredson and Travis Hirschi

Lack of self-control does not require crime and can be counteracted by situational conditions or other properties of the individual. At the same time, we suggest that high self-control effectively reduces the possibility of crime—that is, those possessing it will be substantially less likely at all periods of life to engage in criminal acts.

THE ELEMENTS OF SELF-CONTROL

Criminal acts provide *immediate* gratification of desires. A major characteristic of people with low self-control is therefore a tendency to respond to tangible stimuli in the immediate environment, to have a concrete "here and now" orientation. People with high self-control, in contrast, tend to defer gratification.

Criminal acts provide *easy or simple* gratification of desires. They provide money without work, sex without courtship, revenge without court delays. People lacking self-con-

trol also tend to lack diligence, tenacity, or persistence in a course of action.

Criminal acts are *exciting, risky, or thrilling*. They involve stealth, danger, speed, agility, deception, or power. People lacking self-control therefore tend to be adventuresome, active, and physical. Those with high levels of self-control tend to be cautious, cognitive, and verbal.

Crimes provide *few or meager long-term benefits*. They are not equivalent to a job or a career. On the contrary, crimes interfere with long-term commitments to jobs, marriages, family, or friends. People with low self-control thus tend to have unstable marriages, friendships, and job profiles. They tend to be little interested in and unprepared for long-term occupational pursuits.

Crimes require *little skill or planning*. The cognitive requirements for most crimes are minimal. It follows that people lacking self-control need not possess or value cognitive or academic skills. The manual skills re-

From Michael R. Gottfredson and Travis Hirschi. 1990. *A General Theory of Crime*. Stanford: Stanford University Press. Reprinted by permission of Stanford University Press, © 1990.

quired for most crimes are minimal. It follows that people lacking self-control need not possess manual skills that require training or apprenticeship.

Crimes often result in *pain or discomfort for the victim*. Property is lost, bodies are injured, privacy is violated, trust is broken. It follows that people with low self-control tend to be self-centered, indifferent, or insensitive to the suffering and needs of others. It does not follow, however, that people with low self-control are routinely unkind or antisocial. On the contrary, they may discover the immediate and easy rewards of charm and generosity.

Recall that crime involves the pursuit of immediate pleasure. It follows that people lacking self-control will also tend to pursue immediate pleasures that are *not* criminal: they will tend to smoke, drink, use drugs, gamble, have children out of wedlock, and engage in illicit sex.

Crimes require the interaction of an offender with people or their property. It does not follow that people lacking self-control will tend to be gregarious or social. However, it does follow that, other things being equal, gregarious or social people are more likely to be involved in criminal acts.

The major benefit of many crimes is not pleasure but relief from momentary irritation. The irritation caused by a crying child is often the stimulus for physical abuse. That caused by a taunting stranger in a bar is often the stimulus for aggravated assault. It follows that people with low self-control tend to have minimal tolerance for frustration and little ability to respond to conflict through verbal rather than physical means.

Crimes involve the risk of violence and physical injury, of pain and suffering on the part of the offender. It does not follow that people with low self-control will tend to be tolerant of physical pain or to be indifferent to physical discomfort. It does follow that people tolerant of physical pain or indifferent to physical discomfort will be more likely to engage in criminal acts whatever their level of self-control.

In sum, people who lack self-control will tend to be impulsive, insensitive, physical (as opposed to mental), risk-taking, short-sighted, and nonverbal, and they will tend therefore to engage in criminal and analogous acts. Since these traits can be identified prior to the age of responsibility for crime, since there is considerable tendency for these traits to come together in the same people, and since the traits tend to persist through life, it seems reasonable to consider them as comprising a stable construct useful in the explanation of crime.

THE MANY MANIFESTATIONS OF LOW SELF-CONTROL

Our image of the "offender" suggests that crime is not an automatic or necessary consequence of low self-control. It suggests that many noncriminal acts analogous to crime (such as accidents, smoking, and alcohol use) are also manifestations of low self-control. Our image therefore implies that no specific act, type of crime, or form of deviance is uniquely required by the absence of self-control.

Because both crime and analogous behaviors stem from low self-control (that is, both are manifestations of low self-control), they will all be engaged in at a relatively high rate by people with low self-control. Within the domain of crime, then, there will be much versatility among offenders in the criminal acts in which they engage.

By versatility we mean that offenders commit a wide variety of criminal acts, with no strong inclination to pursue a specific criminal act or a pattern of criminal acts to the exclusion of others. Most theories suggest that offenders tend to specialize, whereby such terms as robber, burglar, drug dealer, rapist, and murderer have predictive or descriptive import. In fact, some theories create offender specialization as part of their explanation of crime. For example, Cloward and Ohlin (1960) create distinctive subcultures of delinquency around particular forms of criminal behavior, identifying subcultures specializing in theft, violence, or drugs. In a related way, books are written about white-collar crime as though it were a clearly distinct specialty requiring a unique explanation. Research projects are undertaken for study of drug use, or vandalism, or teen pregnancy (as though every study of delinquency were not a study of drug use and vandalism and teenage sexual behavior).

The evidence that offenders are likely to engage in noncriminal acts psychologically or theoretically equivalent to crime is, because of the relatively high rates of these "noncriminal" acts, even easier to document. Thieves are likely to smoke, drink, and skip school at considerably higher rates than nonthieves. Offenders are considerably more likely than nonoffenders to be involved in most types of accidents, including household fires, auto crashes, and unwanted pregnancies. They are also considerably more likely to die at an early age.

Good research on drug use and abuse routinely reveals that the correlates of delinquency and drug use are the same. As Akers (1984) has noted, "compared to the abstaining teenager, the drinking, smoking, and drug-taking teen is much more likely to be getting into fights, stealing, hurting other people, and committing other delinquencies." Akers goes on to say, "but the variation in the order in which they take up these things leaves little basis for proposing the causation of one by the other." In our view, the relation between drug use and delinquency is not a causal question. The correlates are the same because drug use and delinquency are both manifestations of an underlying tendency to pursue short-term, immediate pleasure. This underlying tendency (i.e., lack of self-control) has many manifestations, as listed by Harrison Gough (1948:362):

> unconcern over the rights and privileges of others when recognizing them would interfere with personal satisfaction in any way; impulsive behavior, or apparent incongruity between the strength of the stimulus and the magnitude of the behavioral response; inability to form deep or persistent attachments to other persons or to identify in interpersonal relationships; poor judgment and planning in attaining defined goals; apparent lack of anxiety and distress over social maladjustment and unwillingness or inability to consider maladjustment qua maladjustment; a tendency to project blame onto others and to take no responsibility for failures; meaningless prevarication, often about trivial matters in situations where detection is inevitable; almost complete lack of dependability . . . and willingness to assume responsibility; and, finally, emotional poverty.

This combination of characteristics has been revealed in the life histories of the subjects in the famous studies by Lee Robins. Robins is one of the few researchers to focus on the varieties of deviance and the way they tend to go together in the lives of those she designates as having "antisocial personalities." In her words: "We refer to someone who fails to maintain close personal relationships with anyone else, [who] performs poorly on the job, who is involved in illegal behaviors (whether or not apprehended), who fails to support himself and his dependents without outside aid, and who is given to sudden changes of plan and loss of temper in response to what appear to others as minor frustrations" (1978:255).

For 30 years Robins traced 524 children referred to a guidance clinic in St. Louis, Missouri, and she compared them to a control group matched on IQ, age, sex, and area of the city. She discovered that, in comparison to the control group, those people referred at an early age were more likely to be arrested as adults (for a wide variety of offenses), were less likely to get married, were more likely to be divorced, were more likely to marry a spouse with a behavior problem, were less likely to have children (but if they had children were likely to have more children), were more likely to have children with behavior problems, were more likely to be unemployed, had considerably more frequent job changes, were more likely to be on welfare, had fewer contacts with relatives, had fewer friends, were substantially less likely to attend church, were less likely to serve in the armed forces and more likely to be dishonorably discharged if they did serve, were more likely to exhibit physical evidence of excessive alcohol use, and were more likely to be hospitalized for psychiatric problems (Robins 1966:42–73).

Note that these outcomes are consistent with four general elements of our notion of low self-control: basic stability of individual differences over a long period of time; great variability in the kinds of criminal acts engaged in; conceptual or causal equivalence of criminal and noncriminal acts; and inability to predict the specific forms of deviance engaged in, whether criminal or noncriminal. In our view, the idea of an antisocial personality defined by certain behavioral consequences is too positivistic or deterministic, suggesting that the offender must do certain things given his antisocial personality. Thus we would say only that the subjects in question are *more likely* to commit criminal acts (as the data indicate they are). We do not make commission

of criminal acts part of the definition of the individual with low self-control.

Be this as it may, Robins's retrospective research shows that predictions derived from a concept of antisocial personality are highly consistent with the results of prospective longitudinal and cross-sectional research: offenders do not specialize; they tend to be involved in accidents, illness, and death at higher rates than the general population; they tend to have difficulty persisting in a job regardless of the particular characteristics of the job (no job will turn out to be good job); they have difficulty acquiring and retaining friends; and they have difficulty meeting the demands of long-term financial commitments (such as mortgages or car payments) and the demands of parenting.

Seen in this light, the "costs" of low self-control for the individual may far exceed the costs of his criminal acts. In fact, it appears that crime is often among the least serious consequences of a lack of self-control in terms of the quality of life of those lacking it.

THE CAUSES OF SELF-CONTROL

We know better what deficiencies in self-control lead to than where they come from. One thing is, however, clear: low self-control is not produced by training, tutelage, or socialization. As a matter of fact, all of the characteristics associated with low self-control tend to show themselves in the absence of nurturance, discipline, or training. Given the classical appreciation of the causes of human behavior, the implications of this fact are straightforward: the causes of low self-control are negative rather than positive; self-control is unlikely in the absence of effort, intended or unintended, to create it. This assumption separates the present theory from most modern theories of crime, where the offender is automatically seen as a product of positive forces, a creature of learning, particular pressures, or specific defect.

At this point it would be easy to construct a theory of crime causation, according to which characteristics of potential offenders lead them ineluctably to the commission of criminal acts. Our task at this point would simply be to identify the likely sources of impulsiveness, intelligence, risk-taking, and the like. But to do so would be to follow the path that has proven so unproductive in the past, the path according to which criminals commit crimes irrespective of the characteristics of the setting or situation.

We can avoid this pitfall by recalling the elements inherent in the decision to commit a criminal act. The object of the offense is clearly pleasurable, and universally so. Engaging in the act, however, entails some risk of social, legal, and/or natural sanctions. Whereas the pleasure attained by the act is direct, obvious, and immediate, the pains risked by it are not obvious, or direct, and are in any event at greater remove from it. It follows that, though there will be little variability among people in their ability to see the pleasures of crime, there will be considerable variability in their ability to calculate potential pains. But the problem goes further than this: whereas the pleasures of crime are reasonably equally distributed over the population, this is not true for the pains. Everyone appreciates money; not everyone dreads parental anger or disappointment upon learning that the money was stolen.

So, the dimensions of self-control are, in our view, factors affecting calculation of the consequences of one's acts. The impulsive or short-sighted person fails to consider the negative or painful consequences of his acts; the insensitive person has fewer negative consequences to consider; the less intelligent person also has fewer negative consequences to consider (has less to lose).

No known social group, whether criminal or noncriminal, actively or purposefully attempts to reduce the self-control of its members. Social life is not enhanced by low self-control and its consequences. On the contrary, the exhibition of these tendencies undermines harmonious group relations and the ability to achieve collective ends. These facts explicitly deny that a tendency to crime is a product of socialization, culture, or positive learning of any sort.

The traits composing low self-control are also not conductive to the achievement of long-term individual goals. On the contrary, they impede educational and occupational achievement, destroy interpersonal relations, and undermine physical health and economic well-being. Such facts explicitly deny the notion that criminality is an alternative route to the goals otherwise obtainable through legitimate avenues. It follows that people who care about the interpersonal skill, educational and occupational achievement, and physical and economic well-being of those in their care will seek to rid them of these traits.

Two general sources of variation are immediately apparent in this scheme. The first is the variation among children in the degree to which they manifest such traits to begin with. The second is the variation among caretakers in the degree to which they recognize low self-control and its consequences and the degree to which they are willing and able to correct it.

There is good evidence that some of the traits predicting subsequent involvement in crime appear as early as they can be reliably measured, including low intelligence, high activity level, physical strength, and adventuresomeness. The evidence suggests that the connection between these traits and commission of criminal acts ranges from weak to moderate.

Other traits affecting crime appear later and seem to be largely products of ineffective or incomplete socialization. For example, differences in impulsivity and insensitivity become noticeable later in childhood when they are no longer common to all children. The ability and willingness to delay immediate gratification for some larger purpose may therefore be assumed to be a consequence of training. Much parental action is in fact geared toward suppression of impulsive behavior, toward making the child consider the long-range consequences of acts. Consistent sensitivity to the needs and feelings of others may also be assumed to be a consequence of training. Indeed, much parental behavior is directed toward teaching the child about the rights and feelings of others, and of how these rights and feelings ought to constrain the child's behavior. All of these points focus our attention on child-rearing.

CHILD-REARING AND SELF-CONTROL: THE FAMILY

The major "cause" of low self-control thus appears to be ineffective child-rearing. Put in positive terms, several conditions appear necessary to produce a socialized child. Perhaps the place to begin looking for these conditions is the research literature on the relation between family conditions and delinquency. This research (e.g., Glueck and Glueck 1950; McCord and McCord 1959) has examined the connection between many family factors and delinquency. It reports that discipline, supervision, and affection tend to be missing in the homes of delinquents; that the behavior of the parents is often "poor" (e.g., excessive drinking and poor supervision [Glueck and Glueck 1950:110-11]); and that the parents of delinquents are unusually likely to have criminal records themselves. Indeed, according to Michael Rutter and Henri Giller, "of the parental characteristics associated with delin-

quency, criminality is the most striking and most consistent" (1984:182).

Such information undermines the many explanations of crime that ignore the family, but in this form it does not represent much of an advance over the belief of the general public (and those who deal with offenders in the criminal justice system) that "defective upbringing" or "neglect" in the home is the primary cause of crime.

To put these standard research findings in perspective, we think it necessary to define the conditions necessary for adequate child-rearing to occur. The minimum conditions seem to be these: in order to teach the child self-control, someone must (1) monitor the child's behavior; (2) recognize deviant behavior when it occurs; and (3) punish such behavior. This seems simple and obvious enough. All that is required to activate the system is affection for *or* investment in the child. The person who cares for the child will watch his behavior, see him doing things he should not do, and correct him. The result may be a child more capable of delaying gratification, more sensitive to the interests and desires of others, more independent, more willing to accept restraints on his activity, and more unlikely to use force or violence to attain his ends.

When we seek the causes of low self-control, we ask where this system can go wrong. Obviously, parents do not prefer their children to be unsocialized in the terms described. We can therefore rule out in advance the possibility of positive socialization to unsocialized behavior (as cultural or subcultural deviance theories suggest). Still, the system can go wrong at any one of four places. First, the parents may not care for the child (in which case none of the other conditions would be met); second, the parents, even if they care, may not have the time or energy to monitor the child's behavior; third, the parents, even if they care *and* monitor, may not see anything wrong with the child's behavior; finally, even if everything else is in place, the parents may not have the inclination or the means to punish the child.

The Attachment of the Parent to the Child

Our model states that parental concern for the welfare or behavior of the child is a necessary condition for successful child-rearing. Because it is too often assumed that all parents are alike in their love for their children, the evidence directly on this point is not as good or extensive as it could be. However, what exists is clearly consistent with the model. Glueck and Glueck (1950:125–28) report that, compared to the fathers of delinquents, fathers of nondelinquents were twice as likely to be warmly disposed toward their sons and one-fifth as likely to be hostile toward them. In the same sample, 28 percent of the mothers of delinquents were characterized as "indifferent or hostile" toward the child as compared to 4 percent of the mothers of nondelinquents. The evidence suggests that stepparents are especially unlikely to have feelings of affection toward their stepchildren (Burgess 1980), adding in contemporary society to the likelihood that children will be "reared" by people who do not especially care for them.

Parental Supervision

The connection between social control and self-control could not be more direct than in the case of parental supervision of the child. Such supervision presumably prevents criminal or analogous acts and at the same time trains the child to avoid them on his own. Consistent with this assumption, supervision tends to be a major predictor of delinquency, however supervision or delinquency is measured.

Our general theory in principle provides a method of separating supervision as external control from supervision as internal control. For one thing, offenses differ in the degree to which they can be prevented through monitoring; children at one age are monitored much more closely than children at other ages; girls are supervised more closely than boys. In some situations, monitoring is universal or nearly constant; in other situations monitoring for some offenses is virtually absent. In the present context, however, the concern is with the connection between supervision and self-control, a connection established by the stronger tendency of those poorly supervised when young to commit crimes as adults (McCord 1979).

Recognition of Deviant Behavior

In order for supervision to have an impact on self-control, the supervisor must perceive deviant behavior when it occurs. Remarkably, not all parents are adept at recognizing lack of self-control. Some parents allow the child to do pretty much as he pleases without interference. Extensive television-viewing is one modern example, as is the failure to require completion of homework, to prohibit smoking, to curtail the use of physical force, or to see to it that the child actually attends school. (As noted, truancy among second-graders presumably reflects on the adequacy of parental awareness of the child's misbehavior.) Again, the research is not as good as it should be, but evidence of "poor conduct standards" in the homes of delinquents is common.

Punishment of Deviant Acts

Control theories explicitly acknowledge the necessity of sanctions in preventing criminal behavior. They do not suggest that the major sanctions are legal or corporal. On the contrary, as we have seen, they suggest that disapproval by people one cares about is the most powerful of sanctions. Effective punishment by the parent or major caretaker therefore usually entails nothing more than explicit disapproval of unwanted behavior. The criticism of control theories that dwells on their alleged cruelty is therefore simply misguided or ill informed.

Not all caretakers punish effectively. In fact, some are too harsh and some are too lenient. Given our model, however, rewarding good behavior cannot compensate for failure to correct deviant behavior.

REFERENCES

Akers, Ronald. 1984. "Delinquent Behavior, Drugs, and Alcohol: What Is the Relationship?" *Today's Delinquent* 3:19–47.

Burgess, Robert. 1980. "Family Violence," in T. Hirschi and M. Gottfredson (eds.), *Understanding Crime*. Beverly Hills: Sage.

Cloward, Richard, and Lloyd Ohlin. 1960. *Delinquency and Opportunity*. Glencoe, IL: Free Press.

Glueck, Sheldon, and Eleanor Glueck. 1950. *Unraveling Juvenile Delinquency*. Cambridge, MA: Harvard University Press.

Gough, Harrison. 1948. "A Sociological Theory of Psychopathy." *American Journal of Sociology* 53:359–366.

McCord, Joan. 1979. "Some Child-Rearing Antecedents of Criminal Behavior in Adult Men." *Journal of Personality and Social Psychology* 37:1477–1486.

McCord, William, and Joan McCord. 1959. *Origins of Crime*. New York: Columbia University Press.

Robins, Lee. 1966. *Deviant Children Grown Up*. Baltimore: Williams and Wilkins.

———. 1978. "Aetiological Implications in Studies of Childhood Histories Relating to Antisocial Personality," in R. Hare and D. Schalling (eds.), *Psychopathic Behavior*. New York: Wiley.

Rutter, Michael, and Henri Giller 1984. *Juvenile Delinquency*. New York: Guilford.

STUDY QUESTIONS TO PART I

1. Marvin Wolfgang and Franco Ferracuti present seven propositions that are designed to clarify and qualify their subculture of violence theory. Describe how each of these propositions helps to refine the theory so that it is not interpreted simplistically.

2. Elliott Currie rejects the "hard cultural" perspective of Wolfgang and Ferracuti, and others, and replaces it with a "soft cultural" thesis. (a) What is the main difference between the "hard" and the "soft" cultural approaches? (b) Is the "soft cultural" thesis superior to the "hard cultural" perspective? (c) Why or why not?

3. According to Currie, comparing the United States to Japan and European nations helps us understand why violent crime is so much higher in America. (a) What are the key variables in Currie's comparative analysis? (b) How do these variables help predict American and European violent crime rates?

4. How would Lawrence Cohen and Marcus Felson's routine activities theory account for increases and decreases in the crime rate over time?

5. Is routine activities theory applicable to crimes that occur inside the home, such as child abuse and wife beating?

6. In what ways do the neighborhood factors of density, poverty, mixed use, transience, and dilapidation create conditions conducive to crime and disorder, according to Rodney Stark's social disorganization perspective?

7. What types of crime are best explained by Stark's propositions, and what types of crime are not easily explained by his propositions?
8. Describe the five stages that precede an act of homicide, according to David Luckenbill's study.
9. Drawing on Luckenbill's findings, why is it important to study the causes of crime at the microlevel?
10. Michael Gottfredson and Travis Hirschi identify several "elements of self-control," which they derive from ideas about the attractions of crime to persons with low self-control. (a) Are their claims convincing? (b) What evidence is presented to support those claims?
11. Describe the ways in which ineffective child-rearing produces low self-control in children, according to Gottfredson and Hirschi.

INTRODUCTION TO Part Two:
Controversial Crimes

Some crimes are more controversial than others. Part II features readings on a number of crimes for which there is continuing disagreement (1) over whether the act ought to be criminalized at all, (2) over the very nature of the crime, or (3) over the best approach to combating the crime.

The first reading, Norval Morris and Gordon Hawkins' "The Overreach of the Criminal Law," tackles *victimless crimes*. Originally published in 1970, the authors' arguments and proposals are no less relevant today. According to Morris and Hawkins, American criminal law has "overreached" in criminalizing a host of behaviors that are "victimless"—in the sense that they are consensual acts with no complainant and no readily identifiable victim. Criminalizing such things as bigamy, drug use, gambling, prostitution, public drunkenness, sodomy, and other nonpredatory acts interferes with the freedom of citizens, breeds disrespect for the law, provides temptation for organized crime to market illicit goods and services, and invites police corruption (e.g., taking payoffs in return for disregarding these

crimes). While some victimless crimes are deemed immoral by a substantial segment of American society, another segment of the population believes that these activities should be decriminalized, and a smaller number have actually engaged in such prohibited conduct. For example, public support for the legalization of prostitution ranges from a quarter to half the population in various polls, and 18 percent of American men report that they have patronized a prostitute at some time in their lives (Weitzer 2000:2, 164–165).

Victimless crimes are, in short, controversial for many Americans. For Morris and Hawkins, the costs of criminalizing such acts far outweigh any benefits, and they propose decriminalizing such offenses. One obvious way of cutting crime is to reduce the number of acts that are criminalized. Decriminalization would also free police and other criminal justice agencies to concentrate on more serious crimes. Many Americans, however, oppose decriminalizing "victimless" offenses, on the grounds that these crimes (1) are immoral, (2) may cause harm to others (family members, local communities, etc.), or (3) may lead to more serious offending.

"Hate crime" is a relatively new offense category that has recently generated considerable public debate and legislative action in the United States. Forty-five states have passed hate crime laws that increase the punishment for crimes motivated by prejudice toward the victim. In 1997, 9,861 hate crimes were reported to the police: 60 percent were racially motivated, 14 percent were motivated by sexual-orientation bias, and the remainder involved attacks against an ethnic or religious group (FBI 1999:7). James Jacobs and Kimberly Potter examine trends in the political and criminal justice response to hate crimes, and argue that the issue is fraught with problems. Jacobs and Potter contend that the very concept of "hate crime" is problematic, that some hate-crime laws may be unconstitutional, and that punishing a crime more harshly just because it is motivated by prejudice is flawed. Notwithstanding these problems, most politicians believe that hate-crime laws are needed, and growing numbers of offenders are being prosecuted under these laws.

A generation ago, child abuse was not taken seriously by the authorities in the United States. Since then, a sea change has taken place in American views of child abuse and family violence more generally. While some officials continue to downplay the seriousness of domestic violence, the criminal justice system is now much more responsive to victims than it was in the past. In fact, some agencies arguably have gone overboard in their efforts to protect women and children from abuse. One example is the frenzy over child abuse at day care centers that erupted in the 1980s, which involved allegations of satanic ritual abuse of children at some centers. The first major scandal

came to light in 1983 at the McMartin Preschool in Manhattan Beach, California, where 369 children were identified as victims; alleged abuses included the ritualistic ingestion of urine, blood, and human flesh; mutilation of corpses; sexual orgies with day care providers; and many other atrocities (deYoung 1998). Prosecutions of the McMartin staff and their counterparts at several other day care centers featured the sensational testimony of social workers, police officers, and mental health professionals—some of whom appeared on television talk shows and prime-time newsmagazine shows. In the end, the McMartin case and some of the other cases collapsed: Children recanted; charges were dismissed; mistrials were declared; day care providers were acquitted in court; and convictions were overturned (deYoung 1998). None of this implies that child abuse at day care centers is fictional, but only that it appears to be exaggerated. One study of 270 day care centers across the country found that sexual abuse of children at the centers was very rare, affecting only .05 percent of children enrolled at the centers (Leary 1988). The "moral panic" of ritual child abuse during the 1980s demonstrates how easy it was for parents and the authorities to make accusations, sometimes with dubious evidence, and how hard it was for the accused to fight the charges.

This same dynamic is mirrored in how some authorities have handled allegations of child abuse at home, where the accused are parents, relatives, or other persons. Leslie Margolin's chapter, "Child Abuse," examines how social workers reached conclusions that babysitters had abused children under their care. Conditioned by organizational norms and pressures, the social workers Margolin studied made every effort to "discover" child abuse. Staff operated with an overriding presumption against the suspect and in favor of a determination that abuse had taken place. That over half of the suspects either denied the charges or were not interviewed at all did not prevent investigators from labeling them child abusers. The child "victims," by contrast, were viewed as credible only if they made charges of abuse; when they said the accused babysitter was innocent, their testimony was consistently disregarded and explained away by the social workers. As Margolin writes, the "goal of the child abuse investigation is not to determine an individual's guilt or innocence but to find evidence to be used in recording or documenting what is already taken for granted," that abuse indeed occurred.

Insofar as investigators in other cities operate similarly to those studied by Margolin, one clear policy implication is the need to change the way social workers "prove" the existence of child abuse and to more carefully weigh the testimony of all parties involved before rushing to judgment. Again, none of this is to suggest that child abuse is a myth. Quite the contrary: 8 percent of the population reports being a victim of child abuse, according to a 1989 Gallup poll, and there is widespread agreement that child abuse is wrong and must be punished. It is equally important, however, to protect innocent people from being so easily branded as abusers.

School shootings in recent years have generated tremendous public anxiety and outrage, criticisms of school officials for their failure to prevent shootings, and pressure on legislators to pass laws to crack down on youth violence. Each shooting generates renewed calls for more gun control and for more stringent security measures at schools. Despite popular impressions of an epidemic of school violence, there has been no dramatic increase in violent incidents over the past 25 years. Intensive media coverage of school shootings might give the impression that these events occur frequently, but the reading "School Shootings," by Ronald Burns and Charles Crawford, shows that this is not the case. Burns and Crawford argue that the recent spate of school shootings has become a "moral panic," a problem blown way out of proportion by the mass media, politicians, and other claims-makers who seize on such incidents in part because they serve their own interests. The moral panic thesis helps explain why events, like school shootings, that occur rarely have been given so much attention in American society.

"Date rape" may be defined as unconsensual, forced sex, within a dating context. Date rape is more controversial than "stranger rape" because of the relationship between the offender and the victim and the greater difficulty of documenting "lack of consent" in sexual encounters between the two parties. Unlike stranger rapists, who are unknown to the victim, date rapists attack persons they know. Also unlike many stranger rapes that are planned in advance, date rape tends to be unplanned, often resulting from the offender's unmet expectations during the date (similar to "saving face" as a precursor to homicide in Luckenbill's study). Date rape also differs from stranger rape in terms of the response of the criminal justice system. Police, prosecutors, judges, and juries are much more likely to discount victims' allegations in date rape cases, with the result that prosecutors seldom bring charges in these cases, and when they do, convictions are more difficult to obtain than in stranger rape cases (Estrich 1987; Fairstein 1993; Vachss 1993).

Date rape appears to be much more prevalent than is commonly believed, and these attacks are rarely reported to the police. According to the 1999 National Crime Victimization Survey, 47 percent of all female rape victims were attacked by a friend or acquaintance (which includes date rapes), 24 percent were attacked by a family member or another relative, and 28 percent by a stranger (BJS 2000:8). Only 5 percent of date rape victims reported the attack to the police, one study found (Koss et al. 1987).

Eugene Kanin's article, "Date Rape," is a fascinating study that attempts to explain why men rape women on dates, by comparing a sample of male college students who admitted to rape with a sample that had not raped. Rather than being sexually "deprived," the rapists were in fact more sexually active than other college students, but their desire for even more sex left them frustrated. In other words, they were unsatisfied with their frequent sexual achievements and thus inclined to engage in sexual conquests by force. Kanin found that male friends had encouraged these men to expect a great deal of sex, even if it meant using force against some women (see also Schwartz et al. 2001). As Kanin puts it, date rapists experience "socialization in a hypererotic male culture, a culture where sexual success is of paramount importance in the maintenance of self-esteem, and the inability to achieve sexual success" can result in rape.

In Kanin's study, "rape is *primarily* being examined from a sexual perspective rather than from one that views it as an expression of power and aggression." He argues that date rape and stranger rape differ in terms of offenders' motives: Stranger rape is primarily driven by motives of power and domination over victims, whereas date rape has a stronger sexual component. Nevertheless, date rape still involves sexual *conquest* and the use of power to overcome victims. As Kanin himself points out, even in date rape, "the power–aggression compo-

nent is, in one form or another, *ipso facto* present." The idea that power and control are present in all rape situations is widely accepted by criminologists.

Computer crime refers to the use of a computer to intentionally bring harm to a victim and benefit the perpetrator. Victims include businesses, government agencies, and ordinary citizens, and the crimes include spreading computer viruses, theft of credit card and other confidential information, and threats to the operations of public utilities and to national security. Focusing just on the financial costs, the average cost of a computer crime is perhaps 200 times greater than the relatively modest yield from the typical bank robbery.

In their article, "Computer Crime," Stephen Rosoff, Henry Pontell, and Robert Tillman describe several types of offenses—hacking, sabotage, espionage, electronic theft, and embezzlement of funds. With the increasing use of computers, opportunities for these crimes are rising—with growing numbers of victims—and becoming increasingly serious, including cyber attacks on the FBI and other national security agencies. One type of computer crime not discussed in the Rosoff, Pontell, and Tillman article is the use of the Internet to distribute child pornography or to make contact with underage girls and boys for purposes of sexual communication and possibly an illicit rendezvous. The Internet has opened up new opportunities for individuals to engage in crime and other deviant behavior, but it also offers law enforcement agencies new opportunities for surveillance and control of crime.

Corporate crime has never received the same kind of attention as street crime from the public, legislators, or law enforcement. Yet it costs the nation dearly. The financial losses from corporate crime far exceed those of street crimes. The estimated $13.3 billion in annual losses from conventional crime pales in comparison to the costs of corporate crime; the annual toll from antitrust violations alone is estimated at $250 billion (Coleman 1998:9). And corporate crime can also cause illness, injury, and death; in fact, "white-collar criminals probably kill more people than all the violent criminals put together" (Coleman 1998:11), if one considers all the violations of occupational health and safety codes, the manufacture of dangerous products, and illegal pollution of the environment.

The recent scandal over Firestone tires on Ford Explorers, which have been linked to 200 fatalities and 700 injuries after the tires failed, demonstrates how harmful corporate crime can be. The available evidence suggests that both Ford and Firestone knew their products were dangerous, but failed to correct the problems because of financial considerations. Many Americans believe that Ford and Firestone committed crimes: A September 2000 CNN/*USA Today* poll found that 48 percent believed that either Ford or Firestone had engaged in "criminal behavior" that "should be prosecuted in court," while 34 percent disagreed.

The same dynamic—favoring profits over consumer safety—was apparent in the 1970s with another Ford product, the Pinto. The Pinto's design left its gas tank unprotected and prone to puncture in rear-end collisions, converting the car into a firetrap when the leaked gas ignited. The evidence shows that Ford was well aware of the defect and knew that it could be fixed at relatively little cost per car ($11), but to recall the 1.5 million Pintos then on the road would have cost Ford $16.5 million (Cullen, Maakestad, and Cavendar 1987). Ford elected to risk drivers' lives instead of recalling and fixing the cars. In the end, this was a colossal miscalculation: Ford later agreed to recall the cars, and the recall, coupled with several multimillion-dollar judgments in civil suits and the effect of bad publicity on Ford sales, cost the company dearly. History seems to be repeating itself three decades later in the Ford–Firestone scandal. Civil suits by victims' families have been initiated, and sales of Ford Explorers and Firestone tires have plummeted.

Events like these have helped to lower public confidence in big business, and a significant proportion of the American population believes that corporate criminals should be punished more severely than they typically are. In a 1985 opinion poll, for instance, 68 percent of the public felt that the government was not making "enough of an effort to catch white-collar criminals," and 65 percent thought that when they are convicted, the punishment given to white-collar offenders is "too lenient" (only 1 percent thought the punishment "too harsh" and 24 percent considered it "about right"). But what kind of punishment is most appropriate for corporate offenders? John Braithwaite and Gilbert Geis ("Corporate Crime") tackle this question. After describing several important differences between corporate crime and the "traditional" property and violent crimes, they present six propositions regarding the best strategies for combating corporate crime. Whereas the standard criminal justice policies of deterrence, incapacitation, public shaming, and rehabilitation do not seem very effective in reducing recidivism among conventional offenders, Braithwaite and Geis argue that such methods may be very effective when applied to corporate offenders.

When most people think of "crime" they think of predatory street crimes like robbery, rape, and murder. We know from the readings on computer crime and corporate crime that these offenses can be very harmful as well. But there is another type of crime that is serious but often ignored: political crimes committed by the government, or what William Chambliss calls "state-organized crime." Despite the fact that state-sponsored crime victimizes individuals and negatively affects society, the field of criminology has paid scant attention to it. *State-organized crimes* are acts that the law defines as criminal, committed by state officials on behalf of the state, not for their own personal gain. Chambliss describes several instances of American government involvement in criminal activity, including drug smuggling during the Vietnam war, arms smuggling during the infamous Iran-Contra scandal of the mid-1980s, and state-sponsored assassinations of foreign political leaders. He explains these events by identifying contradictions between legal constraints on government action and government officials' pursuit of goals that cannot be achieved through legitimate means. To resolve this dilemma and achieve their goals, government agents sometimes violate the law, with socially harmful and bloody results.

REFERENCES

BJS [Bureau of Justice Statistics]. 2000. *Criminal Victimization in 1999.* U.S. Department of Justice.

Coleman, James William. 1998. *The Criminal Elite: Understanding White-Collar Crime.* New York: St. Martin's Press.

Cullen, Francis T., W. J. Maakstad, and Gray Cavender. 1987. *Corporate Crime under Attack: The Ford Pinto Case and Beyond.* Cincinnati: Anderson.

deYoung, Mary. 1998. "Another Look at Moral Panics: The Case of Satanic Day Care Centers," *Deviant Behavior* 19:257–278.

Estrich, Susan. 1987. *Real Rape.* Cambridge: Harvard University Press.

Fairstein, Linda. 1993. *Sexual Violence.* New York: William Morrow.

FBI. 1999. *Hate Crime Statistics, 1997.* Washington, DC: U.S. Department of Justice.

Koss, Mary P., Christine Gidycz, and Nadine Wisniewski. 1987. "The Scope of Rape," *Journal of Counseling and Clinical Psychology* 55:162–170.

Leary, Warren E. 1988. "Risk of Abuse in Day Care Held Low," *New York Times,* March 22.

Schwartz, Martin, Walter DeKeseredy, David Tait, and Shahid Alvi. 2001. "Male Peer Support and Feminist Routine Activities Theory: Understanding Sexual Assault on the College Campus," *Justice Quarterly* 18:623–649.

Vachss, Alice. 1993. *Sex Crimes.* New York: Random House.

Weitzer, Ronald (ed.). 2000. *Sex for Sale: Prostitution, Pornography, and the Sex Industry.* New York: Routledge.

The Overreach of the Criminal Law

Norval Morris and Gordon Hawkins

Most of our legislation concerning drunkenness, narcotics, gambling, and sexual behavior and a good deal of it concerning juvenile delinquency, is wholly misguided. It is based on an exaggerated conception of the capacity of the criminal law to influence men. We incur enormous collateral disadvantage costs for that exaggeration and we overload our criminal justice system to a degree which renders it grossly defective as a means of protection in the areas where we really need protection—from violence, incursions into our homes, and depredations of our property.

The present "overreach" of the criminal law contributes to the crime problem in the following ways, which will be more fully documented as we deal with particular areas of that overreach:

1. Where the supply of goods or services is concerned, such as narcotics, gambling, and prostitution, the criminal law operates as a "crime tariff" which makes the supply of such goods and services profitable for the criminal by driving up prices and at the same time discourages competition by those who might enter the market were it legal.

2. This leads to the development of large-scale organized criminal groups which, as in the field of legitimate business, tend to extend and diversify their operations, thus financing and promoting other criminal activity.

3. The high prices which criminal prohibition and law enforcement help to maintain have a secondary criminogenic effect in cases where demand is inelastic, as for narcotics, by causing persons to resort to crime in order to obtain the money to pay those prices.

4. The proscription of a particular form of behavior (e.g., homosexuality, prostitution, drug addiction) by the criminal law drives those who engage or participate in it into association with those engaged in other criminal activities and leads to the growth of an extensive criminal subculture which is subversive of social order generally. It also leads, in the

From Norval Morris and Gordon Hawkins. 1970. *The Honest Politician's Guide to Crime Control,* Chicago: University of Chicago Press. Reprinted by permission of the University of Chicago Press and the authors, case of drug addiction, to endowing that pathological condition with the romantic glamour of a rebellion against authority or of some sort of élitist enterprise.

5. The expenditure of police and criminal justice resources involved in attempting to enforce statutes in relation to sexual behavior, drug taking, gambling, and other matters of private morality seriously depletes the time, energy, and manpower available for dealing with the types of crime involving violence and stealing which are the primary concern of the criminal justice system. This diversion and overextension of resources results both in failure to deal adequately with current serious crime and, because of the increased chances of impunity, in encouraging further crime.

6. These crimes lack victims, in the sense of complainants asking for the protection of the criminal law. Where such complainants are absent it is particularly difficult for the police to enforce the law. Bribery tends to flourish; political corruption of the police is invited. It is peculiarly with reference to these victimless crimes that the police are led to employ illegal means of law enforcement.

It follows therefore that any plan to deal with crime in America must first of all face this problem of the overreach of the criminal law, state clearly the nature of its priorities in regard to the use of the criminal sanction, and indicate what kinds of immoral or antisocial conduct should be removed from the current calendar of crime.

DRUNKENNESS

One of every three arrests in America—over two million each year—is for the offense of public drunkenness; more than twice the number of arrests in the combined total for all of the seven serious crimes which the FBI takes as its index crimes (willful homicide, forcible

rape, aggravated assault, robbery, burglary, theft of $50 or over, and motor vehicle theft). The cost of handling each drunkenness case involving police, court, and correctional time has been estimated at $50 per arrest. We thus reach a conservative national estimate of annual expenditure for the handling of drunkenness offenders (excluding expenditure for treatment or prevention) of $100 million. In addition, the great volume of these arrests places an enormous burden on the criminal justice system; it overloads the police, clogs the courts, and crowds the jails.

The extent to which drunkenness offenses interfere with other police activities varies from city to city, but in the majority of cities it involves a substantial diversion of resources from serious crime. Thus, in Washington, D.C., during a nine-month period, it was found that 44 percent of the arrests made by the special tactical police force unit used "to combat serious crime" was for drunkenness. A similar situation exists in relation to correctional systems. In one city it was reported that 95 percent of short-term prisoners were drunkenness offenders. One-half of the entire misdemeanant population consists of drunkenness offenders. Yet the criminal justice system is effective neither in deterring drunkenness nor in meeting the problems of the chronic offenders who form a large proportion of those arrested for drunkenness. All that the system appears to accomplish is the temporary removal from view of an unseemly public spectacle.

We think that the use of the police, the courts, and the prisons on this scale to handle unseemliness at a time when one-third of Americans are afraid to walk alone at night in their own neighborhoods is so ludicrously inept and disproportionate that we need no more than point it out to justify the removal of drunkenness from the criminal justice system. This is not to say that if a person while drunk causes damage to property, steals, or assaults another person he should not be arrested under the appropriate statutes dealing with malicious damage, theft, or assault. But there should always be some specific kind of offensive conduct in addition to drunkenness before the criminal law is invoked.

It is sometimes argued that we have a choice between the criminal law model and the medical model in the treatment of drunkenness. And there is a considerable literature which deals with the dangers of medical authoritarianism. To us this is a false dichotomy; our choice need not be so narrowly restricted. A social welfare model may, in the present state of medical knowledge, be preferable to either the criminal law or the medical model.

For the police lockups, courts, and jails we would substitute community-owned overnight houses capable of bedding down insensible or exhausted drunks. For the police and the paddy wagons we would substitute minibuses, each with a woman driver and two men knowledgeable of the local community in which the minibus will move. A woman is preferred to a man as the driver-radio-operator because it is our experience that the presence of a woman has an ameliorative effect on the behavior of males, even drunken males.

The minibus would tour the skid row area, picking up the fallen drunks and offering to help the weaving, near-to-falling drunks. If there be a protest or resistance by a drunk, cowardice and withdrawal must control our team's actions; if there be assaults or other crimes, a police transceiver will call those who will attend to it; if there be unconsciousness or drunken consent, the minibus will deliver the body to the overnight house.

If there be talk by the drunk the next day of treatment for his social or alcoholic problem, let him be referred, or preferably taken, to whatever social assistance and alcoholic treatment facilities are available. Indeed, let

such assistance be offered if he fails to mention them; but let them never be coercively pressed.

The saving effected by abolishing the costly and pointless business of processing drunkenness cases through the criminal justice system would vastly exceed the cost of providing such facilities and treatment programs for those willing to accept them.

Such a system may be less effective than a medical detoxification model of the type now operating in New York and Saint Louis, but it is clearly cheaper and more humane than our present processes and does not distract the criminal justice system from its proper and important social functions.

NARCOTICS AND DRUG ABUSE

As in the case of drunkenness, so in regard to the use of other drugs, the invocation of the criminal process is wholly inappropriate. Yet at present, although drug addiction itself is not a crime in America, the practical effect of federal and state laws is to define the addict as a criminal. According to FBI arrest data, 162,177 arrests for violations of the narcotic drug laws were made in 1968 [and 1.5 million arrests in 1999]. As the President's Crime Commission report puts it, ". . . the addict lives in almost perpetual violation of one or several criminal laws." Neither the acquisition nor the purchase nor the possession nor the use of drugs should be a criminal offense. This elimination of criminal prosecution provisions should apply to the narcotics (opiates, synthetic opiates, and cocaine), marihuana, hallucinogens, amphetamines, tranquilizers, barbiturates, and the volatile intoxicants.

Those who support the present laws and the traditional methods of enforcement commonly claim a causal connection between drug use and crime. Yet leaving aside crime to raise funds to support the inflated costs of purchasing legally proscribed drugs, the evidence of a causal connection between drug use and crime is slight and suspect.

As with alcohol, the fact that drugs not only release inhibition but also suppress function is commonly ignored. They may well inhibit more crime than they facilitate; heroin for example has a calming depressant effect, and the "drug crazed sex fiend" of popular journalism has no counterpart in reality although the myth dies hard. The prototypal headline, "Addict Rapes Widow" is misleading—the truth would be "Addict Nods While Widow Burns."

There seems to be no doubt, however, that the policy of criminalization and the operations of criminal justice agencies in this field have in themselves been criminogenic without measurably diminishing the extent of the drug problem or reducing the supply of narcotics entering the country. There is substantial evidence that organized criminals engaged in drug traffic have made and continue to make high profits. There is evidence, too, that criminalization of the distribution of drugs has caused much collateral crime with drug addicts, "to support their habits," as the President's Crime Commission puts it, "stealing millions of dollars worth of property every year and contributing to the public's fear of robbery and burglary."

The one certain way totally to destroy the criminal organizations engaged in the narcotics trade and to abolish addict crime would be to remove the controls and make narcotics freely available to addicts. As Harvard economist Thomas C. Schelling puts it, "If narcotics were not illegal, there could be no black market and no monopoly profits, and the interest in 'pushing' it would probably be not much greater than the pharmaceutical interest in pills to reduce the symptoms of common colds."

We do not propose the abolition of all controls over the importation, manufacture, and distribution of drugs, nor the abolition of penalties against those unauthorized persons who trade in drugs for profit; but we are convinced that if addiction were treated as a medical matter this would undercut the illicit traffic and largely eliminate the profit incentive supporting that traffic. The British approach to this problem, which involves the maintenance of strict control over the supply of drugs but leaves the treatment of addicts (including maintenance doses to addicts) in the hands of the medical profession, has resulted in a situation where no serious drug problem exists.

Certain difficulties in the British approach have recently emerged. Heroin addiction has increased with immigration of groups having larger addict subcultures within them and for other reasons. But though the increase, stated as a percentage, seems great, it starts from a base so very much smaller than that in the United States that the figures showing increase misstate the problem. It remains a problem of little social significance. Further, the outlets for medical prescription and administration of drugs need to be better controlled to avoid the development of a black market. But these are details in a scheme of incomparably sounder structure than we have evolved in this country.

With regard to marihuana, it is necessary to say something further. At present marihuana is equated, in law, with the opiates although its use does not lead to physical dependence nor does tolerance and the desired dose increase over time. Further, the risks of crime, accident, suicide, and physical or psychological illness are less than those associated with alcohol.

One of the principal advantages of the decriminalization and the pathologization of addiction is that the "image" of drug taking as an act of adventurous daring conferring status on the taker as a bold challenger of authority, convention, and the Establishment will be destroyed. With punitive laws and the brunt of law enforcement falling heavily on the user and the addict rather than on traffickers, we have created a persecuted minority with its own self-sustaining myths and ideology. The alcoholic, on the other hand, is nowhere seen as a heroic figure in our culture but quite commonly as a person to be pitied and treated as sick. Consequently, no addict subculture with a morale-enhancing, self-justifying ideology and recruitment process has developed in this area.

GAMBLING

Gambling is the greatest source of revenue for organized crime. Estimates of the size of the criminal revenue from gambling in the United States vary from $7 to $50 billion, which means that it is huge but nobody knows how huge. Because statutes in every state, except Nevada, prohibit various forms of gambling, criminals operate behind the protection of a crime tariff which guarantees the absence of legitimate competition. This has led to the development of a powerful and influential vested interest opposed to the legalization of gambling.

Despite sporadic prosecution, the laws prohibiting gambling are poorly enforced and there is widespread disregard for the law. We do not face a choice between abolishing or legalizing gambling; the choice is between leaving gambling and the vast profits which accrue from it in the hands of criminals or citizens taking it over and running it for the benefit of society or, by licensing and taxation measures, controlling it.

The position regarding betting on horse races is highly irrational. In many states those who attend races are allowed to bet on horses and a portion of the money wagered is paid as a tax to the state treasury. Yet it is illegal to accept off-track wagers. But as most people cannot find time to go to the track, such wagers are placed on a scale far exceeding the legitimate ones. The President's Crime Commission cites "estimates by experts" which state that the total involved in off-track betting "is at least two or three times as great" as the total of $5 billion involved in legal betting at race tracks. Yet of the sum of from $10 to $15 billion wagered off-track, nothing at all is forfeit to the state treasury.

Off-track betting can be controlled by the establishment of state-run betting shops as in Australia. Insofar as gambling is harmful, the harm can at least be reduced by fixing limits to wagers and other measures of control. As for other forms of gambling, the Nevada solution whereby the state tax commission administers gambling by supervising a license system under which all applicants have to be cleared by the commission—and state, county, and city taxes and license fees represent a substantial revenue—has operated with success for many years. The infiltration of organized criminals has been blocked by screening all applicants for criminal records. The tax commission employs inspectors and has held hearings and revoked several licenses. The principal lesson to be learned from Nevada is that gambling can be kept clean and does not have to be run by criminals.

DISORDERLY CONDUCT AND VAGRANCY

According to the Uniform Crime Reports, there were nearly 600,000 arrests for disorderly conduct in 1968 [and 655,000 arrests in 1999]. This represents more arrests than for any other crime except drunkenness.

Disorderly conduct statutes vary in their formulation, and the conduct dealt with as disorderly includes a wide variety of petty misbehavior including much that is harmless, although annoying, and not properly subject to criminal control.

Criminal codes and statutes should prohibit specific, carefully defined, serious misconduct so that the police can concentrate on enforcing the law in that context. Disorderly conduct statutes allow the police very wide discretion in deciding what conduct to treat as criminal and are conducive to inefficiency, open to abuse, and bad for police-public relations.

Similar considerations apply to vagrancy. It is a criminal offense in all states, with over 99,000 arrests in 1968 [31,000 in 1999]. Here, however, it is not a question of more rigorously defining the type of behavior to be prohibited but rather of entirely abandoning the vagrancy concept. The commentary to the American Law Institute's Model Penal Code states: "If disorderly conduct statutes are troublesome because they require so little in the way of misbehavior, the vagrancy statutes offer the astounding spectacle of criminality with no misbehavior at all." And the fact is that those statutes, which frequently make it an offense for any person to wander about without being able to give a "good account of himself," burden defendants with a presumption of criminality and constitute a license for arbitrary arrest without a warrant.

Vagrancy laws are widely used to provide the police with justification for arresting, searching, questioning, and detaining persons whom they suspect may have committed or may commit a crime. They are also used, according to the President's Crime Commission task force report on the courts, "by the police to clean the streets of undesirables, to harass persons believed to be engaged in crime and to investigate uncleared offenses." These laws often make possible the conviction of persons without proof of antisocial behavior or intention and in general confer unbounded discretion on the police.

In our view the police need authority to stop any person whom they reasonably suspect is committing, has committed, or is about to commit a crime and to demand his name, address, and an explanation of his behavior—to stop and frisk, now clearly constitutionally permissible. The police need such powers of inquiry to control crime and to protect themselves in dealing with persons encountered in suspicious circumstances, and they should have these powers without having to resort to the subterfuge of vagrancy arrest.

As for such behavior as begging, which is included in many vagrancy statutes, we agree with the American Law Institute's Model Penal Code commentary that "municipalities may properly regulate the use of sidewalks to safeguard against annoying and importunate mendicants and merchants; but such legislation does not belong in the penal code."

SEXUAL BEHAVIOR

With the possible exception of sixteenth-century Geneva under John Calvin, America has the most moralistic criminal law that the world has yet witnessed. One area in which this moralism is most extensively reflected is that of sexual behavior. In all states the criminal law is used in an egregiously wide-ranging and largely ineffectual attempt to regulate the sexual relationships and activities of citizens. Indeed, it is as if the sex offense laws were designed to provide an enormous legislative chastity belt encompassing the whole population and proscribing everything but solitary and joyless masturbation and "normal coitus" inside wedlock.

It is proper for the criminal law to seek to protect children from the sexual depradations of adults, and adults and children from the use of force, the threat of force, and certain types of fraud in sexual relationships. Further, there is some justification for the use of the criminal law to suppress such kinds of public sexual activity or open sexual solicitation as are widely felt to constitute a nuisance or an affront to decency. But beyond this, we recognize that the criminal law is largely both unenforceable and ineffective, and we think that in some areas the law itself constitutes a public nuisance. We shall deal with some of the principal areas of conduct from which the criminal law should be withdrawn in whole or in part; types of behavior which although at present adjudged criminal are more properly regarded as matters of private morals.

Adultery, Fornication, and Illicit Cohabitation

Extramarital intercourse is punishable in the majority of states with penalties ranging from a $10 fine for fornication to five years' imprisonment and a $1,000 fine for adultery. Mercifully, prosecutions are rare. The vast disparity between the number of divorces on the ground of adultery and the minute number of prosecutions for that offense reveals that enforcement is deliberately kept at a microscopic level.

A situation of this kind constitutes a double threat to society. In the first place it provides opportunities for victimization and discriminatory enforcement often provoked by jealousies. In the second place the promulgation of a code of sexual behavior unrelated to actuality (according to Kinsey, 95 percent of the male population is criminal by statutory standards), and its enforcement on a derisory scale, and in arbitrary fashion, cannot but provoke contempt and resentment.

It is one thing to retain laws which, because of difficulty of detection, cannot be rigorously enforced, quite another to preserve those which are not seriously intended to be applied. At a time when it is of considerable importance that the law should mean what it says, anything likely to make citizens take it less than seriously can only be harmful. It is at least a reasonable assumption that anything which provokes cynicism, contempt, derision, indifference, resentment, and hostility toward the law and law enforcement agencies is likely to have undesirable repercussions on behavior. At this time it seems unwise to incur the risk of such costs and for no discernible gain.

Statutory Rape or Carnal Knowledge

Sexual intercourse with a willing female under the statutory age of consent is sometimes referred to as "carnal knowledge," sometimes as "statutory rape." It is usually a felony. The statutory age of consent varies from ten years of age (in Florida, South Dakota, and New Mexico) to eighteen years of age (in New York and thirteen other states) and, in Tennessee, twenty-one years of age. Such variations must confuse the divining rod of the natural lawyer! The maximum penalties range from death (in fifteen states) to ten years' imprisonment (in New York). In general these penalties are exceeded only by those for murder and equaled only by those for forcible rape and kidnapping. In North Carolina and Washington sexual intercourse between an adult female and a male under the age of consent is also statutory rape on the part of the female, but in general, as one textbook puts it, "the criminality of statutory rape seeks to protect the purity of young girls."

A great deal of statutory rape legislation is totally unrealistic in a number of respects. Most age limits were fixed at a time when physical maturity was attained later than it is now. Furthermore, nowadays teenage girls are far more knowledgeable and sophisticated than the law appears to recognize, and the assumption that in cases of consensual intercourse the male is necessarily the initiator and the female always plays a passive, bewildered role is unlikely to correspond closely to reality. Moreover, even if the male genuinely believes, on reasonable grounds, that the girl is over the age of consent, he has, except in California, no defense to a charge of statutory rape; it is thus clear that not only rationality but also justice is sacrificed in the pursuit of purity.

The offense of statutory rape should clearly be abolished and since in all such cases the girl has given her consent—otherwise it would be rape, viking rape not statutory rape—the man's offense should be that of intercourse with a minor. In our view, the function of the law in relation to sexual behavior of this nature should be restricted to providing protection for the immature in cases where there is significant disparity of age between the male and the female.

An abuse of a relation of trust or dependency should be regarded as an aggravating circumstance. This need would be adequately met if the age of consent were fixed at sixteen. The accused should be acquitted if he can establish that he reasonably believed the girl to be past her sixteenth birthday. It should be added that we are speaking of adult criminal liability here; that is, we are not talking about problems of sexual experimentation by youths and criminal liability within whatever is the juvenile court age in any jurisdiction.

Bigamy

Bigamy, the triumph of hope over experience, is contracting a second marriage during the existence of a prior marriage and is a statutory crime. It does not constitute a serious part of the crime problem. We mention it only as an interesting example of the legal stigmatization and punishment of conduct which may (as when both parties are aware of the previous marriage, which is the general situation) harm no one although it offends some religious and moral codes. It may be that a certain amount of wrath on the part of the Deity is engendered but his appeasement is no longer regarded as a function of the criminal law. The bigamous marriage itself is legally a nullity.

In many cases the only antisocial consequences of bigamy are the falsification of state records and the waste of time of the celebrating officer. This problem would be better handled by penalties for false declarations in relation to ceremonies of marriage. Sanctions are to be found in all criminal codes for giving false information in relation to official processes, and deceiving the woman would be an aggravating circumstance relevant to sentencing. If necessary, the maximum punishment for such false declarations could be statutorily increased.

Sodomy and Crimes against Nature

Statutes concerning sodomy and crimes against nature include within their scope such sexual behavior as bestiality, both homosexual and heterosexual anal and oral copulation, and mutual masturbation. These laws receive only capricious and sporadic enforcement, usually, although not exclusively, in regard to such relations outside marriage. Obviously laws of this kind are peculiarly liable to abuse because of the wide discretion involved.

No social interests whatsoever are protected by desultory attempts to impose upon persons adherence to patterns of sexual behavior arbitrarily selected from the great variety which forms our mammalian heritage. Bestiality would be more properly dealt with under statutes relating to cruelty to animals where any cruelty is involved; otherwise, there is no reason to include it within the criminal law.

Homosexual Acts

Homosexual offenses are treated under such titles as sodomy, buggery, perverse or unnatural acts, and crimes against nature. Although the Kinsey report maintains that "perhaps the major portion of the male population, has at least some homosexual experience between adolescence and old age," only a small minority are ever prosecuted and convicted. Yet the law in this area, while not significantly controlling the incidence of the proscribed behavior, not only increases unhappiness by humiliating and demoralizing an arbitrarily selected sample of persons every year and threatening numberless others, but at the same time encourages corruption of both the police and others who discover such relationships by providing opportunities for blackmail and extortion.

As far as the police are concerned, a great deal has been written both about corruption in this area and the degrading use of entrapment and decoy methods employed in order to enforce the law. It seems to us that the employment of tight-panted police officers to invite homosexual advances or to spy upon public toilets in the hope of detecting deviant behavior, at a time when police solutions of serious crimes are steadily declining and, to cite one example, less than one-third of robbery crimes are cleared by arrest, is a perversion of public policy both maleficent in itself and calculated to inspire contempt and ridicule.

In brief, our attitude to the function of the law in regard to homosexual behavior is the same as in regard to heterosexual behavior. Apart from providing protection for the young

and immature, protection against violence, the threat of violence, and fraud, and protection against affronts to public order and decency, the criminal law should not trespass in this area.

Prostitution

Relations with female prostitutes represent a very small part of the total sexual outlet of the male population. The Uniform Crime Report shows 42,338 arrests for "prostitution and commercialized vice" in 1968 [and 92,000 in 1999], but many arrests of prostitutes are included in the yearly arrests for "disorderly conduct," so that the figures cannot be regarded as a meaningful index.

Prostitution is commonly statutorily defined as the indiscriminate offer by a female of her body for sexual intercourse or other lewdness for the purpose of gain and is a criminal offense in all states. The penalties most commonly imposed are fines or short prison sentences.

At one time it was widely believed that most prostitutes were unfortunate women who had been "driven" to a life of prostitution by poverty, bad upbringing, seduction at an early age, or broken marriages, but research suggests that in the majority of cases this way of life is chosen because it offers greater ease, freedom, and profit than available alternatives. There is no evidence that the incidence of neurosis or psychological abnormality is greater among prostitutes than among housewives.

Prostitution is an ancient and enduring institution which has survived centuries of attack and condemnation, and there is no doubt that it fulfills a social function. It is often asserted that prostitution provides an outlet for sexual impulses which might otherwise be expressed in rape or other kinds of sexual crime. No research has been done in this area but the notion has a certain plausibility. It is undeniable, however, that prostitutes are sought out by some men who, because of a physical deformity, psychological inadequacy, or (in the case of foreigners and immigrants) unfamiliarity with the language and customs, find great difficulty in obtaining sexual partners. The Kinsey report states that prostitutes provide a sexual outlet for many persons who without this "would become even more serious social problems than they already are."

The costs of attempting to enforce our prostitution laws have been admirably summarized by Professor Sanford Kadish:

> . . . diversion of police resources; encouragement of use of illegal means of police control (which, in the case of prostitution, take the form of knowingly unlawful harassment arrests to remove suspected prostitutes from the streets; and various entrapment devices, usually the only means of obtaining convictions); degradation of the image of law enforcement; discriminatory enforcement against the poor; and official corruption.

Once again it is our view that the use of law enforcement resources in this way, in a fruitless effort to promote moral virtue, is wasteful and socially injurious. Insofar as prostitution itself is responsible for social harms like the spread of venereal disease, regular compulsory medical inspection would provide better protection than our present haphazard enforcement policies. Moreover, all the evidence indicates that it is ordinary free promiscuity which is more largely responsible for the spread of venereal disease. Insofar as public solicitation constitutes an affront to some persons' susceptibilities, it would be perfectly possible (as has been done in some German cities) for municipal regulation to confine the activities of prostitutes to certain prescribed areas. As in many cases they are already largely confined in this way for purely commercial reasons, this would create few enforcement problems.

CONCLUSION

We recognize that so radical a program as that proposed may be regarded by some as unacceptable and that it could justifiably be said that we have so far ignored a number of legitimate objections to the repeal of criminal laws. Thus Rupert Cross in his admirable paper "Unmaking Criminal Laws" says, "In general the criminal law has selected as proper subjects for its attention those parts of the moral law which are suitable for enforcement by the infliction of punishment following upon a judicial enquiry, and in general the criminal law disregards those parts of the moral law which are unsuitable for enforcement in this way."

He goes on to say that "whenever the repeal of a criminal law is mooted, it is proper to ask" a number of questions, which he lists as follows:

> Would the repeal of the relevant law lead to an increase in the prohibited practice? Would it weaken the moral condemnation of that practice? Is the prohibited practice harmful to other individuals? Is it actually or potentially harmful to society? Is the practice strenuously condemned by public opinion? And, is the criminal sanction effective?

We agree that these are all in some degree relevant questions. They are not, however, questions to which it is possible to give categorical answers in every case. And even if answers can be given it is by no means clear what the practical implications of any particular answer or combination of answers might be. Indeed, it is evident that if one accepts Mill's doctrine that "the only purpose for which power can rightfully be exercised over any member of a civilized community against his will is to prevent harm to others," then the crucial question in this context must be: Is the prohibited conduct harmful to other individuals or to society? If the answer to that question is negative, then questions about whether a repeal of the relevant law might lead to an increase in the prohibited conduct or weaken moral condemnation of it are otiose.

It should be clear, then, that in the light of our definition of the function of the criminal law, in terms of the protection of the lives and property of citizens and the preservation of public order and decency, the sort of restrictions on the use of the criminal sanction we have proposed are not only unobjectionable but desirable. Moreover, we have suggested that even those who do not accept our definition must face the question whether the collateral social costs of endeavoring to preserve the particular prohibitions we have discussed are not excessive.

We have argued that they are excessive, not only in terms of human suffering and the loss of freedom, but also in that in many cases the attempt to use the criminal law to prohibit the supply of goods and services which are constantly demanded by millions of Americans is one of the most powerful criminogenic forces in our society. By enabling criminals to make vast profits from such sources as gambling and narcotics, by maximizing opportunities for bribery and corruption, by attempting to enforce standards which do not command either the respect or compliance of citizens in general, by these and in a variety of other ways we both encourage disrespect for the law and stimulate the expansion of both individual and organized crime to an extent unparalleled in any other country in the world.

Hate Crimes

James B. Jacobs and Kimberly A. Potter

The terms "hate crime" or "bias crime" have established their places in the crime and justice lexicon and appear routinely in the media, scholarly journals, legislation, and judicial opinions. Many advocacy groups, politicians, scholars, and journalists claim that the country is experiencing a hate crime epidemic. A majority of states have enacted substantive hate crime laws or sentence enhancements for crimes motivated by officially disfavored prejudices. A few large police departments have formed bias crime units for investigative and data compilation purposes. In 1990, Congress directed the Department of Justice to provide a nationwide accounting of hate crimes.

The goals of this essay are to assess the definition of "hate crime," to present what is known about its incidence, and to analyze how the criminal justice system is adapting to this new offense.

WHAT IS HATE CRIME?

The term "hate crime" is a misnomer. The term actually refers to criminal behavior motivated, not by hate, but by *prejudice*, although there is undoubtedly some overlap. Generically, "hate crime" is meant to distinguish criminal conduct motivated by prejudices from criminal conduct motivated by lust, jealousy, greed, politics, and so forth. Unlike theft, burglary, or assault, hate crime emphasizes the offender's attitudes, values, and character. Lobbyists for special hate crime laws believe that prejudice is worse than all other criminal motivations (Crocker 1992/93, pp. 491–94).

Whereas the classical and the neoclassical models of criminal justice focus on the crime rather than the criminal, the movement to recognize and label hate crimes strives to make criminals' motivations salient and deter-

From *Crime and Justice*, Vol. 22, Chicago: University of Chicago Press, 1997. Reprinted by permission of the University of Chicago Press and the authors.

minative. Hate crime laws condemn discrimination by criminals in the same way that Title VII of the Federal Equal Employment Opportunity Act condemns discrimination by public and private employers.

For some people, the importance of a hate crime offense category is that it condemns in the moralistic language of the criminal law values and attitudes already condemned via employment, voting rights, and constitutional laws. For others, hate crime laws are important because they punish prejudiced offenders more severely than other offenders who have less abhorrent motivations. Finally, in the context of the identity politics that characterize contemporary American society, minority groups perceive it to be in their interest to emphasize and even exaggerate their victimization (Epstein 1989, p. 20; Jacobs 1992/93, pp. 542–43; Sykes 1992; Sleeper 1993).

At some level of abstraction all crime, or at least a great deal of it, could be said to be motivated by manifest or latent prejudice—against victims because they are tall, short, rich, poor, good-looking, bad-looking, cocky, vulnerable, smart, dumb, members of one gang or another, and so forth. In contemporary American society, however, certain prejudices are officially disfavored—especially those based on race and religion. All hate crime laws include prejudice based on race, color, religion, and national origin (Wang 1995, app. B.). However, only eighteen states and the District of Columbia include gender or sexual orientation bias as a hate crime trigger. Prejudice against Native Americans, immigrants, the physically and mentally handicapped, union members, non-union members, right-to-lifers, and those advocating the right to choose are hardly ever included in hate crime laws (Wang 1995, app. B). Some states punish criminal conduct based on uncommon preju-

dices such as against service in the armed forces (Vermont Stat. Ann. tit. 13, § 1455) or "involvement in civil rights or human rights activities" (Mont. Code Ann. §§ 45-5-221). The District of Columbia has the most all encompassing hate crime statute; it covers religion, national origin, gender and sexual orientation, "personal appearance," "family responsibility," "marital status," and "matriculation." Clearly, the boundaries of hate crime legislation are fixed by political decision rather than by any logical or legal rationale.

The Nature of Prejudice

What does it mean to say that criminal conduct is *motivated* by *prejudice*? A simple definition of prejudice is "a negative attitude or opinion about a particular group or class of people" (*International Encyclopedia of the Social Sciences* 1968, pp. 439–40). Some commentators would include "irrational" as well. It can result from experience or from fantasies and myths. It can be based partly on fact, or it can be completely fictional. Some people admit to their prejudices, and even espouse them as ideologies. Others deny their prejudices, sometimes because they do not recognize them and sometimes because they are ashamed of them. Prejudice can be "subconscious" as well as "conscious." Not infrequently, whether a particular belief or attitude should be labeled as prejudice is a matter on which reasonable people can differ (e.g., Is Z prejudiced if he believes that blacks are more likely to have out-of-wedlock children than whites and Asians and therefore to raise their children less satisfactorily?).

There seems to be no agreement on whether "prejudice" includes a negative attitude toward a people which is based in fact (e.g., X does not like or wish to associate with Libyans, because of their government's sponsorship of international terrorism). Would it be a hate crime if X decided to rob only elderly Asian women because he believed they were likely to resist less than other elderly women? If the definition of prejudice is broad enough, practically everyone could be called prejudiced, or to put the matter differently, practically everyone could be said to hold some prejudiced beliefs and opinions. If so, then every crime in which the perpetrator and victim are members of different groups could potentially be labeled a hate crime.

Causality

For criminal conduct to constitute a hate crime it must be motivated by prejudice; that is, the criminal conduct must be causally related to the prejudice. How strong must that causal relationship be? Must the criminal conduct have been wholly, primarily, or slightly motivated by the disfavored prejudice? The answer determines how much hate crime there is. If a hate crime must have been *wholly* motivated by prejudice, there will be only a very small number of hate crimes—those perpetrated by individuals whose prejudice amounts to an ideology or perhaps an obsession. By contrast, if a hate crime must have been only *in part* motivated by prejudice, a significant percentage (possibly nearly all) of intergroup crimes is potentially classifiable as hate crime.

What percentage of robberies by black perpetrators against white victims might be classified as hate crime if the key question is whether the robbery or choice of robbery victim was *in part* attributable to anti-white prejudice? What percentage of violence by males against females ought to be investigated as possible hate crime if the critical question is whether the perpetrator was *in part* motivated by prejudice against women?

TYPES OF HATE CRIME LAWS

As of spring 1996, the federal government, thirty-six states, and the District of Columbia have passed hate crime laws that fall into three categories: substantive crimes, sentence enhancements, and reporting statutes.

Substantive Hate Crimes

The majority of *substantive* hate crime statutes are based on the Anti-Defamation League's (ADL) Model Hate Crime Law, which establishes a separate "intimidation" offense:

> A person commits the crime of intimidation, if, by reason of actual or perceived race, color, religion, national origin or sexual orientation of another individual or group of individuals, he violates Section ___ of the Penal code (insert code provision for criminal trespass, criminal mischief, harassment, menacing, assault and/or other appropriate statutorily proscribed criminal conduct). Intimidation is a ___ misdemeanor/felony (the degree of the criminal liability should be at least one degree more serious than that imposed for commission of the offense). (Anti-Defamation League 1992, p. 4)

"Intimidation" is the only prosecutable hate crime under the ADL model law. Thus, in the "ADL states," hate crimes are low-level offenses, not the savage violence of organized terror groups but the shoves, pushes, and insults that result from frictions between ordinary, albeit prejudiced people, in a multiethnic, multiracial, multireligious, sexually diverse, and gendered society.

States' hate crime laws differ, not only with respect to which prejudices transform "ordinary" crime into hate crime, but according to which predicate crimes, when motivated by prejudice, qualify as hate crimes. In Pennsylvania and Vermont, for example, *any* offense is a hate crime if motivated by race, religion, national origin, and so forth (Pa. Cons. Stat. § 2710[a]; Vt. Stat. Ann. tit. 13, § 1455). Other states limit hate crimes to certain predicate offenses when motivated by a disfavored prejudice. For example, in New Jersey only simple assault and harassment, when motivated by prejudice, are classified as hate crimes (N.J. Stat. Ann. § 2C:12-1). Illinois designates nine predicate offenses: assault, battery, aggravated assault, misdemeanor theft, criminal trespass to residence, misdemeanor criminal damage to property, criminal trespass to vehicle, criminal trespass to real property, and mob action (Ill. Juris. Crim. Law & Proc. § 61:02).

Oregon provides that a person commits intimidation in the second degree, a misdemeanor, when the offender tampers or interferes with property or subjects an individual to alarm by threatening harm to the individual or his or her property or to a member of the individual's family by reason of race, color, religion, national origin, or sexual orientation. Where the offender causes physical injury to an individual or his or her property or places an individual in fear of imminent serious physical injury by reason of these characteristics, intimidation becomes a felony (Ore. Rev. Stat. Ann. § 166.155[1][c]).

Most hate crime laws (and sentencing enhancement provisions) do not employ the word "motivation." Instead, they speak of a person who commits an offense "because of" or "by reason of" one of the disfavored prejudices. The Washington, D.C., and Florida laws require that the offense "demonstrate prejudice" (D.C. Code Ann. § 22-4001; Fla. Stat. Ann. § 775.085[1]). Some jurisdictions make it an offense (or an aggravating sentencing factor) for a perpetrator to *select* a victim by reason of race, religion, and so forth (Ore.

Rev. Stat. Ann. § 166.155 [1][c]; Cal. Penal Code §§ 422.6, 422.7), or to "intentionally select" the victim based on race (Wisc. Stat. Ann. § 939.645[1][b]). Read literally, this type of statute does not even require a showing of prejudice. Consider a defendant who selected his victim, say, an Asian man, because someone who had just seen the defendant's car broken into told him that the thief was an Asian man, so the defendant attacked the only Asian person in sight. The defendant, although not necessarily prejudiced against Asians, would be guilty of a hate crime because he selected the victim "by reason of" race. If the statute is not meant to cover this situation (which seems likely), then it is no different than a statute that explicitly requires a bias motivation. Lu-in Wang explains that state courts have uniformly interpreted hate crime statutes to require proof of a prejudiced motive (Wang 1995, chap. 10, pp. 16, 34–35).

Hate Crime Sentence Enhancement

A second genre of hate crime law is comprised of statutes that provide sentence enhancements for prejudice-motivated crimes (Wang 1995, chap. 10, p. 22). These statutes either upgrade an existing offense (e.g., Fla. Stat. Ann. § 775.085[1]) or increase the maximum penalty for offenses motivated by prejudice (N.J. Stat. Ann. §§ 2C:43-7, 2C:44-3). The enhancement may apply to all or just to some predicate crimes. Under the Pennsylvania statute, for example, the bias offender is charged with a crime one degree higher than the predicate offense (Pa. Cons. Stat. § 2710[a]). Vermont's statute *doubles* the maximum prison term for bias-motivated crimes; if the maximum term is five years or more, the defendant's bias motivation becomes a factor for consideration by the judge at sentencing (Vt. Stat. Ann. tit. 13, § 1455). In Minnesota, the only bias-motivated crimes subject to enhanced punishment are harassment and stalking (Minn. Stat. Ann. § 609.749). In contrast, Nevada makes twenty crimes subject to enhanced sentences (Nev. Rev. Stat. Ann § 207.185). Florida subjects *any bias-motivated felony or misdemeanor* to enhanced punishment (Fla. Stat. Ann. 775.085[1]).

State laws vary with respect to the magnitude of the enhancement for bias motivation. The aggravated battery statute before the Supreme Court in *Wisconsin v. Mitchell*, 113 S. Ct. 2194 (1993), provided for a two-year maximum prison term, but if the perpetrator was motivated by one of the enumerated prejudices, the maximum punishment soared to seven years.

The federal Violent Crime Control and Law Enforcement Act of 1994 (Pub. L. No. 102–322) mandated a revision of the U.S. sentencing guidelines to provide an enhancement for hate crimes of three offense levels above the base level for the underlying offense. The guideline provides: "If the finder of fact at trial or, in the case of a guilty plea, . . . the court at sentencing determines beyond a reasonable doubt that the defendant intentionally selected any victim or any property as the object of the offense because of the actual or perceived race, color, religion, national origin, ethnicity, gender [not applicable for sex crimes], disability, or sexual orientation of any person, *an additional 3-level enhancement from [the base level offense] will apply*" (60 Fed. Reg., May 10, 1995, p. 25,082; emphasis added). In the case of aggravated assault, for example, the ordinary base level offense of 15 is elevated to 18 and the sentencing range is consequently elevated from 18–24 months to 27–33 months imprisonment.

Hate Crime Reporting Statutes

Many states, as well as the federal government, have enacted hate crime data collection and reporting statutes to generate statistics on the incidence of hate crime (Wang 1995, app. B). Ultimately, these reporting statutes may have more importance than the substantive laws and sentence enhancement statutes. The old sociological adage "what's counted, counts" suggests that the hate crime reporting statutes will reshape the way that Americans think about crime.

The federal Hate Crime Statistics Act of 1990 (HCSA), 28 U.S.C. § 534 (Supp. IV 1992), mandates the collection of nationwide hate crime data in order to help communities, legislatures, and law enforcement personnel appropriately respond to the problem by gathering information on the frequency, location, extent, and patterns of hate crime; increase law enforcement's awareness of and sensitivity to hate crimes in order to improve its response; raise public awareness of the existence of hate crimes; and send a message that the federal government is concerned about hate crime (U.S. Senate 1989, p. 3).

The Act directs the U.S. Department of Justice to collect and report data on hate crimes involving the predicate offenses of murder, non-negligent manslaughter, forcible rape,[1] aggravated assault, simple assault, intimidation, arson, and destruction, damage, or vandalism of property (28 U.S.C. § 534 [Supp. IV 1992]). The attorney general, given discretion by the Act to add to or delete from the list of predicate crimes, added robbery, burglary, and motor vehicle theft (Federal Bureau of Investigation 1990, p. 4).

The HCSA defines a hate crime as "a criminal offense committed against a person or property, which is motivated, in whole or in part, by the offender's bias against a race, religion, ethnic/national origin group, or sexual orientation group." The FBI guidelines implementing the act define "bias" as "a *preformed negative opinion or attitude toward a group of persons based on their race, religion, ethnicity/ national origin, or sexual orientation*" (emphasis added). According to this broad definition, most interracial and other intergroup crimes could be classified as (or certainly be investigated as possible) hate crimes.

The guidelines, although quite thorough, leave much ambiguity. For example, what is meant by "ethnic group or national origin"? Are "Hispanics" or "Latinos" counted as one group for purposes of the HCSA? Would an assault by a Cuban against a Colombian count as a hate crime if the assailant was motivated by a belief that Colombians are importing drugs into the community? Are "Asians" (e.g., Syrians, Indians, Vietnamese, Filipinos, Chinese, and Japanese) an ethnic group? Could conflicts between Chinese-Americans and Vietnamese-Americans or between Palestinians and Kuwaitis qualify as hate crimes?

HATE SPEECH, HATE CRIME, AND THE FIRST AMENDMENT

Defining hate crimes and punishing hate criminals is akin to, but distinct from, the move to criminalize hate speech (Walker 1994; Schweitzer 1995). The anti-hate speech movement asserts that certain kinds of racist, sexist, anti-Semitic, misogynistic, and homophobic expressions and epithets impose emotional damage on persons to whom they are addressed and to other members of the groups to which these persons belong. Therefore, proponents of hate speech restrictions urge that such expressions and epithets be prohibited and that those who utter them be punished (Matsuda 1989; Lawrence 1990). However, hate speech laws have not fared well in the courts, which have declared them unconstitutional on First Amendment grounds (*Doe v. University of Michigan*, 721 F. Supp. 852 [1989] [declaring unconstitutional campus hate speech code]; *UWM Post v. Board of Regents of the*

University of Wisconsin, 774 F. Supp. 1163 [1991] [declaring unconstitutional campus hate speech code]).

There is a lively debate among constitutional lawyers and civil libertarians over whether *hate crime* laws, like hate speech laws, should flunk a First Amendment test (Fleischauer 1990; Gellman 1991, 1992/93; Redish 1992; Gaumer 1994). Those who believe hate crime laws to be constitutional emphasize the familiar speech/conduct distinction in First Amendment law; people are entitled to speak their minds but not to impose physical harm on others in acting out their opinions (Crocker 1992/93, pp. 495–500). They argue that while an individual has a right to his bigoted thoughts, he has no right to act on them. According to this view, hate crime laws punish antisocial conduct just as Title VII provides a remedy against employment discrimination.

Those who believe hate crime laws to be unconstitutional argue that generic criminal law already punishes injurious conduct and that recriminalization or sentence enhancement for the same offense when it is motivated by prejudice amounts to extra punishment for values, thoughts, and opinions which the government deems abhorrent (Freeman 1992/93; Gellman 1992/93; Goldberger 1992/93). These critics ask: if the purpose of hate crimes is to punish more severely offenders who are motivated by disfavored prejudices, is that not equivalent to punishment for "improper thinking?" For example, suppose there are two defendants: A is a white supremacist who only robs black men; B is a communist who only robs rich people. Under the typical hate crime statute, B would be convicted of robbery, while A would be convicted of a hate crime or be subject to a sentence enhancement.

A few scholars have sought to distinguish between different formulations of hate crime offenses (Crocker 1992/93, pp. 495–500; Freeman 1992/93, pp. 582–83). They argue that a hate crime statute that does not use the word "motivation," but that prohibits *selection* of a victim *because of* or *by reason of* the victim's race, religion, or sexual orientation and so forth, has nothing to do with punishing ideas or speech, but punishes conduct. While there may be something to this subtle analytical distinction, most commentators and courts have treated such statutes as requiring proof of prejudiced motivation.

The U.S. Supreme Court so far has struck down one hate crime statute and approved one. In *R.A.V. v. City of St. Paul*, 112 S. Ct. 2538 (1992), the Supreme Court was faced with a constitutional challenge to a local ordinance which provided that "whoever places on public or private property a symbol, object, appellation, characterization or graffiti, including, but not limited to, a burning cross or Nazi swastika, which one knows or has reasonable grounds to know arouses anger, alarm or resentment in others on the basis of race, color, creed, religion or gender commits disorderly conduct and shall be guilty of a misdemeanor" (112 S. Ct. at 2541). R.A.V., a white juvenile, was convicted under the ordinance for burning a cross on a black family's lawn. The justices unanimously agreed that the ordinance violated the First Amendment, but there were at least two different rationales.[2] Justice Scalia's majority opinion pointed out that while the government could criminalize constitutionally unprotected "fighting words" (the ordinance applied only to fighting words), it could not criminalize only those fighting words of which the government disapproved. Thus, "the reason why fighting words are categorically excluded from the protection of the First Amendment is not that their content communicates any particular idea, but that their content embodies a particularly intolerable . . . mode of expressing whatever idea the speaker wishes to convey. St. Paul has not singled out an especially offensive mode of expression. . . . Rather, it has proscribed fighting words of whatever manner that communicate messages of racial, gender or religious intolerance. Selectivity of this sort creates the possibility that the city is seeking to handicap the expression of particular ideas" (112 S. Ct. at 2549).

Justice White's concurrence stated that the ordinance could have been struck down simply by holding "that the St. Paul ordinance is fatally overbroad because it criminalizes not only unprotected expression but expression protected by the First Amendment" (i.e., both fighting and nonfighting words [Justice White concurring at 2550]). Therefore, according to Justice White, the majority need not have addressed whether the ordinance affected content-based discrimination.

In another concurring opinion, Justice Stevens stated that the ordinance did not, as the majority asserted, regulate speech based on the subject matter or viewpoint but distinguished different verbal conduct "on the basis of the *harm* the speech causes" (Justice Stevens concurring at 2570; emphasis in original). According to Justice Stevens, the ordinance did not prevent just one side from "hurling fighting words at the other on the basis of conflicting ideas, but it does bar *both* sides from hurling such words on the basis of the target's 'race, color, creed, religion or gender' " (at 2571 [emphasis in original]). Nevertheless, he concurred on the ground that the ordinance was unconstitutionally overbroad; in other words, the ordinance prohibits both constitutionally unprotected *and* protected speech.

The second hate crime statute to reach the Supreme Court was the sentence enhancement statute challenged in *Wisconsin v. Mitchell*, 113 S. Ct. 2194 (1993). It provided for an enhanced sentence when a person "intentionally selects the person against whom the crime . . . is committed or selects the property which is damaged or otherwise affected . . . because of race, religion, color, disability, sexual orientation, national origin or ancestry of that person or the owner or occupant of that property" (113 S. Ct. at 2197 n.1). Mitchell, a black juvenile, was convicted of aggravated battery and subject to a sentence enhancement for selection of the white victim based on race. Prior to the attack, Mitchell and other black youths were discussing a scene from the movie "Mississippi Burning" which depicted a white man beating a black boy. Mitchell asked the group, "Do you all feel hyped up to move on some white people?" When the victim, a white juvenile, walked by, Mitchell said, "You all want to fuck somebody up? There goes a white boy; go get him." Mitchell and the group beat the boy unconscious (at 2196–97).

The Wisconsin Supreme Court, following the reasoning set forth in *R.A.V.*, struck down the statute for creating a "thought crime" which assigned more severe punishment to offenses motivated by disfavored viewpoints. In a unanimous decision, the U.S. Supreme Court, in an opinion written by Chief Justice Rehnquist, reversed and upheld the statute. The chief justice denied that the First Amendment was implicated by the Wisconsin statute. He distinguished Wisconsin's sentence enhancement law from the *R.A.V.* ordinance on the ground that the St. Paul ordinance was directed at politically incorrect viewpoints, whereas the Wisconsin statute was directed at unprotected criminal conduct that may properly be singled out by the legislature for increased punishment due to the greater harm such crimes are perceived to inflict on victims and society. Rehnquist explained that motive has traditionally been used by sentencing judges in determining sentences. "'Motives are most relevant when the trial judge sets the defendant's sentence, and it is not uncommon

for a defendant to receive a minimum sentence because he was acting with good motives, or a rather higher sentence because of his bad motives' " (Mitchell, at 2199 [quoting LaFave and Scott 1986]). (The Supreme Court did not adopt the subtle argument of some legal scholars that hate crime statutes worded in terms of target *selection* are different from *motivation* statutes.)

The *Mitchell* decision lifted the constitutional cloud from hate crime sentence enhancement statutes. Nevertheless, academic debate among constitutional scholars and civil libertarians continues. The critics insist that there is only a semantic difference between what is constitutionally impermissible under *R.A.V.* and what is constitutionally permissible under *Mitchell*. *R.A.V.*'s cross-burning ordinance could easily be redrafted as a vandalism statute with a penalty enhancement for offenders who select their targets because of race, religion, or sexual orientation.

THE INCIDENCE OF HATE CRIME

There is a consensus among journalists, politicians, and academics that the United States is experiencing an unprecedented "hate crime epidemic" (see Levin and McDevitt 1993; but see Jacobs and Henry 1996). Incredibly, there are no reliable empirical data to support this conclusion. Indeed, until 1990, the only available data were those provided by advocacy groups like the Anti-Defamation League, the Southern Poverty Law Center, and the Gay and Lesbian Anti-Violence Project, all of which lobby for more government attention to hate crimes. In 1990, at the behest of these and other advocacy groups, Congress passed the Hate Crime Statistics Act (Jacobs and Eisler 1993). Because of the conceptual and definitional problems discussed earlier, and implementation problems, the data collected pursuant to HCSA are inadequate and disappointing.

The Hate Crime Epidemic Hypothesis

The "epidemic hypothesis" asserts that *all forms* of prejudice-motivated crime are rising alarmingly. Dozens of newspaper and magazine articles in the last few years have referred to "a hate crime epidemic" (Jacobs and Henry 1996). Many of the academics who have written on the subject begin with the assumption that hate crimes are on the rise and characterize the problem as a crisis or epidemic (*Harvard Law Review* 1988, 1993; Crocker 1992/93; *Santa Clara Law Review* 1994; Lawrence 1994; Smith 1994). Abraham Abramovsky has even asserted that "no one seriously questions the severity of the [hate crime] problem" (Abramovsky 1992).

We believe that there is reason to be skeptical about this epidemic thesis. First, criminologists are (or should be) professionally inured to claims about crime waves (Chaiken and Chaiken 1983, p. 11; Wright 1985). Second, the claim that the incidence of crime between members of different groups stands at an all-time high completely ignores history. A near-genocide against Native Americans, massive violence against blacks, attacks on ethnic and religious groups, and unceasing violence against women and homosexuals are themes that run throughout American history; they are certainly not new. Indeed, it is almost certainly true that there is far less prejudice and intergroup violence now than at most previous points in our history. For example, does anyone really believe that black Americans are now in as much danger from attack by white racists as they were during the Jim Crow era when hundreds of lynchings took place (Ames 1942; Ginzburg 1962)? Is it plausible that there is more virulent anti-Semitism (not to mention anti-Catholicism) now than in the

heyday of Father Coughlin (Desmond 1912)? And could it likely be shown that there is more xenophobic violence against immigrants today than during the Sacco and Vanzetti era (Miller 1969; Alfredo 1987)? The rediscovery of hate crime is probably best explained not by an epidemic of prejudice-motivated violence but by our society's far greater sensitivity to prejudice.

The Advocacy Groups' Hate Crime Data Collection

Advocacy groups that collect and report hate crime statistics use those statistics to further their claims that the racial/religious/sexual orientation group they represent is experiencing unprecedented victimization at the hands of prejudiced criminals. Such claims are used to raise funds and to obtain government support on a whole range of issues.

No advocacy group has made as substantial a commitment to data gathering or has shown as much sophistication as the Anti-Defamation League, nor has any other group been gathering and reporting data for nearly as long. Since 1979, the ADL has published an "annual audit" of "overt acts or *expressions*" of anti-Semitic hostility, which includes criminal offenses, verbal harassment, and distribution of anti-Semitic literature. Many such incidents would not qualify as hate *crimes* under any federal or state statute. The inclusion of noncriminal acts, such as the distribution of anti-Semitic literature, and of acts for which the anti-Semitic motivation is questionable, are primary problems with the ADL's statistics from the standpoint of counting hate crimes.

The ADL's methods of data collection also leave much to be desired. The ADL's audit is based on data provided by its twenty-eight regional offices. The regional offices, in turn, rely on information from individuals and community groups who contact the ADL, newspaper reports, and local law enforcement agencies (Jacobs and Henry 1996). There are a number of obvious problems with such data collection. The sensitivity to perceived anti-Semitic acts or expressions necessarily varies from state to state, and from city to city, as does the willingness of individuals to come forward and report incidents. Further, reliance on newspaper reports also poses problems since newspaper coverage of anti-Semitic incidents varies depending on the size of the newspaper, the readership's concern with anti-Semitism (New Yorkers are more likely to be concerned with anti-Semitism than readers in Fargo, North Dakota), and competition from other high profile news events. Despite such shortcomings, these statistics, as well as others, are constantly used to support the claim that an epidemic of religious, racial, or other bias-motivated violence is plaguing the nation.

The Federal Data Gathering Effort

The 1990 federal Hate Crime Statistics Act mandated that the U.S. Department of Justice collect national hate crime data and publish an annual statistical report. The Act defines hate crime as any one of eight (later increased to eleven) predicate offenses (murder, nonnegligent manslaughter, forcible rape, aggravated assault, simple assault, intimidation, arson, destruction, damage or vandalism of property, robbery, burglary, and motor vehicle theft) "where there is *manifest evidence* of *prejudice* based on race, religion, sexual orientation, or ethnicity." No other predicate offense, even if motivated by one of the officially disfavored prejudices, will be counted as a hate crime. Prejudice is "manifest," according to the FBI guidelines, if "sufficient objective facts [are] present to lead a reasonable and prudent person to conclude that the offender's actions

were motivated, in whole or in part, by bias" (Federal Bureau of Investigation 1990, p. 2). Prejudice which is palpable, even virulent, but not *manifest* on the face of the crime does not transform an ordinary crime into a hate crime.

This data collection system has been fleshed out by FBI *Hate Crime Data Collection Guidelines* and the *Training Guide for Hate Crime Data Collection*, prepared to aid state and local police in implementing the Act. In deciding whether a particular crime should be labeled a hate crime, the Training Guide instructs local police to consider the questions printed below. However, the exercise bristles with ambiguity and subjectivity. The Training Guide does not specify how much weight should be given to each question or how many questions need to be answered affirmatively to qualify criminal conduct as a "hate crime." Moreover, questions 10 and 15 seem to allow for a hate crime label even if the offender's prejudice is not "manifest" under the ordinary definition of the word. We have inserted in italics possible difficulties in interpreting and answering these questions.

1. Is the victim a member of a target racial, religious, ethnic/national origin, or sexual orientation group? *Are all ethnic groups "target" groups? Do "whites" count as a "target racial group"? Do all religious groups?*

2. Were the offender and victim of different racial, religious, ethnic/national origin, or sexual orientation groups? For example, the victim was black and the offenders were white. *What if one of the offenders is from the same group as the victim?*

3. Would the incident have taken place if the victim and offender were of the same race, religion, ethnic group, or sexual orientation?

4. Were biased oral comments, written statements, or gestures made by the offender

which indicate his/her bias? For example, the offender shouted a racial epithet at the victim. *What if the epithet was in response to bias statements or gestures by the victim?*

5. Were bias-related drawings, markings, symbols, or graffiti left at the crime scene? For example, a swastika painted on the door of a synagogue.

6. Were certain items, objects, or things which indicate bias used (e.g., the offenders wore white sheets with hoods covering their faces) or left behind by the offender(s) (e.g., a burning cross was left in front of the victim's residence)?

7. Is the victim a member of a racial, religious, ethnic/national origin, or sexual orientation group which is overwhelmingly outnumbered by members of another group in the neighborhood where the victim lives and the incident took place? This factor loses significance with the passage of time, that is, it is most significant when the victim first moved into a neighborhood and becomes less significant as time passes without incident.

8. Was the victim visiting a neighborhood where previous hate crimes had been committed against members of his/her racial, religious, ethnic/national origin, or sexual orientation group and where tensions remain high against his/her group? *This seems to call for historical data and sociological assessments that would be very difficult to make reliably.*

9. Have several incidents occurred in the same locality at or about the same time, and are the victims all of the same racial, religious, ethnic/national origin, or sexual orientation group?

10. Does a substantial portion of the community where the crime occurred perceive that the incident was motivated by bias? *How could the police make such a determination?*

11. Was the victim engaged in activities promoting his/her racial, religious, ethnic/national origin, or sexual orientation group? For example, the victim is a member of the NAACP, participates in gay rights demonstrations, etc.

12. Did the incident coincide with a holiday relating to, or a date of particular significance to a, racial, religious, or ethnic/national origin group (e.g., Martin Luther King Day, Rosh Hashanah, etc.)?

13. Was the offender previously involved in a similar hate crime or is he/she a member of a hate group? *Searching out the defendant's organizational memberships and magazine subscriptions will set off First Amendment alarms.*

14. Were there indications that a hate group was involved? For example, a hate group claimed responsibility for the crime or was active in the neighborhood.

15. Does a historically established animosity exist between the victim's group and the offender's group? *How shall we answer such questions as whether there is historic animosity between blacks and whites, blacks and Latinos, whites and Latinos, Jews and gentiles, and so forth? Does historical animosity exist between all racial, ethnic, and religious groups or is it more complicated than that?*

16. Is this incident similar to other known and documented cases of bias, particularly in this area? Does it fit a similar modus operandi to these other incidents?

17. Has this victim been previously involved in similar situations?

18. Are there other explanations for the incident, such as a childish prank, unrelated vandalism, etc? *Won't many young hate crime offenders wish to characterize their conduct as pranks?*

19. Did the offender have some understanding of the impact that his/her actions

would have on the victim? *Won't this be difficult to determine? What if the offender is not apprehended or does not make a statement?* (Federal Bureau of Investigation 1991).

In January 1993, the FBI released its first official report, containing nationwide hate crime statistics for 1991 (Federal Bureau of Investigation 1993). It contained data from only thirty-two states; only 2,771 law enforcement agencies (of the 12,805 agencies nationwide reporting to the FBI) participated in the data collection effort, and of these, 73 percent reported no hate crime incidents.

Even though the report found only 4,558 hate crimes nationwide (compared with over 14 million reported crimes), many newspapers cited it as confirming the existence of a hate crime epidemic. A *Houston Chronicle* editorial stated: "The specter of hate is unfortunately alive and well in the United States. . . . The national report reveals a grim picture" (*Houston Chronicle* 1993).

The FBI's second report, covering 1992 hate crimes, contained information from forty-one states and the District of Columbia and found 6,623 hate crimes (Federal Bureau of Investigation 1994). The statistics for 1993 were based on forty-six reporting states and the District of Columbia and reported 7,587 hate crimes (Federal Bureau of Investigation 1995). One newspaper opined that the 1990s may be remembered as "the decade of hate crime" and solemnly reported that "since the federal government began counting hate crimes in January 1991, hate crime has increased" (Rovella 1994, p. A1). The so-called increase could more accurately be attributed to an increase in the number of states submitting data rather than an increased *rate* of hate crimes. Indeed, some states that contributed data in 1990 and 1991 reported decreases for 1993.

PORTRAIT OF HATE CRIMES, HATE CRIMINALS, AND HATE CRIME VICTIMS

The macropicture of the incidence of hate crime in the United States is very sketchy. Even minimally reliable statistics on hate crimes are lacking. Moreover, the problem is not likely to improve because of the ambiguities in defining and the subjectivity in labeling hate crime.

The Typical Hate Crime[3]

The vast majority of reported hate crimes are not committed by organized hate groups and their members, but by teenagers, primarily white males, acting alone or in a group (Goleman 1990, p. C1; McKinley 1990, p. A1; Herek and Berrill 1992, pp. 29–30; Levin and McDevitt 1993, pp. 244–46; New York Police Department 1995). The New York Police Department (NYPD) Bias Unit found that 63.84 percent of hate crime offenders were under the age of nineteen. The San Francisco Community United Against Violence, a gay victim assistance organization, says that the typical "gay basher" is a white male under the age of twenty-one (although there are more black and Latino perpetrators than whites).[4] The FBI statistics do not provide any sociodemographic data on hate crime offenders. The federal data do indicate that the typical hate crime consists of low-level criminal conduct. For 1993, the FBI reported that the most common hate crimes were intimidation (2,239 incidents),[5] destruction/damage/vandalism to property (1,949 incidents), and simple assault (1,249 incidents). There were only fifteen bias-motivated murders and thirteen bias-motivated rapes (Federal Bureau of Investigation 1995). The FBI's data provide information on the rate of apprehension and on the offenders' and victims' race and gender but not on religion, sexual orientation, or other sociodemographic characteristics. A large percentage of hate crime offenders go unapprehended—at least 42 percent. Of apprehended offenders, 51 percent were white and 35 percent were black. According to the FBI's 1993 statistics, vandalism, one of the most common hate crimes, has the lowest rate of apprehension—of 2,294 cases, 1,830 went unsolved. This low rate of apprehension, typical for vandalism offenses, is a significant obstacle to research.

Hate Crime Offenders

For almost every prejudice condemned by hate crime laws, there is a separate, sometimes vast, academic and popular literature. We need to emphasize that only a small minority of offenders are hard-core ideologically committed haters. The typical hate crime offender is an individual, usually a juvenile, who, like the offenders in *Wisconsin v. Mitchell*, holds vague underlying prejudices which on occasion spill over into criminal conduct.

1. *Antiblack Offending*. At certain times and places in American history and society, groups like the Ku Klux Klan have perpetrated systematic and organized violence and terror against blacks. In the post–Civil War era until well into the twentieth century, lynchings reached a pinnacle (Ferrell 1986, p. 92). From 1882 to 1968, 4,743 people were lynched; the vast majority were black. During the peak lynching years, 1889–1918, the five most active lynching states were Georgia (360), Mississippi (350), Louisiana (264), Texas (263), and Alabama (244) (Ferrell 1986, p. 91; Howard 1995, p. 18). In 1892, 200 lynchings occurred in a single year. These numbers include only the recorded lynchings; historians can only speculate on the number of blacks

whose deaths at the hands of lynch mobs went unreported (Ferrell 1986, p. 91). Even today certain skinhead groups on occasion engage in such conduct. The Southern Poverty Law Center's Klanwatch Project releases periodic reports on extremist racist groups and on vicious individual hate crimes (Klanwatch 1987, 1989, 1991). They do not necessarily engage in organized violence but their rhetoric, written and oral, is frightening. More common than the violence of ideologically driven racists is unorganized bullying and situational violence. And a good deal of reported antiblack hate crime could be attributed to repressed prejudice that erupts in the course of encounters based on nonracial issues.

2. *Anti-Asian Offending*. Crime based on prejudice against Asians has generated far less research and writing than crime against blacks. Nevertheless, prejudice and violence against Chinese immigrants early in the century and against Japanese Americans during World War II have been documented (Miller 1969; Saxton 1971; Daniels 1978; Takaki 1989; McWilliams 1944).

In the Congressional hearings leading to passage of the 1990 HCSA, Asian-American advocacy groups appeared before Congress and testified to "the rising tide of violence" against Asian Americans. In a letter to the Senate, the National Democratic Council of Asian and Pacific Americans stated, "Our members in California, Texas, Massachusetts and New York are aware of an increase in violent crimes against Asian and Pacific Americans, most frequently new arrivals from southeast Asia and Korea, often elderly" (letter to Senator Paul Simon from Susan Lee, U.S. Senate 1988).

Anecdotal evidence documents outrageously humiliating and violent anti-Asian attacks. For example, in 1987, a Jersey City gang called "Dot Busters," beat to death Navroze Mody, an Asian Indian American (U.S. Congress 1987, pp. 34–37); in 1989, a Chinese American was murdered following a pool room fight in which he was called "gook," "chink," and blamed for American casualties in Vietnam (U.S. Commission on Civil Rights 1992, pp. 26–31). The 1992 Los Angeles riots revealed virulent anti-Asian, especially anti-Korean prejudice, by blacks. Mobs of blacks burned and looted Korean-owned stores; one looter stated, "Ask them will they hire blacks now" (Griego 1992, p. A2). Similar prejudice, although resulting in less violence, erupted in New York City, Chicago, and Dallas, in the context of black boycotts of Korean stores in the late 1980s and early 1990s (Rieder 1990, p. 16; Papajohn 1993, p. 1). Boycotters in Brooklyn stood in front of Korean stores chanting, "Koreans must go. They should not be here in the first place." The racial tensions caused by the boycotts spilled over into violence when a black youth brutally assaulted an Asian man while yelling, "Koreans go home" (Rieder 1990, p. 16).

3. *Ethnic Offending.* Prejudice and conflict, including the whole panoply of crime and violence, is a major theme in late nineteenth and early twentieth century American society. Italians, Irish, Jews, and Germans all had their ethnic conclaves. During the early part of the century, when such groups were immigrating in large numbers to the United States, they experienced a great deal of xenophobic and prejudice-specific violence and what would now be called hate crime, some of which is well documented (Desmond 1912; Lowenstein 1989; Isolani and Martinelli 1993; Markowitz 1993; Maffi 1995). Similarly, the history of anti-Hispanic, especially anti-Mexican, violence against legal and illegal immigrants has been documented over the last two decades (Prago 1973; Mazon 1984; Alfredo 1987; Pachon 1994).

In recent years, advocacy groups have called attention to anti-Arab violence. Representative Joe Rahall testified that "we are now confronted . . . with a wave of anti-Arab hysteria which is fueled daily by the media in this country . . . and worst of all, this hysteria has manifested itself in terrorist acts on Americans of Arab heritage" (U.S. Congress 1986, p. 2). The American-Arab Anti-Discrimination Committee (ADC) presented examples of anti-Arab hate crimes consisting primarily of vandalism and harassing and threatening phones calls, as well as instances of violence against individuals, such as the pipe bombing murder of Alex Odeh, director of the ADC (pp. 62–64).

4. *Anti–Native American Offending.* Perhaps indicative of how marginal their position is, even among minority groups, there is very little scholarship on anti–Native American hate crimes, although undoubtedly such violence occurs, especially in those states with large Native American populations.

5. *Anti-Semitic Offending.* Anti-Defamation League audits reveal that a significant amount of current anti-Semitism (not necessarily hate crimes) is expressed and perpetrated by black hate mongers, who seem to have a great deal of support in the black community (Anti-Defamation League 1990*a*, 1994). Khalid Abdul Muhammad, spokesman for Nation of Islam leader Louis Farrakhan, claimed that victims of the Holocaust brought it on themselves: "They went in there to Germany the way they do everywhere they go, and they supplanted, they usurped, they turned around, and a German in his own country would almost have to go to a Jew to get money" (Anti-Defamation League 1994). The most dramatic recent black anti-Semitic hate crime was committed in the course of four days of rioting in 1991 in the Crown Heights section of Brooklyn. Chanting "kill the Jews," mobs set fires, destroyed property, and looted stores, and assaulted and harassed citizens, and murdered rabbinical student Yankel Rosenbaum. Over the course of four days

there were 259 calls to 911 regarding property offenses, 192 calls regarding offenses against persons, and 233 calls regarding roving groups of disorderly persons (more than double the number of calls logged during an average four-day period) (Girgenti 1993, p. 126). Nevertheless, the NYPD Bias Investigation Unit identified only twenty-seven bias-motivated incidents (Girgenti 1993, p. 129).

6. *Antiwhite Offending.* In recent years, there has been much more attention to anti-white prejudice among blacks (Box 1993; Welch 1994). According to a recent Klan-watch report, more whites than blacks were the victims of racially motivated murders (nine white and six black hate murder victims) (Box 1993). Further, it is reported that when Louis Farrakhan mentioned Colin Ferguson, the black man who opened fire on a crowded commuter train killing six white passengers, at a rally in New York City the audience broke into a prolonged ovation (Mills 1994, p. 13). In a speech before an audience of 2,000 at Howard University, Nation of Islam spokesman Khalid Muhammad drew similar applause when he stated, "I love Colin Ferguson, who killed all those white folks on the Long Island train" (Melillo and Harris 1994, p. B1). Moreover, literature about the virulently antiwhite, anti-Semitic black radio and press in the New York City area illustrates the climate of antiwhite hate (Sleeper 1990).

There is a dispute about what percentage of black-on-white crime is motivated by prejudice. Some writers seem to bend over backward to explain such crime as economically motivated or the result of repressed rage, but it is hard to see how a good deal of black-on-white street crime is not based, *in part*, on prejudice. Certainly crimes like Colin Ferguson's murder of six white Long Island Rail Road commuters in December 1993 could be considered antiwhite hate crime; Ferguson

was carrying notes expressing hatred for whites, Asians, and conservative blacks. However, commentators disagreed over whether his killing spree should be characterized as hate crime (Wilson 1993, p. A14).

While most black rioting since the 1960s has involved black neighborhoods and black victims, some rioting has been targeted at whites and Asians. For example, the April 1992 Los Angeles riots, in which crowds of blacks erupted in response to the not-guilty verdicts in the trial of police officers accused of beating Rodney King, included numerous antiwhite hate crimes, including the near fatal attack on Reginald Denny and the murders of Howard Epstein and Matthew Haines.[6]

7. *Anti-Gay Offending.* Crimes motivated by sexual-orientation bias have generated a body of research on offenders. Unlike other hate crime offenders, anti-gay offenders are more likely actively to seek out victims by traveling to neighborhoods or locations where gays live or congregate (Levin and McDevitt 1993). Reports and informal surveys indicate that the overwhelming majority of anti-gay offenders are males in their late teens to early twenties (Berk, Boyd, and Hamner 1992, p. 131; Berrill 1992, pp. 29–30; Harry 1992, p. 113). Other common characteristics of anti-gay attacks are that offenders typically act as a group; the offenders and victim are strangers; and offenders appear to have no underlying criminal motive, such as obtaining money or property from the victim (Berk, Boyd, and Hamner 1992, p. 131; Berrill 1993, pp. 156–57).

Joseph Harry categorizes anti-gay hate crime offenders into two classes: the "activists" who seek out homosexual victims by traveling to gay neighborhoods, and the "opportunists" who engage in gay bashing only when the opportunity arises. Harry suggests that four elements must be present in order for gay bashing to occur: "(a) the *institution of gender*, which defines departure from a gender role, and especially sexual departure, as an abomination; (b) *groups of immature males* who feel the need to validate their status as males; (c) *disengagement* by those males from the conventional moral order; and (d) *opportunities for gay-bashing—gay neighborhoods for activists, visibly homosexual persons for opportunists*" (Harry 1992, p. 121).

Richard Berk, Elizabeth Boyd, and Karl Hamner offer a conceptual foundation by categorizing anti-gay hate crimes into three types, with the premise that all hate crimes are "symbolic crimes" (Berk, Boyd, and Hamner 1992, pp. 127–28). A symbolic crime is defined as one in which the key ingredient in choosing the victim is that individual's membership in a particular social category. The first type of hate crime is the "actuarial crime." A good example involves a group of youths who decide to rob a gay man "not because of what his sexual orientation represents to them but because they apply a stereotype to him implying an upper-middle class income and a disinclination to fight back" (p. 128). "Expressive" anti-gay hate crimes, in effect, are a way of conveying the offenders' opinion or worldview. An expressive hate crime may be a way "to teach 'those people' a lesson," or it may simply be a homophobic reaction (p. 129). "Instrumental" hate crimes may be expressive, as well as acting as a means to an end, such as keeping homosexuals from moving into a neighborhood or closing down a gay bar or gathering place (p. 129).

Berk, Boyd, and Hamner suggest a list of empirical attributes of anti-gay hate crimes which may be useful in identifying, labeling, and researching this species of hate crime. Although based on scanty empirical evidence, they came up with the following set of attributes: more than one perpetrator, ranging in age from late teens to early twenties, ratio of perpetrators to victims (two to one), victim is stranger or "distant acquaintance," "location (outside of residences for person crimes)," occurring in the evening and during weekends, perpetrators are male, and no other underlying crime (e.g., robbery). Berk, Boyd, and Hamner acknowledge that this list of attributes may be unreliable given the slim database on anti-gay hate crimes. Further, they state that attributes applicable to anti-gay hate crimes may be irrelevant to anti-Semitic or racial hate crimes (1992, p. 132).

Gregory Herek applied the "functional approach" theory to examine gay bashing and the motivations of antigay offenders. The functional approach assumes that people hold and express certain attitudes because they derive some type of psychological benefit from doing so (Herek 1992, p. 151). "Social-expressive" functions may be affirmed and strengthened through gay bashing. For example, young males may bond and reaffirm their group solidarity by attacking homosexuals. According to Herek, "By clearly differentiating and then attacking an out-group [homosexuals], anti-gay violence can help in-group members [heterosexual males] to feel more positive about their group, and consequently about themselves as well" (p. 160). Similarly, ego-defensive violence provides a means for young males to reaffirm their masculinity, which they perceive to be associated with heterosexuality, by targeting "someone who symbolizes an unacceptable aspect of their own personalities" (p. 161).

Herek's social-expressive and ego-defensive functions are nearly identical to the social identity theory. Social identity theory posits that an individual's self-concept and self-esteem are based on identification with a particular "in-group," which is defined as "any group with which the individuals identifies and feels a sense of membership" (Herek 1992, p. 180). In order to evaluate and make judgments about themselves, individuals compare their own in-group to an "out-group." An out-group can be any group with which the individual does not identify or finds abhorrent. As applied to anti-gay violence, heterosexual males use their negative perception of homosexuals to increase their individual and group self-esteem (p. 182).

8. *Antifemale Offending.* Aggression, including violent crime, by men against women is very common (Rothschild 1993; Pendo 1994). Violence against women and girls is so common that to recognize it as a hate crime category would likely make it the most prevalent type of hate crime. If all rapes were counted as hate crimes, rape would be by far the most common violent hate crime (in 1993, there were 104,806 reported rapes: Federal Bureau of Investigation 1995, p. 23). Additionally, other criminal offenses for which women are the primary victims would also count as hate crimes. For example, the victims of serial murderers are almost always female, while the killers are male (Holmes and DeBurger 1988; Egger 1990, p. 7; Kiger 1990). It is highly plausible that these serial killers are motivated at least in part by antifemale bias.

Women's groups actively campaigned to have crime based on gender prejudice included in hate crime statutes, and in some states (although not in the federal HCSA) they have been successful.

In 1994, Congress passed the Violence Against Women Act of 1994 (Pub. L. No. 103–322), which creates a civil cause of action for victims of gender motivated crimes (although paradoxically, "gender-motivated crime" is not hate crime).[7] Under the statute, a victim may sue the offender for compensatory and punitive damages and injunctive and declaratory relief in federal court.

9. *Organized Hate Groups.* The labeling of various organized groups as hate groups is as fraught with definitional problems and social and political subjectivity as the labeling of individual acts of crime. Consider whether the Nation of Islam, the Jewish Defense League, Act-Up, and the Hell's Angels should be categorized as hate groups? Many commentators loosely label all the militia groups in the West and Midwest as hate groups although some of these groups at least resist the label (Coates 1987; Bennett 1988; Sargent 1995).

Some groups are uncontroversially and avowedly ideologically committed to prejudice—for example, the Ku Klux Klan, the Order, White Aryan Resistance, and small gangs of skinheads. Mark S. Hamm conducted interviews and questionnaires of white supremacist skinheads and their organizations. Hamm differentiates between hate crimes and terrorist acts; hate crimes are motivated by prejudice with no underlying social or political objective, whereas terrorist acts are based on a social or political objective. According to Hamm, "not all acts of terrorism can be considered hate crimes, and hate crimes are not necessarily terrorism unless such prejudicial violence has a political or social underpinning" (Hamm 1993, p. 107). Fifty-eight percent of the 120 self-reported acts of violence by the skinheads Hamm interviewed were not directed at nonwhite individuals (Hamm 1993, p. 109).

Hamm's research presents a picture of two types of skinheads: terrorists (those who have regularly engaged in acts of violence based on prejudice) and nonterrorists (those who have not engaged in acts of violence). Hamm interviewed thirty-six skinheads; he identified twenty-two terrorists and fourteen nonterrorists. Hamm compared the backgrounds and ideologies of the terrorists and nonterrorists. He found that terrorists come from predominantly lower-class backgrounds and that the vast majority of terrorists and nonterrorists came from stable families with whom they got along.

10. *Hate Crime Victims.* Proponents of the new hate crime laws frequently contend that hate crimes are "different" because they inflict more injury to the individual victim and to third persons and community stability than crimes in the same offense category that are attributable to other motivations (Greenawalt 1992/93, pp. 617–28; Garofalo and Martin 1993, pp. 65–66; Marovitz 1993, pp. 49–50).

A 1994 study of hate crime victims by Arnold Barnes and Paul H. Ephross found of fifty-nine hate crime victims of various racial, religious, and ethnic backgrounds that "the predominant emotional responses of hate violence victims appear similar to those of non-hate-crime victims of similar crimes. The behavioral coping responses of hate violence victims are also similar to those used by other victims of crime" (Barnes and Ephross 1994, p. 250). No direct comparison was made of ordinary crime victims; Barnes and Ephross examined the emotional responses of hate crime victims and compared them to common emotional reactions of ordinary crime victims based on existing victimization research and literature. Barnes and Ephross found only one significant difference in hate crime victims' emotional reactions, and this difference pointed to less severe emotional injury: "A major difference in the emotional response of hate violence victims appears to be the *absence of lowered self-esteem*. The ability of some hate violence victims to maintain their self-esteem may be associated with their attribution of responsibility for the attacks to the prejudice and racism of others" (Barnes and Ephross 1994, p. 250, emphasis added).

To date, there is no empirical research comparing the emotional reactions of hate crime victims and ordinary crime victims. Indeed, very little research exists which focuses exclusively on hate crime victims as a separate victim group.

It is frequently asserted that hate crime, or intergroup crime per se, is more traumatic to some or all members of the group of which the victim is a member. But the assertion that hate crime has greater adverse impacts on the victim's community has not been systematically documented. Obviously, a *campaign* of hate crime against a group ("Krystallnacht") will be more traumatic than an individual crime that can be rationalized as aberrational, if the community even finds out about it. Thus, the beating of Rodney King by a group of Los Angeles police officers angered Los Angeles's black community and, after the police were acquitted, touched off rioting in south central Los Angeles. The explosive black violence against Korean stores during the 1992 Los Angeles riots was said to be traumatic for the whole Korean community (Chavez 1994).

It is sometimes asserted, without supporting empirical evidence, that hate crime leads to reprisals and intergroup warfare (Coldren 1993; Greenawalt 1992/93, p. 627). If this is true at all, it only holds for interracial and interethnic violence and not for homophobic, anti-Semitic, and misogynistic crimes.

It is sometimes said that hate crime is more socially destabilizing than ordinary crime (Crocker 1992/93, p. 489; Greenawalt 1992/93, p. 627; Coldren 1993). That proposition is not obviously true. "Ordinary" street crime has devastated America's urban environment over the last several decades; among other things it has been a chief contributor to mass flight to the suburbs. Likewise, drug-related crime and black-on-black violence have been enormously destabilizing for the inner city. All kinds of horrifying crimes—carjackings, arson, drive-by shootings, serial murder—send shock waves through the community.

HATE CRIMES AND THE CRIMINAL JUSTICE SYSTEM

How have the police adapted to the emergence of the new hate crime category? Have they shifted resources into hate crime investigations and away from other kinds of investigations? Has the recognition of hate crimes as a separate genre of crime meant a reordering of police priorities?

Police and Hate Crime Investigation

The New York City Police Department, as well as a few other large police departments, have formed "bias units" to investigate bias crimes. Typically, these units are staffed with officers whose sole responsibilities involve the investigation and labeling of hate crimes (Marx 1986). A police bias unit's responsibility for deciding whether particular crimes are bias motivated is fraught with sensitive, and potentially explosive, social and political ramifications. In New York City, racial groups have been known to mobilize and polarize over labeling or failing to label a crime as a hate crime (Sleeper 1990; Jacobs 1992*a*, 1992*b*, 1993*a*, 1993*b*). During the investigation and trial of the black youths who raped and nearly beat to death a female jogger in Central Park, journalists and some citizens charged that a double standard exists, whereby white-on-black crimes are quickly labeled hate crimes, while black-on-white crimes are explained in different terms (Benedict 1992, pp. 189–251). At the same time, some black observers branded the prosecution of the

youths as itself racist (O'Sullivan 1989, p. 13; Anderson 1990, p. 52). So politically sensitive is the hate crime labeling decision that, in 1987, the NYPD created a Bias Review Panel to review the classification of bias-motivated crimes.

Another obstacle to identifying a bias-motivated offense is failure to apprehend the offender. No arrest is made in the majority of hate crimes; arrests are most rare in low-level offenses like bias-motivated vandalism. In 1990, only 127 of 530 bias offenses in New York City were cleared; of 167 anti-Semitic offenses, there were only sixteen arrests (New York Police Department 1991, p. 44).

In some situations, the victim may misconstrue the offender's motivation or simply be unreliable. The NYPD Bias Unit investigated one case, in which six Hasidic men riding the subway were confronted by a group of black youths. One of the Hasidic men was sprayed with mace and robbed. After investigation, the Bias Unit discovered that fifteen minutes after the Hasidic men were attacked, the same group of black youths attacked and robbed a white man and then a Hispanic man. The Bias Unit concluded that "the groups' actions should not be considered anti-white or anti-religious but totally criminal in nature with robbery as their sole objective" (New York Police Department 1991, p. 24). That conclusion itself seems debatable since the offenders might well have been prejudiced against Jews, whites generally, and Hispanics (if indeed they perceived the Hispanic victim to be Hispanic rather than white).

Prosecuting Hate Crimes

Defendants have been prosecuted for crimes motivated by prejudice long before the emergence of the new hate crime laws. They were prosecuted under "generic" criminal laws, although on conviction prosecutors may have persuaded sentencing judges to treat the defendant's bias motive as an aggravating factor justifying a severe punishment. In a very small number of cases, hate crimes were prosecuted under the federal criminal civil rights act (18 U.S.C. § 241), which criminalizes conspiracies to interfere with constitutional or federal statutory rights.

1. *The Decision to Charge.* Charging a defendant with a hate crime "ups the ante." The prosecutor, in addition to having to prove the underlying offense, shoulders the burden of proving that the defendant is a racist, anti-Semite, or homophobe. Consider the consequences for the prosecution if it had to prove the racism of the defendants in the Rodney King, Reginald Denny, or Yankel Rosenbaum cases (Lorch 1992, p. B3; Praeger 1993, p. 11; Schmich 1993, p. 1). In interracial cases like those, the prosecution usually tries to keep jurors focused on the essential elements of the offense, especially when the defense is intent on "playing the race card" (Jacobs 1992/93, p. 549). If the criminal conduct had been charged as a hate crime, it would have signalled the jurors that this is a "race case" and possibly polarized the jurors along racial lines. That almost certainly would disadvantage the prosecution, at least whenever there is a multiracial jury.

Charging, or failing to charge, a hate crime could place a prosecutor in a "catch-22" situation. The decision to charge or not charge a defendant with a bias crime could provoke anger in the victim's or the defendant's community (Fleisher 1994, p. 28). For example, the failure to bring a hate crime charge in the gang rape and near-fatal beating of the Central Park jogger led some observers to accuse the police and the mayor of adhering to a double standard in labeling hate crimes.

Hate crimes attract more media and community attention than ordinary crimes (see Chermak 1995, pp. 54–55). A prosecutor may desire such publicity in order to placate or attract the support of the victim's community. However, a prosecutor may wish to downplay the defendant's prejudice in order to avoid alienating members of the defendant's community.

2. *The Jury and Hate Crime Trials.* Selecting a jury for a hate crime trial presents unique challenges. How far should the prosecutor go on voir dire to determine whether a prospective juror is not himself or herself prejudiced against the victim's group and is willing and capable of finding the defendant to be prejudiced against the victim's group (Maldonado 1992/93, p. 559)? Some jurors who may be able to find that a defendant, a member of their same racial, ethnic, religious, or sexual orientation group, committed a garden-variety crime, may not be willing to find the defendant guilty of being a racist, anti-Semite, or other type of bigot. The juror, consciously or unconsciously, might see this as an indictment of his or her own prejudices (Jacobson 1977, p. 88; Barkan 1983, p. 28–44; Levine 1992, pp. 169–72).

3. *Proving Prejudice.* In some cases, evidence of bias motivation is "manifest." For example, the defendant may have been screaming racial epithets at the time of the assault or robbery or when taken into custody may confess that his crime was racially motivated. However, even epithets at the crime scene will not invariably mean that the defendant was motivated by prejudice. For example, two individuals may have become embroiled in an argument over a parking place, the victim may have shouted an epithet, and the defendant may have retaliated with an epithet and a punch.

How much evidence is required to prove that a crime was motivated *in part* by prejudice? Would it be sufficient to show that the defendant shouted a racial or religious slur as he fled the crime scene? In an attack on a Hispanic couple by a group of white youths who remained silent during the attack, would it be sufficient to present testimony from a witness who overhead the youths make ethnic slurs an hour (six hours? a day?) before or after the attack?

Where the offense involves more than one perpetrator, the problem of proving motive is more complex. What if only one member of the group shouted an epithet? Can that person's motivation be attributed to the codefendants? Accomplice liability typically requires that the accomplice desire the crime to be committed. Does that include the bias motivation (Fleisher 1994, p. 27)?

Most hate crime statutes do not require proof of *manifest* prejudice. Thus, where manifest prejudice was not evident at the crime scene, the prosecutor may attempt to prove prejudice based on the defendant's character, activities, and pronouncements. In order to prove the defendant's prejudice, a prosecutor may be tempted or pressured to delve into the defendant's beliefs and values, the publications he reads, the organizations to which he belongs, his activities, the backgrounds of his friends. In *People v. Aishman*, 19 Cal. Rep. 444 (1993), the prosecutor introduced as evidence of prejudice the fact that one of the defendants had a swastika and "Thank God I'm White" tattooed on his arms (1993, p. 447). Further, witnesses may be called on to testify about how the defendant told (or laughed at) racist or homophobic jokes, or whether he ever used racial slurs. In *Grimm v. Churchill*, 932 F.2d 674 (1991), the arresting officer testified that Grimm had a history of making racist remarks (pp. 675–76). Similarly, in *People v. Lampkin*, 457 N.E.2d 50 (1983), the prosecution presented as evidence racist statements that the defendant had uttered six years

before the crime for which he was on trial (p. 50). In effect, the trial may turn into an inquisition on the defendant's character, or at least his values and beliefs.

When confronted with such evidence, a defendant may rebut the prosecution's allegations of prejudice by testifying, or having friends testify, that he is not prejudiced (Jacobs 1992/93, p. 551).

Such testimony and cross examination may transform hate crime trials into character tests, which defendants will pass only if they are politically correct multiculturalists. The result of such inquisition-style hate crime trials may be increased polarization of the community and politicization of the criminal justice system. Ironically, the emphasis on hate crimes might generate more intergroup prejudice and conflict.

It is not surprising then that prosecutors infrequently bring hate crime charges. In Kings County (Brooklyn), New York, the Civil Rights Bureau of the district attorney's office received 169 complaints of bias motivated crimes in 1992 (Maldonado 1992/93, p. 555). Of these complaints, twenty-nine were prosecuted through disposition, or about 12 percent (p. 555). Maldonado attributes case mortality primarily to the difficulty of proving a nexus between the underlying crime and the bias motivation of the offender (p. 556).

Sentencing Enhancement Statutes

Hate crime laws that are formulated as sentencing enhancements, rather than as substantive offenses, need not be proved before a jury and therefore do not raise the problems discussed in the last section. Rules governing the admissibility of evidence, especially hearsay evidence, are less stringent at a sentencing hearing than at a trial. Indeed, courts have traditionally permitted the admission of associational and speech-related evidence at sentencing hearings where the evidence bears a direct relation to the crime charge (*Barclay v. Florida*, 1983, p. 939; *Dawson v. Delaware*, 112 S. Ct. 1093 [1992]; *Wisconsin v. Mitchell*, 113 S. Ct. 2194 [1993]).

The federal sentencing guidelines mandate an increased base-level offense score for the underlying crime when the offender had a bias motive. The defendant's prejudice must be shown by a preponderance of the evidence at the sentencing hearing.

SOCIOPOLITICAL SIGNIFICANCE OF HATE CRIME LAWS

The criminal justice system is unlikely to enforce these special laws vigorously for the reasons discussed in the last section. Their importance is greater as symbolic legislation than as crime control (Jacobs 1992/93, 1993*b*).

Civil rights legislation attempts to rectify past wrongs by codifying positive rights, and affirmative action extends preferences to members of historically discriminated against groups. Hate crime statutes transport the civil rights/affirmative action paradigm into the criminal law. The prejudice and discrimination that are condemned are not those of government or private employers but of criminals. Unlike civil rights legislation that makes otherwise lawful conduct (e.g., refusal to hire or promote) unlawful, hate crime laws enhance punishment for conduct that is already criminal. One further asymmetry with the standard civil rights model is that, in the hate crime context, minority group members, especially blacks and Hispanics, constitute a high proportion of offenders.

Politicians are easily convinced to support hate crime laws, because in passing such laws they believe they are sending a message of support to minority communities that demand such signals. They also send a more general message that they are morally correct individuals. Just as it does not take much political courage for politicians to denounce crime, it does not take courage, nor is it politically risky, for most politicians to denounce crime motivated by racism and religious prejudice. Only denunciation of prejudice against homosexuals seems politically risky. Thus, ironically, some politicians cannot or will not condemn crime motivated by prejudice against homosexuality, although this is a classic type of hate crime.

Understood as symbolic politics, the new genre of hate crime laws makes sense, but it ought not to be assumed that such laws will contribute to a more just and harmonious society. Indeed, the formulation and implementation of hate crime laws themselves generate conflict and social strain.

The concept of hate crime is easy to grasp as an ideal type, but it is difficult to effectuate in a workaday criminal justice system. Most putative hate crimes are not ideologically motivated murders, although some of those do occur. Most are low-level crimes committed, like most crime, by non-ideological young men who could be described as alienated, antisocial, impulsive, and frequently prejudiced. Whether it aids understanding of their conduct and of our society to brand them as bigots as well as criminals is not an easy question to answer. Whether so branding them will improve intergroup relations generally is also an open question.

Beyond the problem of definition, labeling particular incidents as hate crimes bristles with subjectivity and potential for bias. Nevertheless, the very existence of the term, the attempt to measure the incidence of hate crime, and the prosecution and sentencing of some offenders under different types of hate crime statutes have already changed how Americans think about the crime problem. At a minimum, the new hate crime laws have contributed further to politicizing the crime problem.

Émile Durkheim and the sociologists and criminologists who have followed in his wake emphasized the social bonding effects of crime. According to Durkheim, in expressing their outrage at the criminal, the society affirms its commitment to common norms and culture. All this now may be changing. Rather than Americans pulling together and affirming their common ground by condemning criminal conduct, they may now increasingly see crime as a polarizing issue that pits one social group against another, thereby further dividing an already fractured society.

NOTES

1. The hate crime sentencing guideline is explicitly inapplicable to sex crimes.
2. The majority opinion was joined by Justices Scalia, Kennedy, Souter, Thomas, and Chief Justice Rehnquist. Justices Blackmun and Stevens filed concurring opinions, in which Justices O'Connor and White joined. For a journalist's account of the facts surrounding the case, see Cleary (1994).
3. Jack Levin and Jack McDevitt (1993) identify and classify three types of hate crimes: thrill-seeking hate crimes, in which the individual acts with a group to achieve acceptance; reactive hate crimes, in which the individual acts to protect himself from perceived threats from outsiders; and mission hate crimes, in which an individual or group targets members of a particular group which is seen as the cause of personal or societal problems. However, these authors do not have data on the relative frequencies of these three types.
4. Fifty-four percent of offenders were identified as twenty-one or under. Ninety-two percent of offenders were male. The racial break-down of offenders was: 40 percent white, 30 percent black, and 23 percent Latino (Herek and Berrill 1992, pp. 29–30).

5. Intimidation is defined as "to unlawfully place another person in reasonable fear of bodily harm through the use of threatening words and/or other conduct, but without displaying a weapon or subjecting the victim to actual physical attack" (Federal Bureau of Investigation 1991).
6. "After Howard Epstein was shot in the head, onlookers, who gathered around his car, broke into applause when someone pointed out that the victim was white" (Lacey and Feldman 1992, p. A1).
7. The act defines a "crime of violence motivated by gender" as a felony "committed because of gender or on the basis of gender, and due, at least in part, to an animus based on the victim's gender" (Section 40302 [d][1]).

REFERENCES

Abramovsky, Abraham. 1992. "Bias Crime: A Call for Alternative Responses." *Fordham Urban Law Journal* 19:875–914.

Alfredo, Mirande. 1987. *Gringo Justice*. Notre Dame, Ind.: University of Notre Dame Press.

Ames, Jessie. 1942. *The Changing Character of Lynching*. Atlanta: Commission on Interracial Cooperation.

Anderson, Lorrin. 1990. "Crime, Race and the Fourth Estate." *National Review* (October 15), p. 52.

Anti-Defamation League. 1989. *Combatting Bigotry on Campus*. New York: Anti-Defamation League.

———. 1990a. *Louis Ferrakhan. The Campaign to Manipulate Public Opinion*. New York: Anti-Defamation League.

———. 1990b. *Liberty Lobby: A Network of Hate*. New York: Anti-Defamation League.

———. 1990c. *Neo-Nazi Skinheads: A 1990 Status Report*. New York: Anti-Defamation League.

———. 1991. *An ADL Special Report: The KKK Today: A 1991 Status Report*. New York: Anti-Defamation League.

———. 1992. *Hate Crimes Statutes: A 1991 Status Report*. New York: Anti-Defamation League.

———. 1994. *ADL Audit of Anti-Semitic Incidents for 1993*. New York: Anti-Defamation League.

Barkan, Steven E. 1983. "Jury Nullification on Political Trials." *Social Problems* 31:28–44.

Barnes, Arnold, and Paul H. Ephross. 1994. "The Impact of Hate Violence on Victims: Emotional and Behavioral Responses to Attacks." *Social Work* 39(3):247–51.

Benedict, Helen. 1992. *Virgin or Vamp: How the Press Covers Sex Crimes*. New York: Oxford University Press.

Bennett, David H. 1988. *The Party of Fear: The American Far Right from Nativism to the Militia Movement*. New York: Vintage.

Berk, Richard A., Elizabeth A. Boyd, and Karl M. Hamner. 1992. "Thinking More Clearly About Hate Motivated Crimes." In *Hate Crimes: Confronting Violence against Lesbians and Gay Men*, edited by Gregory M. Herek and Kevin T. Berrill. London: Sage.

Berrill, Kevin T. 1992. "Anti-Gay Violence and Victimization in the United States: An Overview." In *Hate Crimes: Confronting Violence against Lesbians and Gay Men*, edited by Gregory M. Herek and Kevin T. Berrill. London: Sage.

——— 1993. "Anti-Gay Violence: Causes, Consequences, and Responses." In *Bias Crime: American Law Enforcement and Legal Responses*, edited by Robert J. Kelly. Chicago: Office of International Criminal Justice.

Box, Terry. 1993. "Hate Crimes against Whites Increase: Researchers, Observers Disagree on Meaning of Higher Numbers." *Dallas Morning News* (April 28), p. A1.

Chaiken, Jan M., and Marcia R. Chaiken. 1983. "Crime Rates and the Active Criminal." In *Crime and Public Policy*, edited by James Q. Wilson. San Francisco: ICS Press.

Chavez, Lydia. 1994. "Crossing the Culture Line." *Los Angeles Times Magazine* (August 28), p. 22.

Chermak, Steven M. 1995. *Victims in the News: Crime and the American News Media*. Boulder, Colo.: Westview.

Cleary, Edward J. 1994. *Beyond the Burning Cross: The First Amendment and the Landmark R.A.V. Case*. New York: Random House.

Coates, James. 1987. *Armed and Dangerous: The Rise of the Survivalist Right*. New York: Hill & Wang.

Coldren, J. David. 1993. "Bias Crimes: State Policy Considerations." In *Bias Crime: American Law Enforcement and Legal Responses*, edited by Robert J. Kelly. Chicago: Office of International Criminal Justice.

Crocker, Lawrence. 1992/93. "Hate Crime Statutes: Just? Constitutional? Wise?" *Annual Survey of American Law* 1992/93:485–507.

Daniels, Roger. 1978. *Anti-Chinese Violence in North America*. New York: Arno.

Desmond, Humphrey. 1912. *The A.P.A. Movement*. New York: Arno.

Egger, Steven A. 1990. "Serial Murder: A Synthesis of Literature and Research." In *Serial Murder: An Elusive Phenomenon*, edited by Steven A. Egger. New York: Praeger.

Ehrlich, Howard J. 1973. *The Social Psychology of Prejudice*. New York: John Wiley.

Epstein, Joseph. 1989. "The Joys of Victimhood." *New York Times Magazine* (July 2), p. 20.

Federal Bureau of Investigation. 1990. *Hate Crime Data Collection Guidelines*. Washington, D.C.: U.S. Government Printing Office.

———. 1991. *Training Guide for Hate Crime Data Collection*. Washington, D.C.: U.S. Government Printing Office.

———. 1992a. *Hate Crime Statistics, 1990: A Resource Book*. Washington, D.C.: U.S. Government Printing Office.

———. 1993. Press release. U.S. Dept. of Justice, January 1. Washington, D.C.: U.S. Government Printing Office.

———. 1994. *Hate Crime Statistics, 1992*. Washington, D.C.: U.S. Government Printing Office.

———. 1995. *Hate Crime Statistics, 1993*. Washington, D.C.: U.S. Government Printing Office.

Ferrell, Claudine L. 1986. *Nightmare and Dream: Anti-lynching in Congress, 1917–1922*. New York: Garland.

Fleischauer, Marc L. 1990. "Teeth for a Paper Tiger: A Proposal to Add Enforceability to Florida's Hate Crimes Act." *Florida State University Law Review* 17:697–711.

Fleisher, Marc. 1994. "Down the Passage Which We Should Not Take: The Folly of Hate Crime Legislation." *Journal of Law and Policy* 2:1–53.

Freeman, Steven M. 1992/93. "Hate Crime Laws: Punishment Which Fits the Crime." *Annual Survey of American Law* 1992/93:581–85.

Garofalo, James, and Susan E. Martin. 1993. "The Law Enforcement Response to Bias-Motivated Crimes." In *Bias Crime: American Law Enforcement and Legal Responses*, edited by Robert J. Kelly. Chicago: Office of International Criminal Justice.

Gaumer, Craig Peyton. 1994. "Punishment for Prejudice: A Commentary on the Constitutionality and Utility of State Statutory Responses to the Problem of Hate Crimes." *South Dakota Law Review* 39:1–48.

Gellman, Susan. 1991. "Sticks and Stones Can Put You in Jail, But Can Words Increase Your Sentence? Constitutional and Policy Dilemmas of Ethnic Intimidation Laws." *UCLA Law Review* 39:333–96.

———. 1992/93. "Hate Crime Laws Are Thought Crime Laws." *Annual Survey of American Law* 1992/93:509–31.

Ginzburg, Ralph. 1962. *100 Years of Lynchings.* New York: Lancer.

Girgenti, Richard H. 1993. *A Report to the Governor on the Disturbances in Crown Heights: An Assessment of the City's Preparedness and Response to Civil Disorder*, vol. 1. Albany: York State Division of Criminal Justice Services.

Goldberger, David. 1992/93. "Hate Crimes Laws and Their Impact on the First Amendment." *Annual Survey of American Law* 1992/93:659–80.

Goleman, Daniel. 1990. "As Bias Crime Seems to Rise, Scientists Study Roots of Racism." *New York Times* (May 29), p. C1.

Greenawalt, Kent. 1992/93. "Reflections on Justifications for Defining Crimes by the Category of Victim." *Annual Survey of American Law.* 1992/93:617–28.

Griego, Tina. 1992. "King Case Aftermath." *Los Angeles Times* (May 2), p. A2.

Hamm, Mark S. 1993. *American Skinheads: The Criminology and Control of Hate Crimes.* Westport, Conn.: Praeger.

Harry, Joseph. 1992. "Conceptualizing Anti-Gay Violence." In *Hate Crimes: Confronting Violence against Lesbians and Gay Men*, edited by Gregory M. Herek and Kevin T. Berrill. London: Sage.

Harvard Law Review. 1988. Note. "Combatting Racial Violence: A Legislative Proposal." *Harvard Law Review* 101:1270–86.

———. 1993. Note. "Hate Is Not Speech: A Constitutional Defense of Penalty Enhancement for Hate Crimes." *Harvard Law Review* 106:1314–31.

Herek, Gregory M. 1992. "Psychological Heterosexism and Anti-Gay Violence: The Social Psychology of Bigotry and Bashing." In *Hate Crimes: Confronting Violence against Lesbians and Gay Men*, edited by Gregory M. Herek and Kevin T. Berrill. London: Sage.

Herek, Gregory M., and Kevin T. Berrill, eds. 1992. *Hate Crimes: Confronting Violence against Lesbians and Gay Men.* London: Sage.

Holmes, Ronald M., and J. DeBurger. 1988. *Serial Murder.* Newbury Park, Calif.: Sage.

Houston Chronicle. 1993. "First-Time FBI Report Reveals Prevalence of Malice." (January 11), p. 12.

International Encyclopedia of the Social Sciences. 1st ed. 1968. New York: Macmillan.

Isolani, Paola A. Sensi, and Phylis Cancilla Martinelli. 1993. *Struggle and Success: An Anthology of the Italian Immigrant Experience in California.* New York: Center for Migration Studies.

Jacobs, James B. 1992*a.* "The New Wave of American Hate Crime Legislation." Report from the Institute of Philosophy and Public Policy, College Park, Md., 12:9–12.

———. 1992*b.* "Rethinking the Law against Hate Crimes: A New York City Perspective." *Criminal Justice Ethics* 11:55–61.

———. 1992/93. "Implementing Hate Crime Legislation: Symbolism and Crime Control." *Annual Survey of American Law* 1992/93:541–53.

———. 1993*a*. "Should Hate Be a Crime?" *Public Interest* 3–14.

———. 1993*b*. "The Emergence and Implications of American Hate Crime Jurisprudence." *Israel Yearbook on Human Rights* 22:113–39.

Jacobs, James B., and Barry Eisler. 1993. "The Hate Crime Statistics Act of 1990." *Criminal Law Bulletin* 29:99–123.

Jacobs, James B., and Jessica S. Henry. 1996. "The Social Construction of a Hate Crime Epidemic." *Journal of Criminal Law and Criminology* 86: 366–91.

Jacobson, Garry J. 1977. "Citizen Participation in Policy Making: The Role of the Jury." *Journal of Politics* 39:73–88.

Kiger, Kenna. 1990. "The Darker Figure of Crime: The Serial Murder Enigma." In *Serial Murder: An Elusive Phenomenon*, edited by Steven A. Egger. New York: Praeger.

Klanwatch. 1987. *"Move-In Violence": White Resistance to Neighborhood Integration in the 1980s*. Montgomery, Ala.: Southern Poverty Law Center.

———. 1989. *Intelligence Report #47, Hate Violence and White Supremacy—a Decade of Review, 1980–1990*. Montgomery, Ala.: Southern Poverty Law Center.

———. 1991. *The Ku Klux Klan: A History of Racism and Violence*. Montgomery, Ala.: Southern Poverty Law Center.

Lacey, Marc, and Paul Feldman. 1992. "Delays, Chaos Add to Woes in Solving Riot Homicides." *Los Angeles Times* (June 21), p. A1.

LaFave, Wayne, and Austin W. Scott. 1986. *Substantive Criminal Law*, vol. 1. St. Paul, Minn.: West.

Lawrence, Charles R. III. 1990. "If He Hollers Let Him Go: Regulating Racist Speech on Campus." *Duke Law Journal* 1990:431–83.

Lawrence, Frederick M. 1994. "The Punishment of Hate: Toward a Normative Theory of Bias-Motivated Crimes." *Michigan Law Review* 93:320–81.

Levin, Jack, and Jack McDevitt. 1993. *Hate Crimes: The Rising Tide of Bigotry and Bloodshed*. New York: Plenum.

Levine, James P. 1992. "The Impact of Local Political Cultures on Jury Verdicts." *Criminal Justice Journal* 14:163–80.

Lorch, Donatella. 1992. "2 Crown Heights Deaths Are Still Deeply Mourned." *New York Times* (September 8), p. B3.

Lowenstein, Steven. 1989. *Frankfurt on the Hudson: The German-Jewish Community in Washington Heights*. Detroit: Wayne State University Press.

Maffi, Mario, 1995. *Gateway to the Promised Land: Ethnic Cultures on New York's Lower East Side*. New York: New York University Press.

Maldonado, Migdalia. 1992/93. "Practical Problems with Enforcing Hate Crimes Legislation in New York City." *Annual Survey of American Law* 1992/93:555–61.

Markowitz, Fran. 1993. *Community in Spite of Itself: Soviet Jewish Emigres in New York*. Washington, D.C.: Smithsonian Institute Press.

Marovitz, William A. 1993. "Hate or Bias Crime Legislation." In *Bias Crime: American Law Enforcement and Legal Responses*, edited by Robert J. Kelly. Chicago: Office of International Criminal Justice.

Marx, Gary. 1986. "When Law and Order Works: Boston's Innovative Approach to the Problem of Racial Violence." *Crime and Delinquency* 32: 205–23.

Matsuda, Mari J. 1989. "Public Response to Racist Speech: Considering the Victim's Story." *Michigan Law Review* 87:2320–81.

Mazon, Mauricio. 1984. *The Zoot-Suit Riots*. Austin: University of Texas Press.

McKinley, James C., Jr. 1990. "Tracking Crimes of Prejudice: A Hunt for the Elusive Truth." *New York Times* (June 29), p. A1.

McWilliams, Carey. 1944. *Prejudice—Japanese Americans: Symbol of Racial Intolerance*. Boston: Little, Brown.

Melillo, Wendy, and Hamil Harris. 1994. "Dissent Raised as Ex-Farrakhan Aide Returns to Howard U." *Washington Post* (April 20), p. B1.

Miller, Stuart. 1969. *The Unwelcome Immigrant*. Berkeley: University of California Press.

Mills, Nicolaus. 1994. "The Shame of 'Black Rage' Defense." *Chicago Tribune* (June 6), p. 13.

New York Police Department. 1991. Untitled document. Bias Incident Investigation Unit, September.

———. 1995. *Bias Incident Investigation Unit Year End Report—1995.*

O'Sullivan, John. 1989. "Do the Right Thing— Suppress Crime: Racial Aspects of New York City Crime." *National Review* (October 13), p. 13.

Pachon, Harry. 1994. *New Americans by Choice: Political Perspectives of Latino Immigrants.* Boulder, Colo.: Westview.

Papajohn, George. 1993. "Korean Store Boycott Splits South Siders." *Chicago Tribune* (December 28), p. 1.

Pendo, Elizabeth A. 1994. "Recognizing Violence against Women: Gender and the Hate Crime Statistics Act." *Harvard Women's Law Journal* 17: 157–83.

Praeger, Dennis. 1993. "Blacks and Liberals: The Los Angeles Riots." *Current* (January), p. 11.

Prago, Albert. 1973. *Strangers in Their Own Land.* New York: Four Winds.

Redish, Martin H. 1992. "Freedom of Thought as Freedom of Expression." *Criminal Justice Ethics* 11:29–42.

Rieder, Jonathan. 1990. "Trouble in Store: Beyond the Brooklyn Boycott." *New Republic* (July 2), p. 16.

Rothschild, Eric. 1993. "Recognizing Another Face of Hate Crimes: Rape as a Gender-Bias Crime." *Maryland Journal of Contemporary Legal Issues* 4:231–85.

Rovella, David E. 1994. "Attack on Hate Crime Is Enhanced." *National Law Journal* (August 29), p. A1.

Santa Clara Law Review. 1994. Comment: "Substantive Penal Hate Crime Legislation: Toward Defining Constitutional Guidelines Following the *R.A.V. v. City of St. Paul* and *Wisconsin v. Mitchell* Decisions." *Santa Clara Law Review* 34:711–64.

Sargent, Lyman Tower, ed. 1995. *Extremism in America.* New York: New York University Press.

Saxton, Alexander. 1971. *The Invisible Enemy.* Berkeley: University of California Press.

Schmich, Mary. 1993. "Denny Case: Step Back or Justice?" *Chicago Tribune* (October 20), p. N1.

Schweitzer, Thomas A. 1995. "Hate Speech on Campus and the First Amendment. Can They Be Reconciled?" *Connecticut Law Review* 27:493–521.

Sleeper, Jim. 1990. *The Closest of Strangers: Liberalism and the Politics of Race in New York.* New York: W. W. Norton.

———. 1993. *In Defense of Civic Culture.* Washington, D.C.: The Progressive Foundation.

Smith, David Todd. 1994. "Enhanced Punishment under the Texas Hate Crimes Act: Politics, Panacea, or Pathway to Hell?" *St. Mary's Law Journal* 26:259–305.

Sykes, Charles. 1992. *A Nation of Victims.* New York: St. Martin's.

Takaki, Ronald. 1989. *Strangers from a Different Shore.* Boston: Little, Brown.

U.S. Commission on Civil Rights. 1992. *Civil Rights Issues Facing Asian Americans in the 1990s.* Washington, D.C.: U.S. Commission on Civil Rights.

U.S. Congress. 1987. *Anti-Asian Violence: Hearings before the Subcommittee on Civil and Constitutional Rights of the House Committee on the Judiciary.* 100th Cong., 1st Sess. Washington, D.C.: U.S. Government Printing Office.

U.S. Congress. House of Representatives Committee on the Judiciary. Subcommittee on Criminal Justice. 1986. *Ethnically Motivated Violence against Arab-Americans.* 99th Cong., 2d Sess. Washington, D.C.: U.S. Government Printing Office.

U.S. Senate. Senate Committee on the Judiciary. Subcommittee on the Constitution. 1988. *Hate Crime Statistics Act of 1988.* 100th Cong., 2d Sess. Washington, D.C.: U.S. Government Printing Office.

U.S. Senate. 1989. Senate Report No. 21. 101st Cong., 1st Sess. Washington, D.C.: U.S. Government Printing Office.

Walker, Samuel. 1994. *Hate Speech: The History of an American Controversy*. Lincoln: University of Nebraska Press.

Wang, Lu-in. 1995. *Hate Crimes Laws*. New York: Clark, Boardman, Callaghan.

Welch, Richard F. 1994. "Unchallenged, Black Racism Grows." *Newsday* (February 10), p. 113.

Wilson, Laurie. 1993. "Scholars Say NY Attack Hard to Assess." *Dallas Morning News* (December 9), p. A14.

Wright, Kevin N. 1985. *The Great American Crime Myth*. New York: Praeger.

Child Abuse

Leslie Margolin

METHODS

The idea for this research emerged while I was involved in a study of child abuse by babysitters. As part of that study, I had to read "official" case records documenting that child abuse had occurred. The more records I read, the more it appeared that the social workers devoted a rather large portion of their writing to describing children's injuries, as well as the violent and sexual interactions which often preceded and followed them. By contrast, the alleged perpetrator's intentions, feelings, and interpretations of what happened appeared to occupy a relatively small portion of the documents. This imbalance roused interest in view of the agency's formal regulations that social workers satisfy two criteria to establish that a caregiver committed child abuse: (1) They must establish that a caregiver performed acts which were damaging or exploitive to a child; (2) They must prove that the caregiver *intended* to damage or exploit the child—that the trauma was non-accidental. In the article I examine how social workers managed to label child abusers in a manner consistent with these regulations without appearing to give much weight to subjective factors such as suspects' excuses and justifications.

The sample consisted of 60 case records documenting physical abuse and 60 records documenting sexual abuse. They were randomly selected from all case records of child abuse by babysitters substantiated by a state agency during a two year period (N = 537). A babysitter was defined as someone who took care of a child who was not a member of the child's family, was not a boyfriend or girlfriend of the child's parent, and was not employed in a registered or licensed group care facility.

I do not treat these records as ontologically valid accounts of "what happened"; rather, I treat them as a "documentary reality" (Smith 1974), indicating the ways the social workers who constructed them want to be seen by their superiors. As such, the records

From Leslie Margolin, "Deviance on Record," *Social Problems* v. 39, no. 1 (1992): 58–70. Reprinted by permission of the University of California Press, the Society for the Study of Social Problems, and the author.

provide evidence that the social workers utilized the unstated yet commonly known procedures which represent "good work." The following analysis attempts to make these procedures explicit and to show how the social workers who used them "prove" that child abuse took place by constructing good (bureaucratically sound) arguments supporting the view that a specific person intentionally damaged a child. I also explore the degree to which deviants' excuses, denials, and other accounts were incorporated into these decision processes. Finally, I look at how each type of information—descriptions of the injuries and accounts of what happened—was used as evidence that child abuse occurred and could have only been performed by the person who was labeled.

DISPLAYING VIOLENCE AND SEXUALITY

At the beginning of each record, the social worker described the physical injuries which were believed to have been inflicted on the child by the babysitter. These descriptions did not specify how the child's health or functioning were impaired but were presented as evidence that an act of transformative social import had occurred (cf. Denzin 1989). To illustrate this reporting style, one three-year-old who was spanked by his babysitter was described by the physician as having "a contusion to the buttocks and small superficial lacerations." However, the social worker who used these injuries as evidence of child abuse described them as follows:

> The injuries gave the appearance of an ink blot, in that they were almost mirror images of each other, positioned in the center of each buttock. The bruising was approximately four inches long by about two and a half inches wide, and was dark red on the perimeter and had a white cast to the inside of the bruise.

> There was a long linear line running across the bottom of both buttocks extending almost the entire width of the child's buttock. There was lighter reddish bruising surrounding the two largest bruises on each buttock and faint bluish-red bruising extending up to the lower back. The bruising would be characterized as being red turning to a deeper reddish-purple than true bright red.

This unusually graphic style of presentation gave the bruises a special status. They were no longer simply bruises but were now defined as out of the ordinary, strange, and grotesque. By removing the bruises from everyday experience, the stage was set for redefining the babysitter who supposedly did this to the child. In this manner, a person whose social status had been taken for granted could now be seen as potentially suspicious, foreign, and malevolent (Garfinkel 1956).

A parallel line of reportage was apparent in the sexual abuse cases. To the degree that the available information permitted, reports contained no obscurity in the descriptions of sexual interactions. No detail of what happened appeared too small to be pursued, named, and included in the records as evidence (cf. Foucault 1978). This excerpt from a social worker's recorded interview with an eight-year-old girl illustrates:

> S.W.: How did the bad touch happen? Can you think?
> Child: I can't remember.
> S.W.: Did you ever have to kiss?
> Child: No.
> S.W.: Anybody?
> Child: Uh uh.
> S.W.: Did you have to touch anybody?
> Child: Yeah.
> S.W.: Ah, you had to touch 'em. Where did you have to touch 'em?
> Child: Down below.
> S.W.: Oh, down below. Do you have a word for that body part?

Child: A thing-a-ma-jig.

S.W.: A thing-a-ma-jig. OK, let's look. . . . Is P [the suspect] a man?

Child: Yeah.

S.W.: OK, let's take a look at the man doll. Can you show me on the man doll what part you're talking about?

Child: This part.

S.W.: Oh, the part that sticks out in front. We have another word for that. Do you know the other word for that part?

Child: Dick.

S.W.: Yeah. Dick is another word for it. Another word is penis.

Child: Penis?

S.W.: Yeah.

Child: Oh.

S.W.: Can you tell me what—Did you see his body? Did you see his penis with your eyes?

Child: No.

S.W.: OK. Did he have his pants on or off?

Child: Unzipped.

S.W.: Unzipped. I see. How did his penis happen to come out of his pants?

Child: By the zipper.

S.W.: I see. Who took his penis out of his pants?

Child: He did.

S.W.: What did you have to touch his penis with?

Child: My fingers.

S.W.: I see. How did you know you had to do that?

Child: He told me to.

S.W.: What did he say?

Child: Itch it.

S.W.: Itch it. I see. Did he show you how to itch it? How did he have to itch it? One question at a time. Did he show you how to itch it?

Child: He said just go back.

S.W.: So you showed me that you're kind of scratching on it.

Child: Um hum.

S.W.: Did anything happen to his penis or his thing-a-ma-jig when you did that?

Child: No.

S.W.: OK. When he took his penis out of his pants, how did it look?

Child: Yucky.

S.W.: Yeah, I know you think it's yucky, but um, what does yucky mean? Can you tell me with some other words besides yucky?

Child: Slimy.

S.W.: Looked slimy. OK. Was it big?

Child: Yeah.

S.W.: Was it hard or soft.

Child: Soft and hard.

S.W.: OK. Explain how you mean that. . . .

I offer this dialogue not as evidence that sexual abuse did or did not occur, but rather, to display the means by which equivocal behavior is translated into the "fact" of sexual abuse. Whatever it is that "really happened" to this child, we see that her experience of it is not a concern when "documentation" is being gathered. She is an object of inquiry, not a participant (Cicourel 1968; Smith 1974). Whatever reasons compel social workers to bring her to their offices and ask these questions are their reasons not hers. And as the child learns, even features of the "event"—such as the size, hardness, and overall appearance of a penis—can assume critical importance within interviewers' frames of reference.

While social workers used these details of sexual interactions and injuries to set the stage for the attribution of deviance, I noted four cases in which the analysis of the injuries themselves played a conspicuously larger role in determining who was responsible. In these cases the injured children were too young to explain how their injuries were caused, the babysitters denied causing the injuries, and there were no witnesses. This meant that the only way the investigators were able to label the babysitters as abusive was to argue that the injuries occurred during the time the suspects were taking care of the children. The parents of the injured children testified that the children were sent to the babysitters in good health, without any marks, but returned from the babysitters with a noticeable injury. This allowed the social workers to determine responsibility through the following method: if a babysitter cannot produce any plausible alternative explanation for the child's injuries, the babysitter must be responsible for the injuries.

Since children who had allegedly been sexually abused did not have conspicuous or easily described injuries, attributing sexual abuse on the absence of any plausible alternative explanation for the injury was, of course, impossible. This would appear to severely limit social workers' capacity to document that a babysitter committed sexual abuse when the babysitter denied the charges, when the child was too young to provide coherent testimony, and when there were no other witnesses. However, this was not always the case. Like the investigators described by Garfinkel (1967:18) who were able to determine the cause of death among possible suicides with only "*this* much; *this* sight; *this* note; *this* collection of whatever is at hand," child abuse investigators showed the capacity to "make do" with whatever information was available. In one case of sexual abuse, for example, there were no witnesses, no admission from the suspect, no physical evidence, and no charge from the alleged victim; still, "evidence" was summoned to establish a babysitter's guilt. Here, the social worker cited a four-year-old girl's fears, nightmares, and other "behavior consistent with that of a child who was sexually traumatized by a close family friend." Additionally, the babysitter in question was portrayed as a "type" capable of doing such things:

> Having no physical evidence, and no consistent statement from the alleged victim, I am forced to make a conclusion based on the credibility of the child as opposed to that of the perpetrator. This conclusion is supported by similar allegations against him from an independent source. It is also supported by behavioral indications and what we know of his history.

In a second case, a social worker showed that information pointing to the suspect's homosexuality and history of sexual victimization could be used to support charges of sexual abuse when other kinds of evidence were lacking:

> Although the babysitter denied having sexual contact with this child when interviewed, he did leave a note to the effect that he was attracted to males and thought that he was homosexual, and records indicate that he, himself, was sexually abused at the age of eight. Based on the interview done, the past history, and his own previous victimization, this worker feels that he did, in fact, penetrate and perpetrate himself upon the victim.

In most cases, however, portraying the suspect as a "type" was not critical to the finding of child abuse. The rationale for labeling was primarily constructed out of witnesses' testimony showing "who did what to whom."

USING WITNESSES TO DETERMINE WHO DID WHAT TO WHOM

Since the children and alleged child abusers often had different versions of what happened (40 cases), social workers needed a decision-rule to settle the question of who had the correct story. The rule used for resolving disagreements was fairly simple: The child's version was considered the true one. The children were called "credible" witnesses when describing assaults which were done to them because it was assumed they had nothing to gain by falsely accusing the babysitter. The babysitters, on the other hand, were seen as "non-credible" (when they attempted to establish their innocence) because they had everything to gain by lying. Even children as young as two- and three-years-old were believed in preference to their adult babysitters. In fact, the main reason given for interpreting children as superior witnesses was precisely their youth, ignorance, and lack of sophistication. As one social worker observed, "It's my experience that a four-year-old would not be able to maintain such a consistent account of an incident if she was not telling the truth." Particularly in cases of sexual abuse, it was believed that the younger the witness, the more credible his or her testimony was. Social workers made the point that children who were providing details of sexual behavior would not know of such things unless they had been abused (cf. Eberle and Eberle 1986).

The children's accounts were rejected in only three instances. In one of these cases, two teenage boys claimed they witnessed a babysitter abuse a child as they peered through a window. Both the babysitter and the child said this was not true. The social worker did not feel it was necessary to explain why the babysitter would deny the allegations, but the child's denial was seen as problematic. Therefore, the social worker offered the following rationale for rejecting the child's account: "The child's refusal to say anything is not unusual because her mother was so verbally upset when she was informed of the allegations." A child's version of what happened (his denial of abuse) was rejected in a second case on the grounds that he was protecting a babysitter described as his "best friend." Finally, a 12-year-old female who repeatedly denied that anyone had touched her sexually was seen as non-credible because of her "modesty." As the social worker put it, "She did seem to have a very difficult time talking

about it, and I feel she greatly minimized the incident due to her embarrassment about it."

In general, however, testimony from children was treated as the most credible source of evidence of what happened, since most social workers believe that children do not lie about the abuse done to them. By contrast, babysitters were presented as credible witnesses only when they agreed with the allegations made against them (56 cases). When they testified to the contrary, they were portrayed as biased. What does *not* happen, therefore, is the child implicating someone, the accused saying nothing happened, and the investigator siding with the accused. This suggests an underlying idealization that precedes and supports the ones operating on the surface of most cases: *the accused is guilty.* It goes without saying that this organizational stance runs roughly opposite to the Constitutional one of "innocent until proven guilty."

Here, it might be useful to draw an analogy between the child protection workers' "investigative stance" and that of welfare investigators responsible for determining applicants' eligibility (Zimmerman 1974). In both cases, investigators adopt a thoroughgoing skepticism designed "to locate and display the potential discrepancy between the applicant's [or suspect's] subjective and 'interested' claims and the factual and objective (i.e., rational) account that close observance of agency procedure is deemed to produce" (Zimmerman 1974:131). However, an important difference should be noted: during the conduct of welfare investigations, the investigated party is referred to as the "applicant," indicating that the investigation could end in a determination of either eligibility or ineligibility; by contrast, during the conduct of child abuse investigations, the investigated party is routinely identified as the "perpetrator," suggesting a previously concluded status. To illustrate, these notations documented one worker's activities during the first days of a child abuse investigation:

> 3/24: Home visit with police, interviewed parents, child not at home—perpetrator not in home.
> 3/26: Interview with detective J at Police station with CPI and child. Perpetrator arrested.

While babysitters accused of child abuse may in theory be only "suspects," at the level of practice, they are "perpetrators." This discrepancy between "theory" and "practice" is more than an example of how the formal structures of organizations are accompanied by unintended and unprogrammed structures (Bittner 1965). In this instance, child protection workers are formally enjoined to gather evidence about "perpetrators," not "suspects." Consider these guidelines from the agency's official handbook:

> Information collected from the person [witness] should include precise description of size, shape, color, type, and location of injury. It may be possible to establish the credibility of the child, the responsible caretaker or the *perpetrator* as a source of this information. . . . The *perpetrator* and victim may be credible persons and need to be judged on the basis of the same factors as any other persons. (Italics added.)

The implicit message is that the goal of the child abuse investigation is not to determine an individual's guilt or innocence but to find evidence to be used in recording or "documenting" what is already taken for granted, that parties initially identified as the "perpetrator" and "victim" are in fact the "perpetrator" and "victim." Strictly speaking, then, the goal is not to determine "who did what to whom," since that information is assumed at the outset, but rather, to document that agency rules have been followed, and that the investigation was conducted in a rational, impersonal manner.

DETERMINING INTENTIONALITY

A decision-rule was also needed to determine the babysitter's intentions. While babysitters were portrayed in the allegations as malicious or exploitive, many babysitters offered a different version of their motivations. Among the babysitters accused of physical abuse, 25 acknowledged hitting the children but also claimed they intended no harm. Three said they were having a bad day, were under unusual stress, and simply "lost it." They attributed their violence to a spontaneous, non-instrumental, expression of frustration. For example, one male caregiver took a two-year-old to the potty several times but the child did not go. Later he noticed that the child's diaper was wet; so he hurried him to the potty. However, just before being placed on the potty the child had a bowel movement. At that point the caregiver lost his temper and hit the child.

One woman who was labeled abusive claimed she was ill and never wanted to babysit in the first place. She only agreed to take care of a two-year-old girl because the girl's mother insisted. The mother had an unexpected schedule change at work and needed child care on an emergency basis. The abusive event occurred soon after the babysitter served lunch to the child. While the sitter rested on a couch in the living room, she observed the girl messing with her lunch. The sitter got up and tried to settle the child. When this did not work, she took away the girl's paper plate and threw it in the garbage. At that point the girl began to cry for her mother. The babysitter returned to the living room to lie down on the couch. But the girl followed her, wailing for her mother. When the girl reached the couch, the babysitter sat up and slapped her.

Other babysitters described their violence in instrumental terms: their goal was to discipline the children and not to hurt or injure them. They said that whatever injuries occurred were the accidental result of hitting (in one case, biting) the children harder than they meant to do. Some sitters indicated that the only reason children were injured during a disciplinary action was that the children moved just as they were being hit, exposing a sensitive part of the body to the blow. Others protested that the child's movements made it impossible to aim the blows accurately or to assess how hard they were hitting. In one case, the sitter said she was trying to hit the child across the buttocks with a stick, but the child put her hand across her buttocks to protect herself, receiving "non-intentional" bruising and swelling to the hand. A different sitter asked that the social worker consider that at the time of the violation he did not know it was against the law to beat a child with a belt. Another said he had been given permission to spank the child by the child's mother and was only following her orders. This was confirmed by the mother. After a two-and-a-half-year-old bit another child, his sitter bit him to show him "what it felt like." The sitter argued that she had done this in the past and had even told the child's mother. Thus, she believed that this was tacitly approved. Still another babysitter claimed that he struck the 11-year-old girl who was in his care in self-defense. He said that when he told her it was time for bed she began to bite and kick him. He said her injuries resulted from his efforts to calm and restrain her.

To sift out the babysitters' "official" intentions from the versions offered by the sitters themselves, several social workers explicitly invoked the following reasoning: Physical damage to the child would be considered "intentional" if the acts which produced them were intentional. Thus, a social worker wrote:

> I am concluding that this injury to the child was non-accidental in that the babysitter did have a purpose in striking the child, that purpose being to discipline her in hopes of modifying her behavior.

While close examination of this logic reveals an absurdity (the injury was seen as "intentional" despite the fact that it was produced by an act aimed at an entirely different outcome, "modifying her behavior"), the practical consequence of such a formula was a simple method for determining a suspect's intentions: If a babysitter was known to intentionally hit a child, causing an injury, the social worker could conclude the babysitter intended to cause the injury. Through such a formula, the most common excuse utilized by babysitters to account for their actions, that the injury was the accidental result of a disciplinary action, was interpreted as a confession of responsibility for physical abuse.

To give another example of how this formula provided a short-cut to determining intentionality, one social worker concluded her recording as follows:

> Physical abuse is founded in that the caretaker did hit the child on the face because she was throwing a temper tantrum and left a bruise approximately one inch long under the right eye. This constitutes a non-accidental injury. The bruise is still visible after five days.

In cases involving allegations of physical abuse, the problem of figuring out what the babysitter was really contemplating at the time of the violation never came up as a separate issue because the alleged perpetrator's motivation to injure the child was seen as the operational equivalent of two prior questions, "Does the child have an injury resulting from a blow?" and "Did the babysitter intentionally strike the child?" When each of these questions was answered affirmatively, intent to harm the child was inferred. Thus, it was possible for a social worker to observe, "It was this writer's opinion that the babysitter was surprised at the injury she left on the child by spanking the child," and later conclude, "the injury occurred as a result of a non-accidental incident."

One record included comments from witnesses which stated that a babysitter pushed a five-year-old boy after the child socked a cat. All agreed that the injury was not a direct consequence of the push but resulted when the child lost balance and fell over. Despite the social worker's explicit recognition that the child's injury was neither planned nor anticipated (she wrote that "the injury will probably not be repeated due to the sitter's awareness of the seriousness of disciplining a child by reacting rather than thinking"), the report of physical abuse was, nonetheless, founded "due to the fact that the injury occurred in the course of a disciplinary action."

In another record, a male babysitter admitted to spanking a child, causing red marks on his buttocks. Although the child's father said he "did not believe the sitter meant to spank as hard as he did," and the police officer who was present concluded that "based on the information obtained in this investigation, I could find no intent on the sitter's part to assault this child," the social worker found the determination of physical abuse nonproblematic. Since the child received the injury in the course of a spanking, child abuse occurred.

There were only two cases of sexual abuse in which the alleged abuser acknowledged touching the child in a manner consistent with the allegations, but at the same time

denied sexual intent. In one of these cases, the alleged abuser said he only touched a 10-year-old boy's genitals in the process of giving him a bath. In the other case, the alleged abuser claimed he only touched the girl's body as part of an anatomy lesson, to show her where her rib and pelvic bones were located. Both of these accounts were dismissed as preposterous. The social workers expressed the opinion that sexual intent was the only possible reason anyone would enact the types of behavior attributed to the accused in the allegations. In short, an equation was drawn between specific behaviors attributed to the accused and their states of mind. If it was established that the babysitter behaved toward the child in ways commonly understood as sexual (e.g., fondling), establishing intent, as a separate dimension of the investigation, was seen as redundant. Thus, social workers were able to conclude their investigations of sexual abuse, as one investigator did, by utilizing the following formula: "The child, a credible witness, indicated that her babysitter did fondle her genitals. Therefore, this is a founded case of intent to commit sexual abuse."

To summarize, in cases of both physical and sexual abuse, the intent to commit these acts was seen as a necessary component of the specific behaviors used to accomplish them. Hitting which resulted in an injury was always treated as if it was a direct indicator of the motivation to injure. Similarly, behavior commonly known as "sexual" was always treated as if it was identical with the suspect's intent to sexually exploit. The fact that social workers sometimes described the suspects' surprise and horror at the physical damage their violence caused the child did not make the attribution of "intent to harm" more problematic because suspects' accounts were not organizationally defined as indicators of intent. Motives for child abuse are not features of the perpetrator's psyche, but rather, of the bureaucracy and profession. That 50 of the babysitters labeled as abusive denied performing the actions imputed to them, and another 14 were not interviewed at all (either because they could not be located or refused to speak to the social worker) demonstrated that it was possible to "officially" determine babysitters' intentions without confirmatory statements from the babysitters themselves.

DISCUSSION

Sociologists have often questioned official records on the grounds of their accuracy, reliability, and representativeness. However, the methods through which and by which deviance is routinely displayed in records have rarely been investigated (cf. Cicourel and Kitsuse 1963; Kitsuse and Cicourel 1963). This study has treated as problematic the standardized arguments and evidence which social workers use in official documents to prove that child abuse has taken place. In this regard, child abuse is seen as an accomplishment of a bureaucratic system in which members agree to treat specific phenomena as if they were "child abuse."

The proof of abuse was problematic since more than half of the suspects either denied the accusations or were not interviewed. Social workers "made do" without supportive testimony from suspects by routinely defining them as "non-credible" witnesses. Also, social workers managed to conform to agency regulations requiring proof that suspects intended to harm or exploit children by agreeing to treat specific observables as if they represented the intent to harm or exploit.

Thus, the designation of child abuse was simplified. Testimony from the person most likely to disagree with this label, the accused, did not have to be considered. This is not to say that testimony from the accused might overcome the processes of institutional sense-making. It is to suggest, rather, that defining the accused as non-credible makes the designation of child abuse more "cut and dried," defendable, and recordable, since abuse that might otherwise be denied, excused, or justified, either in whole or in part, can then be fully attributed to suspects.

While it can be argued that simplifying the means by which suspects are labeled is desirable for a society concerned about keeping dangerous people away from children, the negative consequences should be acknowledged. As already shown, individuals who assign child abuse labels have more power than suspects, making it impossible for parties at risk of being labeled to "negotiate" on an equal footing with labelers. Indeed, any disjuncture between suspects' and investigators' versions of "what really happened" do not have to be resolved prior to the attribution of child abuse (cf. Pollner 1987:77–81). Since investigators have the capacity to impose their versions of reality on suspects, the only "resolution" needed from the investigators' perspective entails finding ways to make their decisions defendable in writing.

As might also be expected, the personal, social, and legal stigma resulting from designating this label is enormous. Once the impression has been formed that a person is a child abuser, the expectation exists that he or she will continue to be abusive. Moreover, there is little a person can do to remove this label. It exists as part of a permanent record that can be recalled whenever a person's child care capacities or moral standing are questioned.

While most who write about child abuse are enmeshed in that system, either as practitioners or ideologues and so are strained to defend its existence, in recent years critics have shown concern about the growing numbers of people labeled as child abusers (Besharov 1986; Eberle and Eberle 1986; Elshtain 1985; Johnson 1985; Pride 1986; Wexler 1985).

Most trace this "overattribution" of child abuse to professional and lay people's "emotionally charged desire to 'do something' about child abuse, fanned by repeated and often sensational media coverage" (Besharov 1986:19). However, Conrad and Schneider (1980:270) provide a more general explanation: "bureaucratic 'industries' with large budgets and many employees . . . depend for their existence on the acceptance of a particular deviance designation. They become 'vested interests' in every sense of the term."

It is possible that social agencies geared to controlling child care grow in response to instability in the child care system. This hypothesis warrants attention if for no other reason than that mothers' dramatic increases in labor force participation over the last three decades, and the commensurate increase in young children's time in nonparental care, have closely paralleled the emergence of child abuse as a major social issue. However, this single causal mode of explanation would be more compelling if it were not that history reveals other periods in which institutional momentum developed around "saving children" under a variety of different conditions (Best 1990, Finestone 1976, Platt 1969). This suggests that any explanation of why such social movements wax and wane, taking their particular form at each point in history, needs to account for many interacting factors, including the prevailing moralities and family institutions as well as opportunities for effectively marketing these problems to a wide audience.

REFERENCES

Besharov, Douglas J. 1986. "Unfounded allegations—A new child abuse problem." *The Public Interest* 83:18–33.

Best, Joel. 1990. *Threatened Children: Rhetoric and Concern about Child-Victims.* Chicago: The University of Chicago Press.

Bittner, Egon. 1965. The concept of organization." *Social Research* 32:239–255.

Cicourel, Aaron V. 1968. *The Social Organization of Juvenile Justice.* New York: John Wiley and Sons.

Cicourel, Aaron V., and John I. Kitsuse. 1963. *The Educational Decision-Makers.* New York: Bobbs-Merrill.

Conrad, Peter, and Joseph W. Schneider. 1980. *Deviance and Medicalization.* St. Louis: C. V. Mosby.

Denzin, Norman K. 1989. *Interpretive Interactionism.* Newbury Park, Calif.: Sage.

Eberle, Paul, and Shirley Eberle. 1986. *The Politics of Child Abuse.* Secaucus, N.J.: Lyle Stuart.

Elshtain, Jean Bethke. 1985. "Invasion of the child savers: How we succumb to hype and hysteria." *The Progressive* 49:23–26.

Finestone, Harold. 1976. *Victims of Change: Juvenile Delinquents in American Society.* Westport, Conn.: Greenwood Press.

Foucault, Michel. 1978. *The History of Sexuality.* Vol. 1. New York: Pantheon.

Garfinkel, Harold. 1956. "Conditions of successful degradation ceremonies." *American Journal of Sociology* 61:420–424.

———. 1967. *Studies in Ethnomethodology.* Englewood Cliff, N.J.: Prentice-Hall.

Johnson, John M. 1985. "Symbolic salvation: The changing meanings of the child maltreatment movement." *Studies in Symbolic Interaction* 6:289–305.

Kitsuse, John I., and Aaron, V. Cicourel. 1963. "A note on the use of official statistics." *Social Problems* 11:131–139.

Platt, Anthony M. 1969. *The Child Savers: The Invention of Delinquency.* Chicago: The University of Chicago Press.

Pollner, Melvin. 1987. *Mundane Reason: Reality in Everyday and Sociological Discourse.* Cambridge: Cambridge University Press.

Pride, Mary. 1986. *The Child Abuse Industry.* Westchester, Ill.: Crossway.

Smith, Dorothy E. 1974. "The social construction of documentary reality." *Sociological Inquiry* 44:257–268.

Wexler, Richard. 1985. "Invasions of the child savers: No one is safe in the war against abuse." *The Progressive* 49:19–22.

Zimmerman, Don H. 1974. "Fact as a practical accomplishment." In *Ethnomethodology*, ed. Roy Turner, 128–143. Middlesex, Eng.: Penguin Books.

School Shootings

Ronald Burns and Charles Crawford

Since the recent fervor over school shootings, Americans appear to be gripped with fear. This fear has extended beyond the poor, inner-city neighborhoods, reaching affluent suburbs, towns, and rural areas. An issue that was once thought of as an urban problem has recently touched historically stable suburban and rural communities. For many, the violence suggests a breakdown in the social order, as no place seems safe anymore.

Yet, is the public's fear justified? Have the recent school shootings provided ample evidence that something must be done not only to prevent violence in schools, but all juvenile violence? In the present research we argue that the widespread societal responses to several high profile incidents should be reevaluated, mainly because of the decreasing amount of juvenile violence both within and outside of schools, and especially because of the relatively small numbers of children murdered at school. We argue that the situation evolved largely due to the self-serving interests of several groups in American society. Put simply, we claim that the recent school shootings have resulted in a moral panic.

DEFINING AND IDENTIFYING MORAL PANICS

A moral panic typically focuses on evildoers—or supposed evildoers who come to be defined as the enemy of society. Therefore, in the eyes of the claimsmakers, or moral entrepreneurs (Becker, 1963), these "folk devils," deviants, or outsiders deserve public hostility and punishment.

Goode and Ben-Yehuda (1994) suggest that a moral panic appears when a substantial portion of society feels that particular evildoers pose a threat to the moral order of society. As a result, the general consensus among the group is to "do something" about the issue. A major focus of their reaction "typically in-

From *Crime, Law, and Social Change* 32 (1999): 147–168. Reprinted by permission of Kluwer Academic Publishers and the authors.

volves strengthening the social control apparatus of the society, including tougher or renewed rules, increased public hostility and condemnation, more laws, longer sentences, more police, more arrests, and more prison cells" (Goode and Ben-Yehuda, 1994:30). It is through these, and other efforts, that the "moral order" is to be re-established, or held in check.

How and why a moral panic emerges has been a serious research topic for social scientists for decades. We employ a model based on Goode and Ben-Yehuda's (1994) approach to moral panics which requires a problematic behavior that generates heightened senses of societal concern and hostility, a general societal consensus that the behavior is harmful, and a disproportionate societal interpretation/reaction to the problem.

SCHOOL SHOOTINGS

The United States was shocked on October 1, 1997 when a 16-year-old Pearl, Mississippi student killed his mother and proceeded to his school where he shot nine students. Two of them died, including the boy's ex-girlfriend. Two months later the American public was saddened and became nervous about school violence when a 14-year old boy began shooting at a student prayer circle in West Paducah, Kentucky. Three students were killed and five wounded. Later, in March 1998, four students and one teacher were killed in Jonesboro, Arkansas as they exited West Side Middle School when a fire alarm, deliberately set off by the shooters, went off. Two boys, ages 11 and 13, opened fire on the group of students as they proceeded from the building. Similar incidents occurred around the United States, including situations in Oregon where on May 21, 15-year old Kip Kinkel fired a gun indis-

criminately into a crowded cafeteria at Thurston High School, killing two students and wounding 22 others; and in Edinboro, Pennsylvania where on April 24, a student fatally shot a teacher and wounded two classmates. Perhaps the most prolific incident occurred on April 20, 1999, when two Columbine (CO) High School students opened fire, killing a teacher and 12 classmates before killing themselves. Several high-profile incidents occurring within a short time frame ignited widespread public concern, fear, and reaction.

Concern

Even though fear is not a necessary element of a moral panic, it can be very real to those who see the event(s) or behavior(s) as a serious threat to society. Public concern and fear in response to the school shootings can be observed in several areas. For example, after each of the shooting incidents, various media outlets flooded the public with horrifying accounts. *The New York Times* ran stories about the Oregon shooting for three straight days on the front page. President Clinton used his Saturday radio address to decry the "changing culture that desensitizes our children to violence," and was one of numerous politicians who publicly chastised the entertainment industry for being "irresponsible" and playing a role in the recent school shootings. Daytime television programming was being pre-empted and continuous coverage of the shootings was provided (McFadden, 1998), while funerals for the victims were advertised and broadcast live on the Internet, radio, and closed circuit television (McFadden, 1998; Cart, 1998).

Concern and fear are also evident in the general reactions to the shootings. Among the reactions to the shootings were hiring additional security officers in schools (Sanchez, 1998); installing metal detectors in schools (Page, 1998); keeping schools open evenings and nights and proposals to fund 100,000 "youth counselors" (Willing, 1998); a guidebook compiled by a presidential panel to alert teachers, parents, and students to early warning signs of potential violent behavior and to provide strategies for preventing and responding to violence; the discontinuation of selling toy action figures because the toy's name could provoke reminders of a boy charged in one of the school shootings ("Burger King . . .", 1998); bullet drills in which school children drop and take cover (Tirrell-Wysocki, 1998); requiring at least a few school teachers to carry concealed weapons at school (Page, 1998); efforts by libraries to raise the age at which teenagers may borrow general circulation books to 16 from 13 and issuing special library cards that allow access only to juvenile books (Carvajal, 1999); efforts to include cigarette-style warning labels on violent music, movies and video games (Fiore and Anderson, 1999); and school lockdown procedures (Behrendt, 1998).

Further evidence of the public concern and fear is found in a senior White House advisor's plan to extend the Brady gun control law to juveniles (Burnett, 1998). The advisor apparently was unaware that the application of the Brady Bill to juveniles is virtually impossible as current law already states that no one under age 21 can purchase guns. Comments made by President Clinton and public opinion surveys (both discussed below) also suggest that many Americans were troubled by school violence. Similar to Fritz and Altheide's (1987:478) account of the media's portrayal of the missing children issue, these reactions tended "to focus on the tragedy and suffering of individual children and parents."

Hostility

The hostility displayed by the American public is evident in the punitive, restrictive responses both suggested and implemented in response to the school shootings. Actions included the suspension of bail for students charged with bringing guns to school (Willing, 1998); imposing stiffer penalties against gun owners who fail to keep firearms out of the reach of children (Bendavid, 1998), and a variety of other gun restrictions including criminal background checks for guns purchased at gun shows, and requiring dealers to provide safety devices with all handguns (Fairbank, 1999); requiring that students caught with guns be detained by officials for 72 hours and evaluated ("Keep guns . . .," 1998); making it a felony to expose children to books, movies and video games that contain explicit sex or violence (Carvajal, 1999); and the Senate's Juvenile Crime Bill which calls for $1 billion in Federal grants to toughen prosecution of juvenile crime and efforts to prevent it (Bruni, 1999) and proposes structuring current law to incarcerate youthful offenders, including those charged with acts such as running away from home, with adult offenders (Weisman, 1998). Other proposed efforts include the governmental allocation of $1.5 billion over three years to local and state governments that impose corrective sanctions beginning with young, first-time offenders ("Heading off . . .," 1999); incarcerating the parents of children who are truant from school and/or fining the truant student (MacGregor, 1999); and increasing security measures at the expense of students' rights (McDowell, 1999). Several of these actions had been taken in schools prior to the rash of shootings, however, they mostly focused upon inner-city youths attending urban schools. The recent school shootings generated and directed hostility toward youths, particularly juvenile delinquents, in schools throughout all of the country.

As such, juveniles were feeling the brunt of the "get tough" policies directed towards them, due in part to the recent school shootings. The public hostility was spurred by statements such as those from:

1. Juvenile Magistrate Deborah Robertson who noted that "troublemakers are younger than their counterparts 20 years ago; carrying guns, issuing deadly threats and vandalizing buildings" (McNeil, 1998);

2. Reverend Mark Clark who noted that "Right when it (a school shooting) happened, I wanted to kill that kid, to rip him apart with my bare hands" (Siemaszko, 1998); and

3. President Clinton and various experts who referred to today's youth as a generation desensitized to brutality by its own culture of violent media and seemingly unable or unwilling to take responsibility for their actions (Males, 1998).

Such reactions provide evidence of, and fueled the public's hostility and concern about the incidents, which eventually assisted in legitimizing school shootings as a "social problem."

Disproportionality

Were these massive societal responses to what were indeed heinous, threatening offenses against schoolteachers and students justified? A closer look at statistics regarding juvenile crime and more specifically school violence suggests that what occurred was arguably an overreaction to the situation. For example, consider the following sample of recent findings regarding juvenile crime in the context of the aforementioned societal responses:

- There has been no increase in the number of children under age 13 arrested for homicides in the U.S. In 1965, 25 children under age 13 were arrested for homicides and in 1996 it was 16, a 36 percent decline (Donahue, Vincent and Schiraldi, 1998).
- Overall, fewer than 3 percent of the killings in America in 1996 involved someone under age 18 killing someone else under age 18 (FBI, 1997).
- FBI data suggest that national youth violence arrests went down both in number and in share of total youth arrests between 1992 and 1996 ("Violent youth . . . ," 1998).
- Three of four young murder victims—90% of them under age 12 and 70% of them aged 12–17—are killed by adults, not by juveniles (Males, 1998).

While one cannot discount the substantial increases in juvenile crime during the late 1980s, recent reports suggest that the problem is diminishing. Bernard (1999) suggests that although there exists conflicting trends, the most consistent interpretation is that juvenile crime, with the exception of homicide, has declined by about one-third over the last twenty years. There has been a similar, and probably more pronounced decrease in the amount of school violence. Consider the following:

- There were 55 school shooting deaths in the 1992–1993 school year; 51 in 93–94; 20 in 1994–95; 35 in 1995–96; 25 in 1996–97; and 40 in 1997–98 (Lester, 1998). There are more than 50 million students and more than 80,000 schools across the country (Sanchez, 1998).
- A child's chances of being struck by lightning are greater than the million-to-one odds of being killed in school. The

number of children killed by gun violence in schools is about half the number of Americans killed annually by lightning (Byrne, 1998).

- According to PRIDE, the number of students bringing guns to school dropped from 6 percent in 1993–94 to 3.8 percent in 1997–98 ("1 million . . . ," 1998).
- In Los Angeles, 15,000 people have been murdered during the 1990s. Five occurred at school. Of 1,500 murders in Orange County during the 1990s, none took place at school. Institutions in these areas serve 2 million students, including 700,000 teenagers (Males, 1998).
- The United States has approximately 38 million children between the ages of ten and seventeen who attend roughly 20,000 secondary schools. In 1994, there were no school shootings in which more than a single person was killed; in 1997, there were four; and in 1998 there were two (Glassman, 1998).

Available data from sources such as the Centers for Disease Control, National School Safety Center, National Center for Education Statistics, U.S. Department of Education, and The Sourcebook of Criminal Justice Statistics support the suggestion that the recent school shootings were idiosyncratic events and not part of any recognizable trend. Ironically, the shootings may have received such intense coverage because of the infrequency of these occurrences rather than their frequency (Donohue, Schiraldi, and Ziedenberg, 1998).

Consensus

The recent shootings left many Americans disturbed and fearful for their children's safety. Comments made by President Bill Clinton to members attending the October 15, 1998 White House Conference on School Safety summarize the public's perception of fear and concern regarding the situation ("Federal emergency . . . ," 1998:9A):

> I saw a survey, a public opinion survey a few months ago that asked the American people what they thought the most important story of the first six months of 1998 was, and dwarfing everything else was the concern our people had for the children who were killed in their schools.

Clinton's words reflect the July, 1998 findings of a nationwide study of adults which suggested that 75% of Americans were very seriously concerned about school violence and school shootings with another 15% noting that they were somewhat seriously concerned (Shell Oil Company, 1998). Similarly, Rose and Gallup (1998) noted that there was an 11% increase between 1977 and 1998 in the number of parents who feared for their child's safety while they were at school. In addition to providing supportive evidence regarding the societal *consensus* surrounding the school shooting incidents, such findings could also be used as supporting evidence of the societal *concern* surrounding school violence.

To better understand the situation surrounding the school shooting incidents, we must consider why there was such an overzealous societal reaction to the spate of school shootings. Looking at the interests held by several claimsmakers with regard to the school shooting incidents assists in understanding the societal response. The groups having the greatest interests in the school shooting incidents (whose efforts were largely responsible for the aforementioned responses) include, but are not limited to: (1) proponents of increased punitiveness with regard to juvenile justice (including politicians and legislators), and (2) the media. It has largely been through the actions of these groups that the moral panic surrounding school shootings developed and persevered.

Interests

It should be noted that successful moral panics are not only interest-driven. They are also cultural constructions assembled by cultural entrepreneurs who, among other things, draw on cultural resources to convey compelling narratives, tell riveting stories, and present engaging melodramas. While narratives, stories, and melodramas were indeed present throughout the moral panic surrounding school shootings (largely in the form of accounts concerning the star athlete who wrestled the gun away from one of the shooters, the "heroic" teacher who gave her life to protect her students, and the various discussions surrounding how each of the shooters obtained their respective weapons), we chose to focus upon select groups whose involvement/roles/ participation in addressing the situation was largely encouraged by their personal interests. Such an approach assists in presenting the issue as a moral panic and provides a better understanding of how these particular interest-driven agents can largely impact societal happenings.

Politicians

What, specifically, were the interests of the claimsmakers and how did this social problem fulfill their interests? Through statements such as "there was a time when no one could conceive of students shooting classmates in school, and the public now has a right to be outraged, if not demand from their schools and the children who attend them higher standards of conduct" (Byrd, 1998), and deeming student-criminals "fledgling psychopaths" (Monmaney and Krikorian, 1998), those in favor of increasing the punishments directed toward juvenile criminals were able to use the school shooting incidents to strengthen their arguments. With regard to the interests of politicians, it becomes quite clear why they appear to have a vested interest in promoting tougher legislation surrounding juveniles. Their interests largely lie in the hands of the voters, who, through their "media-filtered and culturally-influenced" understanding of the situation largely support the idea of increased punishment for juvenile delinquents. Schiraldi's (1998) suggestion that fear generates a temptation to reach for simple, often punitive, solutions to complex problems becomes quite apparent in the present situation. In juveniles and more specifically juvenile delinquents, politicians have an ideal target for action.

Increasing the penalties directed towards juvenile delinquents is a no-lose situation for politicians, mainly because such an approach has become popular with the general public. Juveniles are not permitted to vote in popular elections, and they are not likely to develop lobby or special interest groups. Thus, politicians do not fear losing juveniles' votes upon election day nor any threat of opposition. Politicians also enjoy the benefit of our country's historical approach of taking our societal frustrations out upon the marginal, fringe, or deviant classes, rendering juvenile delinquents prime candidates for increased punishments.

Media

Glassman (1998) suggests that in an era of peace and prosperity, the press finds little to excite the imagination, and prey on the fears, of its audience. The school shootings provided a perfect opportunity to reach the public. With the pre-existing general discomfort with juvenile crime, the media recognized and seized an ideal opportunity to continuously cover an issue that personally affects a large audience and involves harms against children. Overwhelming media coverage enabled society to press even harder upon the "juvenile crime panic button."

There is so little we can all agree upon in a pluralistic society. However, when evil is oversimplified (e.g., through sensationalistic media accounts of select horrific incidents) societal agreement becomes feasible, if not likely. Pitting "evil" against "innocents" likely results in societal support, or encouragement for the innocents. Due in part to the media's and popular culture's continued utilization of crime stories to attract customers (Surette, 1992), the general public has developed a "discomfort" with criminals, and in particular, juvenile criminals. The recent reports of school shootings reinforced and legitimized the arguments of those who were previously rallying to increase the punishments for juvenile criminals, while encouraging additional citizens to support their views.

People use the knowledge they obtain from the media to construct an image of the world. However, the news media are frequently chastised for presenting a misleading portrayal of crime, often functioning as a "carnival mirror" (Reiman, 1990) by distorting reality through focusing disproportionately on street crime, particularly violent offenses. Unfortunately, most people learn about crime from the mass media, and because the public rarely has enough information to form opinions independently on many issues, people are often at the mercy of the media, not only for information, but also for interpretation (Graber, 1980). Researchers from the Justice Policy Institute recently accused the media

of creating a dangerous misperception that schools are dangerous (Donahue et al., 1998). They noted that the danger is magnified when the media describe these unusual crime stories as "an all-too-familiar story" or "another in a recent trend," and suggest that the media's fixation on the shootings ignited a "moral panic" among the public and a "fever pitch" among school administrators.

The researchers suggested that the perception of increased school dangers could lead to "counterproductive" new laws and an excessive focus on dangers at school when everyday gun violence outside school is a bigger threat to children (Byrne, 1998). Glassman (1998) added that the media's overreaction to a single school shooting makes the common viewer think that child murders are rampant and an immediate threat to society. The media continually fail to put these events into proper context, even when statistics strongly suggest the problem is blown out of proportion.

DISCUSSION

In discussing the social construction of the missing children problem, Fritz and Altheide (1987:487) note that, "Politicians, moral entrepreneurs, and journalists used the issue for their own purposes." Their argument also applies to the situation surrounding the recent school shootings. For instance, the interaction between the media, politicians, and the general public regarding the school shootings could be depicted in the shape of a triangle, with a constant circular motion encouraging punitive directives to be imposed upon juveniles. Juveniles represent a group which is not directly involved in the motions occurring in the triangle, yet absorb the impact of whatever developments, decisions, and/or laws emerge from the interaction.

The triangular motion is initiated by a harmful event involving juveniles (e.g., a school shooting), and the interaction between the three participants consists of a self-perpetuating cycle in which major actors involved in the situation respond in a manner which encourages subsequent action from the other groups. For example, a school shooting occurs, and the three groups immediately become aware of a problematic social situation. The media seize upon the opportunity to cover a story that will pique the public's interest (mainly due to the involvement of children, violence, and the public's appetite for sensationalism), arguably with the underlying intention of increasing their customer base. The public is disturbed because of the thought "You never know when it's going to be one of your kids," and thus continuously reads, watches, and/or hears about the situation (including analyses from various "professionals" in the field regarding the "problem"), and their concern is compounded by the intense media coverage (Fritz and Altheide, 1987). As a result, they feel that "something needs to be done." Politicians, who recognize their concern for the situation and the public's dependence upon the government to address the situation, use their position to, among other things, pass legislation and make public announcements and appearances about their "tough stance" in regard to the situation. In turn, the politician's tough stance against the problem is covered by the media, which further legitimizes the "problem" and perpetuates the public's concern about the problem. The responses and reactions ultimately result in punitive actions against the evildoers. In the school shooting incidents, juveniles (especially juvenile delinquents) have felt the brunt of the societal response. Figure 1 depicts such a cycle.

With regard to the interaction between politicians and the media, among other things, the media provide a forum for politicians to appear "tough" or portray their actions. Media outlets also enable "issue-identification" by which politicians are able to determine which topics they need to address, as it is these issues which are going to be recognized by the public. In return, politicians provide the media with a sense of legitimization. In other words, through speaking about or responding to an issue being covered by the media, politicians not only provide credible sources, but also enable the issue to seem more "real" or "important" to the public.

The interactions between politicians and the public largely consist of politicians providing the public with information about how they're going to address the problematic situation, and the public providing a sense of direction for politicians. This direction is determined through public opinion polls, general election polls, and various other methods used by politicians to "tap into the public's mind" and see what issues they should be addressing, and how they ought to address the issues. For example, soon after the shootings, policy makers reacted abruptly to what they perceived to be a huge swing in public opinion; a moral panic swept the country as parents and children suddenly feared for their safety at school (Donahue et al., 1998).

Finally, the interaction between the public and the media is based upon, among other things, sensationalism and concern. A school shooting occurs and the general public demonstrates an obvious concern. In response, the media continuously cover the issue. The media tend to focus upon sensationalized stories, or stories they know will pique the public's interest (e.g., violent crime stories), thus meeting their needs while earning a profit and arguably inadvertently altering public perception of these issues. Erikson (1966) suggests that confrontations between deviant offenders and agents of control have always attracted a

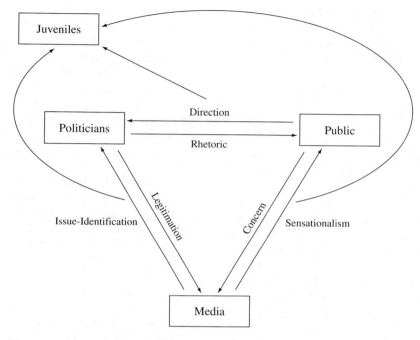

Figure 1. Interactions in the School Shooting Moral Panic

great deal of attention, adding that although we no longer stage the trial and punishment in the market place, popular media outlets such as televisions and newspapers have fulfilled the public's hunger for this information. This portion of the triangle involving the interaction between the media and the public is one that appears to have quite a large effect upon the development of moral panics.

The results of these interactions are often directed toward some group outside of the triangle, which basically has limited, if any, say in what's occurring within the triangle. In the present case, it is juveniles who are outside of the triangle, and thus, have no input regarding the decisions affecting them. Often marginal groups, or those outside of the triangle, are helpless, voiceless beneficiaries of the

punitive, or restrictive, decisions being made within the triangle.

While such a cycle involving the media, government, and public is not necessarily harmful to addressing problematic social issues, concern arises when the foundation of their involvement and concern is predicated upon high-profile, select events which are then incorrectly generalized to suggest a much larger problem. The media's linking of these shootings as "a trend" has tended to exacerbate people's fears about the safety of their children and youth in schools (Donahue et al., 1998). The likely result is misdirected public policy and misguided solutions to safeguard schools, even though the real threat may lie elsewhere. If the groups addressed the incidents in the context of empirically based research, the knee-jerk reaction that we've seen in response to the shootings might have been replaced by more sound, rational, and/or proportionate responses.

CONCLUSION

By no means do we intend to diminish the seriousness of school shootings. We argue that social problems should be addressed through broad assessments of each individual situation, not emotionally charged reactions to isolated incidents. Thus, we question why, instead of recognizing that these incidents occur quite infrequently and that schools are actually one of the safest places a child can be, our society focuses constant attention toward understanding why some juveniles would want to shoot their teachers and fellow students.

Arguably, societal focus is largely dictated by media accounts and political dictates, which could explain the recent fervor surrounding the school shootings. Lester (1998) suggests that the intense media attention given several recent sensational school shootings has left the impression that such fatal attacks are on the rise when the total is actually lower than five years ago. Similarly, Glassman (1998) argues that most people practice a kind of "social synecdoche" in believing that the part equals the whole, that a single shooting (or even several in a year) suggests that child murderers are rampant and something must be done. There is no evidence suggesting that gunfire at school is occurring more frequently today than in the past, yet enormous attention was directed toward the issue. Perhaps societal attention could be better focused elsewhere.

In an insightful analysis of the school shooting situations, Males (1998) compares the harms caused by the shootings to harms inflicted upon children in the home. He cites a study by the United States Advisory Board on Child Abuse and Neglect which noted that approximately 2,000 to 3,000 children are killed each year by parents or guardians, arguing that perhaps the media should focus upon adults killing children instead of children killing children. He adds that approximately three out of four child homicide victims, 90% under the age of twelve and 70% aged twelve to seventeen, are murdered by adults, not other children. When one considers that more children are killed in two days of domestic violence than were killed in all of the recent, high-profile shootings, all of the recent panic seems unimportant (Males, 1998).

REFERENCES

Becker, H. S., *Outsiders: Studies in the Sociology of Deviance*, (London: The Free Press, 1963).

Behrendt, B., "Rampage Spurs Look at Local School Safety," *St. Petersburgh Times* 1998, March 26, p. 1.

Bendavid, N., "Gun Control Backers Unveil Child Safety Bill," *Portland Oregonian* 1998, June 18, p. A8.

Bernard, T., "Juvenile Crime and the Transformation of Juvenile Justice: Is There a Juvenile Crime Wave?," *Justice Quarterly* 1999, 16, 2, 337–356.

Bruni, F., "Senate Votes Gun Curbs, Hours After School Shooting," *The New York Times* 1999, May 21, p. 1.

"Burger King Stops Sale of Toy Because of Name," *Buffalo News* 1998, July 20, p. A4.

Burnett, H. S., "What is a Juvenile Brady Bill?," *Investor's Business Daily* 1998, July 1, p. A32.

Byrd, K. H., "Schools Confront the Threat of Violence: Shootings Last Year Increased Awareness," *The Atlanta Journal* 1998, August 23, p. D1.

Byrne, D., "One Man's Hype Another's Reality," *Chicago Sun-Times* 1998, July 29, p. 39.

Cart, J., "Heroic Teacher, 2 Schoolgirls Buried in Arkansas Funerals: Shannon Wright is Remembered for Shielding a Student from Gunfire. Clinton Talks of the Tragedy During Radio Address from Africa," *Los Angeles Times* 1998, March 29, p. A20.

Carvajal, D., "Full Metal Dust Jacket: Books are Violent, Too," *The New York Times* 1999, June 20, p. 16.

Cohen, S., *Folk Devils and Moral Panics: The Creation of the Mods and Rockers*, (London: MacGibbon and Kee, 1972).

Donahue, E., V. Schiraldi and J. Ziedenberg, "School House Hype: School Shootings and the Real Risks Kids Face in America," *Justice Policy Institute Report* 1998.

Erikson, K. T., *Wayward Puritans*, (New York: John Wiley and Sons, 1966).

Fairbank, K., "Gun Control Legislation Will Still be Approved House Speaker Says," *The Fort Worth Star-Telegram* 1999, June 20, p. 6A.

Federal Bureau of Investigation, *Uniform Crime Reports for the United States—1996*, (Washington, D.C.: U.S. Government Printing Office, 1997).

"Federal Emergency Response Needed to Combat School Violence," *The Dallas Morning News* 1998, October 20, p. 9A.

Fiore, F. and Anderson, N., "House Blasts Hollywood but Fails to Act on Violence Media: Proposal to Put Labels on Music, Movies and Video Games is Rejected. Resolution is Seen as a Warning," *Los Angeles Times* 1999, June 18, p. A-1.

Fritz, N. and D. L. Altheide, "The Mass Media and the Social Construction of the Missing Children Problem," *The Sociological Quarterly* 1997, 28, 4, 473–492.

Glassman, J., ". . . Or a Made-Up Menace?," *The Washington Post* 1998, May 26, p. A17.

Goode, E. and N. Ben-Yehuda, *Moral Panics: The Social Construction of Deviance*, (Malden, MA: Blackwell, 1994).

Graber, D., *Crime News and the Public*, (New York: Praeger, 1980).

"Heading Off Youth Crime," *Los Angeles Times* 1999 April 27, p. B6.

"Keep Guns from Kids, Mom Pleads: Jonesboro Woman Joins Clinton's Safety Effort," *Chicago Tribune* 1998, July 9, p. 18.

Lester, W., "School Gun Deaths Decline: Rural Incidents Drew Attention," *The New Orleans Times-Picayune* 1998, July 30, p. A8.

MacGregor, H., "New Truancy Policy Allows D.A. to Prosecute Students and Their Parents. Education: Intervention Plan will Concentrate on Extreme Cases. Heavy Fines, Community Service and Even Jail Time May Result," *Los Angeles Times* 1999, February 15, p. B-11.

Males, M., "Who's Really Killing Our School Kids?," *Los Angeles Times* 1998, May 31, p. M1.

McDowell, R., "Denver Police Chief Says Students' Rights May be Curbed to Ensure Safety," *The Fort Worth Star-Telegram* 1999, April 20, p. 6A.

McFadden, K., "TV's Coverage of a Tragedy: Readers Share Their Views," *The Seattle Times* 1998, June 1, p. E1.

McNeil, M., "Summit Focuses on Troubled Juveniles: Educators, Officials Try to Figure Out How to Help Kids, Keep Violence Out of Schools," *The Indianapolis Star* 1998, August 6, p. S1.

Monmaney, T. and G. Krikorian, "Violent Culture, Media Share Blame, Experts Say Killings: Spate of Deaths Prompts Many Explanations, Including Emergence of 'Fledgling Psychopaths'," *Los Angeles Times* 1998, p. A16.

"1 Million Toting Guns at School, Survey Finds," *The Atlanta Journal* 1998, June 19, p. A1.

Page, C., "Laws Alone Can't Stop the Killing," *Ft. Lauderdale Sun-Sentinel* 1998, May 28, p. 19A.

Reiman, J., *The Rich Get Richer and the Poor Get Prison, Third Ed.*, (Needham Heights, MA. Allyn & Bacon 1990).

Rose, L. C. and A. M. Gallup, "The 30th Annual Phi Delta Kappa/Gallup Poll of the Public's Attitudes Toward the Public Schools," *Phi Delta Kappan* 1998, September, 80 1, 41–56.

Sanchez, R., "Educators Pursue Solutions to Violence Crisis: As Deadly Sprees Increase, Schools Struggle for Ways to Deal with Student Anger," *Washington Post* 1998, May 23, p. A12.

Schiraldi, V., "Youth Crime is Not Increasing," *The Baltimore Sun* 1998, August 24, p. 7A.

Shell Oil Company, "The Shell Poll: Report Card: Americans Like Local Schools, Worry About Violence," Fall 1998, 1, 1, 1–8.

Siemaszko, C., "Hero Recalls Shootings," *New York Daily News* 1998, May 25, p. 8.

Surette, R., *Media, Crime, and Criminal Justice: Images and Realities*, (Pacific Grove, CA: Brooks/Cole, 1992).

Tirrell-Wysocki, D., "Bullet Drills Teach Students to Drop, Seek Cover," *Ft. Lauderdale Sun-Sentinel* 1998, June 11, p. 5A.

"Violent Youth Crime Down," *USA Today* 1998, April 1, p. 1A.

Weisman, J., "Shooting Revives Drive to Toughen Juvenile Justice," *The Baltimore Sun* 1998, March 25, p. 12A.

Willing, R., "Mayors Take Aim at Violence in Schools," *USA Today* 1998, September 25, p. 7A.

Zelizer, V. A., *Pricing the Priceless Child: The Changing Social Value of Children*, (New York: Basic Books, 1985).

Date Rape

Eugene J. Kanin

In this paper we will study a group of self-disclosed rapists in order to determine whether these men are encountering difficulties in obtaining heterosexual outlets by more conventional means. Our principal objective, then, is to examine the sexual histories of rapists and nonrapists and attempt to determine if the former are more sexually deprived. It is apparent here that rape is *primarily* being examined from a sexual perspective rather than from one that views it as an expression of power and aggression. The assumption of a sexual perspective has its genesis in the nature of these acts and is not an expression of a polemic to cover all rape. Our study of this particular sample reveals all the offenses to have been date rapes and to have occurred only after intensive consensual sexual encounters between the rapists and their victims. We have argued elsewhere that a sexual framework is more appropriate to the facts regarding these men, acknowledging, of course, that

in rape the power-aggression component is, in one form or another, *ipso facto* present (Kanin, 1984) and, in some cases, dominant.

METHOD

We will report on 71 self-disclosed rapists. These 71 men are all white, unmarried college undergraduates who came to our attention as solicited volunteers during the past decade from university classes and campus organizations where this writer has lectured. In all instances, these men voluntarily presented themselves as possible rapists who were amenable to study by interview and questionnaire. Anonymity of response and the option to terminate participation at any time were emphatically stressed.

An issue here concerns the validity of these disclosures and the subsequent attachment of the rape label. For these volunteers to

From Eugene J. Kanin, "Date Rapists," *Archives of Sexual Behavior*, v. 14, no. 3(1985):219–231. Reprinted by permission of Kluwer Academic Publishers and the author.

be accepted as rapists, it was necessary to conform to the legal criterion that penetration was accomplished on a nonconsenting female by employing or threatening force. In every case, a validity check was exercised by having the respondent give two accounts of the assaultive incident, one at the beginning and one at the end of the interview. All 71 cases reported here satisfied these conditions. Fifteen additional volunteered cases were rejected for inclusion in this study because they either failed to conform to the foregoing criterion (13) or decided to discontinue the interview (2). Not one case was excluded on the basis of mendacity. This should be no surprise, since the events reported here could hardly be considered ego enhancing, particularly since they are not being related to select peers.

A short profile of these men and the nature of their assaults is in order to appreciate the assumption of a sexually dominant perspective rather than the currently more popular power-aggression stance. First, these were all cases of date rape. The majority of the pairs had two to five dates together prior to the rape, and most of these pairs had sexually interacted on a prior date(s) in a fashion comparable to the sexual interaction that immediately preceded the rape. Every case of rape followed a fairly intensive bout of sex play, the most common activity being orogenital. Only six men were reported to the police, and in every case the charges were dropped. Thus, these date rapists are not represented in any official tally of rapists. Also crucial to an understanding of these rapists is that only six volunteered that they were recidivists, and all these admitted to but a single prior rape, all under comparable circumstances.

Since there was a conspicuous absence of the use of weapons and fists, it is virtually impossible, in any objective sense, to evaluate realistically the amount of force necessary to have brought these females to victimization. This is due to the fact that the rape interaction would have to take into account the male's execution of force, which usually includes both a physical and verbal dimension, and his companion's interpretation of that force which would result in the victim's determining if sexual compliance were the most judicious adaptation. It was not unusual for some of these men to report that they had exerted greater efforts on dates with other women but were clearly successfully rebuffed, and for some men to express surprise that their partners were so readily intimidated.[1] There is a strong fortuitous factor contributing to these rapes, namely, the interaction stemming from the unique characteristics and perspectives of both the aggressor and the victim.

The control group consists of 227 white, undergraduate, unmarried college males from 15 university classes. The age composition of this group was comparable to that of the rapists. Every male in class at the time of the administration of the schedule cooperated. Eleven schedules were deemed incomplete, and eight others were eliminated because the respondent identified himself as a homosexual. Thirty-six others were excluded from the control group because they indicated that they had engaged in heterosexual encounters with dates where they either tried to gain coitus by employing force or threats or did, in fact, succeed in "forcing" a female to have intercourse. Considering the chance element involved in date rape, viz., that the degree of force necessary to rape successfully may be less important than the nature of the particular victim involved, it was assumed that a high proportion of these men had probably engaged in behavior comparable to our rapists. Therefore, their inclusion would introduce an undesirable bias in the controls. In other words, what we wanted to avoid in our control sample was including men who had been involved in heterosexual performances that could very well have precipitated a rape of the type with which we are dealing.[2]

RESULTS AND DISCUSSION

Sexual Histories

Rape is clearly only one facet of a wide range of erotic activities engaged in by these men. These rapists have had, comparatively speaking, considerably more heterosexual experience, have engaged in a more persistent quest for heterosexual encounters, and have utilized more exploitative techniques in their efforts to gain sexual expression. To be specific, the rapist appears considerably more sexually successful and active. Regarding the incidence of coitus exclusive of the rape experiences, the rapists are more experienced than the controls, 100% and 59%, respectively. It is worth noting that this 100% incidence characterized these men at the time of the rape. In addition, the frequency of consensual heterosexual outlets as estimated by the respondents for the past year are overwhelmingly in favor of the rapist. Heterosexual orgasms resulting from coitus, fellatio, and masturbation average 1.5

per week for the rapists, while the mean for the controls is 0.8 per month. It is obvious that these rapists represent a very sexually active group of young men.

Much of this success can probably be attributed to the fact that these men are sexually predatory, that is, they are much more apt to attempt to precipitate new sexual experiences and to employ a variety of surreptitious seductive techniques. For example, when our respondents were asked the frequency with which they attempt to seduce a new date, 62% of the rapists and 19% of the controls responded "most of the time." The rapists' quests for heterosexual engagements largely borders on a no-holds-barred contest. To illustrate, these men were asked about efforts to gain coital access by employing such methods as trying to intoxicate their companions, threatening to terminate the relationship, falsely promising some sort of relationship permanence, i.e., "pinning," engagement, or marriage, falsely professing love, and threatening to abandon their dates, e.g., make them walk home. Table 1 rather cogently portrays these rapists as most apt to pursue their sexual goals by employing drugging, extortion, fraud, and lying: 93% of the rapists, compared to 40% of the controls, used at least one of these techniques while in college. Crucial to

Table 1. Incidence of Sexual Exploitation Techniques Employed by Rapists and Controls since College Entrance, by Percentage

	RAPISTS (N=71)	CONTROLS (N=227)
Attempt to intoxicate female with alcohol	76[a]	23[b]
Falsely profess love	86	25
Falsely promise "pinning," engagement, or marriage	46	6
Threaten to terminate relationship	31	7
Threaten to leave female stranded	9	0

[a]28% also involved marijuana.
[b]19% also involved marijuana.

the central argument of this paper is the finding that 93% of the rapists, but only 37% of the controls, said that their best friends would "definitely approve" of such tactics for *certain* women. Furthermore, 91% of the rapists, in contrast to 32% of the controls, have had such procedures seriously suggested to them by their best friends as functional for sexual success. Sexual exploitation of the female largely permeates their entire male-female approach. The foregoing is compelling testimony to the fact that those who have been most successful in obtaining heterosexual outlets are also those who resort to deviant means.

Regarding the question of assessing sexual frustration by the criterion of sexual experience, it has usually been assumed that a comparative lack of sexual encounters can be roughly translated into proportional increases of frustration. However, it is necessary first to aspire to a goal in order to experience frustration. If the controls should demonstrate a comparatively lesser interest in sex for whatever reasons, then it would be questionable simply to attribute frustration to those with less experience and sexual satisfaction to those with greater experience. It is plausible, of course, that a male with few, if any, heterosexual outlets can still assess himself as not sexually frustrated. The sexually more successful male, on the other hand, may be experiencing frustration if his aspirations exceed his achievements. Asking the respondents to indicate the degree of satisfaction with which they view their sexual activities of the past year, the rapists with their more extensive experience are more apt to report dissatisfaction than the controls with their comparative lack of sexual activity, 79% and 32%, respectively. These findings suggest that satisfaction with one's sexual activity might be only casually related to one's sexual activities. It will be argued here that the dissatisfaction manifested by the rapists is due to a differential socializa-

tion in a hypererotic male culture, a culture where sexual success is of paramount importance in the maintenance of self-esteem, and the inability to achieve sexual success can, on a select occasion, result in an expression of violence sufficient to achieve rape.

Differential Sexual Socialization: Peer Groups

In trying to conceptualize a socialization process that would increase the likelihood of date rape, it became very apparent from the study of these data that direct tutelage or example, for all practical purposes, be totally excluded. However, it is feasible to think in terms of a sexual socialization that not only would make sex a highly valued and prestigious activity but also would provide justifications for directing sexual efforts toward specific targets. More specifically, sexual socialization can be thought to comprise influences positive to sexual predation, including providing stereotypes of ideal victims, and of the absence of negative definitions that serve to counteract or insulate against the positive "pulls." Agents that could be considered central to providing such definitions would be an individual's peers and family.

An attempt was made to gauge the degree that one's current peer group would condone aggressive and offensive sexual efforts by obtaining the *imputed* reputational consequences of such behavior. The respondents were asked what they thought would be the reputational consequences in the eyes of their best friends "if they found out that you offended a woman by *trying* to force her to have sexual intercourse, during the course of which you used physical force and/or threats." It is patently implicit here that these are not successful efforts and, therefore, that these acts do not constitute forcible rape. The question was phrased so as to apply to aggressions

Table 2. Imputed Positive Reputational Consequences of Aggressively Offending Five Hypothetical Women, by Percentage

	RAPISTS (N = 71)	CONTROLS (N = 227)
Bar "pick-up"	54	16
Woman with "loose" reputation	27	10
Known "teaser"	81	40
Economic exploiter	73	39
A more or less regular date	9	7

committed against five hypothetical women, each possessing a significant characteristic that might affect her attractiveness as an aggression target. Table 2 shows the percentage of rapists and controls who believe that their reputations would be enhanced by aggressing against a woman playing a role with a stereotyped sexual significance in the male world. Although it is apparent that the "teaser" and economic exploiter are prime targets for both groups, positive reputational consequences are dramatically seen as forthcoming from the friends of the rapists. Their erotic subculture has adequately conferred the label of legitimate sexual targets on certain "deviant" females. In a substantial segment of the male culture, four of these women qualify as social deviants by violating expectations in the dating encounter. Essentially, the "pick-up," the "loose woman," and the "teaser" are viewed as upending sexual expectations after "flaunting," "advertising," and "promising" sexual accessibility. The economic exploiter, although less sexually explicit, earns her deviant label by violating reciprocity norms held by some segments of the male culture. In short, these women are seen as not playing by the rules of the game, and, therefore, the man feels justified in suspending the rules regarding his dating conduct. It should be noted that these men are aware that frequent encounters with "rough sex" would evoke suspicion of derangement, even from their close friends.

Only a minority, about 25%, would tell their friends about such encounters. There is, additionally, an anxiety that these aggressions could be status detracting in that they highlight sexual failure and the inability to succeed by more sophisticated means. Essentially, their friends are not seen as rewarding violence; the offensive sexuality that receives acclaim—or at least does not draw opprobrium—is largely due to the "provocative" conduct of the victim.

Not only do these males have associates who they believe would condone aggressive behavior, but they are also subjected to peer influences to be sexually active. Responses to the question, "What degree of pressure do your best friends exert on you to seek sexual encounters?" shows that the rapists are indeed the recipients of such spheres of influence. Table 3 clearly portrays the rapists as receiving such peer enticements, whereas the controls are overrepresented as receiving little or no pressure from their friends. The evidence thus far shows that the rapists have a differential association with close friends who encourage and reward sexual experience and who will also support sexual transgressions on select females.

It is crucial to note that these men did not acquire their aggressive sexuality in college. Although they definitely tended to immerse themselves in an erotic culture that served normative reference-group functions

Table 3.   Degree of Pressure Exerted by Current Friends for Sexual Activity, by Percentage

	RAPISTS (N = 71)	CONTROLS (N = 227)
Great deal or considerable	40	9
Moderate	45	28
Little or none	15	63
Totals	100	100

for them, this current culture functioned as a reference group primarily by supporting and sustaining values acquired prior to college entrance. Of course the newly acquired collegiate friendship groups did serve reference-group functions in that they embellished old values, provided new vocabularies of adjustment, altered old norms, and introduced new norms. If we look at the behaviors of these men while they were still in high school, we find the same peer group phenomenon operating, only in an exaggerated fashion. For example, 85% of the rapists, in contrast to 26% of the controls, reported high school friendships where pressure for heterosexual expression was "great and considerable."

It seems appropriate here to raise the question as to the nature of the perceptions of these respondents regarding their peer group influences. Specifically, it may be charged that these perceptions are largely defensive and, therefore, represent distortions. Our evidence, however, does not lend support to such a hypothesis but rather bolsters the position that the sexual socialization of these rapists was substantially influenced by a supportive hypererotic male culture. This is particularly the case when we examine some of the more concrete behavioral aspects involving the rapists and their close associates. For example, it can be pointed out that the rapists are much more apt to have a history of collaborative sex. Fully 41% of the rapists, but only 7% of the controls, were ever involved in either a "gang-bang" or a sequential sexual sharing of a fe-

male with a male friend. Furthermore, over 67% of the rapists had had intercourse with a female whom a friend had recommended as sexually congenial. Only 13% of the controls indicated that they were ever recipients of such a friendship referral network. Lastly, 21% of the rapists reported that their first female-genital contact, whether manual, oral, or coital, was the direct consequence of having been "fixed-up" by a friend(s). This contrasts rather sharply with the 6% of the controls who reported that such third-party arrangements had entered into their premier episode. All these data confirm these respondents' perceptions that their close associates do indeed represent an active hypererotic influence.

Differential Sexual Socialization: Justifications

An integral aspect of the variety of differential sexual socialization with which we are dealing should involve the provision for a vocabulary of adjustment, a means of justifying behavior. It has been shown that these rapists see their prestige as being enhanced for sexually exploiting select women. It would seem to follow that their associates, those who encourage them to deviate, would provide them with—or reinforce—appropriate vocabularies of adjustment so that they can continue to maintain their conception of themselves as beings of worth and esteem while continuing to exploit and degrade. Such a process would be an essential prerequisite for the maintenance and perpetuation of group values. Approximately 86% of these rapists believe that rape, in the abstract, and not necessarily in their own behavior, can be justified under certain conditions. This contrasts rather sharply with the 19% of the controls who believe in the justifiability of rape. These justifications, as one would expect, are almost completely made up of women viewed as "teasers," economic exploiters, and "loose." The more extensive information gathered through the interviews with the rapists seems to point to a composite of teaser-exploiter-loose as the quintessential deviant dating companion. She is seen as the one who financially extends the man, who enters into sex play with sufficient enthusiasm to convey a presupposition of having "been around," and who insists on stabilizing the sexual aspect of the relationship short of coitus. It should be pointed out, however, that in reality victims only seldom qualify, even under student standards, as economic exploiters but eminently qualify as "teaser-loose" because of the nature of their role in the sexual encounter, namely, one that is consensual and active.

Considering again peer group influence on the ability to perceive a deviant act as justified, it is found that 93% of the rapists who indicated they were recipients of great, considerable, or moderate peer group pressure for sexual activity indicated that rape can be justified. The rapists who reported that their peers exerted little or no pressure for sexual involvement were considerably less apt to believe in the justification of rape, only 45%.

Relative Deprivation

Now that it has been established that these rapists were the recipients of strong social pressures for sexual achievement, it is time to return to the finding that these more experienced men reported a greater incidence of sexual dissatisfaction than the sexually less experienced controls. As previously stated, more extensive sexual experience could readily be associated with greater dissatisfaction if one's peers highly value sexual accomplishment and confer prestige rewards for success. In effect, an exaggerated level of sexual aspiration is introjected from one's erotically oriented significant others, a level that, at best, will be difficult for the majority of college males to maintain continually.

Evidence supporting this position comes from demonstrating that the degree of the rapists' sexual satisfaction with their sexual accomplishment for the previous year appears strongly related to the degree of pressure their friends exert for sexual experience. The rapists show the most pronounced inclination to report sexual satisfaction when little or no group pressure is applied, 71%, while satisfaction is less frequently indicated by the recipients of great, considerable, and moderate pressures, 40%. Although this finding does not prove a causal nexus exists here, it is compatible with "reference group theory."

CONCLUSIONS

These date rapists experienced a differential sexual socialization that resulted in the development of an exaggerated sex impulse and the placing of an inordinately high value on sexual accomplishment. Consequently, a frustration of the aroused impulse led these men to undergo an acute sense of goal deprivation that can best be understood in the context of relative deprivation. Specifically, it is sexually less frustrating to encounter rejection when one's socialization has provided for a lower level of aspiration than when one's socialization has instilled a high expectancy of sexual success (see Kanin, 1967; Chappell et al., 1977). The female's rejection of coital intimacy after rather intensive advanced sexual interaction is primarily the expression of her need to stabilize intimacy for personal reasons, and not to exploit or to be fashionably provocative.[3] The male fails to recognize this. Instead, he focuses on whether her rejection is genuine and/or on the adequacy of his sexual powers, a very likely manifestation of a perceptual defense process. This results in his bewilderment and anxiety. The disregard for her rejection behavior and the subsequent display of aggressive presentations, verbal and physical, intended and/or unintended, readily led to the rape episode on this occasion. The inflicting of punishment or suffering through the rape appears incidental in the vast majority of cases and, at best, serves a secondary function. There is very little evidence here that violence functioned as a sexual stimulant for these men (see Barbaree et al., 1979). The coital experience, the manifest and anticipated benefit, and the accompanying reaffirmation of self-worth, not entirely lost to consciousness, appear to be prime movers for these rapes.

NOTES

1. None of this is to imply that these women were merely being respectably reluctant. All cases where the female metamorphosed into an active participant were discarded, along with cases where she apparently showed no traumatic consequences.
2. In view of the nature of the accidental samples of rapists and controls, all percentages were rounded off, and no tests of statistical significance were employed. Instead, we relied exclusively on the pronounced differences between the rapists and the nonrapists.
3. The great majority of our respondents concurred with this interpretation at the time of the interview.

REFERENCES

Barbaree, H. E., Marshall, W. L., and Lanthier, R. D. (1979). Deviant sexual arousal in rapists. *Behav. Res. Ther.* 17:215–221.

Chappell, D., Geis, G., Schafer, S., and Siegel, L. (1977). A comparative study of forcible rape offenses known to the police in Boston and Los Angeles. In Chappel, D., Geis, R., and Geis, G. (eds.), *Forcible Rape*, Columbia University Press, New York.

Kanin, E. (1967). Reference groups and sex conduct norm violations. *Soc. Quart.* 8:495–504.

Kanin, E. (1984). Date rape: Unofficial criminals and victims. *Victimology*, 9:95–108.

Computer Crime

Stephen M. Rosoff, Henry N. Pontell, and Robert Tillman

Computer crime has been defined broadly as "the destruction, theft, or unauthorized or illegal use, modification, or copying of information, programs, services, equipment, or communication networks."[1] Donn B. Parker, one of the country's leading computer crime researchers, offers a less formal definition of computer crime as any intentional act associated with computers where a victim suffers a loss and a perpetrator makes a gain.[2] Under these definitional guidelines, the following offenses all could be classified as computer crimes: (1) electronic embezzlement and financial theft; (2) computer hacking and malicious sabotage, including the creation, installation, or dissemination of computer viruses; (3) utilization of computers and computer networks for purposes of espionage; (4) use of electronic devices and computer codes for making unauthorized long-distance telephone calls.

How common and how costly has computer crime become? A 1993 survey reports that 70 percent of the more than four hundred companies responding admitted to at least one security infringement in the previous twelve months; 24 percent put the loss per incident at more than $100,000.[3] The head of the group which conducted the survey noted: "The problem is much more serious than expected."[4]

Moreover, computer crime is no longer just an American problem. It has been uncovered in both Canada[5] and Mexico,[6] as well as Western European nations such as the United Kingdom,[7] Sweden,[8] The Netherlands,[9] Germany,[10] and Italy.[11] Viruses have been created in such distant places as Bulgaria and South Africa.[12] Hackers reportedly have proliferated in France and Israel,[13] India and Singapore,[14] as well as the former Soviet Union (where they are called *chackers*).[15] Likewise, computer

From *Profit Without Honor: White-Collar Crime and the Looting of America*, pp. 365–396, Prentice Hall, 1998. Reprinted by permission of Pearson Education, Inc.

security has become a major concern in Japan[16] and Australia.[17] And in one especially malignant use of computer technology, an Argentine kidnapping ring illegally accessed financial records to determine how much ransom money potential victims could afford to pay.[18]

Regarding cost, estimates of annual losses due to computer crime range from $550 million (National Center for Computer Crime Data) to $15 billion (Inter-Pact computer security organization)[19] or even more. This remarkably wide range of estimates no doubt reflects the substantial variation which exists in defining what qualifies as computer crime. For instance, about 14 million federal tax returns are now filed electronically. A 1993 report by the General Accounting Office warns the IRS of its potential vulnerability to a number of new fraud schemes.[20] Should this be classified as tax evasion or computer crime? Dealers in child pornography now use private computer bulletin board services to advertise materials and exchange information.[21] Can this really be considered computer crime? Organized crime syndicates and illegal drug cartels routinely employ computers to launder money. Since the computer has become an indispensable tool of money-laundering, should all those billions of dollars be considered part of the cost of computer crime? The truth is that there is little consensus in these matters. In fact, some experts have adopted a so-called "agnostic" position that the true cost is unknowable.

Another gray area is that of software piracy. No one knows the total cost of this offense, but it is certainly in the billions. Based on their 1985 survey of forty-five thousand households, McGraw-Hill Information Systems conservatively estimates that there is one pirated copy of software for every authorized copy.[22] An overseas dealer, for example, was selling pirated copies of the popular *Lotus 1-2-3* spreadsheet software (which usually retails for around $200) for $1.50![23] To put it in perspective, this means that for every $100 in pirated Lotus sales generated by this dealer, MicroPro, the manufacturer of Lotus, lost nearly $15,000 in legitimate sales.

There is in addition surely a huge "dark figure" of unreported computer crimes. "Because of public humiliation, liability issues, and security inadequacies, many corporations do not report computer crime losses, especially large ones."[24] The fear of "copycat" incidents also probably discourages the reporting of security breaches.[25] Furthermore, when it is information that is stolen, rather than money, the loss may be incalculable in terms of dollars. Finally, the estimation of computer crime losses perhaps is most complicated by the clandestine nature of the crimes themselves. The most talented electronic thieves are able to cover up all traces that a crime has been committed. As the president of a major computer security consulting firm has noted: "We only read about the failed computer criminals. The really successful ones are never detected in the first place."[26]

However, even if the actual computer crime loss figure can only be guessed, no one questions that the losses are enormous. A survey by Com-Sec, an organization of computer security professionals, reports that 36 of 300 companies responding (12 percent) acknowledged losses of $100,000 or more in just the first three months of 1993, with another 42 (14 percent) losing between $10,000 and $100,000. For the preceding year, 69 percent of respondents admitted security problems, with 53 percent of those problems resulting in losses of at least $10,000.[27] Once more, the findings far exceeded the predictions of the startled investigators.

EMBEZZLEMENT AND FINANCIAL THEFT

According to recent FBI statistics, the average armed bank robbery nets $3,177.[28] The Data Processing Management Association reports that the average computer crime loss may be as high as $500,000.[29] This great disparity reveals that while there are physical limitations to the potential payoff available to the blue-collar robber—large amounts of money have weight and take up space—the white-collar thief who can access the appropriate computer can steal a fortune without moving anything heavier than some decimal points. As if to demonstrate this lack of physical limitations, a gang of rogue employees in a major railroad's computerized inventory center once stole two hundred boxcars by permanently keeping them under repair.[30] As a 1991 report by the National Research Council warns: "The modern thief can steal more with a computer than with a gun."[31] In addition, bank robbers must face the prospect of getting shot at; not so the computer criminal. Dillinger never had it so good.

One of the most famous bank-related computer crimes, however, did involve the physical movement of hard cash. For three years, beginning in 1970, the chief teller at the Park Avenue branch of New York's Union Dime Savings Bank embezzled over $1.5 million from hundreds of accounts. Despite having no formal computer training, he was able to shift nonexistent money around from account to account, falsifying quarterly interest payments and satisfying visiting auditors with remarkable ease. So slick were his manipulations that reportedly, he had difficulty explaining the intricacies of his crime to the bank's executives after his arrest.[32] He eventually served fifteen months of a twenty-month sentence. At last report, he was driving a taxicab in New Jersey. None of his pilfered funds has ever been recovered.

His eventual downfall happened almost by accident—as a by-product of an entirely different case. A routine police raid on a "bookie joint" revealed that he had been betting as much as $30,000 a day on sporting events. "If his indiscreet bookmakers had not kept his name in their files, he might well have kept up his embezzlement for quite a while longer than he did."[33]

It is interesting to note that the Union Dime Savings case serves as a perfect model of Donald Cressey's earlier research on the social psychology of embezzlement. According to Cressey, embezzlers typically go through a three-stage process. In stage 1, they are faced with what they perceive to be an unshareable financial problem, that is, a need for money which they cannot share with spouses, relatives, or friends. A $30,000-a-day gambling habit on an $11,000 a year salary[34] would certainly seem to qualify in this regard. In stage 2, they recognize an opportunity to solve their problem secretly. This opportunity rests in the positions of trust which they hold. A position of chief teller, of course, would provide just such an opportunity. Finally, in stage 3, they manage to avoid internalizing a criminal identity by rationalizing their acts as borrowing rather than stealing.[35] It is the curse of compulsive gamblers like the Union Dime teller to continue expecting a financial recovery, even as the debts keep mounting. As we shall see, such labored rationalization is a recurring theme among computer criminals.

In 1991, someone, believed to be an employee, used the computer in the payroll department of a prestigious New York bank to steal $25 million without leaving a trace. As of this writing, the case remains unsolved—not because there are no suspects, but because there are too many. "[H]undreds of employees had access to the same data that appear to have made at least one of them very rich."[36]

But not all electronic embezzlers work for banks. An employee in the computer center of a big-city welfare department once stole $2.75 million, over a nine-month period, by entering fraudulent data into the computerized payroll system and thereby creating a phantom work force complete with fake social security numbers. He would intercept the weekly paychecks "earned" by the fictitious crew, endorse and cash them, and dream of early retirement. He was uncovered only when a police officer found a fistful of phony checks in his illegally parked rental car.[37]

As we have already noted, some embezzlers have employed a Trojan horse—the "bad" program concealed inside the "good" program—as a means of diverting cash into fraudulent accounts. A common variation on this method involves a practice known as the *salami* technique. This type of fraud has been around for many years and was known in the precomputer era as "rounding down."[38] Salami techniques divert (or, in keeping with the metaphor, "slice off") very small amounts of assets from very large numbers of private accounts. The stolen assets are so small, sometimes a few cents or even just a fraction of a cent per transaction, that they do not make a noticeable dent in any single account.[39]

How many people, after all, will bother to stoop down to retrieve a dropped penny? But when multiplied over a million or so bank transactions at computer speed, these "dropped pennies" can turn into tens or hundreds of thousands of dollars—well worth stooping for. For example, in the 1980s an employee at an investment firm used a computer to set up false accounts and filled them by diverting three-tenths of a cent interest from actual accounts.[40]

One of the more spectacular salami-type embezzlements took place in California at around the same time as the Union Dime Savings case. Over a six-year period, the chief ac-

countant for a large produce company siphoned more than $1.5 million from his employers. While studying computer technology, he developed a program able to add small sums to disbursement accounts in payment of phony produce orders.[41] He later claimed that his motivation was simply to receive a promised annual bonus of which he felt he had been cheated. He decided he was entitled to three-quarters of 1 percent of the company's gross, and he began looting the company at exactly that rate. "He did this by devising a special algorithm—a set of rules for making calculations—which he used as a master program to alter the company's accounting data in the computer."[42] Because this firm grossed $30 million a year, pennies became dollars and dollars became a fortune.

When he eventually was arrested and tried, he pleaded *nolo contendere* (no contest), perhaps expecting the same sort of typically light sentence his counterpart at Union Dime Savings was to receive. Instead, he was sentenced to ten years in San Quentin and served just over five. Upon release, he became—what else?—a computer consultant.

The stark difference in the punitive sanctions meted out in these two roughly equivalent embezzlement cases underscores how confused the general public often is about computer crime. Depending upon how a prosecutor chooses to present a case, a jury is apt to perceive a computer criminal as anything from a pathetic "nerd" gone bad to an electronic terrorist threatening the very foundation of the American way of life.

Sometimes embezzlers are not low- or mid-level employees of a company, but those at the very top. This certainly would apply to the notorious Equity Funding scandal. This case well illustrates the lack of definitional consensus regarding computer crime. Because the Equity Funding case is considered by some to be mainly one of securities fraud, rather than true computer fraud, many analyses of computer crime never mention Equity Funding—although it is arguably one of the most costly frauds ever perpetrated.

In the 1970s, the Los Angeles-based insurance firm and mutual fund company programmed its computer to issue insurance policies on people who did not exist and then sell those fake policies to other companies, through a system of reinsurance customarily employed in that business to spread actuarial risk and increase cash flow.[43] This was done to inflate the price of Equity Funding stock which had begun to fall after a spectacular run-up in the early 1960s. The scheme grew over time to epic proportions. Fictitious policy holders, or persons already dead, were carrying $3.2 billion in life insurance. Some of the conspirators were skimming from the resale proceeds, and other conspirators were skimming from the skimmers.

It has been observed that as computer crimes go, the Equity Funding fraud was not a particularly sophisticated one and would have been uncovered sooner or later, if only because there were just too many people involved.[44] The most effective computer crimes probably are the work of a single individual or at most a small gang. Moreover, because the fraud was conducted by management itself, there was little incentive to conceal the misuse of the computer from company officials. In the final analysis, Equity Funding was simply a gigantic "pyramid scam" run amok.[45]

When the computer fraud is committed by someone from outside the victimized organization, embezzlement becomes theft. Here again, banks are a frequent target. In 1980, for example, the Wells Fargo bank of San Francisco lost $21 million allegedly to two boxing promoters who used a computer for illegal EFTs (Electronic Fund Transfers).[46] In 1988, the First National Bank in Chicago lost $55 million through a fraudulent wire transfer.[47] In absolute terms, this is a great deal of money; but, in relative terms, it hardly makes a ripple in the more than $1 trillion that is transferred electronically by American banks each day.[48]

Probably the best-known EFT case is that of Stanley Mark Rifkin, who stole $10.2 million from California's Security National Bank in less than an hour.[49] Rifkin was a computer programmer who was creating a back-up system for Security National's wire room—the bank's communication center from where between $2 billion and $4 billion are transferred every day. The purpose of the back-up system was to allow the bank to continue making EFTs even if the primary system crashed.[50] Rifkin, of course, had to learn the system intimately, and, as his education continued, he began to think about robbing the bank. On October 25, 1978, he stole an employee access code from the wall of the wire room, walked to a nearby telephone booth, and transferred the $10.2 million to a New York bank and then to Switzerland. The next day, the cash was converted into diamonds.[51]

Rifkin may have been a brilliant computer programmer, but he turned out to be an inept criminal. He was arrested ten days later after attempting to sell some diamonds in Beverly Hills. He was convicted in March, 1979, and received a sentence of eight years in federal prison.

More recently, beginning in the mid-1980s, officials in several states began uncovering a simple but alarmingly effective form of electronic bank robbery. An individual would open an account and eventually receive computer-coded deposit slips. Near the beginning of a month, he or she then would place some of those deposit slips on the counter where blank deposit slips normally would be. When customers unknowingly used them, the money would be deposited in the criminal's account. By the time the irate customers questioned their monthly bank statements, the thieves had emptied their accounts and were nowhere to be found.[52]

Another form of electronic larceny came to light in 1987, when nine Pittsburgh teenagers were arrested for computer fraud. They had made thousands of dollars in purchases using stolen credit card numbers. They had obtained these numbers by using their PCs to break into the files of a West Coast credit card authorization service, which provided them with a lengthy list of valid credit card numbers and expiration dates.[53]

In 1993, one of the most brazen computer crimes in memory occurred in Connecticut. Two ex-convicts built a homemade automatic teller machine, wheeled it into a shopping mall, and planted it there for sixteen days. The bogus machine even contained money for its users, thus enhancing its seeming legitimacy. But despite its clever masquerade, it was yet another species of Trojan horse, designed to copy secret access codes from customers' ATM cards. This allowed the criminals to withdraw more than $100,000 from banks in six states.[54] They were arrested two months later on a variety of fraud, theft, and conspiracy charges.

HACKING

The pioneer hackers of the 1960s and 1970s probably exemplified Edwin Lemert's classic concept of primary deviance,[55] that is, their conduct would have been described by observers as norm violating. Of course, computers were so new then, there may have been few clear norms to violate. If their intent was not to destroy private files, could they be considered vandals? If their intent was not to steal data, could they be considered thieves? Perhaps the least ambiguous way to characterize them was as trespassers.

On the other hand, there was likely little, if any, of Lemert's notion of secondary deviance,[56] that is, no deviant self-identity on the parts of the hackers themselves. Indeed, their mastery of skills that may have seemed more magic than science to the general public endowed them with a sense of intellectual elitism. As one author, commenting on the first generation of hackers, has observed: "[T]o be a computer hacker was to wear a badge of honor."[57]

Hackers, particularly those of the nondestructive, nonlarcenous ilk, might be thought of as a deviant subculture. They ascribe to a set of norms, which apparently they take very seriously, but which often conflicts with the norms of the dominant society. They have their own peculiar code of ethics. For instance, they believe computerized data are public property and that passwords and other security features are only hurdles to be jumped in pursuit of these communal data.[58] They even appear to adhere to an ultimate proscription: "Hackers will do just about anything to break into a computer except crashing a system. That's the only taboo."[59]

Another way of looking at young hackers is from the perspective of Sykes and Matza's well-known "drift" theory of delinquency.[60] Hackers might be viewed in this manner as fundamentally conforming youths who drift into occasionally deviant behavior through the use of such "neutralizations" as the claim that they are only trying to expose lax security systems[61] or merely learn more about computers.[62] These may seem like weak rationalizations, but more than one young hacker has justified his misconduct on those very grounds.

Furthermore, even the most benign intentions can go terribly awry. A group of seven Milwaukee high school students, devoted electronic joy riders who called themselves the "414" gang, learned this lesson in 1983. They were from all accounts nice young men—Eagle Scouts, exemplary students. But, in the name of fun-and-games, they managed to break into a file at the Los Alamos, New Mexico, nuclear weapons facility and also erase a file at New York's Memorial Sloan-Kettering Cancer Center.[63] When they were apprehended, they denied any illegality in their actions. Their public statements seemed to be drawn directly from Sykes and Matza's inventory of neutralization techniques: "[I]t's not our fault" (denial of responsibility); "We didn't intend harm" (denial of injury); "There was no security" (denial of victim).[64]

Like the fabled sorcerer's apprentice, the 414s became intoxicated with their inordinate power and failed to contemplate maturely the consequences of their actions. This sort of irresponsibility has been the hackers' bane from the very beginning. If there is such a construct as "white-collar delinquency," teenage hackers are its embodiment.

Beyond the fun-and-games, however, there is a dark side to hacking, personified by a second generation of hackers whose intentions are undeniably malicious. One such hacker revealed this dark side in an article he wrote under the ominous pen name Mr. X:

> I can turn off your electricity or phone, destroy your credit rating—even take money out of your bank account—without ever leaving the keyboard of my home computer. And you would never know I was the one ruining your life![65]

If one doubts the plausibility of Mr. X's frightening boast, consider that in 1985 seven New Jersey teenagers were arrested for stealing $30,000 worth of computer equipment, which they had billed to total strangers on "hacked" credit card numbers.[66] Hackers have

also invaded credit files[67]—including those at TRW, the nation's largest credit information storage system.[68] Anyone who has ever been victimized in this manner has experienced the living hell of the credit pariah. If one's credit rating is sabotaged, one can no longer apply for a mortgage or loans of any kind. Even renting an apartment may become impossible.[69]

The infamous case of Kevin Mitnick is a good example of how a hacker can degenerate from prankster to public enemy. Like many computer wizards, he began his criminal career in high school by breaking into the school's main computer system. Later, he managed to hack into the central computer of the entire Los Angeles Unified School District. After dropping out of school in 1981, at the age of seventeen, he was arrested as part of a hacker ring that had stolen key manuals from Pacific Telephone. Mitnick was prosecuted as a juvenile and placed on probation. The following year, he was in trouble again. This time he used publicly available computers at the University of Southern California to break into numerous systems—including some at the U.S. Department of Defense. His probation was revoked, and he spent six months in a California Youth Authority facility.[70]

Up to this point, Mitnick arguably was still more aging "brat" than criminal. He had not yet stolen money or damaged data; but a manifest pattern of escalation already was emerging. In 1988, Mitnick, now twenty-five, was arrested for repeatedly breaking into a computer software system at the Digital Equipment Corporation in Massachusetts. He copied the software, which had cost DEC more than $1 million to develop. He further cost DEC more than $4 million in downtime. And if this were not enough, Mitnick had also broken into the computer system at Leeds University in England by telephone, using the sixteen unauthorized MCI long-distance telephone account numbers in his possession.[71]

He was denied bail and spent seven and one-half months in jail awaiting trial—a very unusual fate for a white-collar criminal. So frightened were the authorities of Mitnick's skills and potential for electronic vengeance that all his telephone calls had to be dialed by others. Finally, Mitnick entered into a plea bargain and, in 1989, received a one-year sentence to be followed by entry into a rehabilitation program for computer addiction.

More recently, a group of young hackers, ranging in age from eighteen to twenty-two and calling themselves by such exotic names as Phiber Optik, Acid Phreak, Outlaw, and Scorpion,[72] were arrested in 1992 for corrupting the databases of some of the largest corporations in America. The MOD, alternately known as the Masters of Destruction[73] or the Masters of Deception,[74] allegedly stole passwords and technical data from Pacific Bell, NYNEX, and other telephone companies, Martin Marietta, ITT, and other Fortune 500 companies, several big credit agencies, two major universities, and the Educational Broadcasting Network.[75] The damage caused by these hackers was extensive. One company alone, Southwestern Bell, suffered losses of $370,000.[76]

In what resembles a high-tech parody of urban gang warfare, the MOD apparently were motivated by a fierce competition with a rival "gang," the Legion of Doom.[77] Donn B. Parker, who once interviewed Phiber Optik,[78] has noted the importance of one-upmanship in the hacker subculture: "Computer hacking is a meritocracy. You rise in the culture depending on the information you can supply to other hackers."[79]

One of the most disturbing aspects of malicious hacking involves the area of national security. In 1983, for example, a nineteen-year-old UCLA student used his PC to break into a Defense Department international communications system.[80] In 1991, a gang of Dutch hackers managed to crack Pacific Fleet computers during the Persian Gulf War.[81] More recently still, two young hackers broke into computers at the Boeing Corporation—a major defense contractor[82]—and later used their home PCs to examine confidential government agency files.[83] A 1993 report from the American military's inspector-general found "serious deficiencies in the integrity and security" of a Pentagon computer used to make $67 billion a year in payments.[84] Members of Congress have expressed great concern over such stories, calling for tougher sanctions and the federalization of all computer crime.

Another reason for so much congressional anxiety is the threat of pernicious computer viruses—once a rare phenomenon, now, some claim, approaching epidemic proportions. A virus is an instructional code lodged in a computer's disk operating system that is designed to copy itself over and over. When the infected computer comes in contact with an uninfected piece of software, the virus is transmitted. "In today's computer culture, in which everybody from video gamesters to businessmen trade computer disks like baseball cards, the potential for widespread contagion is enormous."[85]

For example, in 1988, a previously unknown virus infected over one hundred thousand PC disks across the United States, including about ten thousand at George Washington University alone. Embedded in the virus was the cryptic message, WELCOME TO THE DUNGEON.[86] It turned out to be the creation of two brothers operating a computer store in Pakistan. Under a bizarre retailing philosophy that might best be described as schizoid vigilantism, they were selling pirated software, then punishing their customers for buying it.[87]

Some viruses are relatively innocuous, such as the so-called Peace virus. Designed by a twenty-three-year-old Arizona programmer, it showed up on the screens of thousands of Macintosh computers in 1987, flashed a single peace message, then erased itself and disappeared.[88]

Certain viruses might even be described as playful:

> A rogue program that made the rounds of Ivy League schools featured a creature inspired by *Sesame Street* called the Cookie Monster. Students trying to do useful work would be interrupted by persistent messages saying: "I want a cookie." In one variation, the message would be repeated with greater and greater frequency until users typed the letters C-O-O-K-I-E on their terminal keyboards.[89]

Far less playful, however, is the Rock Video virus that entertains unsuspecting users with an animated image of Madonna—then erases all their files and displays the ignominious taunt, YOU'RE STUPID.[90]

Sadly, most viruses wreak havoc without even offering glimpses of glamorous rock stars as compensation. In 1988, Robert Morris, a Cornell University graduate student, planted the infamous Internet virus which infected a vast network of six thousand computers stretching from Berkeley to Princeton to M.I.T. and caused at least a quarter of a million dollars in damage.[91] Morris was sentenced to three years probation, fined $10,000, and ordered to perform four hundred hours of community service.[92] This comparatively light sentence was received with hostility by some members of both the computer community and the general public. Sanctioning renegade hackers remains a controversial topic, since they are characteristically so far removed from any popular criminal stereotype.

On the other hand, Morris's offense was hardly trivial. It has been reported that when the Internet virus entered the computers at the Army's Ballistic Research laboratory in Maryland, system managers feared the United States had been invaded.[93]

Some other viruses appear deceptively benign. In December, 1987, a seemingly harmless "Christmas Tree" virus, designed by a German student, was loosed on a worldwide IBM network. Instructions to type the word "Christmas" would flash on a terminal screen. Users who complied with this innocent-sounding request tripped a virus that ultimately infected 350,000 terminals in 130 countries. IBM had to shut down its entire electronic mail system for two days to contain the spread.[94]

Viruses are sometimes placed in so-called "time bombs." In other words, the virus program contains delayed instructions to go off at some future date. An early example was the Jerusalem virus, so named because it was discovered at Hebrew University. This virus, which had the potential to cause a computer to lose all its files instantly, was set to go off on the fortieth anniversary of the State of Israel. Fortunately, the virus was eradicated well before that date.[95] Additional examples are the Joshi virus, which instructed the user to type "Happy Birthday Joshi" and was set to activate on January 5, 1993, and the Casino virus, set to activate on January 15, April 15, and August 15, 1993. Casino is a particularly odd virus which challenges the user to a slot-machine game and damages files if the user loses.[96]

Probably the best-known prosecution involving a computer virus was that of Donald Burleson in Texas. He worked in the computer room of a Fort Worth securities-trading firm and was responsible for assuring that the company's password system operated properly.

Burleson, a man of unconventional political beliefs, was a member of a fanatical tax protest movement. He argued frequently with his employers over the issue of federal withholding tax, which he insisted not be deducted from his paycheck. In 1985, when his employers learned he was planning to sue them to force them to stop withholding his taxes, he was fired. Before turning in his keys, the enraged Burleson planted a "worm." A worm is similar to a virus, except it is not contagious and only infects its host computer.

A few days later, the director of accounting discovered to his horror that "168,000 commission records no longer existed on the computer—they had been deleted from the system!"[97] This, of course, would make the month's payroll impossible to calculate. Burleson was arrested and became the first person ever tried for sabotage by virus.[98] He was convicted in 1988, fined $12,000, and placed on seven years probation.[99]

Except for precipitating the first "virus trial," the Burleson case does not seem, upon reflection, especially remarkable. Yet it was a media sensation. This may be explained in part simply by its timing. Just a few months earlier, "the Christmas Tree virus had embarrassed IBM and introduced readers to the concept of viruses as a type of computer crime."[100] For whatever reason, computer viruses subsequently have captured the public's imagination. Perhaps the term itself, with its mad scientist imagery and plague like connotation, has generated a strange blend of fright and titillation. In any event, the media seldom underplay a virus story. Studies reveal that the level of public interest in viruses is a direct function of increasing or decreasing media attention.[101]

Critics of the media have argued that the virus "epidemic" has been overblown; that there are more problematic computer crime issues worthier of public concern. They cite as an example of alleged "media hype" the Michelangelo virus, which was supposed to infect millions of computers worldwide on March 6, 1992 (Michelangelo's birthday), and erase everything it touched. "In the end, scattered copies of Michelangelo were found— but nowhere near the millions predicted."[102]

ESPIONAGE

While computer viruses generally receive substantial media attention, statistics reveal that the misuse of computers as tools for industrial, political, and international espionage may be a cause for greater concern. Industrial espionage exploded during the 1980s, perhaps increasing by an estimated 75 percent or more.[103] A data loss protection consultant in Houston has observed that the percentage of his firm's jobs in which electronic eavesdropping devices turned up quadrupled (5 percent to 20 percent) in the single year 1983.[104] In a sensational representation of that "golden age" of computer espionage, a major FBI sting operation in 1982 targeted more than twenty employees of the Hitachi and Mitsubishi corporations of Japan, who were suspected of stealing data from IBM.[105]

In 1992 American companies suffered losses from computer-related industrial espionage exceeding $1 billion. It is estimated that more than 85 percent of these crimes were committed or aided by employees—sometimes to settle a grudge, sometimes simply to make some money.[106] For example, employees with access to equipment and passwords can download strategic data or client lists and sell them to unscrupulous competitors. Because of the number of company insiders with such access, as well as the number of predatory outsiders capable of breaking through passwords and cracking data encryption, many computer networks have proven vulnerable to spying and data theft.[107]

A Canadian-based computer company filed a $5 million lawsuit in 1992 against a former employee, alleging that he copied the firm's entire customer database and used it to establish his own competing business.[108] At about that same time, computerized trade-secret data were stolen from a California technology company.[109] Six months later, the head of a rival firm and a former employee of the victimized firm were indicted on charges of conspiracy and data theft.[110] These criminal indictments were considered precedent-setting because electronic industrial espionage cases traditionally had been fought in the civil court arena.[111]

Occasionally, industrial espionage and virus infection are melded into a single computer crime. Consider the plight of the head of a British technology company whose latest product was sabotaged with a software virus by a rival exhibitor during a 1993 trade show for potential customers. In an open letter to an industry journal, this embittered executive talks about his experience with white-collar crime in a tone more suggestive of a street crime victim:

> There is a fair chance that whoever planted the virus is reading this. So to him I have a private message. Whoever you are, I understand why your bosses told you to do it. Nevertheless, it was vandalism, you tried to wreck something which is very valuable to me, and I won't stand for it. I'm going to pursue this with the full weight of the law, and if I ever find out who you are, may God help you.[112]

A dramatic example of political espionage occurred in New York in 1992. The confidential medical records of a congressional candidate were hacked from a hospital computer by an unknown party and sent to a tabloid newspaper. Those records revealed that the candidate once had attempted suicide,

and this information soon was published in a front-page story. The candidate won the election, despite the publicity regarding her medical history, but the personal aftermath of this electronic invasion of her privacy serves as a reminder of why this chapter is as much about victims as villains. "It caused me a lot of pain," she would later say, "especially since my parents didn't know."[113]

Computer crime in the area of international espionage is more difficult to assess. Since by definition this brand of white-collar crime often involves material classified as secret by the government, details of certain cases probably have been concealed from public scrutiny. A few stories, however, have been reported by the media.

The most widely chronicled computer espionage case is that of the so-called "Hanover Hackers" in 1989. A group of young West German men were arrested for selling American military data to the Soviet KGB in exchange for cash and cocaine. This spy ring consisted of five members of West Germany's notorious Chaos Computer Club, which had achieved European hacking stardom in 1987 by breaking into two NASA computers.[114] The most proficient member of the Hanover group, twenty-four-year-old Markus Hess, had illegally accessed a computer at the Lawrence Berkeley Laboratory on the University of California campus and had used that computer as a launch pad to access U.S. military computers at sites such as the Pentagon, the White Sands Missile Range, and the Redstone Missile Base.[115]

Of the five original Hanover Hackers, the youngest one was not charged in exchange for testifying; another was burned to death in what was either a hideous suicide or a brutal murder. The remaining three who stood trial were convicted in 1990. Germany was reuniting, the cold war was winding down, and no one seemed particularly anxious to lock the defendants up and throw away the key. That they sold classified computer data to the Russians was undeniable; but just how valuable those data were was not at all clear. For one thing, the relatively small payments they received did not seem commensurate with a major espionage success. When the U.S. National Security Agency assessed the damage, one of their scientists observed in a memo: "Looks like the Russians got rooked."[116] In one of those truth-is-stranger-than-fiction twists, that scientist was Robert Morris, Sr., whose son had released the Internet virus eighteen months earlier.

The sentences handed down ranged from one year and eight months to two months. All the defendants were put on probation, because their drug problems had, in the opinion of the judges, clouded their judgment and mitigated their responsibility.[117]

International computer espionage in the United States appears to be taken more seriously than in Europe. Indeed, it has been called the single most important security issue of the 1990s.[118] This concern may have originated in the early 1980s, when the Reagan administration withdrew funding for an international research center in Vienna, because its computers were tied in to other research centers in both the United States and the Soviet Union. A fear was expressed that this connection might have allowed the Russians to log in to American computers and scan for classified data.[119]

Under the Computer Fraud and Abuse Act of 1986, it is illegal to tamper with any computer system used by the federal government or by government contractors. The act empowers the FBI to investigate the damage, destruction, or alteration of any data stored in such systems.[120] A representative case occurred in 1990 when personal computers at NASA and the EPA were infected with the SCORES virus, although the FBI ultimately turned this case over to local police because of difficulty in proving the suspect's intent to contaminate government computers.[121]

The first indictment of an American hacker on espionage charges occurred in 1992. The accused spy was a computer programmer from California. He allegedly stole secret Air Force flight orders for a military exercise at Fort Bragg, North Carolina.[122] Although the value of this material to the international intelligence community is dubious, the illegal possession of classified computer data is considered espionage, "even if no attempt is made to pass it to a foreign government."[123]

NOTES

1. Perry, Robert L. *Computer Crime*. New York: Franklin Watts, 1986.
2. Parker, Donn B. *Fighting Computer Crime*. New York: Scribners, 1983.
3. *PC User*. "Security Survey Reveals Huge Financial Losses," April 21, 1993: p. 20.
4. Ibid.
5. Wood, Chris. "Crime in the Computer Age," *Maclean's* 101, January 25, 1988: 28–30.
6. Sherizen, Sanford. "The Globalization of Computer Crime and Information Security." *Computer Security Journal* 8, 1992: 13–19.
7. Sykes, John. "Computer Crime: A Spanner in the Works." *Management Accounting* 70, 1992: p. 55. This article notes the exploits of England's "Mad Hacker."
8. Saari, Juhani. "Computer Crime—Numbers Lie." *Computers & Security* 6, 1987: 111–117.
9. Norman, Adrian R. D. *Computer Insecurity*. London: Chapman and Hall, 1989.
10. Hafner, Katie, and Markoff, John. *Cyberpunk*. New York: Touchstone, 1991.
11. Rockwell, Robin. "The Advent of Computer Related Crimes." *Secured Lender* 46, 1990: pp. 40, 42.
12. Sherizen, op. cit.
13. Major, Michael J. "Taking the Byte out of Crime: Computer Crime Statistics Vary as

Much as the Types of Offenses Committed." *Midrange Systems* 6, 1993: 25–28.

14. Gold, Steve. "Two Hackers Get Six Months Jail in UK." *Newsbytes*, May 24, 1993: 1–2.
15. Sherizen, op. cit.
16. Ibid.
17. Hooper, Narelle. "Tackling the Techno-Crims." *Rydge's*, September, 1987: 112–119.
18. Sherizen, op. cit.
19. Major, op. cit.
20. Quindlen, Terry H. "IRS Computer Systems Are Catching More Fishy Tax Returns: GAO Praises Agency for Reeling in Electronic Cheaters But Urges Tighter Controls." *Government Computer News* 12, 1993: p. 67.
21. Torres, Vicki. "New Puzzle: High-Tech Peophilia." *Los Angeles Times*, March 5, 1993: p. B3.
22. Francis, Dorothy. *Computer Crime,* New York: Dutton, 1987.
23. Elmer-DeWitt, Phillip. "Invasion of the Data Snatchers." *Time* 132, September 26, 1988: 62–67.
24. Ibid., p. 25.
25. Didio, Laura. "Security Deteriorates as LAN Usage Grows." *LAN Times* 7, 1993: 1–2.
26. Quoted in Schuyten, Peter J. "Computers and Criminals." *New York Times*, September 27, 1979: p. D2.
27. Didio, op. cit.
28. U.S. Department of Justice. "FBI Uniform Crime Reports 1991" in *Crime in the United States 1991*, 1992: p. 13.
29. Nawrocki, Jay. "There Are Too Many Loopholes: Current Computer Crime Laws Require Clearer Definition." *Data Management* 25, 1987: 14–15.
30. Brandt, Allen. "Embezzler's Guide to the Computer." *Harvard Business Review* 53, 1975: 79–89.
31. Bass, Frank. "Potential for Computerized Fraud Growing, Say Experts." *Houston Post*, August 14, 1991: pp. A1, A8.
32. Whiteside, Thomas. *Computer Capers: Tales of Electronic Thievery, Embezzlement, and Fraud.* New York: Thomas Y. Crowell, 1978.
33. Ibid.
34. Conklin, John E. *"Illegal But Not Criminal": Business Crime in America.* Engle-

wood Cliffs, New Jersey: Prentice Hall, 1977.
35. Cressey, Donald R. *Other People's Money: A Study in the Social Psychology of Embezzlement.* Belmont, California: Wadsworth, 1971.
36. Violino, Bob. "Are Your Networks Secure?" *Information Week*, April 12, 1993: p. 30.
37. Brandt, op. cit.
38. Francis, op. cit.
39. Ibid.
40. Ibid.
41. Whiteside, op. cit.
42. Ibid., p. 93.
43. Seidler, Lee. *The Equity Funding Papers: The Anatomy of a Fraud.* New York: Wiley, 1977.
44. Whiteside, op. cit.
45. Ibid.
46. Thornton, Mary. "Age of Electronic Convenience Spawning Inventive Thieves." *Washington Post*, May 20, 1984: A1, A8–A9.
47. Violino, op. cit., 30–33.
48. Adam, John A. "Data Security." *IEEE Spectrum* 29, 1992: 18–20. See also Sherizen, Sanford. "Future Bank Crimes." *Bank Systems & Technology* 26: 60, 62.
49. Schuyten, op. cit.
50. Bloombecker, Buck. *Spectacular Computer Crimes.* Homewood, Illinois: Dow Jones-Irwin, 1990.
51. Ibid.
52. Thornton, op. cit.
53. Roberts, Ralph, and Kane, Pamela. *Computer Security.* Greensboro, North Carolina: Compute! Books, 1989.
54. *Houston Chronicle.* "Duo Arrested in Phony Teller Machine Scheme." June 30, 1993: p. 6A.
55. Lemert, Edwin M. *Human Deviance, Social Problems, and Social Control.* Englewood Cliffs, New Jersey: Prentice Hall, 1967.
56. Ibid.
57. Hafner and Markoff, op. cit., p. 11.
58. McEwen, J. Thomas. "Computer Ethics." *National Institute of Justice Reports*, January/February 1991: 8–11.
59. Ibid., p. 9.

60. Sykes, Gresham M., and Matza, David. "Techniques of Neutralization: A Theory of Delinquency." *American Sociological Review* 22, 1957: 664–666.

61. Kabay, Mich. "Computer Hackers Are No Vigilantes." *Computing Canada* 18, 1992: p. 36.

62. Keefe, Patricia. "Portraits of Hackers as Young Adventurers Not Convincing." *Computerworld* 26, 1992: p. 33.

63. O'Driscoll, Patrick. "At 17, a Pro at Testifying on Computers." *USA Today*, September 26, 1983: p. 2A.

64. Quoted in Francis, op. cit., p. 28.

65. Quoted in Francis, op. cit., p. 35.

66. Ibid.

67. Van Brussel, Carolyn. "Arrest of N.Y.C. Hackers Hailed as 'Breakthrough.'" *Computing Canada* 18, 1992: p. 1.

68. Benedetto, Richard. "Computer Crooks Spy on Our Credit." *USA Today*, July 22–24, 1984: p. 1A.

69. Kirvan, Paul. "Is a Hacker Hovering in Your Horoscope?" *Communications News* 29, 1992: p. 48.

70. Rebello, Kathy. "'Sensitive Kid' Faces Trial." *USA Today*, February 28, 1989: 1B–2B.

71. Ibid.

72. Brown, Bob. "Indictment Handed Down on 'Masters of Disaster.'" *Network World* 29, 1992: p. 34.

73. Moses, Jonathan M. "Wiretap Inquiry Spurs Computer Hacker Charges." *Wall Street Journal*, July 9, 1992: p. B8.

74. Thyfault, Mary E. "Feds Tap into Major Hacker Ring." *Information Week*, July 13, 1992: p. 15.

75. Schwartau, Winn. "Hackers Indicted for Infiltrating Corporate Networks." *Infoworld* 14, 1992: p. 56. See also Daly, James. "Frustrated Hackers May Have Helped Feds in MOD Sting." *Computerworld* 26, 1992: p. 6.

76. Schwartau, op. cit. See also *Wall Street Journal*. "Hackers Plead Guilty." March 22, 1993: p. B2; and *Wall Street Journal*.

"Hacker is Sentenced." June 7, 1993: p. B2.

77. Tabor, Mary B. W. "Urban Hackers Charged in High-Tech Crime." *New York Times*, July 23, 1992: p. A1. For a detailed account of the rivalry between the Masters of Destruction and the Legion of Doom see Sterling, Bruce. *The Hacker Crackdown*. New York: Bantam Books, 1992.

78. Littman, Jonathan. "Cyberpunk Meets Mr. Security." *PC-Computing* 5, 1992: 288–293.

79. Quoted in Francis, op. cit., p. 25.

80. Meddis, Sam. "Lawmakers: Pull Plug on Hackers." *USA Today*, November 4, 1983: 3A.

81. *USA Today*. "Blabbermouth Computers." July 27, 1993: p. 8A.

82. *New York Times*. "US Charges Young Hackers." November 15, 1992: p. 40.

83. *Government Computer News*. "Feds Charge 2 in Computer Break-in." November 23, 1992: p. 8.

84. Collins, Chris. "Hackers' Paradise." *USA Today*, July 6, 1993: p. 5A.

85. Elmer-DeWitt, op. cit.

86. Ibid., 62–67.

87. Ibid.

88. Ibid.

89. Ibid., p. 66.

90. Ibid.

91. Bloombecker, op. cit.

92. Hafner and Markoff, op. cit.

93. Ibid.

94. Bloombecker, op. cit.

95. Elmer-DeWitt, op. cit.

96. Daly, James. "Viruses Ringing in the New Year." *Computerworld* 27, 1992: p. 79.

97. Bloombecker, op. cit.

98. Lewyn, Mark. "First 'Computer Virus' Trial Starts Today." *USA Today*, September 6, 1988: p. 3B.

99. Lewyn, Mark. "Computer Verdict Sets 'Precedent.'" *USA Today*, September 27, 1988: p. 1A.

100. Bloombecker, op. cit., p. 104.

101. Zalud, Bill. "Doing the Virus Hustle." *Security* 27, 1990: 42–44.

102. Burgess, John. "Viruses: An Overblown Epidemic?" *Washington Post*, December 30, 1992; F1, F3.
103. Friedman, Jon, and Meddis, Sam. "White-Collar Crime Cuts into Companies' Profits." *USA Today*, August 30, 1984: p. 3B.
104. Ibid.
105. Parker, 1983, op. cit.
106. Rothfeder, Jeffrey. "Holes in the Net." *Corporate Computing* 2, 1993: 114–118.
107. Violino, op. cit.
108. Buchok, James. "$5M Suit Filed Over Database Copying Claim." *Computing Canada* 18, 1992: 1–2.
109. O'Connor, Rory J. "High-Tech Cops Wade Through Digital Dump of Information." *San Jose Mercury News*, October 24, 1992: 10D–11D.
110. Groves, Martha. "2 Indicted on Trade-Secret Theft Charges." *Los Angeles Times*, March 5, 1993: p. D1.
111. Ratcliffe, Mitch. "Symantec Execs Face Felony Rap in Borland Case." *MacWEEK* 7, 1993: 1–2.
112. "Jules." "On the Use of Weapons." *EXE* 10, 1993: 52–53.
113. Hasson, Judi. "Access to Medical Files Reform Issue." *USA Today*, July 27, 1993: 1A–2A.
114. Hafner and Markoff, op. cit.
115. Stoll, Clifford. *The Cuckoo's Egg*. New York: Doubleday, 1989.
116. Hafner and Markoff, op. cit.
117. Stoll, op. cit.
118. Ibid.
119. Hafner and Markoff, op. cit.
120. Belts, Mitch. "Recovering From Hacker Invasion." *Computerworld* 27, 1993: p. 45.
121. *Houston Post*. "Dallas Police Investigate Suspect in Spreading of Computer Virus." December 29, 1990: p. 19.
122. Markoff, John. "Hacker Indicted on Spy Charges." *New York Times*, December 8, 1992: p. 13.
123. Ibid., p. 13.

Corporate Crime

John Braithwaite and Gilbert Geis

Criminal justice interventions to reduce street crime, whether mediated by principles of deterrence, rehabilitation, or incapacitation, can at best have only modest effects on the rate of offending. It will be argued in this paper that, in contrast, deterrence, rehabilitation, and incapacitation are viable strategies for fighting crime in the suites. This argument will be advanced in the context of a more general set of propositions asserting that the conventional wisdom of criminology with respect to traditional crime should be inverted with corporate crime.

There also is a broader purpose in our presenting the six propositions which follow. We seek to establish that corporate crime is a conceptually different phenomenon from traditional crime. Corporate crime is defined as conduct of a corporation, or of individuals acting on behalf of a corporation, that is proscribed and punishable by law. The propositions that follow specify reasons why principles developed in relation to traditional crime should not be assumed to apply to corporate offenses. Once the domains are accepted as conceptually separate, the burden of proof shifts; the opponent of legislation to control corporate crime must show why caveats from traditional criminal law should be regarded as relevant to the control of corporate crime.

SIX BASIC PROPOSITIONS

Proposition 1 With most traditional crimes, the fact that an offense has occurred is readily apparent; with most corporate crimes, the effect is not readily apparent.

When one person murders another, the corpse is there for people to see; or at least the

From John Braithwaite and Gilbert Geis, "On Theory and Action for Corporate Crime Control," *Crime & Delinquency*, vol. 28, (1982): 292–314. Reprinted by permission of Sage Publications, © 1982.

fact that a person has disappeared is readily apparent. When, on the other hand, a miner dies from a lung disease, people may never appreciate that he has died because his employer violated mine safety regulations. Inevitably, most such violations are undetected.[1] People who pay more to go to a movie because of price fixing among theater owners will not be aware that they have been victims of a crime. When taxes go up because Defense Department officials have accepted bribes to purchase more expensive ships or missiles than the country needs, no one knows that a crime has occurred and that we all have been its victims.

Such is the limited power of individuals for ill that when they perpetrate a traditional crime there is usually only one victim (or, at most, there are only a few victims) for each offense. These individual victims become acutely aware that another person has dealt them a blow. The structural reality of much corporate crime, in contrast, is one of diffuse effects. A million one-dollar victimizations will not generate the kind of public visibility that a single million-dollar victimization will.

Even when the effects of corporate crime are concentrated rather than diffuse, victim awareness is often not there. If a consumer pays an extra thousand dollars for a used car that has had its odometer turned back, he will almost never be aware of the fraud.[2] The consumer might think that he has been sold a lemon, but not that he has been a victim of business crime. Similarly, when patients die from using a dangerous drug that was approved by health authorities on the strength of a bribe from a pharmaceutical company, a practice common in many countries,[3] the crime is not apparent. Low visibility also follows from the fact that often the only witnesses to a crime are themselves implicated in the offense.[4]

This first proposition has important implications for the difference between how law enforcers must go about controlling corporate versus traditional crime. Traditional crime control is reactive. The police normally do not investigate until a citizen reports a victimization. For corporate crimes, whose visibility is almost invariably masked through being embedded in an ongoing transaction, the reactive model must be discarded for a proactive enforcement stance.

Proposition 2   Once an offense becomes apparent, apprehending a suspect can be difficult with traditional crime, but is almost always easy with corporate crime.

When a house is robbed, or when a car is reported as missing, it is often a difficult job for the police to find the burglar or the car thief. Great public expense is incurred to achieve unremarkable clearance rates for these types of offenses. In contrast, in the unlikely event that a sick worker discovers his illness is the result of an industrial health violation at work, almost by definition the law enforcement agency can identify a corporate suspect—the worker's employer. Similarly, if it is discovered that a bribe has been passed to secure a particular defense contract, there is an immediate suspect, the corporation that benefits from the contract. There was no need for the police to print "Wanted" posters or to set up roadblocks to find the corporate suspect when it was discovered that bribes were accepted in many countries throughout the world to secure sales of Lockheed aircraft.

This second proposition more than counterbalances the first in its implications for the potential effectiveness of corporate crime control. Corporate crime investigators cannot enjoy the luxury of sitting back in their offices waiting for the telephone to ring to notify them of the offense, but they are saved the tribulations of identikit photos, fingerprinting, and all the other paraphernalia that burden police in pursuit of traditional types of suspects.

With the use of proactive enforcement, there are many ways in which the disadvantage of invisibility could be swamped by the advantage to the enforcement agency of not having to apprehend the suspect. Although odometer frauds are invisible to the victims, representatives of law enforcement agencies could readily observe the mileage readings of cars standing in used car lots and then check back with the former owners to establish the mileage readings at the time of sale. If the enforcement agency were in a position to deliver the cars to the company itself, it would not even have to rely on the memory of the former owners.

Our first two propositions together may constitute an argument for tactics that might involve or border on entrapment. Nevertheless, it is an argument that demands consideration in corporate crime cases. Under the reactive enforcement model for traditional crimes, entrapment is hardly necessary. Law enforcement agencies have quite enough offenses reported to them and need not create more. Should they decide that they do want to create more offenses, given how little the police know about who is committing most of them, deciding whom to entrap would be difficult.

In contrast, if one accepts the inevitability of a proactive enforcement model for white collar crime, investigators may have little choice but to create their own offenses. For some types of white collar crimes, entrapment may be one of the few ways of doing this. The present authors differ with respect to the FBI's tactics in the ABSCAM case; but consider the options available for the conviction of political bribe takers. The FBI does not have citizens calling the agency claiming to be victims of political bribes, yet it does have intelligence on who the corrupt politicians are. Such intelligence rarely is sufficient to sustain criminal charges. The use of entrapment ruses for corrupt politicians may be more necessary and less indiscriminate than is the entrapment of, say, drug users by the offer of a deal. It can also be argued that holders of public office and the primary beneficiaries of the economic system have a special obligation to obey the law and to resist temptation.

Readers may conclude that entrapment is unacceptable with respect to either white collar or traditional crime. However, the balance of considerations that lead to this conclusion under the proactive model of white collar crime enforcement should be very different than the factors weighed for the types of offenses that can be handled under the reactive model.

Proposition 3 Once the suspect has been apprehended, proving guilt is usually easy with traditional crime, but almost always difficult with corporate crime.

Especially for less serious traditional crimes, the police have little difficulty in obtaining a conviction, particularly when they are willing to plea bargain. Once the police have made up their minds that a person is guilty and deserves to go to court, a conviction usually will follow.[5] When enforcement officers decide that a corporation probably is guilty of an offense and deserves to go to court, a conviction is usually *not* the result. Indeed, it does not normally eventuate that the matter *will* go to court.[6] The high costs to the state of corporate prosecutions, which work against pursuing the case in court, may be not only financial (e.g., legal fees) but also political (e.g., votes and campaign contributions, which may produce understandable caution among conservative bureaucrats in dealing with powerful actors).

Even where these costs are deemed to be bearable, the government will often lose in court because the complexity of the law[7] or the complexity of the company's books[8] makes it impossible to prove the case beyond reasonable doubt. There is a considerable difference, for instance, between convicting a corporation that takes money by fraud and convicting an individual who takes it at the point of a gun: "Criminal intent is not as easily inferred from a taking executed through a market transaction, as it is from a taking by force."[9] Corporations, unlike individuals, have the resources to employ the legal talent to exploit this inherent complexity. Good lawyers who use complexity to cast "reasonable doubt" on the applicability of existing statutes to the behavior of their client also use complexity to protract proceedings and thereby push up the cost disincentives for the prosecution to continue with formal proceedings.[10]

In addition to the complexity of the law and the complexity of the books, there is the complexity of the organizational reality of corporate action. Every individual in a large organization can present a different version of what company policy was, and individual corporate actors can blame others for their own actions (x says he was following y's instructions, y says that x misunderstood instructions she had passed down from z, ad infinitum). So how can either company policy or any individual company employee be guilty?[11] Even if this is not what actually happened,[12] it is difficult for the prosecution to prove otherwise.

There is, in addition, the complexity of science. Pollution, product safety, and occupational safety and health prosecutions typically turn on scientific evidence that the corporation caused certain consequences. In cases that involve scientific dispute, proof beyond reasonable doubt is rarely, if ever, possible. Science deals in probabilities, not certainties. The superstructure of science is erected on a foundation of mathematical statistics which estimate a probability that inferences are true or false. Logically, proof beyond reasonable doubt that a "causes" b is impossible. It is always possible that an observed correlation between a and b is explained by an unknown third variable, c. The scientist can never eliminate all the possible third variables. Hence, to require proof beyond reasonable doubt that a violation of the Food, Drug and Cosmetic Act caused an observed level of drug impurity, which in turn caused fifty deaths, is to require the impossible.[13]

The problem is illustrated by the federal OSHA statute. It requires proof that the violation was willful and caused death before a criminal conviction can stand. OSHA counsel explained to one of the authors that when fifty-one Research-Cottrell workers were killed by the collapse of scaffolding for a water tower, the fact that OSHA regulations had been violated was clear, the fact that workers died was clear, but proving beyond reasonable doubt that it was the violations (rather than other factors) that caused the scaffolding to collapse was another matter. The complexity of the forces that caused the scaffolding to collapse was such that it was represented by a computer simulation. OSHA counsel decided, undoubtedly correctly, that a computer simulation was more complexity than any jury could stand.

That the complexity of corporate crime and the power and legal resources of the defendants make convictions much more difficult than with traditional crime hardly needs to be belabored. This difficulty rather than the low visibility of offenses (Proposition 1) is the real stumbling block to effective corporate crime control. Consequently, it will be the barriers to conviction rather than those to discovery and apprehension that will be the focus of reforms considered in the final part of the paper.

Proposition 4 Once an offender has been convicted, deterrence is doubtful with traditional crime, but may well be strong with corporate crime.

Specific must be distinguished from general deterrence. The former refers to the deterrence of the offender who is actually convicted. The case for specific deterrence is weak with traditional crime. Offenders who are incarcerated may be more embittered than deterred by the experience. They appear less likely to learn the error of their ways while in prison than to learn better ways of committing crimes. This is not likely to be true of persons convicted of corporate crime. A feature that distinguishes traditional from corporate crime is that the illegitimate skills (e.g., safecracking) involved in the former are learned in criminal settings (e.g., prison), while the illegitimate skills (e.g., concealing transactions in books of account) of the corporate criminal are learned in legitimate noncriminal settings. While the illegitimate skills of burglars may be developed while they are incarcerated, those of crooked accountants will simply become increasingly out of date as they languish in prison.

A major risk in apprehending the traditional criminal is that the stigmatizing process will push him further and further into a criminal self-concept. This is the contention of labeling theory. Evidence such as that from the Cambridge longitudinal study of delinquency[14] has been interpreted as support for the labeling hypothesis. This study showed that boys who were apprehended for and convicted of delinquent offenses became more delinquent than boys who were equally delinquent to begin with but who escaped apprehension.

These labeling arguments cannot readily be applied to corporate offenders. They are likely to regard themselves as unfairly maligned pillars of respectability, and no amount of stigmatization is apt to convince them otherwise. One does meet people who have a mental image of themselves as a thief, a safecracker, a prostitute, a pimp, a drug runner, and even a hit man, but how often does one meet a person who sees himself as a corporate criminal? The young black offender can often enhance his status back on the street by having done some time, but the reaction of the corporate criminal to incarceration is shame and humiliation.

Such an observation has important implications. Although the labeling hypothesis makes it unwise to use publicity as a tool to punish juvenile delinquents, it is sound deterrence to broadcast widely the names of corporate offenders. Corporations and their officers are genuinely afraid of bad publicity arising from their illegitimate activities.[15] They respond to it with moral indignation and denials, not with assertions that "if you think I'm bad, I'll really show you how bad I can be," as juvenile delinquents sometimes do.

Individual corporate criminals are also more deterrable because they have more of those valued possessions that can be lost through a criminal conviction, such as social status, respectability, money, a job, and a comfortable home and family life. As Geerken and Gove hypothesize, "the effectiveness of [a] deterrence system will increase as the individual's investment in and rewards from the social system increase."[16] Clinard and Meier, moreover, place particular emphasis on the "future orientation" of white collar criminals:

> Punishment may work best with those individuals who are "future oriented" and who are thus worried about the effect of punishment on their future plans and their social status rather than being concerned largely with the present and having little or no concern about their status. For this reason gang boys may be deterred by punishment less strongly than the white-collar professional person.[17]

In general, the arguments about the deterrability of individuals convicted of corporate crimes are equally applicable to the corporations themselves. Corporations are future oriented, concerned about their reputation, and quintessentially rational. Although most individuals do not possess the information necessary to calculate rationally the probability of detection and punishment,[18] corporations have information-gathering systems designed precisely for this purpose. Hence, conclude Ermann and Lundman, "business concerns have regularly engaged in price fixing . . . under the correct assumption that the benefits outweigh the costs."[19]

The specific deterrent value of fines can be questioned for both traditional[20] and corporate[21] offenders. A large fine imposed upon a poor property offender might leave him little option but to steal again so as to be able to pay the fine. With corporations the problem is to be able to set a fine large enough to have a deterrent effect.

> The $7 million fine which was levied against the Ford Motor Company for environmental violations was certainly more than a slap on the wrist, but it rather pales beside the estimated $250 million loss which the company sustained on the Edsel. Both represent environmental contingencies which managers are paid high salaries to handle. We know they handled the latter—the first seven years of the Mustang more than offset the Edsel losses. One can only infer that they worked out ways to handle the fine too.[22]

Although the fine itself may be an ineffective deterrent when used against the corporate criminal, other sanctions associated with the prosecution—unfavorable publicity, the harrowing experience for the senior executive of days under cross-examination, the dislocation of top management from their normal duties so that they can defend the corporation against public attacks—can be important specific deterrents.

General deterrence is an effect more difficult to establish empirically. General deterrence refers to the consequences of a conviction for those who are not caught, but who through observing the penalties imposed on others decide not to violate the law. The state of the evidence on general deterrence for common crime, and how scholars interpret that evidence, is in turmoil. It seems fair to say, however, that there has been a growing disillusionment with how much crime prevention can be achieved through deterrence, particularly of offenders from lower socioeconomic levels. Disillusionment has progressed so far that, whereas once the conventional wisdom of conservative criminology demanded that high imprisonment rates be justified by deterrence, now incarceration conventionally is based on the idea of just deserts.

The evidence on the deterrent effects of sanctions against corporate crime is not nearly so voluminous, but the consensus among scholars is overwhelmingly optimistic concerning general deterrence.[23] This may in part reflect an uncritical acceptance of the empirically untested assumption that because corporate crime is a notably rational economic activity, it must be more subject to general deterrence.

However, the faith in the efficacy of general deterrence for corporate crime is not totally blind, as can be illustrated by a number of instances of corporate reaction to enforcement strategies. For example, business executives in Australia were asked whether the introduction of the Australian Trade Practices Act of 1974, with its relatively severe penalties, affected their behavior.[24] Survey respondents claimed that the legislation caused them to abandon certain price-fixing agreements with competitors and introduce antitrust "compliance programs." A more sophisticated study by Block et al. found that U.S. Justice Department antitrust prosecutions in the bread industry had significant and notable specific and general deterrent effects on price fixing. The degree of deterrence was surprising, given that bread price fixers have never been sent to jail and that fines average only 0.3 percent of the annual sales of the colluding firms. The Block et al. data suggest that deterrence is mainly mediated by civil treble damage suits that follow in the wake of criminal conviction.[25]

The most impressive evidence is from Lewis-Beck and Alford's study of United States coal mine safety enforcement.[26] Using a multiple interrupted time series analysis, these authors were able to show that the considerable increases in enforcement expenditure which followed the toughening of the mine safety legislation in 1941 and 1969 were both associated with dramatic reductions in coal mine fatality rates. The cosmetic 1952 Federal Coal Mine Safety Act, which actually arrested the rate of increase in Bureau of Mines enforcement expenditures, had no effect on fatality rates. Controls introduced into the regression models refute an interpretation that the historical trends are the result of technological advances in mining, changes in mine size, or variations in the types of mining operations. The most parsimonious interpretation of the data is that the rate of deaths from coal mine accidents is less than one-quarter of the rate of fatal accidents occurring before the 1941 legislation because of the deterrent effects of law enforcement.

Proposition 5   Although incapacitation is not apt to be very effective or acceptable for controlling traditional crime in a humane society, it can be a highly successful strategy in the control of corporate crime.

Traditional criminals can be incapacitated if the society is willing to countenance severe solutions. If we execute murderers, they will never murder again; or we can lock them up and never let them out. Pickpockets can be incapacitated by our cutting off their hands. Most contemporary societies are not prepared to resort to such barbaric methods. Instead, the widely used punishment is imprisonment for periods of months or years. Yet only partial incapacitation is in effect while the offender is incarcerated. Offenders continue to murder, to rape, and to commit a multitude of less serious offenses while they are in prison. Indeed, the chances of being a victim of homicide in the United States are five times as high for white males inside prison as for those outside. And the partial incapacitation of prison lasts only as long as the sentence.

The limits of incapacitation as a policy become more apparent when we ask who is to be incapacitated. A substantial body of evidence shows that no matter how we attempt to predict dangerousness, the success rate is very low.[27] Any policy of selective incarceration to "protect society" will result in prisons full of "false positives."

Incapacitation is more workable with corporate criminals because their kind of criminal activity is dependent on their being able to maintain legitimacy in formalized roles in the economy. We do not have to cut off the hands of surgeons who increase their income by having patients undergo unnecessary surgery. All we need do is deregister them. Similarly, we can prevent people from acting in such formal roles as company directors, product safety managers, environmental engineers, lawyers, and accountants swiftly and without barbarism. Should we want only short-term incapacitation, we can, as Stone advocates, prohibit a person "for a period of three years from serving as officer, director, or consultant of any corporation. . . ."[28] Moreover, an incapacitative court order could be even more finely tuned. The prohibition could be against the person's serving in any position entailing decision making that might influence the quality of the environment. Corporate crime's total dependence on incumbency in roles in the economy renders possible this tailor-made incapacitation. It makes the shotgun approach to incapacitation for common crimes look very crude indeed. However, the substitution problems that plague traditional incapacitative models are also a major constraint on the efficacy of incapacitating individuals who have been responsible for corporate crime. If, for example, the corporation is committed to cutting corners on environmental emissions, it can replace one irresponsible environmental engineer with another who is equally willing to violate the law.

This is where court orders to incapacitate the whole organization become necessary. Capital punishment for the corporation is one possibility: The charter of a corporation can be revoked, the corporation can be put in the hands of a receiver, or it can be nationalized. Although corporate capital punishment is not as barbaric as execution of individual persons, it is an extreme measure which courts undoubtedly would be loath to adopt, especially considering the unemployment caused by terminating an enterprise (although this does not apply to nationalizing it). Even though court-ordered corporate death sentences may be politically unrealistic, there are cases where regulatory agencies through their harassment of criminal corporations have bankrupted fairly large concerns.

A less draconian remedy is to limit the charter of a company by preventing it from continuing those aspects of its operations where it has flagrantly failed to respect the law. Alternatively, as part of a consent decree, a corporation could be forced to sell that part of its business which has been the locus of continued law violation. The participation of the regulatory agency in the negotiations would serve to ensure that the sale was to a new parent with an exemplary record of compliance.[29] This kind of remedy becomes in-creasingly useful in an era when the diversified conglomerate is the modal form of industrial organization. Forcing a conglomerate to sell one of its divisions would, in addition to having incapacitative effects, be a strong deterrent in cases where the division made sound profits. Deterrence and incapacitation can be achieved without harm to the economy or to innocent employees.

Effective incapacitative strategies for corporate crime are, therefore, possible. All that is required is for legislatures, courts, and regulatory agencies to apply them creatively, to overcome the conservatism that leaves them clinging to the failed remedies carried over from traditional crime. The goal of incapacitation illustrates better than any other how the effective and just means for achieving criminal justice goals cannot be the same with corporate crime as with traditional crime. Consider, for example, the application to the Olin Mathieson Chemical Corporation of a law that forbids offenders convicted of a felony from carrying guns. Mintz has described what happened after Olin Mathieson was convicted of conspiracy concerning bribes to get foreign aid contracts in Cambodia and Vietnam:

> It happened that there was a law which said in essence that a person who had been convicted of a felony could not transport a weapon in interstate commerce. This created a legal problem for Olin, because it had been convicted of a felony, was in the eyes of the law a person and had a division that made weapons for use by the armed forces. Congress resolved the dilemma by enacting a law that, in effect, got Olin off the hook.[30]

Here we are struck by the absurdity of automatically applying to corporations an incapacitative policy designed for individuals. It will be argued later that this absurdity of applying law governing the behavior of individuals to the crimes of collectivities is the fundamental impediment to effective corporate crime control.

Proposition 6   Even though rehabilitation has failed as a doctrine for the control of traditional crime, it can succeed with corporate crime.

The disenchantment of criminologists in the past two decades with rehabilitation as a response to traditional crime has been even more profound than has the disillusionment with deterrence. The high tide of this change was the publication of the massive and detailed review of the effectiveness of correctional rehabilitation programs by Lipton, Martinson, and Wilks.[31] Even though Martinson stated at a later time that the review should not be used to justify a wholesale rejection of rehabilitation as a goal for the criminal justice system, the raw data which aroused the mood of pessimism are still there for all to see; and since the publication of the review there has hardly been a flood of studies showing that rehabilitative programs really do reduce crime.

There is little reason to suspect that individuals responsible for corporate crime, or white collar crime generally, should be any more amenable to rehabilitation than are traditional offenders. As Morris noted,

> What would Jimmy Hoffa discuss with his caseworker, in or out of prison, relevant to Hoffa's psyche or the manipulation of power within a union? A discussion between Spiro Agnew and his probation officer, had any unfortunate been appointed to that task, is even more mind boggling.[32]

Although rehabilitating individuals would seem as unpromising with corporate as with traditional offenders, rehabilitating the corporation itself is a different matter. Many corporate crimes arise from defective control systems, insufficient checks and balances within the organization to ensure the law is complied with, poor communication, and inadequate standard operating procedures which fail to incorporate safeguards against reckless behavior.[33] Sometimes these organizational defects are intentional, manifesting a conscious decision by the corporate hierarchy to turn a blind eye to corner cutting in order to get results.[34] Sometimes the defects reflect sloppiness or managerial negligence. The chief executive of a pharmaceutical company, for example, might consciously ignore a situation in which his quality control director was overruled by the production manager when a batch of drugs was rejected for want of purity. If the organization were reformed so that the person responsible for achieving production targets was no longer able to overrule quality control, and if only the chief executive officer could reverse a quality control finding, and then only in writing, the chief executive could no longer turn a blind eye to avoid the situation.

Regulatory agencies have an arsenal of weapons with which to force corporations to correct criminogenic policies and practices. They can insist upon, for example, abolition of off-the-books accounts, multiple approvals for specified actions, routine reporting of certain matters to committees of outside directors, and the establishment of internal compliance groups who report directly to the board with recommendations for sanctioning individuals who fail to abide by corporate policies. Rehabilitation is a more workable strategy with corporate crime than with traditional crime because criminogenic organizational structures are more malleable than are criminogenic human personalities. A new internal compliance group can be put in place much more readily than can a new superego. Moreover, state-imposed reorganization of the structure of a publicly traded company is not so unconscionable an encroachment on individual freedom as is state-imposed rearrangement of a psyche.

Hopkins, in the only systematic published study of the rehabilitation of corporate offenders, concluded that most companies prosecuted under the consumer protection provisions of the Australian Trade Practices Act introduced at least some measures to ensure that the offense did not recur.[35] Case studies based on interviews by Fisse and one of the present authors with executives involved in major corporate crimes in America confirm Hopkins's finding. In the aftermath of public disclosure of corporate crimes and the ensuing scandals, many, although not all, corporations changed internal policies and procedures to reduce the probability of reoffending. Much of this corporate rehabilitation undoubtedly took place because of prodding by regulatory agencies. Large corporations tend to be responsive to the demands of regulators in making internal reform following the unveiling of a corporate crime in part because they want the pressure exerted by regulators to cease.

A number of formal mechanisms can be used to bring about corporate rehabilitation: consent decrees negotiated with regulatory agencies[36]; probation orders placing the corporation under the supervision of an auditor, environmental expert, or other authority who would ensure that an order to restructure compliance systems was carried out[37]; or suspended sentencing of convicted corporations by the courts, contingent on their producing a report on the weaknesses of their old compliance systems and implementing new ones.[38]

DISCUSSION

It has been argued that the largely discredited doctrines of crime control by public disgrace, deterrence, incapacitation, and rehabilitation could become highly successful when applied to corporate crime. More generally, it has been argued that when the accumulated insight of criminology tells us that something is true of traditional crime, in many respects we can expect the opposite to be true of corporate crime.

Hence, there is reason for optimism that where we have failed with street crime, we might succeed with suite crime. Because corporate crime is more preventable than other types of crime, the persons and property of citizens can be better protected; and restitution is a more viable goal for corporate than for traditional criminal law. Convicted corporations generally have a better capacity than do individuals to compensate the victims of their crimes.

Even though corporate crime is potentially more preventable and its victims are more readily compensated, there is no guarantee that either prevention or restitution will happen under traditional legal systems. This is because of our third proposition: Convictions are extremely difficult in complex cases involving powerful corporations. There are at least two ways of dealing with this problem. One is for regulatory agencies to achieve the goals of deterrence, incapacitation, and rehabilitation by nonprosecutorial means. They readily can do this if they have sufficient bargaining power. Consider the tactics of the Securities and Exchange Commission in the foreign bribery scandals of the latter half of the 1970s. In many cases the agency may have effected significant deterrence through the adverse publicity that followed public disclosure of the largest scandals, a modicum of incapacitation in cases where corporations forced responsible senior executives into early retirement, and a considerable amount of rehabilitation through consent orders that mandated audit committees of outside directors, outlawed off-the-books accounts, and led to other reforms which, although far from eliminating the prospect of bribery, certainly made it a much riskier and therefore less rational business practice.[39] At the same time, criticism of the agency on a number of grounds regarding the small number of cases referred to the Justice Department for prosecution assuredly was justified.

In an illuminating article detailing why law enforcers so often choose to practice informal enforcement, Schrag discusses why he abandoned the prosecutorial stance that he brought to his position as head of the enforcement division of the New York City Department of Consumer Affairs.[40] A variety of frustrations, especially the use of delaying tactics by company lawyers, led to substitution of a "direct action" model for the "judicial" model. Nonlitigious methods which were increasingly used included threats and use of adverse publicity, revocation of licenses, direct contact of consumers to warn them of company practices, and pressure exerted on reputable financial institutions and suppliers to withdraw support of the targeted company. As Schrag points out, the dilemma of the direct action model is that it gets results without any regard for the due process rights of targeted "offenders."

An alternative to substituting the direct action for the judicial model is to reform the law so that the conviction of guilty corporations is made easier. The precise nature of such reform is beyond the scope of the present paper. What we have attempted is to establish a case for the premise to undergird such a program of law reform: *The fact that a principle has been found to be justified in dealing with traditional crime is not a satisfactory rationale for its application to corporate crime.* If valid, the six propositions in this paper force the conclusion that corporate crime is a conceptually quite different domain from traditional crime. Consequently, we should never reject a strategy for controlling corporate crime merely because that strategy has been found wanting, on the grounds of either justice or efficacy, with traditional crime.

NOTES

1. Joel Swartz, "Silent Killers at Work," *Crime and Social Justice*, Summer 1975, pp. 15–20; W. G. Carson, "White-Collar Crime and the Enforcement of Factory Legislation," *British Journal of Criminology*, October 1970, pp. 383–98.
2. John Braithwaite, "An Exploratory Study of Used Car Fraud," in *Two Faces of Deviance*, Paul R. Wilson and John Braithwaite, eds. (St. Lucia, Australia: University of Queensland Press, 1978), pp. 101–22.
3. John Braithwaite, *Corporate Crime in the Pharmaceutical Industry* (London, England: Routledge and Kegan Paul, in press), ch. 2.
4. John Hagan, Ilene H. Nagel, and Celesta Albonetti, "Differential Sentencing of White-Collar Offenders," *American Sociological Review*, December 1980, pp. 802–20.
5. Only 2.8 percent of defendants in cases terminated before United States district courts in 1977 were found not guilty. *Sourcebook of Criminal Justice Statistics—1979* (Washington, D.C.: Law Enforcement Assistance Administration, 1980), p. 555.
6. Clinard et al., *Illegal Corporate Behavior*, p. 291; Carson, "White-Collar Crime and the Enforcement of Factory Legislation"; Ross Cranston, *Regulating Business: Law and Consumer Agencies* (London, England: Macmillan, 1979).
7. Adam Sutton and Ron Wild, "Corporate Crime and Social Structure," in *Two Faces of Deviance*, Wilson and Braithwaite, eds., pp. 177–98; John Braithwaite, "Inegalitarian Consequences of Egalitarian Reforms to Control Corporate Crime," *Temple Law Quarterly*, vol. 53, no. 4 (1980), pp. 1127–46.
8. Adam Sutton and Ron Wild, "Companies, the Law and the Professions: A Sociological View of Australian Companies Legislation,"

in *Legislation and Society in Australia*, Roman Tomasic, ed. (Sydney, Australia: Allen and Unwin, 1979), pp. 200–13; Abraham J. Briloff, *Unaccountable Accounting* (New York: Harper and Row, 1972).

9. Gilbert Geis and Herbert Edelhertz, "Criminal Law and Consumer Fraud: A Sociolegal View," *American Criminal Law Review*, Summer 1973, p. 1006. See Holland v. U.S., 348 U.S. 121, 139–40 (1954); U.S. v. Woodner, 317 F.2d 649, 651 (2d Cir. 1963).

10. Mark J. Green, *The Other Government: The Unseen Power of Washington Lawyers*, rev. ed. (New York: W. W. Norton, 1978).

11. It may be that individual corporate actors are following standard operating procedures which were written by a committee, many of whose members are now retired, deceased, or working elsewhere. Consider Simeon M. Kriesberg, "Decisionmaking Models and the Control of Corporate Crime," *Yale Law Journal*, July 1976, pp. 1091–129.

12. In *Corporate Crime in the Pharmaceutical Industry*, Braithwaite concludes that many corporations present to the outside world a picture of diffused accountability for law observance, while ensuring that lines of accountability are in fact clearly defined for internal compliance purposes.

13. See the discussion of this problem in relation to the Abbott case study, ibid., ch. 4.

14. Donald J. West and David P. Farrington, *The Delinquent Way of Life* (New York: Crane Russak, 1977).

15. W. Brent Fisse, "The Use of Publicity as a Criminal Sanction against Business Corporations," *Melbourne University Law Review*, June 1971, pp. 250–79.

16. Michael R. Geerken and Walter R. Gove, "Deterrence: Some Theoretical Considerations," *Law & Society Review*, Spring 1975, p. 509. See also Franklin E. Zimring and Gordon J. Hawkins, *Deterrence: The Legal Threat in Crime Control* (Chicago: University of Chicago Press, 1973), pp. 127–28; Johannes Andenaes, "Deterrence and Specific Offenses," *University of Chicago Law Review*, Spring 1971, p. 545.

17. Marshall B. Clinard and Robert F. Meier, *Sociology of Deviant Behavior*, 5th ed. (New York: Holt, Rinehart and Winston, 1979), p. 248.

18. Dorothy Miller et al., "Public Knowledge of Criminal Penalties: A Research Report," in *Theories of Punishment*, Stanley Grupp, ed. (Bloomington: Indiana University Press, 1971), pp. 205–26.

19. M. David Ermann and Richard J. Lundman, "Deviant Acts by Complex Organizations: Deviance and Social Control at the Organizational Level of Analysis," *Sociological Quarterly*, Winter 1978, p. 64.

20. Jocelynne A. Scutt, "The Fine as a Penal Measure in the United States of America, Canada and Australia," in *Die Geldstrafe im Deutschen und Auslandischen Recht*, Hans-Heinrich Jescheck and Gerhardt Grebing, eds. (Baden-Baden, Germany: Nomos Verlagsgesellschaft, 1978), pp. 1062–181.

21. Trevor Nagel, "The Fine as a Sanction against Corporations" (Ph.D. diss., University of Adelaide Law School, 1979); Laura Shill Schrager and James F. Short, "Toward a Sociology of Organizational Crime," *Social Problems*, April 1978, pp. 407–19.

22. Edward Gross, "Organizations as Criminal Actors," in *Two Faces of Deviance*, Wilson and Braithwaite, eds., p. 202.

23. Clinard, *Black Market*; Marshall B. Clinard and Peter C. Yeager, *Corporate Crime* (New York: Free Press, 1980); Saxon, *White-Collar Crime*; Gilbert Geis, "Criminal Penalties for Corporate Criminals," *Criminal Law Bulletin*, June 1972, pp. 377–92; Developments in the Law: "Corporate Crime"; Richard A. Posner, *Antitrust Law: An Economic Perspective* (Chicago: University of Chicago Press, 1976); Kenneth Elzinga and William Briet, *The Antitrust Penalties: A Study in Law and Economics* (New Haven, Conn.: Yale University Press, 1976); Stephen A. Yoder, "Criminal Sanctions for Corporate Illegality," *Journal of Criminal Law and Criminology*, Spring 1978, pp. 40–58.

24. G. deQ. Walker, "The Trade Practices Act at Work," in *Australian Trade Practices*, John

P. Nieuwenhuysen, ed. (London, England: Croom Helm, 1976), pp. 146–47.

25. Michael K. Block, Frederick C. Nold, and Joseph G. Sidak, "The Deterrent Effect of Antitrust Enforcement," *Journal of Political Economy*, June 1981, pp. 429–45.

26. Michael S. Lewis-Beck and John R. Alford, "Can Government Regulate Safety? The Coal Mine Example," *American Political Science Review*, September 1980, pp. 745–56.

27. Ernst A. Wenk, James O. Robison, and Gerald W. Smith, "Can Violence Be Predicted?" *Crime and Delinquency*, October 1972, pp. 393–402; Joseph Cocozza and Henry J. Steadman, "Prediction in Psychiatry: An Example of Misplaced Confidence in Experts," *Social Problems*, February 1978, pp. 267–76; Murray L. Cohen, A. Nicholas Groth, and Richard Siegel, "The Clinical Prediction of Dangerousness," *Crime & Delinquency*, January 1978, pp. 28–39; Simon Dinitz and John P. Conrad, "Thinking about Dangerous Offenders," *Criminal Justice Abstracts*, March 1978, pp. 99–130; John Monahan, "The Prediction of Violent Criminal Behavior: A Methodological Critique and Prospectus," in *Deterrence and Incapacitation*, Blumstein, Cohen, and Nagin, eds., pp. 244–69.

28. Stone, *Where the Law Ends*, pp. 148–49.

29. The coal industry is a classic illustration of how some corporations are well known to have a superior record of compliance compared with the performance of others. Generally, it is the mines owned by the large steel corporations, with the safety compliance systems they bring from their parent industry, that have superior safety performance. In 1978–79 Westmorland Coal Co. had an injury incidence rate seven times as high as the rate in mines owned by U.S. Steel. Ben A. Franklin, "New Effort to Make Mines Safer," *New York Times*, Nov. 22, 1980, pp. L29, L32.

30. Morton Mintz, *By Prescription Only* (Boston: Houghton-Mifflin, 1967), p. 383j.

31. Douglas Lipton, Robert Martinson, and Judith Wilks, *The Effectiveness of Correctional Treatment: A Survey of Treatment Evaluation Studies* (New York: Praeger, 1975).

32. Norval Morris, *The Future of Imprisonment* (Chicago: University of Chicago Press, 1974), p. 20.

33. Hopkins, "Anatomy of Corporate Crime"; Braithwaite, *Corporate Crime in the Pharmaceutical Industry*.

34. Stone, *Where the Law Ends*, pp. 199–216.

35. Hopkins, "Anatomy of Corporate Crime."

36. This technique has been particularly popular with the United States Securities and Exchange Commission. For a more refined version of this general approach, see Fisse's development of the idea of court-imposed "preventive orders." W. Brent Fisse, "Responsibility, Prevention and Corporate Crime," *New Zealand Universities Law Review*, April 1973, pp. 250–79.

37. Comment: "Structural Crime and Institutional Rehabilitation: A New Approach to Corporate Sentencing," *Yale Law Journal*, December 1979, pp. 353–75; John Collins Coffee, Jr., "Corporate Crime and Punishment: A Non-Chicago View of the Economics of Criminal Sanctions," *American Criminal Law Review*, Spring 1980, pp. 419–78.

38. Fisse suggests adjournment of sentence as a "back-door to enter the internal affairs of an offender" by reference to Trade Practices Commission v. Pye Industries Sales Pty. Ltd., A.T.P.R. 40-089 (1978); W. Brent Fisse, "Criminal Law and Consumer Protection," in *Consumer Protection Law and Theory*, Anthony J. Duggan and Leanna W. Darvall, eds. (Sydney, Australia: Law Book Co., 1980).

39. Edward D. Herlihy and Theodore A. Levine, "Corporate Crisis: The Overseas Payment Problem," *Law and Policy in International Business*, vol. 8, no. 4 (1976), pp. 547–629. Note also Arthur F. Mathews, "Recent Trends in SEC Requested Ancillary Relief in SEC Level Injunctive Actions," *Business Lawyer*, March 1976, pp. 1323–52.

40. Schrag, "On Her Majesty's Secret Service."

State-Organized Crime

William J. Chambliss

There is a form of crime that has heretofore escaped criminological inquiry, yet its persistence and omnipresence raise theoretical and methodological issues crucial to the development of criminology as a science. I am referring to what I call "state-organized crime."

STATE-ORGANIZED CRIME DEFINED

The most important type of criminality organized by the state consists of acts defined by law as criminal and committed by state officials in the pursuit of their job as representatives of the state. Examples include a state's complicity in piracy, smuggling, assasinations, criminal conspiracies, acting as an accessory before or after the fact, and violating laws that limit their activities. In the latter category would be included the use of illegal methods of spying on citizens, diverting funds in ways prohibited by law (e.g., illegal campaign contributions, selling arms to countries prohibited by law, and supporting terrorist activities).

State-organized crime does not include criminal acts that benefit only individual officeholders, such as the acceptance of bribes or the illegal use of violence by the police against individuals, unless such acts violate existing criminal law and are official policy. For example, the current policies of torture and random violence by the police in South Africa are incorporated under the category of state-organized crime because, apparently, those practices are both state policy and in violation of existing South African law. On the other hand, the excessive use of violence by the police in urban ghettoes is not state-organized crime for it lacks the necessary institutionalized policy of the state.

From *Criminology*, v. 27, No. 2 (1989): 183–207. Reprinted by permission of the American Society of Criminology and the author.

SMUGGLING

Smuggling occurs when a government has successfully cornered the market on some commodity or when it seeks to keep a commodity of another nation from crossing its borders. In the annals of crime, everything from sheep to people, wool to wine, gold to drugs, and even ideas, have been prohibited for either export or import. Paradoxically, whatever is prohibited, it is at the expense of one group of people for the benefit of another. Thus, the laws that prohibit the import or export of a commodity inevitably face a built-in resistance. Some part of the population will always want to either possess or to distribute the prohibited goods. At times, the state finds itself in the position of having its own interests served by violating precisely the same laws passed to prohibit the export or import of the goods it has defined as illegal.

Narcotics and the Vietnam War

Sometime around the eighth century, Turkish traders discovered a market for opium in Southeast Asia (Chambliss, 1977; McCoy, 1973). Portuguese traders several centuries later found a thriving business in opium trafficking conducted by small ships sailing between trading ports in the area. One of the prizes of Portuguese piracy was the opium that was taken from local traders and exchanged for tea, spices, and pottery. Several centuries later, when the French colonized Indochina, the traffic in opium was a thriving business. The French joined the drug traffickers and licensed opium dens throughout Indochina. With the profits from those licenses, the French supported 50% of the cost of their colonial government (McCoy, 1973:27).

When the Communists began threatening French rule in Indochina, the French government used the opium profits to finance the

war. It also used cooperation with the hill tribes who controlled opium production as a means of ensuring the allegiance of the hill tribes in the war against the Communists (McCoy, 1973).

The French were defeated in Vietnam and withdrew, only to be replaced by the United States. The United States inherited the dependence on opium profits and the cooperation of the hill tribes, who in turn depended on being allowed to continue growing and shipping opium. The CIA went a step further than the French and provided the opium-growing feudal lords in the mountains of Vietnam, Laos, Cambodia, and Thailand with transportation for their opium via Air America, the CIA airline in Vietnam.

Air America regularly transported bundles of opium from airstrips in Laos, Cambodia, and Burma to Saigon and Hong Kong (Chambliss, 1977:56). An American stationed at Long Cheng, the secret CIA military base in northern Laos during the war, observed:

> . . . so long as the Meo leadership could keep their wards in the boondocks fighting and dying in the name of, for these unfortunates anyway, some nebulous cause . . . the Meo leadership [was paid off] in the form of a carte-blanch to exploit U.S.-supplied airplanes and communication gear to the end of greatly streamlining the opium operations. (Chambliss, 1977:56).

This report was confirmed by Laotian Army General Ouane Rattikone, who told me in an interview in 1974 that he was the principal overseer of the shipment of opium out of the Golden Triangle via Air America. U.S. law did not permit the CIA or any of its agents to engage in the smuggling of opium.

After France withdrew from Vietnam and left the protection of democracy to the United States, the French intelligence service that preceded the CIA in managing the opium smuggling in Asia continued to support part of its clandestine operations through drug trafficking (Kruger, 1980). Although those operations are shrouded in secrecy, the evidence is very strong that the French intelligence agencies helped to organize the movement of opium through the Middle East (especially Morocco) after their revenue from opium from Southeast Asia was cut off.

In 1969 Michael Hand, a former Green Beret and one of the CIA agents stationed at Long Cheng when Air America was shipping opium, moved to Australia, ostensibly as a private citizen. On arriving in Australia, Hand entered into a business partnership with an Australian national, Frank Nugan. In 1976 they established the Nugan Hand Bank in Sydney (Commonwealth of New South Wales, 1982a, 1982b). The Nugan Hand Bank began as a storefront operation with minimal capital investment, but almost immediately it boasted deposits of over $25 million. The rapid growth of the bank resulted from large deposits of secret funds made by narcotics and arms smugglers and large deposits from the CIA (Nihill, 1982).

In addition to the records from the bank that suggest the CIA was using the bank as a conduit for its funds, the bank's connection to the CIA and other U.S. intelligence agencies is evidenced by the people who formed the directors and principal officers of the bank, including the following:

- Admiral Earl F. Yates, president of the Nugan Hand Bank was, during the Vietnam War, chief of staff for strategic planning of U.S. forces in Asia and the Pacific.
- General Edwin F. Black, president of Nugan Hand's Hawaii branch, was commander of U.S. troops in Thailand during the Vietnam War and, after the war, assistant army chief of staff for the Pacific.

- General Erle Cocke, Jr., head of the Nugan Hand Washington, D.C., office.
- George Farris, worked in the Nugan Hand Hong Kong and Washington, D.C. offices. Farris was a military intelligence specialist who worked in a special forces training base in the Pacific.
- Bernie Houghton, Nugan Hand's representative in Saudi Arabia. Houghton was also a U.S. naval intelligence undercover agent.
- Thomas Clines, director of training in the CIA's clandestine service, was a London operative for Nugan Hand who helped in the takeover of a London-based bank and was stationed at Long Cheng with Michael Hand and Theodore S. Shackley during the Vietnam War.
- Dale Holmgreen, former flight service manager in Vietnam for Civil Air Transport, which became Air America. He was on the board of directors of Nugan Hand and ran the bank's Taiwan office.
- Walter McDonald, an economist and former deputy director of CIA for economic research, was a specialist in petroleum. He became a consultant to Nugan Hand and served as head of its Annapolis, Maryland, branch.
- General Roy Manor, who ran the Nugan Hand Philippine office, was a Vietnam veteran who helped coordinate the aborted attempt to rescue the Iranian hostages, chief of staff for the U.S. Pacific command, and the U.S. government's liaison officer to Philippine President Ferdinand Marcos.

On the board of directors of the parent company formed by Michael Hand that preceded the Nugan Hand Bank were Grant Walters, Robert Peterson, David M. Houton, and Spencer Smith, all of whom listed their address as c/o Air America, Army Post Office, San Francisco, California.

Also working through the Nugan Hand Bank was Edwin F. Wilson, a CIA agent involved in smuggling arms to the Middle East and later sentenced to prison by a U.S. court for smuggling illegal arms to Libya. Edwin Wilson's associate in Mideast arms shipments was Theodore Shackley, head of the Miami, Florida, CIA station.[1] In 1973, when William Colby was made director of Central Intelligence, Shackley replaced him as head of covert operations for the Far East; on his retirement from the CIA William Colby became Nugan Hand's lawyer.

In the late 1970s the bank experienced financial difficulties, which led to the death of Frank Nugan. He was found dead of a shotgun blast in his Mercedes Benz on a remote road outside Sydney. The official explanation was suicide, but some investigators speculated that he might have been murdered. In any event, Nugan's death created a major banking scandal and culminated in a government investigation. The investigation revealed that millions of dollars were unaccounted for in the bank's records and that the bank was serving as a money-laundering operation for narcotics smugglers and as a conduit through which the CIA was financing gun smuggling and other illegal operations throughout the world. These operations included illegally smuggling arms to South Africa and the Middle East. There was also evidence that the CIA used the Nugan Hand Bank to pay for political campaigns that slandered politicians, including Australia's Prime Minister Witham (Kwitny, 1977).

Michael Hand tried desperately to cover up the operations of the bank. Hundreds of documents were destroyed before investigators could get into the bank. Despite Hand's efforts, the scandal mushroomed and eventually Hand was forced to flee Australia. He managed this, while under indictment for a rash of felonies, with the aid of a CIA official who flew to Australia with a false passport and accompanied him out of the country. Hand's father, who lives in New York, denies knowing anything about his son's whereabouts.

Thus, the evidence uncovered by the government investigation in Australia linked high-level CIA officials to a bank in Sydney that was responsible for financing and laundering money for a significant part of the narcotics trafficking originating in Southeast Asia (Commonwealth of New South Wales, 1982b; Owen, 1983). It also linked the CIA to arms smuggling and illegal involvement in the democratic processes of a friendly nation. Other investigations reveal that the events in Australia were but part of a worldwide involvement in narcotics and arms smuggling by the CIA and French intelligence (Hougan, 1978; Kruger, 1980; Owen, 1983).

Arms Smuggling

One of the most important forms of state-organized crime today is arms smuggling. To a significant extent, U.S. involvement in narcotics smuggling after the Vietnam War can be understood as a means of funding the purchase of military weapons for nations and insurgent groups that could not be funded legally through congressional allocations or for which U.S. law prohibited support (NARMIC, 1984).

In violation of U.S. law, members of the National Security Council (NSC), the Department of Defense, and the CIA carried out a plan to sell millions of dollars worth of arms to Iran and use profits from those sales to support the Contras in Nicaragua (Senate Hearings, 1986). The Boland amendment, effective in 1985, prohibited any U.S. official from directly or indirectly assisting the Contras. To circumvent the law, a group of intelligence and military officials established a "secret team" of U.S. operatives, including Lt. Colonel Oliver North, Theodore Shackley, Thomas Clines, and Maj. General Richard Secord, among others (testimony before U.S. Senate, 1986). Shackley and Clines, as noted, were CIA agents in Long Cheng; along with Michael Hand they ran the secret war in Laos, which was financed in part from profits from opium smuggling. Shackley and Clines had also been involved in the 1961 invasion of Cuba and were instrumental in hiring organized-crime figures in an attempt to assassinate Fidel Castro.

Senator Daniel Inouye of Hawaii claims that this "secret government within our government" waging war in Third World countries was part of the Reagan doctrine (the *Guardian*, July 29, 1987). Whether President Reagan or then Vice President Bush were aware of the operations is yet to be established. What cannot be doubted in the face of overwhelming evidence in testimony before the Senate and from court documents is that this group of officials of the state oversaw and coordinated the distribution and sale of weapons to Iran and to the Contras in Nicaragua. These acts were in direct violation of the Illegal Arms Export Control Act, which made the sale of arms to Iran unlawful, and the Boland amendment, which made it a criminal act to supply the Contras with arms or funds.

The weapons that were sold to Iran were obtained by the CIA through the Pentagon. Secretary of Defense Caspar Weinberger ordered the transfer of weapons from Army stocks to the CIA without the knowledge of Congress four times in 1986. The arms were then transferred to middlemen, such as Iranian arms dealer Yaacov Nimrodi, exiled Iranian arms dealer Manucher Ghorbanifar, and Saudi

Arabian businessman Adman Khashoggi. Weapons were also flown directly to the Contras, and funds from the sale of weapons were diverted to support Contra warfare. There is also considerable evidence that this "secret team," along with other military and CIA officials, cooperated with narcotics smuggling in Latin America in order to fund the Contras in Nicaragua.

In 1986, the Reagan administration admitted that Adolfo Chamorro's Contra group, which was supported by the CIA, was helping a Colombian drug trafficker transport drugs into the United States. Chamorro was arrested in April 1986 for his involvement (Potter and Bullington, 1987:54). Testimony in several trials of major drug traffickers in the past 5 years has revealed innumerable instances in which drugs were flown from Central America into the United States with the cooperation of military and CIA personnel. These reports have also been confirmed by military personnel and private citizens who testified that they saw drugs being loaded on planes in Central America and unloaded at military bases in the United States. Pilots who flew planes with arms to the Contras report returning with planes carrying drugs.

At the same time that the United States was illegally supplying the Nicaraguan Contras with arms purchased, at least in part, with profits from the sale of illegal drugs, the administration launched a campaign against the Sandanistas for their alleged involvement in drug trafficking. Twice during his weekly radio shows in 1986, President Reagan accused the Sandanistas of smuggling drugs. Barry Seal, an informant and pilot for the Drug Enforcement Administration (DEA) was ordered by members of the CIA and DEA to photograph the Sandanistas loading a plane. During a televised speech in March 1986, Reagan showed the picture that Seal took and said that it showed Sandinista officials loading a plane with drugs for shipment to the United States. After the photo was displayed, Congress appropriated $100 million in aid for the Contras. Seal later admitted to reporters that the photograph he took was a plane being loaded with crates that did not contain drugs. He also told reporters that he was aware of the drug smuggling activities of the Contra network and a Colombian cocaine syndicate. For his candor, Seal was murdered in February 1987. Shortly after his murder, the DEA issued a "low key clarification" regarding the validity of the photograph, admitting that there was no evidence that the plane was being loaded with drugs.

Other testimony linking the CIA and U.S. military officials to complicity in drug trafficking includes the testimony of John Stockwell, a former high-ranking CIA official, who claims that drug smuggling and the CIA were essential components in the private campaign for the Contras. Corroboration for these assertions comes also from George Morales, one of the largest drug traffickers in South America, who testified that he was approached by the CIA in 1984 to fly weapons into Nicaragua. Morales claims that the CIA opened up an airstrip in Costa Rica and gave the pilots information on how to avoid radar traps. According to Morales, he flew 20 shipments of weapons into Costa Rica in 1984 and 1985. In return, the CIA helped him to smuggle thousands of kilos of cocaine into the United States. Morales alone channeled $250,000 quarterly to Contra leader Adolfo Chamorro from his trafficking activity. A pilot for Morales, Gary Betzner, substantiated Morales's claims and admitted flying 4,000 pounds of arms into Costa Rica and 500 kilos of cocaine to Lakeland, Florida, on his return trips. From 1985 to 1987, the CIA arranged 50 to 100 flights using U.S. airports that did not undergo inspection.

The destination of the flights by Morales and Betzner was a hidden airstrip on the ranch of John Hull. Hull, an admitted CIA agent, was a primary player in Oliver North's plan to aid the Contras. Hull's activities were closely monitored by Robert Owen, a key player in the Contra supply network. Owen established the Institute for Democracy, Education, and Assistance, which raised money to buy arms for the Contras and which, in October 1985, was asked by Congress to distribute $50,000 in "humanitarian aid" to the Contras. Owen worked for Oliver North in coordinating illegal aid to the Contras and setting up the airstrip on the ranch of John Hull.

According to an article in the *Nation*, Oliver North's network of operatives and mercenaries had been linked to the largest drug cartel in South America since 1983. The DEA estimates that Colombian Jorge Ochoa Vasquez, the "kingpin" of the Medellin drug empire, is responsible for supplying 70% to 80% of the cocaine that enters the United States every year. Ochoa was taken into custody by Spanish police in October 1984 when a verbal order was sent by the U.S. Embassy in Madrid for his arrest. The embassy specified that Officer Cos-Gayon, who had undergone training with the DEA, should make the arrest. Other members of the Madrid Judicial Police were connected to the DEA and North's arms smuggling network. Ochoa's lawyers informed him that the United States would alter his extradition if he agreed to implicate the Sandanista government in drug trafficking. Ochoa refused and spent 20 months in jail before returning to Colombia. The Spanish courts ruled that the United States was trying to use Ochoa to discredit Nicaragua and released him (*The Nation*, September 5, 1987).

There are other links between the U.S. government and the Medellin cartel. Jose

Blandon, General Noriega's former chief advisor, claims that DEA operations have protected the drug empire in the past and that the DEA paid Noriega $4.7 million for his silence. Blandon also testified in Senate committee hearings that Panama's bases were used as training camps for the Contras in exchange for "economic" support from the United States. Finally, Blandon contends that the CIA gave Panamanian leaders intelligence documents about U.S. senators and aides; the CIA denies these charges (*Christian Science Monitor*, February 11, 1988:3).

Other evidence of the interrelationship among drug trafficking, the CIA, the NSC, and aid to the Contras includes the following:

- In January 1983, two Contra leaders in Costa Rica persuaded the Justice Department to return over $36,000 in drug profits to drug dealers Julio Zavala and Carlos Cabezas for aid to the Contras (Potter and Bullington, 1987:22).
- Michael Palmer, a drug dealer in Miami, testified that the State Department's Nicaraguan humanitarian assistance office contracted with his company, Vortex Sales and Leasing, to take humanitarian aid to the Contras. Palmer claims that he smuggled $40 million in marijuana to the United States between 1977 and 1985 (*Guardian*, March 20, 1988:3).
- During House and Senate hearings in 1986, it was revealed that a major DEA investigation of the Medellin drug cartel of Colombia, which was expected to culminate in the arrest of several leaders of the cartel, was compromised when someone in the White House leaked the story of the investigation to the *Washington Times* (a conservative newspaper in Washington, D.C.), which published the story on July 17, 1984. According to

DEA Administrator John Lawn, the leak destroyed what was "probably one of the most significant operations in DEA history" (Sharkey, 1988:24).
- When Honduran General Jose Buseo, who was described by the Justice Department as an "international terrorist," was indicted for conspiring to murder the president of Honduras in a plot financed by profits from cocaine smuggling, Oliver North and officials from the Department of Defense and the CIA pressured the Justice Department to be lenient with General Buseo. In a memo disclosed by the Iran-Contra committee, North stated that if Buseo was not protected "he will break his longstanding silence about the Nic[araguan] resistance and other sensitive operations" (Sharkey, 1988:27).

On first blush, it seems odd that government agencies and officials would engage in such wholesale disregard of the law. As a first step in building an explanation for these and other forms of state-organized crime, let us try to understand why officials of the CIA, the NSC, and the Department of Defense would be willing to commit criminal acts in pursuit of other goals.

WHY?

Why would government officials from the NSC, the Defense Department, the State Department, and the CIA become involved in smuggling arms and narcotics, money laundering, assassinations, and other criminal activities? The answer lies in the structural contradictions that inhere in nation-states (Chambliss, 1980).

As Weber, Marx, and Gramsci pointed out, no state can survive without establishing legitimacy. The law is a fundamental cornerstone in creating legitimacy and an illusion (at least) of social order. It claims universal principles that demand some behaviors and prohibit others. The protection of property and personal security are obligations assumed by states everywhere both as a means of legitimizing the state's franchise on violence and as a means of protecting commercial interests (Chambliss and Seidman, 1982).

The threat posed by smuggling to both personal security and property interests makes laws prohibiting smuggling essential. Under some circumstances, however, such laws contradict other interests of the state. This contradiction prepares the ground for state-organized crime as a solution to the conflicts and dilemmas posed by the simultaneous existence of contradictory "legitimate" goals.

The military-intelligence establishment in the United States is resolutely committed to fighting the spread of "communism" throughout the world. This mission is not new but has prevailed since the 1800s. Congress and the presidency are not consistent in their support for the money and policies thought by the frontline warriors to be necessary to accomplish their lofty goals. As a result, programs under way are sometimes undermined by a lack of funding and even by laws that prohibit their continuation (such as the passage of laws prohibiting support for the Contras). Officials of government agencies adversely affected by political changes are thus placed squarely in a dilemma: If they comply with the legal limitations on their activities they sacrifice their mission. The dilemma is heightened by the fact that they can anticipate future policy changes that will reinstate their resources and their freedom. When that time comes, however, programs adversely affected will be difficult if not impossible to re-create.

A number of events that occurred between 1960 and 1980 left the military and the CIA with badly tarnished images. Those events and political changes underscored their vulnerability. The CIA lost considerable political clout with elected officials when its planned invasion of Cuba (the infamous Bay of Pigs invasion) was a complete disaster. Perhaps as never before in its history, the United States showed itself vulnerable to the resistance of a small nation. The CIA was blamed for this fiasco even though it was President Kennedy's decision to go ahead with the plans that he inherited from the previous administration. To add to the agency's problems, the complicity between it and ITT to invade Chile and overthrow the Allende government was yet another scar (see below), as was the involvement of the CIA in narcotics smuggling in Vietnam.

These and other political realities led to a serious breach between Presidents Kennedy, Johnson, Nixon, and Carter and the CIA. During President Nixon's tenure in the White House, one of the CIA's top men, James Angleton, referred to Nixon's national security advisor, Henry Kissinger (who became secretary of state) as "objectively, a Soviet Agent" (Hougan, 1984:75). Another top agent of the CIA, James McCord (later implicated in the Watergate burglary) wrote a secret letter to his superior, General Paul Gaynor, in January 1973 in which he said:

> When the hundreds of dedicated fine men and women of the CIA no longer write intelligence summaries and reports with integrity, without fear of political recrimination—when their fine Director [Richard Helms] is being summarily discharged in order to make way for a politician who will write or rewrite intelligence the way the politicians want them written, instead of the way truth and best judgment dictates, our nation is in the deepest of trouble and freedom itself was

never so imperiled. Nazi Germany rose and fell under exactly the same philosophy of governmental operation. (Hougan, 1984: 26–27)

McCord (1974:60) spoke for many of the top military and intelligence officers in the United States when he wrote in his autobiography: "I believed that the whole future of the nation was at stake." These views show the depth of feeling toward the dangers of political "interference" with what is generally accepted in the military-intelligence establishment as their mission (Goulden, 1984).

When Jimmy Carter was elected president, he appointed Admiral Stansfield Turner as director of Central Intelligence. At the outset, Turner made it clear that he and the president did not share the agency's view that they were conducting their mission properly (Goulden, 1984; Turner, 1985). Turner insisted on centralizing power in the director's office and on overseeing clandestine and covert operations. He met with a great deal of resistance. Against considerable opposition from within the agency, he reduced the size of the covert operation section from 1,200 to 400 agents. Agency people still refer to this as the "Halloween massacre."

Old hands at the CIA do not think their work is dispensable. They believe zealously, protectively, and one is tempted to say, with religious fervor, that the work they are doing is essential for the salvation of humankind. With threats from both Republican and Democratic administrations, the agency sought alternative sources of revenue to carry out its mission. The alternative was already in place with the connections to the international narcotics traffic, arms smuggling, the existence of secret corporations incorporated in foreign countries (such as Panama), and the established links to banks for the laundering of money for covert operations.

STATE-ORGANIZED ASSASSINATIONS AND MURDER

Assassination plots and political murders are usually associated in people's minds with military dictatorships and European monarchies. The practice of assassination, however, is not limited to unique historical events but has become a tool of international politics that involves modern nation-states of many different types.

In the 1960s a French intelligence agency hired Christian David to assassinate the Moroccan leader Ben Barka (Hougan, 1978:204–207). Christian David was one of those international "spooks" with connections to the DEA, the CIA, and international arms smugglers, such as Robert Vesco.

In 1953 the CIA organized and supervised a coup d'etat in Iran that overthrew the democratically elected government of Mohammed Mossadegh, who had become unpopular with the United States when he nationalized foreign-owned oil companies. The CIA's coup replaced Mossadegh with Reza Shah Pahlevi, who denationalized the oil companies and with CIA guidance established one of the most vicious secret intelligence organizations in the world: SAVAK. In the years to follow, the shah and CIA-trained agents of SAVAK murdered thousands of Iranian citizens. They arrested almost 1,500 people monthly, most of whom were subjected to inhuman torture and punishments without trial. Not only were SAVAK agents trained by the CIA, but there is evidence that they were instructed in techniques of torture (Hersh, 1979:13).

In 1970 the CIA repeated the practice of overthrowing democratically elected governments that were not completely favorable to U.S. investments. When Salvador Allende was elected president of Chile, the CIA organized a coup that overthrew Allende, during which he was murdered, along with the head of the military, General Rene Schneider. Following Allende's overthrow, the CIA trained agents for the Chilean secret service (DINA). DINA set up a team of assassins who could "travel anywhere in the world . . . to carry out sanctions including assassinations" (Dinges and Landau, 1980:239). One of the assassinations carried out by DINA was the murder of Orlando Letellier, Allende's ambassador to the United States and his former minister of defense. Letellier was killed when a car bomb blew up his car on Embassy Row in Washington, D.C. (Dinges and Landau, 1982).

Other bloody coups known to have been planned, organized, and executed by U.S. agents include coups in Guatemala, Nicaragua, the Dominican Republic, and Vietnam. American involvement in those coups was never legally authorized. The murders, assassinations, and terrorist acts that accompany coups are criminal acts by law, both in the United States and in the country in which they take place.

More recent examples of murder and assassination for which government officials are responsible include the death of 80 people in Beirut, Lebanon, when a car bomb exploded on May 8, 1985. The bomb was set by a Lebanese counterterrorist unit working with the CIA. Senator Daniel Moynihan has said that when he was vice president of the Senate Intelligence Committee, President Reagan ordered the CIA to form a small antiterrorist effort in the Mideast. Two sources said that the CIA was working with the group that planted the bomb to kill the Shiite leader Hussein Fadallah (*New York Times*, May 13, 1985).

A host of terrorist plans and activities connected with the attempt to overthrow the Nicaraguan government, including several murders and assassinations, were exposed in an affidavit filed by free-lance reporters Tony Avirgan and Martha Honey. They began investigating Contra activities after Avirgan was injured in an attempt on the life of Contra leader Eden Pastora. In 1986, Honey and Avirgan filed a complaint with the U.S. District Court in Miami charging John Hull, Robert Owen, Theodore Shackley, Thomas Clines, Chi Chi Quintero, Maj. General Richard Secord, and others working for the CIA in Central America with criminal conspiracy and the smuggling of cocaine to aid the Nicaraguan rebels.

A criminal conspiracy in which the CIA admits participating is the publication of a manual, *Psychological Operation in Guerrilla Warfare*, which was distributed to the people of Nicaragua. The manual describes how the people should proceed to commit murder, sabotage, vandalism, and violent acts in order to undermine the government. Encouraging or instigating such crimes is not only a violation of U.S. law, it was also prohibited by Reagan's executive order of 1981, which forbade any U.S. participation in foreign assassinations.

The CIA is not alone in hatching criminal conspiracies. The DEA organized a "Special Operations Group," which was responsible for working out plans to assassinate political and business leaders in foreign countries who were involved in drug trafficking. The head of this group was a former CIA agent, Lou Conein (also known as "Black Luigi"). George Crile wrote in the *Washington Post* (June 13, 1976):

> When you get down to it, Conein was organizing an assassination program. He was frustrated by the big-time operators who were just too insulated to get to . . . Meetings were held to decide whom to target and what method of assassination to employ.

Crile's findings were also supported by the investigative journalist Jim Hougan (1978: 132).

It is a crime to conspire to commit murder. The official record, including testimony by participants in three conspiracies before the U.S. Congress and in court, make it abundantly clear that the crime of conspiring to commit murder is not infrequent in the intelligence agencies of the United States and other countries.

It is also a crime to cover up criminal acts, but there are innumerable examples of instances in which the CIA and the FBI conspired to interfere with the criminal prosecution of drug dealers, murderers, and assassins. In the death of Letellier, mentioned earlier, the FBI and the CIA refused to cooperate with the prosecution of the DINA agents who murdered Letellier (Dinges and Landau, 1980:208–209). Those agencies were also involved in the cover-up of the criminal activities of a Cuban exile, Ricardo (Monkey) Morales. While an employee of the FBI and the CIA, Morales planted a bomb on an Air Cubana flight from Venezuela, which killed 73 people. The Miami police confirmed Morales's claim that he was acting under orders from the CIA (Lernoux, 1984:188). In fact, Morales, who was arrested for overseeing the shipment of 10 tons of marijuana, admitted to being a CIA contract agent who conducted bombings, murders, and assassinations. He was himself killed in a bar after he made public his work with the CIA and the FBI.

OTHER STATE-ORGANIZED CRIMES

Every agency of government is restricted by law in certain fundamental ways. Yet structural pressures exist that can push agencies to go beyond their legal limits. The CIA, for example, is not permitted to engage in domestic intelligence. Despite this, the CIA has opened and photographed the mail of over 1 million private citizens (Rockefeller Report, 1975: 101–115), illegally entered people's homes, and conducted domestic surveillance through electronic devices (Parenti, 1983:170–171).

Agencies of the government also cannot legally conduct experiments on human subjects that violate civil rights or endanger the lives of the subjects. But the CIA conducted experiments on unknowing subjects by hiring prostitutes to administer drugs to their clients. CIA-trained medical doctors and psychologists observed the effects of the drugs through a two-way mirror in expensive apartments furnished to the prostitutes by the CIA. At least one of the victims of these experiments died and others suffered considerable trauma (Anderson and Whitten, 1976; Crewdson and Thomas, 1977; Jacobs 1977a, 1977b).

The most flagrant violation of civil rights by federal agencies is the FBI's counterintelligence program, known as COINTELPRO. This program was designed to disrupt, harass, and discredit groups that the FBI decided were in some way "un-American." Such groups included the American Civil Liberties Union, antiwar movements, civil rights organizations, and a host of other legally constituted political groups whose views opposed some of the policies of the United States (Church Committee, 1976). With the exposure of COINTELPRO, the group was disbanded. There is evidence, however, that the illegal surveillance of U.S. citizens did not stop with the abolition of COINTELPRO but continues today (Klein, 1988).

DISCUSSION

Elsewhere I have suggested a general theory to account for variations in types and frequency of crime (Chambliss, 1988). The starting point for that theory is the assumption that in every era political, economic, and social relations contain certain inherent *contradictions*, which produce *conflicts* and *dilemmas* that people struggle to resolve. The study of state-organized crime brings into sharp relief the necessity of understanding the role of contradictions in the formation and implementation of law.

Contradictions inherent in the formation of states create conditions under which there will be a tendency for state officials to violate the criminal law. State officials inherit from the past laws that were not of their making and that were the result of earlier efforts to resolve conflicts wrought by structural contradictions (Chambliss, 1980; Chambliss and Seidman, 1982). The inherited laws nonetheless represent the foundation on which the legitimacy of the state's authority depends.

Law is a two-edged sword; it creates one set of conflicts while it attempts to resolve another. The passage of a particular law or set of laws may resolve conflicts and enhance state control, but it also limits the legal activities of the state. State officials are thus often caught between conflicting demands as they find themselves constrained by laws that interfere with other goals demanded of them by their roles or their perception of what is in the interests of the state. There is a contradiction, then, between the legal prescriptions and the agreed goals of state agencies. Not everyone caught in this dilemma will opt for violating the law, but some will. Those who do are the perpetrators, but not the cause, of the persistence of state-organized crime.

CONCLUSION

Data on contemporary examples of state-organized crime are difficult to obtain. The data I have been able to gather depend on sources that must be used cautiously. Government hearings, court trials, interviews, newspaper accounts, and historical documents are replete with problems of validity and reliability. In my view they are no more so than conventional research methods in the social sciences, but that does not alter the fact that there is room for error in interpreting the findings. It will require considerable imagination and diligence for others to pursue research on this topic and add to the empirical base from which theoretical propositions can be tested and elaborated.

We need to explore different political, economic, and social systems in varying historical periods to discover why some forms of social organization are more likely to create state-organized crimes than others. We need to explore the possibility that some types of state agencies are more prone to engaging in criminality than others. It seems likely, for example, that state agencies whose activities can be hidden from scrutiny are more likely to engage in criminal acts than those whose record is public. This principle may also apply to whole nation-states: the more open the society, the less likely it is that state-organized crime will become institutionalized.

NOTES

1. It was Shackley who, along with Rafael "Chi Chi" Quintero, a Cuban-American, forged the plot to assassinate Fidel Castro by using organized-crime figures Santo Trafficante, Jr., John Roselli, and Sam Giancana.

REFERENCES

Anderson, Jack, and Lee Whitten. 1976. The CIA's "sex squad." *The Washington Post*, June 22:B13.

Chambliss, William J. 1977. Markets, profits, labor and smack. *Contemporary Crises* 1:53–57.

———. 1980. On lawmaking. *British Journal of Law and Society* 6:149–172.

———. 1988. *Exploring Criminology.* New York: Macmillan.

Chambliss, William J., and Robert B. Seidman. 1982. *Law, Order and Power.* Rev. ed. Reading, Mass.: Addison-Wesley.

Church Committee. 1976. Intelligence Activities and the Rights of Americans. Washington, D.C.: Government Printing Office.

Commonwealth of New South Wales. 1982a. New South Wales Joint Task Force on Drug Trafficking. Federal Parliament Report. Sydney: Government of New South Wales.

———. 1982b. Preliminary Report of the Royal Commission to Investigate the Nugan Hand Bank Failure. Federal Parliament Report. Sydney: Government of New South Wales.

Crewdson, John M., and Jo Thomas. 1977. Abuses in testing of drugs by CIA to be panel focus. *The New York Times,* September 20.

Dinges, John, and Saul Landau. 1982. The CIA's link to Chile's plot. *The Nation,* June 12:712–713.

Goulden, Joseph C. 1984. *Death Merchant: The Brutal True Story of Edwin P. Wilson.* New York: Simon and Schuster.

Hersh, Seymour. 1979. Ex-analyst says CIA rejected warning on Shah. *The New York Times,* January 7:A10. Cited in Piers Beirne and James Messerschmidt, *Criminology.* New York: Harcourt Brace Jovanovich, forthcoming.

Hougan, Jim. 1978. *Spooks: The Haunting of America—The Private Use of Secret Agents.* New York: William Morrow.

———. 1984. *Secret Agenda: Watergate, Deep Throat, and the CIA.* New York: Random House.

Jacobs, John. 1977a. The diaries of a CIA operative. *The Washington Post,* September 5:1.

———. 1977b. Turner cites 149 drug-test projects. *The Washington Post,* August 4:1.

Klein, Lloyd. 1988. Big Brother Is Still Watching You. Paper presented at the annual meetings of the American Society of Criminology, Chicago, November 12.

Kruger, Henrik. 1980. *The Great Heroin Coup.* Boston: South End Press.

Kwitny, Jonathan. 1987. *The Crimes of Patriots.* New York: W. W. Norton.

Lernoux, Penny. 1984. The Miami connection. *The Nation,* February 18:186–198.

McCord, James W., Jr., 1974. *A Piece of Tape.* Rockville, Md.: Washington Media Services.

McCoy, Alfred W., 1973. *The Politics of Heroin in Southeast Asia.* New York: Harper & Row.

NARMIC. 1984. Military Exports to South Africa: A Research Report on the Arms Embargo. Philadelphia: American Friends Service Committee.

Nihill, Grant. 1982. Bank links to spies, drugs. *The Advertiser,* November 10:1.

Owen, John. 1983. *Sleight of Hand: The $25 Million Nugan Hand Bank Scandal.* Sydney: Calporteur Press.

Parenti, Michael. 1983. *Democracy for the Few.* New York: St. Martin's.

Potter, Gary W., and Bruce Bullington. 1987. Drug Trafficking and the Contras: A Case Study of State-Organized Crime. Paper presented at annual meeting of the American Society of Criminology, Montreal.

Rockefeller Report. 1975. Report to the President by the Commission on CIA Activities within the United States. Washington, D.C.: Government Printing Office.

Senate Hearings. 1986. Senate Select Committee on Assassination, Alleged Assassination Plots Involving Foreign Leaders. Interim Report of the Senate Select Committee to Study Governmental Operations with Respect to Intelligence Activities. 94th Cong., 1st sess., November 20. Washington, D.C.: Government Printing Office.

Sharkey, Jacqueline. 1988. The Contra-drug trade eff. *Common Cause Magazine,* September-October: 23–33.

Turner, Stansfield. 1985. *Secrecy and Democracy: The CIA in Transition.* New York: Houghton Mifflin.

STUDY QUESTIONS TO PART II

1. Norval Morris and Gordon Hawkins advocate decriminalizing several types of victimless crimes. (a) Describe their reasoning for decriminalization. (b) How convincing are the arguments and evidence they marshall in support of decriminalization, for each of the crimes discussed? (c) How would Morris and Hawkins respond to the counterargument that these acts should be prohibited on moral grounds?

2. According to James Jacobs and Kimberly Potter, the concept of "hate crime" is problematic. Based on the authors' critique, write an essay describing the main problems with the idea of hate crime.

3. (a) What data source was used in Leslie Margolin's study of child abuse? (b) What additional source of data could be used to enhance or cross-check the information gathered by Margolin?

4. Based on Margolin's essay, describe the main problems with the procedures used by social workers to reach their conclusions that child abuse occurred, and give one example from the case records to illustrate these problems.

5. According to Ronald Burns and Charles Crawford, the problem of school shootings has become a "moral panic" in America. (a) What is a moral panic? (b) What evidence is presented in the article that a moral panic has clouded the issue of school shootings? (c) What are the motives or interests of politicians and media organizations involved in perpetuating the panic over school shootings?

6. Based on Eugene Kanin's study, what are the main differences between college students who have engaged in date rape and those who have not?

7. Based on the reading "Computer Crime," describe the ways in which computer crime may be considered serious and harmful crime.

8. According to John Braithwaite and Gilbert Geis, corporate crime differs from traditional crime in several ways, and these differences mean that traditional crime-control methods might be more successful with respect to corporate crime than conventional crime. (a) Describe the authors' six propositions that address this issue. (b) Evaluate the authors' arguments in support of their propositions: Are they convincing?

9. William Chambliss uses the concept of "structural contradictions" to explain state-organized crime. (a) What does he mean by "contradiction"? (b) Discuss how the idea of contradiction can be used to explain one of the instances of state-organized crime described in his article.

INTRODUCTION TO Part Three: Controversial Crime-Fighting Methods

Some crime-fighting methods are very controversial, so much so that we can question whether they do more harm than good. The readings in Part III focus on several of these disputed laws and practices: racial profiling by the police, the expansion of paramilitary police units, zero-tolerance law enforcement, punitive drug policies, new controls on sex offenders, "three strikes and you're out" laws, DNA testing, gun control, the treatment of juvenile offenders, and the death penalty.

Racial profiling has become one of the most hotly contested practices in criminal justice, attracting critical attention from the media, civil rights groups, and politicians. Some maintain that racial profiling is pervasive (ACLU 1999), while others claim that profiling is a "myth" (MacDonald 2001). *Racial profiling* generally refers to police actions toward citizens that are based on the citizen's race. One type of profiling occurs when officers stop African American motorists either without observing any wrongdoing or under the pretext of a minor traffic infraction, to justify the stop, when the real

reason is either sheer racial harassment or the belief that the stop might uncover evidence of criminality. Police officers tend to presume that race correlates with criminal propensity—specifically, that African Americans are more likely than other races to be carrying drugs or guns or to have been involved in some other criminal activity. Police therefore believe that their discriminatory stops are rational, not invidious. But many others believe that such stops are unjustifiable and do much more harm than good. Most Americans (90 percent) disapprove of racial profiling by the police (Weitzer and Tuch 2002).

The practice is troubling in several respects: It inevitably ensnares more innocent people than criminals; it generates distrust of the police among those who have been stopped; and it increases the chances of confrontations between police officers and black motorists. It is also troubling because it appears to be fairly widespread. In a recent opinion poll, 40 percent of blacks felt that they had, at some time, been stopped by the police because of their race. Young black males appear to be the prime targets: 73 percent of black men ages 18 to 34 said they had been stopped because of their race, compared to only 11 percent of white males in that age group (Weitzer and Tuch 2002).

In his article, "Racial Profiling," David Harris presents evidence documenting racial bias in police stops and shows how the experience of being stopped not only affects those who are stopped but also has a ripple effect on the black community in general, increasing blacks' distrust of the police (see also Harris 1997; Weitzer 1999).

A policing problem that has attracted far less public attention than racial profiling is the growing *militarization* of police departments in the United States. Police paramilitary units (PPUs) have proliferated in recent years, and their activities have expanded to the degree that they sometimes overlap or interfere with routine police practices. Peter Kraska and Victor Kappeler's article, "Militarizing American Police," shows how PPUs have contributed to a broader shift toward more aggressive and obtrusive police practices at the same time that many police departments are embracing the opposite style: community policing.

Evidence of a broader militarization of police practices is found in the authors' examination of how paramilitary units are most frequently deployed. Today, they are seldom used for traditional special operations duties—such as hostage situations, civil disturbances, and barricaded persons—but very frequently deployed in drug raids and other high-risk warrant work. Paramilitary units are increasingly used to execute search warrants and arrest warrants, duties previously handled by regular police officers.

Another example of the "normalization" of PPUs is their growing use in proactive patrol work in high crime areas. In some cities, the units patrol in full tactical gear, looking for signs of drug or gang activity and responding aggressively when they observe such activity. In the past, it was thought that regular police patrols were sufficient for this kind of work and that supplementing them with paramilitary units would risk alienating the community, whose residents might feel they were under military occupation. Some police chiefs still refuse to deploy their paramilitary squads in patrol work for precisely these reasons.

Kraska and Kappeler are disturbed by this escalating militarization of policing in America. Not only can it interfere with conventional policing and undermine community policing, but paramilitary units sometimes intimidate and endanger law-abiding people. Moreover, the squads no longer simply respond to emergency situations, as the authors point out: ". . . most PPUs proactively seek out and manufacture highly dangerous situations."

Some cities have adopted the philosophy of *zero-tolerance policing* as a crime-fighting strategy. Zero tolerance means that police officers fully enforce the laws and pay just as much attention to minor offenses as to serious crimes. Underlying the notion of zero tolerance is the popular "broken windows" thesis, first proposed by James Q. Wilson and George Kelling. Wilson and Kelling (1982) argued that petty crimes and signs of neighborhood decay (graffiti, abandoned cars, broken windows) will become only more widespread if left unchecked, and ultimately will lead to more serious crime in a community—hence, the need for police to remove graffiti and abandoned cars and to arrest people for minor crimes such as panhandling, vandalism, prostitution, drinking or urinating in public, and so forth. The broken windows/zero-tolerance perspective is derived from social disorganization theory, as presented in Rodney Stark's reading in Part I.

Under Mayor Rudolph Giuliani, New York City implemented the broken windows/zero-tolerance approach, and arrests for misdemeanors increased by about 50 percent. Judith Greene's article analyzes the effects of zero tolerance in New York in comparison with San Diego, a city that embraced a quite different style: community policing. First, Greene documents some major consequences of New York's approach, including the fact that citizen complaints about police misconduct rose substantially after zero tolerance was implemented, especially among blacks and Latinos. Second, New York was by no means unique in lowering its crime rate during the 1990s. Other cities, including San Diego, which did not adopt zero tolerance, also experienced substantial declines in violent crime. Both cities saw crime drop about the same amount from 1990 to 1995, yet *arrests* in New York rose while arrests in San Diego fell, and citizen *complaints* against the police increased in New York but decreased in San Diego. Greene concludes that these differences in arrest patterns and citizen complaints indicate that community policing "can provide effective crime control through more efficient and humane methods" than New York's aggressive zero-tolerance strategy.

The nature and extent of America's drug problem, and what to do about it, are highly politicized issues. Our drug policy has always been controversial, but policies have changed over time. The sweeping prohibitionist approach, popular in the country since Reagan's war on drugs in the mid-1980s, stands in stark contrast to the trend toward decriminalization that took place in the 1970s. In 1972 a blue-ribbon commission appointed by President Nixon recommended the decriminalization of marijuana possession (National Commission 1972). The commission proposed that the penalty for possession of a small amount of marijuana (one ounce or less) be limited to a token fine ($100 or less) and confiscation of the drug. Nixon rejected the report, but 11 states passed laws in the 1970s modeled on the commission's recommendations. The states ranged from conservative (Mississippi, Nebraska, North Carolina) to more liberal (Minnesota, Oregon, New York) and represented every region of the country. The prospects for further decriminalization were dampened with the election of Ronald Reagan in 1980. His administration launched a robust anti-drug crusade, which effectively ended the decriminalization trend and resulted in passage of harsher drug laws.

This background offers a useful, contrasting frame of reference for critically evaluating the current state of American drug policy. Peter Reuter's essay tracks the increasing "punitive trend" in drug control, which he argues is overwhelmingly dominated by the influence of drug policy "hawks." Their triumph has effectively preempted serious discussion of alternative policies, increased the number of persons incarcerated for drug offenses, and created other collateral costs and harms.

The hawks are hardly representative of the nation: Public opinion in America is divided on the drug issue. According to a February 2001 Pew Research Center poll, 46 percent of Americans think the "possession of small amounts of marijuana" should not be a crime, while 49 percent think it should be a crime. And one-third of adults say they have used the drug at some time, according to a September 1999 Gallup poll.

There also have been some significant countertrends to the dominant punitive trend. In January 2001, for example, a drug policy commission created by the Governor of New Mexico recommended the repeal of mandatory minimum sentences for all drug offenses, as well as the complete decriminalization of possession of one ounce or less of marijuana by persons aged 18 and over; use of marijuana would be allowed in private places, but public use would trigger a civil penalty (Drug Policy Advisory Group 2001). In two states, Arizona in 1996 and California in 2000, voters approved ballot propositions that eliminated incarceration for persons convicted of drug possession a first or second time, and replaced it with probation and mandatory treatment.

Nine states have passed medical marijuana laws, despite opposition from the federal government, and four-fifths of Americans believe that people should be allowed to use marijuana for medical purposes if a physician prescribes it, according to a March 2001 Fox News poll. Opponents believe medical marijuana is a thinly disguised strategy on the part of advocates whose hidden agenda is broader legalization of the drug, but most Americans are fully supportive of medical marijuana, and it is likely that the number of states permitting such use will continue to grow.

These alternative developments are noteworthy, but at this point in time they remain fairly isolated exceptions to the overall punitive trend in drug policy documented in Peter Reuter's article.

How should sex offenders be treated after they have served their prison sentences? Should they be subjected to further confinement in a state mental hospital and detained there until they can prove they are no longer dangerous? Fifteen states now have "sexually violent predator" statutes that allow for post-prison commitment to a mental hospital, despite the opposition of the American Psychiatric Association, which maintains that this is a criminal justice issue, not a mental health issue.

Alternatively, should sex offenders be publicly identified and subjected to stringent control in the communities in which they reside after being released from prison? The Megan's Laws that have swept the country in recent years require sex offenders to register with local authorities, and require some type of community notification once a released offender has taken up residence in a particular community. The federal government and every state have enacted such laws, whose purpose is to provide communities with information about sex offenders in order to better protect children. The public overwhelmingly endorses these laws: 9 out of 10 Americans approve of community notification of released sex offenders, according to a 1994 Gallup poll.

The laws apply to child molesters, rapists, and other sex offenders, but they vary from state to state in the method of notification: whether the names, addresses, and photos of the offenders are accessible only if a person visits a police station, mailed to all residents of the immediate neighborhood in which the offender lives, or publicized more widely—by being posted on the Internet, printed in a newspaper, or available by calling a 900 telephone number. Some cities have taken extreme action. In Corpus Christi, Texas, a judge recently ordered sex offenders on probation to post yard signs at their homes that read "DANGER. Registered Sex Offender Lives Here," and to affix bumper stickers to their cars that warn, "DANGER. Registered Sex Offender in Vehicle" (Duggan 2001). The judge acknowledged that the warnings could incite violent attacks, but he insisted that protecting children was more important.

Community notification raises several thorny issues:

- Should sex offenders be singled out for post-incarceration, secondary punishment, and official stigmatization when other criminals are not? Courts have held that community notification is not really "punishment" but rather "regulation" of offenders' conduct—hence, not violating the prohibition on double jeopardy.
- Do the notification laws intrude on privacy rights? Courts have generally upheld the laws against constitutional challenges, ruling that the offenders' privacy rights are outweighed by community rights to public safety.
- Does notification create unwarranted fear and loathing in communities where sex offenders live, and does it prompt residents to take the law into their own hands—engaging in harassment, efforts to drive individuals out of the community, or vigilante attacks? In interviews with released sex offenders in Wisconsin, all of them expressed concern for their personal safety and 3 percent reported that they had been the target of vigilante violence. Most had suffered in other ways as a result of community notification: 83 percent had been excluded from a residence, 77 percent had endured threats or harassment, 67 percent reported emotional harm to their family members, 67 percent had been ostracized by neighborhood residents or acquaintances, and 50 percent had lost their jobs (Zevitz and Farkas 2000).

Another problem is that these laws seem to assume that sex offenders cannot be rehabilitated and reintegrated into a community. Lois Presser and Elaine Gunnison address this problem in the article reprinted here. They find that sex offender notification laws, while often presented as an example of "community justice," actually contradict core principles of community justice. Community justice seeks to increase citizens' safety in their neighborhoods and also aims to prevent crime by addressing the problems that give rise to crime. "Restorative community justice" goes a step further by attempting to repair the damage caused by crime, both healing victims and reintegrating offenders. Presser and Gunnison's analysis of sex offender notification shows that it fails on all counts. It does little if anything to enhance residents' safety, to prevent sex crimes, to meet victims' needs, or to rehabilitate and reintegrate offenders. Instead, notification has the opposite effect on offenders—isolating, stigmatizing, and debilitating them.

"Three strikes and you're out" laws are the latest chapter in America's "get tough" approach to crime, and these laws are very popular with the public. Fully 86 percent of Americans support laws requiring life imprisonment for anyone convicted of a third violent felony, according to a 1994 ABC News/*Washington Post* poll.

The majority of states now have three strikes laws, though they vary considerably from state to state. Most states define "strikeable" offenses as violent crimes like murder, robbery, and rape, but some states include nonviolent offenses like burglary, drug sales, and embezzlement. Most require a conviction on a third offense before a life sentence is triggered, but eight states require only two offenses before the offender "strikes out."

In their article, "Three Strikes Laws," James Austin, John Clark, Patricia Hardyman, and Alan Henry focus on the toughest three-strikes law in the country: California's. The state is unique in allowing the third strikeable offense to be *any* felony; other states stipulate that the third strike must be a violent felony. Conviction on a third strike-able offense triggers a mandatory 25-years-to-life sentence, and the California law also doubles the sentence for second strike offenders, double what they would have received had it been their first conviction. California holds the distinction of having charged far more offenders under its three strikes law than any other state.

California counties vary tremendously in their application of the law. Prosecutors retain some discretion in invoking the law, including a determination as to whether a three-strikes charge serves the "interests of justice" in a particular case. Some counties have applied the law strictly, while others have applied it more selectively. In fact, counties with the highest use of three strikes powers invoke the law between 3 and 12 times more often than the lowest sentencing counties (Males and Macallair 1999).

Perhaps the most important finding in the Austin study is the number of second- and third-strike offenders who have been sentenced for *nonviolent offenses*. About 80 percent of second strikers and 60 percent of third strikers were convicted and sentenced for nonviolent crimes. Some of these offenses involved simple drug possession, while others hardly seem serious enough to warrant life imprisonment. Although the majority of Californians approve of some three strikes law, many believe it should be restricted to violent felonies, not just any felony. But calls for the law to be amended to cover only violent felons have not been successful.

Three strikes laws were intended to help reduce crime rates, serving as a deterrent to would-be repeat offenders. Have the laws reduced crime? Austin compared three states with three-strikes laws to three states

without them. Crime trends in the six states did not support the prediction that three-strikes laws help to reduce crime. The state where three strikes has been implemented most aggressively, California, "has shown no superior reduction in crime rates." Have California's counties or cities that vigorously apply the law fared better in reducing crime than counties and cities that make more selective use of the law? Analyses by Austin and other researchers (Males and Macallair 1999) of aggressive and lenient counties found no evidence that crime rates were affected by three strikes sentencing. As Males and Macallair (1999) conclude, "Data clearly show that counties that vigorously and strictly enforce the 'three strikes' law did not experience a decline in any crime category relative to more lenient counties." The same conclusion can be drawn at the city level: An analysis of the state's 10 largest cities found no difference in crime rate reductions between the cities, again challenging the notion that aggressive application of the law will help to reduce crime (Stolzenberg and D'Alessio 1997).

The use of DNA testing in the criminal justice system has been all the rage during the past decade. Most people see only benefits from its use in helping to convict suspects, close cases that have remained unsolved for years, and free wrongly convicted people. But there is a darker side to DNA testing that has generated some concern.

All 50 states now have statutes authorizing police agencies to operate DNA databases for criminals and to pool their data into the FBI's national database, CODIS. The laws vary, however, in the types of offenses covered. About half the states require DNA samples not only from felons but also from certain types of misdemeanants; all states take DNA samples from convicted sex offenders, while some also require samples from those convicted of robbery, assault, kidnapping, or burglary; Massachusetts orders DNA samples for 33 crimes, including something as minor as prostitution; Louisiana law covers persons *arrested* for but not convicted of sex offenses; and Illinois retains DNA profiles even for persons whose convictions have been overturned (Gugliotta 1999; Kimmelman 2000). New York Mayor Rudolph Giuliani once proposed that the state should sample every newborn infant!

Clearly, DNA testing constitutes a major expansion of governmental power, and the question is: Where do we draw the line? Concerns have been raised about the constitutionality of DNA testing, about the possibility that states may fail to destroy DNA samples after they have been tested, and about the need for strict privacy protections governing the information contained in DNA databases, including prohibitions on the use of DNA profiles for anything other than matching them with material collected at crime scenes.

Paul Tracy and Vincent Morgan ("DNA Testing") are strong advocates of the use of DNA testing for known offenders and for exonerating people wrongly convicted of crimes. DNA testing in these cases serves the twin goals of the criminal justice system: crime control and justice. But Tracy and Morgan are critical of the costly proliferation of DNA databases and their use in all manner of crime. They view the astronomical costs involved as grossly disproportionate to the benefits. DNA databases, they argue, will not help to resolve most property crimes or the less serious crimes such as vandalism, prostitution, and drunk driving. At best, they will help to resolve *some* murders, rapes, and other serious crimes, but even here their impact will be limited. Tracy

and Morgan question whether the huge expense involved in DNA extraction from crime scenes, DNA testing of suspects, and the creation and maintenance of DNA databases is a cost-effective way to spend scarce criminal justice resources.

Gun control ranks as one of the most contested issues in American politics. Organizations on both sides of the issue, such as Handgun Control and the National Rifle Association, are locked in an ongoing war over guns, pouring millions of dollars every year into their public education campaigns and lobbying efforts. Most Americans support tighter restrictions on guns: A 1999 Gallup poll found that 87 percent approve of mandatory background checks for persons who wish to buy a gun at a gun show; 85 percent support mandatory safety locks on handguns; 79 percent want all firearms registered. Also popular are 5-day waiting periods for purchasing a gun, a nationwide ban on assault rifles (77 percent), and a ban on gun sales by mail order or over the Internet (66 percent), according to a 1999 ABC News/*Washington Post* poll.

Much of the public's perception of guns and gun control policies is influenced by the claims of advocates in opposing camps and politicians who see political advantage in propagating a particular "solution" to the gun problem. In this politically charged environment, there is a clear need for scientific analyses of the impact of guns on crime rates and on the kinds of policies that might reduce gun violence. Drawing on social science evidence, Philip Cook and Mark Moore ("Gun Control") sketch the various dimensions of gun use and gun control in the United States. They carefully evaluate an array of gun control policies and proposals and estimate their chances of reducing gun availability and the criminal use of guns. After reviewing the evidence, Cook and

Moore propose a package of reforms that might help reduce gun violence.

The juvenile justice system is in a state of crisis. Its caseload has increased dramatically in recent years; it is adjudicating a growing number of violent offenders; and a significant number of juveniles are being transferred out of juvenile court to the adult, criminal courts. Indeed, the traditional rationale for a separate juvenile court—that children are immature and therefore ought to be treated differently than adults when they break the law—is eroding. A Gallup poll in 2000 reported that 65 percent of Americans believed that juveniles between the ages of 14 and 17 who commit violent crimes should be treated the same as adults, whereas only 24 percent thought they should get more lenient treatment in a juvenile court. And a 1999 survey by the Pew Research Center found that 73 percent favored laws that would result in more juveniles, ages 14 and over, being tried as adults. Forty-six states now permit juveniles to be tried as adults, and 14 states stipulate mandatory transfer to adult court for certain offenses (*Washington Post,* November 5, 1999).

What happens to juveniles who are convicted of crimes in criminal courts? They do not serve longer sentences than they would have received in the juvenile system, but they do tend to reoffend at a higher rate than if they remained in the juvenile system. Research in Florida found that youths transferred to adult court were a third more likely to recidivate than their counterparts in the juvenile system, who were matched by offense type. The former reoffended more often, more rapidly, and more seriously than did youths in juvenile facilities (Bishop et al. 1996). The same authors also interviewed youths sent to adult prison and those sent

to a maximum-risk juvenile detention facility. Two-thirds of the youths in prison believed that they would reoffend after release, and 40 percent said that other prisoners had taught them new ways to commit crime.

These findings raise questions about the wisdom of trying juveniles as adults and incarcerating them in prison. Nevertheless, Barry Feld ("Abolish the Juvenile Court") argues that there are many reasons why we should scrap the entire juvenile court and try all juveniles in criminal courts—provided that we also introduce major procedural and substantive changes in the way juveniles are treated in criminal courts to accommodate their youthful status. For example, Feld advocates a "youth discount" in the sentences given to offenders—an age-based sliding scale of punishments reflecting the lesser culpability of the youngest offenders. At the same time, he wants to maintain separate correctional facilities for juveniles and adults. Juveniles should be *tried* in criminal courts, but those who are convicted and given a custodial sentence should not be *incarcerated* with adults, because they risk being victimized by adult inmates and because incarceration with adults interferes with juveniles' rehabilitation and increases their chances of reoffending. Feld presents a wide-ranging critique of the existing juvenile justice system and a provocative defense of his proposal to abolish the juvenile court.

Capital punishment is perhaps the single most hotly debated issue in American criminal justice. Michael Radelet and Marian Borg ("The Death Penalty") examine the major arguments for and against the death penalty. They find that two of the traditional justifications for capital punishment—deterrence and incapacitation—are not supported by research studies, while a third—

retribution or "just deserts"—may have some logical deficiencies but is not really amenable to scientific verification or falsification because it is essentially a moral position. Arguments against the death penalty include racial bias, financial costs, caprice and inconsistency, and miscarriages of justice. The social science evidence reviewed by the authors indicates that these are indeed serious problems. The United States features (1) *national* variation in where capital punishment is permitted (12 states have no death penalty), (2) disparities *between states* that permit capital punishment (some Southern states use it frequently, other states have not used it since 1976), (3) disparities *within states* from jurisdiction to jurisdiction, and (4) disparities *within jurisdictions* from case to case. Moreover, whether one receives the death penalty is less a function of the crime committed than the quality of the defendants' legal counsel, the discretion of local prosecutors, and the race of the offender and the victim. African Americans are more likely than whites to receive the death penalty, and persons whose victim is white are more likely to receive the death penalty than killers of blacks.

Wrongful convictions are another problem. Between 1973 and 2001, 96 people were released from death row due to evidence of their innocence, according to the Death Penalty Information Center. Some of these prisoners were released within a few days of being executed! And one study suggests that at least 25 innocent people were executed during the 20th century (Radelet and Bedau 1998). Recent research also finds a stunning error rate in capital cases. A study of 5,760 capital cases nationwide between 1973 and 1995 found "epidemic" error rates in the sentences imposed (Lieb-

man et al. 2000). Appellate courts found serious errors in fully *two-thirds* of these cases. After new trials, 7 percent of the defendants were exonerated, 75 percent were resentenced to a term less than death, and 18 percent were resentenced to death. The most common errors were incompetent defense lawyers and police and prosecutors who suppressed evidence. In 37 percent of the cases, appeals courts later ruled that defense attorneys had performed so poorly that the defendant did not receive a proper defense, and in 16 percent prosecutors had suppressed mitigating or exculpatory evidence.

The level of public support for the death penalty is declining. A *Washington Post* poll in April 2001 found that 63 percent of Americans favor the death penalty for persons convicted of murder, down from 77 percent in 1996. However, general questions asking respondents whether they "favor" or "support" the death penalty mask important qualifications and concerns that are revealed in answers to more specific questions. When respondents are given the alternative of a life sentence without possibility of parole, support for the death penalty drops to about 50 percent. And if a majority of Americans support the death penalty in principle, many are deeply concerned about the way in which it is applied: 63 percent believe capital punishment is unfair because of geographical differences in its use (ABC News/*Washington Post* poll, 2001); 50 percent believe that the death penalty is applied unequally to blacks and whites convicted of the same crime (Gallup poll, 2001); 68 percent believe that poor people are more likely than higher income people to receive the death penalty (Gallup poll, 2001); and fully 80 percent believe that an innocent person has been executed in the U.S. in the past five years (CNN/*USA Today*/Gallup poll, 2000). Because of these concerns, a growing number of Americans now favor a moratorium on the death penalty until questions about its fairness can be resolved: 72 percent subscribed to this view in a March 2001 opinion poll by Peter Hart Research Associates. The same survey found that 91 percent endorsed mandatory access to DNA testing for all defendants in capital cases and 84 percent favored a requirement that court-appointed attorneys have prior experience in trying capital cases and be certified to try such cases by the local bar association.

The United States is now almost alone (along with Japan) among democratic nations in its use of capital punishment. Radelet and Borg document a worldwide trend toward abolition of the death penalty, and they predict that the United States will eventually follow suit, bringing the country in line with the international trend. In the meantime, some reforms might render the death penalty less capricious and more reliable. A number of prominent organizations have called for a moratorium on the death penalty until fundamental changes are made in the way it is administered. The American Bar Association passed a resolution in 1997 calling for the suspension of executions until procedures are implemented to "minimize the risk" of executing innocent persons and to ensure that the penalty is "administered fairly and impartially, in accordance with due process." Previous ABA resolutions have called for a ban on execution of mentally retarded persons and persons under 18 years of age, elimination of racial discrimination in capital sentencing, and improvements in the quality of defense counsel in capital cases. Similarly, a bipartisan panel of experts, the Committee to Prevent Wrongful Executions

(2001), recently issued a report urging Congress and state legislatures to make it easier for convicts to get new trials based on newly discovered evidence; increase competency standards and resources for defense lawyers who represent defendants in capital cases; eliminate the death penalty for the mentally retarded and juveniles; create safeguards to prevent racially discriminatory application of the death penalty; and make routine use of DNA evidence in capital cases where it may help to establish guilt or innocence. As indicated above, there is considerable public support for these remedial measures.

REFERENCES

ACLU [American Civil Liberties Union]. 1999. *Driving While Black*. New York: ACLU.

Bishop, Donna, Charles Frazier, Lonn Lanza-Kaduce, and Lawrence Winner. 1996. "The Transfer of Juveniles to Criminal Court: Does it Make a Difference?" *Crime and Delinquency* 42:171–191.

Committee to Prevent Wrongful Executions. 2001. *Mandatory Justice: Eighteen Reforms to the Death Penalty*. Washington, DC: Constitution Project.

Drug Policy Advisory Group. 2001. *Report and Recommendations*. Office of the Governor, State of New Mexico.

Duggan, Paul. 2001. "The Sex Offender Down the Street," *Washington Post*, May 29.

Gugliotta, Guy. 1999. "A Rush to DNA Sampling," *Washington Post*, July 7.

Harris, David. 1997. "'Driving While Black' and All Other Traffic Offenses," *Journal of Criminal Law and Criminology* 87:544–582.

Kimmelman, Jonathan. 2000. "Just a Needle-Stick Away," *The Nation*, November 27.

Liebman, James S., Jeffrey Fagan, Valerie West, and Jonathan Lloyd. 2000. "Capital Attrition:

Error Rates in Capital Cases, 1973–1995," *Texas Law Review* 78:1839–1865.

MacDonald, Heather. 2001. "The Myth of Racial Profiling," *City Journal* (New York), 11 (Spring).

Males, Mike, and Dan Macallair. 1999. *Striking Out: The Failure of California's "Three Strikes and You're Out" Law.* San Francisco: Justice Policy Institute.

National Commission on Marijuana and Drug Abuse. 1972. *Marijuana: A Signal of Misunderstanding.* Washington, DC: U.S. Government Printing Office.

Radelet, Michael L., and Hugo Adam Bedau. 1998. "The Execution of the Innocent," *Law and Contemporary Problems* 64:105–124.

Stolzenberg, Lisa, and Steward D'Alessio. 1997. "Three Strikes and You're Out," *Crime and Delinquency* 43:457–469.

Weitzer, Ronald. 1999. "Citizens' Perceptions of Police Misconduct: Race and Neighborhood Context," *Justice Quarterly* 16:819–846.

Weitzer, Ronald, and Steven Tuch. 2002. "Perceptions of Racial Profiling: Race, Class, and Personal Experience," *Criminology* 40:435–456.

Wilson, James Q., and George Kelling. 1982. "Broken Windows: The Police and Neighborhood Safety," *Atlantic Monthly*, March: 29–83.

Zevitz, Richard G., and Mary Ann Farkas. 2000. "Sex Offender Community Notification: Assessing the Impact in Wisconsin," *Research in Brief*, National Institute of Justice. Washington, DC: U.S. Department of Justice.

Racial Profiling

David A. Harris

It has happened to actors Wesley Snipes, Will Smith, Blair Underwood, and LeVar Burton. It has also happened to football player Marcus Allen, and Olympic athletes Al Joyner and Edwin Moses. African-Americans call it "driving while black"—police officers stopping, questioning, and even searching black drivers who have committed no crime, based on the excuse of a traffic offense.

Data on this problem are not easy to come by. This is, in part, because the problem has only recently been recognized beyond the black community. It may also be because records concerning police conduct are either irregular or nonexistent. But it may also be because there is active hostility in the law enforcement community to the idea of keeping comprehensive records of traffic stops. In 1997, Representative John Conyers of Michigan introduced H.R. 118, the Traffic Stops Statistics Act, which would require the Department of Justice to collect and analyze data on all traffic stops around the country—including the race of the driver, whether a search took place, and the legal justification for the search.[1] When the bill passed the House with unanimous, bipartisan support the National Association of Police Organizations (NAPO), an umbrella group representing more than 4,000 police interest groups across the country, announced its strong opposition to the bill.[2] Officers would "resent" having to collect the data, a spokesman for the group said. Moreover, there is "no pressing need or justification" for collecting the data.[3] In other words, there is no problem, so there is no need to collect data. NAPO's opposition was enough to kill the bill in the Senate in the 105th Congress. As a consequence, there is now no requirement at the federal level that law enforcement agencies collect data on traffic stops that include race. Thus, all of the data gathering so far has been the result of statistical inquiry in lawsuits or independent academic research.

NEW JERSEY

The most rigorous statistical analysis of the racial distribution of traffic stops was performed in New Jersey by John Lamberth of Temple University. In the late 1980s and early 1990s, African-Americans often complained that police stopped them on the New Jersey Turnpike more frequently than their numbers on that road would have predicted. Similarly, public defenders in the area had observed that "a strikingly high proportion of cases arising from stops and searches on the New Jersey Turnpike involve black persons."[4] In 1994, the problem was brought to the state court's atten-

From David A. Harris, "The Stories, the Statistics and the Law: Why 'Driving While Black' Matters," *Minnesota Law Review* v. 84, no. 1 (Dec. 1999): 265–326. Reprinted by permission of the author.

tion in *State v. Pedro Soto*,[5] in which the defendant alleged that he had been stopped because of his ethnicity.[6] The defendant sought to have the evidence gathered as a result of the stop suppressed as the fruit of an illegal seizure. Lamberth served as a defense expert in the case. His report is a virtual tutorial on how to apply statistical analysis to this type of problem.[7]

The goal of Lamberth's study was "to determine if the State Police stop, investigate, and arrest black travelers at rates significantly disproportionate to the percentage of blacks in the traveling population, so as to suggest the existence of an official or de facto policy of targeting blacks for investigation and arrest."[8] To do this, Lamberth designed a research methodology to determine two things: first, the rate at which blacks were being stopped, ticketed, and/or arrested on the relevant part of the highway, and second, the percentage of blacks among travelers on that same stretch of road.

To gather data concerning the rate at which blacks were stopped, ticketed and arrested, Lamberth reviewed and reconstructed three types of information received in discovery from the state: reports of all arrests that resulted from stops on the turnpike from April of 1988 through May of 1991, patrol activity logs from randomly selected days from 1988 through 1991, and police radio logs from randomly selected days from 1988 through 1991.[9] Many of these records identified the race of the driver or passenger.

Then Lamberth sought to measure the racial composition of the traveling public on the road. He did this through a turnpike population census—direct observation by teams of research assistants who counted the cars on the road and tabulated whether the driver or another occupant appeared black. During these observations, teams of observers sat at the side of the road for randomly selected periods of 75 minutes from 8:00 a.m. to 8:00 p.m.[10] To ensure further precision, Lamberth also designed another census procedure—a turnpike violation census. This was a rolling survey by teams of observers in cars moving in traffic on the highway, with the cruise control calibrated and set at five miles per hour above the speed limit. The teams observed each car that they passed or that passed them, noted the race of the driver, and also noted whether or not the driver was exceeding the speed limit.[11]

The teams recorded data on more than forty-two thousand cars.[12] With these observations, Lamberth was able to compare the percentages of African-American drivers who are stopped, ticketed, and arrested, to their relative presence on the road. This data enabled him to carefully and rigorously test whether blacks were in fact being disproportionately targeted for stops.

By any standard, the results of Lamberth's analysis are startling. First, the turnpike violator census, in which observers in moving cars recorded the races and speeds of the cars around them, showed that blacks and whites violated the traffic laws at almost exactly the same rate; there was no statistically significant difference in the way they drove.[13] Thus, driving behavior alone could not explain differences in how police might treat black and white drivers.[14] With regard to arrests, 73.2% of those stopped and arrested were black, while only 13.5% of the cars on the road had a black driver or passenger.[15] Lamberth notes that the disparity between these two numbers "is statistically vast."[16] The number of standard deviations present—54.27—means that the probability that the racial disparity is a random result "is infinitesimally small."[17] Radio and patrol logs yielded similar results. Blacks are approximately 35% of those stopped,[18] though they are only 13.5% of those on the road—19.45 standard deviations.[19] Considering all stops in all three types of records surveyed, the chance that 34.9% of the cars combined would have black drivers or occupants "is substantially less than one in one billion."[20] This led Lamberth to the following conclusion:

> Absent some other explanation for the dramatically disproportionate number of stops of blacks, it would appear that the race of the occupants and/or drivers of the cars is a decisive factor or a factor with great explanatory power. I can say to a reasonable degree of statistical probability that the disparity outlined here is strongly consistent with the existence of a discriminatory policy, official or de facto, of targeting blacks for stop and investigation. . . . Put bluntly, the statistics demonstrate that in a population of blacks and whites which is (legally) virtually universally subject to police stop for traffic law violation, (cf. the turnpike violator census), blacks in general are several times more likely to be stopped than non-blacks.[21]

MARYLAND

A short time after completing his analysis of the New Jersey data, Lamberth also conducted a study of traffic stops by the Maryland State Police on Interstate 95 between Baltimore and the Delaware border.[22] In 1993, an African-American Harvard Law School graduate named Robert Wilkins filed a federal lawsuit against the Maryland State Police. Wilkins alleged that the police stopped him as he was driving with his family, questioned them and searched the car with a drug-sniffing dog because of their race.[23] When a State Police memo surfaced during discovery instructing troopers to look for drug couriers who were described as "predominantly black males and black females,"[24] the State Police settled with Wilkins. As part of the settlement, the police agreed to give the court data on every stop fol-

lowed by a search conducted with the driver's consent or with a dog for three years. The data also were to include the race of the driver.

With this data, Lamberth used a rolling survey, similar to the one in New Jersey, to determine the racial breakdown of the driving population. Lamberth's assistants observed almost 6,000 cars over approximately 42 randomly distributed hours. As he had in New Jersey, Lamberth concluded that blacks and whites drove no differently; the percentages of blacks and whites violating the traffic code were virtually indistinguishable. More importantly, Lamberth's analysis found that although 17.5% of the population violating the traffic code on the road he studied was black, more than 72% of those stopped and searched were black. In more than 80% of the cases, the person stopped and searched was a member of some racial minority.[25] The disparity between 17.5% black and 72% stopped includes 34.6 standard deviations.[26] Such statistical significance, Lamberth said, "is literally off the charts.[27] Even while exhibiting appropriate caution, Lamberth came to a devastating conclusion:

> While no one can know the motivation of each individual trooper in conducting a traffic stop, the statistics presented herein, representing a broad and detailed sample of highly appropriate data, show without question a racially discriminatory impact on blacks . . . from state police behavior along I-95. The disparities are sufficiently great that taken as a whole, they are consistent and strongly support the assertion that the state police targeted the community of black motorists for stop, detention, and investigation within the Interstate 95 corridor.[28]

OHIO

In the Spring of 1998, several members of the Ohio General Assembly began to consider whether to propose legislation that would require police departments to collect data on traffic stops. But in order to sponsor such a bill, the legislators wanted some preliminary statistical evidence—a prima facie case, one could say—of the existence of the problem. This would help them persuade their colleagues to support the effort, they said. I was asked to gather this preliminary evidence. The methodology used here presents a case study in how to analyze this type of problem when the best type of data to do so is not available.

In the most fundamental ways, the task was the same as Lamberth's had been in both New Jersey and Maryland: use statistics to test whether blacks in Ohio were being stopped in numbers disproportionate to their presence in the driving population. Doing this would require data on stops broken down by race, and a comparison of those numbers to the percentage of black drivers on the roads. But if the goal was the same, two circumstances made the task considerably more difficult to accomplish in Ohio. First, Ohio does not collect statewide data on traffic stops that can be correlated with race. In fact, no police department of any sizeable city in the state keeps any data on all of its traffic stops that could be broken down by race. Second, the state legislators wanted some preliminary statistics to demonstrate that "driving while black" was a problem in all of Ohio, or at least in some significant—and different—parts of the whole state. While Lamberth's stationary and rolling survey methods worked well to ascertain the driving populations of particular stretches of individual, limited access highways, those methods were obviously resource- and labor-intensive. Applying the same methods to an entire city—even a medium-sized one—would entail duplicating the Lamberth approach on many major roads to get a complete picture. It would be impractical, not to mention prohibitively expensive, to do this in communities across an entire state. Thus, different methods had to be found.

To determine the percentage of blacks stopped, data was obtained from municipal courts in four Ohio cities.[29] Municipal courts in Ohio handle all low-level criminal cases and virtually all of the traffic citations issued in the state. Most of these courts also generate a computer file for each case, which includes the race of the defendant as part of a physical description. This data provided the basis for a breakdown of all tickets given by the race of the driver.

The downside of using the municipal court data is that it only includes stops in which citations were given. Stops resulting in no action or a warning are not included. In all likelihood, using tickets alone might underestimate any racial bias that is present because police might not ticket blacks stopped for non-traffic purposes. Since using tickets could underestimate any possible racial bias, any resulting calculations are conservative and tend to give law enforcement the benefit of the doubt. Similarly, the way the racial statistics are grouped in the analysis is also conservative because the numbers are limited to only two categories of drivers: black and nonblack. In other words, all minorities other than African-Americans are lumped together with whites, even though some of these other minorities, notably Hispanics, have also complained about targeted stops directed at them. Using conservative assumptions means that if a bias does show up in the analysis, we can be relatively confident that it actually exists.[30]

The percentage of all tickets in 1996, 1997, and the first four months of 1998[31] that were issued to blacks by the Akron, Dayton, and Toledo Police Departments and all of the police departments in Franklin County[32] are set out in Table 1.

With ticketing percentages used as a measure of stops, attention turns to the other number needed for the analysis: the presence of blacks in the driving population. Given the

Table 1.   Ticketing of African-Americans for 1996, 1997, and 1998*

CITY	PERCENTAGE OF ALL TICKETS IN CITY ISSUED TO AFRICAN-AMERICANS
Akron	37.6%
Toledo	30.8%
Dayton	50.0%
*Columbus/Franklin County***	25.2%

*Through April 30, 1998.
**Data for Franklin County include 1996 and 1997, but not 1998, and include tickets issued by all law enforcement units in the county, not just the city of Columbus.

concerns about the use of Lamberth's method in a statewide, preliminary study, another approach—a less exact one than direct observation, to be sure, but one that would yield a reasonable estimate of the driving population—was devised. Data from the U.S. Census breaks down the populations of states, counties, and individual cities by race and by age. This data is readily available and easy to use.[33] Using this data, a reasonable basis for comparing ticketing percentages can be constructed: blacks versus nonblacks in the *driving age population*. This was done by breaking down the general population by race and by age. By selecting a lower and upper

age limit—fifteen and seventy-five, respectively for driving age, the data yield a reasonable reflection of what we would expect to find if we surveyed the roads themselves. The data on driving age population can also be sharpened by using information from the National Personal Transportation Survey,[34] a study done every five years by the Federal Highway Administration of the U.S. Department of Transportation. The 1990 survey indicates that 21% of black households do not own a vehicle.[35] If the driving age population figure is reduced by 21%, this gives us another baseline with which to make a comparison to the ticketing percentages. Both baselines—black driving age population, and black driving age population less 21%—for Akron, Dayton, Toledo, and Franklin County are set out in Table 2.

The ticketing percentages in Table 1 and the baselines in Table 2 can then be compared by constructing a "likelihood ratio" that will show whether blacks are receiving tickets in numbers that are out of proportion to their presence in the driving age population and the driving age population less 21%. The likelihood ratio will allow the following sentence to be completed: "If you're black, you're _____ times as likely to be ticketed by this police

Table 2.   Population Baselines

CITY	BLACK DRIVING AGE POPULATION* (PERCENTAGE OF CITY TOTAL)	BLACK DRIVING AGE POPULATION, LESS 21% OF BLACK HOUSEHOLDS WITHOUT VEHICLES**
Akron	22.7%	17.9%
Toledo	18%	14.2%
Dayton	38%	30.0%
*Columbus/Franklin County****	16%	12.6%

*Source: U.S. Census Bureau.
**Source: Federal Highway Admin., U.S. Dep't of Transp., *1995 National Personal Transportation Survey*, (visited Sept. 27, 1999) <http://www.bts.gov/ntda/npts>; Letters from Eric Hill, Research Associate, Center for Urban Transportation, to David A. Harris (Sept. 28 & Oct. 9, 1998).
***Data for all of Franklin County, not just the city of Columbus.

Table 3. Likelihood Ratio "If You're Black, You're _____ Times as Likely to Get a Ticket in This City Than if You Are Not Black"

CITY	BLACK DRIVING AGE POPULATION*	BLACK DRIVING AGE POPULATION, LESS 21% OF BLACK HOUSEHOLDS WITHOUT VEHICLES**
Akron P.D.	2.05	2.76
Toledo P.D.	2.04	2.67
Dayton P.D.	1.67	2.32
Columbus/Franklin County***	1.77	2.34

*Source: U.S. Census Bureau.
**Source: Federal Highway Admin., U.S. Dep't of Transp., *1995 National Personal Transportation Survey*, (visited Sept. 27, 1999) <http://www.bts.gov/ntda/npts>; Letters from Eric Hill, Research Associate, Center for Urban Transportation, to David A. Harris (Sept. 28 & Oct. 9, 1998).
***Includes all police agencies in Franklin County, not just Columbus.

department than if you are not black." A likelihood ratio of approximately one means that blacks received tickets in roughly the proportion one would expect, given their presence in the driving age population. A likelihood ratio of much greater than one indicates that blacks received tickets at a rate higher than would be expected. Using both baselines—the black driving age population, and the black driving age population less 21%—the likelihood ratios for Akron, Dayton, Toledo and Franklin County are presented in Table 3.

Table 4 combines population baselines from Table 2 and likelihood ratios from Table 3.

The method used here to attempt to discover whether "driving while black" is a problem in Ohio is less exact than the observation-based method used in New Jersey and Maryland. There are assumptions built into the analysis at several points in an attempt to arrive at reasonable substitutes for observation-based data. Since better data do not exist, all of the assumptions made in the analysis

Table 4. Combined Population Baselines and Likelihood Ratios

CITY	BLACK DRIVING AGE POPULATION*	BLACK DRIVING AGE POPULATION, LESS 21% OF BLACK HOUSEHOLDS WITHOUT VEHICLES**
Akron	22.7%	17.9%
	2.05	2.76
Toledo	18%	14.2%
	2.04	2.67
Dayton	38%	30.0%
	1.67	2.32
Columbus/Franklin County***	16%	12.6%
	1.77	2.34

*Source: U.S. Census Bureau.
**Source: Federal Highway Admin., U.S. Dep't of Transp., *1995 National Personal Transportation Survey*, (visited Sept. 27, 1999) <http://www.bts.gov/ntda/npts>; Letters from Eric Hill, Research Associate, Center for Urban Transportation, to David A. Harris (Sept. 28 & Oct. 9, 1998).
***Data for all of Franklin County, not just the city of Columbus.

involve some speculation. But all of the assumptions are conservative, calculated to err on the side of caution. According to sociologist and criminologist Joseph E. Jacoby, the numbers used here probably are flawed because blacks are probably "at an even greater risk of being stopped" than these numbers show.[36] For example, blacks are likely to drive fewer miles than whites, which suggests that police have fewer opportunities to stop blacks for traffic violations.[37] In statistical terms, the biases in the assumptions are additive, not offsetting.

What do these figures mean? Even when conservative assumptions are built in, likelihood ratios for Akron, Dayton, Toledo, and Franklin County, Ohio, all either approach or exceed 2.0. In other words, blacks are about twice as likely to be ticketed as nonblacks. When the fact that 21% of black households do not own a vehicle is factored in, the ratios rise, with some approaching 3.0. Assuming that ticketing is a fair mirror of traffic stops in general, the data suggest that a "driving while black" problem does indeed exist in Ohio. There may be race-neutral explanations for the statistical pattern, but none seem obvious. At the very least, further study—something as accurate and exacting as Lamberth's studies in New Jersey and Maryland—is needed.

WHY IT MATTERS: THE CONNECTION OF "DRIVING WHILE BLACK" TO OTHER ISSUES OF CRIMINAL JUSTICE AND RACE

The interviews excerpted here show that racially biased pretextual traffic stops have a strong and immediate impact on the individual African-American drivers involved. These stops are not the minor inconveniences they might seem to those who are not subjected to them. Rather, they are experiences that can wound the soul and cause psychological scar tissue to form. And the statistics show that these experiences are not simply disconnected anecdotes or exaggerated versions of personal experiences, but rather established and persistent patterns of law enforcement conduct. It may be that these stops do not spring from racism on the part of individual officers, or even from the official policies of the police departments for which they work. Nevertheless, the statistics leave little doubt that, whatever the source of this conduct by police, it has a disparate and degrading impact on blacks.

But racial profiling is important not only because of the damage it does, but also because of the connections between stops of minority drivers and other, larger issues of criminal justice and race. Put another way, "driving while black" reflects, illustrates, and aggravates some of the most important problems we face today when we debate issues involving race, the police, the courts, punishment, crime control, criminal justice, and constitutional law.

The Impact on the Innocent

The Fourth Amendment to the United States Constitution prohibits unreasonable searches and seizures, and specifies some of the requirements to be met in order to procure a warrant for a search. Since 1961—and earlier in the federal court system—the Supreme Court has required the exclusion of any evidence obtained through an unconstitutional search or seizure.

I wish to point out a major difference between the usual Fourth Amendment cases and the most common "driving while black" cases. *While police catch some criminals through the use of pretext stops, far more innocent people are likely to be affected by these practices than criminals.* Indeed, the black community as a whole undoubtedly needs the protection of the police more than other segments of society because African-Americans are more likely than others to be victims of crime. Ironically, it is members of that same community who are likely to feel the consequences of pretextual stops and be treated like criminals. While whites who have done nothing wrong generally have little need to fear constitutional violations by the police, this is decidedly *untrue* for blacks. Blacks attract undesirable police attention whether they do anything to bring it on themselves or not. This makes "driving while black" a most unusual issue of constitutional criminal procedure: a search and seizure question that directly affects a large, identifiable group of almost entirely innocent people.

The Criminalization of Blackness

The fact that the cost of "driving while black" is imposed almost exclusively on the innocent raises another point. Recall that by allowing the police to stop, question, and sometimes even search drivers without regard to the real motives for the search, the Supreme Court has, in effect, turned a blind eye to the use of pretextual stops on a racial basis. That is, as long as the officer or the police department does not come straight out and say that race was the reason for a stop, the stop can always be accomplished based on some other reason—a pretext. Police are therefore free to use blackness as a surrogate indicator or proxy for criminal propensity. While it seems unfair to view *all* members of one racial or ethnic group as criminal suspects just because *some* members of that group engage in criminal activity, this is what the law permits.

Stopping disproportionate numbers of black drivers because some small percentage are criminals means that skin color is being used as evidence of wrongdoing. In effect,

blackness itself has been criminalized. And if "driving while black" is a powerful example, it is not the only one. For instance, in 1992, the city of Chicago enacted an ordinance that made it a criminal offense for gang members to stand on public streets or sidewalks after police ordered them to disperse.[38] The ordinance was used to make over forty-five thousand arrests of mostly African-American and Latino youths[39] before Illinois courts found the ordinance unconstitutionally vague. In June of 1999, the U.S. Supreme Court declared the law unconstitutional, because it did not sufficiently limit the discretion of officers enforcing it.

The arrests under the Chicago ordinance share something with "driving while black": in each instance, the salient quality that attracts police attention will often be the suspect's race or ethnicity. An officer cannot know simply by looking whether a driver has a valid license or carries insurance, as the law requires, and cannot see whether there is a warrant for the arrest of the driver or another occupant of the car. But the officer *can* see whether the person is black or white. And, as the statistics presented here show, police use blackness as a way to sort those they are interested in investigating from those that they are not. As a consequence, every member of the group becomes a potential criminal in the eyes of law enforcement.

Rational Discrimination

When one hears the most common justification offered for the disproportionate numbers of traffic stops of African-Americans, it usually takes the form of rationality, not racism. Blacks commit a disproportionate share of certain crimes, the argument goes. Therefore, it only makes sense for police to focus their efforts on African-Americans. It only makes sense to focus law enforcement efforts and resources where they will make the most difference. In other words, targeting blacks is the rational, sound policy choice. It is the efficient approach, as well.

As appealing as this argument may sound, it is fraught with problems because its underlying premise is dubious at best. Government statistics on drug offenses, which are the basis for the great majority of pretext traffic stops, tell us virtually nothing about the racial breakdown of those involved in drug crime. Thinking for a moment about arrest data and victimization surveys makes the reasons for this clear. These statistics show that blacks are indeed overrepresented among those arrested for homicide, rape, robbery, aggravated assault, larceny/theft, and simple assault crimes.[40] Note that because they directly affect their victims, these crimes are at least somewhat likely to be reported to the police and to result in arrests. By contrast, drug offenses are much less likely to be reported, since possessors, buyers, and sellers of narcotics are all willing participants in these crimes. Therefore, arrest data for drug crimes is highly suspect. These data may measure the law enforcement activities and policy choices of the institutions and actors involved in the criminal justice system, but the number of drug arrests does not measure the extent of drug crimes themselves. Similarly, the racial composition of prisons and jail populations or the racial breakdown of sentences for these crimes only measures the actions of those institutions and individuals in charge; it tells us nothing about drug activity itself.

Other statistics on both drug use and drug crime show something surprising in light of the usual beliefs many hold: blacks may *not*, in fact, be more likely than whites to be involved with drugs. Lamberth's study in Maryland showed that among vehicles stopped and searched, the "hit rates"—the percentage of vehicles searched in which drugs were found—were statistically indistinguishable for blacks and whites.[41] There is also a considerable amount of data on drug use that belies the standard beliefs. The percentages of drug users who are black or white are roughly the same as the presence of those groups in the population as a whole. For example, blacks constitute approximately twelve percent of the country's population. In 1997, the most recent year for which statistics are available, thirteen percent of all drug users were black.[42] In fact, among black youths, a demographic group often portrayed as most likely to be involved with drugs, use of all illicit substances has actually been *consistently lower* than among white youths for *twenty years running*.[43]

Nevertheless, many believe that African-Americans and members of other minority groups are responsible for most drug use and drug trafficking. Carl Williams, the head of the New Jersey State Police dismissed by the Governor in March of 1999, stated that "mostly minorities" trafficked in marijuana and cocaine, and pointed out that when senior American officials went overseas to discuss the drug problem, they went to Mexico, not Ireland. Even if he is wrong, if the many troopers who worked for Williams share his opinions, they will act accordingly. And they will do so by looking for drug criminals among black drivers. Blackness will become an indicator of suspicion of drug crime involvement. This, in turn, means that the belief that blacks are disproportionately involved in drug crimes will become a self-fulfilling prophecy. Because police will *look* for drug crime among black drivers, they will *find* it disproportionately among black drivers. More blacks will be arrested, prosecuted, convicted, and jailed, thereby reinforcing the idea that blacks constitute the majority of drug offenders. This will provide a continuing motive and justification for stopping more black drivers as a rational way of using resources to catch the most criminals. At the same time, because police will focus on black drivers, white drivers will receive less attention, and the drug dealers and possessors among them will be apprehended in proportionately smaller numbers than their presence in the population would predict.

The upshot of this thinking is visible in the stark and stunning numbers that show what our criminal justice system is doing when it uses law enforcement practices like racially-biased traffic stops to enforce drug laws. African-Americans are just 12% of the population and 13% of the drug users, but they are about 38% of all those arrested for drug offenses, 59% of all those convicted of drug offenses, and 63% of all those convicted for drug trafficking. While only 33% of whites who are convicted are sent to prison, 50% of convicted blacks are jailed, and blacks who are sent to prison receive higher sentences than whites for the same crimes. For state drug defendants, the average maximum sentence length is fifty-one months for whites and sixty months for blacks.[44]

The Expansion of Police Discretion

Police have nearly complete discretion to decide who to stop. According to all of the evidence available, police frequently exercise this discretion in a racially-biased way, stopping blacks in numbers far out of proportion to their presence on the highway. Law enforcement generally sees this as something positive because the more discretion officers have to fight crime, the better able they will be to do the job.

Police discretion cannot be eliminated; frankly, even if it could be, this would not necessarily be a desirable goal. Officers need discretion to meet individual situations with judgment and intelligence, and to choose their responses so that the ultimate result will make sense. Yet few would contend that police discretion should be *limitless*. But this is exactly what the pretextual stop doctrine allows. Since *everyone* violates the traffic code at some point, it is not a matter of *whether* police can stop a driver, but *which driver* they want to stop. Police are free to pick and choose the motorists they will pull over, so factors other than direct evidence of law breaking come into play. In the "driving while black" situation, of course, that factor is race. In other law enforcement areas in which the state has nearly limitless discretion to prosecute, the decision could be based on political affiliation, popularity, or any number of other things. What these arenas have in common is that enforcement depends upon external factors, instead of law breaking.

Distortion of the Social World

"Driving while black" distorts not only the perception and reality of the criminal justice system, but also the social world. For example, many African-Americans cope with the possibility of pretextual traffic stops by driving drab cars and dressing in ways that are not flamboyant so as not to attract attention. More than that, "driving while black" serves as a spatial restriction on African-Americans, circumscribing their movements. Put simply, blacks know that police and white residents feel that there are areas in which blacks "do not belong." Often, these are all-white suburban communities or upscale commercial areas. When blacks drive through these areas, they may be watched and stopped because they are "out of place." Consequently, blacks try to avoid these places if for no other reason than that they do not want the extra police scrutiny. It is simply more trouble than it is worth to travel to or through these areas. While it is blacks themselves who avoid these communities, and not police officers or anyone else literally keeping them out, in practice it makes little difference. African-Americans do not enter if they can avoid doing so, whether by dint of self-restriction or by government policy.

Undermining Community-Based Policing

Though the term sometimes seems to have as many meanings as people who use it, community policing does have some identifiable characteristics. The idea is for the police to serve the community and become part of it, not to dominate it or occupy it. To accomplish this, police become known to and involved with residents, make efforts to understand their problems, and attack crime in ways that help address those difficulties. The reasoning is that if the police become part of the community, members of the public will feel comfortable enough to help officers identify troubled spots and trouble makers.

As difficult as it will be to build, given the many years of disrespect blacks have suffered at the hands of the police, the community must feel that it can trust the police to treat them as law-abiding citizens if community policing is to succeed. Using traffic stops in racially disproportionate numbers will directly and fundamentally undermine this effort. Why should law-abiding residents of these communities trust the police if, every time they go out for a drive, they are treated like criminals? If the "driving while black" problem is not addressed, community policing will be made much more difficult and may even fail. Thus, aside from the damage "driving while black" stops inflict on African-

Americans, there is another powerful reason to change this police behavior: it is in the interest of police departments themselves to correct it.

WAYS TO ADDRESS THE PROBLEM

With the Supreme Court abdicating any role for the judiciary in regulating these police practices under the Fourth Amendment, leadership must come from other directions and other institutions. What other approaches might be fruitful sources of change?

The Traffic Stops Statistics Act

At the beginning of the 105th Congress, Representative John Conyers of Michigan introduced House Bill 118, the Traffic Stops Statistics Act of 1997.[45] This bill would provide for the collection of several categories of data on each traffic stop, including the race of the driver and whether and why a search was performed. The Attorney General would then summarize the data in the first nationwide, statistically rigorous study of these practices. The idea behind the bill was that if the study confirmed what people of color have experienced for years, it would put to rest once and for all the idea that African-Americans who have been stopped for "driving while black" are exaggerating isolated anecdotes into a social problem. Congress and other bodies might then begin to take concrete steps to channel police discretion more appropriately. The Act passed the House of Representatives in March of 1998 with bipartisan support, and then was referred to the Senate Judiciary Committee. When police opposition arose, the Senate took no action and the bill died at the end of the session. Congressman

Conyers reintroduced the measure in April of 1999.[46]

The Traffic Stops Statistics Act is a very modest bill, a first step toward addressing a difficult problem. It mandated no concrete action on the problem; it did not regulate traffic stops, set standards for them, or require implementation of particular policies. It was merely an attempt to gather solid, comprehensive information, so that discussion of the problem could move ahead beyond the debate of whether or not the problem existed. Still, the bill attracted enough law enforcement opposition to kill it. But even if the Act did not pass the last Congress and subsequent bills also fail, it seems to have had at least one interesting effect: it has inspired action at the state and local level.

State Legislation

As important as national legislation on this issue would be, congressional action is no longer the only game in town. In fact, efforts are underway in a number of states to address the problem. [By mid-2001, thirteen states had laws that took some kind of action on racial profiling.]

While all of these measures differ in their particulars, they are all variations on Representative Conyers' bill—they mandate the collection of data and analyses of these data.

Local Action

Of course, legislative action is not required for a police department to collect data and to take other steps to address the "driving while black" problem. When a department realizes that it is in its own interest to take action, it can go ahead without being ordered to do so.

This is precisely what happened in San Diego, California. In February 1999, Jerome Sanders, the city's Chief of Police, announced that the department would begin to collect data on traffic stops, without any federal or state requirement.[47] The Chief's statement showed a desire to find out whether in fact the officers in his department were engaged in enforcing traffic laws on a racially uneven basis. If so, the problem could then be addressed. If the numbers did not show this, the statistics might help to dispel perceptions to the contrary.

Thus far, San Diego, San Jose, Oakland, and Houston are the largest urban jurisdictions to do this, but they are not alone. Police in over thirty other cities in California, as well as departments in Michigan, Florida, Washington and Rhode Island, are also collecting data. Police departments, not courts, are in the best possible position to take action—by collecting data, by re-training officers, and by putting in place and enforcing policies against the racially disproportionate use of traffic stops. Taking the initiative in this fashion allows a police department to control the process to a much greater extent than it might if it is mandated from the outside. And developing regulations from inside the organization usually will result in greater compliance by those who have to follow these rules—police officers themselves.[48] This represents a promising new approach to the problem. The police must first, of course, realize that there is a problem, and that doing something about it is in their interest.

Litigation

Another way to address racial profiling is to bring lawsuits under the Equal Protection Clause and federal civil rights statutes. In *Whren*, the U.S. Supreme Court said that under the Fourth Amendment of the U.S. Constitution courts can no longer suppress evidence in pretextual stop cases. But the Court did leave open the possibility of attacking racially-biased law enforcement activity under the Equal Protection Clause with civil suits. There are a number of such suits around the country that are either pending or recently concluded, including cases in Maryland, Florida, Indiana, and Illinois.

It is important not to underestimate the difficulty of filing a lawsuit against a police department alleging racial bias. These cases require an "attractive" plaintiff who will not make a bad impression due to prior criminal record, current criminal involvement, or the like. They also require a significant amount of resources. For this reason, organizations interested in this issue, particularly the American Civil Liberties Union, have taken the lead in bringing these cases. Last but not least, it takes a plaintiff with guts to stand up and publicly sue a police department in a racially-charged case. Most people would probably rather walk away from these experiences, no matter how difficult and humiliating, than get into a legal battle with law enforcement.

CONCLUSION

Everyone wants criminals caught. Few feel this with more urgency than African-Americans, who are so often the victims of crime. But we must choose our methods carefully. As a country, we must strive to avoid police practices that impose high costs on law abiding citizens, and that skew those costs heavily on the basis of race.

NOTES

1. *See* Traffic Stops Statistics Act of 1997, H.R. 118, 105th Cong. (1997). The bill was re-introduced in 1999 as the Traffic Stops Statis-tics Study Act, H.R. 1443, 106th Cong. (1999). The new bill limits data collection to a national sample of police departments.

2. Robert L. Jackson, "Push Against Bias in Traffic Stops Arrested," *Los Angeles Times*, June 1, 1998, A5.

3. Jackson 1998.

4. John Lamberth. 1996a. *Revised Statistical Analysis of the Incidence of Police Stops and Arrests of Black Drivers/Travelers on the New Jersey Turnpike Between Exits or Interchanges 1 and 3 from the Years 1988 Through 1991.*

5. 734 A.2d 350.

6. *Soto* was a criminal case; the defendant and the others joining his motion had been stopped and contraband seized from them, resulting in their arrests. *See id.* at 352. There is no doubt that now this claim would not succeed if based on the Fourth Amendment to the Federal Constitution. Under *Whren v. U.S.*, the Fourth Amendment would play no part in the decision because the motivation of the officer is immaterial, as long as a traffic offense was, in fact, committed. 517 U.S. 806, 813 (1996). As the case was eventually decided, the trial court granted the motion to suppress based on New Jersey's own law and constitution. *See Soto*, 734 A.2d at 352.

7. Lamberth, 1996a.

8. Lamberth 1996a:2.

9. Lamberth 1996a:3–6.

10. Lamberth 1996a:6–7.

11. Lamberth 1996a:14.

12. Lamberth 1996a:9.

13. Lamberth 1996a:26.

14. Lamberth's finding was supported by the testimony of several state police supervisors and officers. All said that blacks and whites drive indistinguishably. *See Soto*, 734 A.2d, 354.

15. *See Soto* 352.

16. Lamberth, 1996a:20.

17. Lamberth, 1996a:21.

18. This does not count those who are stopped *and arrested*.

19. Lamberth, 1996a:24.

20. Lamberth, 1996a:25.

21. Lamberth 1996a:25–26, 28.
22. John Lamberth. 1996b. Report, *Wilkins v. Maryland State Police*, Civil No. MJG-93-468.
23. David A. Harris, 1997. "Driving While Black and All Other Traffic Offenses: The Supreme Court and Pretextual Traffic Stops," *Journal of Criminal Law and Criminology*, 87:544–582.
24. Criminal Intelligence Report from Allegany County Narcotic Task Force to Maryland State Police (Apr. 27, 1992).
25. Lamberth 1996b, at 5 tbl.1.
26. Lamberth 1996b, at 9. Statewide, State Police found drugs on virtually the same percentages of black and white drivers. This means that even though blacks were much more likely to get stopped and searched than whites were, they were no more likely to have drugs, putting the supposed justification for these stops in grave doubt.
27. Lamberth 1996b, at 9.
28. Lamberth 1996b, at 9–10.
29. Data from Akron Municipal Court, Dayton Municipal Court, Toledo Municipal Court, and Franklin County Municipal Court, which includes Columbus, were used.
30. For at least Toledo and Akron, these numbers represent the total number of traffic *cases*, not individual tickets; some cases include more than one ticket given to the driver on the same occasion. By sheer coincidence, the data for Toledo were produced twice—first, tabulating all *tickets*, and then all *cases*. The data tabulating cases came to me by accident. The data were different; in the data on tickets, blacks were 35% of those ticketed; in the data concerning cases, blacks were 31%. These data showed that blacks were more likely than nonblacks to receive more than one ticket in the same stop, an interesting fact in its own right. Because I am interested in measuring traffic *stops* and am using ticketing only as a way to estimate stops, I have used the data on cases; after all, even if more than one ticket is issued in any given encounter, the driver was only stopped once. It is of course possi-

ble that the fact that blacks receive more than one ticket per incident more often than whites is itself a reflection of race-based policing, but there may be other factors at work here as well, such as the fact that blacks tend to drive older cars than whites that may have more obvious safety violations, or the fact that blacks use seat belts less often than whites. Therefore, for purposes of this study, I have chosen to treat this difference as if it is not evidence of racial bias.
31. Data from Franklin County Municipal Court include only the years 1996 and 1997, but none from 1998.
32. Franklin County Municipal Court data include all communities in the county, not just Columbus, but were not listed in a way that allowed separate numbers to be broken out for individual police departments. *See* Memorandum from Michael A. Pirik, Deputy Chief Clerk, Franklin County Municipal Court, to David Harris (Aug. 28, 1998).
33. The data in this portion of the study were obtained from the Census Bureau's website: <http://www.census.gov>.
34. Federal Highway Admin., U.S. Dep't of Transp., *1995 Nationwide Personal Transportation Survey* <http://www.bts.gov/ntda/npts>.
35. Letter from Eric Hill, Research Associate, Center for Urban Transportation Research, to David A. Harris (Oct. 9, 1998).
36. E-mails from Joseph E. Jacoby, Bowling Green State University, to David A. Harris (Feb. 2 & 3, 1999).
37. Federal Highway Admin., 1995 (reporting that whites average 4.4 vehicle trips daily and blacks average 3.9).
38. Chicago Gang Congregation Ordinance, Chicago Mun. Code § 8-4-015 (1992).
39. Joan Biskupic, "High Court to Review Law Aimed at Gangs," *Washington Post,* Dec. 7, 1998, at A4 (reporting that while the law was enforced, 45,000 people, mostly African-Americans and Hispanics, were arrested); David G. Savage, "High Court May Move Back on 'Move On' Laws," *Los Angeles Times*, Oct. 5, 1998.

40. Bureau of Justice Statistics, 1997. *Source Book of Criminal Justice Statistics* 1997, U.S. Department of Justice, at 338.

41. Lamberth, 1996b, 7–8.

42. Substance Abuse and Mental Health Servs. Nat'l Admin., U.S. Dep't. of Health and Human Servs., *National Household Survey on Drug Abuse, Preliminary Results from 1997*, 13, 58.

43. National Inst. on Drug Abuse, *Drug Use Among Racial/Ethnic Minorities*, (1997) (showing past-year use of marijuana, inhalants, cocaine, and LSD by black twelfth graders lower than use by whites in every year from 1977 to 1997, and tobacco use by blacks lower since 1982); Bureau of Justice Statistics, U.S. Dep't of Justice, *Drugs, Crime, and the Justice System* (1992).

44. Bureau of Justice Statistics, 1997, at 338, 426, 428.

45. Traffic Stops Statistics Act of 1997, H.R. 118, 105th Cong. (1997).

46. Traffic Stops Statistics Study Act of 1999, H.R. 1443, 106th Cong. (1999).

47. Michael Stetz & Kelly Thornton, 1999. "Cops to Collect Traffic-Stop Racial Data," *San Diego Union-Trib.*, Feb. 5:A1.

48. Wayne R. LaFave, 1990. "Controlling Discretion by Administrative Regulations: The Use, Misuse, and Nonuse of Police Rules and Policies in Fourth Amendment Adjudication," *Michigan Law Review*, 89.

Militarizing American Police

Peter B. Kraska and Victor E. Kappeler

The military and police comprise the state's primary use-of-force entities, the foundation of its coercive power (Bittner 1970; Enloe 1980; Kraska 1994; Turk 1982). A close ideological and operational alliance between these two entities in handling domestic social problems usually is associated with repressive governments. Although such an alliance is not normally associated with countries like the United States, reacting to certain social problems by blurring the distinction between military and police may be a key feature of the post-Cold War United States.

IGNORING POLICE/MILITARY CONNECTIONS

Scant attention has been paid to the emerging overlaps between police and military functions in the post-Cold War era (Kraska 1993). In the last decade most police academics have fixated on the professed turn toward community and problem-oriented policing. While transfixed on the "velvet glove," few have inquired into the possibility of a simultaneous strengthening of the "iron-fist" as a type of "backstage" phenomenon (Manning 1977; Crime and Social Justice 1983). Despite the overtly militaristic

nature of U.S. police paramilitary units (PPUs), and their continued growth since the early 1970s, little academic research or discussion examines these units.

Underlying the inattention paid to PPUs might be the assumption that they are sociologically and politically insignificant. Initially these units constituted a small portion of police efforts and were limited to large urban police departments. The constructed and publicly understood role of PPUs was confined to rare situations involving hostages, terrorism, or the "maniac sniper." Despite the camouflage of these common assumptions, there have been recent unmistakable signs of intensifying military culture in police departments. Although these units are highly secretive about their operations, obvious expressions of militarism are found throughout contemporary policing in the form of changing uniforms, weaponry, language, training, and tactics (Kraska 1996).

Distinguishing Characteristics of PPUs

As opposed to traditional police, paramilitary units can be distinguished in the following ways. PPUs are equipped with an array of

From *Social Problems* v. 44, No. 1. (February 1997): 1–18. Reprinted by permission of the University of California Press, the Society for the Study of Social Problems, and the authors.

militaristic equipment and technology. They often refer to themselves in military jargon as the "heavy weapons units," implying that what distinguishes them from regular police is the power and number of their weapons. The weapon most popular among these units is the Heckler and Koch MP5 submachine gun; its notoriety originates from elite military "special operations" teams, such as the "Navy Seals." The MP5's direct connection to elite military teams, its imposing futuristic style, an aggressive marketing and training program conducted by the Heckler and Koch corporation, and a host of hi-tech accessories such as laser sights and sound suppressers, all solidify this weapon's central place in police paramilitary subculture (Kraska 1996). Other weapons include tactical, semi-automatic shotguns, M16s, sniper rifles, and automatic shotguns referred to as "street-sweepers."

PPUs have an array of "less-than-lethal" technology for conducting "dynamic entries" (e.g., serving a search warrant). These include percussion grenades (explosive devices designed to disorient residents), stinger grenades (similar devices containing rubber pellets), CS and OC gas grenades (tear gas), and shotgun launched bean-bag systems (nylon bags of lead shot). "Dynamic entries" require apparatuses for opening doors, including battering rams, hydraulic door-jamb spreaders, and C4 explosives. Some PPUs purchase and incorporate a range of "fortified tactical vehicles," including military armored personnel carriers and specially equipped "tactical cruisers."

A PPU's organizational structure is modeled after military and foreign police special operations teams in that they operate and train collectively under military command structure and discipline (Jefferson 1990). These teams wear black or urban camouflage "battle dress uniforms (BDUs)," lace-up combat boots, full body armor, Kevlar helmets, and sometimes goggles with "ninja" style hoods. Team members place a high premium on group solidarity and view themselves as "elite" officers, a view supported and promoted by police management (Kraska and Paulsen 1996).

Traditionally, PPU work differed significantly from routine policing. The bulk of these units formed in the late 1960s and early 1970s to respond to civil riots, terrorism, barricaded suspects, and hostage situations. Today, it is all but impossible to differentiate most PPUs by their work, except that it tends to be what each department defines as "high-risk." High-risk activities are generally defined as those situations that require a squad of police officers trained to be use-force-specialists. These squads have an intensified operational focus on either the threatened or the actual use of collective force.

Despite these distinguishing characteristics, PPUs could indeed be considered inconsequential and perhaps functional if they handled only the narrowly defined terrorist or barricaded suspect situations, were housed in the largest departments under tight control, and had little impact on the operations and culture of their departments. However, the authors' ethnographic studies revealed a different set of circumstances (Kraska 1996; Kraska and Paulsen 1996), raising numerous research questions amenable to a national police survey.

METHODOLOGY

We constructed a 40-item survey (98 variables) to examine the growth and normalization of military tactics and ideology among and within United States law enforcement agencies. The instrument sought basic demographic information on the responding police agencies, and included an option for respondents to list their identity and phone number. It also sought both descriptive and longitudinal data on the formation, prevalence, uses, and activities of PPUs as they relate to the U.S. military. Finally, we solicited attitudinal information regarding the respondents' rationales for using PPUs.

Our sampling frame was all United States law enforcement agencies, excluding federal agencies, servicing jurisdictions of 50,000 or more citizens and employing at least 100 sworn officers. This list yielded a population of 690 law enforcement agencies across the states, representing all the various political subdivisions of state and local government. Because we could not determine whether four agencies identified in our sampling frame existed, they were excluded from the mailing.

An initial mailing of the survey was sent to the entire population of police agencies in January, 1996. This mailing included a letter of introduction, along with a copy of the survey instrument. Because of the secretive and suspicious character of police agencies (Manning 1978; Skolnick 1966; Westley 1956) and the difficulty in researching highly sensitive topics associated with policing (Kraska and Kappeler 1995), the introductory letter was written on a recognized sponsor's letterhead. This letter was signed by the principal researcher (first author) as well as the director of the professional organization that agreed to sponsor the research. It also noted the researchers' university affiliation.[1] The language used in the survey encouraged respondents to recognize the study as administratively oriented. This orientation, coupled with the authors' familiarity with PPU rhetoric and the promise of confidentiality and anonymity, likely provided a level of occupational comfort to the respondents.

Within four weeks, the first mailing yielded 413 responses, a 61 percent response rate. After approximately five weeks, a second wave of surveys was mailed to the remaining 281 non-respondents. The second mailing stressed the high level of participation among other law enforcement agencies and it urged cooperation from those departments without a PPU. After approximately 6 weeks, this follow-up mailing yielded an additional 135 responses for a total response rate of 79 percent.

The researchers selected 81 of the respondents that provided identification and telephone information for unstructured follow-up phone interviews. Forty agencies that used their PPU for proactive patrol work were selected at random; the remainder were called to have police officials elaborate on their responses. Each phone interview began with an introduction and a brief verification of the data provided on the written survey. We then explored the more sensitive and controversial aspects of PPUs. Interviews lasted between five minutes and one hour—the majority about 20 minutes.

ESCALATING AND NORMALIZING PPUs

Of the 548 departments responding, 89.4 percent had a police paramilitary unit. Over 20 percent of those departments without a unit said they were "planning on establishing one in the next few years." Although most departments formed their units in the 1970s, the percentage of police departments with PPUs has grown steadily (see Figure 1). In 1982, about 59 percent of the police departments surveyed had a PPU. By 1990, this figure had increased to 78 percent, and by 1995 it reached 89 percent. The bulk of the newer units were from smaller municipalities and state police agencies.[2]

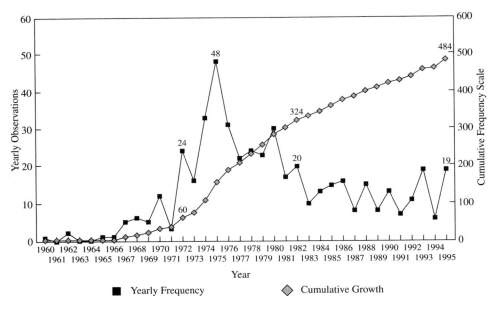

Figure 1. Year PPU Formed and Cumulative Growth

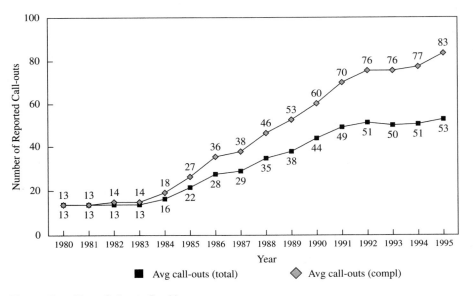

Figure 2. Mean Call-outs Per Year

Of course an increase in the number of PPUs, although an important indication of police militarization, means little without examining longitudinally the activities of these paramilitary units. Given the traditional role of PPUs, we might expect only a limited number of "deployments" in cases of barricaded suspects or civil demonstrations. Figure 2 reports on the mean "call-outs"—all emergency or high-risk deployments of the PPUs—for each of the years between 1980 and 1995. This graph depicts two sets of call-out data. The first includes all departments which provided call-out data for any of the years between 1980–1995 (marked as "total"). The second includes only those departments that had PPUs before 1980, and that provided complete data for all the years 1980–1995 (marked as "compl").

Regarding the "total" data set, between 1980–1983 the mean number of call-outs was fairly constant and minimal, with about 13 call-outs on average per year, or approximately one PPU deployment per month. The level of police paramilitary unit activity more than doubled by 1986, almost tripled by 1989, and quadrupled by 1995. If we only include those departments that have had PPUs since 1980 (marked as "compl"), and that provided complete data from 1980–1995 (n=193), we find that the rise in paramilitary police activity is even more pronounced—a 538 percent increase.

This enormous growth in PPU activity documents an unprecedented yet little noticed phenomenon in U.S. policing—a dramatic increase in paramilitary policing activity. Moving from one call-out per month to four or five may only indicate a dramatic increase in the number of traditional PPU activities rather than normalization of these units into mainstream policing. Although we could not expect departments to provide data on the types of call-outs for every year, we did ask them for

1995 data on "barricaded persons," "hostage situations," "terrorist activity," "dangerous warrants," "civil disturbances," and "other activities." Of the total number of call-outs (n=25,201), civil disturbances accounted for 1.3 percent (n=338), terrorist incidents .09 percent (n=23), hostage situations 3.6 percent (n=913), and barricaded persons 13.4 percent (n=3,880). Respondents reported that the majority of call-outs were to conduct what the police call "high risk warrant work," mostly "drug raids." Warrant work accounted for 75.9 percent (n=19,125) of all paramilitary activity in 1995.

As shown in Figure 3, police using PPUs "proactively" for high-risk warrant work surged in the late 1980s and early 1990s. Phone interviews provided the researchers with insights into the significance of this phenomenon. Both large and small departments, with the exception of those few PPUs that have remained true to their original purpose (about 10 percent), gave essentially the same account. The drug war of the late 1980s and early 1990s required the servicing of an unprecedented number of search warrants and a lesser number of arrest warrants. Rather than reactively responding to traditional crimes such as robbery, the police can go into the population and proactively produce cases against an almost limitless number of drug users and low-level dealers (Barnett 1987)— hence, the dramatic increase in "call-outs." Most traditionally reaction-oriented PPUs enthusiastically accepted the new function of executing large numbers of warrants; many PPUs now conduct between 200–700 warrants/drug raids a year.

According to our respondents, "warrant work" consists almost exclusively of what police call "no-knock entries." Generally a search warrant is obtained through either a police informant or a tip from a neighbor. After securing a warrant, the paramilitary unit

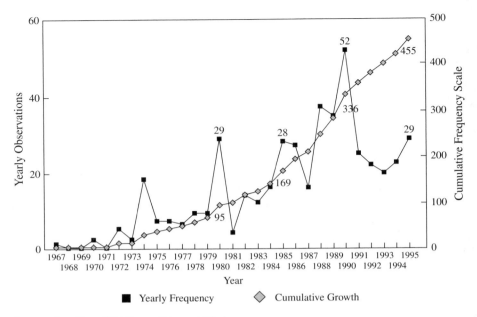

Figure 3. Year PPU Began Warrant Work

conducts a "dynamic entry," generally on a private residence. Some departments claimed that these "drug raids" do not even require a warrant if the police have reason to believe that waiting for a warrant would endanger lives or lead to the destruction of evidence.[3] As one commander described these operations, "our unit storms the residence with a full display of weaponry so we can get the drugs before they're flushed."[4] Some of the PPU commanders stressed that this type of proactive policing—instigated not by an existing high-risk situation but one generated by the police themselves—is highly dangerous for both PPU members and citizens.

A police official from a large southwestern police department explained: "In the early 90s we conducted 500 drug raids a year; things got way too dangerous and we cut way back." In this department, a team of ex-PPU members took over the warrant work after

forming their own narcotics PPU. A specific incident led to this captain's negative view of drug raids:

> We did a crack-raid and got in a massive shoot-out in an apartment building. Shots were fired and we riddled a wall with bullets. An MP5 round will go through walls. When we went into the next apartment where the bullets were penetrating, we found a baby crib full of holes; thank god those people weren't home.

The interviewees also stressed that confiscating guns and money in these drug raids is as important as confiscating drugs. Several commanders noted how confiscated assets sometimes fund the purchase of new paramilitary equipment. It is critical to recognize, therefore, that doing "warrant work" is not just the perfunctory serving of a warrant subsequent to an in-depth investigation. Rather, it has become a proactive tool through which the police gather evidence and crudely conduct an investigation into suspected illegal activity. Marx (1988) has drawn considerable attention to police undercover narcotics investigations in the war on drugs. Few have noted this proactive policing tactic, perhaps more prevalent than undercover work, of PPUs conducting military-style investigatory drug raids on private residences.

These data demonstrate movement toward the normalization of paramilitary police groups. Another change that further substantiates the militarization of policing is patrol work. A recent article in a popular police magazine indicates just such a phenomenon. Police in Fresno, California pursue the goal of "proactive policing" by responding to what the article termed their inner-city "war zone" with a 40-man SWAT team, equipped with full military garb and weaponry. The objective of this full-time patrol-unit is to "suppress" the gang, drug, and crime problems. The article claims great success for this approach and sees it as an inevitable trend:

> The general consensus has been that SWAT teams working in a proactive patrol-type setting does work. Police officers working in patrol vehicles, dressed in *urban tactical gear* and armed with automatic weapons are here—and they're here to stay (Smith 1995:82; emphasis added).

Although we assumed the Fresno police department was an aberration, we still asked in the survey, "Is your department using the tactical operations unit as a proactive patrol unit to aid high crime areas?" Out of the 487 departments responding to this question, more than 20 percent (n=107) responded affirmatively. Using a PPU for patrol work was not limited to large metropolitan cities. Forty-

seven percent (n=50) of the departments using their PPU for proactive patrol work served populations between 50,000 and 250,000; 20 percent (n=21) served populations between 50,000 and 100,000.

Figure 4 illustrates the year when each department began using its PPU for proactive patrol work. The graph shows a precipitous rise in normalizing paramilitary teams into patrol work. Since 1982, there has been a 292 percent increase (from 24 to 94) in the number of departments using PPUs for proactive patrol. Just since 1989, the number of departments deploying PPUs in this manner has doubled. As an indication of this trend continuing, 61 percent of the respondents agreed that: "Tactical Operations Units should be deployed to patrol high crime areas."

As Figure 4 shows, a few departments have used PPUs as patrol units since the late 1960s and early 1970s. Early PPUs sometimes engaged in "saturation patrol" of high crime areas, often in plain-clothes and unmarked cars. The question we needed answered, and one that was too threatening to ask in the survey itself, was whether the PPU patrolled in full "tactical gear" like the Fresno police department.

Forty departments that answered affirmatively to the patrol question were randomly selected for telephone interviews. We asked about their garb, weaponry, and tactics. Different departments employ a variety of methods, ranging from full military-like, aggressive patrol as found in Fresno (n=21), to patrol officers not dressed in full tactical gear but "slung with MP5s" (n=9), to PPU members in plain-clothes and standard police revolvers, carrying their full tactical gear and weaponry in car trunks (n=10). Some departments rotated these approaches depending on circumstances. One highly acclaimed community policing department described their latest approach:

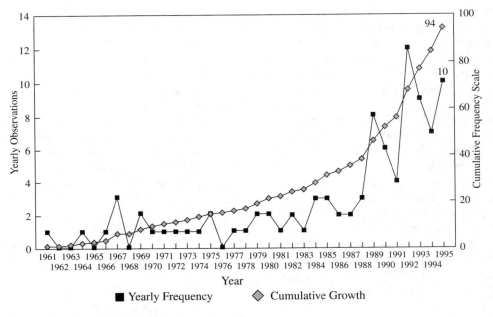

Figure 4. Year PPU Began Pro-Active Control

We're into saturation patrols in hot spots. We do a lot of our work with the SWAT unit because we have bigger guns. We send out two, two-to-four-men cars, we look for minor violations and do jump-outs, either on people on the street or automobiles. After we jump-out the second car provides periphery cover with an *ostentatious display of weaponry*. We're sending a clear message: if the shootings don't stop, we'll shoot someone [emphasis added].

Another commander described how his "progressive" police chief purchased a "SWAT bus" so that 30 tactical officers in full military gear could be deployed to "hot spots" throughout the city. "They geared up every night—30 officers every night for four months." One mid-west police department that services a community of 75,000 people patrols in full-tactical gear using a military armored personnel carrier (termed a "peace-keeper") as their transport vehicle. The PPU commander described their approach as targeting:

suspicious vehicles and people. We stop anything that moves. We'll sometimes even surround suspicious homes and bring out the MP5s. We usually don't have any problems with crack-heads cooperating.[5]

Two departments admitted they funded these very expensive operations with federal monies allocated for community policing programs—either by using these funds for overtime pay to PPU officers, or by hiring community policing officers and then transferring personnel to staff new PPU positions.

It is critical to note that several of the PPU commanders interviewed were shocked, and others displeased, to hear that other departments were patrolling in full tactical gear.

One commander stressed that the practice not only would be offensive to the community he serves but, "operationally stupid. I realize some departments do that crap, it's just showing off—intimidation with no purpose." Another commander who disapproved of the practice did admit that his PPU members repeatedly request to wear their black BDUs on patrol. As he put it, "I can't blame them, we're a very elite unit, they just want to be distinguishable."

The elite self-perception and status granted these police units stems from the high status military special operations groups have in military culture (Gibson 1994; Kraska 1996). Although the shared culture between the police and military seems obvious, little evidence supported the notion that these two use-of-force institutions were connected materially and operationally. However, field research uncovered a pattern of former and reserve soldiers intimately involved in police special operations units, as well as active-duty soldiers "cross-training" with paramilitary police officers (Kraska 1996). This survey, therefore, inquired into the training activities of PPUs and its connection to the U.S. armed forces. While "training" may seem to be a purely technical exercise, it actually plays a central role in paramilitary subculture (Gibson

1994). Training constructs and reinforces the "dangerousness" of the group's work, the importance of feeling and thinking as a team, the belief that this elite team is doing "real" police work (see Kappeler et. al 1994), and the "pleasure" that comes from playing out "warrior fantasies" (Gibson 1994; Kraska 1996). An entire "tactical" culture revolves around PPU training in which units from all over the United States, sometimes from other countries, join together in annual training competitions. Interagency training is also prevalent; our survey found that 63 percent of PPUs provide training to other police agencies.

With regard to PPU's material connection with the U.S. armed forces, departments were asked first to identify the sources of training which were influential during the start-up period of their PPU. As seen in Table 1, almost 46 percent drew expertise from "police officers with special operations experience in the military." Similarly, 43 percent trained with "active-duty military experts in special operations." We then asked respondents to check those sources that currently provide training for the department's PPU. Table 1 shows that 30 percent of the departments received training from "police officers with special operations experience in the military," and almost 46 percent "trained with

Table 1. Past and Current PPU Connections to the U.S. Military*

Past Connection to Military		Yes	
	%		n
Police with Special Ops. Exp.	45.7		219
Military Special Ops. Training	42.8		205
Current Connection to Military		Yes	
	%		n
Police with Special Ops. Exp.	30.0		146
Military Special Ops. Training	45.7		222

*excludes 11 non-respondents for the "past connection" category and four non-respondents for the "current connection" category.

active-duty military experts in special operations."

Because 23 of the respondents wrote in the margin of the instrument that they train with either "Navy Seals" or "Army Rangers," we attempted to ascertain in phone interviews the extent and nature of this training. One respondent revealed the connection:

> We've had special forces folks who have come right out of the jungles of Central and South America. These guys get into the real shit. All branches of military service are involved in providing training to law enforcement. U.S. Marshalls act as liaisons between the police and military to set up the training—our go-between. They have an arrangement with the military through JTF-6 [joint task force 6]. . . . I just received a piece of paper from a four-star general who tells us he's concerned about the type of training we're getting. We've had teams of Navy Seals and Army Rangers come here and teach us everything. We just have to use our judgment and exclude the information like: "at this point we bring in the mortars and blow the place up."

During the late 1980s drug war, the Bush administration established several Department of Defense "Joint Task Forces" responsible for coordinating drug interdiction operations at the borders, abroad, and domestically (Kraska 1993). This arrangement required substantial overlap and cooperation between the military and civilian police forces, to the point of having the armed forces' elite special operations teams cross-train with U.S. civilian police forces.

IMPLICATIONS

Our research found a sharp rise in the number of police paramilitary units, a rapid expansion in their activities, the normalization of paramilitary units into mainstream police work, and a close ideological and material connection between PPUs and the U.S. armed forces. These findings provide compelling evidence of a national trend toward the militarization of U.S. civilian police forces and, in turn, the militarization of corresponding social problems handled by the police.[6] The data also reveal a continuing upward trend in proactive paramilitary policing activities. It is important to review some policy-specific dangers associated with the rise and normalization of paramilitary policing.

First, the militarism inherent in PPUs escalates to new heights the cynical view that the most expedient route to solving social problems is through military-style force, weaponry, and technology. Second, the heightened ethos of militarism in these "elite" police units is potentially infectious for the police institution; many police departments have created specialized PPUs for patrol, narcotics, and gang "suppression." According to some commanders, PPUs are also the testing ground for incorporating tactical equipment, such as percussion grenades, into mainstream policing. Third, despite the belief among tactical officers that PPUs enhance officer and citizen safety, numerous incidents and common sense raise questions about the dangerousness of these units to officers and citizens.[7] Contemporary PPUs do not just react to pre-existing emergencies that might require highly trained teams of police officers. Instead, most PPUs proactively seek out and even manufacture highly dangerous situations. Finally, paramilitary policing is not just an urban "inner-city" phenomenon. These units target what the police define as high crime or disorderly areas, which most often are poor neighborhoods, whatever the city's size.

NOTES

1. Sponsorship was limited to the use of the association's letterhead. The association did not provide any resources nor did it have any input into the project beyond its initial approval. Without the endorsement of a recognized law enforcement organization, the response rate would likely have been significantly lower.

2. Results from research just completed indicate an even more rapid growth in PPUs in smaller county and municipal police departments (departments serving populations between 25,000 and 50,000 with less than 150 officers). In 1985, 31 percent of these departments had a paramilitary unit; by 1995, 69 percent had a fully staffed paramilitary unit.

3. The PPU in Chapel Hill, North Carolina conducted a crack-raid of an entire block in an African-American neighborhood. The raid, termed "Operation Redi-Rock," resulted in the detention and search of up to 100 people, all of whom were African-American (whites were allowed to leave the area). No one was ever prosecuted for a crime (Barnett v. Karpinos 1995).

4. According to our interviews the majority of warrants served by PPUs are executed as dynamic, no-knock entries. While constitutional provisions of the Fourth Amendment are intended to constrain and limit the situations and methods used in police searches, courts have endorsed the use of PPUs to serve routine search and arrest warrants (Kappeler 1993). Courts are more than willing to issue "no-knock if necessary" warrants, particularly in cases characterized as drug-related (Moss v. City of Colorado Springs, 1989; King v. Marmon, 1992). The ease with which police can obtain no-knock warrants and the almost unlimited "reasonable" justifications for deviating from the knock and announce requirement (Collier v. Locicero, 1993) partly account for increases in dynamic no-knock entries. The "if neces-

sary" clause of the no-knock warrant has also given the police greater autonomy in how these raids are conducted. It is not uncommon for warrants to be issued based on fictitious police informants (Streetman v. Jordan, 1990; Hervey v. Estes, 1995), false or misleading information provided by police (Williams v. City of Detroit, 1994), or an officer's sole testimony concerning the detection of drug orders (U.S. v. Riveria, 1979). The growing list of exceptions to the Fourth Amendment's warrant requirement provides the police with near unlimited discretion in making the decision of whether to conduct a raid. Police now use the "administrative search exception" to the warrant requirement to conduct warrantless raids (Hamilton v. Lokuta, 1992). These raids often target locations deemed by the police to be community problems such as exotic dance halls, "drughouses," private birthing clinics, or people the police previously, and often unsuccessfully investigated (Hummel-Toner v. Strope, 1994; Hamilton v. Lokita, 1992; Turner v. Upton County, Texas, 1990).

5. One PPU commander was overt about the intersection of militarism and racial bias in their paramilitary patrol work when he stated: "When the soldiers ride in you should see those blacks scatter."

6. We are not asserting that militarization is the only trend in policing, or even the predominant trend. As Manning (1995:609) states," . . . policing is fragmented and polyphonic, contains a variety of discourses, and symbolizes various aims and values."

7. Seven of the police departments surveyed had sharp declines in PPU activity in the last few years. We called these departments out of curiosity and they explained that there had been a controversy over the PPU killing or wounding innocent people, sometimes while at the wrong residence, or instances where team members were shot by "friendly fire." These departments' chiefs "temporarily" cut-back on using the PPUs proactively.

REFERENCES

Barnett, Randy E. 1987. "Curing the drug-law addiction: The harmful side effects of legal prohibition." In *Dealing With Drugs: Consequences of Governmental Control*, ed. Ronald Hamowy, 73–102. San Francisco: Pacific Research Institute for Public Policy.

Bittner, Egon. 1970. *The Functions of Police in Modern Society*. Chevy Chase, Md.: National Clearinghouse for Mental Health.

Crime and Social Justice Associates. 1983. *The Iron Fist and Velvet Glove: An Analysis of the U.S. Police*, 3rd ed. San Francisco: Garret Press.

Enloe, Cynthia. 1980. *Police, Military and Ethnicity*. New Brunswick, N.J.: Transaction.

Gibson, James W. 1994. *Warrior Dreams: Manhood in Post-Vietnam America*. New York: Hill and Wang.

Jefferson, Tony. 1990. *The Case Against Paramilitary Policing*. Bristol, Penn.: Open University Press.

Kappeler, Victor E. 1993. *Critical Issues in Police Civil Liability*. Prospect Heights Ill.: Waveland Press.

Kappeler, Victor E., Richard D. Sluder, and Geoffrey P. Alpert. 1994. *Forces of Deviance: Understanding the Dark Side of Policing*. Prospect Heights, Ill.: Waveland Press.

Kraska, Peter B. 1993. "Militarizing the drug war: A sign of the times." In *Altered States of Mind: Critical Observations of the Drug War*, ed. Peter B. Kraska, 159–206. New York: Garland.

———. 1994. "The police and military in the post-Cold War era: Streamlining the state's use of force entities in the drug war." *Police Forum* 4:1–8.

———. 1996. "Enjoying militarism: Political/personal dilemmas in studying U.S. police paramilitary units." *Justice Quarterly* 13:405–429.

Kraska, Peter B., and Victor E. Kappeler. 1995. "To serve and pursue: Exploring police sexual violence against women." *Justice Quarterly* 12:85–112.

Kraska, Peter B., and Derek Paulsen. 1996. "Forging the iron first inside the velvet glove: A case study in the rise of U.S. paramilitary units." Presented at the Academy of Criminal Justice Sciences meeting in Las Vegas, Nevada.

Manning, Peter K. 1977. *Police Work: The Social Organization of Policing*. Cambridge, Mass.: MIT Press.

———. 1978. "The police: Mandate, strategies and appearances." In *Policing: A View From the Street*, eds. P.K. Manning and J. Van Maanen, 7–32. Chicago: Goodyear.

———. 1995. "Book review: Forces of Deviance." *Justice Quarterly* 12:605–610.

Marx, Gary T. 1988. *Undercover Policing: Police Surveillance in America*. Berkeley: University of California Press.

Skolnick, Jerome H. 1966. *Justice Without Trial: Law Enforcement in a Democratic Society*. New York: John Wiley and Sons.

Smith, C. D. 1995. "Taking back the streets." *Police Magazine* 19:36–40.

Turk, Austin. 1982. *Political Criminality: The Defiance and Defense of Authority*. Beverly Hills: Sage Publications.

Westley, W. A. 1956. "Secrecy and the Police." *Social Forces* 34:254–257.

LEGAL CITES

Barnett v. Karpinos, 460 S.E.2d 208 (N.C. App. 1995).

Bonner v. Anderson 81 F.3d 472 (4th Cir. 1996).

Collier v. Locicero, 820 F.Supp. 673 (D.Conn. 1993).

Hale v. Townley, 19 F.3d 1068 (5th Cir. 1994).

Hamilton v. Lokuta, 803 F.Supp. 82 (E.D. Mich. 1992).

Hervey v. Estes, 65 F.3d 784 (9th Cir. 1995).

Hummel-Toner v. Strope, 25 F.3d 647 (8th Cir. 1994).

King v. Marmon, 793 F.Supp. 1030 (D. Kan. 1992).

McGovern v. City of Minneapolis, 480 N.W.2d 121 (Minn.App. 1992).

Moss v. City of Colorado Springs, 871 F.2d 112 (10th Cir. 1989).

Streetman v. Jordan, 918 F.2d 555 (5th Cir, 1990).

Turner v. Upton County, Texas, 915 F.2d 133 (5th Cir. 1990).

U.S. v. Riveria, 595 F.2d 1095 (5th Cir. 1979).

Williams v. City of Detroit, 843 F.Supp. 1183 (E.D.Mich. 1994).

Zero Tolerance Policing

Judith A. Greene

The 1998 New York City Mayor's Management Report lists many concrete improvements in the quality of life in New York City, which Mayor Rudy Giuliani believes have been won directly through the New York Police Department's targeted approach to crime control—now held up by many observers as the epitome of "zero-tolerance" policing. During the first half of 1997, New York City was ranked 150th out of 189 U.S. cities with populations of more than 100,000 for its Federal Bureau of Investigation (FBI) Index Crime rate.[1] In 1993, the year Giuliani was elected mayor, New York City had been ranked 87th on this list.

The Mayor's office reports that from 1993 to 1997 the number of felony complaints in New York City dropped by 44.3 percent: a 60.2 percent drop in murders and nonnegligent homicides, a 12.4 percent drop in forcible rape, a 48.4 percent drop in robbery, and a 45.7 drop in burglary. Mayor Giuliani points out that New York City is responsible for a large share of the overall crime reduction for the country as a whole. Comparing data from cities of more than 100,000 population for the first half of 1997 with data from these cities in the first half of 1993, the mayor's management report asserts that New York City accounted for 32 percent of the overall drop in FBI Index Crimes, 29 percent of the drop in murders, and 44 percent of the drop in larceny/thefts (New York City Mayor's Office of Operations 1998).

The Mayor's office credits the New York Police Department's (NYPD's) "Compstat"[2] system for much of the progress made in reducing crime. Compstat was introduced by Police Commissioner William Bratton, who had served as commissioner for the first 27 months (from January 1994 to April 1996) of Giuliani's first term as mayor. The Compstat system puts up-to-date crime data into the hands of NYPD managers at all levels and bolsters a department-wide process for precinct-level accountability in meeting the department's crime-reduction goals.

As described in Bratton's recent book, *Turnaround: How America's Top Cop Reversed the Crime Epidemic* (Bratton 1998, p. 224), the Compstat system is built on four concepts: (1) accurate and timely intelligence, (2) rapid deployment of personnel and resources, (3) effective tactics, and (4) relentless follow-up and assessment. Compstat is the engine that drives "zero-tolerance" policing in New York City, and it is at the heart of the strategic organizational changes that Bratton introduced when he took command of the NYPD in 1994 (Silverman 1997a).

Zero-tolerance policing puts major emphasis on the kinds of "quality-of-life" issues

From *Crime and Delinquency*, Vol. 45 No. 2 (April 1999):171–187. Reprinted by permission of Sage Publications © 1999.

that set the drumbeat rhythm for Giuliani's 1993 mayoral campaign. The "Squeegee Men" (beggars who accosted drivers in their cars to scrub their windshields and panhandle for cash), the petty drug dealers, the graffiti scribblers, and the prostitutes who ruled the sidewalks in certain high-crime neighborhoods all were targeted in candidate Giuliani's campaign promise to reclaim the streets of New York for law-abiding citizens.

Prior to his election, Giuliani's professional career had been spent in law enforcement. It is no coincidence that these types of disorderly persons and small-time criminals exactly fit the flesh-and-blood profile of the "broken windows" theory of policing—an approach first promoted in 1982 by James Q. Wilson and George Kelling. The broken windows theory holds that if not firmly suppressed, disorderly behavior in public will frighten citizens and attract predatory criminals, thus leading to more serious crime problems.[3]

Although "reclaiming the open spaces of New York" was but one of six specific crime strategies that Bratton designed and introduced to reshape the goals of the NYPD,[4] it was moved quickly to the front of the line when city officials began to make the claim that the Giuliani administration's police reforms were *causing* the decreases in crime. Cracking down hard on the most visible symbols of urban disorder proved to be a powerful political tool for bolstering Giuliani's image as a highly effective mayor. The speed with which the city's crime statistics have fallen has been taken by many to prove that Wilson and Kelling are correct and that serious crime problems can be quelled by mounting a large-scale attack on petty crime and disorderly behavior through a broken windows, zero-tolerance strategy.

To at least some extent, rhetorical emphasis on the broken windows theory has served to obscure the truly phenomenal record that William Bratton set in managing organizational change within the NYPD. As chief executive officer of one of the world's largest police agencies, he introduced new management tools, techniques, and technology at lightning speed and moved quickly to decentralize authority and to wrest decision-making power away from headquarters brass and move it out to the precinct and borough commands. He broke down a maze of bureaucratic barriers—pushing, prodding, and (when necessary) replacing personnel. He was able to integrate many of the police functions previously held by specialized units so as to empower patrol officers to move directly to address drug and gun crimes in the neighborhoods they serve (Silverman 1997a).

But Bratton's concept and style of police management has driven the NYPD a distinct and substantial distance apart from the community policing concepts that have been used to reshape and redirect police services in many other American cities. Moreover, some of these cities are closely rivaling the crime-reduction record set in New York City.

In a 1996 lecture sponsored by the Heritage Foundation, Bratton discussed the flaws that he perceives in the community policing initiatives of the early 1990s. He argued that community policing in New York was hampered by a lack of attention to those quality-of-life issues that cause widespread fear of crime among the public and by an unwieldy and highly centralized, overspecialized police bureaucracy. Bratton had served from 1990 to 1992 as chief of the New York Transit Police (the agency then responsible for patrolling the city's vast subway system), and he had observed the NYPD's community policing effort up close. At Transit, he pursued a successful quality-of-life policing campaign that consisted of large-scale arrests of young New Yorkers for fare evasion, which he credits with greatly reducing more serious subway crime (Bratton 1996).

Once recruited by Mayor-elect Giuliani to serve as commissioner of the NYPD, Bratton used his prior experience combating subway crime as a springboard into a citywide campaign to aggressively apprehend the perpetrators of quality-of-life crimes on the streets. Bratton's managerial reforms were brilliantly innovative, using up-to-the-minute technology. But at the neighborhood level, his crime-fighting strategies were grounded in traditional law enforcement methods and in relentless crackdown campaigns to arrest and jail low-level drug offenders and other petty perpetrators. His efforts to decentralize and devolve decision-making authority downward have relocated power at the precinct command level rather than empowering patrol officers to plan and implement crime prevention efforts in partnership with the communities they serve.

Bratton's crime-prevention concepts are more often cloaked in military campaign metaphors—"in New York City, we now know where the enemy is" (Bratton 1996)—than in the public-health/epidemiological images now more common is community-focused prevention efforts elsewhere. And his quality-of-life law-enforcement style was hyperaggressive. In *Turnaround*, Bratton (1998) describes how his school truancy program grabbed so many school-age kids off the streets that "we had to set up 'catchment' areas in school auditoriums and gymnasiums" (p. 225). He retooled New York City's drug enforcement effort to target more muscle toward low- and middle-level dealers, and he lifted a longstanding police policy that discouraged drug enforcement arrests by patrol officers—freeing them to seek warrants, make narcotics arrests, and go after those they suspected of drug dealing for quality-of-life violations to sweep them off the streets and into the jails (Bratton 1998, p. 227).

Bratton attacked the legal restrictions that had impeded aggressive enforcement against those deemed disorderly. He "took the handcuffs off" the police department and unleashed patrol officers to stop and search citizens who were violating the most minor laws on the books (e.g., drinking a beer or urinating in public), to run warrant checks on them, or just to pull them in for questioning about criminal activity in their neighborhood. If, in the course of such an incident, a weapon was found and confiscated, Bratton asserts that it was lawful prevention of crime "before it happened" (Bratton 1998, p. 229).

If, as its keystone crime-prevention strategy, New York City has turned away from community policing and chosen instead a zero-tolerance campaign that is heavily reliant on traditional methods of law enforcement to eradicate quality-of-life problems, what negative consequences have resulted from this choice? And which New Yorkers have borne the brunt of these negative consequences?

Joel Berger—a prominent New York City civil rights attorney who represents alleged victims of police misconduct and abuse in New York City—reports that legal filings of new civil rights claims against the police for abusive conduct have increased by 75 percent in the city over the last four years.[5] Berger says that the largest increase in new claims of this type occurred during the most recent fiscal year, indicating that the problem of police brutality is getting worse, not better (interview with Joel Berger, May 4, 1998).

Amnesty International has reported that police brutality and unjustifiable use of force is a widespread problem in New York City (Amnesty International 1996). There is a wealth of documentation to support the charge that police misconduct and abuse have increased under the Giuliani administration's zero-tolerance regime. The total number of citizen complaints filed annually with the Civilian Complaint Review Board (CCRB) increased more than 60 percent between 1992 and 1996.

Joel Berger says that during the first year of the Giuliani administration, the number of complaints filed by citizens before the CCRB that involved incidents where no arrest was made or summons issued showed a sudden and sharp increase. The proportion of "general patrol incidents"—that is, civilian complaints associated simply with routine police contacts (involving no suspicion of criminal activity, no hot pursuit, no arrest or summons)—among all complaints increased from 29 percent for the last year of the Dinkins administration to 58 percent under Mayor Giuliani. After 1994, the CCRB stopped distinguishing this particular type of complaint from others (interview with Joel Berger, May 4, 1998).

Complaints by citizens in New York City about police misconduct and abuse, and the response to these complaints by the New York City CCRB and the NYPD, have been the subject of hot debate between some resistant city officials and those who advocate for a more effective process to increase police accountability for abuse of citizens. From the start, Mayor Giuliani resisted the effort to establish an independent CCRB. By the time it was set up, its budget had been slashed by 17 percent (about a million dollars) as compared with the police department-based civilian complaint unit it had replaced (Siegel and Perry 1997, p. 2).

According to New York City Public Advocate Mark Green, recent CCRB complaint data suggest that the problem of police misconduct is disproportionately concentrated in New York City's high-crime minority neigh-

borhoods. Nine out of 76 precincts account for more than 50 percent of the increase in CCRB complaints since 1992; 21 precincts account for more than 80 percent. Mark Green charges that those precincts with the highest incidence of misconduct "appear to have disproportionately higher percentages of African American and Latino residents" (Green 1997, p. 4). Norman Siegel—director of the New York Civil Liberties Union (NYCLU) and a harsh critic of the mayor on these issues—has presented data showing that three quarters of all CCRB complaints are filed by African Americans and Latinos. He reports that African Americans (who make up 29 percent of the city's population) filed 53 percent of all complaints in 1996 (Siegel and Perry 1997, p. 13).

Moreover, the vast majority of complaints filed with the CCRB are never substantiated, and the small portion that are substantiated usually do not result in proper disciplinary actions. In the first eight months of last year, only 8 percent of the 3,991 cases filed with the CCRB were substantiated. Furthermore, Public Advocate Mark Green has complained that so few substantiated cases ever result in charges brought or disciplinary actions taken by the police department that the civilian complaint process is a sham (Green 1997).

This brief review of the downside *costs* that many New Yorkers argue have been incurred through the city's reliance on a highly aggressive, traditional law-enforcement style of policing begs the *benefits* question: Is there hard evidence that this strategy has been truly effective in reducing crime? How valid are the claims made by Mayor Giuliani that his police policies are responsible for the city's remarkable crime reduction record?

The declining crime rate that New Yorkers are enjoying has not happened in a vacuum, nor is it as exceptional as some New

York officials suggest. Many urban communities across America have experienced reductions in crime during the same time period, and it is highly likely that there are numerous factors—beyond zero-tolerance policing—that might be contributing to these remarkable declines in some of the nation's largest cities.

Serious violent crime rates have been falling for the nation as a whole. The National Crime Victimization Survey crime-trends data (1973–1996) published by the Bureau of Justice Statistics indicate that rapes declined 60 percent from 1991 to 1996, whereas robberies began to decline more recently; robberies were down 17 percent from 1994 to 1996. Aggravated assaults declined by 27 percent from 1993 to 1996. The victimization data show that total violent crime was down 19 percent from 1994 to 1996. Data from the National Center for Health Statistics indicate that the nation's homicide rate fell by 10 percent from 1991 to 1995. Property crimes are also on the decline for the nation as a whole, according to the National Crime Victimization Survey. The rates reported for total property crime show a 25 percent decline from 1991 to 1996 (National Center for Health Statistics 1998; National Crime Victimization Survey 1998).

One city located at the opposite end of the country from New York has taken a distinctly different path in pursuit of crime prevention and effective policing. Whereas New York City's index crime rate ranks 150th in a list of 189 American cities with populations of more than 100,000, San Diego ranks nearby at 145th (New York City Mayor's Office of Operations 1998). San Diego and New York City have enjoyed virtually equal reductions in rates of serious crime over the first half of the 1990s. From 1990 to 1995, a period when the NYPD gained a 39.5 percent increase in the number of sworn officers, New York City's reduction in crime was 37.4 percent, whereas San Diego's was 36.8 percent, but during this same

period the increase in sworn officers on the San Diego police force *was only 6.2 percent*. According to San Diego police officials, this is a far more favorable "yield" in terms of crimes reduced per each additional officer (San Diego Police Department 1998).

San Diego's police executives began to experiment with a form of community policing—the Neighborhood Policing Philosophy as they term it—in the late 1980s. In 1993, they laid the groundwork for a department-wide restructuring process coupled with an effort to retrain the entire force in problem-oriented (as opposed to incident-based) policing methods. Two key concepts of neighborhood policing in San Diego—as described by San Diego Police Department (SDPD) officials—are that police and citizens share responsibility for identifying and solving crime problems and that law enforcement is one important tool for addressing crime, but it is not an end in itself.

The emphasis of the San Diego neighborhood-policing approach is on creating problem-solving partnerships and fostering connections between police and community for sharing information, working with citizens to address crime and disorder problems, and tapping other public and private agencies for resources to help solve them. The types of activities fostered by the neighborhood policing strategy in San Diego resemble many that are common elements of community policing elsewhere, such as the following:

- support for "neighborhood watch" and citizen patrol groups that look for suspicious activity, identify community problems, and work on crime prevention projects;
- use of civil remedies and strict building code enforcement to abate nuisance properties and close down "drug houses"; and

- collaboration with community organizations and local business groups to clean up, close down, or redesign specific locations and properties that repeatedly attract prostitution, drug, and gang problems.

The role of organized neighborhood volunteers in efforts to impact local crime problems—and thus national crime patterns—is too often overlooked or misunderstood. There are important differences between community *policing* and community *participation*,[6] yet San Diego seems to be striving to integrate these distinct, semiautonomous crime prevention tools. The SDPD has recruited and trained a pool of more than 1,000 citizen volunteers who perform a broad array of crime prevention and victim assistance services.

The restructuring of police services in San Diego has involved a geographic consolidation of 68 existing patrol sectors and a reconfiguration of their boundaries to correspond to 99 distinct neighborhoods defined by community residents. Laptop computers equipped with mapping software are now being introduced to automate field reporting and to put up-to-date crime and calls-for-service data into the hands of patrol officers (San Diego Police Department 1997).

Descriptions of the neighborhood policing approaches given by police executives in San Diego are different in tone and texture from the terms in which Giuliani and Bratton have described New York City's policing strategies. A comparison of arrest patterns in recent years offers concrete evidence that these two approaches differ markedly in fact. New York City's data show increases in arrests both for felonies and misdemeanors from 1993 to 1996, whereas San Diego arrest data show declines.

Data from the New York State Department of Criminal Justice Services from 1993 through 1996 show that arrests in New York City rose by 23 percent across the board. Reflecting the broken windows, zero-tolerance policing strategy introduced by Bratton, misdemeanor arrests rose by 40 percent—led by drug arrests, which were increased by 97 percent over this period.

Arrest statistics provided by the SDPD for this same period show a marked contrast, reflecting the contrasting philosophy of neighborhood policing adopted in that city.

Across the board, arrests have fallen in San Diego by 15 percent, whereas reductions for key indicators of crime (homicides and FBI Index Crimes) closely rival the crime reductions in New York City. Total complaints

Table 1. Adult Arrests in New York City

	1993	1994	1995	1996
Total arrests	255,087	307,802	316,690	314,292
Total felony arrests	125,684	138,043	135,141	132,601
Felony drug arrests	39,298	44,442	43,698	45,312
Total misdemeanor arrests	129,403	169,759	181,549	181,691
Misdemeanor drug arrests	27,446	42,546	52,891	54,133
Misdemeanor DWI arrests	5,621	5,628	5,763	4,624
Other misdemeanor arrests	96,335	121,585	122,895	122,934

NOTE: DWI = driving while intoxicated.

Table 2.   Adult Arrests in San Diego

	1993	1994	1995	1996
Total arrests	56,631	55,887	55,909	48,264
Total felony arrests	17,007	17,135	16,854	13,825
Felony drug arrests	5,808	6,432	6,685	5,034
Total misdemeanor arrests	39,624	38,752	39,055	34,439
Misdemeanor drug arrests	7,099	8,313	7,965	6,352
Misdemeanor DWI arrests	3,782	3,649	3,749	3,545
Other misdemeanor arrests	28,743	26,790	27,341	24,542

NOTE: DWI = driving while intoxicated.

filed during this period with the SDPD regarding police misconduct fell from 552 in 1993 to 508 in 1996 (interview with John Welter, June 1998).

Zero-tolerance policing in New York City uses the Compstat system to direct hyper-aggressive crime-control tactics toward high-crime "hot spots," and city officials have been quick to claim credit for a dramatic drop in crime. Yet, the sharp contrast in arrest patterns and citizen complaints between New York City and San Diego offers compelling evidence that cooperative police-community problem solving can provide effective crime control through more efficient and humane methods. Moreover, the San Diego strategy seems better designed to support and sustain vital elements of community social organization that can inhibit criminality and build safer neighborhoods over the long run.

NOTES

1. This is a crime indicator (the number of crimes per 100,000 persons) calculated from the Federal Bureau of Investigation's national crime data system, which is used to produce national reports on the number of selected offenses—murder and nonnegligent manslaughter, robbery, forcible rape, aggravated assault, burglary, larceny/theft, motor vehicle theft, and arson—known to the police.

2. "Compstat" is an abbreviation for "computer statistics" (Bratton 1998, p. 233).

3. Bratton (1998) presents a synopsis of the broken windows theory as follows: "Just as unrepaired broken windows can signal to people that nobody cares about a building and lead to more serious vandalism, untended disorderly behavior can also signal that nobody cares about the community and lead to more serious disorder and crime" (p. 152).

4. The other five strategies were "getting guns off the streets of New York," "curbing youth violence in the schools and on the streets," "driving drug dealers out of New York," "breaking the cycle of domestic violence," and "reducing auto-related crime in New York" (Silverman 1997b, p. 101).

5. Until 1996, Joel Berger served as senior litigator in New York City's Corporation Counsel's Office. He was responsible for monitoring police brutality cases and deciding which defendants would be represented by lawyers in his office.

6. Whereas community policing engages neighborhood residents in identification of crime problems and in planning crime-control strategies, community participation entails residents becoming directly involved in crime prevention activities and in effecting structural solutions to the neighborhood problems that give rise to crime.

REFERENCES

Amnesty International. 1996. "Police Brutality and Excessive Force in the New York City Police Department." Amnesty International Report 51/36/96, June.

Bratton, William. 1996. "Cutting Crime and Restoring Order: What America Can Learn From New York's Finest." *Heritage Lecture*, No. 573, Washington, DC.

———. 1998. *Turnaround: How America's Top Cop Reversed the Crime Epidemic*. New York: Random House.

Green, Mark. 1997. "Testimony of the Public Advocate before the New York City Council Committee on Public Safety," September 11.

National Center for Health Statistics. 1998. *Homicide Rates from the Vital Statistics*. Washington, DC: Department of Justice, Bureau of Justice Statistics.

National Crime Victimization Survey. 1998. *Crime Trends, 1973–1996*. Washington, DC: Department of Justice, Bureau of Justice Statistics.

New York City Mayor's Office of Operations. 1998. *The Mayor's Management Report: Preliminary Fiscal 1998 Summary Volume*. New York: Mayor's Office of Operations.

San Diego Police Department. 1997. *Briefing Book* (Narrative Report). San Diego, CA: San Diego Police Department Information Services Division.

———. 1998. *Changes 1990 to 1995* (Data Chart). San Diego, CA: San Diego Police Department Information Services Division.

Siegel, Norman and Robert A. Perry. 1997. *A Fourth Anniversary Overview of the Civilian Complaint Review Board*. New York: New York Civil Liberties Union.

Silverman, Eli B. 1997a. "Crime in New York: A Success Story." *Public Perspective*, June/July:3–5.

———. 1997b. "Revolutionizing the Police: Fighting Crime in New York City." *Security Journal* 9:101–4.

The Punitive Trend
of American Drug Policy

Peter Reuter

Drug policy has generated two debates. The more elevated one concerns the retention of our current prohibitions, the legalization debate. Though it has occasionally impinged on the rhetoric of political discussion, as in the attack against legalization in the introduction to the first *National Drug Strategy*, this debate remains largely a parlor sport for intellectuals, divorced from the policy-making process. The more consequential, albeit less lofty, debate has been that between what are usually called the supply-side advocates and the demand-side advocates. The supply-siders, with former National Drug Control Director William Bennett as their most articulate spokesman, seek continued expansion of the nation's effort to imprison drug sellers and detect and punish (in various ways) drug users, while denying that they are slighting demand-side considerations.[1] The demand-side advocates, led by Senator Joseph Biden, while generally accepting the need for "vigorous enforcement," argue that current resource commitments to programs directly aimed at demand (prevention and treatment) are grossly underfunded and should be massively increased, even if this is at the expense of enforcement.[2]

Neither debate is satisfactory. The legalization debate is too focused on extremes, excluding the possibility of compromise. It is strident, with both sides casting aspersion on the values of the other. On the other hand, the debate between the supply and demand-siders is too narrow, allowing only minor programmatic tinkering.

Borrowing liberally from the classic essay of Nye, Allison, and Carnesale on approaches to preventing nuclear war,[3] I propose to combine the two debates on drug policy into a three-sided discussion among hawks (supply-side advocates), doves (legalizers), and owls (bold demand-side advocates) about the nature of the drug problem and the consequences of different approaches to controlling it.[4]

Drug policy debates have been conducted largely in terms of images. The hawks point to the immediacy of the problems in the streets (particularly the carnage surrounding drug distribution) and reasonably (though in intemperate tones) ask whether efforts at drug prevention or treatment offer any reasonable hope for controlling those markets and associated violence in the near future. They note the apparently low success rates of drug treatment

From Peter Reuter, "Hawks Ascendant: The Punitive Trend of American Drug Policy," *Daedalus* v. 121, no. 3, (Summer 1992): 15–52. Reprinted by permission of Daedalus.

programs; many programs show relapse rates of more than 60 percent.[5] Prevention programs aimed at seventh graders (the most commonly targeted grade) will reduce the number of adult drug addicts only with a five to ten year lag. Finally, they argue that effective prevention and treatment require intense enforcement, both to make drugs difficult to obtain (driving users into treatment) and to make drug use appear legally risky (reinforcing prevention messages).[6]

The doves' message is even clearer than that of the hawks. After defending themselves from the charge that they condone the use of drugs by asserting that society should strive to reduce use of all dangerous psychoactive drugs[7] including alcohol and cigarettes, they go on to argue that most of the current evils associated with drugs arise from the prohibitions and enforcement of those prohibitions. The violence, overdoses, and massive illegal incomes that are such a prominent part of our current concerns with psychoactive drugs are not consequences of the nature of the drugs themselves but rather of the conditions of use that society has created. Doves are strong on critiques of the current regime[8] but rather weak in describing their preferred alternatives. However, they are clear that criminal prohibitions should play no role in society's efforts to keep use of psychoactive drugs to a minimum.[9]

The current owls are less eloquent. They argue that drug enforcement has proven a failure. The intensification of enforcement throughout the 1980s failed to stem a massive growth in the nation's drug problems. Enforcement does not go to the root of the problem; with a loss of faith in source country control programs (such as crop eradication and crop substitution),[10] the root of the problem is now seen to be the initiation of new users in the United States and the failure to provide good quality treatment for addicts. Prevention and treatment receive a derisory

share of what the nation spends to control its drug problems. Public treatment programs, faced with the most difficult clients, have far fewer resources to spend on those clients than do private treatment programs.[11] Success in reducing the nation's drug problem requires a change in spending priorities. *Sotto voce*, at most, they also suggest that intense drug enforcement increases crime and may exacerbate health problems related to drug use; however, they believe in the value of the criminal prohibition and significant enforcement against drug dealers.

This essay has two goals. The first is to describe the increasing success of the hawks. To an extraordinary degree, they have taken control of drug policy and given it a distinctively punitive hew. The second goal is the more difficult one, namely to suggest that the hawks may have gone too far. The punishment is expensive, not so much in money terms (though the sums are no longer trivial, even in an inflation-adjusted Everett Dirksen sense) as in terms of the human costs of locking up many people for relatively minor offenses and not locking up many others for more serious offenses. Intense enforcement also increases the harms caused by drug users to themselves and others.

The differences among the three positions (summarized very crudely in Table 1, borrowed again from Nye, Allison, and Carnesale) in part come from different views of what constitutes the drug problem and the sources of that problem. For hawks, the heart of the matter is the threat to youth and to American values; drug use means an abandoning of concern with others, and focusing on short-term pleasures for oneself. It is a lack of clarity about values in society and a failure to ensure that drug use is punished that leads to so many young people becoming regular users of psychoactives. The violence and health damage are merely the visible emblems of a

Table 1. Drug War Strategies: Hawks, Owls, and Doves

POSITION	NATURE OF DRUG PROBLEM	EXPLANATION FOR DRUG USE	POLICY EMPHASIS	CONSEQUENCE OF FAILURE
HAWKS	Amorality of Drug Users & Sellers	Selfishness, Lack of Clear Social Values	Tough Enforcement	Violence, Repression
OWLS	Addiction, Disease	Adverse Social Conditions	Prevention, Treatment, Prohibition	Continuation of Present Problems
DOVES	The Bad Effects of Prohibition	Pleasures from Drugs	Legalize, Inform	Large Increase in Drug Abuse

more fundamental problem. The first *National Drug Control Strategy* says it eloquently: For "most drug users" use is the result of a "human flaw" that leads them to pursue "a hollow, degrading and deceptive pleasure." What is required is "a firm moral stand that using drugs is wrong and should be resisted." If values are the heart of the matter, then all institutions of society must join in the fight; the 1992 *Strategy* says "[T]he family, neighborhood, community, church, school and workplace must be very active in this effort. If they are not, they implicitly signal to young people that drug use is not to be taken seriously, at least not seriously enough to do anything about it."

Doves believe that individuals use psychoactive substances because they provide pleasure and that society should minimize the harm that results from the use of such substances without criminalizing the choice of a particular substance. Psychoactive drugs can harm individuals and society has a responsibility to inform adolescents about the consequences of choosing drugs and to help those who become dependent deal with the problem. But the criminal law makes those tasks more difficult as well as imposing direct costs on society.

Owls focus on the damage arising from heavy drug use by a relatively small number of those who become dependent. The health consequences are given considerable weight. Again, drug use is regarded as evil in and of itself but, in my preferred version, attention is given to the evils created by enforcement. Criminal law may be an important tool for minimizing the damage done by dangerous and attractive psychoactives in a world of imperfect decisionmakers but enforcement is not a good in itself; indeed, one wants the lowest level of enforcement compatible with keeping initiation down and encouraging the dependent to seek treatment.[12] Drug control is also not the only goal, and higher drug use may be accepted in return for better performance with respect to some other social goal, such as reduced spread of HIV infection.

No one can describe, even very roughly, the consequences of doubling the number of treatment slots available for addicts without insurance coverage for such treatment, or what would happen if we were to increase the number of drug arrests by 25 percent. Over five years, would these result in declines of 20 percent in the extent of heroin addiction or in drug related homicides? What else might occur as a consequence, positive or negative, of these actions? The doves may be correct that many of the current evils are the consequence of prohibition but they have little basis for suggesting the consequence of the removal of those prohibitions on either the extent of use or the way that users would behave in a legalized regime.[13]

But whatever the shakiness of the arguments and evidence of the various positions, the simple truth is that the hawks have prevailed; indeed their ascendance still seems to be increasing. Thus the next section deals mainly with their position, describing the many dimensions of their success. The section entitled "Changing Patterns of Drug Use and Related Problems," summarizes what has happened to the drug problem since 1980, pointing to the mixed record of success of American drug policy. A later section presents what we can reasonably claim to know about "the consequences of toughness," both good and bad. It also includes a brief survey of the experiences of Western Europe, to show what other approaches are possible. The concluding section begins with a short excursion into the political dynamics of the drug issue, explaining why the hawks almost always win, and then speculates about the likely future of US drug policy.

THE TRIUMPH OF THE HAWKS

Many have noted that American drug policy has traditionally been heavily dependent on criminal law when compared to most other Western societies. Particularly in the last decade, the hawks have been in soaring ascendance. Though they grumble about the lack of severity in punishment of drug users and dealers, they have managed to massively increase funding for such punishment, to expand the scope of efforts to detect drug users in many settings and to intensify the severity of penalties imposed on those convicted of selling or using drugs.

Budgets, Legislation, and Programs

Budget allocations help make the point. The federal budget for drug control has increased substantially over the last decade; in constant dollars it has risen from $1.5 billion in fiscal year 1980 to $6.7 billion in fiscal year 1990. Throughout that period it has been dominated by enforcement programs; the share going to such programs never fell below 70 percent and rose as high as 80 percent. The federal drug control budget in 1990 allocated only 29 percent of total expenditures to treatment and prevention.

Even this understates the extent of the hawks' budgetary dominance. State and local governments spend more in total than the federal government (even eliminating federal pass-throughs) but allocate a still smaller share to treatment and prevention programs. It is difficult to assemble a national drug control budget, since most state and local drug enforcement is carried out by nonspecialized law enforcement agencies and the allocation of their budgets to drug control has a very judgemental element. My own estimate is that in 1990, state and local governments spent roughly $18 billion on drug control and 80 percent of that went for enforcement.[14] This suggests a 1990 national drug control budget of $28 billion for all levels of government, with 75 percent going to enforcement.[15] Less than $5 billion went to treatment, compared to over $20 billion spent on enforcement of various kinds, mostly at the local level. Indeed, the treatment figure may have been only $3 billion, though there may be another $2 billion of private funding through health insurance.

Budget allocation is of course only one measure of the hawks' triumph. Legislatures throughout the country, with the US Congress very much in the vanguard, have dramatically increased the sentences for drug offenses, though prison overcrowding has undercut the effectiveness of these sentencing statutes. For example, in the 1988 Anti-Drug Abuse Control Act, Congress raised the mandatory sentence for selling 50 grams of crack to five years. The state of Michigan has imposed mandatory life imprisonment without parole for those convicted of selling 650 grams of cocaine. Congress has required that states impose various penalties, such as loss of drivers' licenses, for persons convicted of drug offenses, including simple possession of marijuana; federal highway funds are to be withheld from states that do not impose such penalties.

Drug testing programs have become almost ubiquitous in many institutional settings, with an emphasis on penalty rather than treatment for those who test positive. For example, many of the new Intensively Supervised Probation programs require frequent drug testing though providing few of their clients with access to drug treatment.[16] The federal government has imposed drug testing on much of its civilian work force, while perhaps half of large corporations test job applicants for drug use.

I include the recent decisions by the Drug Enforcement Administration (DEA) and by the Public Health Service (PHS) to disallow use of marijuana for medical purposes, even on an experimental basis, as reflecting the hawkishness of current policies. DEA is responsible for the scheduling of drugs; marijuana is currently classified as Schedule I (high abuse potential, no currently accepted medical use in treatment). A number of organizations initiated a suit in 1972 seeking to have the drug reclassified as Schedule II, allowing it to be prescribed. They claimed that marijuana can alleviate nausea associated with chemotherapy as well as relieve glaucoma; it

now also appears that marijuana can improve the appetite of AIDS patients. The PHS has, for the last year, allowed "compassionate" approval of marijuana prescriptions, produced on the government's marijuana farm in Mississippi, for thirteen patients.

In March 1992, the head of DEA once again refused to reschedule marijuana and the PHS announced the end of the compassionate exemption program. Both agencies deny that they had any concern with the symbolic effect of allowing marijuana to be used for therapeutic purposes.[17] On the basis of conversations with various government officials and other observers, I disbelieve that claim, though I can offer no documentary backing for this. The official argument asserts that there is no credible evidence that marijuana, as opposed to synthetic drugs containing some of its active ingredients, has greater therapeutic value. In large part this reflects the lack of research on the topic. The PHS rejection flew in the face of a survey of oncologists that found a majority who believed that marijuana should be available on prescription.[18] Indeed, that survey found that almost half of the oncologists responding currently advised their patients to use marijuana, even though the drug was not legally available. The DEA Administrator's decision reversed a remarkably strongly worded decision by the administrative law judge that the Schedule I classification was "unreasonable, arbitrary and capricious." The head of the Public Health Service did suggest that it would send a "wrong signal" to hand out a drug that can cloud judgement with respect to automobile driving or sexual behavior.[19]

The rejection of experimentation with marijuana for therapeutic purposes has an earlier parallel in the rejection of heroin for treatment of pain. In many other nations, heroin is routinely provided for relief of pain in terminal cancer patients; here it remains on Schedule I, not allowed for any medicinal use in treatment. There is a genuine controversy about whether other synthetic opiates might not be more effective in each of the possible circumstances that heroin is a candidate pain reliever. However, the evidence for the effectiveness of heroin is strong enough that it might be left to the individual physician to decide; leakage to the illicit market is likely to provide only a negligible supplement to existing supplies.

Marijuana's "signal" value has also been emphasized by the concerted effort to reverse the decriminalization statutes that were passed in thirteen states in the 1970s. William Bennett appeared before a number of state legislatures to argue for recriminalization and was successful in Alaska in 1990.

Increasing Punitiveness

One symbol of the hawks' success is that they have managed to sustain the belief that drug sellers and users are at low risk from law enforcement, a belief that has helped promote more stringent sentencing statutes. They have emphasized stories about arrested drug sellers returning to the streets more rapidly than the police who arrested them and not getting jailed until they have been convicted numerous times. The truth is more complicated. By contemporary American standards, drug selling has become quite risky and drug use may be very risky for certain classes of users.

All this depends on a great deal of speculative arithmetic, which is only summarized here.[20] Enforcement intensity is a function not simply of the total number of arrests or imprisonments for drug offenses but of the ratio of such figures to the number of drug offenses. It is hard to find good measures of the number of such offenses but if the rise in illicit drug episodes, in Drug Abuse Warning Network (DAWN), is taken as a surrogate, then it rose

faster than arrests or imprisonments from 1980 to 1985 but not as rapidly from 1985 to 1990. Moreover, most drug arrests probably did not lead to serious penal sanction in the first period but in the second half of the 1980s aggressive arrest policies at last led to large increases in the number of incarcerations. Thus it is likely that the intensity of enforcement decreased, at least for cocaine offenses, in the first half of the 1980s but then rose in the second half of that decade.

So far I have not made much of differences among drugs. Law and policy appropriately make such distinctions, though not necessarily in appropriate ways. Enforcement has been quite drug specific and the impacts differ by drugs. Most attention in this section will be given to cocaine but it is worth noting marijuana enforcement patterns as well. In contrast to cocaine, marijuana enforcement became more stringent throughout the decade as usage dropped.

Enforcement has increased massively in absolute terms. The number of state and local arrests for drug offenses increased rapidly, from 581,000 in 1980 to 1,090,000 in 1990. The composition of these arrests changed in an important way over the same period. Whereas the 1980 total was dominated by arrests for marijuana (70 percent) and possession (82 percent) offenses, in 1990 heroin/cocaine[21] arrests had come to exceed the number for marijuana (591,000 versus 391,000) and distribution arrests now accounted for a much larger share than in 1980 (27 percent versus 18 percent). In effect, the average seriousness of arrest offense has increased sharply.

Arrest is only the first step in the criminal justice process; it is conviction and sentence that provide the principal punishment, though arrest itself can lead to seizure of drugs and other assets. At the national level we cannot systematically trace through the disposition of arrests prior to 1986. We have to rely on fragments of data collected for a few states on an occasional basis to get a sense of how many drug offenders were imprisoned during the earlier years.

The best data cover felony drug arrests in California; Table 2 shows the disposition of these arrests in 1980, 1985, and 1990.

The number of felony drug arrests disposed of increased by about 21,000 in each half of the decade. What changed dramatically was the disposition of those arrests. The percentage convicted rose, particularly after 1985, and the percentage of convictions resulting in prison sentence went up dramatically. The total number of persons sent to prison for drug offenses rose threefold between 1980 and 1985 and tripled again in the following five years; over the entire decade the figure rose from less than 1,000 to over 10,000. A focus simply on the number of drug arrests fails to capture the increasing stringency of enforcement.

Nationally the only available data on the sentencing for felony drug convictions cover 1986 and 1988.[22] In that two year period there was a very sharp increase (from 135,000 to 225,000, approximately a 70 percent rise) in the number of persons convicted of felony

Table 2. Disposition of California Felony Drug Arrests, 1980, 1985, 1990

	1980	1985	1990
Felony Arrests Disposed of Number	40,451	63,766	84,538
Convicted	18,800	30,100	53,200
(percent of arrests)	(45)	(48)	(63)
Number to State Prisons	921	3,366	10,494
(percent of convicted)	(5)	(11)	(20)
Number to Jail	9,700	22,500	33,900
(percent of convicted)	(52)	(75)	(64)

Source: Unpublished tabulations, California Bureau of Criminal Statistics

drug trafficking or possession charges.[23] The number receiving state prison sentences (i.e., more than twelve months) rose from 49,900 to 92,500, though there was a modest decline in their expected time served from twenty-two months to twenty months.[24] In 1988 drug offenses accounted for approximately one-third of all felony convictions in state courts.[25]

The most recent year for which available data permit rough estimates of prison and jail years meted out for drug felonies by state courts is 1988. About 90,000 persons were sentenced to prison, and another 65,000 were sentenced to local jails. The federal court system also imposes punishment on drug dealers. Though federal drug convictions constitute a small share of the total, the average time served for those incarcerated is much higher than for state sentenced offenders, reflecting mandatory penalties for many drug selling offenses of ten years or more and no parole. In 1988 federal courts generated an estimated 50,000 years of expected prison time for drug dealers, compared to only one-tenth that amount in 1980. That reflected increasing numbers of convictions, rising sentence length and, most significantly, a rise in the share of sentences that the inmate expected to serve; this last was the result of the imposition of sentencing guidelines and the abolition of federal parole. The total of federal and state incarceration figures for 1988 was about 200,000 cell years; this is perhaps ten times the 1980 figure.

CHANGING PATTERNS OF DRUG USE AND RELATED PROBLEMS

By historic and international standards, use of illegal psychoactive drugs in the United States in the early 1990s is extraordinarily high.[26] Moreover, that drug use is associated with more severe and diverse problems than those associated with illegal drugs in other periods or societies. It is almost certain nevertheless that the prevalence of drug use has declined sharply from the dizzying heights of the early to mid-1980s and is likely to continue to decline. These two discordant facts present a dilemma in assessing the effectiveness of current policies. Should we focus on the high absolute levels, and conclude that these policies have failed, or on the declines and conclude that they are finally succeeding?

The Prevalence of Drug Use

The broad population surveys, of the household population and of high school seniors, tell a consistent story.[27] Initiation into drug use (as measured, for example, by the percentage of successive cohorts of 18 year olds reporting use in past year) escalated rapidly in the late 1970s and early 1980s and then began to decline by 1986 or slightly earlier. The peaks were alarming; in 1978, 11 percent of high school seniors reported using marijuana on a daily basis in the previous month. Every number is now down sharply from its peak; for example, by 1991 less than 2 percent of seniors reported daily use in the previous month.

The declines, as reported in the surveys, have been surprisingly evenly spread across age/race/sex groups. The surveys also have shown a complex and changing relationship between education and drug use. In 1985 prevalence rates among males born between 1959 and 1964 were very similar for high school graduates and for dropouts; indeed the former showed slightly higher rates for both recent use (past thirty days) and past use (last twelve months). By 1990 the rates had fallen much more sharply for the high school graduates, particularly for past use. Differences in the declines for recent use were less marked, perhaps because this included more people who were habituated to drug use. The emerg-

ing negative correlation between education and cocaine use is consistent with the changes in cigarette use.[28]

The surveys provide mixed support for hypotheses about higher rates of drug use among African-Americans and Hispanics. The high school senior surveys consistently show sharply higher prevalence rates among whites.[29] However, the National Household Survey shows higher rates for African-Americans; in the age group 26–34 for example, in 1990, the percentage reporting some use of an illegal drug in previous month was 13.7 percent, compared to 9.5 percent for white respondents.[30]

The broad surveys can reasonably claim to provide a valid measure of trends in the extent of drug use among the general population, though they have serious weaknesses even in that role. Increased stigmatization of drug use reduces the willingness of respondents to report that they are actually users; however, that stigmatization also reduces the extent of use. Thus the surveys may exaggerate the downward trend in use but it is unlikely that they misrepresent the direction.

But no one doubts that the broad population surveys miss a great deal of the most important behavior, namely frequent drug use. There are at least three reasons for this. First, the surveys do not include some critical populations in their sampling frames (for example, the homeless[31] and prisoners) who are believed to have high rates of drug abuse. Moreover, the size of these noncovered populations has risen and their composition has changed; both populations now seem to include higher percentages with drug abuse problems than they did in 1980. Second, those who use drugs frequently, even if formally included in the sampling frame, are likely to be more difficult to reach because they behave more erratically. Third, the response rate for the survey has declined from 83 percent in 1985 to 79 percent in 1990; this nonresponse increase may well be related to increased disapproval of drug use and thus lower willingness to even participate in a survey.

Moreover, the credibility of the surveys as a good representation of the nation's drug problems was undermined in the late 1980s by the dramatic discrepancy between the most publicized findings of those surveys and public perception of the changing problem. While the surveys pointed to substantial declines in drug use, it was widely believed that the drug problem was getting a great deal worse. The surveys also pointed to quite modest numbers of persons with severe drug problems; for example, the number of persons using cocaine weekly or more frequently was estimated at less than 1 million, which seemed inconsistent with the severity of cocaine-related problems.

Two official indicators supported the popular beliefs. DAWN reported data on the involvement of drugs in Emergency Room (ER) cases and in Medical Examiners' (ME) reports on deaths. DAWN, in contrast to the survey data, showed dramatic increases in cocaine mentions throughout the 1980s; the total number rose more than tenfold between 1980 and 1988. Beginning in 1988, the Drug Use Forecasting (DUF) system collected data on the prevalence of recent drug use by arrestees in twenty major cities, relying on analysis of urine specimens. It found very high rates of drug use in the arrested population and produced estimates of the number of frequent users that were very much higher than those derived from the household survey. Moreover, both DAWN and DUF pointed to a concentration of problems in the inner city. DAWN which increasingly measures the extent of drug dependence,[32] also suggested that whatever is happening to drug use generally, the number of cocaine dependent persons rose substantially between 1980 and 1990.[33]

In summary, these, and other data, suggest that the number of drug users has declined since the peak of the early to mid-1980s. However, there has been a much slighter, and later, decline in the numbers experiencing, and causing, significant problems related to their own frequent use of drugs. An increasing share of the drug abusing population is found among the inner-city poor, as the more educated became more concerned about the health consequences of drug use. The poorer users are criminally active; their criminal activity is exacerbated by this drug use. That has enormous consequences for the politics of drug policy.

Costs

It is all very well to have estimates of the numbers of drug users and abusers. What costs, social and economic, should we attach to these figures? How significant is this problem?

The federal government has sponsored a series of four estimates of the economic cost of drug abuse.[34] For 1985, the estimated economic cost was $44 billion, compared to $70 billion for alcohol abuse and $103 billion for mental illness. It is hard to know what to make of these numbers, even if taken at face value, but the simple truth is that they are essentially irrelevant for our purposes because they are dominated by what the government spends to control the problem and they miss major elements of the social costs associated with illicit drugs. Particularly troubling is the treatment of the cost of crime associated with drug abuse. This is estimated to be $13 billion, of which 90 percent is public expenditures on law enforcement; the loss of safety and amenity is treated as zero. Yet in terms of dollars that individuals would be willing to spend to have lower crime rates in their community, that cost might well be much larger than the figures cited above.[35]

Estimates of the number of drug users is probably not a good metric for scaling the drug problem. After all, as even William Bennett noted in the introduction to the first *National Drug Strategy*, most drug using careers are short, with only a few episodes involving drugs other than marijuana and are ended without requiring any treatment. Estimates that large numbers experiment with drugs or use drugs on an occasional basis does not mean that use of illicit drugs constitutes a major problem. Alternatively put, is there a credible base for the popular fears that briefly made drugs the leading social problem in 1988 and 1989?

Some drugs such as LSD and PCP can cause substantial and lasting damage to an individual who uses them just once; this, however, is an extremely rare event for cocaine, heroin or marijuana. It seems likely that the vast majority of those who use these latter drugs only a few times suffer little harm as a consequence. The external costs of their use in aggregate may be high, if for example they provide a substantial share of the total market for illicit drugs and that market generates violence and corruption, but the costs to the individuals look modest. Moreover, it seems likely that occasional users actually account for a small share of total consumption, so that it is also unlikely that they impose high external costs through their contribution to the violence and disorder surrounding markets.

It is appropriate then to focus on those who are drug abusers in order to obtain an understanding of the costs to individuals. The standard comparison of morbidity and mortality suggests that illicit drugs present only a moderately serious problem. Compared to alcohol or tobacco, the numbers of users, abusers, premature deaths, and disease associated with all illegal drugs together is small. Tobacco accounts for about 400,000 premature deaths annually, alcohol for about 100,000. It would be hard to sustain a figure of more than 20,000 premature deaths from the direct effects of illegal drugs; even if half of all homicides are drug related, the figure is still barely 30,000.[36] Nor are the figures for morbidity impressive. With a base of frequent users of no more than 3 million, the health effects are tiny compared to those associated with the 50 million regular cigarette smokers and the 10 million heavy drinkers. On the grounds of the health costs, it could scarcely be claimed that use of illicit psychoactives constitutes a social problem of the first order.

Yet there are other, distinctive and important problems associated with illegal drugs. Alcohol is comparable to cocaine in its individual criminogenic consequences. Of those sentenced to jail terms in 1989, 29 percent reported being under the influence of alcohol (and not drugs) at the time of the offense, compared to 15 percent reporting being under the influence of drugs alone; another 12 percent reported being under the influence of both.[37] However, the high price of cocaine and the extensive illegal markets associated with it have engendered crime and violence that have sources other than the direct effect of the drugs themselves. For example, Goldstein found that the majority of drug related homicides in New York were the result of "systemic" violence (for example, disputes over territories or contractual disagreements) rather than of the psychoactive effect of the drug or the need to obtain money to purchase drugs.[38] In some cities it is claimed that half of all homicides are drug related, though the criteria used to make the classification are quite murky. Moreover, the earnings from drug markets are believed to have been important in increasing the lethality of guns used in urban crime. That lethality may have contributed to the rise in killings of innocent bystanders.

The spread of HIV through needle sharing and other drug related behaviors (such as the extreme promiscuity of crack users) is another hard-to-value consequence of drug use.[39] Over one-quarter of AIDS cases include intravenous drug use as a primary risk factor and that percentage is rising. Curiously, though, in most of Western Europe, a concern with AIDS has been a principal influence on drug policy; in the United States it has been treated as almost a separate policy arena.[40] In particular, it has not been given much attention in the debates with which this paper is concerned.

In the last few years, a great deal of attention has been given to the phenomenon of "crack babies," who are severely damaged by the cocaine use of their mothers during pregnancy. From an official high of 375,000 in the first *National Strategy*, the estimated number of babies annually affected by mother's drug use has fallen to 30,000–50,000. Moreover, it is no longer so clear that the damage suffered by most of these babies is very long-lasting. The problem is an emotionally very troubling one but may be rare in most populations.

Corruption is another cost associated with drug prohibition and its enforcement. Though there are spectacular and troubling instances of such corruption, such as that involving the homicide squad in the Miami Police Department in the mid-1980s and the more recent convictions of numerous deputies in the Los Angeles Sheriff's department, the revealed corruption seems fairly opportunistic and small scale, certainly when compared with that surrounding the enforcement of gambling laws in the 1940s and 1950s.[41]

It is difficult then to say much about the real social costs of drug use and abuse. Vio-

lence, AIDS, corruption, and crack babies are all important and distinctive consequences of drug use under current conditions. There is enough of each of them to make understandable the public panic of the late 1980s. They have all become familiar enough to make equally understandable the declining concern of the last two years. That latter effect has been hastened by the fact that the most visible effects are highly concentrated in inner-city communities.

Knowing the scale of the social costs generated by drugs is important for determining what society should be willing to sacrifice in order to attain the goal of reduced use and abuse. Our inability to provide meaningful measures, along with the visibility and drama of illegal drugs, facilitates the task of those who would have the nation become harshly punitive.

THE CONSEQUENCES OF TOUGHNESS

To what extent can it be shown that reductions in drug use have been accomplished by the general toughening of society's approach to drug control? What are other negative consequences of toughness? Unfortunately, discussion of these issues must be highly speculative since there is little research on which to draw.

The punitive approach should reduce drug use and abuse by making drugs more expensive and/or less accessible. This will drive addicts into treatment and discourage adolescents from initiating use. Intense enforcement should also increase disapproval of drugs, which will lead current users to desist earlier. The available evidence suggests that intensified enforcement has had modest success in raising drug prices and has not reduced already limited access for the middle class. Disapproval of drug use has increased, and that may well have reduced initiation, but it is unlikely that this disapproval is a function of enforcement stringency.

It is even harder to determine the costs of heavy enforcement, in other than budgetary terms. Drug enforcement bears particularly heavily on the African-American population. Large numbers of young poorly educated males are being locked up for long periods in institutions that do little to rehabilitate them. Tough enforcement may also exacerbate various harms of drug use.

The latter brings us to the issue of harm reduction, the European term for the more pragmatic approach to drug problems that takes account of the fact that goals of drug control can conflict with other social goals. The concluding part of this section describes what that approach entails, how (and why) it has been implemented elsewhere, and its possible application in the United States.

Prices, Attitudes, and Prevalence

Price is determined by the interaction of supply and demand. If the demand for cocaine was declining in the second half of the 1980s, as suggested by the surveys, the rising numbers entering treatment and increasing imprisonment rates, then, absent tougher enforcement, prices might have been expected to fall during that period. In fact we observe a complex pattern, with retail cocaine prices declining until 1988 and then rising for the next two years.

The failure of cocaine prices to collapse may be evidence of the effectiveness of stringent enforcement. Certainly the margins for different actors in the trade remain high and, if 1988 District of Columbia data are any guide, provide substantial wage levels (approximately $30 per hour for low level participants

in 1988). But the price increase that has been achieved is surprisingly modest; late 1990 prices were perhaps 25 percent above their 1988 nadir and close to their levels of 1986 in nominal dollars. This may reflect a growing correlation between selling and heavy use. Adult cocaine retailers are frequent users themselves; if a significant portion of their earnings from this activity go to support their own consumption, then enforcement risks will have less effect on prices.

Marijuana seems to represent more of a success for enforcement. Its price is sharply higher than ten years ago, even after adjusting for potency increases and inflation. Interdiction may well have played a role; Colombia, the low cost producer of marijuana, no longer services the US market, as a consequence of increasingly effective interdiction. The primary sources are Mexico and the United States itself, both of which are very high cost producers. Moreover, the price increase has occurred over a period during which all the indicators point to a substantial decline in demand, making even clearer the impact of enforcement.

There is only one measure of availability, which comes from the High School Senior Survey. Respondents are asked whether it would be "easy," "very easy," etc. to get a particular drug. In 1980, 48 percent said that it was easy or very easy for them to get cocaine; by 1990 the figure was 59 percent. It declined for the first time in 1991, perhaps reflecting the falling demand among the seniors; with markedly fewer buyers in this population, the market may work less smoothly. In any case, if availability is a measure of enforcement success, then it certainly has lagged the increasing toughness by a long time. Marijuana availability as measured in the same survey, has remained essentially unchanged since the survey began in 1975; each year 80 to 85 percent report that marijuana is readily available or available.

These data make it difficult to evaluate enforcement success. In the legal market, where cocaine is available as a local anesthetic, it sells for $4 per pure gram, compared to the $130 on the streets. It is not readily available for many segments of the population. Marijuana prices are high by historical and international standards; indeed high enough to perhaps encourage more use of other drugs, such as alcohol and cocaine. The question is whether less rigorous enforcement, with fewer dealers incarcerated, would much reduce price or increase availability.

A striking feature of the general population surveys over the 1980s was the changing attitude toward both the dangers and perceived popularity of drug use. Whereas in 1980, only 31 percent of high school seniors believed that using cocaine once or twice was very risky, that percentage had risen to 59 percent in 1990; for marijuana the figures were 15 percent in 1980 and 37 percent in 1990. The responses stressed health dangers rather than legal dangers.

Fewer respondents also saw drug use as the norm. Whereas in 1980, 76 percent disapproved of using cocaine once or twice, the 1990 figure was 92 percent. The most sophisticated analysis of the high school senior survey data has found that it is these attitudinal changes which best explain declining drug use.[42]

As mentioned earlier, the evidence suggests that drug use has declined more sharply among those who have graduated from high school than those who have not. At the same time, it appears that enforcement risks have increased more for the less educated. It may well be that the more educated have greater sensitivity to the threat of arrest but the evidence is against enforcement as the primary engine for reduced drug use.

Incapacitation

Over the second half of the 1980s there was a dramatic increase in the number of prison and jail inmates, continuing a trend that goes back to the mid-1970s. Between the end of 1985 and the end of 1990, that figure increased from 750,000 (including federal, state, and local correctional facilities) to 1,200,000. The incarcerated population became richer in drug users over that time; in 1988 nearly one-third of those sent to state prison were convicted of drug offenses, compared to only 23 percent in 1986. Moreover, the data from local urinalysis programs suggests that the percentage of those imprisoned on nondrug charges who were drug users also rose. Taking account of both the increasing population of prisoners and the rising share that were drug users, perhaps a total of 450,000 additional drug users were removed from the population that might be involved in regular use or selling of drugs.[43]

What are the effects of this increase? In the context of an estimated 2 to 3 million frequent drug users, that is a substantial change and may do much to explain the decline in various indicators, including both DAWN and DUF. That is, declines in the numbers of persons showing up in emergency rooms for drug related problems or in the percentage of arrestees testing positive for drugs may reflect not just declines in drug using behavior but also the incapacitation of large numbers of drug users. The gains then are contingent on continued incarceration, given the lack of effective treatment in most prison facilities.

Other Consequences

A standard charge against the war on drugs is that it is racist and has led to a serious erosion of civil liberties. It is certainly true that African-Americans make up an extraordinarily high proportion of those charged with drug offenses, even when compared to their proportion in criminal offenses generally or to their share of the population of frequent drug users. That does not imply racism on the part of police or courts but it does point to the possibility of selective enforcement.

Table 3 provides data on the high and growing fraction of drug arrestees who are categorized as Black in the Uniform Crime Reports.

That share has increased dramatically over the ten years from 1980 to 1990, from less than one-fourth to more than two-fifths. The percentage has risen much faster for drug offenses than for others, including the more serious (represented by "Crime Index" offenses).

The emphasis on crack seems to have exacerbated this tendency. For example, the Minnesota legislature in 1989 raised the maximum penalty for possession of 3 grams of crack to twenty years; the same quantity of cocaine powder involved a maximum of five years. As it turned out, 96.6 percent of those charged with crack possession were African-American; for powder cocaine the figure was about 20 percent. The Minnesota Supreme Court overturned the statute for that reason in 1991.[44]

The high and rising drug arrest rates for African-Americans represents another dilemma for drug policy. It is in poorer sections of large cities, with high percentages of young African-American males, that the problems of disorder and violence surrounding drug distribution are most acute. These are the communities that have the greatest need for active drug enforcement. Yet that enforcement, responsive to community concerns, results in the incarceration of alarmingly high percentages of young males from the same communities.

This brings us to another concern, namely that those who are locked up are unimportant figures in the drug trades and that their sentences are too severe for the crime, particularly when prisons are regarded as more likely to worsen an inmate's behavior than to rehabilitate him. The contention about the role of those locked up is almost irrefutable because of the highly pyramided nature of the drug trade. Cocaine enters this country in 100 kilogram lots and sells in 1 gram units; under reasonable assumptions about how many others a wholesale dealer is willing to transact with, there are about 1,000 retailers for each importer. Thus most of those who are locked up must be retailers and their support personnel. There simply aren't 100,000 significant figures in the cocaine trade; indeed, there probably aren't more than 10,000 whose removal would make the trade go somewhat slower.[45]

Those locked up receive long sentences now, particularly at the federal level. The expected time served for conviction on a drug trafficking offense in federal court is over six years. Though federal courts confront the highest level dealers, they also sentence numerous minor agents of these dealers, such as the Colombian sailors who transport cocaine from that country. The sentences received by these agents are not light. Indeed, a horrible irony of the existing federal sentencing guidelines is that the only mitigating circumstance for shortening of the mandatory sentences is effective cooperation with the prosecutor.

Table 3. Race Characteristics of Arrestees

	PERCENT BLACK		
	1980	1985	1990
All Offenses	24.5	26.6	28.9
Crime Index	32.8	33.7	34.4
Drug Abuse	23.6	30.0	40.7

Source: *Uniform Crime Reports.*

Unimportant agents such as sailors have little to offer, whereas the principal figures in seller networks can, if they choose, provide valuable information.

At the state level the average sentences are not particularly long by contemporary US standards but as we saw above, about 90,000 persons received sentences of at least one year for drug offenses in 1988. At a time of overcrowded prisons, even one uncomfortable with the level of incarceration in the United States must ask whether the space could not be allocated more sensibly for more serious offenses.

One response to this is that those sentenced for drug offenses are also involved in more serious offenses; the drug selling is merely a marker for these other crimes. Little data are available on this matter. In the District of Columbia in a sample of drug dealers on probation in 1988, only 5 percent reported a violent offense in the previous six months. Indeed, drug selling in that sample looked very much like a substitute for other kinds of income generating (and sometimes violent) crimes.

The issue here is that of the seriousness of the offense. Legislatures have been impressed by claims that drugs cause great harm and have consequently demanded that the criminal justice system treat this as a serious offense. As always, it is a question of emphasis and allocation of resources but I confess that it is not clear to me that marijuana selling, or even possession with intent to distribute cocaine, should necessarily lead to lengthy incarceration, particularly at a time when punishment capacity is stretched so thin. That so many of those being locked up in state prisons and local jails for drug offenses are African-Americans makes it particularly important that we judge whether this incarceration is necessary.

Moreover, there are other harms that may be exacerbated by tough enforcement. Frequent harassment of street drug sellers increases the incentives to use violence for the maintenance of market share. More variability in the purity of heroin, resulting from occasional large seizures, may cause more overdoses. Stringent enforcement has raised marijuana potency, while head shop laws prevent marijuana users from using water pipes; marijuana is consumed in the most harmful possible manner.

The list of conjectured harms from intense enforcement can be extended. How significant each of them is and what they amount to in the aggregate is impossible to even guess at. I believe though that they are troubling enough that one needs to consider whether there is an alternative approach to drug control that takes them into account.

Harm Minimization and Aggressive Owls

The reality and rhetoric of drug policy in most of Western Europe is very different from that in the United States. The crime consequences of drug use are given far less attention, though property crime is often believed to be substantially raised by drug addiction. The health consequences dominate discussion in most of Europe, though that has led to only a moderate hatching of doves. Syringe exchange schemes, scarcely permitted even on a pilot basis here, have become common in Britain, the Netherlands, Italy, and the German cantons of Switzerland. Spain and the Netherlands, with very different social policies toward drug use generally, have given the criminal law a minor role in dealing with drug users.

The discussion of drug policy in Europe, outside of Scandinavia, is dominated by debate about harm minimization rather than minimizing the prevalence of drug use. Cannabis use, outside of Scandinavia, is almost entirely ignored. The emergence of AIDS has been the catalytic force. As the Advisory Council on the Misuse of Drugs in Great Britain said in a 1988 report, "HIV is a greater threat to public and individual health than drug misuse."[46] Policy measures that might increase the extent of drug use but lower the prevalence of HIV are likely to be endorsed under this hierarchy of values.

The policy view extends though to more than just AIDS related matters. If tough enforcement lessens the likelihood of drug addicts seeking treatment, then less stringent enforcement might be preferred. Some Europeans even talk about police making harm minimization choices in their tactics, for example using selective enforcement to focus on heroin injectors rather than heroin smokers, since smoking poses lower risk of both HIV and hepatitis B.

The difference in policy tone between Europe and the United States is importantly affected by the much lower prevalence of violence associated with drug distribution and use in Europe. That in turn may reflect simply the lower level of violence in European crime generally. Without that violence it is much easier to see health measures as the most appropriate response.

How successful have harm minimization policies been? Precisely because they are more concerned with reducing harms than drug use, they cannot be judged simply by the extent of drug use that they have engendered. The Dutch make a reasonable case that their very conscious adoption of the harm minimization approach has permitted their addicts to lead healthier and less crime ridden lives than their counterparts in the United States. However, the much more generous income

support schemes available to prime age males in Holland may be more significant here than any facet of targeted drug policy.

THE POLITICAL DYNAMICS OF DRUG POLICY

The success of the hawks is in part a function of how the drug problem has been characterized in the United States. So long as crime is the dominant part of the public image of the problem, then law enforcement is plausibly the most appropriate response. Drugs are produced by evil syndicates (the Medellin cartel), sold by ruthless gangs who kill innocent bystanders and generate fabulous incomes for the sellers (media stories about inner-city kids earning $1,000 a day)[47] operating in settings that generate neighborhood fear and disorder (street corners and crack houses); so runs the standard version of the problem.

The media reporting of the "drug crisis" has undoubtedly helped here. An analysis of prime-time network news bulletins in 1988 found that illegal drugs were the second most frequently mentioned item. Most of those news stories dealt with the drama of crime associated with drugs; few of the stories concerned drug treatment or prevention. The standard media mention of the issue is drugs and crime, rather than addiction to psychoactive substances of varying legal status.

All this has made it difficult for owls or doves to win the debate. No member of Congress has had political problems as the result of pressing for tougher penalties or expanded enforcement. The risks in arguing for more lenient punishment of drug users or dealers are clearly very serious, in face of popular opinion inflamed to believe in the need for toughness. It is depressing to note that a 1986 "Sense of Congress" resolution demanding the additions to the federal drug control budget be split evenly between enforcement and demand-side programs has led only to a modest shift in the balance of funding, even as federal drug budgets have rapidly escalated.

CONCLUSION

A particularly disturbing aspect of the current situation is the difficulty of dismantling the punitive apparatus that has been assembled since the mid-1980s. With declines in drug involvement among American youth likely to continue for some years, the justification for the draconian sentences at the federal level, with their personal and fiscal costs, will be even harder to sustain. The problem is increasingly that of the adult drug addicts who became dependent during the heroin epidemic of 1967–1973 or the cocaine epidemic of the 1980s.

Yet the political forces are not favorable to changing this bent in the near future. The doves are likely to be pushed back to the fringe status they held until 1987. Their appearance on center stage was fueled by the pervasive sense of despair in the late 1980s that the nation's drug problem was continuing to worsen despite tough and intrusive control. That sense of despair has lessened, reflecting at last the great decline in initiation into drug use among the vast middle class of the nation. Notwithstanding the rhetoric of liberals and conservatives alike that it is "everybody's problem," drugs now seem to be moving to another entry on the long list of ills that emanate from the inner city and poor minority populations in particular. Hawkishness may not have been the primary cause for the diminution of the problem but nonetheless the diminution occurred during the hawks' ascendancy, so that hawks find it easy to claim that

"toughness worked." Those who argue that the problem also worsened during the earlier ascendancy of the hawks will find a small audience. Calls for major changes in policy, in particular for the legal availability of what have come to be seen as "devil drugs," no matter how stringent the associated regulation, will also have limited appeal.

Owls may do better than doves. The imagery of war ought to work in their favor; victory is often followed by a period of humanitarian outreach by the winning side, an effort to help the casualties of war. The continuing decline in initiation among America's youth will make ever clearer that the drug problem is mostly the dangerous behavior of a relatively small number of adults, caught in the cocaine epidemic of the 1980s. Maybe locking them up will start to look more expensive and less attractive than developing better quality health and social services aimed at reducing their drug use and at improving their social functioning. Owls, even if their message lacks the simplicity and clarity of the competing birds, may yet come to dominate the aviary.

NOTES

1. Punishing drug users should reduce demand; to that extent the "supply-sider" label has an element of exaggeration.
2. This debate was given its most explicit formulation in the congressional debate on the 1988 Omnibus Anti-Drug Control Act.
3. Joseph Nye, Graham Allison, and Albert Carnesale, "Analytic Conclusions: Hawks, Doves and Owls," in Allison, Nye, and Carnesale, eds., *Hawks, Doves and Owls: An Agenda for Avoiding Nuclear War* (New York: W.W. Norton, 1985), 206–22.
4. Nye et al.'s tripartite division added owls to the conventional hawks and doves. Whereas

hawks believed that war could be avoided only if both sides have enough weapons to impose unacceptable damage on the other and doves believed that disarmament was essential to prevention of nuclear war, owls believed in confidence building measures and other elements of process, rather than the scale and comparability of nuclear arsenals as the key to peace.

5. The most appropriate measurement of treatment success is a vexed issue. Does one include the large number of persons who drop out early in a particular program, perhaps because they decide that other programs are more suitable? What constitutes success: abstinence or improved social functioning? The authoritative review is Dean Gerstein and Hendrick Harwood, eds., *Treating Drug Problems* (Washington, D.C.: National Academy Press, 1990).

6. The argument is made most explicitly in reports of the Office of National Drug Control Policy. See *National Drug Strategy* (1989 and 1990) and *White Paper on Drug Treatment*, 1990.

7. I shall not deal with the fringe dove movement that emphasizes the positive effects of psychoactive drugs. Thomas Szaz is probably the leading intellectual evangelist of this group; see Thomas Szaz, *Ceremonial Chemistry: The Ritual Persecution of Drugs, Addicts and Pushers* (Garden City, N.Y.: Anchor Books, 1974).

8. Ethan Nadelmann, "America's Drug Problem," *Bulletin of the American Academy of Arts and Sciences* 45 (3) (December 1991): 24–40.

9. Most acknowledge an exception for children; criminal prohibitions for the sale to children is a staple of dove advocacy.

10. Recent statements of this pessimism include Peter Andreas, Eva Bertram, Morris Blachman, and Kenneth Sharpe, "Dead-End Drug Wars," *Foreign Policy* 85 (Winter 1991–1992); and *The Andean Initiative: Squeezing a Balloon*, Report prepared by the staff of the House Judiciary Committee's Subcom-

mittee on Crime and Criminal Justice, February 24 1992.

11. Gerstein and Harwood, *Treating Drug Problems.*

12. Mark Kleiman, *Against Excess: Drug Policy for Results* (New York: Basic Books, 1992).

13. James Q. Wilson, "Drugs and Crime," in Michael Tonry and James Q. Wilson, eds., *Drugs and Crime* (Chicago: University of Chicago Press, 1990).

14. To estimate the share of criminal justice expenditures accounted for by drug enforcement, I separated police, courts, and corrections. The share of police expenditures on the drug "account" was measured by the ratio of drug selling arrests to Part I arrests plus drug selling arrests. For courts it was the ratio of drug felony convictions to all felony convictions. Finally, for prisons I used the share of all commitments to prison that were for drug offenses. These are all crude estimates. The only systematic effort to measure state and local expenditures on drug enforcement by police, Gerald Godshaw, Ross Pancoast, and Russell Koppel, *Anti-Drug Law Enforcement Efforts and Their Impact* (Bala Cynwyd, Pa.: Wharton Econometric Forecasting Associates, 1987), showed an even higher share of the police expenditures going to that effort in 1985 and 1986.

15. It is striking just how state and local governments have succeeded in keeping the public debate focused on the federal budget allocation. State and local expenditures on treatment and prevention have been growing very slowly compared to those of the federal government, even though these services are delivered almost exclusively by the lower levels of government.

16. Joan Petersilia, Joyce Peterson, and Susan Turner, *Intensive Probation and Parole: Research Findings and Policy Implications* (Santa Monica, Calif.: RAND Corporation, 1992).

17. *New York Times*, March 22, 1992.

18. Richard Doblin and Mark Kleiman, "Marijuana as an Antiemetic Medicine: A Survey

of Oncologists' Experiences and Attitudes," *Journal of Clinical Oncology* 9 (July 1991).

19. "Out of Joint," *New Republic*, July 15 & 22, 1991.

20. Peter Reuter, "On the Consequences of Toughness," in Krauss, Melvyn, and Edward Lazear, eds., *Drug Policy in America: The Search for Alternatives* (Stanford, Calif.: Hoover Institution Press, 1991).

21. The Uniform Crime Reports system of the FBI combines heroin and cocaine arrests into a single category. It is generally believed that the increase in this category throughout the 1980s was dominated by an increase in cocaine related arrests.

22. Bureau of Justice Statistics, *Felony Sentences in State Courts* (Washington, D.C.: 1989, 1990).

23. Since these possession charges were prosecuted as felonies, they are presumably possession with intent to distribute rather than simple possession offenses, which in most states are misdemeanors only.

24. The declining average time served probably reflects two phenomena. The first is simply prison overcrowding, which has led to a reduction in the share of sentence actually served. The second is that the rapid increase in the number of drug offenders receiving prison sentences means that some are now being imprisoned for less severe offenses.

25. All of these dispositional data, both national and Californian, bear on felonies, primarily related to distribution and/or manufacture. There are literally no published data concerning the sentences received by those arrested on simple possession charges.

26. Mark Kleiman sensibly notes that this kind of statement ignores the prevalence of alcohol use. It may well be that the average hours of intoxication per citizen is no higher in the United States than in nations, such as France, where alcohol is more widely abused. Without denying the relevance of that measure, there are distinctive problems arising from use of illegal substances and it is worth considering differences among societies in the extent of that use.

27. During the 1980s, the National Institute on Drug Abuse funded three surveys of drug use in the household population; that survey has been conducted annually since 1990. Each year since 1975 the University of Michigan has surveyed a sample of approximately 16,000 high school seniors.

28. Thirty years ago smoking was not associated with social class. It is now. In 1980, a quarter of professional men smoked, a third of white collar men and almost half of blue collar men . . ." Thomas Schelling, "Addictive Drugs: The Cigarette Experience," *Science* 255 (January 24, 1992): 430–31.

29. Nor is this simply explained by higher drop out rates among African-Americans, which would suggest that the high school senior population was a more select group within their age cohort when compared to the white seniors. Drop-out rates in recent years have been almost equal for the two populations.

30. That difference is particularly striking since the percentage of incarcerated males aged 26–34 is much higher for African-Americans than for the rest of the population. The incarcerated males are much more likely to be drug users than the nonincarcerated; if the two ethnic groups have the same prevalence rate overall, the nonincarcerated African-American rate should be lower than the white rate. Note that these are all unadjusted rates; the differences should not be ascribed to ethnicity but may be a function of urbanness, education, employment rates, etc.

31. In 1991, the survey for the first time included homeless in shelters.

32. The DAWN reports include data on the patient's motive for using the drug. In 1983, 42 percent reported that they took cocaine for its psychic effects (i.e. for pleasure) and 47 percent reported dependence. By 1989, 63 percent of those episodes involving cocaine were classified as drug dependence and for only 28 percent was "psychic effects" the motive for taking the drug.

33. The number of DAWN cocaine mentions flattened out in 1988 and then fell by about 25 percent between the second and third

quarters of 1989. The numbers then rose over the following two years, close to their prior peak. Little effort has been made to understand these changes, which may be affected by shifts in emergency room policies during an urban health care financing crisis, or by alterations in the behavior of addicts rather than by their numbers.

34. The most recent is Dorothy Rice, Sander Kelman, Leonard Miller, and Sarah Dunmeyer, *Economic Costs of Alcohol Abuse, Drug Abuse and Mental Illness, 1985* (Rockville, Md.: Alcohol, Mental Health and Drug Abuse Administration, 1990).

35. To get a sense of this, the reader should consider what would happen to the value of her house if the crime rate in the surrounding area reached a figure comparable to that on Capitol Hill in Washington, D.C.

36. A better measure is Years of Life Lost (YLL) which takes account of how premature a death is; for example, the average YLL is higher for alcohol than cigarettes, since lung cancer typically strikes its victims in late middle age, while many alcoholics die in early middle age. DAWN data suggest a much higher average YLL (i.e. earlier age of death) for illicit drugs but even that would not raise the significance of illegal drugs to that of either alcohol or tobacco.

37. Bureau of Justice Statistics, *Profile of Jail Inmates, 1989* (April 1991).

38. Paul Goldstein, H. H. Brownstein, P. J. Ryan, and P. A. Belluci, "Crack and Homicide in New York, 1988," *Contemporary Drug Problems* (1990).

39. Medical costs for treatment and lost wages capture only the direct costs; the increased

fear associated with sexual intercourse is an instance of those indirect consequences that seem both difficult to value and potentially very important.

40. See the recent complaints by the National Commission on AIDS about lack of drug treatment capacity, *The Twin Epidemics of Substance Use and HIV* (1991), 7–10.

41. Peter Reuter, "Police Regulation of Illegal Gambling: Frustrations of Symbolic Enforcement," *Annals of the American Academy of Political Science* (July 1984).

42. Jerald G. Bachman, Lloyd D. Johnston, and Patrick M. O'Malley, "Explaining the Recent Decline in Cocaine Use Among Young Adults: Further Evidence that Perceived Risks and Disapproval Lead to Reduced Drug Use," *Journal of Health and Social Behavior* 31 (June 1990).

43. If 45 percent of the 1985 incarcerated population were drug users and the figure for 1990 were 65 percent, then the total number of drug users locked up rose from about 350,000 to 800,000. Both percentages seem fairly conservative.

44. *Washington Post*, December 14, 1991, A10.

45. This is not to say that the more senior figures are at low risk. Indeed, it seems unlikely that one could operate as long as five years in most American cities in the high levels of the drug market without facing substantial risk of long term imprisonment.

46. The Advisory Council on the Misuse of Drugs, *Report: AIDS and Drug Misuse* (London: HMSO).

47. See for example the alarmist cover story in *Time*, May 9, 1988, 21–33.

Sex Offender Notification and Community Justice

Lois Presser and *Elaine Gunnison*

Sex offender notification, also called community notification, is the law in all but a few American states (Pearson 1998). The ubiquity of notification laws is matched only by the controversy surrounding them. Their fairness and consequences have been hotly contested in the courts and in the press. Following suit, criminologists have examined notification almost exclusively in terms of fairness and consequences, the latter being a matter of speculation rather than empirical inquiry (Finn 1997; Freeman-Longo 1996). Questions about underlying principles have received little scholarly attention.

Sex offender notification is commonly aligned with the contemporary trend toward community justice. Supporters of notification claim that the laws empower private citizens to protect themselves. They refer to notification as "community management of offenders" (Beatty 1997, p. 20) and "a form of community policing" (Lieb 1996, p. 299). Yet the extent to which notification truly is community justice has not been examined.

Though the term *community justice* is used broadly, it is possible to identify two unifying principles. First, community justice helps citizens increase their own safety (Moore 1992; Zehr 1995). Second, community justice looks to the roots of crime problems, seeking to prevent crime before it occurs (Office of Justice Programs [OJP] 1998; Oliver 1998).

On the surface, sex offender notification legislation seems like a community justice initiative. The laws allegedly involve citizens in crime prevention by supplying them with information about known sex offenders (Beatty 1997; Goodman 1996). However, the alliance between sex offender notification and community justice is an odd one. The supporter of notification seems more like a retributivist than a problem solver.

This article examines what sex offender notification shares with community justice and what it does not. We contend that notification is not community justice, though it has appropriated some of its rhetoric. Sex offender notification differs from community justice in terms of the following: (1) views of crime, (2) the nature of citizen participation, (3) problem-solving orientations, (4) treatment of victims' needs, (5) willingness to understand offenders, (6) shaming of offenders, and (7) extension of state control.

From Lois Presser and Elaine Gunnison, "Strange Bedfellows: Is Sex Offender Notification a Form of Community Justice?" *Crime and Delinquency,* Vol. 45 No. 3 (July 1999): 299–315. Reprinted by permission of Sage Publications, © 1999.

BACKGROUND

Restorative Community Justice

Restorative justice is a branch of the community justice movement. The two movements are so closely related that the term *restorative community justice* is popular (Young 1995), and our discussion of community justice will center on restorative justice.

Restorative justice stresses the need to repair the harms caused by crime and to reintegrate victims, offenders, and communities. Programs based on restorative justice include victim-offender mediation, family group conferencing, and sentencing circles. To varying degrees, all involve healing dialogue and communal participation.

Sex Offender Notification

The sex offender notification movement is a more recent development than restorative justice, though its historical antecedents include sweeping legislation against rape beginning in the late 1970s (Caringella-MacDonald and Humphries 1991). Washington state was the first to pass a notification statute in 1989. The notification movement gained momentum with the 1994 enactment of New Jersey's Megan's Law, a legislative response to the rape and murder of 7-year-old Megan Kanka by a paroled sex offender (Goodman 1996; Rudin 1996). The New Jersey law also provided for involuntary civil commitment for the most serious offenders, a DNA database, and similar "containment" strategies (Goodman 1996). The nationwide influence of the New Jersey law was so great that notification laws are now known generically as Megan's Laws.

Notification laws were a supplement to registration laws, which require offenders just released from prison to register with local law enforcement agencies. A "perception that registration alone is inadequate to protect the public against released sex offenders" prompted notification of community members (Finn 1997, p. 2). That perception was fed by heinous cases, such as the victimization of Megan Kanka. The Kanka case roused citizen activism to "prevent a recurrence of such a tragedy" (Brooks 1996, p. 56). A federal Megan's Law followed in May 1996. The law mandated the public release of information about offenders by the states, in part by relaxing confidentiality restrictions.

Two types of procedures are invoked by notification laws: one for assessing offender risk and one for disseminating information about offenders. Risk is assessed differently across the states. Some states (e.g., California) rely solely on criminal history. Some defer to the determination of one law enforcement official, such as the county prosecutor (Pearson 1998). Some (e.g., Georgia) automatically subject certain sex offenders, such as pedophiles, to notification requirements. Finally, some states use actuarial risk assessment instruments (Canestrini 1998; Goodman 1996). However risk is assessed, a three-tier risk typology is commonly applied that consists of low (Tier 1), moderate (Tier 2), and high (Tier 3) risk (Goodman 1996).

Methods of notification vary across states and communities, as local law enforcement officials devise "their own notification plan based on the offender's criminal behavior and the make-up of the community" (Finn 1997, p. 5). There are roughly three notification categories: active notification, limited disclosure, and passive notification, which roughly correspond with the three risk tiers (Goodman 1996). For the Tier 3 offender, only active notification delivers information to citizens without their asking for it. The public is notified through virtually any available means, including clothing labels, visits from police officers, newspaper ads, and the internet. With limited disclosure, generally for the Tier 2 offender, only some organizations (like schools) are notified. For the Tier 1 offender, passive notification requires citizens to obtain information themselves.

According to federal law, persons convicted of any criminal offense against a minor, or a sexually violent offense against any victim, are subject to registration and notification for 10 years. The sexually violent predator, so classified by the court and a board of experts, is subject to these requirements for life (Feinberg 1998).

Sex Offender Notification and the Restorative Justice Ideal

The sex offender notification movement draws ideologically from a restorative justice ideal, which states that a more just society will be achieved through community problemsolving. In addition, the benefits of community justice will be reaped at the local level (Van Ness and Strong 1997). The language of the notification movement underscores these two basic concepts: community and problemsolving.

In the notification literature, it is "everyday citizens" who will "build a world worthy of our children" (Wetterling 1998, p. 6). Teir and Coy (1997) observe that notification "relies solely upon self-help" (p. 406), thus down-playing the role of government. Public safety is supposedly achieved "through the sharing of information and education" by community members (Center for Sex Offender Management [CSOM] 1997, p. 5). Communities are held responsible for sex offender recidivism; when it occurs, the families of victims "are left questioning whether the community and *its* [italics added] criminal

justice system let them down" (Teir and Coy 1997, p. 405).

Sex offender notification is designed to allow citizens to "actively participate in reclaiming the safety of their neighborhoods, cities and towns" (Beatty 1997, p. 20). Legislation is sometimes tied to communitybuilding activities. The Megan Kanka Foundation, which provides information on notification policies, also offers scholarships to high school students who "show leadership in community service" (Megan Nicole Kanka Foundation 1997). Notification laws occasion greater dialogue between citizens and criminal justice personnel, such that "a problemsolving relationship develops between criminal justice professionals and local residents" (CSOM 1997, p. 5).

The ideology of communities obtaining justice has been adopted, but has restorative justice been achieved? To answer this question, we compare restorative justice and sex offender notification in terms of seven conceptual themes.

THEMES OF RESTORATIVE COMMUNITY JUSTICE AND SEX OFFENDER NOTIFICATION

Views of Crime

Supporters of both the restorative justice and the sex offender notification movements allege that certain truths about crime are the starting point of their efforts. Community justice deals with particular conflicts between people, rejecting abstract views of crime (Zehr 1995). Notification advocates claim that they have taken a good, hard look at the facts about sexual violence and, particularly in view of recidivism data, they have designed realistic policies (see Wetterling 1998).

We contend that the notification movement has focused on some realities about sex crime to the exclusion of others. The process by which offenders are deemed dangerous is problematic. Standardized assessment instruments are frequently used, but they tend to overestimate risk (Van Ness and Strong 1997; Wright, Clear, and Dickson 1984). Inaccurate determinations have resulted, such that the New Jersey Supreme Court ruled that these assessment tools should not be relied on exclusively (Cooper 1998).

Moreover, the classification process pares the identity of the sex offender down to offending alone. That is, other life roles that the offender might play (e.g., parent or friend) are discounted. Sex offender becomes a master status; the diversity of behaviors and identities of those persons labeled sex offender are obscured. The master status is difficult to escape and, most often, the offender must actively seek relief from notification requirements. The label may have lasting effects, as there are no "ceremonies to decertify deviance" before the community (Braithwaite and Mugford 1994, p. 141).

Reports of high recidivism rates that are impervious to treatment (e.g., Furby, Weinrott, and Blackshaw 1989) are used by notification supporters to justify the extreme measures that have been proposed for dealing with sex offenders, such as chemical castration. In 1997, when the U.S. Supreme Court ruled that states can indefinitely confine sex offenders, the majority opinion was that some of these persons "suffer from a volitional impairment rendering them dangerous beyond their control" (Mishra 1997, p. 2). Yet recent research suggests that treatment, especially cognitive-behavioral approaches coupled with relapse prevention, can be effective in reducing recidivism (Marshall and Pithers 1994). Furthermore, recidivism rates may be lower than is commonly believed. Lotke (1996) reports that untreated sex offenders sentenced to prison have a recidivism rate of 18.5 percent, compared with 25 percent for drug offenders and 30 percent for (nonsexually) violent offenders.

Another myth nurtured by notification advocates is that sex offenses are carried out by persons who are strangers to the victims. But in nearly 75 percent of sexual assault and rape cases and in 90 percent of those involving children, the victim knew the offender (Greenfeld 1997). Forty-three percent of victims under age 12 were assaulted by family members (Chaiken 1998). With an emphasis on "outing" the dangerous stranger, notification laws perpetuate a false sense of security that all sex offenders are known to the authorities (Finn 1997) and ignore the social and family structures within which most offenders live. The idea that "people who harm us are not of us" justifies notification and other divisive policies (Clear 1994, p. 149).

Citizen Participation

Citizen participation in crime control is central to the rhetoric of both movements. However, their rationales for participation and the forms it has taken differ markedly.

Rationale for participation. In the restorative justice model, citizen participation in crime control strengthens communities. Crimes create opportunities for citizen involvement in matters of personal importance and for clarification of social norms (Christie 1977). Community building is as important a goal as problem solving (Harris 1991; McKnight 1995).

In contrast, notification assumes a strictly utilitarian rationale for citizen participation. The community represents "more eyes monitoring released offenders" (Beatty 1997,

p. 20). Lawmakers and law enforcement officials set the boundaries for formal processes of notification, and citizens are expected to act on the information provided. According to notification advocates, government is not to blame if offenders are denied jobs and housing, for these are "the normal societal consequences of committing a heinous crime" and not "requirements of or the intent of notification laws" (Sacco 1998, pp. 51–52). The state thus disowns responsibility for postnotification community conduct. Citizens determine most of the ways in which offenders are responded to day to day, and the government only steps in to restore peace. It is neither the duty nor the concern of citizens to achieve peace. This recipe for community action is the virtual opposite of that proposed by restorative justice, where citizens restore peace between victims and offenders and the government supervises how offenders are treated (Van Ness and Strong 1997, pp. 38–39).

Participation of victims, offenders, and other citizens. The involvement of victims is central to the restorative justice model, which explicitly calls for "comprehensive changes to expand victim involvement in the criminal justice process" (Van Ness and Strong 1997, p. 150). These changes include new, formal roles for victims from investigation to postsentence supervision of offenders. By comparison, though victims helped launch notification legislation in some states, their involvement soon became superfluous. For example, in Washington state the early influence of victims' groups was great, but their policy preferences were later ignored (Scheingold, Olson, and Pershing 1994, p. 747).

Offenders are essential actors in both restorative justice and notification processes. Restorative justice programs ask offenders to perform community service, pay restitution, and/or apologize to their victims and commu-

nities. Notification requires only that offenders register with the government, which is easy to avoid. A California study found that 75 percent of sex offenders in the state had failed to register (Montana 1996).

Restorative justice has evolved from the grass roots; that is, the work of community members (e.g., victims' and offenders' friends and neighbors) and organizations (e.g., churches) has been as instrumental in its development as the government. Citizens design programs, act as mediation or conference facilitators, arrange community service for offenders, and offer aid to victims and offenders (Van Ness and Strong 1997).

Conversely, notification laws maintain the dominance of the criminal justice system. Particular agents of the system assess the risk that an offender poses (Goodman 1996), after which information is disclosed or withheld by public officials. Activism stirred by notification law has taken several forms. Most commonly, it involves organized campaigns to alert the community to the presence of a sex offender. Citizens have also organized protests against the individual, involving a range of activities, both nonviolent and violent. Offenders and their families have been "picketed, leafleted, stoned, pummeled with eggs, threatened, or had signs posted outside their residences" (Rudin 1996, p. 7). A lesser number have been victims of vigilante attacks (Stadler 1995). These different forms of participating all seek the goal of exiling the offender. Rather than a means to "social cohesion," citizen participation is "an instrument of divisiveness" (Grabosky 1992, p. 267).

Problem Solving

Notification laws are a proactive and apparently new response to a social problem, so they seem like solutions. But in fact, the sex offender is defined as the problem to be solved. Because the offender is allegedly unalterable, so too is the problem (see Furby et al. 1989; Mishra 1997). Strategies for dealing with the sex offender problem emphasize containment (English, Pullen, and Jones 1997; Myers 1996). The problem can only be checked and its effects mitigated rather than averted. A sense of hopelessness thus shapes notification policies, which offer little in the way of suggested action for concerned citizens. Whereas notification laws "clearly affirm the desire for protection from assaultive and predatory behavior . . . they do not suggest what communities should do once they are notified that sex offenders live in their neighborhoods" (CSOM 1997, p. 7).

Restorative justice approaches to sex crimes aspire to eradicate the root causes of those crimes. They have been influenced by feminist thought, which holds that the problem of sex crime is rooted in general cultural codes; thus, it is these codes that must be transformed (Carrington and Watson 1996). Rather than a more effective crackdown on particular incidents, policing sexual violence demands the dispelling of oppressive myths and the development of new norms. Myths that facilitate sex crimes include the idea that, absent clear and abundant evidence of coercion or resistance, participation in sexual activity was probably consensual. Such beliefs are widespread. For example, most junior high school students surveyed in a Rhode Island study agreed that it is acceptable for a man to force a woman to have sexual intercourse under certain circumstances, which included spending money on a date, having dated one person exclusively for more than six months, and being married (Caringella-MacDonald and Humphries 1991, pp. 101–102). These findings contradict "the perception that rape is an isolated problem amenable to security and criminal justice solutions" (Caringella-MacDonald and Humphries 1991, p. 106). As

Braithwaite and Mugford (1994) note, "attacking deeper structures of inequality is more important" (p. 156) than individual intervention.

Sex offender notification fails to consider the societal basis of the offender's conduct, with the result that the problem of sexual violence is left unexamined and unchanged. Notification not only neglects the root causes of sexual violence but also diverts attention away from them. The public "is relieved of having to make connections between the root causes of antisocial and sexually violent acts and the kind of social-change alternatives that actually could make our communities more just and safe" (Knopp 1991, p. 183). In fact, controlling sexual violence by making life miserable for the offender is a contradiction, because sexual violence and notification laws share the logic of dominating and harming another (Clear 1994; Harris 1991). The "oppressive institutions of patriarchy and . . . punishment" are inseparable (Knopp 1991, p. 181).

The sex offender notification movement has attended to neither causes nor, for that matter, solutions. Notification laws were passed hastily, without planning (Rudin 1996). Pallone (1995) describes how New Jersey legislators enacted Megan's Law without hearings on alternative proposals or "even a cursory reconstructive analysis" (p. 10) of the events that led to Megan Kanka's victimization to inform action.

It is true that vigilantism has been widely condemned by notification advocates (Beatty 1997; Hanley 1998). However, official reports tend to frame vigilantism as the result of misinformation about the laws (Hanley 1998). Sacco (1998) speculates that "the likelihood of vigilantism will decrease as notification becomes more common" (p. 51). On the other hand, a view is emerging of vigilantism as a "logical outcome of telling people that an evil menace lurks next door" (Prentky 1996, p. 296). The compatibility of notification law with violent responses is noted by opponents and proponents alike (Allen 1998). Notification law, so prescriptive about other procedures, offers few suggestions as to what citizens should do about sexual violence, with the possible result that tolerance of vigilantism is fostered.

Helping Victims

Restorative justice and sex offender notification share a concern about the crime victim. In the restorative model, sanctions for offenders should be designed to meet victims' needs (Zehr 1995). Notification laws were lobbied for by victims' groups (Scheingold et al. 1994), and some were named after victims of sexual violence (Rudin 1996; Wetterling 1998). But in fact, the notification movement offers little aid to victims.

Like offenders, victims of sex crimes need to be reintegrated into society. In addition to damage to self-image, relationships, and employability (Van Ness and Strong 1997), sex crime victims are prone to "shame, self-blame, fear, developmental crises, post-traumatic stress disorder" (English et al. 1997, p. 3). When restorative justice entails an apology from the offender and community condemnation of the crime, victims receive "powerful affirmation of the respect for (him or her) as a person" (Braithwaite and Mugford 1994, p. 155). Clear (1994) suggests that condemning the offender as opposed to the offense can negatively affect the victim, upholding "the idea that moral worth is a product of judgements" (p. 133) and thus that the victim's worth is similarly prone to degradation by others.

Sex crimes cause particular harm to children (English et al. 1997) who then need

special services, especially when incest has occurred. Kreindler and Armstrong (1983) point out that "incest is a family affair rather than just the expression of one family member's psychopathology" (p. 555). They highlight the discrepancy between what the child and his or her family need and what they inevitably receive. Treatment should be "as nonthreatening as possible" for all involved, or "the intervention may be more damaging than the experience itself, particularly if the child ends up in care, the father in prison, and the family on welfare" (Kreindler and Armstrong 1983, p. 560). Often when incest is discovered and the offender is incarcerated, the child victim is made a scapegoat for the family's resultant problems, which, in turn, instills guilt and self-hatred. It should also be noted that incest victims are themselves publicly identified by notification, causing a second form of violation (Pearson 1998).

Female rape victims are often held responsible for the violation. In court, their character and behavior are considered relevant (Spears and Spohn 1997). Sex offender notification laws have done nothing to change the sociolegal context within which the female victim's credibility is questioned. Ironically, this is the context in which sex offender notification might effect change, because notification is a legal practice.

Notification laws do not directly address the needs of victims after the crime has occurred (Klein 1998), except by prohibiting offender contact with victims (Shapiro 1998). This neglect might be explained by the legal context of notification. The focus of criminal law remains firmly on the offender and protection of society, not the assistance to victims (Dow 1989, p. 373). Neglect of victims also follows from the warlike mentality of notification law. Victims are not people with needs but rather recruits into battle, "used by the prosecution for their own adversarial purposes" (Knopp 1991, p. 182).

Understanding Offenders

Trying to understand offenders is part of the problem-solving orientation of community justice. In stark contrast, an effort to understand sex offenders is not part of the notification agenda, which is primarily focused on exiling them.

Understanding why offenders offend allows for effective interventions. For example, many sex offenders were themselves victims of sexual assault, and "addressing the psychological harm done to offenders in the past may help to reduce the harm they inflict on others in the future" (Lotke 1996, p. 1). Compassionate treatment approaches do not preclude efforts to encourage offenders to take responsibility for their offending. Rather, acceptance of responsibility is a first step in the most promising treatments. The second step involves "understanding the sequence of thoughts, feelings, events, high-risk circumstances, and arousal stimuli that (precede) their sexual assaults" (Knopp 1991, p. 191). This understanding is followed by training on how to interrupt the cycle and the teaching of new attitudes and behaviors.

By contrast, the notification movement considers the offender the enemy in a battle of rights and interests (Shapiro 1998). In this light, notification laws represent mastery over dark forces. Megan's Law "tips the balance in favor of the innocent victims of sex crimes rather than the perpetrators" (Goodman 1996, p. 797). The efforts that followed Megan Kanka's victimization are constructed as "an inspiring story of tragedy fueling a passionate fight for the protection of children from sexual predators" (Megan Nicole Kanka Foundation 1997, p. 1). Paradoxically, with the whole

community poised for battle against the offender, he or she is more likely to try to distance himself or herself psychologically from the offense. Responsibility is avoided as "unconsciously or even consciously (offenders) work to insulate themselves from the victim" (Zehr 1995, p. 41). Notification facilitates that insulating process by positioning the offender as adversary. To relieve the discomfort of constant shame, the offender likewise may "reject the rejectors," viewing the law-abiding community as adversaries (Braithwaite and Mugford 1994; see also Sherman 1993).

Shaming Offenders

Both notification and restorative justice processes shame the offender. Braithwaite (1989) commends the sort of shaming used by restorative justice programs, in which offenders are subsequently reintegrated into the community. Offenders are shown that "they are not what they do (hence) they can be better than what they do" (Wylie 1998, p. 57). Conversely, notification rebukes both offender and offense, which may foster "adoption of a delinquent identity" (Braithwaite and Mugford 1994, p. 146).

Clinical knowledge about sexual deviance suggests that notification is likely to be counterproductive. Censure may encourage retreat into denial and defensiveness (Kreindler and Armstrong 1983; see also Braithwaite and Mugford 1994; Kear-Colwell and Pollock 1997; Sherman 1993). Pedophiles in particular may respond to notification by reoffending, because they are often loners who find companionship in children instead of adults. Montana (1996) notes that "by ostracizing sex offenders, community members may reinforce their attraction toward children" (p. 585). Furthermore, the stress of public exposure may provoke reoffense, and its threat may keep offenders from seeking treatment (CSOM 1997).

Social Control

Both restorative justice and sex offender notification negotiate new combinations of social control. Restorative justice purportedly substitutes informal for formal social control over offenders (Christie 1977; Stuart 1997). The notification movement seeks a net increase in both formal and informal social control over offenders.

Restorative justice may lead to more control over more people, despite its professed intentions. First, the net of social control may be widened if persons whom the formal justice system would have dismissed (e.g., petty offenders) are sanctioned (Dittenhoffer and Ericson 1983; Levrant, Cullen, Fulton, and Wozniak 1999). Second, by adding restorative conditions to probation terms, more opportunities are provided to "fail" and to be incarcerated for violation. Third, state control is exercised if parties to mediation are pressured to reconcile with one another (Brown 1994; Levrant et al. 1999; Pavlich 1996).

Net widening is regarded as a potential problem by many restorative justice advocates (Immarigeon and Daly 1997; Umbreit and Zehr 1995–1996; Van Ness and Strong 1997). Others minimize the seriousness of net widening on the grounds that, whatever the systemic effect, "it is just and right for the offender to be confronted with the personal impact of her or his crime" (Coates and Gehm 1989; see also Braithwaite and Daly 1994; Stuart 1997).

For the notification movement, extending social control over sex offenders is the manifest goal. Notification generalizes the incapacitive functions of the prison beyond the

prison and, indeed, beyond the dominion of government. Empirical evidence of net widening as a result of notification laws is not available, though it seems highly likely that it does occur. Probation and parole conditions are directly widened by the legislation. There is no shortage of volunteers to police those conditions (see Nieves 1998, p. 17). With neighbors alert to any presumed evidence of criminality, the offender stands a good chance of returning to court on a violation. It is not at all clear that society is better off with this brand of justice or if its main accomplishment is simply to "ensure that their problems will have solutions" (Feeley and Simon 1992, p. 456).

SUMMARY AND CONCLUSIONS

Sex offender notification is a flawed strategy for controlling sex crime. It reflects a skewed view of sex offenders and, lacking a plan for problem solving, it encourages citizen action in the form of vigilantism. Notification relies on stigma, such that offenders are likely to retreat into denial and eventually to recidivate (Kear-Colwell and Pollock 1997).

Notification has been promoted as a community justice initiative. The insight that notification shares little with community justice highlights the fact that something is missing in the restorative community justice movement. Namely, it is not meeting the needs of communities threatened by sexual violence. Harris (1987) articulates the movement's general strategy: to do what is possible and postpone the toughest challenges. She advises fellow advocates to "not allow the most difficult cases to stand in the way of more rapidly evolving better approaches for the rest" (p. 35).

That pragmatic strategy was a good one for a time, considering the movement's broad goals and formidable obstacles. Following this plan, community groups are "doing *something* [italics added]" (Caringella-MacDonald and Humphries 1991, p. 109). However, there is now an urgent need for programs for sex offenders: the notification movement makes this clear. Most mediation programs in the United States exclude violent cases (Hughes and Schneider 1989; Lerman 1984; Rowe 1985). Treatment is critical, but restorative justice programs have often failed to consider current knowledge about offender treatment (Levrant et al. 1999). If restorative justice cannot change serious sex offenders, then incapacitation—through confinement or registration and notification—would seem the only legitimate means available for protecting society.

Though restorative programs for sex offenders are in short supply, a few have been developed that emphasize both treatment and restorative justice principles. One such program is The Safer Society sponsored by an association of churches, which calls for offender-specific interventions including "restraint of the few" very serious sex offenders (Knopp 1991, p. 185). The restraint used should be "the least restrictive and most humane option for the shortest period of time in the most remedial and restorative environment" (Knopp 1991, p. 186). Above all, The Safer Society emphasizes early intervention with youth who show signs of sexual aggression and educational programs that teach non-sexist values.

Other innovations are on the horizon. Some victim-offender mediation programs in Canada and England have surrogate victims meet with sex offenders so that certain benefits of encounter are realized without added trauma to victims (Zehr 1995, p. 206). Victim-sensitive sex offender therapy, developed by Walter Berea, considers the victim's needs at each of three offender treatment phases (Zehr 1995, p. 207). Finally, Braithwaite and Daly (1994) call for a pyramid of responses to rape and other violence between intimates that applies family group conferencing in combination with law enforcement responses. A succession of responses, both formal/legal and informal/communitarian, is "more practical and more decent" than formal sanctions alone (Braithwaite and Daly 1994, p. 201). What these interventions to sex crime have in common is a practical agenda for meeting the needs of victims, offenders, and communities, often using community resources.

Research on effective treatment for sex offenders of all types should be a priority of government and the scientific community. Too little is known about what works with sex offenders (Quinsey 1998, p. 415). In addition, the effects of notification on positive community outcomes, such as citizens' sense of empowerment, should be studied to reveal what the notification movement is doing right. These aspects of the notification movement can help shape new programs more consistent with peacemaking. Though strange bedfellows, sex offender notification and restorative community justice might become friends yet.

REFERENCES

Allen, Mike. 1998. "Killing Shows Connecticut the Limits of Its 'Megan's Law.'" *New York Times*, August 28, p. A19.

Beatty, David. 1997. "Community Notification—It's the Right Thing To Do." *Corrections Today* 59:20.

Braithwaite, John. 1989. *Crime, Shame and Reintegration*. Cambridge, UK: Cambridge University Press.

Braithwaite, John and Kathleen Daly. 1994. "Masculinities, Violence, and Communitarian Control." Pp. 189–213 in *Just Boys Doing Business? Men,*

Masculinity and Crime, edited by T. Newburn and B. Stanko. London: Routledge.

Braithwaite, John and Stephen Mugford. 1994. "Conditions of Successful Reintegration Ceremonies." *British Journal of Criminology* 34:139–71.

Brooks, Alexander D. 1996. "Megan's Law: Constitutionality and Policy." *Criminal Justice Ethics* 15:56–66.

Brown, Jennifer Gerarda. 1994. "The Use of Mediation to Resolve Criminal Cases: A Procedural Critique." *Emory Law Journal* 43:1247–1309.

Canestrini, Kathy. 1998. "The Method of Risk Assessment Used for the New York State Sex Offender Registration Act." *National Conference on Sex Offender Registries Proceedings.* Washington, DC: Bureau of Justice Statistics.

Caringella-MacDonald, Susan and Drew Humphries. 1991. "Sexual Assault, Women, and the Community." Pp. 98–113 in *Criminology as Peacemaking*, edited by H. E. Pepinsky and R. Quinney. Bloomington: Indiana University Press.

Carrington, Kerry and Paul Watson. 1996. "Policing Sexual Violence: Feminism, Criminal Justice and Governmentality." *International Journal of the Sociology of Law* 24:253–72.

Center for Sex Offender Management (CSOM). 1997. *An Overview of Sex Offender Community Notification Practices: Policy Implications and Promising Approaches.* Silver Springs, MD: Author.

Chaiken, Jan M. 1998. "Sex Offenders and Offending: Learning More From National Data Collection Programs." *National Conference on Sex Offender Registries.* Washington, DC: Bureau of Justice Statistics.

Christie, Nils. 1977. "Conflict As Property." *British Journal of Criminology* 17:1–15.

Clear, Todd R. 1994. *Harm in American Penology: Offenders, Victims, and Their Communities.* Albany: State University of New York Press.

Coates, Robert B. and John Gehm. 1989. "An Empirical Assessment." Pp. 251–63 in *Mediation and Criminal Justice: Victims, Offenders and Community*, edited by M. Wright and B. Galaway. London: Sage Ltd.

Cooper, Scott A. 1998. "Community Notification and Verification Practices in Three States." *National Conference on Sex Offender Registries.* Washington, DC: Bureau of Justice Statistics.

Dittenhoffer, Tony and Richard V. Ericson. 1983. "The Victim/Offender Reconciliation Program: A Message to Correctional Reformers." *University of Toronto Law Journal* 33:315–47.

Dow, David R. 1989. "Individuals, Government, and Rights: A Reply to Cathleen Herasimchuk." *South Texas Law Review* 30:369–85.

English, Kim, Suzanne Pullen, and Linda Jones. 1997. "Managing Adult Sex Offenders in the Community—A Containment Approach" [On-line]. *National Institute of Justice Research in Action.* Washington, DC: National Institute of Justice. Available: http://www.ncjrs.org/txtfiles/sexoff.txt.

Feeley, Malcolm M. and Jonathan Simon. 1992. "The New Penology: Notes on the Emerging Strategy of Corrections and Its Implications." *Criminology* 30:449–74.

Feinberg, Donna. 1998. "Justice Department Guideline Changes and Clarifications." *National Conference on Sex Offender Registries.* Washington, DC: Bureau of Justice Statistics.

Finn, Peter, 1997. *Sex Offender Community Notification.* Washington, DC: National Institute of Justice.

Freeman-Longo, Robert E. 1996. "Feel Good Legislation: Prevention or Calamity." *Child Abuse & Neglect* 20:95–101.

Furby, Lita, Mark R. Weinrott, and Lyn Blackshaw. 1989. "Sex Offender Recidivism: A Review." *Psychological Bulletin* 105:3–30.

Goodman, Elga A. 1996. "Megan's Law: The New Jersey Supreme Court Navigates Uncharted Waters." *Seton Hall Law Review* 26:764–802.

Grabosky, Peter N. 1992 "Law Enforcement and the Citizen: Non-Governmental Participants in Crime Prevention and Control." *Policing & Society* 2:249–71.

Greenfeld, Lawrence A. 1997. *Sex Offenses and Offenders: An Analysis of Data on Rape and Sexual Assault.* Washington, DC: Bureau of Justice Statistics.

Hanley, Robert. 1998. "Attorney General Seeks to Combat Vigilantism: Effort to Clear Up 'Megan's Law' Confusion." *New York Times*, June 18, p. B5.

Harris, M. Kay. 1987. "Exploring the Connections Between Feminism and Justice." *National Prison Project Journal* (Fall):33–35.

———. 1991. "Moving into the New Millenium: Toward a Feminist Vision of Justice." Pp. 83–97 in *Criminology as Peacemaking*, edited by H. E. Pepinsky and R. Quinney. Bloomington: Indiana University Press.

Hughes, Stella P. and Anne L. Schneider. 1989. "Victim-Offender Mediation: A Survey of Program Characteristics and Perceptions of Effectiveness." *Crime & Delinquency* 35:217–33.

Immarigeon, Russ and Kathleen Daly. 1997. "Restorative Justice: Origins, Practices, Contexts, and Challenges." *International Community Corrections Association (ICCA) Journal on Community Corrections* (December):13–18.

Kear-Colwell, Jon and Phillip Pollock. 1997. "Motivation or Confrontation: Which Approach to the Child Sex Offender?" *Criminal Justice & Behavior* 24:20–33.

Klein, Lloyd. 1998. "Do Ask, Do Tell: Assessing Implications of Community Notification Requirements Within Sexual Offender Legislation." Pp. 177–91 in *Current Issues in Victimology Research*, edited by L. J. Moriarity and R. J. Jerin. Durham, NC: Carolina Academic Press.

Knopp, Fay Honey 1991. "Community Solutions to Sexual Violence." Pp. 181–93 in *Criminology as Peacemaking*, edited by H. E. Pepinsky and R. Quinney. Bloomington: Indiana University Press.

Kreindler, Simon, and Harvey Armstrong. 1983. "The Abused Child and the Family." Pp. 545–64 in *Psychological Problems of the Child in the Family*, 2d ed., edited by P. D. Steinhauer and Q. Rae-Grant. New York: Basic Books.

Lerman, Lisa G. 1984. "Mediation of Wife Abuse Cases: The Adverse Impact of Informal Dispute Resolution on Women." *Harvard Women's Law Journal* 7:57–113.

Levrant, Sharon, Francis T. Cullen, Betsy Fulton, and John F. Wozniak. 1999. "Reconsidering

Restorative Justice: The Corruption of Benevolence Revisited." *Crime & Delinquency* 45:3–27.

Lieb, Roxanne. 1996. "Community Notification Laws: 'A Step Toward More Effective Solutions.' " *Journal of Interpersonal Violence* 11:298–300.

Lotke, Eric. 1996. "Sex Offenders: Does Treatment Work?" *Issues and Answers: Research Update* (April) Washington, DC: National Center on Institutions and Alternatives.

Marshall, W. L. and W. D. Pithers. 1994. "A Reconsideration of Treatment Outcome With Sex Offenders." *Criminal Justice & Behavior* 21:10–27.

McKnight, John. 1995. *The Careless Society: Community and Its Counterfeits*. New York: Basic Books.

Megan Nicole Kanka Foundation. 1997. *Abuse/Incest Support*. Trenton, NJ: Author.

Mishra, Raja. 1997. "What Can Be Done?: Society Struggles With the Treatment of Sex Offenders." *Detroit Free Press*, July 15 [On-line]. Available: http://www.freep.com/news/health/qsex15.htm.

Montana, Jenny A. 1996. "An Ineffective Weapon in the Fight Against Child Sexual Abuse: New Jersey's Megan's Law." *Journal of Law & Policy* 3:569–604.

Moore, Mark Harrison. 1992. "Problem-solving and Community Policing." Pp. 99–158 in *Modern Policing: Crime and Justice, A Review of Research*, vol. 15, edited by M. Tonry and N. Morris. Chicago: University of Chicago Press.

Myers, John E. B. 1996. "Societal Self-Defense: New Laws to Protect Children From Sexual Abuse." *Child Abuse & Neglect* 20:255–58.

Nieves, Evelyn. 1998. "Watching 'Megan's Law' in Practice." *New York Times*, January 4, p. 17.

Office of Justice Programs (OJP). 1998. *Attorney General Encourages Community Leaders to Focus on Community Justice*. Washington, DC: Author.

Oliver, Willard M. 1998. *Community-Oriented Policing: A Systematic Approach to Policing*. Upper Saddle River, NJ: Prentice Hall.

Pallone, Nathaniel J. 1995. "A View From the Front Line." *Criminal Justice Ethics* 14:9–11.

Pavlich, George. 1996. "The Power of Community Mediation: Government and Formation of Self-Identity." *Law & Society Review* 30:707–33.

Pearson, Elizabeth A. 1998. "Status and Latest Developments in Sex Offender Registration and Notification Laws." *National Conference on Sex Offender Registries*. Washington, DC: Bureau of Justice Statistics.

Prentky, Robert A. 1996. "Community Notification and Constructive Risk Reduction." *Journal of Interpersonal Violence Commentary* 11:295–98.

Quinsey, Vernon L. 1998. "Treatment of Sex Offenders." Pp. 403–25 in *The Handbook of Crime & Punishment*, edited by M. Tonry. New York: Oxford.

Rowe, Kelly. 1985. "The Limits of the Neighborhood Justice Center. Why Domestic Violence Cases Should Not Be Mediated." *Emory Law Journal* 34:855–910.

Rudin, Joel B. 1996. "Megan's Law: Can It Stop Sexual Predators—and at What Cost to Constitutional Rights?" *Westlaw Criminal Justice* 11:1–18.

Sacco, Dena T. 1998. "Arguments Used to Challenge Notification Laws—and the Government's Response." *National Conference on Sex Offender Registries*. Washington, DC: Bureau of Justice Statistics.

Scheingold, Stuart A., Toska Olson, and Jana Pershing. 1994. "Sexual Violence, Victim Advocacy, and Republican Criminology: Washington State's Community Protection Act." *Law & Society Review* 28:729–63.

Shapiro, Florence. 1998. "The Big Picture of Sex Offenders and Public Policy." *National Conference on Sex Offender Registries*. Washington, DC: Bureau of Justice Statistics.

Sherman, Lawrence W. 1993. "Defiance, Deterrence, and Irrelevance: A Theory of the Criminal Sanction." *Journal of Research in Crime & Delinquency* 30:445–73.

Spears, Jeffrey W. and Cassia C. Spohn. 1997. "The Effect of Evidence Factors and Victim Characteristics on Prosecutors' Charging Decisions in Sexual Assault Cases." *Justice Quarterly* 14:501–24.

Stadler, Matthew. 1995. "Staking the Predator." *New York Times*, November 7, p. A23.

Stuart, Barry. 1997. *Building Community Justice Partnerships: Community Peacemaking Circles*. Ottawa, Canada: Report of the Ministry of Justice.

Teir, Robert and Kevin Coy. 1997. "Approaches to Sexual Predators: Community Notification and Civil Commitment." *New England Journal of Criminal & Civil Confinement* 23:405–26.

Umbreit, Mark S. and Howard Zehr. 1995–1996. "Family Group Conferences: A Challenge to Victim-Offender Mediation?" *VOMA Quarterly* 7:4–8.

Van Ness, Daniel and Karen Heetderks Strong. 1997. *Restoring Justice*. Cincinnati, OH: Anderson.

Wetterling, Patty. 1998. "The Jacob Wetterling Story." *National Conference on Sex Offender Registries*. Washington, DC: Bureau of Justice Statistics.

Wright, Kevin N., Todd R. Clear, and Paul Dickson. 1984. "Universal Applicability of Probation Risk-Assessment Instruments: A Critique." *Criminology* 22:113–34.

Wylie, Mary Sykes. 1998. "Secret Lives: Pedophelia and the Possibility of Forgiveness." *Family Therapy Networker* (November/December):39–59.

Young, Marlene A. 1995. *Restorative Community Justice: A Call to Action*. Washington, DC: National Organization for Victim Assistance.

Zehr, Howard. 1995. *Changing Lenses: A New Focus for Crime and Justice*. Scottdale, PA: Herald Press.

Three Strikes Laws

James Austin, John Clark, Patricia Hardyman, and D. Alan Henry

In 1993, an initiative was placed on the ballot in the state of Washington to require a term of life imprisonment without the possibility of parole for persons convicted for a third time of certain specified violent or serious felonies. This action was fueled by the tragic death of Diane Ballasiotes who was murdered by a convicted rapist who had been released from prison. Shortly thereafter, Polly Klass was kidnapped and murdered by a California-released inmate who also had an extensive prior record of violence. The rallying cry of "three strikes and you're out" caught on, not only with Washington and California voters, who passed their ballot measures by wide margins, but with legislatures and the public throughout the country. By 1997, 24 other states and the Federal government enacted laws using the "three strikes and you're out" phrase. In 1994, President Clinton received a long standing ovation in his State of the Union speech when he endorsed three strikes as a federal sentencing policy (Gest, 1994).

The three strikes movement is the most recent anti-crime policy to sweep the United States. Such reforms have included the Scared Straight Shock Incarceration programs in the 1970s, boot camps, mandatory minimum sentencing for certain crimes (e.g. use a gun go to prison), and truth in sentencing (Surette, 1996). These often short-lived campaigns have widespread appeal to a disenchanted public who, through the media, have perceived the criminal justice system as overly lenient and incapable of protecting them from violent offenders. Highly publicized cases where the courts or correctional officials have allowed violent and habitual offenders to be released from prison only to commit yet another violent crime have fueled the public's appetite for harsher sentencing policies to correct a criminal justice system run amok.

The theoretical justification for such policies, and in particular, three strikes and you're out, is grounded in the punitive ideologies of deterrence, incapacitation, and/or just deserts. General deterrence is achieved by delivering swift, certain, and severe punishment (life imprisonment without parole) to habitual offenders in order to suppress the criminal tendencies of potential habitual criminals (for a summary of this literature, see Zimring and Hawkins, 1973 and Gibbs, 1975). Knowing that the next conviction will result in life imprisonment, the offender would weigh the consequences of committing another offense or living a crime-free life to avoid such punishment. In order for this sequence of events to occur, two critical but highly questionable conditions must exist: (1) offenders must be well informed of the new sentencing policy and (2) they must believe there is a high prob-

From *Punishment and Society* v. 1, no. 2 (1999): 131–162. Reprinted by permission of Sage Publications © 1999.

ability of arrest and conviction should one's criminal activities persist.

Incapacitation effects may be realized by accurately targeting habitual or career offenders who are unamenable to deterrence and rehabilitation, and must be permanently separated from society. This perspective was popularized by RAND's research in the 1970s and 1980s on habitual offenders. Peter Greenwood (Greenwood with Abrahamse, 1982) and Joan Petersilia (Petersilia et al., 1978) were early advocates of sentencing reforms that would isolate and incapacitate habitual offenders. This perspective assumed that (1) the courts could readily identify the so called "career offender" and (2) the offender's career will continue unabated over time.

Both assumptions have been widely criticized. Previous studies have documented that the courts and social scientists have not yet been able to accurately identify the so-called rate offender without also punishing an equal or higher number of "false positives." Indeed, Greenwood's own but less publicized research discredited his claim that career offenders can be identified or that they even exist. Second, reforms such as "three strikes" run counter to knowledge that criminals' careers are strongly impacted by age. As noted by the national panel on criminal careers:

> From the perspective of incapacitation, prison capacity is used inefficiently if offenders are imprisoned beyond the time their criminal activity would have terminated if they were free on the street. Therefore, it is reasonable to ask whether "habitual-offender" laws, which mandate very long sentences, may result in incarceration of offenders well after they ceased to be serious risks. (Blumstein et al., 1986:15)

It should be added here that incapacitation effects of a three strikes law on crime rates must be viewed as long term if the goal is simply to extend incarceration. Assuming that some portion of the targeted offenders are already being incarcerated, the added benefits are not realized until the offender's "normal" release date has been extended. For example, if the targeted group already serves 10 years, the crime reduction effects will not occur for 10 years after the bill's passage.

The last possible justification for this policy is straightforward with wide public and political appeal—punishment or just deserts. As Shichor and Sechrest noted (1996), three strikes and you're out, in its purest form, is "vengeance as public policy." This ideology requires no empirical validation or justification. As Greenwood and his RAND colleagues (the same scholars who had advocated selective incapacitation as a viable sentencing policy) note in their analysis of the California three strikes law:

> It is the "right thing to do." Aside from the savings and other effects, justice demands that those who repeatedly cause injury and loss to others have their freedom revoked. (Greenwood et al., 1996)

This article examines this highly popular movement from two perspectives. First, review of the various three strikes laws passed by the states since 1993 is presented. This analysis will show, among other things, that only California passed a three strikes law that was designed to have a substantial impact on the criminal justice process. But, given the importance of the California effort to truly implement a three strikes law on a widespread basis, the remainder of the article examines the impact to date of the California law on the courts, prison population, and crime.

THE VARIOUS FORMS OF THREE STRIKES LEGISLATION

As of 1996, 24 states and Congress had adopted some form of three strikes legislation. Table 1 summarizes the key provisions of these laws based on a national assessment completed in 1996 (Clark et al., 1997). Although there are variations among the states in how they decided the rules of the three strikes game, there are some common themes. Table 2 gives a more detailed picture of strikeable offenses in Washington and California.

First, in terms of what constitutes a strike, the vast majority of states include on their list of "strikeable" offenses violent felonies such as murder, rape, robbery, arson, and assaults, and some states also include non-violent charges. Some states have included other charges, such as:

- the sale of drugs in Indiana;
- any drug offense punishable by imprisonment for more than five years in Louisiana;
- the sale of drugs to minors, burglary, and weapons possession in California;
- escape in Florida;
- treason in Washington;
- embezzlement and bribery in South Carolina.

There are also variations in the number of strikes needed to be out, with two strikes bringing about some sentence enhancement in eight states.[1] California's law is unique in that it allows for any felony conviction for any felony crime to be counted if the offender has a prior initial conviction for its list of strikeable crimes.

The laws also differ regarding the length of imprisonment that is imposed when the offender "strikes out" although most are designed to incapacitate the offender for extremely long periods of time. For example, mandatory life sentences with no possibility of parole are imposed when "out" in Georgia, Montana, Tennessee, Louisiana, South Carolina, Indiana, New Jersey, North Carolina, Virginia, Washington, and Wisconsin.[2] In three states, parole is possible after an offender is "out," but only after a significant period of incarceration. In New Mexico, such offenders are not eligible for parole until after serving 30 years, while those in Colorado must serve 40 years before parole can be considered. In California, a minimum of 25 years must be served before parole eligibility.

Connecticut, Kansas, Arkansas, and Nevada have recently enacted laws enhancing the possible penalties for multiple convictions for specified serious felonies but leave the actual sentence to the discretion of the court. Several states, Florida, North Dakota, Pennsylvania, Utah, and Vermont, provide ranges of sentences for repeat offenders that can extend up to life when certain violent offenses are involved.

Comparison with Pre-existing Provisions

To understand the potential symbolic nature of these laws, one must consider how each state sentenced repeat violent offenders *prior to* the enactment of three strikes. In other words, did the new legislation successfully close a loophole in the state's criminal sanctioning authority as hoped, or was the new law in effect targeting a population already covered by existing laws?

In general, it was the latter condition that existed in all of the states. As shown in Table 3, provisions were already in place to enhance penalties for repeat offenders in all 24 of the three strike states before the passage of the latest three strike legislation. In four of

Table 1.   Variations in State Strike Laws

STATE	STRIKE ZONE	STRIKES NEEDED TO BE "OUT"	MEANING OF "OUT"
Arkansas	Murder, kidnapping, robbery, rape, terrorist act	Two	Not less than 40 years in prison; no parole
	First degree battery, firing gun from vehicle, use of prohibited weapon, conspiracy to commit: murder; kidnapping; robbery; rape; first degree battery; first degree sexual abuse	Three	Range of no parole sentences, depending on the offence
California	Any felony if one prior felony conviction from list of strikeable offenses (See Table 2)	Two	Mandatory sentence of twice the term for the offense involved
	Any felony if two prior felony convictions from list of strikeable offenses	Three	Mandatory indeterminate life sentence, with no parole eligibility for 25 years
Colorado	Any class 1 or 2 felony or any Class 3 felony that is violent	Three	Mandatory life in prison with no parole eligibility for 40 years
Connecticut	Murder, attempted murder, assault with intent to kill, manslaughter, arson, kidnapping, aggravated sexual assault, robbery, first degree assault	Three	Up to life in prison
Florida	Any forcible felony, aggravated stalking, aggravated child abuse, lewd or indecent conduct, escape	Three	Life if third strike involved first degree felony, 30–40 years if second degree felony, 10–15 years if third degree felony
Georgia	Murder, armed robbery, kidnapping, rape, aggravated child molesting, aggravated sodomy, aggravated sexual battery	Two	Mandatory life without parole
	Any felony	Four	Mandatory maximum sentence for the charge
Indiana	Murder, rape, sexual battery with weapon, child molesting, arson, robbery, burglary with weapon or resulting in serious injury, drug dealing	Three	Mandatory life without possibility of parole
Kansas	Any felony against a person	Two	Court may double term specified in sentencing guidelines
	Any felony against a person	Three	Court may triple term specified in sentencing guidelines
Louisiana	Murder, attempted murder, manslaughter, rape, armed robbery, kidnapping, any drug offense punishable by more than five years, any felony punishable by more than 12 years	Three	Mandatory life in prison with no parole eligibility

Table 1. Variations in State Strike Laws (*continued*)

STATE	STRIKE ZONE	STRIKES NEEDED TO BE "OUT"	MEANING OF "OUT"
	Any four felony convictions if at least one was on the above list	Four	Mandatory life in prison with no parole eligibility
Maryland	Murder, rape, robbery, first or second degree sexual offense, arson, burglary, kidnapping, carjacking, manslaughter, use of firearm in felony, assault with intent to murder, rape, rob, or commit sexual offense	Four, with separate prison terms served for first three strikes	Mandatory life in prison with no parole eligibility
Montana	Deliberate homicide, aggravated kidnapping, sexual intercourse without consent, ritual abuse of a minor	Two	Mandatory life in prison with no parole eligibility
	Mitigated deliberate homicide, aggravated assault, kidnapping, robbery	Three	Mandatory life in prison with no parole eligibility
Nevada	Murder, robbery, kidnapping, battery, abuse of children, arson, home invasion	Three	Life without parole: with parole possible after 10 years; or 25 years with parole possible after 10 years
New Jersey	Murder, robbery, carjacking	Three	Mandatory life in prison with no parole eligibility
New Mexico	Murder, shooting at or from vehicle and causing harm, kidnapping, criminal sexual penetration, armed robbery resulting in harm	Three	Mandatory life in prison with parole eligibility after 30 years
North Carolina	47 violent felonies; separate indictment required finding that offender is violent habitual offender	Three	Mandatory life in prison with no parole eligibility
North Dakota	Any Class A, B, or C felony	Two	If second strike was for Class A felony, court may impose extended sentence of up to life; if Class B felony, up to 20 years; if Class C felony, up to 10 years
Pennsylvania	Murder, voluntary manslaughter, rape, involuntary deviate sexual intercourse, arson, kidnapping, robbery, aggravated assault	Two	Enhanced sentence of up to 10 years
	Same offenses	Three	Enhanced sentence of up to 25 years
South Carolina	Murder, voluntary manslaughter, homicide by child abuse, rape, kidnapping, armed robbery, drug trafficking, embezzlement, bribery, certain accessory and attempted offenses	Two	Mandatory life in prison with no parole eligibility
Tennessee	Murder, especially aggravated kidnapping, especially aggravated robbery, aggravated rape, rape of a child, aggravated arson	Two, if prison term served for first strike	Mandatory life in prison with no parole eligibility

(*continued*)

Table 1. Variations in State Strike Laws (*continued*)

STATE	STRIKE ZONE	STRIKES NEEDED TO BE "OUT"	MEANING OF "OUT"
	Same as above, plus rape, aggravated sexual battery, aggravated robbery, especially aggravated burglary, child abuse and aggravated sexual exploitation of child	Three, if separate prison terms served	Mandatory life in prison with no parole eligibility for first two strikes
Utah	Any first or second degree felony	Three	Court may sentence from five years up to life
Vermont	Murder, manslaughter, arson causing death, assault and robbery with weapon or causing bodily injury, aggravated assault, kidnapping, maiming, aggravated sexual assault, aggravated do-mestic assault, lewd conduct with child	Three	Court may sentence up to life in prison
Virginia	Murder, kidnapping, robbery, carjacking, sexual assault, con-spiracy to commit any of above	Three	Mandatory life in prison with no parole eligibility
Washington	Charges listed in Table 2	Three	Mandatory life in prison with no parole eligibility
Wisconsin	Murder, manslaughter, vehicular homicide, aggravated battery, abuse of children, robbery, sexual assault, taking hostages, kidnap-ping, arson, burglary	Three	Mandatory life in prison with no parole eligibility

these states, Louisiana, South Carolina, Tennessee, and Maryland, the mandatory penalty for a person found to be a repeat violent offender—life in prison without the possibility of parole—already existed and remained unchanged, but the definition of such an offender was expanded under the new legislation.

The definition of a repeat offender was expanded in two additional states, with the penalties remaining the same (Vermont and North Dakota). In at least one state, the definition of a repeat violent offender remained essentially the same (third conviction for a violent offense), but the punishment was enhanced. Virginia moved from providing no pa-role eligibility for those convicted of three separate violent felonies, no matter the sentence, to mandating life sentences with no parole eligibility for this group. In some states, the changes involved both expanding the definitions of repeat violent offenders and enhancing the sentences. For example, the habitual offender statute in effect in California prior to the enactment of the three strikes law mandated a sentence of life imprisonment with first parole eligibility after 20 years for persons convicted for the third time of a listed violent offense where separate prison terms were served for the first two convictions. It also provided that, upon the fourth conviction

Table 2. Washington and California Strikeable Offenses

WASHINGTON	CALIFORNIA
Any class A felony	Murder
Conspiracy or solicitation to commit class A felony	Voluntary manslaughter
Assault in the second degree	Rape
Child molestation in the second degree	Lewd act on child under 14
Controlled substance homicide	Continual sexual abuse of child
Extortion in the first degree	Forcible penetration by foreign object
Incest against a child under age 14	Sexual penetration by force
Indecent liberties	Forcible sodomy
Kidnapping in the second degree	Forcible oral copulation
Leading organized crime	Robbery
Manslaughter in the first or second degree	Assault with a deadly weapon on peace officer
Promoting prostitution in the first degree	Assault with a deadly weapon by inmate
Rape in the third degree	Assault with intent to rape or rob
Robbery in the second degree	Any felony resulting in bodily harm
Sexual exploitation	Arson causing bodily injury
Vehicular assault	Exploding device with intent to injure or murder
Vehicular homicide when caused by impaired or reckless driver	Kidnapping
Any other class B felony with sexual motivation	Mayhem
Any other felony with deadly weapon	Arson
	Residential burglary
	Grand theft with firearm
	Drug sales to minors
	Any felony with deadly weapon
	Any felony where firearm used
	Attempt to commit any of these offenses

for such a felony in which three separate prison terms had been served, the offender was to be sentenced to life without parole.

In summary, from a national perspective, the "three strikes and you're out" movement was largely symbolic. It was not designed to have a significant impact on the criminal justice system. The laws were crafted so that in order to be 'struck out' an offender would have to be convicted two or more often three times for very serious but rarely committed crimes. Most states knew that very few offenders have more than two prior convictions for these types of crimes. More significantly, all of the states had existing provisions which allowed the courts to sentence these types of offenders for very lengthy prison terms. Con-

sequently, the vast majority of the targeted offender population was already serving long prison terms for these types of crimes. From this perspective, the three strikes law movement is much ado about nothing and is having virtually no impact on current sentencing practices. The only noted exception to the national trend is California, which is the subject of the rest of the article.

A CLOSER LOOK AT THE CALIFORNIA EXPERIENCE

Two provisions in the California law make it one of the most severe in the country. First, the law provides for a greatly expanded "strike

Table 3. Comparison of New Strike Laws with Pre-existing Sentencing Provision

STATE	FEATURES OF NEW STRIKE LEGISLATION	YEAR IMPLEMENTED	FEATURES OF PRE-EXISTING SENTENCING LAWS
Arkansas	Range of no parole sentences starting at 40 years for second conviction for specified violent felonies; no parole sentences for third conviction for other specified felonies	1995	Extended prison terms for repeat offenders, broken down by seriousness of new conviction and number of prior convictions
California	Mandatory doubling of sentence for any felony if one prior serious or violent felony conviction; mandatory life for any third felony if two prior serious or violent felony convictions	1994	Life with no parole eligibility before 20 years for third violent felony conviction where separate prison terms were served for the first two convictions; life without parole for fourth violent felony conviction
Colorado	Mandatory life in prison with no parole eligibility for 40 years for third conviction for Class 1 or 2 felony or Class 3 felony that is violent	1994	Mandatory tripling of presumptive sentence for third conviction for any Class 1, 2, 3, 4, or 5 felony
Connecticut	Up to life in prison for third conviction for many violent offenses	1994	Upon second violent felony conviction in which period of imprisonment was served for the first, court could sentence as Class A felony
Florida	Added new category of "violent career criminal" to existing Habitual Offender statute; for third conviction for specified violent offense, life if first degree felony, 30–40 years if second degree felony, 10–15 years for third degree felony	1995	Categories of habitual felony offender, and habitual violent offender; range of enhanced sentences
Georgia	Mandatory life without parole for second specified violent felony conviction	1995	Upon fourth felony conviction, offender must serve maximum time imposed, and not be eligible for parole until maximum sentence served
Indiana	Mandatory life without parole for third specified violent felony conviction	1994	Habitual offender law requiring enhanced sentencing upon third felony conviction
Kansas	Allows court to double sentencing guidelines for second and third convictions for many "person felonies"	1994	No provisions for enhancing sentences on guidelines for repeat offenders
Louisiana	Mandatory life without parole for third specified felony conviction or for fourth conviction for specified felonies	1994	Same law, except that, for fourth felony conviction, at least two of the convictions must have been among listed violent or drug offenses
Maryland	Life without parole for fourth violent felony conviction for which separate prison terms were served for the first three	1994	Same law, except that carjacking and armed carjacking were not on the list of offenses receiving this sentence

Table 3. Comparison of New Strike Laws with Pre-existing Sentencing Provision (*continued*)

STATE	FEATURES OF NEW STRIKE LEGISLATION	YEAR IMPLEMENTED	FEATURES OF PRE-EXISTING SENTENCING LAWS
Montana	Mandatory life without parole for second conviction for certain offenses and third conviction for other offenses	1995	Persistent offender statute allowing extended sentence of five to 100 years, to be served consecutively to any other sentence, for person convicted of any felony with one or more prior felony convictions
Nevada	Range of options for enhancing sentence upon third conviction for violent felony	1995	Same options, but upon conviction for violent felony if three prior felony convictions of any kind
New Jersey	Mandatory life without parole for third conviction for certain violent felonies	1995	Rarely invoked 'persistent offender' provision allowing sentence of one degree higher than the conviction offense upon third felony conviction for first, second, or third degree felony
New Mexico	Mandatory life with parole eligibility after 30 years for third violent felony conviction	1994	Mandatory increased sentence of one year upon second felony conviction, of four years upon third, and of eight years upon fourth or more
North Carolina	Mandatory life without parole for third conviction for violent offense	1994	"Habitual Criminal" statute mandating an additional consecutive term of 25 years upon third conviction for any felony, with the court specifying minimum number of years to be served before parole eligibility
North Dakota	Enhanced sentences for second conviction for Class A, B, or C felony	1995	Enhanced sentences for second conviction for only Class A or B felony
Pennsylvania	Mandatory minimum enhanced sentence of 10 years for second conviction for crime of violence; and for 25 years for third such conviction⁴	1995	Mandatory minimum enhanced sentence of five years for second or subsequent conviction for certain specified crimes of violence
South Carolina	Mandatory life without parole for second conviction for specified felonies	1995	Mandatory life without parole for third conviction for same specified felonies
Tennessee	Mandatory life without parole for second conviction for designated violent felonies; same for third conviction for other violent felonies	1995	Mandatory life without parole for third violent felony conviction
Utah	Second and third degree felonies sentenced as first degree felons, and first degree felons not eligible for probation if have two prior convictions for any felonies and a present conviction for a violent felony	1995	Second and third degree felonies receive enhanced sentence of five years to life if have two prior convictions at least as severe as second degree felonies

(*continued*)

Table 3. Comparison of New Strike Laws with Pre-existing Sentencing Provision (*continued*)

STATE	FEATURES OF NEW STRIKE LEGISLATION	YEAR IMPLEMENTED	FEATURES OF PRE-EXISTING SENTENCING LAWS
Vermont	Up to life with no probation eligibility or suspended sentence and no early release for third conviction for crime of violence; up to life for fourth felony conviction of any kind	1995	Up to life for fourth felony conviction
Virginia	Mandatory life without parole upon third conviction for specified violent felonies	1994	No parole eligibility if convicted of three separate violent felonies or drug distribution charges
Washington	Mandatory life without parole upon third conviction for specified violent felonies	1993	Number of prior convictions factored into Offender Score on state's Sentencing Guidelines
Wisconsin	Mandatory life without parole upon third conviction for specified serious offenses	1994	For repeat felony offenders, up to ten years can be added to sentences of ten years or more; six years can be added to sentences of one to ten years

zone," or charges that constitute a strike. The strike zone for the first two strikes, listed in Table 1, is similar to that in other states—serious and violent felonies. The third strike in California, however, is *any* felony—a provision found in no other state's strike law. Persons with two or more convictions for qualifying offenses who are convicted of a third felony of any kind are to be sentenced to an indeterminate term of life in prison. The minimum term is calculated as the greater of: three times the term otherwise provided for the current conviction; 25 years; or the term provided by law for the current charge plus any applicable sentence enhancements.[3]

Second, the California law contains a two strike penalty in which a person convicted of *any* felony who has one prior conviction for a strikeable offense is to be sentenced to double the term provided for the offense, and must serve at least 80 percent of the sentence before being released from prison. Under California's criminal code, nonstrike inmates typically serve less than half their sentence. Only

six other states have two strike provisions, all of which limit the offenses that trigger a strike penalty to those that are serious or violent (Clark et al., 1997).

The intent of the legislature in enacting the law is stated explicitly in the statute as being "to ensure longer prison sentences and greater punishment for those who commit a felony and have been previously convicted of serious and/or violent felony offenses" (Penal Code §667(b)). The law was designed to limit the discretion of system officials by prohibiting plea bargaining (Penal Code §667(g)). Also, if the offender is to be sentenced as a second or third striker, the law mandates that the court may not grant probation, suspend the sentence, place the offender on diversion, or commit the offender to any facility other than a state prison (Penal Code §667(c)(2) and (c)(4)).

Even with these explicitly stated limitations on discretion, the law conveys a great deal of authority to the prosecutor to determine the ultimate sentence that the offender will receive if convicted. While the law requires that the prosecution provide evidence of each prior conviction for a qualifying offense, it permits the prosecutor to discount a prior conviction for a qualifying offense if there is insufficient evidence to prove the prior conviction, or if the prosecutor believes that a two or three strike sentence would not be "in the furtherance of justice" (Penal Code §667(f)(2)). It is this latter clause that allows individual district attorneys throughout the state to establish their own policies on how the law should be applied.

Given its broad scope and the fact that it was so much more stringent than pre-existing repeat offender sentencing provisions,[4] concerns were raised by officials in California that the new law would have a substantial impact on the criminal justice system at the local and state levels. Judges might tend to set higher bails on strike defendants because the longer potential sentences may create an incentive to flee to avoid prosecution, thus increasing the number of pretrial detainees being admitted to local jails. Defendants facing strike charges might demand jury trials—with nothing to gain by pleading guilty—resulting in the courts becoming backlogged with pending trials, causing long delays in case processing. This delay would increase the length of stay of pretrial detainees, exacerbating already serious overcrowding problems in local jails (Austin, 1994).

At the state level, attention was focused on the potential impact of the new law on the prison system. The California Department of Corrections (CDC) projected that the prison inmate population would more than double in five years from its 1993 level of 115,534 to 245,554 by 1999—with 80,000 of these additional inmates being second or third strikers. The "stacking effect" of so many prisoners who would have to remain in prison by virtue of the law would result in a prison population of approximately 500,000 inmates by the year 2035 of which half would be second and third strikers (California Department of Corrections). RAND projected that the prison population would quickly rise to over 350,000 by the year 2000 and eventually plateau at nearly 450,000 (Greenwood et al., 1996). As of 1998, over 40,000 offenders have been sentenced to California's prisons under the two or three strike provision.

Impact of California's Law on the Courts

The law has generated much publicity for the harsh sentences that have been imposed for offenses that are portrayed as minor,[5] and a great deal of litigation in the California appellate courts (these cases are compiled and summarized in Couzens, 1997). Among the many constitutional issues the courts have had to address are: whether the law is unconstitutionally vague, whether the sentences required by the law constitute cruel and unusual punishment, whether requiring strike offenders to serve 80 percent of their sentences through limitation on good time credits that do not extend to non-strike offenders is a violation of equal protection, and whether counting as a strike a prior conviction that occurred before the enactment of the law violates ex post facto constitutional provisions. On each of these issues, the courts have been ruling that the law meets state and federal constitutional requirements.

Several legal issues have arisen that ultimately were resolved by the California Supreme Court. The state's highest court has ruled that out-of-state prior convictions for offenses with comparable elements to offenses that are strikes in California should count as prior strikes,[6] as should prior juvenile adjudications if the juvenile was at least 16 years of age when the offense was committed.[7]

Two other issues regarded the discretion retained by the court under the law given its clear mandatory sentencing language. One of these issues concerned what are known as "wobblers." A wobbler offense is one where the judge, by statute, has discretion to sentence either as a felony or misdemeanor. Taking a case in which one Court of Appeal had overturned a trial court's decision to declare a charge in a strike case a misdemeanor (several other Courts of Appeal had affirmed that a trial court retained the right to do this under the three strikes law), the Supreme Court ruled in *People* v. *Superior Court (Alvarez)* that nothing in either the legislature's or the electorate's version of the law limits the judge's statutory discretion regarding wobblers. The court did state, however, that it would be an abuse of discretion on the part of a trial judge to reduce a felony to a misdemeanor just to avoid the two or three strike penalty. The trial court must consider the defendant's background and the nature of the offense in exercising this discretion.[8]

The other issue relating to the court's discretion arose when a trial court decided, over the prosecutor's objections, to discount a prior felony conviction in a three strike case and sentenced the defendant to six years in prison. The prosecution appealed, arguing that the court had no authority under the three strikes law to discount prior convictions, that discretion rested solely with the prosecution. The Court of Appeal agreed and overturned the trial court's decision. The California Supreme Court, in *People* v. *Superior Court (Romero)*, sided with the trial court, ruling that nothing in the law denies judges this authority. The Supreme Court also suggested, but did not rule, that any law that would deny judges this authority would violate the separation of powers.[9]

The first three of these decisions drew little concern about changing the way the law was being applied throughout the state since there was little division on the issues presented in these cases in the lower courts. But the *Romero* decision, which was issued in June 1996, had the potential to create an enormous impact. The appellate courts, which published more than 20 opinions on the issue of judicial authority to disregard prior convictions, were sharply divided. Many ruled that judges had no authority to disregard prior convictions, several that such authority did exist, and some that such authority existed, but in very limited circumstances (Couzens, 1996). By the time the Supreme Court's decision was announced, the law had been in effect for over two years and 16,000 offenders had been sentenced under its provisions. The decision in *Romero* was met with concerns that many of these offenders would have to be brought back to court from prison for re-sentencing. Concern was also expressed by many political leaders that the Supreme Court was substantially "watering down" the three strikes law by giving back to judges the discretion that the law originally was intended to limit. In the aftermath of *Romero*, the actions of trial judges have quieted these concerns. Judges have not been bringing offenders back in large numbers for re-sentencing, and have been using their authority to strike priors sparingly.[10]

Given the broad scope of the strike law, state agencies in California began analyzing the impact the law was having on local systems statewide soon after the law went into effect. A survey done by the Administrative Office of the California Courts approximately a year and a half after the strike law took effect showed the impact that the law was having on the work of the municipal and superior courts. The survey found that 67 percent of responding municipal courts noted an increase in the number of preliminary hearings because of the three strikes law. Forty-six percent of the courts noted an increase in the length of the preliminary hearing, and 40 percent reported more pre-preliminary hearing appearances (Administrative Office of the Courts, 1996).

More recent data show, however, that the number of superior court preliminary hearings are actually decreasing statewide. There was a 13 percent increase in the number of felony trials between FY 1993–4 and FY 1994–5, the first full year that the law was in effect, even though there was only a 2 percent increase in felony filings during the same period. Moreover, the felony trial rate grew by 4 percent the following year, while felony filings decreased by 3 percent (Judicial Council of California, *1996 Annual Report*). However, the following year showed declines in the number of preliminary hearings, felony cases filed and felony trials. If one looks at just the rate of trials per 100 felony cases filed, there has been no change since 1988.

As expected, the trial rate for felony non-strike cases is 4 percent, compared to 9 percent for second strike cases, and 41 percent for third strike cases.[11] But, because the two and three strike cases represent such a small percentage of all trials, the law has not had a major impact on the overall trial rate.

Variation by Counties in Application of the Law

One of the major findings was that the application of the law by county prosecutors varied considerably. As noted above, the law's provision that allowed prosecutors to drop charges or not request application of the two or three strikes provision in the "interest of justice" afforded them great discretion in deciding whether to charge a defendant with a two or three strike provision in the "interest of justice."

The use of this discretion was most dramatic in San Francisco. From the outset, application of the law was controversial. When the strike law was on the ballot as Proposition 184 in November 1994, San Francisco voters were the only ones to reject the measure. Because of this public sentiment against the law, the San Francisco District Attorney's office ran into several problems in obtaining strike convictions in the months immediately following the enactment of the law. For example, in the first strike case that was set to be prosecuted, the victim, a 71-year-old woman whose car was broken into, refused to testify against the defendant when she learned that he/she was facing a mandatory life sentence as a third striker (San Francisco *Daily Journal*, April 25 1994). Just days later, a municipal court judge, in a case involving a wobbler, reduced a felony charge to a misdemeanor, exposing the defendant to a maximum sentence of one year in jail, rather than the 25-year to life sentence that the District Attorney's office was seeking (San Francisco *Daily Journal*, April 28 1994). As a result of these early and highly publicized cases, the District Attorney's office began discounting prior convictions in a number of cases.

In his successful 1995 campaign to become District Attorney, former defense lawyer Terence Hallinan openly criticized the strike law and its interpretation by the current District Attorney. Once in office, one of Hallinan's first actions was to announce a new policy on strike cases: using the discretion conveyed by the law to the District Attorney to discount prior strikes "in the furtherance of justice," strike penalties would no longer be sought for persons charged with non-violent offenses (San Francisco *Daily Journal*, February 25 1996). Cases of strike defendants, i.e. those with the requisite history of convictions for strikeable offenses, who are charged with violent crimes are reviewed by a committee of assistant district attorneys to determine whether strike penalties will be sought.

The same phenomenon was noted by Malcolm Feeley and Sam Kamin in their early study of the effects of the California law in San Francisco and Alameda counties:

> The Alameda County prosecutor's office is even more direct (than San Francisco) in its adaptive response to the law it did not want. According to Chief Deputy Richard Igelhart, a case will not be brought as a third strike unless the current felony is either serious or violent despite the fact that the language of the statute mandates the charging of any felony as a third strike. (Feeley and Kamin, 1996)

The opposite political sentiments surfaced in the high three strikes counties. Unlike San Francisco and Alameda, the local district attorneys vowed strictly to enforce the law and charge all defendants as second and third strike offenders if their prior records so indicated. For example, the written policy of the Los Angeles District Attorney's office on filing and prosecuting strike cases reads: "Only in *rare* [emphasis in original] instances should the prosecution move to dismiss a prior felony conviction allegation under the 'in the furtherance of justice' standard" of the strike law. Furthermore, such action should be taken only when the sentence that would be imposed under the strike law "would result in a miscarriage of justice." Dismissing a prior record can be done only with the written approval of the head deputy in charge of the branch District Attorney's office (Special Directive 94-04 of the Los Angeles County District Attorney's Office, May 2, 1994).

The initial decision to adhere to the law in some counties resulted in some pressures within the courts to cope with the added workloads. In Los Angeles, officials reported that both the number of preliminary hearings held in strike cases and the length of time required to conduct them have increased. As more de-fendants facing strikes are demanding preliminary hearings, and prosecutors and defenders are litigating more vigorously at these hearings, judges and attorneys report that it can take longer to move these cases out of municipal court and on to a superior court calendar. It was also reported that more motions tend to be filed in strike cases in municipal courts.

One of the responses the system developed was to expand and improve an Early Disposition Program in [Los Angeles] municipal courts. Senior level deputy district attorneys and assistant public defenders review felony cases coming into the municipal court, identifying those that might be resolved easily at an early point. Once the two parties agree on those cases, the pretrial services program conducts an extensive record check of the defendants, who are then brought before the court within 48 hours of the initial municipal court appearance for a disposition hearing. A version of this program had been operating in some of the county's 24 municipal courts before the strike law, but it did not exist in the largest municipal court, which handles half of the felony cases filed in the county. A year after implementation of the program in that court, approximately 220 cases per month were reaching early resolution.

A second response is a Delay Reduction Program, which began in March 1996. This program involves a concerted effort by superior and municipal court judges to process cases in an expedient manner. Under the program, prospective attorneys must provide assurance at the outset that they will be able to proceed to trial within 60 days of superior court arraignment. Those who cannot are not appointed. The program also limits the number of continuances, requires that all pretrial motions be made in writing, and that disclosure of discovery materials be made at least 30 days before the trial. The program's goal, based on standards of the American Bar Association, is to have 90 percent of cases resolved in the first 120 days.

The impact of these two programs—which are aimed at all felony cases, not just those that are strikes—has been dramatic. In July 1995, there were 3500 felony cases pending in superior court, the highest number ever. By March 1996, the inventory of pending cases was cut to 2700. By June 1996, it was down to 2100 cases, and, in January 1997, to 1800. Furthermore, in July 1995, there were 1300 cases on the superior court calendar that were over 120 days old. By January 1997, there were only 600 such cases. In July 1995, up to 30 percent of civil court time was being spent conducting criminal trials. By January 1997, this figure had been cut to 4 percent.

While neither of these programs directly addressed strike cases, the philosophy of the officials who planned and implemented them was that the problems brought about by the strike cases would, to an extent, take care of themselves if the system could develop more efficient processing of all cases.

Impact on State Prison Systems

California officials and others overestimated the impact of the state's strike law on the prison system. Although the sheer number of cases sentenced under the law is significantly higher than for any other state, the numbers are not as great as originally projected.

As expected, there was a dramatic increase in the first 12 months that the law was in effect, but the number of admissions has leveled off and even declined slightly.

The primary cause of the missed projections appears to be that planners miscalculated how judges would sentence second strikers. Under California law, when sentencing an offender, the court may choose a sentence that falls within three ranges: low, mid, and high. If the sentencing range for an offense was five

to 10 years, the low end of the range would be five to six years, the mid range seven to eight years, and the high end nine to 10 years. In making its projections, the CDC originally assumed that judges would sentence second strikers at the midpoint of the sentencing range provided for each crime within the California Penal Code. However, CDC analysis of the sentences imposed on second strikers has shown that approximately 60 percent are being sentenced at the low end. The result has been shorter than expected sentence lengths and, consequently, shorter lengths of stay.

Who Are the Strikers?

Contrasting the attributes of inmates sentenced under the strike laws in California with those sentenced under a more "traditional" three strikes law like Washington state illustrates more clearly how each state's strike zone as defined by their laws produces very different types of offenders sent to prison (Table 4). As expected, in Washington state, all but three of the 97 strike inmates had been sentenced for crimes against persons, reflecting the state's statutory three strikes provisions. However, the vast majority of California second and third strike inmates have been sentenced for nonviolent crimes. Approximately 80 percent of the California two strikers were committed for a nonviolent offense and 60 percent of the three strikers. The fact that so many of these offenders have committed nonviolent crimes is a reflection of California's law that allows for a second or third strike to be imposed for "any felon" if the first or second prior conviction was a strikeable offense. The fact that Washington's inmates are older is reflective of the state's more narrow strike zone in that they must have two prior convictions for serious crimes which generally result in a prison term.

Table 4.   Washington and California Prison Admissions, as of September 1998

CHARACTERISTIC	WASHINGTON THREE STRIKES		CALIFORNIA TWO STRIKES		CALIFORNIA THREE STRIKES	
	N	%	N	%	N	%
Intake	115	100.0	37,271	100.0	4613	100.0
Gender						
Male	113	98.3	35,474	95.2	4561	98.9
Female	2	1.7	1797	4.8	52	1.1
Average age (years)	38		33		36	
Race/ethnicity						
Black	41	35.7	13,704	36.8	2025	43.9
Hispanic	3	2.6	12,200	32.7	1202	26.1
White	67	58.3	9908	26.6	1202	26.1
Other	4	3.5	1459	3.9	179	3.9
Current offense						
Person	108	93.9	7265	19.5	1785	38.7
Property	7	6.1	13,662	36.7	1483	32.1
Drugs	0	0.0	11,728	31.5	888	19.3
Other	0	0.0	3895	10.5	400	8.7

Source: California Department of Corrections and Washington Department of Corrections.
Note: Because of missing data on current offense for California cases, the numbers do not total 37,271 and 4613 two and three strike inmates.

Table 5 presents a more detailed analysis of the types of offenses for which California inmates have been convicted as either a two or three striker.[12] The most frequent crime for these inmates is drug possession with over 10,000 prison admissions. Over 600 inmates have been sentenced to 25 years to life as three strikers for drug possession and another 1500 for property crimes.

To understand better the types of crimes these individuals were committing, interviews were conducted with 100 inmates at selected CDC facilities. The sample was stratified by the type of crime they committed and whether or not they were a two or three striker. Although the sample is not strictly a random sample, it did permit one to understand better the types of crimes these inmates have been convicted of.

While space does not permit a full accounting of all of these cases, five cases, which were typical of the cases we examined, are detailed below.

- *Person offense—carjacking—three strikes.* While attempting to steal a parked truck, the offender reportedly held the owner at bay with a buck knife. He fled on a freeway and was apprehended. No physical injuries or vehicle damage were reported. The offender was sentenced to 27 years to life with a minimum term of 22.95 years. The offender was employed at the time of arrest earning between $300 and $500 per week net.

- *Property offense I—possession of cellular telephone to defraud telephone company—three strikes.* The offender was in

Table 5.   Type of Crime for 2 and 3 Strikers Admitted to Prison, as of September 1998

OFFENSE	2 STRIKERS		3 STRIKERS		TOTAL	
	N	%	*N*	%	*N*	%
Totals	37,271	100.0	4613	100.0	41,884	100.0
Person crimes	7265	19.5	1785	38.7	9050	21.6
Homicide	325	0.9	174	3.8	499	1.2
Robbery	2816	7.6	827	17.9	3643	8.7
Assault	2949	7.9	432	9.4	3381	8.1
Rape	98	0.3	71	1.5	169	0.4
Kidnapping	84	0.2	44	1.0	128	0.3
Other sex crimes	697	1.9	237	5.1	934	2.2
Property crimes	13,662	36.7	1483	32.1	15,145	36.2
Burglary	4981	13.4	860	18.6	5841	13.9
Grand theft	1017	2.7	53	1.1	1070	2.6
Petty theft with prior	3932	10.6	246	5.3	4178	10.0
Receiving stolen property	1221	3.3	115	2.5	1336	3.2
Vehicle theft	1640	4.4	151	3.3	1791	4.3
Forgery/fraud	616	1.7	39	0.8	655	1.6
Other property	255	0.7	19	0.4	274	0.7
Drug crimes	11,728	31.5	888	19.3	12,616	30.1
Possession	9494	25.5	635	13.8	10,129	24.2
Sales/manufacturing	2234	6.0	253	5.5	2487	5.9
Other crimes	3895	10.5	400	8.7	4295	10.3
Possession of weapon	2484	6.7	263	5.7	2747	6.6
DUI (Driving Under the Influence)	344	0.9	19	0.4	363	0.9
Other	1067	2.9	118	2.6	1185	2.8
Missing	721	1.9	57	1.2	778	1.9

possession of a cellular phone that when used would be associated with a different number and individual. Telephone calls billed to the victim represent the harm imposed in this case. The offender will serve at least 25.6 years. The offender was employed earning $873 each week.

- *Property offense II—petty theft—three strikes.* The offender received a sentence of 27 years to life for attempting to sell stolen batteries to a retail merchant. The loss to the victim (cost of batteries) is

$90. The offender was collecting disability pay at the time of arrest.

- *Drug offense—sale of marijuana—two strikes.* The offender sold a $5 bag of marijuana to an undercover police officer. The offense did not involve harm to person or to property. The offender will be incarcerated for at least five years.

- *Other offense—reckless driving, evading the police—three strikes.* The offender reportedly rolled his vehicle through a stop sign, panicked when police responded, and led police on a one hour chase. He "decided to ride it out . . . [to] smoke [his] cigarettes and run out of gas." Police apprehended the offender after blowing out the tires on his vehicle. No victim was involved in this case. The offender received a sentence of 25 years to life of which he must serve 20 years.

The majority of drug offenses are either simple possession or possession with intent to sell. Of the inmates interviewed that had been convicted of a drug crime, only one was convicted of sale/possession of more than $20 worth of cocaine or marijuana. The typical

drug offender sold one or two "rocks" of cocaine to an undercover police officer. Similarly, property offenders tended to be engaged in petty but persistent crimes where there was little loss to the victim. The incarceration costs associated with these offenders in most cases dwarf the costs of their crimes—especially the drug and property crimes (see Table 6).

Impact on Crime Rates

In this section, we consider the immediate impact of strike laws on the rate of reported index crimes for California as compared to

Table 6. California Correctional Costs for Strikers and Non-strikers, 1996

OFFENSE TYPE	CDC COST PER YEAR ($)	MEAN MINIMUM TIME TO SERVE IN YEARS[a]	TOTAL ESTIMATED CDC COST PER OFFENDER ($)
3 strikers			
Personal	21,509	48.2	1,036,519
Property	21,509	31.1	669,360
Drugs	21,509	21.9	471,477
Others	21,509	24.9	535,144
2 strikers			
Personal	21,509	9.0	193,151
Property	21,509	3.7	80,013
Drugs	21,509	3.5	75,712
Other	21,509	3.1	65,602
Non-strikers			
Personal	21,509	2.5	53,773
Property	21,509	1.3	26,886
Drugs	21,509	1.2	26,026
Other	21,509	1.0	21,509

Note:
[a] For the strikers, this column represents the average minimum time to serve by offense category. Among the strikers, personal offenders must serve at least 85 percent of the imposed sentence, while all others must serve at least 80 percent of the imposed sentence. Therefore for the personal offender, for example, we multiplied the average sentence imposed on 3 Strikers convicted of a personal offense (56.7 years) times 85 percent to obtain the minimum time to serve. For the non-strikers, the figures represent actual average time served in CDC for those first released to parole during 1996. While these figures ought to represent only non-strikers, it is possible that a minimal number of strikers may have been paroled during this time and included in this population. Time served data for the non-strikers was obtained from CDC Report, "Time served on prison sentence: felons first released to parole by offense, calendar year 1996" (May 1997).

other states and within California [for] five counties that have applied the law in a very different manner. Already we have found a strong variation in how the law has been applied within California since its enactment in 1994. Although the number of post-implementation years is relatively short (three to four years) to perform time series analysis, a preliminary analysis of a natural experiment is emerging which allows one to make some preliminary but tentative analysis of the relative effects of three strikes legislation on public safety. Two counties (San Francisco and Alameda) are clearly the more lenient jurisdictions that have chosen not to apply the law as designed. The other three counties (Los Angeles, Sacramento and San Diego) are more conforming to the law and have applied it far

more frequently than the other two. If the law has crime control effects, one would hypothesize that crime rates would fall more quickly or sharply in the latter three counties as compared to the other two.

Figure 1 shows the rate of reported crimes per 100,000 persons for five California counties and statewide, based upon the California Crime Index (CCI) from 1990–7.[13] Consistent with national as well as state level trends, each of the five counties experienced decreasing crime rates over the eight-year period. The largest reductions in overall crime rates have occurred in San Diego, Los Angeles, and San Francisco with crime rates dropping by over 30 percent during the eight-year period. In Alameda County, total crime also dropped (from 3327 per 100,000 in 1990 to

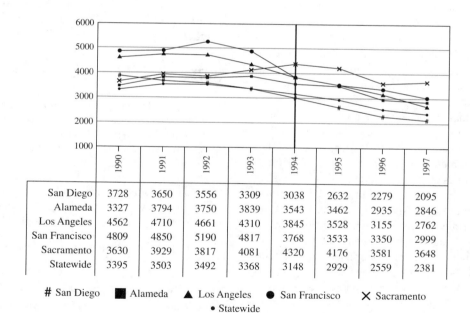

	1990	1991	1992	1993	1994	1995	1996	1997
San Diego	3728	3650	3556	3309	3038	2632	2279	2095
Alameda	3327	3794	3750	3839	3543	3462	2935	2846
Los Angeles	4562	4710	4661	4310	3845	3528	3155	2762
San Francisco	4809	4850	5190	4817	3768	3533	3350	2999
Sacramento	3630	3929	3817	4081	4320	4176	3581	3648
Statewide	3395	3503	3492	3368	3148	2929	2559	2381

\# San Diego   ■ Alameda   ▲ Los Angeles   ● San Francisco   ✗ Sacramento
       • Statewide

Figure 1. Reported Crime per 100,000 Across Selected California Counties, California Crime Index: 1990–7
Source: California Uniform Crime Reports 1990–7.

2846 in 1997) but at a far slower rate. Sacramento County, on the other hand, experienced increases in crime rates between 1991 and 1993, but by 1997 had returned to levels comparable to 1990. These data suggest no clear pattern of crime reduction occurring in relation to the application of California's three strike laws, with crime rates being driven by factors other than the aggressive strike prosecution policies pursued in Los Angeles, San Diego, and Sacramento counties.

The same conclusion can be stated by looking only at violent crime rates. Overall, there was an 18.5 percent reduction in violent offenses reported to police between 1990 and 1996 statewide. Los Angeles and San Francisco posted substantial declines in their rates of violent crime. Alameda County was the only county within our sample that recorded a net increase (from 907 to 1016) in violent acts reported to police between 1990–6. However, violent offenses have been declining in Alameda since 1994.

UCR index crime data from six strike states—California, Washington, Georgia, Texas, Massachusetts, and Michigan—were also collected and analyzed. The first three states are states that adopted three strikes laws and have had them in place since 1993 or 1994. The other three states reflect states that did not adopt three strikes legislation but had similar crime rates at the time that California, Georgia and Washington adopted their bills. As shown in Figure 2, all six states showed trends in their crime rate patterns which are not consistent with those who argued that adoption of these laws would produce independent effects on crime reduction. Admittedly, this analysis is simplistic from a methodological perspective as it does not control for all of the factors that have been shown to be related to crime rates. It could also be that the so-called non-three strike states had adopted other legislative reforms that served the same purpose of targeting habitual offenders. Moreover, there is no reason for Washington and Georgia to even assume that their laws would have an impact as they were largely symbolic to begin with. Only California could possibly argue that three strikes might have an impact on its crime problem.

Overall rates of crime as well as the violent crime rate in the United States declined during the first half of this decade. This downturn in crime was evident as early as 1993; in many states, crime rates were dropping well before then. Many other social, economic, and public policy factors have been cited as contributing to changes in crime rates (Austin and Cohen, 1996). The bottom line is that California, which is the only state to aggressively implement a three strikes law, has shown no superior reductions in crime rates. Furthermore, within California, counties that have vigorously implemented the law also show no superior decreases in crime rates as compared to other counties.

NOTES

1. The eight states are Arkansas, California, Georgia, Kansas, Montana, Pennsylvania, South Carolina, and Tennessee.

2. Virginia law does provide for the release of prisoners 65 years of age and older who have served a specified period of imprisonment, and a North Carolina law, separate from the three strikes statute, entitles those sentenced to life without parole to a review of their sentences after serving 25 years.

3. California law provides for several sentence enhancements, based on either the circumstances of the offense or the offender's prior criminal record. For example, any person convicted of a serious felony who has prior convictions for serious felonies is to receive a five-year sentence enhancement for each such prior conviction. This enhancement is added on after the strike sentence has been

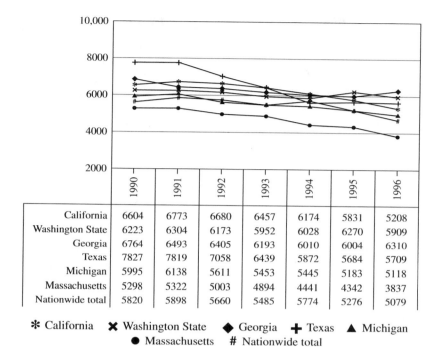

	1990	1991	1992	1993	1994	1995	1996
California	6604	6773	6680	6457	6174	5831	5208
Washington State	6223	6304	6173	5952	6028	6270	5909
Georgia	6764	6493	6405	6193	6010	6004	6310
Texas	7827	7819	7058	6439	5872	5684	5709
Michigan	5995	6138	5611	5453	5445	5183	5118
Massachusetts	5298	5322	5003	4894	4441	4342	3837
Nationwide total	5820	5898	5660	5485	5774	5276	5079

✳ California   ✕ Washington State   ◆ Georgia   ✛ Texas   ▲ Michigan
● Massachusetts   # Nationwide total

Figure 2.   Offenses Reported per 100,000 Across Selected States, FBI Index of Crimes: 1990–6
Source: Uniform Crime Reports for the United States 1990–6.
Note: California, Washington State and Georgia are all states with three strikes and you're out laws. Michigan, Texas and Massachusetts do not have three strikes and you're out laws.

calculated, and must be served consecutively (California Penal Code §667(a)).

4. A version of the three strikes and you're out law was in effect in California prior to March 1994, although it was not labeled as such and was substantially less severe than the new law. The pre-existing version mandated a life sentence with no parole eligibility for 20 years for persons convicted for the third time of specified violent offenses when separate prison terms were served for the first two. The law also provided for a life sentence with no parole eligibility upon the fourth such conviction in which three separate prison terms had been served. In addition, the pre-existing law contained sentencing enhancements related to repeat offending.

5. When a sentence of 25 years to life was imposed on an offender who broke into a restaurant and stole four cookies and on another who stole a slice of pizza, the national news media were there to report it.

6. *People* v. *Hazleton*, Calif. SupCt, No. S051561.

7. *People* v. *Davis*, Calif. SupCt, No. S053934.

8. *People* v. *Superior Court (Alvarez)*, Calif. SupCt, No. S053029.

9. *People* v. *Superior Court (Romero)*, Calif. SupCt, No. S045097.

10. For example, in Santa Clara and Contra Costa Counties, judges were discounting priors in about 5 percent of strike cases. In Los Angeles County, the discount rate has been approximately 14 percent (*San Francisco Recorder*, 1997).

11. These figures represent the medium trial rates for 19 California superior courts which could provide the AOC with these data.

12. The California law requires two strikers to receive sentences twice as long as normally expected and to serve 80 percent of their sentences less pretrial custody credits. Three strikers must serve their entire sentences. Prior to the law's enactment, inmates served slightly less than 50 percent of their sentences.

13. California Crime Index includes the number of reported homicides, forcible rapes, robberies, aggravated assaults, burglaries, and motor vehicle thefts. The FBI UCR includes homicide, forcible rape, robbery, aggravated assault, burglary, larceny theft, motor vehicle theft, and arson (California Department of Justice, 1995).

REFERENCES

Administrative Office of the Courts (1996) *The Impact of the Three Strikes Law on Superior and Municipal Court: Survey no. 2, July–December 1995.* Sacramento, CA: California Administrative Office of the Courts.

Austin, J. (1994) "'Three strikes and you're out': The likely consequences on the courts, prisons, and crime in California and Washington State," *St Louis University Public Law Review* XIV(1).

Austin, J. and Cohen, R. (1996) *Are Crime Rates Declining?* San Francisco, CA: National Council on Crime and Delinquency Focus.

Austin, J., Clark, J., Henry, D. A. and Hardyman, P. (forthcoming) *The Impact of Three Strikes and You're Out in Three States.* Washington, DC: National Institute of Justice.

Blumstein, A., Cohen, J., Roth, J. A. and Visher, C., eds. (1986) *Criminal Careers and "Career Criminals."* Washington, DC: National Academy Press.

California Department of Justice (1995) *California Criminal Justice Profile 1995.* Sacramento, CA: Division of Criminal Justice Information Services, Criminal Justice Statistics Center.

Clark, J., Austin, J. and Henry, D. A. (1997) "Three strikes and you're out: a review of state legislation," *Research in Brief*, US Department of Justice, National Institute of Justice, September.

Couzens, Judge J. R. (1996) "To strike or not to strike; that is the question," *Court News*, Judicial Council of California, February–March.

Couzens, Judge J. R. (1997) *The Three Strikes Sentencing Law.* Auburn, CA: Placer County Superior Court.

Gest, T. (1994) "Reaching for a new fix to an old problem," *US News & World Report*, 7 February: 9.

Gibbs, J. P. (1975) *Crime, Punishment and Deterrence.* New York: Elsevier.

Greenwood, P. W. with Abrahamse, A. (1982) *Selective Incapacitation.* Report prepared for the National Institute of Justice. Santa Monica, CA: RAND.

Greenwood, P. W. et al. (1996) "Estimating benefits and costs of calculating new mandatory-sentencing law," in David Shichor and Dale K. Sechrest (eds.) *Three Strikes and You're Out: Vengeance as Public Policy.* Thousand Oaks, CA: Sage.

Petersilia, J., Greenwood, P. W. and Lavin, M. (1978) *Criminal careers of habitual felons.* Washington, DC: National Institute of Law Enforcement and Criminal Justice.

San Francisco Recorder (1997) "The '3 strikes' crisis that didn't happen," 23 January.

Shichor, D. and Sechrest, D. K., eds. (1996) *Three Strikes and You're Out: Vengeance as Public Policy.* Thousand Oaks, CA: Sage.

Surette, R. (1996) "News from nowhere, policy to follow: Media and the social construction of 'three strikes and you're out,' " in David Shichor and Dale K. Sechrest (eds.) *Three Strikes and You're Out: Vengeance as Public Policy.* Thousand Oaks, CA: Sage.

Zimring, F. E. and Hawkins, G. J. (1973) *Deterrence: The Legal Threat in Crime Control.* Chicago: Chicago University Press.

DNA Testing

Paul E. Tracy and Vincent Morgan

The current proliferation of DNA databases and their likely further expansion raise three significant policy issues and attendant questions. First, how do we utilize this new technology, while protecting against misuse and abuse? The question is really much more complex than this, and it certainly covers a multitude of sub-issues. At the essential core of this issue is the same question which appears in virtually every facet of our daily lives today. Science and technology are progressing at exponential rates, while the ordinary citizen struggles to keep up; so, what happens when technology, and the manifold advances it spawns, transcends society's ability to regulate such technology? Further, in the absence of a serious and well-informed debate about the advisability and demonstrative value of putting into practice whatever advances new technologies may provide, will particular interest groups exert unchallenged influence, if not complete hegemony in a particular area, and successfully lobby for very large expenditures of public financing?

In order to address the first issue properly, the investigation of a second issue requires careful and immediate attention. Although technology makes certain advances possible, are these advances truly necessary?

Moreover, will they produce the alleged benefits and if so, at what cost? This paper will not attempt to solve this dilemma in a macro context. Rather, our interest centers on the forensic application of DNA technology, and in particular, the construction of scientific databases that contain such information. In the past few years, supporters of DNA testing for forensic applications have made remarkable claims about the potential of DNA testing as a crime fighting tool and have touted DNA as the next great breakthrough since fingerprints. It should be noted at the outset that we have no quarrel with DNA testing per se. The scientific community has conclusively demonstrated the reliability and validity of DNA testing and that the "matching" of an evidence sample with that taken from a suspect for purposes of exclusion versus inclusion can be highly successful. Further, although at one time there was considerable debate about the admissibility of DNA evidence, the point is now moot.

Assuming that DNA databases are indeed valuable in the fight against crime, and can be administered in a cost-effective fashion, a final remaining issue arises concerning appropriate regulations surrounding DNA database construction, maintenance, and

From Paul E. Tracy and Vincent Morgan, "Big Brother and His Science Kit," *Journal of Criminal Law & Criminology,* v. 90, no. 2(2000): 635–690. Reprinted by permission of Paul Tracy. Originally published by Northwestern University School of Law.

access. As will be shown below, since there are various schemes concerning who should be required by statute to contribute DNA samples, this question indeed poses significant legal and ethical issues which must not be ignored or dismissed amidst the fervor surrounding the alleged benefits of DNA testing.

The FBI maintains two DNA analysis units. DNA Analysis Unit I performs laboratory testing on evidence samples taken from violent crime scenes. Body fluids and fluid stains are examined serologically and then the DNA is characterized through RFLP and/or PCR testing. In 1996, the FBI opened another unit, DNA Analysis Unit II, which uses mitochondrial DNA testing on evidence samples when the sample is degraded or contains an insufficient amount of DNA for either RFLP or PCR testing.[1] Second, the FBI operates the Combined DNA Index System (CODIS) which began as a pilot project in 1990. CODIS is a software-based system which uses two indices to facilitate violent crime investigations.[2] Third, the DNA Identification Act of 1994 authorized the FBI to establish further DNA indices.[3] The Convicted Offender Index contains DNA profiles of felons convicted of violent crimes and sex offenses, while the Forensic Index contains DNA profiles from crime scenes.[4] The CODIS software permits DNA samples across the two indices to be compared for possible matches thereby facilitating criminal investigations.[5] Fourth, in October 1998, the FBI announced its newest tool—the National DNA Index System (NDIS).[6] The NDIS is an electronic system that will allow federal, state, and local law enforcement agencies to contribute DNA samples to the national database and thereby enhance the investigation of violent crimes.[7] Fifth, the FBI will soon inaugurate a Federal Convicted Offender DNA Database. The Anti-Terrorism and Effective Death Penalty Act of 1996 authorized the FBI to implement a sup-plement to CODIS by requiring federal prisoners, who are convicted of an offense against a minor or a sexually violent offense to provide a DNA sample prior to release from a federal correctional institution.[8]

DNA EFFECTIVENESS: THEORY VS. REALITY

How DNA Databases Are Theoretically Supposed to Work

Once a DNA sample intended for storage in a DNA database is obtained, it is sent to a DNA laboratory for processing. Once it has been analyzed, the results are stored in a central database. After this process is completed, the results of every DNA specimen in that database can be compared with every other sample in the database, and these samples can also be checked against new samples taken from people, crime scenes, or otherwise obtained elsewhere.

Pure Effectiveness

Clearly, because the DNA databases are relative newcomers to the fight against crime, they have yet to make a significant impact on crime rates. This should not, however, be viewed as a failure, at least at this early juncture in their history. Due to the very nature of a database, its utility theoretically increases proportionally as the amount of data contained in it expands. Therein lies the problem: DNA analysis is still quite time consuming, and this has led to a massive backlog of unanalyzed samples in our nation's crime laboratories. This backup may contain as many as 450,000 samples waiting to be analyzed.[9] As of the date of this writing, the Texas Department of Public Safety had analyzed just over one-half of the samples it had received. As these backlogs begin to recede, the effectiveness of the databases will continue to rise. Crime labs across the country are continuing to expand and upgrade their existing technology, and the technology itself is rapidly progressing.[10]

Nationwide, the FBI database has produced some 583 cold hits to date.[11] The National FBI database (CODIS) currently contains DNA samples from over forty-two states, and is expected to include DNA from all fifty states within the near future.[12] England, which started its DNA database before the FBI, has had over 28,000 matches.[13] The scope of Britain's database is considerably wider in terms of whose DNA is included than that of most United States jurisdictions,[14] and it already has more than 360,000 samples indexed and on file.[15] It is expected to eventually encompass more than one third of all English men between the ages of sixteen and thirty.[16]

These isolated successes of DNA databases are interesting and laudatory. However, they do not provide systematic, conclusive, and widespread evidence that such databases, especially the expanded or "all-inclusive" variety, will be proven useful in the fight against crime. Are we to conclude that these few examples will increase dramatically as the databases proliferate and become interconnected? In order to address this fundamental question, we provide data below that exposes the usefulness of DNA databases to a proper scientific test on data concerning law enforcement as well as prosecutorial functions in the fight against crime.

DNA Effectiveness: Law Enforcement

There are two basic applications for DNA in law enforcement, and these two widely divergent applications must be differentiated so that the proper focus of our inquiry will be clear. First, there is DNA testing concerning known suspects and evidence samples. Here, the DNA extracted from bodily fluids or tissue found at a crime scene (e.g., blood or semen), or a victim's DNA extracted from residue left on an offender (e.g., the victim's blood) are compared to determine if there is a match. It would seem that in the absence of other explanatory information, a DNA match or non-match would be dispositive of the suspect's involvement in or his/her innocence of the crime. We wholeheartedly and unequivocally endorse this particular use of DNA testing with known offenders, and further, encourage its use as broadly as possible. The only meaningful caveats we would offer involve proper training for crime-scene technicians and laboratory personnel as well as sound certification policies and well-conceived oversight and monitoring processes for both evidence collection and subsequent DNA testing.[17]

However, a second (and highly touted) use of DNA concerns the construction of massive DNA databases to facilitate what we shall refer to as the "DNA mining process." As noted above, the logic behind DNA databases appears convincing, and concomitantly, such databases are touted as major crime fighting tools. It would seem to make sense that all that society needs do to fight crime effectively is: (1) capture the DNA from known offenders (the exact selection of offenders remains open to debate); (2) store the DNA in a database; and (3) compare the offender bank DNA with that taken from crime scenes. The promised results of course will be the identification and subsequent arrest of a suspect and his or her successful prosecution owing to the DNA match, a result which would not have been possible but for the DNA database. However, when one examines the nature and distribution of crime, the presumed usefulness of DNA databases as a crime control measure may not only be far from obvious or certain, but may turn out to be grossly exaggerated. We thus turn to a consideration of crime events and their susceptibility to DNA applications in law enforcement.

EFFECTIVENESS TEST #1: UCR INDEX CRIMES   Clearly, the vast majority of serious crime is committed against property and not people. Unfortunately, the overwhelming majority of all police responses involve a property offense in which the victim seldom, if ever, sees or confronts the offender, and very likely has no idea who the offender may be. Further, it is highly likely that these voluminous property offenses do not occur with much trace evidence (even fingerprints) left at the scene, evidence which the police actually collect and upon which they can subsequently base their investigation.

We come then to the issue of *Effectiveness Test #1*. In order for the UCR Index crimes to represent viable candidates for being solved by "DNA mining," there would have to be careful and painstaking crime scene investigation. In particular, the crime scene response would have to include forensic technicians and crime scene technicians (or "criminalists," as they are often called) who would scour the crime scene looking for trace evidence like blood, other bodily fluids, tissue, hair, etc., which carries the DNA of the perpetrator. Thus, the success of the DNA mining expedition for crime-fighting depends on three fundamental prerequisites: First, the criminal has to leave evidence behind at the crime scene, or on the person or clothing of the victim, that contains the criminal's DNA. Second, a trained technician must search the crime scene for this evidence. Third, the DNA-bearing evidence has to be, in fact, found, collected, and be of sufficient quantity and quality to permit DNA testing.

Let us be realistic here about the likelihood of these three prerequisites actually taking place, rather than permit ourselves to be swept up in the euphoria exemplified by the proponents of DNA mining. What do the groups of serious offenses classified by FBI as Index offenses tell us? The answer is straightforward—that DNA databases will not be greatly successful in increasing the extent to which police solve the vast majority of Index crimes. There are two principal and inescapable reasons for this conclusion. First, law enforcement already does a more than creditable job (i.e., greater than 50% clearance) of solving three out of the four violent Index crimes (66.1% of murders; 50.8% of rapes; and 58.5% of aggravated assaults). Second, as we have shown, the vast majority of Index crimes are property offenses, and this offense type does not carry a high potential for beneficial DNA testing, owing to the fact that the usual property offense crime scene is not likely to have the perpetrator's DNA, and even if it does, such evidence will hardly be looked for, let alone collected and tested for comparison to the databases.

EFFECTIVENESS TEST #2: NON-INDEX CRIMES   The argument could be made that Index crimes are not the only offenses worthy of consideration, that there are countless other felonies which come to the attention of the police, for which DNA mining would be beneficial. These other offenses are known as "Non-Index" crimes.[18] They are deemed to be less serious than Index offenses, and, accordingly, the FBI does not publish counts concerning the number of such offenses that are reported to the thousands of law enforcement agencies across the country.[19] The FBI does, however, publish data concerning the arrests of suspects for Non-Index events.

The vast majority of arrests, 82.2%, concern Non-Index, or less serious, offenses; of these, only 10.7% concern crimes against persons.[20]

Regarding *Effectiveness Test #2*, the conclusion is as inescapable as was the case for *Test #1*. Law enforcement activity produces arrests for Non-Index crimes, which involve "other" crimes much more often (87%) than for violent crimes (13%). To what extent, then, will DNA mining be beneficial for the vast majority of Non-Index crimes? Realistically, the answer must be that DNA testing is quite irrelevant for these offenses. These are, by all accounts, less serious crimes, and local law enforcement hardly has the necessary resources to treat these offenses as though they require the intensive crime scene effort that is usually reserved for violent crimes against the person.

DNA Effectiveness: Prosecution The other stage of the criminal justice system for which DNA mining (and the DNA databases) could be most beneficial concerns the prosecution of criminal defendants. Just because DNA mining might not dramatically increase the rate at which crimes are solved by the police, there are still advantages to the prosecutorial use of DNA results. DNA could produce the following benefits: (1) convictions could be more likely; (2) convictions without undue plea-bargaining could occur more often; (3) some, if not many, defendants may even plead guilty in the face of such strong forensic evidence; (4) some defendants who might not otherwise be brought to trial could be convicted; and (5) some suspects would be exonerated before trial, thus sparing the necessity of a trial—both the expense as well as unnecessary discomfort and embarrassment for the wrongfully accused. Naturally, this list is not meant to be exhaustive, but merely suggestive of DNA's potential in court. It would seem, therefore, that DNA use by prosecutors would be universally high as it would be difficult to assemble reasons to the contrary.

Table 1 provides the results of three years worth of data from an ongoing Bureau of Justice Statistics study of the nation's pros-

Table 1. Prosecutorial Use of DNA Evidence: 1992–1996

POPULATION SERVED	PERCENT OF OFFICES USING DNA		
	1992	1994	1996
All Offices	25%	42%	49.2%
500,000 or More	n.a.	95%	n.a.
Under 500,000	n.a.	47%	n.a.
Part-Time Office	n.a.	23%	n.a.
1,000,000 or More	n.a.	n.a.	100.0%
250,000 to 999,999	n.a.	n.a.	97.6%
Under 250,000	n.a.	n.a.	56.4%
Part-Time Office	n.a.	n.a.	15.3%

Sources: John M. Dawson et al., *Prosecutors in State Courts, 1992, Bureau Just. Stat. Bull.*, Dec. 1993, at 1; Carol J. De-Frances et al., *Prosecutors in State Courts, 1994, Bureau Just. Stat. Bull.*, Oct. 1996, at 4; Carol J. DeFrances et al., *Prosecutors in State Courts, 1996, Bureau Just. Stat. Bull.*, July 1998, at 6.

ecutors' offices.[21] The data displayed are from the last three installments of the research: 1992, 1994, and 1996. Overall, the results indicate that the use of DNA by prosecutors increased from 25% in 1992 to 42% in 1994, then to 49.2% in 1996.[22] In the 1994 survey, the data were available by size of office, and these results show that when the prosecutor's office serves a very large population (500,000 citizens or more), almost all such offices (95%) use DNA as compared to the offices serving smaller populations (47% for populations under 500,000, and 23% for a part-time office). The 1996 survey provides a different population breakdown with four categories rather than three. Again we see that as the population served increases, there is a corresponding increase in DNA use by the prosecution. The use of DNA ranges from 100% for populations of one million or greater, to 97.6% for populations of 250,000–999,999, to 56.4% for jurisdictions with populations under 250,000, and finally, to 15.3% for part-time offices.

Table 2 provides data from the 1996 survey concerning how prosecutors used DNA evidence. Overall, the results show that less than half of all prosecutors (49.2%) use DNA in any manner. More particularly, only 41.1% use DNA evidence during plea negotiations, while even less, 34.2%, use DNA at trial. With respect to DNA use by type of crime charged, the data once again suggest that use is limited and generally restricted to two offenses. That is, 27.5% of prosecutors use DNA evidence for murder and non-negligent manslaughter cases, while 42.7% use such evidence in sex offenses. The remaining three offense types show extremely low levels of DNA use: aggravated assault—4.2%; robbery—2.9%; and burglary—2.7%.

There are, however, two basic findings that are readily apparent in the data when population groupings are considered. These findings suggest population differentials in the use of DNA evidence, and they also suggest that there are distinct crime-type differences. First, like the result concerning whether DNA was used at all (Table 1), the type of use varies by size of population served. The two larger population groups (1 million or more and 250,000–999,999) make extensive use of DNA at both trial and during plea negotiations. On the other hand, the two smaller groupings (less than 250,000 and part-time offices) are much less likely to use DNA at trial or during plea negotiations. Second, the data also display very significant crime type variation in the use of DNA. That is, the two larger population groups use DNA evidence at a substantial rate for murder or non-negligent manslaughter (93.8% and 87.5%) and sex offenses (100% and 96.4%), but the two smaller population groups do not use DNA evidence in the majority of cases for either murder or non-negligent manslaughter (28.8% and 4.2%) or sex offenses (46.5% and 15.3%). Additionally, the data confirm our suspicion that other crime types beyond homicides and rapes are not readily susceptible to DNA evidence. That is, for neither aggravated assault, robbery, nor burglary do any of the prosecution groups exceed 36.4% in the use of DNA. In fact, from 79% to 100% of the time, the various offices do not use DNA evidence for two major violent crimes (robbery and aggravated assaults) or a major property crime (burglary).

These results are highly pertinent to the question of DNA effectiveness, as even those prosecution offices (i.e., the two largest

Table 2. Prosecutorial Use of DNA Evidence by Population Group, Stage of Case, and Offense, 1996

| | POPULATION SERVED BY PROSECUTOR | | | | |
USE OF DNA	ALL	1,000,000+	250,000 TO 999,999	LESS THAN 250,000	PART TIME
Used Any Time	49.2%	100.0%	97.6%	56.4%	15.3%
Plea Negotiations	41.1%	90.9%	84.1%	48.3%	9.8%
Trial	34.2%	100.0%	91.8%	36.7%	9.8%
Murder/Manslaughter	27.5%	93.8%	87.5%	28.8%	4.2%
Sex Offense	42.7%	100.0%	96.4%	46.5%	15.3%
Aggravated Assault	4.2%	36.4%	13.7%	4.2%	0.0%
Robbery	2.9%	15.2%	13.7%	2.6%	0.0%
Burglary	2.7%	21.2%	12.6%	2.3%	0.0%

Source: Carol J. DeFrancis & Greg W. Steadman, *Prosecutors in State Courts, 1996, Bureau Just. Stat. Bull.*, July 1998, at 6.

groups) that use DNA evidence extensively do not use such evidence beyond the two most serious crime types.

We come then to *Effectiveness Test #3*. As was the case previously with respect to law enforcement, the federal government's own data regarding prosecutors would suggest that DNA is not used by a majority of prosecutors' offices. There were population differentials showing greater use in the most populous areas. However, the extensive use by prosecutors serving the largest population groupings must be discounted by the fact that these offices handle only about one-third of the serious crime in the United States. The vast majority of crime, about 64%, occurs in smaller jurisdictions—jurisdictions served by prosecutor units that do not rely on DNA evidence to a great extent, either at trial or during plea negotiations, regardless of the severity of the crime being prosecuted. Our analysis of the available data leads us to one inescapable conclusion: DNA use is a big city or large county phenomenon, but the majority of crime is committed and prosecuted elsewhere.

Cost-Effectiveness

DNA mining has been shown above, at least anecdotally, to have the capability to match crime scene evidence with known offender samples. With respect to routine police and prosecutorial functions, however, DNA evidence is not being used extensively. Further, there appear to be distinct limitations to its capability to fight crime on any large scale, especially at the law enforcement and investigatory stages. Thus, it may seem unnecessary to consider cost-effectiveness. But, since DNA mining is here to stay, and its use appears likely to expand even further to include more and more donors (arrestees, convicted felons, perhaps even the general public) it is important to assess whether using DNA testing is

cost-effective. At some point, consideration of allocating scarce law enforcement resources must be factored into the DNA mining equation, especially if successful "hits" remain few and far between. The alternative, of course, is that an overabundance of public expenditures might be allocated to DNA mining, even though it is not nearly as effective as has been claimed. There are several issues that warrant careful study in this regard. First, are DNA databases cost-effective right now? If not, will they be cost-effective at some point in the future? Even if such expenditures are the most efficient use of the resources allocated to crime fighting, do we really have sufficient resources to make the necessary and substantial fiscal outlays in order to capitalize on these new technologies?

The answers to all of these questions and more control the debate over whether allocating funds to these databases make economic sense. In one sense, however, it seems ludicrous to talk about cost-effectiveness at all when one reviews the anecdotal evidence of databases that have provided the only means for solving some crimes. What is the value of solving a brutal rape of two young sisters who were forced to watch as the perpetrator violently assaulted one and then the other? It seems that almost any amount of money could be justified as a reasonable expenditure. But, isolated successes are not the proper framework for examining the cost-effectiveness of DNA databases. The proper focus should be whether society is better off by spending money on these databases, which, as has been demonstrated above, may have a very low yield, as opposed to allocating the resources to other crime-fighting techniques.

As DNA laboratories all over the nation continue to upgrade existing technology, the capital investments will likely decline. Once these laboratories are fully equipped to handle DNA analysis on a large scale, the marginal cost of each analysis should decrease accordingly. It currently costs approximately $50 to construct a DNA profile from a sample.[23] This year alone, the National Institute of Justice has begun distribution of $5 million in grants to speed DNA analysis technology.[24] The National Commission on the Future of DNA Evidence has predicted that it would cost an estimated $22 million just to analyze the existing nationwide backlog of DNA samples.[25] New York City Police Commissioner Howard Safir has proposed taking a DNA sample from "anyone who is arrested for anything."[26] It has been estimated that this would cost New York City alone some $18.25 million per year.[27] If this were expanded on a nationwide basis, it would result in about 15.3 million additional tests each year. When multiplied by the cost of each test, this additional expense would come to some $765 million annually (adjusted downward, of course, for offenders with multiple arrests).

These figures may seem daunting, but again, when compared to the costs of crime each year, and when compared to the efficacy of existing crime-fighting techniques, these expenditures may well be justified to some observers. It is also widely accepted that the costs of DNA testing will continue to decrease as technology improves.[28] Moreover, the increased use of DNA evidence could conceivably reduce the costs associated with traditional police investigations.[29] Further, the utility of DNA as evidence should reduce backlogs in our court systems, and may serve to deter recidivism, thereby further justifying the expenditure on a cost-effectiveness basis.[30] The use of DNA has been touted as one of the most effective tools our law enforcement agencies have ever had to fight crime. It is also claimed that DNA databases might diminish the cost of policing, investigating, and prosecuting criminal cases. These and other benefits make the expense seem more than worthwhile despite DNA mining's limited direct effect on crime-solving thus far.

It is difficult to locate precise figures on the cost of constructing and maintaining the current databases, and further, it remains unclear which category of offenders (or even people generally), and consequently, how many people, will have to contribute their DNA to the various databases. Notwithstanding the above limitations, we can offer a close examination concerning the cost-effectiveness of one of the newest databases to come on the scene: the Federal Convicted Offender DNA Database. The FBI has recently been authorized to implement a DNA database of data collected prior to release from a federal correctional institution from federal offenders convicted of an offense against a minor or a sexually violent offense.[31] The FBI, in its budget request for fiscal year 2000, advised the House Committee on Appropriations that it would require $5,336,000 to implement the new federal database.[32] We are curious, if not very skeptical. Why will it cost such a substantial amount of money to add yet another database? Is there not a principle of "economy of scale" by which supplementing an already existing database (i.e., CODIS) could be accomplished without duplicating costs? Perhaps it is because there will be a considerable number of federal inmates subjected to the new program, thereby justifying the high cost.

In order to estimate the number of federal inmates who qualify for the new DNA database, we draw upon the federal government's own data sources. The Bureau of Justice Statistics has published two specialized reports on sex offenders: one on child victimizers[33] and another on sex offenders generally.[34] These reports virtually ignore sex offenders under federal custody, with the exception that there is one reference noting that about 1%

(875) of federal inmates in 1994 were serving time for a sex offense involving a victim who was a minor.[35] Thus, not even the federal government's own specialized reports pay much attention to that segment of the sex offender population that is currently in federal custody. There are, however, other sources from which to validate the small number of such offenders. The Federal Justice Statistics Database provides the following counts of sex offenders under federal custody: 1997—871 inmates (113 rapists and 758 other sex offenders); 1996—811 inmates (123 rapists and 688 other sex offenders); and 1995—731 inmates (120 rapists and 611 other sex offenders).[36] Since the new database will likely collect inmates' DNA prior to release, the number of eligible inmates exiting the federal prison system each year becomes crucial to prospectively estimate the workload of the new database. The number of sex offenders exiting federal prison in recent years are: 1997—348 inmates (28 rapists and 320 other sex offenders); 1996—328 inmates (22 rapists and 306 other sex offenders); and 1995—249 inmates (29 rapists and 220 other sex offenders).[37]

It should be very clear that, when compared to other offender groups, these numbers are extraordinarily small. For the last three years for which the above data are available, on average there were 811 sex offenders in federal custody, and 308 such offenders were released each year.[38] According to the Federal Bureau of Prisons home page on the Internet, the official population count as of September 2, 1999 was 116,775 inmates.[39] Using the Bureau of Justice Statistics 1% estimate, there would be 1,168 sex offenders in custody. Thus, we ask again, why such a substantial line item for a new database which will involve such a small number of offenders? Using the industry rate of $50 per DNA test from a blood sample, it would cost about

$584,000 to test every federal inmate currently in custody, or alternatively, it would cost about $154,000 to test the 308 or so who would be expected to be released in any given year. One certainly wonders why the budget request asked for $5.3 million. In the final analysis, it would appear that the new Federal Convicted Offender DNA Database will hardly be cost-effective. We should all look forward to seeing whether such an extravagant budget is accompanied by significant crime reduction. Of course, if the analyses reported herein are any indication, we will all be very disappointed in the results.

It would seem that, given the questionable effectiveness of DNA in forensic settings, especially with respect to the value of DNA databases, public officials would be hesitant, or at least proceed slowly, in proposing costly DNA databases. However, as we will show in the following section, there has indeed been a rush to judgment that such databases are highly desirable, if not fundamentally necessary, in the fight against criminals.

FUTURE DNA MINING?

Convicted sex-offenders? No problem here. They're all a bunch of sick recidivists anyway. All convicted felons? Sure, why not? Maybe they'll think twice next time. All people arrested? Well, it's a little tougher here, but sure, the cops are good guys and they can't arrest you without probable cause anyway. Everyone at birth or when we get our driver's license renewed? Well, maybe this is what is needed to end crime altogether. After all, if everybody knows that their DNA is on file and, consequently, that they will be caught every time for every crime, then no one would commit crimes. This hypothetical debate is happening in state legislatures everyday. This section of the paper is devoted to the future of DNA databases.

What the Future May Hold

Possible Scenarios Although, in theory, there would seem to be an infinite number of possible DNA database systems which can be developed to take advantage of DNA technology and provide fertile ground for DNA mining, in reality, there are really just seven likely outcomes.

NO DNA DATABASES AT ALL The option of no DNA databases at all seems highly unlikely now that every state in the union has a DNA database system either in operation or under development. Given the alleged advantages that DNA has for crime-solving activities, and its secondary effects on crime prevention, one would not be too adventuresome to predict that these databases are here to stay whether we like it or not.

JUST SEX OFFENDERS This was the early trend, but as advancements in DNA technology continue—and they will—it remains to be seen whether DNA databases will continue to be limited to just these types of offenders. If society's goal is to prevent and catch this type of criminal activity, then it serves its purpose well.

ALL PERSONS CONVICTED OF FELONY OF-FENSES This trend is becoming more popular, as it meshes nicely with the "get tough" on crime mentality among the general population. Further, it catches some criminals who would not otherwise be included under the sex offender-based programs. For example, if a criminal was to rape and kill his victim, this is likely to be classified as a murder, and not a sex offense. Thus, the offender would not be subject to inclusion in the database, even though this is precisely the type of heinous crime that the sex-offender database was designed to prevent.

ALL PERSONS CONVICTED Under such a system, every conviction would result in a DNA database record. This might have a real and substantial impact on a person's desire to commit future criminal acts. However, it is not clear that this would be worth the considerable expense and effort such an undertaking would entail. As technology becomes cheaper, faster, and more user friendly, it might make such programs less cost-prohibitive. One has to wonder how useful the inclusion of someone who was arrested for a so-called "victimless" crime, such as gambling, would be.

ALL PERSONS ARRESTED FOR FELONY OF-FENSES The problem here, and with any other system which does not require a conviction, is that it has a tremendous potential for abuse. Where there is no judicial check on the intake process, it is difficult to convince those who view privacy as one of our most cherished rights that DNA testing is appropriate in this situation. This is particularly true today as we have increasingly looked to courts, and not legislatures, as the primary guardians of our liberties.

ALL PERSONS ARRESTED Soon to take effect in Louisiana, and proposed in New York City, this is the current outer-limit of DNA databases. To date, no system has pushed farther than this. This makes sense, but perhaps only because the next alternative, total population inclusion, is a daunting prospect indeed. Thus, this appears to be our current limit for the use of DNA databases. From one perspective, taking DNA from all arrestees may enable police to solve crimes where only biological evidence was left. A criminal who is arrested for one crime may be wanted in connection with other crimes, but solely on the basis of DNA evidence recovered from a crime scene. This would allow law enforcement authorities to clear many unsolved crimes, which is obviously a tremendous benefit to society. From another perspective, our criminal justice system is based on the concept that we are innocent until proven guilty. Thus, it seems perhaps a little too intrusive to take DNA samples simply on the basis of suspected criminal activity.

TOTAL POPULATION INCLUSION   The final alternative is a database with a record of the DNA profiles of all people. First, the logistical problems here are enormous. How should this category be defined? Every person in the state? A national database with every American citizen? Taken at birth? What about those already born? Does everybody have to give a sample at the local police station? Where do we get the funding for this? Who would be in charge of it? How do we deal with illegal aliens? What about resident aliens? Tourists? Obviously, we cannot force other countries to maintain such a database, nor could we force them to share the data with our law enforcement agencies. The international aspects alone present almost insurmountable obstacles to the successful implementation of such a system.

These various scenarios follow a clearcut progression. A sex-offender-only database seems virtually unobjectionable. The conviction-based databases seem a little more expansive, but still they do not seem particularly troubling. After all, a judge or jury found the accused guilty. That should be enough. The arrest-based systems are the current thresholds, but here, we have no assurance of guilt, only suspicion. With the total population database, even if one takes cost out of the equation, it still seems a little too futuristic. Something about it just seems contrary to our notions of individual autonomy, and our sense of personal privacy.

Aside from pure privacy concerns, there are legitimate fears about misuse of these databases. Other concerns such as the integrity of the DNA analysis process, and whether we should now revisit heretofore accepted rules regarding things such as statutes of limitations are key issues which must be resolved.[40]

Once the DNA is on file, concerns arise as to what other uses it may be put to. To allay these concerns, almost every DNA database statute on the books contains provisions to avoid such improper usage. Rhode Island's DNA database act provides: "DNA samples and DNA records collected under this chapter shall never be used . . . for the purpose of obtaining information about physical characteristics, traits or predispositions for disease.[41] Texas has an explicit prohibition against the use of genetic data by insurance companies for illegitimate purposes. Article 21.73 of the Texas Insurance Code states: "A group health benefit plan issuer may not use genetic information to reject, deny, limit, cancel, refuse to renew, increase the premiums for, or otherwise adversely affect eligibility for or coverage under the group health benefit plan."[42] The statute further holds refusal to submit to a genetic test may also not be used in the same manner.[43] Moreover, such prohibitions do not apply only to people already born. The statute also mandates that "[n]o issuer of a group health benefit plan shall use genetic information to coerce or compel a pregnant woman to have an induced abortion."[44]

EXISTING STATE OF THE LAW

Given the proliferation of DNA databases and the proposals for wide expansion, it is desirable to review briefly the statutes and regulations already "on the books" as of the time of this writing. In so doing, we can examine the extent to which such statutes are uniform, if not identical, thus providing, regardless of jurisdiction, standardized procedures and policies concerning database information. On the other hand, anomalous provisions should be identified and their possible implications raised.

In addition to the FBI's DNA database, every state in the union has established a DNA database in one form or another. This is likely due, at least in part, to the availability of federal funding for such endeavors. As a condition of the federal government's support, each state's database must meet certain criteria. For example, in order to receive a grant, the state must require that DNA samples be obtained from "each person convicted of a felony of a sexual nature."[45] Further, each state must require that its standards for the processing and analysis of such specimens are consistent with those established by the Director of the FBI. These various statutes are generally the same for the most part, but there is substantial variance as to what groups of people are forced to provide samples for inclusion in a database.

Based on the variety among them, it is hazardous to generalize about all states. However, the databases can fairly be divided into two broad groups.[46] These groups are: (1) states which include DNA only from persons with convictions for felony sexual offenses;[47] and (2) states which include DNA from persons with convictions for some or all of the state's felony offenses.[48] The reason that these two classifications were chosen is that it enables one to understand the expansionist tendencies regarding these databases. Typically, they were set up in order to target sex offenders only. However, they have tended to gradually expand to encompass ever broader segments of the population.[49]

There are two states, however, which flatly do not fall within this rubric. Louisiana and Iowa have statutes in a class all by themselves. Louisiana currently has the most expansive statute on the books. Beginning on September 1, 1999, all persons "arrested for a felony sex offense or other specified offense shall have a DNA sample drawn or taken at the same time he is fingerprinted pursuant to the booking procedure."[50] As the statute now reads, a person can be forced to submit a DNA sample merely for being arrested for a simple assault. Under Louisiana law, a person who commits a simple assault "shall be fined not more than two hundred dollars, or imprisoned for not more than ninety days, or both."[51]

Iowa's DNA database system is different than every other state as well. The legislature deferred to the law enforcement divisions of the state, and allowed almost total freedom for the attorney general, courts, and parole boards[52] to define what offenses should trigger inclusion in the DNA database. The Attorney General shall "adopt rules . . . for the purpose of classifying felonies and indictable misdemeanors which shall require the offender to submit a physical specimen for DNA profiling. Factors to be considered shall include the deterrent effect of DNA profiling, the likelihood of repeated violations, and the seriousness of the offense."[53]

Database Issues

While the list detailed below is by no means exhaustive, it does raise a number of important topics relating to the mechanics of these databases. Consider the following questions:

1. Who has access to these databases?

Most states restrict access to law enforcement agencies, court proceedings, and to a defendant in connection with the defense of the charge(s) that gave rise to the DNA sample.

2. What security measures are commonly utilized?

Most states have penalties designed to combat unauthorized use and tampering.

3. Does the statute grant immunity to those who draw samples?

Over thirty states allow some form of immunity, both from criminal and civil liability arising out of the taking of a sample. However, the jurisdictions are about evenly split on whether the immunity covers negligence.

4. Is reasonable force allowed to obtain a sample?

Missouri is one of only eight states that allow the use of reasonable or necessary force to obtain a sample from uncooperative subjects.

5. Does the statute allow the charging of fees for the expense of analyzing the DNA?

Like more than one dozen states, South Carolina allows for costs to be assessed against an offender.

6. Does the statute allow for expunction of DNA records?

Over three dozen states have included expunction provisions expressly related to the DNA database.

The statutes as a whole have many similarities, but there are key distinctions among them. The fact that these statutes are subject to almost constant revision presents a rather large obstacle to a comprehensive survey, and due to the rapidly changing nature of these laws, any comparative study is really more like a photograph that freezes a moment in time.

CONCLUSION

We have no quarrel whatsoever with the earliest and most basic of DNA applications in the criminal law: known suspect testing and post-conviction relief. We agree that there is unparalleled value to the use of DNA testing to match a particular suspect's DNA with that extracted from trace evidence left behind at a crime scene. Similarly, can there be a more justice-oriented application for DNA than to use its exculpatory capabilities to exonerate persons who were wrongfully accused and convicted? Each of these DNA applications should be used as extensively as possible, not only as effective crime control measures, but more importantly, as definitive tests of whether an accused, or even a previously convicted person, is actually innocent.

Beyond these two applications of DNA testing per se, however, our inquiry concerning the spreading craze over DNA databases as a crime control measure does not offer similar support. In fact, the analysis reported here of the best available government crime data raises serious concerns that DNA databases are proliferating and becoming ever more inclusive, and the costs associated with collecting, testing, and storing the information are rising into the hundreds of millions of dollars. These developments are occurring all across the country despite the absence of convincing evidence that the DNA mining process will strike gold as proponents have claimed.

We have demonstrated that DNA databases will not be greatly successful in increasing the extent to which police solve the vast majority of the seven FBI Index crimes. This was shown to be the case because the vast majority of Index crimes are property offenses, and this type of offense does not carry a high potential for beneficial DNA testing because the usual property offense crime scene is not likely to contain the perpetrators' DNA, and even if it does, such evidence will seldom be looked for, let alone collected and tested for comparison with the DNA databases. We also showed that DNA mining will be even less beneficial for solving the vast majority of Non-Index crimes. Again, we argued that the millions of less serious Non-Index crime scenes hardly ever contain DNA-related evidence. We further argued that even if such crime scenes did contain DNA evidence, local law enforcement hardly has the necessary resources to treat these offenses as though they deserved the intensive crime scene effort that is usually reserved for serious violent crimes against the person. In this regard, we noted that it is often difficult enough to convince the police to dust for fingerprints at a residential burglary, because the police know that their search will likely be futile. Imagine, therefore, trying to convince police to search the crime scene (usually outside) of a robbery for such evidence as the perpetrator's hair, tissue, or other residual evidence.

We also considered the value of DNA database evidence to the prosecutorial function. We found that DNA evidence is not used by a majority of prosecutors' offices across the country. We did find that "big city" prosecutors relied heavily on DNA evidence both at trial and during plea negotiations. However, this extensive use pattern in the most populous areas must be discounted by the fact that these offices handle only about one-third of the serious crime in the United States. That is, the vast majority of crime, about 64%, occurs in smaller jurisdictions, which are served by prosecutor units that do not rely heavily on DNA evidence, either at trial or during plea negotiations, regardless of the severity of the crime being prosecuted. We found that prosecutorial use of DNA is clearly a big city or large county phenomenon, but the majority of crime is committed and prosecuted elsewhere, thus diminishing the value of DNA as a crime control measure at the macro level. Further, we also found that even among the big city prosecutors, DNA evidence use was restricted to mostly homicides, rapes, and other very serious offenses.

We also considered the cost-effectiveness of DNA databases. Here the results were quite convincing. At present, the DNA extrac-

tion process is a highly expensive and time-consuming process when considered in the aggregate. The costs associated with increased testing, especially the increased testing necessitated by the more "inclusive" DNA database proposals, are astronomical when compared to the expected crime level benefits associated with the databases. Are DNA databases and their direct and more indirect or diffuse costs the most effective way to spend scarce criminal justice resources? At this point, the answer must be no.

Last, we considered various future scenarios and proposals for various DNA database configurations. These proposals include very specific eligibility criteria, like persons convicted of sex offenses or violent crimes, but they also include more expansive criteria like persons arrested, the general public, or even newborns as has been endorsed by Mayor Giuliani of New York City.[54] We argued that there are actual financial costs, as well as ethical and civil liberty costs associated with these ever expanding DNA database proposals. The only reason to bear the manifold costs associated with DNA databases is if, and only if, it can be shown that a particular database configuration will be demonstratively successful in solving crimes or easing prosecutions which would not be possible otherwise.

NOTES

1. *Scientific Analysis Section*, (last modified Feb. 20, 1999) <http://www.fbi.gov/programs/lab/org/sciana.htm>.
2. *The National DNA Index System* (Oct. 13, 1998) <http://www.fbi.gov/pressrm/pressrel/pressre198/dna.htm> (FBI Press Release).
3. 42 U.S.C. § 14132 (1994).
4. *The National DNA Index System.*

5. Ibid.
6. Ibid.
7. Ibid.
8. Statement of Louis J. Freeh, Dir., Fed. Bureau of Investigation, *Hearings on President's Fiscal Year 2000 Budget, Before the House Comm. on Appropriations, Subcomm. for the Dept's of Commerce, Justice, and State, the Judiciary, and Related Agencies,* 106th Cong. (1999).
9. Richard Willing, "With DNA Databases on Fast Track, Legal Questions Loom," *USA Today,* Mar. 1, 1999, at 5A.
10. Robin Lloyd, "Lab on a Chip May Turn Police Into DNA Detectives," *Wash. Post,* Mar. 1, 1999, at A3.
11. Lloyd, 1999.
12. Ibid.
13. Nicholas Wade, "National DNA Database to Debut as Anti-Crime Tool" *Dallas Morning News,* Oct. 12, 1998, at A1.
14. The English system allows for samples to be taken on arrest.
15. Victor Weedn and John Hicks, "The Unrealized Potential of DNA Testing," National Institute of Justice, 1998.
16. Ibid.
17. National Institute of Justice, Certification of DNA and Other Forensic Specialists (1995).
18. Federal Bureau of Investigation, *Uniform Crime Reports,* 1997.
19. Ibid.
20. Ibid.
21. Bureau of Justice Statistics, *Prosecutors in State Courts,* 1993, 1996, and 1998.
22. Prosecutors use DNA to enhance plea negotiations and, of course, obtain convictions at trial.
23. National Commission on the Future of DNA Evidence.
24. Ibid.
25. Kendall Anderson. "Panel Debates Taking DNA upon Arrest," *Dallas Morning News,* Mar. 2, 1999, at A13.
26. Stevenson Swanson, "Ideas for Widespread DNA 'Fingerprinting' Stir Debate," *Dallas Morning News,* Feb. 7, 1999, at A15.
27. National Commission on the Future of DNA Evidence.
28. Weedn and Hicks.
29. Ibid.
30. W. VA. CODE § 15-2B-2 (Supp. 1999) (legislative findings that DNA databases may serve to discourage recidivism).
31. 42 U.S.C. § 14132 (1994).
32. Ibid.
33. Lawrence Greenfeld, *Child Victimizers: Violent Offenders and Their Victims,* Bureau of Justice Statistics, 1996.
34. Lawrence Greenfeld, *Sex Offenses and Offenders,* Bureau of Justice Statistics, 1997.
35. Ibid.
36. *Federal Justice Statistics Resource Center (FJSRC)* (last modified Jan. 5, 2000) <http://fjsrc.urban.org/Index.shtml>.
37. Ibid.
38. Ibid.
39. *Federal Bureau of Prisons* (visited Sept. 2, 1999) <http://www.bop.gov/>.
40. Under proper conditions, DNA residue can remain viable for thousands of years. David Fisher, *Hard Evidence* (1995) (on the ability to reopen unsolved cases years later now that DNA technology can generate leads).
41. R.I. GEN. LAWS § 12.1.5-10(4) (1999).
42. TEX. INS. CODE ANN. art. 21.73 § 3(a) (West Supp. 1998).
43. Ibid. § 3(e).
44. Ibid. § 8(b).
45. Weedn and Hicks.
46. The FBI database should be categorized in the second group, as it takes DNA samples from "persons convicted of crimes." 42 U.S.C. § 14132(a)(1) (1998).
47. ALA. CODE § 15-20-22 (1999).
48. ARK. CODE ANN. § 12-12-1103 (Michie 1999).
49. Barry Steinhardt, Address to the National Commission on the Future of DNA Evidence (Mar. 1, 1999).
50. LA. REV. STAT. ANN. § 15:603-609(A) (West 2000). "Other specified offense" includes crimes ranging in seriousness from murder to simple assault. *Id.* § 15:603.

51. LA. REV. STAT. ANN. § 14:38 (West 1997).

52. IOWA CODE § 13.10, 901.2, 906.4 (1995).

53. IOWA CODE § 13.10 (1999).

54. Bruce Lambert, "Giuliani Backs DNA Testing of Newborns for Identification," *New York Times,* Dec. 17, 1998, at B4.

Gun Control

Philip J. Cook and Mark H. Moore

The purpose of this chapter is to set out a framework for thinking about the steps that should be taken in the search for an effective gun control policy. We begin with a review of the noncontroversial facts about trends in gun ownership and use and the reasons why Americans are inclined to arm themselves. A discussion follows of the more controversial issue of whether guns influence levels or seriousness of crime. We then identify the important values at stake in adopting any gun control policy and go on to describe the existing policies and the mechanisms by which they and other such measures have their effect. Finally, we make recommendations about promising next steps.

GUN OWNERSHIP: USE AND MISUSE

Guns are versatile tools with many uses, so their broad appeal is not surprising. They are an especially common feature of rural life, in which wild animals provide both a threat and an opportunity for sport. As America has become more urban and more violent, however, the demand for guns has become increasingly motivated by the need for protection against other people.

Patterns of Gun Ownership

The General Social Survey by the National Opinion Research Center found that 41% of American households include at least one firearm. Approximately 29% of adults say that they personally own a gun. These percentages reflect an apparent *decline* in the prevalence of gun ownership since the 1970s (Cook & Ludwig, 1996).

Although the prevalence of gun ownership has declined, it appears that the number of guns in private hands has been increasing rapidly. Since 1970, total sales of new guns have accounted for more than half of all the guns sold during this century, and the total now in circulation is on the order of 200 million (Cook & Ludwig, 1996).

Uses of Guns Against People

A great many Americans die by gunfire. The gun death counts from suicide, homicide, and accidents have totaled more than 30,000 for

From Philip Cook and Mark Moore, "Guns, Gun Control, and Homicide," in M. Dwayne Smith & Margaret Zahn (eds.), *Studying and Preventing Homicide,* Thousand Oaks: Sage, 1999. Reprinted by permission of Sage Publications.

every year since 1972. In 1994, there were approximately 39,000 firearms deaths, a rate of 15 per 100,000 U.S. residents. All but 2,200 of these deaths were either homicides or suicides (Violence Policy Center, 1997).

Criminal homicide and other criminal uses of guns cause the greatest public concern. Gun accident rates have been declining steadily during the past two decades, and suicide seems a threat only to those whose loved ones are at risk. There has been little variation in homicide rates since 1970, with the homicide rate per 100,000 fluctuating between 8.1 and 10.6. Of these, 60% to 70% were committed with guns, mostly (80%) handguns. The peak rates, occurring in 1980 and 1991, were about the same magnitude (Federal Bureau of Investigation, 1971–1997).

Homicide is not a democratic crime. Both victims and perpetrators are vastly disproportionately male, black, and young. With respect to the victims, homicide is the leading cause of death for black males aged 15 to 34, whose victimization rate (in 1994) was 9.5 times as high as for white males and black females in this age range and nearly 50 times as high as for white females. (The evidence suggests that most victims in the high-risk category are killed by people with the same demographic characteristics.) About 75% of the homicide victims in this age group were killed with firearms. Thus, we see a remarkable disparity between the demography of gun sports and of gun crime: Sportsmen are disproportionately older white males from small towns and rural areas, whereas the criminal misuse of guns is concentrated among young urban males, especially minorities. Young black men have suffered the greatest increase in homicide rates since 1985; by 1994, the homicide victimization rate for 15- to 24-year-olds in this group had tripled, reaching 160 per 100,000 (Centers for Disease Control and Prevention, 1997).

Of course, most gun crimes are not fatal. For every gun homicide victim, there are roughly six gun crime victims who receive a less-than-mortal wound (Cook, 1985) and many more who are not wounded at all. Indeed, the most common criminal use of guns is to threaten, with the objective of robbing, raping, or otherwise gaining the victim's compliance. Relatively few of these victims are physically injured, but the threat of lethal violence and the potential for escalation necessarily make these crimes serious. According to the 1994 National Crime Victimization Survey (NCVS), there were 316,000 gun robberies, 727,000 aggravated assaults (of which 94,000 caused injury), and 25,000 rapes in that year, for a total estimated volume of gun crimes of about 1,068,000 (Bureau of Justice Statistics, 1997, Table 66). For each of these crime types, guns are used in only a fraction of all cases. When a gun is used, it is almost always a handgun, which accounts for upwards of 92% of these crimes.

Gun Use as Self-Defense

Although guns do enormous damage in crime, they also provide some crime victims with the means of escaping serious injury or property loss. The NCVS is generally considered the most reliable source of information on predatory crime because it has been in the field more than two decades and incorporates the best thinking of survey methodologists. From this source, it appears that use of guns in self-defense against criminal predation is rather rare, occurring on the order of 100,000 times per year (Cook, Ludwig, & Hemenway, 1997). Of particular interest is the likelihood that a gun will be used in self-defense against an intruder. A study using NCVS data (Cook, 1991) found that only 3% of victims were able to deploy a gun against someone who broke in (or attempted to do so) while they were at home. Remembering that 40% of all households have a gun, we conclude that it is rare for victims to be able to deploy a gun against intruders even when they have one available.

INSTRUMENTALITY AND AVAILABILITY OF FIREARMS

An overriding issue in the gun control debate is "Do guns kill people?" or "Do people kill people?" In murder trials, the killer's motivation and state of mind are explored thoroughly, whereas the type of weapon—usually some type of gun—is often treated as an incidental detail. Yet there is compelling evidence that the *type of weapon matters a great deal* in determining whether the victim lives or dies and therefore becomes a homicide victim. This means that depriving potentially violent people of guns probably can save lives, an essential tenet of the argument for restricting gun availability. But then a second question arises: How can we use the law to deprive violent people of guns if such people are not inclined to be law-abiding? The saying "If guns are outlawed, only outlaws will have guns" may ring true.

Instrumentality

The first piece of evidence is that robberies and assaults committed with guns are more likely to result in the victim's death than are similar violent crimes committed with other weapons.

Fatality rates do not by themselves prove that the type of weapon has an independent causal effect on the probability of death. Possibly, the type of weapon is simply an indicator of the assailant's intent, and it is the intent, rather than the weapon, that determines whether the victim lives or dies. In this view,

the gun makes the killing easier and hence is the obvious choice if the assailant's intent is indeed to kill. The overriding assumption is that if no gun were available, most would-be killers would still find a way (Wolfgang, 1958; Wright, Rossi, & Daly, 1983).

Perhaps the most telling response to this argument comes from Franklin Zimring (1968, 1972; see also Zimring & Hawkins, 1997), who concluded that there actually is a good deal of overlap between fatal and nonfatal attacks; even in the case of earnest and potentially deadly attacks, assailants commonly lack a clear or sustained intent to kill. Zimring's argument in a nutshell is that homicide is, in effect, a by-product of violent crime. Although the law determines the seriousness of the crime by whether the victim lives or dies, the outcome is not a reliable guide to the assailant's intent or state of mind.

In sum, we postulate that the type of weapon deployed in violent confrontations appears to matter in several ways. Because guns provide the power to kill quickly, at a distance, and without much skill or strength, they also provide the power to intimidate other people and gain control of a violent situation. When there is a physical attack, then the lethality of the weapon is an important determinant of whether the victim survives. But when the assailant's purpose is robbery, intimidation, or self-defense rather than inflicting injury, then a gun appears to be more effective than other weapons in achieving that purpose, and without actual use of violence. These hypothesized effects receive support from the empirical work that has been published in this area, but the current state of that evidence surely leaves room for doubt.

Availability

If the type of weapon transforms violent encounters in important ways, as suggested in the preceding discussion, then the extent to which guns are available to violence-prone people is a matter of public concern. *Availability* can be thought of relative to time, expense, and other costs. Violent confrontations often occur unexpectedly, and in such cases the weapons that will be used are among those that are close at hand; the relevant question is whether a gun is *immediately* available. Logically, the next question concerns the likelihood that a gun will be present *when* a violent confrontation occurs. In particular, do the costs of obtaining a gun and keeping it handy influence the likelihood of gun use in violence?

Arthur L. Kellermann and his associates (1992, 1993) provide evidence on the importance of the first issue, immediate availability. In case control studies of violent events occurring in the home, they found that the likelihood of both suicide and homicide is greatly elevated by the presence of a gun in the home. Kellermann et al. selected each "control" from the same neighborhood as that in which the killing occurred, and, through their matching criteria and use of multivariate statistical techniques, attempted to control for other differences between the suicide/homicide cases and cases used as controls. There is no guarantee that this effort to control for other factors that might be confounded with gun possession was successful, so the proper interpretation of these findings remains controversial. If we accept the authors' interpretation, then two propositions follow.

1. If a member of the household owns a gun, then at-home suicide attempts and armed assaults are more likely to involve a gun than otherwise.

2. A gun is more deadly than other weapons would have been in these circumstances (an instrumentality effect).

Extending these propositions, we can ask whether the extent to which guns are readily available in a community influences the likelihood of weapons used in violent crime (and suicide). The prevalence of gun ownership differs rather widely across urban areas, from around 10% in the cities of the Northeast to more than 50% in the Mountain states. The overall prevalence of gun ownership has been found to be highly correlated with the percentage of homicides, suicides, and robberies that involve guns in these cities (Cook, 1979, 1985). Therefore, where gun ownership is prevalent in the general population, guns tend to be prevalent in violence.

A natural explanation for this pattern is differences among cities in their *scarcity* of guns. Predatory criminals obtain most of their guns from acquaintances, family members, drug dealers, thefts from homes and vehicles, and other street sources, rather than from licensed dealers (Decker, Pennell, & Caldwell, 1997; Sheley & Wright, 1995; Smith, 1996). The ease of making such a "connection" will be greater in a city in which guns are prevalent. Further, the black markets for guns, which are the ultimate source for perhaps half or more of the crime guns, will tend to be more active in cities in which gun ownership is prevalent (Moore, 1981; Wright & Rossi, 1986).

It is not just street criminals who carry guns; sometimes their potential victims do as well. The practice of going armed in public has been facilitated in recent years by changes in a number of state laws governing concealed-carry licensing; by 1997, a majority of states had liberal provisions that enable most adults to obtain a license to carry. A controversial study by two economists (Lott & Mustard, 1997) found evidence that states that liberalized their concealed-carry regulations enjoyed a reduction in violent crime rates, presumably because some would-be assailants feared that potential victims might be armed. Black and Nagin (in press), however, using the same data, conclude that there is no evidence of a deterrent effect (see also McDowall, Loftin, & Wiersema, 1995). Stronger conclusions will have to await better evidence.

GUNS AND PUBLIC POLICY: THE VALUES AT STAKE

Guns have many uses, all of which have legitimacy to the people who use them in those ways. Society as a whole, however, values some uses less highly than do the individual owners. The result is a "great American gun war," a continuing debate and political struggle to determine which uses will be protected and which should be sacrificed to achieve some greater social good. Much of the rhetoric in the debate stems from three broad perspectives that will be considered in the following sections.

The Public Health Perspective

The essence of the public health framework is whether a proposed control measure would reduce the incidence of injury and death. There is little concern with the value of sporting uses of guns. From this perspective, the modest pleasures associated with recreational shooting and the dubious benefits from self-defense should yield to society's overwhelming interest in reducing gun deaths. Preserving life is the paramount value in this scheme.

The Welfare Economics Framework

The welfare economics framework is similar to that of the public health framework but has a wider array of consequences and greater attention to individual preferences. It leads us to view the gun "problem" as the harm inflicted on others, with much less attention to suicides and self-inflicted accidents. The uses seen as socially detrimental are virtually the same as those that are prohibited by law. There is no presumption within this framework, however, that punishing criminal uses is an adequate response; consequently, there remains the possibility that the benefits of preemptive controls on guns, such as a ban on carrying concealed handguns, would outweigh the costs. The costs of such controls include the public costs of enforcement and the private costs of compliance (or evasion) of these regulations.

In this calculus of cost and benefit, where does self-defense fit in? For most gun owners, the possibility that the gun will prove useful in fending off a robber or burglar is one source of its value.

Some writers have even argued that the private valuation of guns in this respect understates their public value because the widespread possession of guns has a *general* deterrent effect on crime (Kleck, 1991; Snyder, 1993). Indeed, one survey of imprisoned felons found that a paramount concern in doing their crimes was the prospect of meeting up with an armed victim (Wright & Rossi, 1986). Not known, however, is whether the predominant effect on criminal behavior is desisting, displacement to victims who are not likely to be armed, or a change in technique.

The "Rights and Responsibilities" Perspective

The welfare economics framework helps organize the arguments pro and con for gun controls and suggests a procedure for assigning values. But for those who believe in the "right" to bear arms, it is not a completely satisfactory approach. The debate about gun control can and should be conducted, at least in part, in the context of a framework that defines the appropriate relationship between the individual, the community, and the state.

Much in the foreground of this debate lies the Second Amendment to the U.S. Constitution, which states, "A well regulated militia, being necessary to the security of a free State, the right of the people to keep and bear arms, shall not be infringed." The proper interpretation of this statement has been contested in recent years. The U.S. Supreme Court has not chosen to clarify the matter, having ruled only once during this century on a Second Amendment issue—and that on a rather narrow technical basis. Indeed, no federal court has ever overturned a gun control law on Second Amendment grounds.

ALTERNATIVE GUN CONTROL POLICIES

Commerce in guns and the possession and use of guns are regulated by federal, state, and local governments. To assess the options for reform, it is first helpful to understand the current array of controls and why they fail to achieve an acceptably low rate of gun violence.

The Current Array of Policies

The primary objective of federal law in regulating firearms is to insulate the states from one another, so that restrictive laws adopted in some states are not undercut by the greater availability of guns in other states. The Gun Control Act of 1968 established the framework for the current system of controls on gun transfers. All shipments of firearms (including mail-order sales) are limited to federally licensed dealers who are required to obey applicable state and local ordinances. There are also restrictions on sales of guns to out-of-state residents.

Federal law also seeks to establish a minimum set of restrictions on acquisition and possession of guns. The Gun Control Act of 1968 stipulates several categories of people who are denied the right to receive or possess a gun, including illegal aliens, convicted felons and those under indictment, and people who have at some time been involuntarily committed to a mental institution. Persons with a history of substance abuse are also prohibited from possessing a gun. Dealers are not allowed to sell handguns to persons younger than 21 years old or to sell long guns to those younger than 18, although there is no federal prohibition of gun *possession* by youth. These various prohibitions are implemented by a requirement that the buyer sign a form stating that he or she does not fall into any of the proscribed categories. In 1993, Congress adopted the Brady Bill, which requires dealers in states without screening systems for handgun buyers to enforce a 5-day waiting period between the purchase and transfer of a handgun. The dealers are required to notify law enforcement officials shortly after the purchase so that a background check can be run on the buyer.

State and local legislation tends to make a sharp distinction between keeping a gun in one's home or business and carrying a gun in public. All but a few states either ban concealed weapons entirely or require a special license for carrying concealed weapons (although many states have recently eased the requirements for obtaining a license). Local ordinances typically place additional restrictions on carrying and discharging guns inside city limits.

Facing a daunting array of possibilities for legislation, policymakers need guidance on which approaches hold the most promise of reducing firearms violence and at what cost to legitimate owners. Reliable information is difficult to obtain; still, some evidence is available concerning which general approaches show the most promise. In searching for worthwhile reforms, we find it useful to classify alternative gun control measures into three categories: (a) those designed to affect the supply and overall availability of guns, (b) those designed to influence who has these weapons, and (c) those designed to affect how the guns are used by the people who have them.

Reducing Overall Supply and Availability

Many gun control measures focus on the supply and availability of the guns themselves (or, in one imaginative leap, on the ammunition that makes them deadly). The basic idea is that if guns (or ammunition) become less readily available, or more expensive to purchase, then some violence-prone people will decide to rely on other weapons instead, and gun violence will be reduced.

Many commentators have suggested that this approach is doomed by the huge arsenal of guns currently in private hands. How can we discourage violence-prone people from obtaining guns when there are already enough in circulation to arm every teenager and adult in the country? In response, we note that the number of guns in circulation is only indirectly relevant to whether supply restrictions can hope to succeed; of direct consequence is the *price* and *difficulty* of obtaining a gun. Our discussion of availability in a previous section helps establish the evidence on these matters—availability *does* seem to matter, even within the current context of widespread private ownership.

Basic economic reasoning suggests that if the price of new guns is increased by amending the federal tax or other means, the effects will ripple through all the markets in which guns are transferred, including the black market for stolen guns (Cook & Leitzel,

1996). If the average prices of guns go up, some people—including some violence-prone people—will decide that there are better uses for their money. Others will be discouraged if, in addition to raising the money price, the time or risk required to obtain a gun increases. Although there are no reliable estimates of the elasticity of demand for guns by youths, we believe that youths, in particular, are likely to be more responsive to price than to more remote costs (such as the possibility of arrest and punishment). Those who argue that youthful offenders will do whatever is necessary to obtain their guns may have some hard-core group of violent gang members and drug dealers in mind but surely not the much larger group of kids who rarely get into serious trouble (see Sheley & Wright, 1995; Smith, 1996).

At present, a substantial increase in the federal tax on the purchase of firearms is under discussion for the first time in memory. Potentially even more important is the growing possibility of successful tort litigation against manufacturers of cheap concealable handguns, which, if successful, would raise the price of even the cheapest guns (Teret, 1986). Another approach to raising prices, however, is to impose safety requirements on gun manufacturers. Proposals in this area include "childproofing" guns so that they are inoperable by children; requiring that domestically manufactured guns meet the same safety requirements as imports, including protections against accidental discharge; and requiring safety devices such as trigger locks and loaded chamber indicators (Teret & Wintemute, 1993). As it is now, firearms manufacturers are remarkably free of safety regulation, in part because the Consumer Product Safety Commission has no authority over personal firearms. Although such regulations may be welcomed by gun buyers who are seeking some protection against gun accidents, they would have little direct effect on suicide and criminal misuse of firearms. To the extent that complying with such regulations made guns more costly, however, there could be some indirect effect comparable with raising the federal tax (Cook & Leitzel, 1996).

A more far-reaching proposal is to encourage the manufacture of guns that are "personalized," in the sense that they would be equipped with an electronic sensing device that would recognize a ring on the owner's finger, or even the owner's fingerprint. Such devices are currently under development. If they prove reliable, law enforcement agencies may adopt them to protect officers from being assaulted with their own guns. If all new handguns were equipped with such devices, it would gradually reduce the number of gun accidents and reduce the profitability of stealing guns.

Restricting Access

The second broad class of gun control policy instruments is designed to influence who has access to different types of weapons. The intuitive notion here is that if we could find a way to keep guns out of the hands of "bad guys" without denying access to the "good guys," then gun crimes would decrease without infringing on the legitimate uses of guns. The challenges for this type of policy are, first, to decide where to draw the line and, second, to develop effective barriers to prevent guns from crossing this line.

A fundamental premise underlying much gun legislation holds that owning a gun is a right granted to all adults unless they do something to disqualify themselves, such as committing a serious crime. A different approach is to treat gun ownership as a privilege, as is the case, say, with driving a vehicle on public highways. Similar to driving privileges, one eminently sensible requirement for those

who seek to acquire a gun is that they demonstrate knowledge of how to use it safely and legally. It is an intriguing possibility that such a requirement would engender considerable growth in the National Rifle Association's safety training programs because many of those wishing to qualify for a license would need to enroll in such a course.

Wherever the line is drawn, there is the serious problem of defending it against illegal transfers. That task is currently done poorly. The major loopholes stem from the widespread abuse of the federal licensing system, the lack of effective screening of those who seek to buy guns from dealers, a vigorous and largely unregulated "gray" market by which used guns change hands, and an active black market supplied by theft, scofflaw gun dealers (those who knowingly violate the terms of their license on a frequent basis), and interstate gunrunning operations.

Federal Licensing System The U.S. Bureau of Alcohol, Tobacco, and Firearms (ATF) is the agency charged with the regulation of federally licensed gun dealers. It is a small agency whose jurisdiction includes not only regulatory inspections of gun dealers but also criminal investigations of violations of federal gun laws. As well, it is responsible for the regulatory surveillance and criminal investigation of the explosives, alcohol, and tobacco industries. Obtaining a federal dealer's license from ATF was formerly just a matter of paying a small fee and filling out a form, and in 1993 there were 260,000 people who had done so—far more than were genuinely in the business of selling guns to the public. ATF at that time lacked the authority and resources to screen applicants effectively or to inspect their operations after issuing the license (Violence Policy Center, 1992). In response to this problem, recent changes in application requirements, combined with the hefty increase in fee mandated by the Brady Law, have had the effect of reducing the number of federal licensees to about 100,000 (as of 1997) and greatly enhancing ATF's ability to serve its regulatory function.

Screening People who seek to buy handguns from a dealer are required to submit to state permit requirements or, if there are none, to a 5-day waiting period required by federal law. If the dealer and purchaser comply with this requirement, there is some chance that disqualified buyers will be identified and screened out. But felons, youths, and others who are not permitted to purchase a gun can ask a qualified friend or relative to make a "straw man" purchase from a dealer on their behalf or find a scofflaw dealer who is willing to sell guns off the books. Most common of all is simply to purchase a gun from a nondealer.

Black and Gray Markets There is a remarkably active and open market for used guns that is largely unregulated, a market through which buyers and sellers find each other through "gun shows," word of mouth, or the classified ads. These transactions are often entirely legal; someone who sells a gun or two on occasion is not subject to any federal requirements except that they not knowingly sell to a felon, illicit drug user, or other person prohibited from possessing a gun.

In considering intervention strategies, it is useful to distinguish between transfers that move guns from the licit to the illicit sectors and transfers within the illicit sector (Koper & Reuter, 1996). In the former category are sales by scofflaw dealers and theft from legitimate owners, whereas the latter includes the active but highly disorganized black market for guns in which kids and criminals frequently buy

and sell (Cook, Molliconi, & Cole, 1995; Kennedy, 1994).

Perhaps the best hope for reducing gun trafficking to youths and criminals is a multifaceted enforcement and regulatory effort aimed primarily at reducing the flow of guns from the licit to the illicit sector. On the regulatory side, the main objective is to rein in scofflaw dealers, which most states have left to the federal ATF. ATF's capacity to act effectively has been strengthened in recent years by the great reduction in the number of licensed dealers resulting from changes in ATF licensing procedures and the increase in the initial license fee from $30 to $200 that was required in the Brady Bill. ATF is also beginning to exploit gun-tracing data to identify dealers who are frequently involved in selling guns that are used in crime. Further regulatory efforts to discourage gunrunning include the requirement that dealers report multiple purchases and the prohibition adopted by several states on the sale of more than one handgun to a customer per month.

Designing policies to reduce theft is conceptually more difficult, yet with an estimated 500,000 guns transferred this way each year (Cook & Ludwig, 1996), it is just as important. To reduce this source of crime guns, it may be possible to impose some obligation on gun dealers and gun owners to store their weapons securely (as we now do on pharmacists who sell abusable drugs) and to step up enforcement against fences who happen to deal in stolen guns.

Considering its various components, the illicit gun market is best seen as a relatively large number of persons engaging in relatively unspecialized enterprises. The type of enforcement that would be appropriate in attacking such markets is probably a high-volume "buy and bust" operation (Moore, 1983). Law enforcement agencies may be reluctant to launch an operation of this sort, given the danger inherent in dealing with guns and the legal difficulties in proving that the guns they are buying are in fact stolen and being sold illegally. Consequently, the possibilities for choking off supply to the illicit sector appear more promising than attempting to disrupt their activities.

Controlling Uses

The third broad class of gun control policy instruments is concerned with limiting unsafe and criminal uses of guns. Most prominent are provisions for increasing prison sentences when a gun is used in a crime. One clear advantage of this approach as compared with other gun policies is that it does not impinge on legitimate uses of guns. A recent analysis of crime trends in jurisdictions that adopted such sentencing provisions provides evidence that they may be effective in reducing the homicide rate (McDowall, Loftin, & Wiersema, 1992a).

Another and far more controversial tactic is to focus local law enforcement efforts on illegal possession and carrying. The potential effectiveness of this approach is suggested by the success of the Bartley-Fox Amendment in Massachusetts (Pierce & Bowers, 1981). This sort of gun enforcement typically requires proactive police efforts, and there is considerable variation among police departments in how much effort they direct to halting illegal possession and gun carrying (Moore, 1980). The controversy about enforcement stems in part from the concern that police, if sufficiently motivated, may conduct illegal searches in the effort to get guns off the street. More fundamental is that treating illegal carrying as a serious crime puts in jeopardy millions of otherwise law-abiding people who carry guns for self-protection. Nonetheless, gun-oriented patrol tactics appear to have the potential to reduce gun violence (Sherman, Shaw, & Rogan, 1995).

Rather than a general effort to get guns off the streets, a more focused effort can be directed at prohibiting guns in particularly dangerous locations such as homes with histories of domestic violence, bars with histories of drunken brawls, parks in which gang fights tend to break out, and schools in which teachers and students have been assaulted. Often, in seeking to reduce the presence of weapons in these particularly dangerous places, groups other than the police may be mobilized to help make the laws effective. Victimized spouses or their advocates might help enforce rules against guns in violence-prone households, liquor-licensing agencies might be enlisted to help keep guns out of bars, recreation departments might be mobilized to reduce gun carrying in public parks, and so on. The point is that there may be some particular hot spots for gun offenses that could be targeted as places to concentrate gun enforcement efforts much as we focus on keeping guns and bombs out of airplanes.

CONCLUSION: WHAT'S TO BE DONE?

Given the important value conflicts and empirical uncertainties surrounding gun control policies, some caution in recommending public or governmental action is warranted. But recommending caution is far from recommending *inaction*. Indeed, we think that it is time to get on with the business of actively exploring alternative gun control initiatives to develop more effective interventions than those on which we now rely. The goal of gun control policy during the next decade should be to develop and evaluate specific gun control measures that can reduce gun crimes, suicides, and accidents while preserving as much legitimate use of guns as possible. There is no reason to believe that there is a single best policy. Rather, we should be looking for a combination of policies that address the full array of gun "problems."

Action at the Federal Level

The federal government is best positioned to make guns more valuable and harder to obtain, while insulating the states from one another's supply of guns. Among the next steps that appear most promising are these:

1. Raise the tax on guns and ammunition to make the cost of acquiring and owning particular types of guns more accurately reflect the social costs and benefits of having them. For instance, we favor converting the current excise tax, which is proportional to the wholesale price, to a flat tax. Cheap handguns do as much damage as expensive ones. On the one hand, we recognize that this tax is regressive and will be particularly burdensome on poorer people who want a gun. On the other hand, the benefit of such a tax, reductions in gun crimes and accidents, will be disproportionately experienced by the poor, who are vastly overrepresented among the victims of gunshot wounds and deaths.

2. Require all gun transfers to pass through federally licensed dealers, with the same screening and paperwork provisions as if the gun were being sold by the dealer.

3. Step up criminal enforcement efforts against gunrunning operations.

4. Provide funding and technical know-how to enhance the quality and completeness of state and federal criminal records files and facilitate access by law enforcement agencies to these files.

5. Enhance cooperation with the local law enforcement efforts in investigating and prosecuting those who deal in stolen guns.

6. Mandate that new guns meet minimum safety requirements to reduce gun accidents while encouraging research in devices to personalize guns.

Action at the State Level

A battle in the state arena looms over the extent of liability for manufacturers, sellers, and owners of guns when a gun is used to injure someone. Lawsuits based on a variety of liability theories are moving through the courts. The implicit threat posed by these lawsuits is that if manufacturers and sellers are held responsible for the damage done by handguns, the monetary liability would be prohibitive. This possibility is appealing to those who are impatient with the more moderate results achievable through the political process.

Action at the Metropolitan or Municipal Level

Perhaps the greatest opportunities to work on reducing gun violence in the immediate future lie in the cities in which the toll of gun violence is so high. Working against effective gun legislation at this level are a persistent fear of crime and the fervent belief by some that a gun will provide protection. Thus, one important goal of gun control policy at the local level should be not to simply reduce the availability of guns but to find other, less socially costly means that people can use to produce security and reduce fear. In many cities, this is one of the important goals of shifting to a strategy of community policing. To the extent that efforts associated with this strategy help diminish fear of crime, these measures might also reduce the perceived need for individual gun ownership; with that accomplished, an increase in the range of feasible and desirable gun control policies might become possible.

The particular targets of city efforts against gun violence that seem important to us are these:

1. Reducing gun carrying by offenders on city streets.

2. Reducing youth access to and use of all types of weapons.

3. Keeping guns out of places that have records of violent conflicts such as rowdy bars, homes in which domestic violence often occurs, and other community hot spots.

Exactly how to accomplish these particular objectives remains unclear, but it is not hard to list particular actions one could imagine police departments undertaking. Indeed, bringing gun crime down would be a good exercise in problem solving to turn over to an innovative police agency.

The challenge of implementing effective gun control measures in the United States is daunting in the face of the considerable uncertainty about what works, especially when coupled with the profound national disagreement about which values concerning guns are most important. Still, with continuing attention to the evidence generated by the state and local innovations, and a vigorous public dialogue on the importance of both rights and responsibilities in this arena, there is every hope of doing better. There is little doubt that one of the benefits of such success would be a reduced rate of homicide in the United States.

REFERENCES

Black, D., & Nagin, D. (1998). Do "right-to-carry" laws deter violent crime? *Journal of Legal Studies, 26*, 209–220.

Blumstein, A. (1995). Youth violence, guns, and the illicit-drug industry. *Journal of Criminal Law and Criminology, 86*, 10–36.

Bureau of Justice Statistics. (1997). *Criminal victimization in the United States, 1994* (NCJ-162126). Washington, DC: Government Printing Office.

Centers for Disease Control and Prevention. (1997). CDC WONDER [On-line]. Available: http://wonder.cdc.gov/WONDER

Cook, P. J. (1976). A strategic choice analysis of robbery. In W. Skogan (Ed.), *Sample surveys of the victims of crimes* (pp. 173–187). Cambridge, MA: Ballinger.

Cook, P. J. (1979). The effect of gun availability on robbery and robbery murder: A cross section study of fifty cities. In R. H. Haveman & B. B. Zellner (Eds.), *Policy Studies Review Annual* (Vol. 3, pp. 743–781). Beverly Hills, CA: Sage.

Cook, P. J. (1985). The case of the missing victims: Gunshot woundings in the National Crime Survey. *Journal of Quantitative Criminology, 1*, 91–102.

Cook, P. J. (1991). The technology of personal violence. In M. H. Tonry (Ed.), *Crime and justice: A review of research* (Vol. 14, pp. 1–71). Chicago: University of Chicago Press.

Cook, P. J., & Leitzel, J. A. (1996). Perversity, futility, jeopardy: An economic analysis of the attack on gun control. *Law and Contemporary Problems, 59*, 91–118.

Cook, P. J., & Ludwig, J. (1996). *Guns in America: Results of a comprehensive national survey on firearms ownership and use.* Washington, DC: Police Foundation.

Cook, P. J., Ludwig, J., & Hemenway, D. (1997). The gun debate's new mythical number: How many defensive gun uses per year? *Journal of Policy Analysis and Management, 16*, 463–469.

Cook, P. J., Molliconi, S., & Cole, T. B. (1995). Regulating gun markets. *Journal of Criminal Law and Criminology, 86*, 59–92.

Decker, S. H., Pennell, S., & Caldwell, A. (1997). *Illegal firearms: Access and use by arrestees.* Washington, DC: National Institute of Justice.

Federal Bureau of Investigation. (1971–1997). *Crime in the United States: Uniform crime reports.* Washington, DC: Government Printing Office.

Fingerhut, L. A. (1993). Firearm mortality among children, youth, and young adults 1–34 years of age, trends and current status: United States, 1985–90. *Advance data from vital and health statistics* (No. 231). Hyattsville, MD: National Center for Health Statistics.

Karlson, T. A., & Hargarten, S. W. (1997). *Reducing firearm injury and death: A public health sourcebook on guns.* New Brunswick, NJ: Rutgers University Press.

Kellermann, A. L., Rivara, F. P., Rushforth, N. B., Banton, J. G., Reay, D. T., Francisco, J. T., Locci, A. B., Prodzinski, J. P., Hackman, B. B., & Somes, G. (1993). Gun ownership as a risk factor for homicide in the home. *New England Journal of Medicine, 329,* 1084–1091.

Kellermann, A. L., Rivara, F. P., Somes, G., Reay, D., Francisco, J., Banton, J., Prodzinski, J., Fligner, C., & Hackman, B. B. (1992). Suicide in the home in relation to gun ownership. *New England Journal of Medicine, 327,* 467–472.

Kennedy, D. M. (1994). Can we keep guns away from kids? *The American Prospect, 18,* 74–80.

Kennedy, D. M., Piehl, A. M., & Braga, A. A. (1996). Youth violence in Boston: Gun markets, serious youth offenders, and a use-reduction strategy. *Law and Contemporary Problems, 59,* 147–196.

Kleck, G. (1991). *Point blank: Guns and violence in America.* New York: Aldine de Gruyter.

Kleck, G., & Patterson, E. B. (1993). The impact of gun control and gun ownership levels on violence rates. *Journal of Quantitative Criminology, 9,* 249–287.

Koper, C. S., & Reuter, P. (1996). Suppressing illegal gun markets: Lessons from drug enforcement. *Law and Contemporary Problems, 59,* 119–143.

Lott, J. R., Jr., & Mustard, D. B. (1997). Crime, deterrence and right-to-carry concealed handguns. *Journal of Legal Studies, 26,* 1–68.

McDowall, D., Loftin, C., & Wiersema, B. (1992a). A comparative study of the preventive effects of mandatory sentencing laws for gun crimes. *Journal of Criminal Law and Criminology, 83,* 378–394.

McDowall, D., Loftin, C., & Wiersema, B. (1992b). *The incidence of civilian defensive firearm use.* Unpublished manuscript, University of Maryland-College Park, Institute of Criminal Justice.

McDowall, D., Loftin, C., & Wiersema, B. (1995). Easing concealed firearms laws: Effects on homicide in three states. *Journal of Criminal Law and Criminology, 86,* 193–206.

Moore, M. H. (1980). Police and weapons offenses. *Annals of the American Academy of Political and Social Science, 452,* 22–32.

Moore, M. H. (1981). Keeping handguns from criminal offenders. *Annals of the American Academy of Political and Social Science, 455,* 92–109.

Moore, M. H. (1983). The bird in hand: A feasible strategy for gun control. *Journal of Policy Analysis and Management, 2,* 185–195.

Pierce, G. L., & Bowers, W. J. (1981). The Bartley-Fox Gun Law's short-term impact on crime in Boston. *Annals of the American Academy of Political and Social Science, 455,* 120–137.

Sheley, J. F., & Wright, J. D. (1995). *In the line of fire: Youth, guns, and violence in urban America.* New York: Aldine de Gruyter.

Sherman, L., Shaw, J. W., & Rogan, D. P. (1995). *The Kansas City gun experiment.* Washington, DC: National Institute of Justice.

Smith, M. D. (1996). Sources of firearm acquisition among a sample of inner-city youths: Research results and policy implications. *Journal of Criminal Justice, 24,* 361–367.

Smith, M. D., & Feiler, S. M. (1995). Absolute and relative involvement in homicide offending: Contemporary youth and the baby boom cohorts. *Violence and Victims, 10,* 327–333.

Snyder, J. R. (1993). A nation of cowards. *The Public Interest, 113,* 40–55.

Teret, S. P. (1986). Litigating for the public's health. *American Journal of Public Health, 76,* 1027–1029.

Teret, S. P., & Wintemute, G. (1993). Policies to prevent firearm injuries. *Health Affairs, 12*(4), 96–108.

Violence Policy Center. (1992). *More gun dealers than gas stations.* Washington, DC: Author.

Violence Policy Center. (1997). *Who dies?* Washington, DC: Author.

Wolfgang, M. E. (1958). *Patterns in criminal homicide.* Philadelphia: University of Pennsylvania Press.

Wright, J. D., & Rossi, P. H. (1986). *Armed and considered dangerous: A survey of felons and their firearms.* Hawthorne, NY: Aldine.

Wright, J. D., Rossi, P. H., & Daly, K. (1983). *Under the gun: Weapons, crime, and violence in America.* Hawthorne, NY: Aldine.

Wright, J. D., Sheley, J. F., & Smith, M. D. (1992). Kids, guns, and killing fields. *Society, 30*(1), 84–89.

Zimring, F. E. (1968). Is gun control likely to reduce violent killings? *University of Chicago Law Review, 35*, 21–37.

Zimring, F. E. (1972). The medium is the message: Firearm caliber as a determinant of death from assault. *Journal of Legal Studies, 1*, 97–124.

Zimring, F. E., & Hawkins, G. (1997). *Crime is not the problem: Lethal violence in America*. New York: Oxford University Press.

Abolish the Juvenile Court

Barry C. Feld

Within the past three decades, judicial decisions, legislative amendments, and administrative changes have transformed the juvenile court from a nominally rehabilitative social welfare agency into a scaled-down, second-class criminal court for young people. These reforms have converted the historical ideal of the juvenile court as a social welfare institution into a penal system that provides young offenders with neither therapy nor justice. The substantive and procedural convergence between juvenile and criminal courts eliminates virtually all the conceptual and operational differences in strategies of criminal social control for youths and adults. No compelling reasons exist to maintain separate from an adult criminal court a punitive juvenile court whose only remaining distinctions are its persisting procedural deficiencies. Rather, states should abolish juvenile courts' delinquency jurisdiction and formally recognize youthfulness as a mitigating factor in the sentencing of younger criminal offenders. Such a policy would provide younger offenders with substantive protections comparable to those afforded by juvenile courts, ensure greater procedural regularity in the determination of guilt, and avoid the disjunctions in social control caused by maintaining two duplicative and inconsistent criminal justice systems.

TRANSFORMED BUT UNREFORMED: THE RECENT HISTORY OF THE JUVENILE COURT

The Juvenile Court

Ideological changes in cultural conceptions of children and in strategies of social control during the nineteenth century led to the creation of the juvenile court in 1899. The juvenile court reform movement removed children from the adult criminal justice and corrections systems, provided them with individualized treatment in a separate system, and substituted a scientific and preventative alternative to the criminal law's punitive policies. By separating children from adults and providing a rehabilitative alternative to punishment, juvenile courts rejected both the criminal law's jurisprudence and its procedural safeguards such as juries and lawyers. Judges conducted confidential and private hearings, limited public access to court proceedings and court records, employed a euphemistic vocabulary to

From "Abolish the Juvenile Court: Youthfulness, Criminal Responsibility, and Sentencing Policy" *Journal of Criminal Law and Criminology,* 88, (Fall 1997): 68–136. Reprinted by permission of Northwestern University, School of Law.

minimize stigma, and adjudicated youths to be delinquent rather than convicted them of crimes. Under the guise of *parens patriae*, the juvenile court emphasized treatment, supervision, and control rather than punishment. The juvenile court's "rehabilitative ideal" envisioned a specialized judge trained in social science and child development whose empathic qualities and insight would enable her to make individualized therapeutic dispositions in the "best interests" of the child. Reformers pursued benevolent goals, individualized their solicitude, and maximized discretion to provide flexibility in diagnosis and treatment of the "whole child." They regarded a child's crimes primarily as a symptom of her "real needs," and consequently the nature of the offense affected neither the degree nor the duration of intervention. Rather, juvenile court judges imposed indeterminate and nonproportional sentences that potentially continued for the duration of minority.

Progressives situated the juvenile court on a number of cultural and criminological fault lines and institutionalized several binary conceptions for the respective justice systems: either child or adult, either determinism or free will, either treatment or punishment, either procedural informality or formality, and either discretion or the rule of law. Serious youth crime challenges these dichotomous constructs. The recent procedural and substantive convergence between juvenile and criminal courts represent efforts to modify the Progressives' bifurcation between these competing conceptions of children and crime control.

Constitutional Domestication of the Juvenile Court

In *In re Gault* [1967], the Supreme Court began to transform the juvenile court into a very different institution than the Progressives contemplated. The Supreme Court engrafted some formal procedures at trial onto the juvenile court's individualized treatment sentencing schema. Although the Court did not intend its decisions to alter juvenile courts' therapeutic mission, in the aftermath of *Gault*, judicial, legislative, and administrative changes have fostered a procedural and substantive convergence with adult criminal courts. Several subsequent Supreme Court decisions furthered the "criminalizing" of the juvenile court. In *In re Winship*, the Court required states to prove juvenile delinquency by the criminal law's standard of proof "beyond a reasonable doubt." In *Breed v. Jones*, the Court applied the constitutional ban on double jeopardy and posited a functional equivalence between criminal trials and delinquency proceedings.

Gault and *Winship* unintentionally, but inevitably, transformed the juvenile court system from its original Progressive conception as a social welfare agency into a wholly owned subsidiary of the criminal justice system. By emphasizing criminal procedural regularity in the determination of delinquency, the Court shifted the focus of juvenile courts from paternalistic assessments of a youth's "real needs" to proof of commission of a crime. By formalizing the connection between criminal conduct and coercive intervention, the Court made explicit a relationship previously implicit, unacknowledged, and deliberately obscured.

In *McKeiver v. Pennsylvania*, however, the Court denied to juveniles the constitutional right to jury trials in delinquency proceedings and halted the extension of full procedural parity with adult criminal prosecutions. Without elaborating on or analyzing the distinctions, *McKeiver* relied on the rhetorical differences between juvenile courts' *treatment* rationale and criminal courts' *punitive* purposes to justify the procedural disparities between the two settings. Because *McKeiver* endorsed a treatment justification for its decision, the right to a jury trial provides the crucial legal condition precedent to punish youths explicitly in juvenile courts. Several recent juvenile justice legislative reforms provide some youths with a statutory right to a jury in order to expand the punitive sentencing options available to juvenile court judges.

Transformation of the Juvenile Court

In the decades since *Gault*, legislative, judicial, and administrative changes have modified juvenile courts' jurisdiction, purpose, and procedures and fostered their convergence with criminal courts. These inter-related developments—increased procedural formality, removal of status offenders from juvenile court jurisdiction, waiver of serious offenders to the adult system, and an increased emphasis on punishment in sentencing delinquents—constitute a form of criminological "triage," crucial components of the criminalizing of the juvenile court, and elements of the erosion of the theoretical and practical differences between the two systems. This triage strategy removes many middle-class, white, and female noncriminal status offenders from the juvenile court, simultaneously transfers persistent, violent, and disproportionally minority youths to criminal court for prosecution as adults, and it imposes increasingly punitive sanctions on those middle-range delinquent criminal offenders who remain under the jurisdiction of the juvenile court. As a result of these implicit triage policies, juvenile courts increasingly function similarly to adult criminal courts.

Status Offenses Legislative recognition that juvenile courts often failed to realize their benevolent purposes has led to a strategic retrenchment of juvenile courts' jurisdiction over noncriminal misconduct such as truancy or incorrigibility, behavior that would not be a crime if committed by an adult. In the 1970s, critics objected that juvenile courts' status jurisdiction treated noncriminal offenders indiscriminately like criminal delinquents, disabled families and other sources of referral through one-sided intervention, and posed insuperable legal issues for the court. Judicial and legislative disillusionment with juvenile courts' responses to noncriminal youths led to diversion, deinstitutionalization, and decriminalization reforms that have removed much of the "soft" end of juvenile court clientele.

Waiver of Juvenile Offenders to Adult Criminal Court A second jurisdictional change entails the criminalizing of serious juvenile offenders as courts and legislatures increasingly transfer chronic and violent youths from juvenile to criminal courts for prosecution as adults. Transfer laws simultaneously attempt to resolve both fundamental crime control issues and the ambivalence embedded in our cultural construction of youth. The jurisprudential conflicts reflect many of the current sentencing policy debates: the tensions between rehabilitation or incapacitation and retribution, between basing decisions on characteristics of the individual offender or the seriousness of the offense, between discretion and rules, and between indeterminacy and determinacy. Waiver laws attempt to reconcile the contradictions posed when the child is a criminal and the criminal is a child. What legal processes, crime control policies, and substantive criteria best enable decision makers to select from among the competing cultural images of youths as responsible and culpable offenders and as immature and salvageable children?

In most states, judges decide whether a youth is a criminal or a delinquent in a waiver hearing and base their discretionary assessments on a juvenile's "amenability to treatment" or "dangerousness." The inherent subjectivity of waiver criteria permits a variety of racial inequalities and geographic disparities to occur when judges attempt to interpret and apply these vague laws. When judicial waiver decisions, legislatively excluded offenses, or prosecutorial charging decisions focus on violent young offenders, these youths often receive substantially longer sentences as criminals than do their delinquent counterparts who remain in juvenile court simply because of their new-found "adult" status.

In response to the rise in youth homicide and gun violence in the late 1980s, almost every state has amended its waiver statutes and other provisions of their juvenile codes in a frantic effort to "get tough" and to stem the tide. These recent changes signal a fundamental inversion in juvenile court jurisprudence from treatment to punishment, from rehabilitation to retribution, and from immature child to responsible criminal. Legislatures increasingly use age and offense criteria to redefine the boundaries of adulthood, coordinate juvenile transfer and adult sentencing practices, and reduce the "punishment gap." The common overarching legislative strategy reflects a jurisprudential shift from the *principle of individualized justice* to the *principle of offense*, from rehabilitation to retribution, and an emphasis on the seriousness of the offense rather than judges' clinical assessments of offenders' "amenability to treatment." State legislative amendments use offense criteria either as dispositional guidelines to structure and limit judicial discretion, to guide prosecutorial charging decisions, or automatically to exclude certain youths from juvenile court jurisdiction.

Regardless of the details of these legislative strategies, the efforts to "crack down" and to "get tough" repudiate rehabilitation and judicial discretion, narrow juvenile courts' jurisdiction, base youths' "adult" status increasingly on the offense charged, and reflect a shift toward more retributive sentencing policies. Whether the legislature makes the forum decision by excluding offenses or the prosecutor does so on a discretionary basis via concurrent jurisdiction, these laws reduce or remove both discretionary judicial authority and juvenile courts' clientele. Offense exclusion rejects juvenile courts' philosophical premise that they can aid youth and denies them the opportunity to try without regard to the "real needs" of the offending youth. Finally, the legal shift to punish more young offenders as adults exposes at least some youths to the possibility of capital punishment for the crimes they committed as juveniles.

Although legislatures and courts transfer youths to criminal court so that they may receive longer sentences as adults than they could in the juvenile system, chronic property offenders constitute the bulk of juveniles judicially waived in most states, and they often receive shorter sentences as adults than do property offenders retained in juvenile court. By contrast, youths convicted of violent offenses in criminal courts appear to receive substantially longer sentences than do their retained juvenile counterparts. For youths and adults convicted of comparable crimes, both types of disparities—shorter sentences for waived youths than for retained juveniles adjudicated for property offenses and dramatically longer sentences for waived youths than for retained juveniles convicted for violent crimes—raise issues of sentencing policy fairness and justice. No coherent policy rationales justify either type of disparity. Rather, some youths experience dramatically different consequences than do other offenders simply because of the disjunction between two separate criminal justice systems.

Sentencing Delinquent Offenders

The same jurisprudential shifts from offender to the offense and from treatment to punishment that inspire changes in waiver policies increasingly affect the sentences that juvenile court judges impose on serious delinquent offenders as well.

The same public impetus and political pressures to waive the most serious young offenders to criminal courts also impel juvenile courts to "get tough" and punish more severely the remaining criminal delinquents, the residual "less bad of the worst." Several indicators reveal whether a juvenile court judge's disposition punishes a youth for his past offense or treats him for his future welfare. Increasingly, juvenile court legislative purpose clauses and court opinions explicitly endorse punishment as an appropriate component of juvenile sanctions. Currently, nearly half of the states use determinate or mandatory minimum sentencing provisions that base a youth's disposition on the offense she committed rather than her "real needs" to regulate at least some aspects of sentence duration, institutional commitment, or release. Empirical evaluations of juvenile courts' sentencing practices indicate that the present offense and prior record account for most of the explained variance in judges' dispositions of delinquents and reinforce the criminal orientation of juvenile courts. Finally, evaluations of conditions of confinement and treatment effectiveness belie any therapeutic "alternative purpose" to juvenile incarceration. In short, all these indicators consistently reveal that *treating* juveniles closely resembles *punishing* adults. A strong, nationwide policy shift both in theory and in practice away from therapeutic dispositions toward punishment or incapacitation of young offenders characterizes sentencing practice in the contemporary juvenile court.

Procedural Justice in Juvenile Courts

Procedure and substance intertwine inextricably in juvenile courts. The increased procedural formality since *Gault* coincides with the changes in legal theory and administrative practice from therapeutic, individualized dispositions toward more punitive, offense-based sentences. Indeed, *Gault*'s procedural reforms may have encouraged these changes by legitimating punishment.

Although the formal procedures of juvenile and criminal courts have converged under *Gault*'s impetus, a substantial gulf remains between theory and reality, between the "law on the books" and the "law in action." Theoretically, the Constitution and state juvenile statutes entitle delinquents to formal trials and assistance of counsel. But, the actual quality of procedural justice differs considerably from theory; a gap persists between "rhetoric" and "reality." Despite the criminalizing of juvenile courts, most states provide neither special procedures to protect youths from their own immaturity nor the full panoply of adult procedural safeguards. Instead, states treat juveniles just like adult criminal defendants when treating them equally places youths at a practical disadvantage, and use less effective juvenile court safeguards when those deficient procedures provide an advantage to the state.

JURY.   Although the right to a jury trial is a crucial procedural safeguard when states punish offenders, the vast majority of jurisdictions uncritically follow *McKeiver*'s lead and deny juveniles access to juries. Because judges and juries decide cases and apply *Winship*'s "reasonable doubt" standard differently, it is easier to convict youths in juvenile court than in criminal court with comparable evidence. Moreover, *McKeiver* simply ignored the reality that juries protect against a weak or biased judge, inject the community's values into the law, and increase the visibility and accountability of justice administration. These protective functions acquire even greater importance in juvenile courts, which typically labor behind closed doors immune from public scrutiny.

On the other hand, several states have recently enacted legislation to increase the sentencing authority and punishment capacities of juvenile courts. These "blended" sentences begin with a youth's trial in juvenile court and then authorize the judge to impose enhanced sentences beyond those used for ordinary delinquents. All the variants of "blended jurisdiction" provide these "intermediate" youths with adult criminal procedural safeguards, including the right to a jury trial. Once a state provides a youth with the right to a jury trial and other criminal procedural safeguards, it preserves the option to punish explicitly, as well as to extend jurisdiction for a period of several years or more beyond that available for ordinary delinquents. Thereby the state also gains greater flexibility to treat a youth. Finally, these statutes recognize the futility of trying to rationalize social control in two separate systems. These "blended" jurisdictional provisions represent a significant procedural and substantive convergence with an erosion of the differences between juvenile and criminal courts. They provide a conceptual alternative to binary waiver statutes by recognizing that adolescence comprises a developmental continuum that requires an increasing array of graduated sanctions for youths and procedural equality with adults to reflect the reality of punishment.

COUNSEL.   Procedural justice hinges on access to and the assistance of counsel. Despite *Gault*'s formal legal changes, the promise of quality legal representation remains unrealized for many juveniles. In several states, half or less of all juveniles receive the assistance of counsel to which the Constitution and state statutes entitle them. Moreover, rates of representation vary substantially within states and suggest that differences in rates of appointment of counsel reflect judicial policies to discourage representation. The

most common explanation for why so many juveniles are unrepresented is that judges find that they waived their right to counsel. Courts typically use the adult legal standard of "knowing, intelligent, and voluntary" under the "totality of the circumstances" to gauge the validity of juveniles' waivers of rights. Because juveniles possess less ability than adults to deal effectively with the legal system, formal equality results in practical procedural inequality.

THE INHERENT CONTRADICTION OF THE JUVENILE COURT

The foregoing jurisdictional, jurisprudential, and procedural changes have transformed the juvenile court from its original model as a social service agency into a deficient second-rate criminal court that provides young people with neither positive treatment nor criminal procedural justice. It effectively punishes young offenders but uses procedures under which no adult would consent to be tried if she faced the prospect of confinement in a secure facility.

Social Welfare Versus Penal Social Control

The juvenile court treatment model constitutes an inappropriate policy response to young offenders. If we formulated a child welfare policy *ab initio*, would we choose a juvenile court as the most appropriate agency through which to deliver social services, and make criminality a condition precedent to the receipt of services? If we would not create a court to deliver social services, then does the fact of a youth's criminality confer upon a court any special competency as a welfare agency? Many young people who do not commit crimes desperately need social services, and many youths who commit crimes do not require or will not respond to social services. In short, criminality represents an inaccurate and haphazard criterion on which to allocate social services. Because our society denies adequate help and assistance to meet the social welfare needs of all young people, the juvenile court's treatment ideology serves primarily to legitimate the exercise of judicial coercion of some *because of their criminality*.

Quite apart from its unsuitability as a social welfare agency, the individualized justice of a rehabilitative juvenile court fosters lawlessness and thus detracts from its utility as a court of law as well. Despite statutes and rules, juvenile court judges make discretionary decisions effectively unconstrained by the rule of law. If judges intervene to meet each child's "real needs," then every case is unique and decisional rules or objective criteria cannot constrain clinical intuitions. The *idea* of treatment necessarily entails individual differentiation, indeterminacy, a rejection of proportionality, and a disregard of normative valuations of the seriousness of behavior. But, if judges possess neither practical scientific bases by which to classify youths for treatment nor demonstrably effective programs to prescribe for them, then the exercise of "sound discretion" simply constitutes a euphemism for idiosyncratic judicial subjectivity. Racial, gender, geographic, and socioeconomic disparities constitute almost inevitable corollaries of a treatment ideology that lacks a scientific foundation. At the least, judges will sentence youths differently based on extraneous personal characteristics for which they bear no responsibility. At the worst, judges will impose haphazard, unequal, and discriminatory punishment on similarly situated offenders without effective procedural or appellate checks.

Is the discretion that judges exercise to classify for treatment warranted? Do the suc-

cesses of rehabilitation justify its concomitant lawlessness? Do the incremental benefits of juvenile court intervention outweigh the inevitable inequalities and racial disparities that result from the exercise of individualized discretion? Evaluations of the effectiveness of juvenile court intervention on recidivism rates counsel skepticism about the availability of programs that consistently or systematically rehabilitate juvenile offenders. The inability to demonstrate significant treatment effects may reflect methodological flaws, poorly implemented programs, or, in fact, the absence of effective methods of treatment. In the face of unproven efficacy and inadequate resources, the possibility of an effective rehabilitation program constitutes an insufficient justification to confine young offenders "for their own good" while providing them with fewer procedural safeguards than those afforded adults charged, convicted, and confined for crimes.

The juvenile court predicates its procedural informality on the assumptions that it provides benign and effective treatment. The continuing absence or co-optation of defense counsel in many jurisdictions reduces the likelihood that juvenile courts will adhere to existing legal mandates. The closed, informal, and confidential nature of delinquency proceedings reduces the visibility and accountability of the justice process and precludes external checks on coercive interventions. So long as the mythology prevails that juvenile court intervention constitutes only benign coercion and that, in any event, children should not expect more, youths will continue to receive the "worst of both worlds."

Failure of Implementation Versus Conception

The fundamental shortcoming of the juvenile court's welfare idea reflects a failure of conception rather than simply a failure of implementation. The juvenile court's creators envisioned a social service agency in a judicial setting and attempted to fuse its welfare mission with the power of state coercion. The juvenile court idea that judicial-clinicians successfully can combine social welfare and penal social control in one agency represents an inherent conceptual flaw and an innate contradiction. Combining social welfare and penal social control functions in one agency ensures that the court does both badly. Providing for child welfare is a societal responsibility rather than a judicial one. In practice, juvenile courts subordinate welfare concerns to crime control considerations.

The conflicted impulses engendered between concern for child welfare and punitive responses to criminal violations form the root of the ambivalence embedded in the juvenile court. The hostile reactions that people experience toward other peoples' children, whom they regard as a threat to themselves and their own children, undermine benevolent aspirations and elevate concerns for their control. Juvenile justice personnel simultaneously profess child-saving aspirations but more often function as agents of criminal social control.

The juvenile court inevitably subordinates social welfare to criminal social control because of its built-in penal focus. Legislatures do not define juvenile courts' social welfare jurisdiction on the basis of characteristics of children for which they are not responsible and for which effective intervention could improve their lives. If states defined juvenile courts' jurisdiction on the basis of young people's needs for social welfare, then they would declare a broad category of at-risk children who are eligible for public assistance.

Instead, states' juvenile codes define juvenile courts' jurisdiction based on a youth committing a crime, a prerequisite that detracts from a compassionate response. Unlike disadvantaged social conditions that are not their fault, criminal behavior represents the one characteristic for which adolescent offenders do bear at least partial responsibility. As long as juvenile courts define eligibility for "services" on the basis of criminality, they highlight that aspect of youths which rationally elicits the least sympathy and ignore personal circumstances or social conditions that evoke a desire to help. Thus, the juvenile courts' defining characteristic simply reinforces the public's antipathy to young people by emphasizing that they are law violators. Recent changes in juvenile court waiver and sentencing policies to emphasize punishment, "accountability," and personal responsibility further reinforce juvenile courts' penal foundations and reduce the legitimacy of youths' claims to compassion or humanitarian assistance.

YOUTHFULNESS, CRIMINAL RESPONSIBILITY, AND SENTENCING POLICY: YOUNG OFFENDERS IN CRIMINAL COURTS

Once we uncouple social welfare from penal social control, then no need remains for a separate juvenile court for young offenders. We can try all offenders in criminal court with certain modifications of substantive and procedural criminal law to accommodate younger defendants. Some proponents of juvenile courts properly object that criminal courts suffer from profound deficiencies: crushing caseloads, ineffective attorneys, insufficient sentencing alternatives, coercive plea bargains, and assembly line justice. Unfortunately, these shortcomings equally characterize juvenile courts as well. Others argue that because no social or political will exists to reform or provide resources for criminal courts, then juvenile court abolitionists must demonstrate conclusively their irremediable bankruptcy before remitting youths to the criminal courts that inspired their creation. In short, few juvenile court proponents even attempt any longer to defend the institution on its own merits but only to justify it by comparison with criminal courts, which they contend are worse.

If the child is a criminal and the "real" reason for formal intervention is criminal social control, then states should abolish juvenile courts' delinquency jurisdiction and try young offenders in criminal courts alongside their adult counterparts. But, if the criminal is a child, then states must modify their criminal justice system to accommodate the youthfulness of some defendants. Before prosecuting a child as a criminal in an integrated court, a legislature must address issues of substance and procedure. Substantive justice requires a rationale to sentence younger offenders differently, and more *leniently*, than older defendants, a formal recognition of *youthfulness as a mitigating factor in sentencing*. Procedural justice requires providing youths with full procedural parity with adult defendants and additional safeguards to account for the disadvantages of youth in the justice system. Taken in combination, these substantive and procedural modifications can avoid the "worst of both worlds," provide youths with protections functionally equivalent to those accorded adults, and do justice in sentencing.

Substantive Justice—Juveniles' Criminal Responsibility

Questions about youths' accountability or criminal responsibility arise at two different stages in the justice system—either when deciding guilt or when imposing a sentence. In the former instance, questions of responsibility focus on the minimum age at which the state may find a person guilty of an offense. In making judgments about criminal responsibility, the criminal law's *mens rea* construct fo-

cuses narrowly on cognitive ability and capacity to make choices and excludes from consideration the goals, values, emotions, or psychological development that motivate a person's choices. In the absence of insanity, compulsion, or some cognizable legal excuse, any actor who has the capacity to choose to act otherwise than the way she did possesses criminal responsibility. For questions of criminal responsibility and guilt, the common law's insanity and infancy *mens rea* defenses provide most of the answers. These doctrines excuse from criminal liability only those who lack the requisite criminal intent, the *mens rea*, because of mental illness or immaturity. Because these *mens rea* defenses effectively excuse an offender when the state cannot prove a crucial element of the offense (i.e., criminal intent), the common law employs a very low cognitive threshold—knowledge of "right from wrong"—to establish criminal guilt.

Quite apart from decisions about guilt or innocence, individual accountability and criminal responsibility also relate to questions of disposition or sentence. Even if a court finds a youth criminally responsible for causing a particular harm, should the criminal law treat a 14-year-old as the moral equivalent of a 24-year-old and impose an identical sentence, or should youthfulness mitigate the severity of the consequences? "Old enough to do the crime, old enough to do the time" provides an overly simple answer to a complex, normative, moral, and legal question. If political "sound bites" do not capture adequately the complexity of a youth sentencing policy, then on what principled bases should we distinguish between the two in sentencing?

Contemporary juvenile courts typically impose shorter sentences on serious young offenders than adult offenders convicted of comparable crimes receive. These shorter sentences enable young offenders to survive the mistakes of adolescence with a semblance of life chances intact. The juvenile court reifies the idea that young people bear less criminal responsibility and deserve less punishment than adults. Shorter sentences recognize that young people *do differ somewhat* from adults. These differences stem from physical, psychological, or developmental characteristics of young people and are by-products of the legal and social construction of youth. Youthfulness provides a rationale to mitigate sentences to some degree without excusing criminal conduct. But, shorter sentences for young people do not require a separate justice system in which to try them. Both juvenile and adult courts separate adjudication of guilt or innocence from sentencing, confine consideration of individual circumstances largely to the latter phase, and criminal courts may impose lenient sentences on young offenders when appropriate.

A variety of doctrinal and policy reasons justify sentencing young people less severely than their adult counterparts. The common law's infancy *mens rea* defense antedated positive criminology's deterministic assumptions and recognized that young people may lack criminal capacity. The classical criminal law assumed that rational actors make blameworthy choices and deserve to suffer the consequences of their freely chosen acts. The common law recognized and exempted from punishment categories of persons who lacked the requisite moral and criminal responsibility, for example, the insane and the young. It conclusively presumed that children less than 7 years old lacked criminal capacity and treated those 14 years of age and older as fully responsible. Between the ages of 7 and 14 years, the law rebuttably presumed criminal incapacity. The common law infancy gradations reflect developmental differences that render youths less *culpable* or criminally responsible than their adult coun-

terparts and provide a first approximation of a rationale for shorter sentences for youths than for adults. Juvenile court legislation simply extended upward by a few years the general presumption of youthful criminal irresponsibility and incapacity.

The extent to which young offenders, like adults, deserve punishment hinges on the meaning of culpability. Respect for the integrity of the individual provides the underlying rationale of *deserved punishment*. Blaming a culpable actor for her voluntary choice to do wrong and giving her the consequences that her choice deserves respects her integrity as a morally responsible individual. Deserved punishment emphasizes censure and condemnation for blameworthy choices. As long as the criminal law rests on a moral foundation, the idea of blameworthiness remains central to ascribing guilt and allocating punishment. Penalties proportionate to the seriousness of the crime reflect the connection between conduct, choice, and blameworthiness.

Because commensurate punishment proportions sanctions to the seriousness of the offense, it shifts the analytical focus to the meaning of *seriousness*. Two elements—harm and culpability—define the seriousness of an offense. Evaluations of harm focus on the nature and degree of injury inflicted, risk created, or value taken. A perpetrator's age has little bearing on assessments of harmfulness. But evaluations of seriousness also include the quality of the actor's choice to engage in the criminal conduct that produced the harm. Just deserts theory and criminal law grading principles base the degree of deserved punishment on an actor's culpability. For example, a person may cause the death of another individual with premeditation and deliberation, intentionally, "in the heat of passion," recklessly, negligently, or accidentally. The criminal law treats the same objective consequence or harm, the death of another person, very differently depending on the nature of the choice made.

Youthfulness acquires special salience when gauging the culpability of choices—the blameworthiness of acting in a particular harm-producing way. In a framework of deserved punishment, it would be fundamentally unjust to impose the same penalty on offenders who do not share equal culpability. If young people are neither fully responsible nor the moral equals of adults, then they do not deserve the same legal consequences even for their blameworthy misconduct.

Responsibility for choices hinges on cognitive and volitional competence. Do young offenders make criminal choices that constitute the moral equivalents of those made by more mature actors? If one focuses narrowly only on the capacity to make instrumental choices to do wrong, then we could view even very young actors as criminally responsible. For example, a 6-year-old child can act purposively to "steal" the toy of a friend even though she "knows" and can articulate that such conduct is "wrong." When young children make voluntary and instrumental choices to engage in prohibited conduct, they possess some moral ability to understand its wrongfulness and require discipline to hold them accountable and to teach them the consequences of violating rules. However, despite their ability to make reasoned choices and engage in goal-oriented behavior, we do not regard them as full moral agents. The criminal law regards young actors differently exactly because they have not yet fully internalized moral norms, developed sufficient empathic identification with others, acquired adequate moral comprehension, or had sufficient opportunity to develop the ability to restrain their actions. They possess neither the rationality—cognitive capacity—nor the self-control—volitional capacity—to equate their criminal responsibility with that of adults.

Toward a Youth Sentencing Policy Rationale Certain characteristic developmental differences between adolescents and adults distinguish their quality of judgment, psychosocial maturity, and self-control and justify a different criminal sentencing policy for younger offenders. Youths differ from adults on several dimensions that directly affect their degree of criminal responsibility and deserved punishment: breadth of experience, short-term versus long-term temporal perspective, attitude toward and acceptance of risk, and susceptibility to peer influences. These developmentally unique attributes affect young peoples' capacity to comprehend fully the consequences of their actions and their empathic identification with others. Moreover, it takes time and experience to develop the capacity to exercise self-control. While young offenders possess sufficient understanding and culpability to hold them accountable for their acts, their choices are less blameworthy than those of adults because of truncated self-control. Their crimes are less blameworthy not simply because of reduced culpability and limited appreciation of consequences but because their life situations have understandably limited their capacity to learn to make fully responsible choices.

Administering Youthfulness as a Mitigating Factor at Sentencing: The "Youth Discount"

Implementing a youth sentencing policy entails legal, moral, and social judgments. Because of developmental differences and the social construction of adolescence, younger offenders are less criminally responsible than more mature violators. But, they are not so essentially different and inherently incompetent as the current legal dichotomy between juvenile and criminal court suggests. In view of the developmental psychological research that suggests several ways in which youths systematically differ from adults, should the criminal law adopt a "youth-blind" stance and treat 14-year-olds as the moral equivalent of adults for purposes of sentencing, or should it devise a youth sentencing policy that reflects more appropriately the developmental continuum?

Shorter sentences for reduced responsibility represents a more modest and attainable reason to treat young offenders differently than adults than the rehabilitative justifications advanced by Progressive child savers. In this context, adolescent criminal responsibility represents a global judgment about the degree of youths' deserved punishment rather than a technical legal judgment about whether or not a particular youth possessed the requisite *mens rea* or mental state defined in the criminal statute. If adolescents as a class characteristically exercise poorer judgment than do adults, then sentencing policies can reduce the long-term harm that they cause to themselves. Protecting young people from the full penal consequences of their poor decisions reflects a policy to preserve their life chances for the future when they presumably will make more mature and responsible choices. Such a policy simultaneously holds young offenders accountable for their acts because they possess sufficient culpability and yet mitigates the severity of consequences because their choices entail less blameworthiness than those of adults.

Criminal courts in some jurisdictions already consider "youthfulness" in the context of aggravating and mitigating factors and may impose shorter sentences on a discretionary basis. Although the federal sentencing guidelines explicitly reject youthfulness as a justification to sentence outside of the guidelines range, sentencing statutes in some states recognize youthfulness as a mitigating factor at sentencing. However, states that consider youthfulness as a mitigating factor simply treat it as one element to be weighed with other aggravating and mitigating factors in deciding what sentence to impose on an individual.

A statutory sentencing policy that integrates youthfulness, reduced culpability, and restricted opportunities to learn self-control with principles of proportionality would provide younger offenders with categorical fractional reductions of adult sentences. Because youthfulness constitutes a universal form of "reduced responsibility," states should treat it unequivocally as a mitigating factor without regard to nuances of individual developmental differences.

This categorical approach would take the form of an explicit youth discount at sentencing. A 14-year-old offender might receive, for example, 25–33% of the adult penalty, a 16-year-old defendant 50–60%, and an 18-year-old adult the full penalty, as presently occurs. The "deeper discounts" for younger offenders correspond to the developmental continuum and their more limited opportunities to learn and exercise responsibility. A youth discount based on reduced culpability functions as a sliding scale of diminished responsibility. Just as adolescents possess less criminal responsibility than do adults, 14-year-old youths should enjoy a greater mitigation of blameworthiness than would 17-year-olds. Because the rationale for youthful mitigation rests on reduced culpability and limited opportunities to learn to make responsible choices, younger adolescents bear less responsibility and deserve proportionally shorter sentences than older youths. The capacity to learn to be responsible improves with time and experience. With the passage of time, age, and opportunities to develop the capacity for self-control, social tolerance of criminal deviance and claims for mitigation decline.

Discounted sentences that preserve younger offenders' life chances require that the maximum sentences they receive remain substantially below those imposed on adults. For youths below the age of 14, the common law infancy *mens rea* defense would acquire new vitality for proportionally shorter "discounted" sentences or even noncriminal dispositions.

The rationale for a youth discount also supports requiring a higher in/out threshold of offense seriousness as a prerequisite for imprisonment. Because juveniles depend on their families more than do adults, removal from home constitutes a more severe punishment. Because of differences in "subjective time," youths experience the duration of imprisonment more acutely than do adults. Because of the rapidity of developmental change, sentences of incarceration are more disruptive for youths than for adults. Thus, states should require a higher threshold of offense seriousness and a greater need for social defense before confining a youth than might be warranted for an older offender.

Only the states whose criminal sentencing laws provide realistic, humane, and determinate sentences that enable a judge actually to determine "real-time" sentences can readily implement a proposal for explicit fractional reductions of youths' sentences. One can only know the value of a youth discounted sentence in a sentencing system in which courts know in advance the standard or "going rate" for adults. In many jurisdictions, implementing a youth discount would require significant modification of the current criminal sentencing statutes, including presumptive sentencing guidelines with strong upper limits on punishment severity, elimination of all mandatory minimum sentences, and some structured judi-

cial discretion to mitigate penalties based on individual circumstances. In short, a criminal sentencing system itself must be defensible in terms of equality, equity, desert, and proportionality. Attempts to apply idiosyncratically youth discounts within the flawed indeterminate or draconian mandatory minimum-sentencing regimes that currently prevail in many jurisdictions runs the risk simply of reproducing all their existing inequalities and injustices.

Individualization Versus Categorization Youthful development is highly variable. Young people of the same age may differ dramatically in their criminal sophistication, appreciation of risk, or learned responsibility. Chronological age provides, at best, a crude and imprecise indicator of maturity and the opportunity to develop a capacity for self-control. However, a categorical youth discount that uses age as a conclusive proxy for reduced culpability and a shorter sentence remains preferable to an "individualized" inquiry into the criminal responsibility of each young offender. The criminal law represents an objective standard. Attempts to integrate subjective psychological explanations of adolescent behavior and personal responsibility into a youth sentencing policy cannot be done in a way that can be administered fairly without undermining the objectivity of the law. Developmental psychology does not possess reliable clinical indicators of moral development or criminal sophistication that equate readily with criminal responsibility or accountability. For young criminal actors who possess at least some degree of criminal responsibility, relying on inherently inconclusive or contradictory psychiatric or clinical testimony to precisely tailor sanctions hardly seems worth the judicial burden and diversion of resources that the effort would entail. Thus, for ease of administration, age alone provides the most useful criterion on which to allocate mitigation.

A youth discount that bases fractional reductions of sentences on age as a proxy for culpability also avoids the conceptual and administrative difficulties of a more encompassing subjective inquiry into diminished responsibility, a "rotten social background," or "social adversity." The juvenile courts' treatment ideology mistakenly denies that young people are morally responsible actors whom the law may hold accountable for their behavior.

A youth sentencing policy requires formal mitigation to avoid the undesirable forced choice between either inflicting undeservedly harsh punishments on less culpable actors or "doing nothing" about the manifestly guilty. A formal policy of youthful mitigation provides a buffer against the inevitable political pressure to ratchet-up sanctions every time youths sentenced leniently subsequently commit serious offenses. The idea of deserved punishment also limits the imposition of too little punishment as well as too much. Although the overall cardinal scale of penalties for juveniles should be considerably less than that for adults, a failure to sanction when appropriate, as juvenile court treatment ideology may dictate in some instances, can deprecate the moral seriousness of offending.

Youth and Group Crime

Young offenders commit crimes in groups to a much greater extent than do adults. While the law treats all participants in a crime as equally responsible and may sentence them alike, young people's susceptibility to peer group influences requires a more nuanced assessment of their degree of participation, personal responsibility, and culpability. The group nature of youth crime affects sentencing policy in several ways. The presence of a social audience of peers may induce youths to participate in

criminal behavior that they would not engage in if alone. Even though the criminal law treats all accomplices as equally guilty as a matter of law, they may not all bear equal responsibility for the actual harm inflicted and may deserve different sentences. To some extent, state criminal sentencing laws already recognize an offender's differential participation in a crime as a "mitigating" factor. Similarly, some states' juvenile court waiver laws and juvenile sentencing provisions also focus on "the *culpability* of the child in committing the alleged offense, including the level of the child's participation in planning and carrying out the offense." Thus, the group nature of adolescent criminality requires some formal mechanism to distinguish between active participants and passive accomplices with even greater "discounts" for the latter.

Integrated Criminal Justice System

A graduated age-culpability sentencing scheme in an integrated criminal justice system avoids the inconsistencies and injustices associated with the binary either-juvenile-or-adult drama currently played out in judicial waiver proceedings and in prosecutorial charging decisions. It also avoids the "punishment gap" when youths make the transition from the one justice system to the other. Depending on whether or not a judge or prosecutor transfers a case, the sentences that violent youths receive may differ by orders of magnitude. Moreover, appellate courts eschew proportionality analyses and allow criminal court judges to sentence waived youths to the same terms applied to adults without requiring them to consider or recognize any differences in their degree of criminal responsibility. By contrast, waived chronic property offenders typically receive less severe sanctions as adults than they would have received as persistent offenders in the juvenile system. As the sentencing principles of juvenile courts increasingly resemble more closely those of criminal courts, the sentence disparities that follow from waiver decisions become even less defensible.

An integrated criminal justice system eliminates the need for transfer hearings, saves the considerable resources that juvenile courts currently expend ultimately to no purpose, reduces the punishment gap that presently occurs when youths make the passage from the juvenile system, and ensures similar consequences for similarly situated offenders. Adolescence and criminal careers develop along a continuum. But the radical bifurcation between the two justice systems confounds efforts to respond consistently and systematically to young career offenders.

Integrated Record Keeping The absence of an integrated record-keeping system that enables criminal court judges to identify and respond to career offenders on the basis of their cumulative prior record constitutes one of the most pernicious consequences of jurisdictional bifurcation. Currently, persistent young offenders may "fall between the cracks" of the juvenile and criminal systems, often at the age at which career offenders approach their peak offending rates. A unified criminal court with a single record-keeping system can maintain and retrieve more accurate criminal histories when a judge sentences an offender. Although a youth discount provides appropriate leniency for younger offenders, integrated records would allow courts to escalate the discounted sanctions for chronic and career young offenders.

Decriminalize "Kids' Stuff" Despite juvenile courts' overcrowded dockets and inadequate treatment resources, their procedural deficiencies and informality allow them to process delinquents too efficiently. Expedited procedures, fewer lawyers and legal challenges, and greater flexibility allow juvenile

courts to handle a much larger number of cases per judge than do criminal courts and at lower unit cost. Merging the two systems would introduce an enormous volume of cases into an already overburdened criminal justice system that barely can cope with its current workload. Legislators and prosecutors forced to allocate scarce law enforcement resources would use the seriousness of the offense to rationalize charging decisions and "divert" or "decriminalize" most of the "kids' stuff" that provides the grist of the juvenile court mill until it became chronic or escalated in severity. Unlike a rehabilitative system inclined to extend its benevolent reach, an explicitly punitive process would opt to introduce fewer and more criminally "deserving" youths into the system.

Age-Segregated Dispositional Facilities and "Room to Reform" Questions about young offenders' criminal responsibility and length of sentence differ from issues about appropriate places of confinement or the services or resources the state should provide to them. Even explicitly punitive sentences do not require judges or correctional authorities to confine young people with adults in jails and prisons, as is the current practice for waived youths, or to consign them to custodial warehouses or "punk prisons." States should maintain separate age-segregated youth correctional facilities to protect both younger offenders and older inmates. Even though youths may be somewhat responsible for their criminal conduct, they may not be the physical or psychological equals of adults in prison. While some youths may be vulnerable to victimization or exploitation by more physically developed adults, other youths may pose a threat to older inmates. Younger offenders have not learned to "do easy time," pose more management problems for correctional administrators, and commit more disciplinary infractions while they serve their sentences. Existing juvenile detention facilities, training schools, and institutions provide the option to segregate inmates on the basis of age or other risk factors. Some research indicates that youths sentenced to juvenile correctional facilities may recidivate somewhat less often, seriously, or rapidly than comparable youths sentenced to adult facilities. However, these findings provide modest support for a separate youth correctional system rather than for an entirely separate juvenile justice system.

Virtually all young offenders return to society, and the state should provide them with resources for self-improvement on a voluntary basis because of its basic responsibility to its citizens and its own self-interest. If a state fails to provide opportunities for growth and further debilitates already disadvantaged youths, it guarantees greater long-term human, criminal, and correctional costs.

The Death Penalty

Michael L. Radelet and Marian J. Borg

In a monumental 1972 decision by the US Supreme Court, all but a few death penalty statutes in the United States were declared unconstitutional (*Furman v. Georgia*, 408 US 238). Consequentially, each of the 630 or so inmates then on America's death rows was resentenced to life imprisonment. The nine opinions in the case, decided by a 5–4 vote, remain the longest ever written by the Supreme Court. Four years later, defying predictions that the United States would never again witness executions (Meltsner 1973:290–92), the Supreme Court reversed its course toward abolition by approving several newly enacted capital statutes (*Gregg v. Georgia*, 428 US 153). By mid-1999 there were some 3500 men and 50 women (including 65 juveniles whose capital offenses predated their eighteenth birthdays) on death rows in 38 states and two federal jurisdictions (NAACP Legal Defense Fund 1999). Another 550 death row inmates had been executed in the two preceding decades (Death Penalty Information Center 1999).

The goal of this paper is to review recent social science research that has examined various dimensions of capital punishment. We organize this review by examining how the public debate on the death penalty in the United States has changed over the past quarter century. We attempt to show that arguments supporting the death penalty today, compared to 25 years ago, rely less on such issues as deterrence, cost, and religious principles, and more on grounds of retribution. In addition, those who support the death penalty are more likely today than in years past to acknowledge the inevitability of racial and class bias in death sentencing, as well as the inevitability of executing the innocent. We suggest that many of these arguments have changed because of social science research and that the changing nature of the death penalty debate in this country is part of a worldwide historical trend toward abolition of capital punishment.

Public opinion on the death penalty in America over the past 50 years has vacillated. Support decreased through the 1950s and until 1966, when only 47% of the American public voiced support; since 1982 about three quarters of the population has favored capital punishment (Ellsworth & Gross 1994). In 1991, Gallup found that 76% of Americans favored the death penalty; in 1994 support had reached 80% (Gallup & Newport 1991:44, Gillespie 1999). More recent data indicate that public approval for the death penalty has peaked, and even decreased a bit in recent years. By 1999, support for capital punishment had dropped to 71% (Gillespie 1999).

From "The Changing Nature of the Death Penalty," *Annual Review of Sociology* v. 26 (2000): 43–61. Reprinted by permission of Annual Review of Sociology.

DETERRENCE

In the early 1970s, the top argument in favor of the death penalty was general deterrence. This argument or hypothesis suggests that we must punish offenders to discourage others from committing similar offenses; we punish past offenders to send a message to potential offenders. In a broad sense, the deterrent effect of punishment is thought to be a function of three main elements: certainty, celerity, and severity. First, people do not violate laws if they are certain that they will be caught and punished. Second, celerity refers to the elapsed time between the commission of an offense and the administration of punishment. In theory, the more quickly a punishment is carried out, the greater its deterrent effect. Third, the deterrent effect of a punishment is a function of its severity. However, over the last two decades more and more scholars and citizens have realized that the deterrent effect of a punishment is not a consistent direct effect of its severity—after a while, increases in the severity of a punishment no longer add to its deterrent benefits. In fact, increases in a punishment's severity have decreasing incremental deterrent effects, so that eventually any increase in severity will no longer matter. If one wishes to deter another from leaning on a stove, medium heat works just as well as high heat.

Writing in a special issue of the *Annals of the American Academy of Political and Social Science* devoted to the death penalty in 1952, criminologist Robert Caldwell asserted, "The most frequently advanced and widely accepted argument in favor of the death penalty is that the threat of its infliction deters people from committing capital offenses" (Caldwell 1952:50–51). While some econometric studies have claimed to find deterrent effects (e.g., Ehrlich 1975), these studies have been sharply criticized (e.g., Klein et al. 1978).

Overall, the vast majority of deterrence studies have failed to support the hypothesis that the death penalty is a more effective deterrent to criminal homicides than long imprisonment. As two of this country's most experienced deterrence researchers conclude after their review of recent scholarship, "The available evidence remains 'clear and abundant' that, as practiced in the United States, capital punishment is not more effective than imprisonment in deterring murder" (Bailey & Peterson 1997:155).

There is widespread agreement among both criminologists and law enforcement officials that capital punishment has little curbing effect on homicide rates that is superior to long-term imprisonment. In a recent survey of 70 current and former presidents of three professional associations of criminologists (the American Society of Criminology, the Academy of Criminal Justice Sciences, and the Law and Society Association), 85% of the experts agreed that the empirical research on deterrence has shown that the death penalty never has been, is not, and never could be superior to long prison sentences as a deterrent to criminal violence (Radelet & Akers 1996). Similarly, a 1995 survey of nearly 400 randomly selected police chiefs and county sheriffs from throughout the United States found that two thirds did not believe that the death penalty significantly lowered the number of murders (Radelet & Akers 1996).

Opinion polls show that the general public is gradually learning the results of this body of research. According to a 1991 Gallup Poll, only 51% of Americans believed the death penalty had deterrent effects, a drop of 11% from 1985 (Gallup & Newport 1991). By 1997 this had fallen to 45% (Gross 1998:1454). In short, a remarkable change in the way the death penalty is justified is occurring. What was once the public's most widely cited justification for the death penalty is today rapidly losing its appeal.

INCAPACITATION

A second change in death penalty arguments involves the incapacitation hypothesis, which suggests that we need to execute the most heinous killers in order to prevent them from killing again. According to this view, we need the death penalty to protect the public from recidivist murders. On its face it is a simple and attractive position: No executed prisoner has ever killed again, and some convicted murderers will undoubtedly kill again if, instead of being executed, they are sentenced to prison terms.

Research addressing this issue has focused on calculating precise risks of prison homicides and recidivist murder. This work has found that the odds of repeat murder are low, and that people convicted of homicide tend to make better adjustments to prison (and, if released, exhibit lower rates of recidivism) than do other convicted felons (Bedau 1982a, 1997b, Stanton 1969, Wolfson 1982). The best research on this issue has been done by James Marquart and Jonathan Sorensen, sociologists at Sam Houston State University, who tracked down 558 of the 630 people on death row when all death sentences in the United States were invalidated by the Supreme Court in 1972. Contrary to the predictions of those who advocate the death penalty on the grounds of incapacitation, Marquart and Sorensen found that among those whose death sentences were commuted in 1972, only about one percent went on to kill again. This figure is almost identical with the number of death row prisoners later found to be innocent (Marquart & Sorensen 1989). Interpreted another way, these figures suggest that 100 prisoners would have to be executed to incapacitate the one person who statistically might be expected to repeat. Arguably, today's more sophisticated prisons and the virtual elimination of parole have reduced the risks of repeat homicide even further.

While the incapacitation argument might have made sense in an era when there were no prisons available for long-term confinement, the empirical evidence suggests that today's prisons and the widespread availability of long prison terms are just as effective as capital punishment in preventing murderers from repeating their crimes. Still, incapacitation is the second most popular reason for favoring the death penalty. In a 1991 national poll, for example, 19% of death penalty supporters cited incapacitation as a reason for favoring the death penalty (Gross 1998:1454). But in the last two decades it has become clear that if citizens are convinced that convicted murderers will never be released from prison, support for the death penalty drops dramatically.

The public opinion polls presented at the beginning of this paper measure support for the death penalty in the abstract, not support for the death penalty as it is actually applied. A key factor that has changed in sentencing for capital crimes since the *Furman* decision in 1972 has been the increased availability of "life without parole" as an alternative to the death penalty. Today, at least 32 states offer this option (Wright 1990), although it is clear that most citizens and jurors do not realize this and vastly underestimate the amount of time that those convicted of capital murders will spend in prison (Fox et al. 1990–1991:511–15, Gross 1998:1460–62). Another segment of the population realizes that life without parole is an alternative to the death penalty, but in spite of this, believe that future political leaders or judges will find ways to release life-sentenced inmates.

Nonetheless, when asked about support for the death penalty given an alternative punishment of life without parole, public support for the death penalty plummets. In Florida, for example, where those convicted of first-degree murder must be sentenced either to life without parole or to the death penalty, only 50% of the public polled in 1998 expressed support for the death penalty given the former alternative, and 44% of the respondents supported the idea of entirely banning the death penalty given the life without parole option (Griffin 1998). Nationally, the 1999 Gallup Poll found that 56% of the respondents supported the death penalty given the alternative of life without parole—a vast difference from the "overwhelming support" that many erroneously believe the death penalty enjoys. As more and more Americans learn that, absent the death penalty, those convicted of capital crimes will never be released from prison, further withering of death penalty support seems likely.

CAPRICE AND BIAS

As new death penalty laws were being passed in the 1970s to replace those invalidated by the *Furman* decision, many thought that the death penalty could be applied in a way that would avoid the arbitrariness and racial and class bias that had been condemned in *Furman* (Bedau 1982b, Black 1981). However, research conducted in the years since has all but unanimously concluded that the new laws have failed to achieve this goal.

Most of these analyses conclude that for crimes that are comparable, the death penalty is between three and four times more likely to be imposed in cases in which the victim is white rather than black (Baldus & Woodworth 1998, Baldus et al 1990, Bowers et al 1984, Gross & Mauro 1989, Radelet & Pierce 1991). In a 1990 review of 28 studies that had examined the correlation between race and death sentencing in the United States post-1972, the US General Accounting Agency (1990:6) concluded:

> the synthesis [of the 28 studies reviewed] supports a strong race of victim influence. The race of offender influence is not as clear cut and varies across a number of dimensions. Although there are limitations to the studies' methodologies, they are of sufficient quality to support the syntheses' findings.

The problem continues to be documented in research published in the 1990s. Again, race-of-victim effects are regularly found (e.g., Keil & Vito 1995), although some research, such as an extensive study just completed by David Baldus and his colleagues in Philadelphia (Baldus et al 1998), also finds race-of-defendant effects.

By any measure, the most comprehensive research ever produced on sentencing disparities in American criminal courts is the work of David Baldus and his colleagues conducted in Georgia in the 1970s and 1980s (Baldus et al 1990). After statistically controlling for some 230 variables, these researchers concluded that the odds of a death sentence for those who kill whites in Georgia are 4.3 times higher than the odds of a death sentence for those who kill blacks. Attorneys representing Georgia death row inmate Warren McCleskey took these data to the Supreme Court in 1987, claiming unfair racial bias in the administration of the death penalty in Georgia. But the Court rejected the argument, as well as the idea that a statistical pattern of bias could prove any bias in McCleskey's individual case (*McCleskey v. Kemp*, 481 U.S. 279, 1987).

The vote in the McCleskey case was 5 to 4. Interestingly, the decision was written and the deciding vote cast by Justice Lewis Powell, who was then serving his last year on the Court. Four years later, Powell's biographer asked the retired justice if he wished he could change his vote in any single case. Powell replied, "Yes, *McCleskey v. Kemp*." Powell, who voted in dissent in *Furman* and in his years on the Court remained among the justices who regularly voted to sustain death sentences, had changed his mind. "I have come to think that capital punishment should be abolished . . . [because] it serves no useful purpose" (Jeffries 1994:451–52). Had Powell had this realization a few years earlier, it is quite likely that, as in 1972, the death penalty would have been abolished, at least temporarily.

In effect, the *McCleskey* decision requires that defendants who raise a race claim must prove that race was a factor in their individual cases, and that as far as the courts are concerned, the statistical patterns indicating racial bias are basically irrelevant. In later years, the "Racial Justice Act," which would have required courts to hold hearings to examine statistical patterns of disparities in capital cases, failed to gain congressional approval (Bright 1995:465–66).

Two ways in which possible bias and arbitrariness in the death penalty can be reduced are through the provision of effective counsel to the poor and the careful use of executive clemency powers. Again, social science research addressing these issues has identified problems.

Research on the quality of attorneys provided to indigent defendants charged with capital offenses has relied on case-study methodology and examination of statutory law or customary procedures used to attract and compensate counsel. Stephen Bright has documented dozens of cases in which death sentences were given despite the fact that the defense attorneys were drunk, using drugs, racist against their own clients, unprepared or outright unqualified to practice criminal law, or otherwise incompetent (Bright 1997a, b). In

several cases, the defense attorney slept during the trail—giving a new meaning to the term "dream team" (Bright 1997b:790, 830). State governments are increasingly appointing attorneys in capital cases who submit the lowest bids; typically, attorneys are compensated at less than the minimum wage (Bright 1997b:816–21). As a result, those sentenced to death are often distinguishable from other defendants convicted of murder not on the basis of the heinousness of the crime, but instead on the basis of the quality of their defense attorneys.

A possible remedy for these failures at trial is executive clemency. Executive clemency can be used not only to remove bias and arbitrariness, but also to correct mistakes (e.g., when doubts exist about the prisoner's guilt, or when previously unknown or underweighted mitigation—such as evidence of mental illness or retardation—emerges), or to reward rehabilitation. Again, social science research in this area suggests the ineffectiveness of executive clemency in achieving these goals. Compared to the years before the 1972 *Furman* decision, clemency today is rarely granted (Bedau 1990–1991). Between 1972 and the end of 1992, only 41 death sentences in American jurisdictions were commuted to prison terms through power of executive clemency (Radelet & Zsembik 1993), and an average of just over one per year has been granted since. Of the 51 commutations granted through mid-1999, only six were granted on grounds of "equity."

Public opinion on the death penalty shows that while most Americans recognize the problems of race and class bias, they do not view such discrimination as a reason to oppose the death penalty. In the 1999 Gallup Poll, for example, 65% of the respondents agreed that a poor person is more likely than a person of average to above-average income to receive the death penalty for the same crime

(Gillespie 1999). Half the respondents believed that black defendants are more likely than whites to receive a death sentence for the same crime. Despite recognizing these inequities, 71% of those polled favored the death penalty.

COST

A fourth way in which death penalty arguments have changed in the past 25 years involves the issue of its fiscal costs. Two decades ago, some citizens and political leaders supported the death penalty as a way of avoiding the financial burdens of housing inmates for life or long prison terms. A 1985 Gallup Poll found that 11% of those supporting the death penalty cited the high fiscal costs of imprisonment as a reason for their positions (Gallup Report 1985).

Since then, however, research has firmly established that a modern death penalty system costs several times more than an alternative system in which the maximum criminal punishment is life imprisonment without parole. This research has been conducted in different states with different data sets by newspapers, courts and legislatures, and academics (see reviews in Bohm 1998, Dieter 1997, Spangenberg & Walsh 1989). Estimates by the *Miami Herald* are typical: $3.2 million for every electrocution versus $600,000 for life imprisonment (von Drehle 1988). These cost figures for capital punishment include expenses for not only those cases that end in execution, but also the many more cases in which the death penalty is sought that never end with a death sentence, and cases in which a death sentence is pronounced but never carried out. They also include the costs both for trials and for the lengthy appeals that are necessary before an execution can be authorized. Consequently, the cost issue today has be-

come an anti-death penalty argument, albeit of debatable strength. Absent the death penalty, its critics argue, states would have more resources to devote to the ends the death penalty is allegedly designed to pursue, such as reducing high rates of criminal violence or rendering effective aid to families of homicide victims. Those in favor of capital punishment, however, would argue that its retributive benefits are worth the costs.

MISCARRIAGES OF JUSTICE

Death penalty arguments are changing in a fifth way: Death penalty retentionists now admit that as long as we use the death penalty, innocent defendants will occasionally be executed. Until a decade ago, the pro-death penalty literature took the position that such blunders were historical oddities and could never be committed in modern times. Today the argument is not over the existence or even the inevitability of such errors, but whether the alleged benefits of the death penalty outweigh these uncontested liabilities. Several studies conducted over the last two decades have documented the problem of erroneous convictions in homicide cases (Givelber 1997, Gross 1996, Huff et al. 1996, Radelet et al. 1992). Since 1970 there have been 80 people released from death rows in the United States because of innocence (Death Penalty Information Center 1999; for a description of 68 of these cases, see Bedau & Radelet 1987, Radelet et al. 1996).

The cases of those wrongly sentenced to death and who were totally uninvolved in the crime constitute only one type of miscarriage of justice. Another (and more frequent) blunder arises in the cases of the condemned who, with a more perfect justice system, would have been convicted of second-degree murder or manslaughter, making them innocent of first degree murder. For example, consider the case of Ernest Dobbert, executed in Florida in 1984 for killing his daughter. The key witness at trial was Dobbert's 13-year-old son, who testified that he saw his father kick the victim (this testimony was later recanted). In a dissent from the Supreme Court's denial of certiorari written just hours before Dobbert's execution, Justice Thurgood Marshall argued that while there was no question that Dobbert abused his children, there was substantial doubt about the existence of sufficient premeditation to sustain the conviction for first-degree murder. "That may well make Dobbert guilty of second-degree murder in Florida, but it cannot make him guilty of first-degree murder there. Nor can it subject him to the death penalty in that State" (*Dobbert v. Wainwright*, 468 U.S. 1231, 1246 (1984)). If Justice Marshall's assessment was correct, then Dobbert was not guilty of a capital offense, and—in this qualified sense—Florida executed an innocent man.

In other cases, death row inmates have indeed killed someone, but, again, a more perfect system for deciding who should be convicted and who should die would have found these defendants not guilty because of insanity or self-defense, or because the killing was, in reality, an accident. Examined in this way, the class of "wrongful convictions" extends far beyond the group of those convicted who were legally and factually innocent of the crime.

THE GROWING FOCUS ON RETRIBUTION

Thus far we have argued that in the last two dozen years, debates over deterrence, incapacitation, cost, fairness, and the inevitability of executing the innocent have all been either neutralized or won by those who stand opposed to the death penalty. But while death penalty advocates increasingly acknowledge that these traditional justifications are growing less persuasive, in their place we have witnessed the ascendancy of what has become the most important contemporary pro-death penalty argument: retribution. Here one argues that justice requires the death penalty. Those who commit the most premeditated or heinous murders should be executed simply on the grounds that they deserve it (Berns 1979, van den Haag 1997, 1998). Life without parole, according to this view, is simply insufficient punishment for those who commit the most heinous and premeditated murders.

Retributive arguments are often made in the name of families of homicide victims, who are depicted as "needing" or otherwise benefitting from the retributive satisfaction that the death penalty promises. Perhaps the question most frequently posed to death penalty opponents during debates is "How would you feel if your closest loved one was brutally murdered?" For example, one of the most memorable and damaging questions of the 1988 presidential campaign was raised by Cable News Network (CNN) correspondent Bernard Shaw during the second debate between candidates George Bush and Michael Dukakis, when Shaw asked Dukakis whether his opposition to the death penalty would be swayed if someone raped and murdered his wife.

Those who oppose capital punishment can reasonably respond by pointing out that the death penalty offers much less to families of homicide victims than it first appears. For example, by diverting vast resources into death penalty cases—a small proportion of all homicide cases—the state has fewer resources for families of noncapital homicide victims and for more effective assistance for families of all homicide victims. Or, one could argue that the death penalty hurts families of homicide victims in cases in which the killer is *not* sentenced to death, since the prison sentence risks making them feel as if their loved one's death was not "worth" the life of the killer. Or, one could argue that the death penalty serves to keep the case open for many years before the execution actually occurs, often through resentences or retrials, continuously preventing the wounds of the family of the victim from healing. Motivated by a desire to express these arguments, an organization of families that oppose the death penalty, Murder Victims Families for Reconciliation (now located in Cambridge, MA) was formed in 1976. They and other groups of "homicide survivors" have regularly pointed out that the scholarly community has devoted very little attention to families of homicide victims (for an exception, see Vandiver 1998). Indeed, we are aware of no research specifically studying the short-term and long-term effects of the execution of a killer on the family of the homicide victim, or on the family of the executed inmate. On the other hand, the scholarship of Robert Johnson (1981, 1998a, 1998b) and others (e.g., Cabana 1996) gives readers some insights into what prison life in general, and life on death row in particular, is like. The conclusions of these researchers lend credence to those who argue that in some respects, life imprisonment without parole can be even worse than execution.

Unlike the arguments reviewed above, retribution is a non-empirical justification and thus all but impossible to test with empirical data. After all, there are no mathematical formulae available or on the horizon that can tell us precisely (or even roughly) how much of a given punishment a murderer—or any other offender—"deserves." In the end, the calculation of how much punishment a criminal "deserves" becomes more a moral and less a criminological issue.

To the extent that the death penalty is justified on moral (retributive) grounds, it is paradoxical that much of what can be called the "moral leadership" in the United States is already opposed to the death penalty. Leaders of Catholic, most Protestant, and Jewish denominations are strongly opposed to the death penalty, and most formal religious organizations in the United States have endorsed statements in favor of abolition (American Friends Service Committee 1998).

Consequently, no longer are Old Testament religious arguments in favor of the death penalty widely used or heard. In the late 1990s the Catholic Church and its leader, Pope John Paul II, are increasingly speaking out against the death penalty.

There is also evidence that the general public recognizes some limits to retributive punishments. In 1991, the Gallup Poll asked respondents which method of execution they preferred. After all, if one were *really* retributive, and if people like Oklahoma City bomber Timothy McVeigh *really* got what they "deserved," the preferred method might be slow boiling or public crucifixion. Yet, 66% of the respondents favored lethal injection, an increase of ten points from six years earlier (Gallup & Newport 1991:42). This preference likely reflects, at least in part, the belief that inmates might suffer too much in electric chairs and gas chambers. In contrast, lethal injection offers an ostensibly less painful death. In fact, death penalty opponents often argue against the use of lethal injection on the grounds that this method makes executions more palatable to the public by creating the appearance that the inmate is simply being put to sleep (Schwarzschild 1982).

A similar pattern in public opinion regarding execution methods is found in Florida, where one inmate burst into flames while sitting in the electric chair in 1990, and another did the same in 1997 (Borg & Radelet 1999, Denno 1997). Again, an ardent retributivist would shrug her shoulders at such painful botches and argue that while indeed these may be unfortunate, botched executions are not especially troubling. But contrary to the retributive hypothesis, half of the respondents polled in Florida in 1998 favored lethal injection, and only 22% the electric chair (10% chose "either" and 16% favored "neither") (Judd 1998). And in 1998, 77% of Floridians expressed support for the idea of allowing the condemned to choose between electrocution and lethal injection (Griffin 1998). Historically, these tendencies are not unique. The search for more "humane" methods of execution dates back at least to the eighteenth century when the guillotine was adopted because of botched beheadings (Laurence 1960), and to the nineteenth century when the electric chair was introduced as a "humane" remedy for botched hangings. Nonetheless, the concern to reduce the prisoner's suffering is inconsistent with the idea that we need the death penalty on the grounds of retributive justice.

TRENDS TOWARD ABOLITION

The above changes in death penalty debates come at a time when there is a relatively rapid worldwide movement away from the death penalty. In 1998, five countries combined for over 80% of the world's executions—China, the Democratic Republic of the Congo, Iran, Iraq, and the United States (Amnesty International 1999:15). These first four are countries with whom, normally, the United States does not share domestic policies.

Hugo Adam Bedau, the dean of American death penalty scholars, has argued that the history of the death penalty in the United States over the past two centuries is a history of its gradual retraction. Among specific changes that mark the path toward the decline of the death penalty have been:

> The end of public executions and of mandatory capital sentencing, introduction of the concept of degrees of murder, development

of appellate review in capital cases, decline in annual executions, reduction in the variety of capital statutes, experiments with complete abolition, even the search for more humane ways to inflict death as a punishment (Bedau 1982a:3–4).

With over 3500 men and women currently sentenced to death in the United States, it is quite easy for those who oppose the death penalty to preach doom and gloom. However, Bedau's observations invite students of the death penalty to take a long-term historical view. With such a lens, the outlook for abolition is more optimistic.

A century ago, only three countries had abolished the death penalty for all crimes; by the time of *Furman* in 1972 the number had risen to nineteen. But since then the number of abolitionist countries has tripled. By the end of 1998, 67 countries had abolished the death penalty for all offenses, fourteen more retained it only for "exceptional" crimes (i.e., during wartime), and 24 others had not had an execution in at least ten years. All fifteen members of the European Union have abolished the death penalty, and the Council of Europe, with 41 members, has made the abolition of the death penalty a condition of membership. In the first decision ever made by the newly constituted South African Constitutional Court in 1995—that country's Supreme Court—the death penalty was abolished as "cruel, inhuman and degrading" (Sonn 1996). Russia, a country that was among the world's leaders in executions in the early 1990s, announced in 1999 that it, too, was abolishing the death penalty (Amnesty International 1999:16). In June 1999 President Boris Yeltsin commuted over 700 death sentences to terms of imprisonment. Clearly, in a comparatively short historical time span, more than half of the countries in the world have abolished the death penalty, and the momentum is unquestionably in the direction of total worldwide abolition.

The above is not meant to suggest the absence of countries that continue to swim against the tide of worldwide abolition. Internationally, the death penalty is slowly expanding in a few countries, such as the Philippines, Taiwan, Yemen, and the English-speaking Caribbean (Amnesty International 1999). In the United States, both Congress and the Supreme Court are increasingly restricting access to federal courts by inmates contesting their death sentences (Freedman 1998, Yackle 1998). Few would disagree with the prediction that the next few years will be busy ones for America's executioners.

On the other hand, as the 1990s draw to a close, more and more countries are signing international treaties that abolish or restrict the death penalty (Schabas 1997). For the third year in 1999, the UN Commission on Human Rights, headquartered in Geneva, passed a resolution calling for a moratorium on death sentencing. The resolution was cosponsored by 72 states (compared to 47 in 1997) (Amnesty International 1999:16). Although the total abolition of the death penalty is its ultimate goal, the resolution encourages a strategy of "progressively restricting the offenses for which the death penalty can be imposed" (*New York Times* 1999a:A4). Toward this end, the 1999 resolution reaffirms an international ban on executions of those under 18, those who are pregnant, and those who are suffering from mental illness. The resolution also calls for non-death penalty nations to refuse to extradite suspects to countries that continue to use executions as a form of punishment.

Other calls for moratoriums on death sentencing are also being made. In May 1999, the Nebraska legislature passed a resolution calling for a two-year moratorium on executions because of questions of equity in the administration of its state's death penalty. This resolution was vetoed by the governor, but later the legislature unanimously overrode the governor's veto of that part of the legislation that allocated some $165,000 to study the issue (Tysyer 1999). In March 1999, the Illinois House of Representatives passed a similar resolution calling for a moratorium on executions; authorities in that state have acknowledged that 12 prisoners have been sent to death row in the past two decades who turned out to be innocent (*New York Times* 1999b). Finally, in February 1997, on behalf of its 400,000 members, the normally conservative House of Delegates of the American Bar Association called for a moratorium on the death penalty. The House of Delegates cited four principal reasons: the lack of adequate defense counsel, the erosion of state post-conviction and federal habeas corpus review, the continuing problem of racial bias in the administration of the death penalty, and the refusal of states and the courts to take action to prevent the execution of juveniles and the mentally retarded. Although the resolution cannot be seen as a statement of opposition to the death penalty per se, it is an attempt by the House of Delegates to bring these serious problems to the attention of legislators and the American public. What effect this resolution will have, of course, remains unknown.

CONCLUSION

We organized this discussion by examining six issues that have traditionally framed death penalty debates, paying particular attention to the social scientific literature that has evaluated each one. Our discussion suggests that changes in the discourse of capital punishment have evolved partly in response to the findings of this research. We conclude with three observations derived from the foregoing discussion.

First, the past two dozen years have witnessed significant changes in the nature of death penalty debates. Those who support the death penalty are less likely, and indeed less able, to claim that the death penalty has a deterrent effect greater than that of long imprisonment, or that the death penalty is cheaper than long imprisonment, or that it gives significant incapacitative benefits not offered by long imprisonment. Fewer and fewer religious leaders adopt a pro-death penalty position, and advocates of capital punishment have been forced to admit that the death penalty continues to be applied with unacceptable arbitrariness, as well as racial and class bias. A fair assessment of the data also leads to the conclusion that as long as the executioner is in the state's employ, innocent people will occasionally be executed. Increasingly, the best (and arguably the sole) justification for the death penalty rests on retributive grounds.

Second, at the same time as American discourse on the death penalty is changing, there is an accelerating worldwide decline in the acceptance of capital punishment. Indeed, the trend toward the worldwide abolition of the death penalty is inexorable. To be sure, the immediate future will continue to bring high numbers of executions in American jurisdictions. In all probability, these will increase over the numbers witnessed today. Nonetheless, taking a long-term historical view, the trend toward the abolition of the death penalty, which has now lasted for more than two centuries, will continue. Things could change quickly; the final thrust might come from conservative politicians who turn against the death penalty in the name of fiscal austerity, religious principles (e.g., a consistent "pro-life" stand), responsible crime-fighting, or genuine concern for a "smaller" government. Public support for the death penalty might also drop if there emerged absolute incontrovertible proof that an innocent prisoner had been executed. For those who oppose the death penalty, the long-term forecast should fuel optimism.

Finally, our review sends a positive message to criminologists and other social scientists who often feel as if their research is ignored by the public and by policy makers. As our review suggests, changes in the nature of death penalty debates are a direct consequence of social scientists' close and careful examination of the various dimensions of these arguments. Scholars have examined questions of deterrence, race, cost, methods of execution, innocence, juror decision-making, and the political and social environments in which death penalty legislation has emerged (Mello 1999, Tabak 1999). Clearly, this is one area of public policy where social science research is making a slow but perceptible impact.

REFERENCES

Acker, J., Bohm, R., & Lanier, C. 1998. *America's Experiment with Capital Punishment.* Durham: Carolina Acad. Press.

American Friends Service Committee. 1998. *The Death Penalty: The Religious Community Calls for Abolition.* Philadelphia: Am. Friends Service Com.

Amnesty International. 1999. *Amnesty International Report 1999.* London: Amnesty Int. Publ.

Bailey, W. C., & Peterson, R. D. 1997. Murder, capital punishment, and deterrence: a review of the literature. See Bedau 1997a, pp. 135–61.

Baldus, D. C., & Woodworth, G. 1998. Race discrimination and the death penalty: an empirical and legal overview. See Acker et al. 1998, pp. 385–415.

Baldus, D. C., Woodworth, G., & Pulaski, C. A., Jr. 1990. *Equal Justice and the Death Penalty: A Legal and Empirical Analysis.* Boston: Northeastern Univ. Press.

Baldus, D. C., Woodworth, G., Zuckerman, D., Weiner, N. A., & Broffitt, B. 1998. Racial discrimination and the death penalty in the post-*Furman* era: an empirical and legal overview, with recent findings from Philadelphia. *Cornell L. Rev.* 83:1638–770.

Bedau, H. A. 1982a. *The Death Penalty in America.* New York: Oxford Univ. Press. 3rd ed.

Bedau, H. A. 1982b. Deterrence: problems, doctrines, and evidence. See Bedau 1982a, pp. 95–103.

Jeffries J. C. Jr. 1994. *Justice Lewis E. Powell, Jr.: A Biography.* New York: Charles Scribner's Sons.

Johnson, R. 1981. *Condemned to Die: Life Under Sentence of Death.* New York: Elsevier.

Johnson, R. 1998a. *Death Work: A Study of the Modern Execution Process.* Belmont, CA: West/Wadsworth. 2nd ed.

Johnson, R. 1998b. Life under sentence of death: Historical and contemporary perspectives. See Acker et al. 1998, pp. 507–25.

Judd, A. 1998. Poll: Most favor new execution method. *Gainesville Sun*, Feb. 18.

Keil, T. J., & Vito, G. F. 1995. Race and the death penalty in Kentucky murder trials: 1976–1991. *Am. J. Crim. Justice* 20:17–36.

Klein, L. R., Forst, B., & Filatov, V. 1978. The deterrent effect of capital punishment: an assessment of the estimates. In *Deterrence and Incapacitation: Estimating the Effects of Criminal Sanctions on Crime Rates*, ed. A. Blumstein, J. Cohen, D. Nagin, pp. 336–60. Washington, DC: Natl. Acad. Sci.

Kroll, M. 1997. Death penalty monolith begins to crack *El Hispano,* Aug. 27.

Laurence, J. 1960. *The History of Capital Punishment.* Secaucus, NJ: Citadel Press.

Marquart, J. W., & Sorensen, J. R. 1989. A national study of the *Furman*-commuted inmates: Assessing the threat to society from capital offenders. *Loyola of Los Angeles Law Rev.* 23:101–20.

Mello, M. 1999. The real capital punishment: the (shotgun) marriage between social science and litigation, and the inviting footnote in *Brown v. Texas. Crim. Law Bull.* 35:107–26.

Meltsner, M. 1973. *Cruel and Unusual: The Supreme Court and Capital Punishment.* New York: Random House.

NAACP Legal Defense Fund. 1999. *Death Row, USA* (Spring). New York: NAACP Legal Defense Fund.

New York Times. 1999a. U.N. panel votes for ban on death penalty. *NY Times*, Apr. 29.

New York Times. 1999b. *Innocents on Death Row* (editorial). *NY Times*, May 23.

Peterson, R. D., & Bailey, W. C. 1998. Is capital punishment an effective deterrent for murder? An examination of social science research. See Acker et al. 1998, pp. 157–82.

Radelet, M. L., & Akers, R. L. 1996. Deterrence and the death penalty. The views of the experts. *J. Crim. Law Criminol.* 87:1–16.

Radelet, M. L., Lofquist, W. S., & Bedau, H. A. 1996. Prisoners released from death rows since 1970 because of doubts about their guilt. *Cooley Law Rev.* 13:907–66.

Radelet, M. L., & Pierce, G. L. 1991. Choosing those who will die: Race and the death penalty in Florida. *Florida Law Rev.* 43:1–34.

Radelet, M. L., & Zsembik, B. A. 1993. Executive clemency in post-*Furman* capital cases. *Univ. Richmond Law Rev.* 27:289–314.

Schabas, W. A. 1997. *The Abolition of the Death Penalty in International Law.* Cambridge, UK: Cambridge Univ. Press.

Schwarzschild, H. 1982. Homicide by injection. *NY Times*, Dec. 23.

Sonn, F. A. 1996. Keynote address: The ideals of a democracy. *Cooley Law Rev.* 13:853–61.

Spangenberg, R. L., & Walsh, E. R. 1989. Capital punishment or life imprisonment: some cost considerations. *Loyola of Los Angeles Law Rev.* 23:45–58.

Stanton, J. M. 1969. Murderers on parole. *Crime Delinq.* 15:149–55.

Tabak, R. 1999. How empirical studies can affect positively the politics of the death penalty. *Cornell Law Rev.* 83:1431–47.

Tysyer, R. 1999. Death penalty study OK'd. *Omaha World Herald*, May 28.

US General Accounting Agency. 1990. *Death Penalty Sentencing: Research Indicates Pattern of Racial Disparities* (GGD-90-57). Washington, DC: General Accounting Agency.

van den Haag, E. 1997. The death penalty once more. See Bedau 1997a, p. 445–56.

van den Haag, E. 1998. Justice, deterrence, and the death penalty. See Acker et al. 1998, pp. 139–56.

Vandiver, M. 1998. The impact of the death penalty on the families of homicide victims and of condemned prisoners. See Acker et al. 1998, pp. 477–505.

von Drehle, D. 1988. Capital punishment in paralysis. *Miami Herald*, Jul. 10, p. 1.

Wolfson, W. 1982. The deterrent effect of the death penalty upon prison murder. See Bedau 1982a, pp. 159–80.

Wright, J. H., Jr. 1990. Life-without-parole: an alternative to death or not much of a life at all? *Vanderbilt Law Rev.* 43:529–68.

Yackle, L. W. 1998. The American Bar Association and federal habeas corpus. *Law Contemp. Problems* 61:171–92.

STUDY QUESTIONS TO PART III

1. Describe the evidence presented by David Harris that documents the practice of racial profiling by the police.
2. Racial profiling not only affects the drivers who are stopped but also has larger consequences, according to Harris. What are those larger consequences?
3. What corrective measures does Harris advocate to reduce racial profiling?
4. Peter Kraska and Victor Kappeler identify several problems with the proliferation of police paramilitary units in the United States. Discuss these problems and indicate why the authors consider these squads a cause for concern.
5. Judith Greene evaluates New York City's zero-tolerance style of policing. (a) Describe the zero-tolerance model. (b) Identify one negative consequence of this approach. (c) Compare and contrast New York's and San Diego's policing styles and their consequences.
6. Discuss the various dimensions of the "punitive trend" in American drug policy, as discussed by Peter Reuter.
7. Based on the reading by Lois Presser and Elaine Gunnison, describe the various ways in which community notification laws for released sex offenders contradict the principles of "community justice."
8. Three-strikes laws are popular with the American public, but they have not lived up to predictions. Based on the reading by James Austin and colleagues, describe the impact of three-strikes laws, especially in California.
9. According to Paul Tracy and Vincent Morgan, what major questions remain to be answered with respect to the steady growth of DNA testing in America?
10. What evidence do Tracy and Morgan present to support their argument that widespread DNA testing is not cost effective?
11. Describe the gun control reforms that Philip Cook and Mark Moore suggest may help to reduce gun problems in America, at the federal, state, and municipal levels.
12. According to Barry Feld, what major problems with America's juvenile courts justify abolishing these courts?
13. What kinds of changes does Feld propose in the ways the criminal courts handle juvenile cases, to ensure that juveniles are treated properly?
14. Michael Radelet and Marian Borg review six arguments in favor and against the death penalty. Summarize each argument and then evaluate the merits of each with the help of the social science findings presented by the authors.

Bedau, H. A. 1990–1991. The decline of executive clemency in capital cases. *NY Univ. Rev. Law & Soc. Change* 18:255–72.

Bedau, H. A. 1997a. *The Death Penalty in America.* New York: Oxford Univ. Press.

Bedau, H. A. 1997b. Prison homicides, recidivist murder, and life imprisonment. See Bedau 1997a, pp. 176–82.

Berns, W. 1979. *For Capital Punishment: Crime and the Morality of the Death Penalty.* New York: Basic Books.

Black, C. L. 1981. *Capital Punishment: The Inevitability of Caprice and Mistake.* New York: WW Norton. 2nd ed.

Bohm, R. M. 1998. The economic costs of capital punishment: Past, present, and future. See Acker et al. 1998, pp. 437–58.

Bohm, R. M. 1999. *Deathquest: An Introduction to the Theory and Practice of Capital Punishments in the United States.* Cincinnati, OH. Anderson.

Borg, N. J., & Radelet, M. L. 1999. On botched executions. In *Routes to Abolition: The Law and Practice of the Death Penalty*, ed. P. Hodgkinson, W. Schabas.

Bowers, W. J., Pierce, G. L., McDevitt, J. F. 1984. *Legal Homicide: Death As Punishment in America, 1864–1982.* Boston: Northeastern Univ. Press.

Bright, S. B. 1995. Discrimination, death and denial: the tolerance of racial discriminati of the death penalty. *Santa Clara Law Rev.* 35:433–83.

Bright, S. B. 1997a. Counsel for the poor: the death sentence not for the worst crime but for the worst lawyer. See Bedau 1997a, pp. 275–309.

Bright, S. B. 1997b. Neither equal nor just: The rationing and denial of legal services to the poor when life and liberty are at stake. *Annu. Survey Am. Law* 1997:783–836.

Cabana, D. A. 1996. *Death At Midnight: The Confession of an Executioner.* Boston: Northeastern Univ. Press.

Caldwell, R. G. 1952. Why is the death penalty retained? *Annu. Rev. Am. Acad. Polit. Soc. Sci.* 284:45–53.

Death Penalty Information Center. 1999. http://www.essential.org/dpic/.

Denno, D. 1997. Getting to death: Are executions constitutional? *Iowa Law Rev.* 82:319–464.

Dieter, R. C. 1997. Millions misspent: What politicians don't say about the high costs of the death penalty. See Bedau 1997a, pp. 401–10.

Ehrlich, I. 1975. The deterrent effect of capital punishment: A question of life and death. *Am. Econ. Rev.* 65:397–417.

Ellsworth, P. C., & Gross, S. R. 1994. Hardening of the attitudes: Americans' views on the death penalty. *J. Soc. Issues* 50:19–52.

Fox, J. A., Radelet, M. L., & Bonsteel, J. L. 1990–1991. Death penalty opinion in the post-*Furmant* years. *NY Univ. Rev. Law & Soc. Change* 18:499–528.

Freedman, E. 1998. Federal habeas corpus in capital cases. See Acker et al 1998, pp. 417–26.

Gallup Report. 1985. Support for death penalty highest in half-century. *Gallup Report* Nos. 232 & 233:3–13.

Gallup, A., Newport, F. 1991. Death penalty support remains strong. *Gallup Poll Monthly.* June: No. 309:40–45.

Gillespie, M. 1999. Public Opinion supports death penalty. http://www/gallup.com/POLL ARCHIVES/990219b.htm.

Givelber, D. 1997. Meaningless acquittals, meaningful convictions: Do we reliably acquit the innocent? *Rutgers Law Rev.* 49:1317–96.

Griffin, M. 1998. Voters approve of death penalty: the support would be weaker if Florida voters were certain that killers would be locked up forever, a poll found. *Orlando Sentinel*, Apr. 23. p. D1.

Gross, S. R. 1996. The risks of death: Why erroneous convictions are common in capital cases. *Buffalo Law Rev.* 44:469–500.

Gross, S. R. 1998. Update: American public opinion on the death penalty—it's getting personal. *Cornell Law Rev.* 83:1448–75.

Gross, S., & Mauro, R. 1989. *Death & Discrimination: Racial Disparities in Capital Sentencing.* Boston: Northeastern Univ. Press.

Huff, C. R., Rattner, A., & Sagarin, E. 1996. *Convicted But Innocent: Wrongful Conviction and Public Policy.* Thousand Oaks, CA: Sage.